THE NEW NEWS

The New News offers an approachable, practical guide to the 21st-century newsroom, equipping journalists with the skills needed to work expertly, accurately, and efficiently across multiple media platforms.

Emphasizing the importance of verification and authentication, the book shows how journalists adapt traditional practices of information-gathering, observation, interviewing, and newswriting for online publications. The text includes comprehensive coverage of key digital and multimedia competencies – capturing multimedia content, "doing" data journalism, reporting with mobile equipment, working in teams, participating with global audiences, and building a personal brand.

Features developed exclusively for this book include innovative visuals showing the multimedia news structures and workflows used in modern newsrooms; interviews with prominent journalists about their experiences in contemporary journalism; a glossary of up-to-date terms relevant to online journalism; and practical exercises and activities for classroom use, as well as additional downloadable online instructor materials.

The New News provides excellent resources to help journalism students and early-career professionals succeed in today's digital networked news industry.

The authors are donating all royalties to nonprofit LION's programs to support local online news publications.

Joan Van Tassel, Ph.D. (Annenberg School for Communications/USC, 1988) is an educator, author, and journalist. She's written seven research-based books about the information, telecommunication, and entertainment industries, including *Managing Media: Making, Marketing, & Moving Digital Content*.

Dr. Van Tassel taught journalism at National University, Pepperdine University, and UCLA Extension School. She produced news, documentaries, and TV movies for CBS, NBC, ABC, and PBS. Her work won numerous awards, including the Cable Industry Book Award, an Emmy nomination, the Kenny Rogers/UN Prize, Los Angeles and San Diego Press Club Awards, and New Media Institute Standard of Excellence.

Mary Murphy is an Associate Professor at the USC Annenberg School for Communication and Journalism. A Press Club award-winning journalist in print, TV, and online, she was on the staff of *Esquire*, *New York*, *New West*, and *TV Guide* magazines, and the *St. Louis Post-Dispatch* and the *Los Angeles Times*. She was an on-air correspondent for *Entertainment Tonight*.

Currently, she writes a blog for TheWrap.com and other digital publications. She co-authored *Blood Cold*, an investigation of the Robert Blake case, and is working on another book about Hollywood.

Murphy sits on the Boards of Directors of the Broadcast Television Critics Association and Fordham/Marymount University.

Joseph Schmitz, Ph.D. (Annenberg School for Communications/USC, 1990) is an educator, researcher, and author. Joe developed and tested the Social Influence Model of Communication Technology. He chaired the International Communication Association's Communication and Technology Division. Schmitz was the co-principal investigator and primary research methodologist for National Science Foundation, Technology Opportunity, and US-EU Trans-Atlantic grants. He helped develop the City of Santa Monica's innovative Public Electronic Network.

Schmitz taught research methods and organizational communication at Pepperdine University, The University of Southern California, Tulsa University, and Western Illinois University. Joe collaborated with students to frame important questions and guide their discoveries toward logical, fact-based empirical answers.

THE NEW NEWS

THE JOURNALIST'S GUIDE TO PRODUCING DIGITAL CONTENT FOR ONLINE & MOBILE NEWS

Joan Van Tassel, Mary Murphy & Joseph Schmitz

NEW YORK AND LONDON

First published 2020
by Routledge
52 Vanderbilt Avenue, New York, NY 10017

and by Routledge
2 Park Square, Milton Park, Abingdon, Oxon, OX14 4RN

Routledge is an imprint of the Taylor & Francis Group, an informa business

© 2020 Joan Van Tassel, Mary Murphy, & Joseph Schmitz

The right of Joan Van Tassel, Mary Murphy, & Joseph Schmitz to be identified as authors of this work has been asserted by them in accordance with sections 77 and 78 of the Copyright, Designs and Patents Act 1988.

All rights reserved. No part of this book may be reprinted or reproduced or utilised in any form or by any electronic, mechanical, or other means, now known or hereafter invented, including photocopying and recording, or in any information storage or retrieval system, without permission in writing from the publishers.

Trademark notice: Product or corporate names may be trademarks or registered trademarks, and are used only for identification and explanation without intent to infringe.

Library of Congress Cataloging-in-Publication Data
Names: Van Tassel, Joan M., author. | Murphy, Mary, 1944- author. |
   Schmitz, Joseph, 1942- author.
Title: The new news : the journalist's guide to producing digital content
   for online & mobile news / Joan Van Tassel, Mary Murphy, Joseph Schmitz.
Description: New York : Routledge, 2020. | Includes bibliographical
   references and index.
Identifiers: LCCN 2020008455 | ISBN 9780240824185 (paperback) |
   ISBN 9780367508692 (hardcover) | ISBN 9781003051596 (ebook)
Subjects: LCSH: Online journalism. | Journalism–Technological innovations.
Classification: LCC PN4784.O62 V46 2020 | DDC 070.4–dc23
LC record available at https://lccn.loc.gov/2020008455

ISBN: 978-0-367-50869-2 (hbk)
ISBN: 978-0-240-82418-5 (pbk)
ISBN: 978-1-003-05159-6 (ebk)

Typeset in Sabon
by Swales & Willis, Exeter, Devon, UK

Visit the eResources: www.routledge.com/9780240824185

Dedication

Joan Van Tassel
To Gordon, Karen, Bailey, and Emmy Van Tassell,
Sisters Nancy Van Tassel and Elaine Baer
and Walter H. Annenberg for providing for my graduate education

Mary Murphy
To my family, Nick, Meg and Brett, Sean and Caroline,
the students at the USC Annenberg School for Communication and Journalism,
and Clancy Imislund

Joseph Schmitz
To my parents, Joe and Betty Schmitz – fierce doers and readers
To my two sons, Joseph and Karl, and their families
To the USC Annenberg School for Communication faculty – teachers and mentors *par excellence*
To my research methods students – who taught me how to coach others' discoveries

CONTENTS

Acknowledgments   ix
List of Figures   xi
List of Tables   xv
Preface   xvii

  Introduction: The Gist   1

PART I: NEWS NOW   5

1 Be Here Now: The View From 30,000 Feet   7

2 News by the Numbers   31

3 Journalists @Work: Remix & Reboot   53

PART II: REPORTING: PARTNERING WITH PROCESSORS   79

4 Wwword Slinging: Online Story Structures & Strategies   81

5 News Gathering and Reporting: New Tech, New Tricks   117

6 News Gathering and Reporting: Time-Honored Techniques & Tools   151

7 In Verification Veritas   187

8 Acquiring Story Assets   227

PART III: THE DIGITAL ASSEMBLY LINE: NEWSROOMS TO NEWS PAGES   261

9 Processing Workflows: Transforming Assets Into Content   263

10 Packaging Assets & Publishing Articles   301

11 Mobile Journalism: News on the Move   331

12 Journalism: "It's A Grand, Grand Caper."   355

Glossary   375
Works Cited   403
Index   431

ACKNOWLEDGMENTS

It gives us great pleasure to write this section of the textbook because it means so much to authors and the people who help them – and there were many. Let us begin by thanking Margaret Farrelly, Editor of Media and Journalism Studies at Taylor & Francis, for leading this project to the finish line. At USC, we acknowledge the wonderful work of Christina Campodonico. So: To all of you, thank you!

Focal Press commissioned this textbook due to the efforts of Acquisitions Editor, Megan Ball, Associate Acquisitions Editors Michele Cronin, Katy Morrissey, and Deirdre Byrne. Brianna Bemel devoted many hours to making suggestions for its early development. After Focal Press became an imprint of Taylor & Francis, Ross Wagenhofer, Editor of Broadcasting and Communication, graciously helmed the effort. Nicole Salazar was wonderfully supportive, bringing efficiency and attention to detail throughout a long process. Carlin Reagan and Matthew Scott provided able assistance.

Special thanks go to Editorial Assistant Priscille Biehlmann for all she did to bring this project to print. And we're grateful to Copy Editor Martin Pettitt, whose sensibilities, eagle eyes, and patience were invaluable. The exceptional work of Jess Bithrey and Swales & Willis helped immeasurably with the production of the text. We also want to acknowledge the contributions of the anonymous reader who provided such excellent feedback. The helpful comments improved every chapter in the book, and for that we extend our grateful appreciation.

Thank you to all the journalists who took the time to give us interviews for this book. They are a busy lot and we are grateful. In the writing of the book, Dr. Neal Krawetz, an expert on forensic methods of authenticating pictures, examined an early draft about this topic. He kindly sent us a careful and complete response, teaching us quite a bit about the metadata accompanying photographs and correcting our errors.

Finally, we thank those companies and organizations, especially Wikimedia Commons and the Creative Commons License that let us reprint the graphic content. Many of the points we addressed might have remained trapped in text, without these permissions given that let us put pictures to print.

Joan Van Tassel: I am grateful to all those people who gave me knowledge and inspiration. At the beginning of my work as an author at Focal Press, I must give a tip of the hat to then-Editor Marie Lee, now Executive Editor at MIT Press, for giving me a chance. Thank you! And I am deeply indebted to Tim Vos for allowing me to participate in the University of Missouri, Columbia Conference on Digital Disruption to Journalism and Mass Communication. I learned a great deal from the wonderful researchers and papers I heard there.

I could not have devoted so much time to this text without considerable support from so many people at National University, where I taught strategic communications and journalism. Chancellor Michael Cunningham, then-Provost Debra Bean, Deans

Carol Richardson and Karla Berry, and Chair Janet Baker gave generously of release time and financial support. I fondly recall all the encouragement and understanding of Louis Rumpf, Sara Ellen Amster, Sara Kelly, Laine Goldman, Federica Fornaciari, and Peter Serdyukov. And I received so much help from Karen Goldman.

Finally, I acknowledge the privilege of studying at the Annenberg School for Communications at the University of Southern California. I am forever grateful to my mentors and teachers there: Peter Clarke, Susan Evans, Peter Monge, Janet Fulk, Joseph Schmitz, Everett Rogers, Elihu Katz, and Daniel Dayan. The opportunity to study there for five years changed my life.

Mary Murphy: I want to acknowledge Christina Campodonico and all my fellow journalists who are riding with the technological changes to our reporting way of life.

Joseph Schmitz: I'm grateful to Joan Van Tassel and Mary Murphy for bringing me into their important project. Sharing ideas and writing the book has been deeply informative, satisfying, and fun.

Like Joan, my teachers and mentors from the Annenberg School for Communications at the University of Southern California transformed me and my views of the world in unexpected ways. Janet Fulk, Everett Rogers, Peter Monge, Elihu Katz, Tom Cummings, and Ron Rice at USC literally changed my life's trajectory, as did Ken Phillips in the City of Santa Monica. Their gift of agency – to share interesting and impactful ideas with others – lets us empower people far beyond our own limited horizons of time and space. Thank you.

It's also been a huge privilege to work with so many eager, thoughtful undergraduate students – especially "my" research methods crews.

FIGURES

1.1	On the job, on the scene	12
1.2	Student protesters in Tehran, Iran, 2009	13
1.3	News now	15
1.4	M2M and verification meet head-on	18
1.5	Bots gain followers quickly	26
2.1	Growth of number of internet users, 2011–2016	34
2.2	Secretary of State Michael R. Pompeo conducts a press gaggle	40
2.3	Forces influencing the competitiveness of a market	43
3.1	Legacy newspaper newsroom and early digital newsroom, before IT integration	65
3.2	The BBC Newsroom	66
3.3	Oh, wow! So that's virtual reality!	69
3.4	Augmented reality that you can share with your friends	69
3.5	Journalist and newsroom adaptation to emotional events	72
4.1	Immersed in content on their mobile phones	83
4.2	The inverted pyramid	89
4.3	Comparing structures of reports and narratives	90
4.4	Tools of the trade: peg, hook, and angle	93
4.5	Take Bessie to the bank	98
4.6	Contexts of a school board meeting	99
4.7	The news feature structure	102
4.8	Cave painting from Lascaux, France	103
4.9	Narrative structure	107
5.1	Don't let this be you	119
5.2	Screenshot: Wikipedia homepage on the day it went dark	126
5.3	Online record of bankruptcy filings in Davidson County, Middle Tennessee District	126
5.4	How validity and reliability affect gathered data	135
6.1	Strong south-westerly winds ripple the water	157
6.2	Hi, I'm a dog	159
6.3	Buzz Bissinger makes a point	162
6.4	User interface, Tails Operating System	180
7.1	Created, 1894: Charges of fake news and sensationalism are not new	189
7.2	Triangulation in navigation	195
7.3	Protess method information source categories	199
7.4	Screenshot: Whois domain lookup page	207

7.5	Analog and digital: Two ways to measure and present the same underlying reality	208
7.6	Making continuous information into discrete digital data	209
7.7	Metadata makes life easier	209
7.8	Screenshot: Home page with input fields for www.fotoforensics.com	211
7.9	Screenshots: Metadata structural file, IPTC, and EXIF	212
7.10	Blue eye	215
7.11	Recreation of opening shot of film, "The Blair Witch Project"	217
7.12	Where is he? A green screen lets editors substitute any image behind the person	217
8.1	The difference between design of a newspaper front page and the *Daily Breeze* online homepage	230
8.2	Preparing to acquire multimedia story assets	234
8.3	Controlling lens settings	237
8.4	Rule of thirds, vertical and horizontal	238
8.5	Example of shallow depth of field and bokeh	239
8.6	Microphone pickup patterns	248
8.7	Handheld microphone	248
8.8	Lavalier microphones	249
8.9	Shotgun microphones	249
8.10	Clipping in audio is worse than in football	250
9.1	Transforming information to news	265
9.2	Pre-processing workflow: Getting ready to get rolling	267
9.3	Story structuring apps: Mindmap and timeline software	268
9.4	Copy processing workflow	273
9.5	Watch those hyphens: This headline went viral on the Net	273
9.6	Mind-map or workflow process diagram of annotated story outline	275
9.7	Photo processing workflow	276
9.8	Cropping to the story	277
9.9	Histograms of cropped grayscale image, before and after adjustment	278
9.10	Original photo and photo corrected for exposure and detail	278
9.11	Video asset processing workflow	281
9.12	Editing workflow for video and audio	283
9.13	Details of sweetening workflow	284
9.14	Audio-only processing workflow	286
9.15	Effect of polio vaccine on incidence of polio worldwide	287
9.16	Data processing work flow	288
10.1	Structure of Alciato's "Emblems"	303
10.2	End-to-end online news content editorial workflow	304
10.3	From story to narrative	306
10.4	Storyboarding the multimedia story	307
10.5	The linear-embedded article structure	308
10.6	Hierarchical narrative article structure	309
10.7	Nonlinear narrative article structure	310
10.8	Workflow to assemble the online news package	310
10.9	Technology in online publishing, distribution, and consumption	315
10.10	Web home page wireframe and article page mockup	317

FIGURES

10.11	Chartbeat dashboard mockup	322
10.12	Eye-tracking user scanning: The F-pattern	323
10.13	Eye-tracking user scanning: The Z-pattern	323
11.1	Diffusion of Innovations: How new ideas and products spread	333
11.2	Smartphones give users a gazillion ways to share content	337
11.3	Users just say no!	337
11.4	Workflow for mojos in the field	339
11.5	Newsrooms can reach mobile users who are in a GPS-defined area	340
11.6	Welcome to 5G wireless infrastructure!	342
11.7	Mobile users like short *and* long-form stories	345
11.8	How mobile users check out content	346
11.9	New techs, new models – new screen sizes	346
11.10	A general systems model of newsroom workflow	350
12.1	Russia invades Ukraine, May 24, 2018	357
12.2	News: Breaking it or faking it?	360
12.3	Artificial intelligence model: Based on brain neural networks	363
12.4	Open up the inverted pyramid to add a "methods" graf	368
12.5	Journalists build a personal brand on social media	368
12.6	Protests in Ferguson, Missouri	370
12.7	Two tweets from journalists (both women)	372

TABLES

1.1	Digital changes everything	15
2.1	Percentage of U.S. adults reached each week and size of audience/user base, by consumer device category	35
3.1	Ten roles of the press	55
3.2	Differences in news production between traditional and digital, online organizations	60
4.1	Ten stories journalists can tell with data	110
5.1	Information-gathering method, reporting strategy, and article type	119
5.2	The Guardian game buttons: Reader assessment of expense claim	137
6.1	Interview preparations	163
6.2	Interviewing with Tech: Cues, pros and cons	164
7.1	Metadata types and sources	210
7.2	An informal translation of technical jargon	212
7.3	Finding fakery	215
9.1	Fictitious aircraft flights at the Santa Monica Airport (SMO)	290
10.1	Story and structure	304
10.2	Comparison of communication affordances between non-interactive media and networked digital media	312
10.3	Affordances play well together	314
10.4	Parsing the micro-promotion	320

PREFACE

The authors honor the dedication of journalists who struggle to deliver accurate, timely information about the novel coronavirus pandemic to the people they serve. Their commitment to informing the public about this global catastrophe and its consequences, even as reporting itself carried risks for them and their families, is truly heroic.

DAVID FALLIS, APRIL 5, 2020, DEPUTY EDITOR FOR INVESTIGATIONS, *WASHINGTON POST*

The novel coronavirus pandemic brings into sharp relief the critical need for what we do as journalists. We are the eyes and ears of the public, gathering information and distilling it into stories so readers can make informed decisions. I believe our mission, especially in the investigative field, is to serve the public interest, writing stories that reveal otherwise hidden, obscure, or unrecognized information. The pandemic only reinforces this.

When the pandemic struck with its full force, our entire investigative unit – 21 writers and 4 editors spread across the quick-strike and long-term teams – shifted to virus-related reporting. The challenge for us is that the pandemic is a moving target. As soon as we publish, the framing has changed. We realize that pandemic stories, about topics such as the lack of widespread virus testing, will likely be revisited again and again at successively deeper levels in the months and years to come. Our strategy is to investigate and write the most authoritative account possible in the moment and then move on to the next story target.

The pandemic reminds me in some ways of *The Washington Post* newsroom response after 9/11 – all hands on deck for months after that day of the attacks. The key difference, however, is that the pandemic is a breaking news event that repeats and redefines itself day after day. The number of people the virus has infected and killed continues to grow. We have no idea when we will reach the turning point.

Physically, all of us within *The Washington Post* are working remotely from our homes, which complicates everything. We only see one another virtually, and we only do so in scheduled conversations by videoconferencing. All of us have loved ones that we care about and we have our own safety and health to look after. Some of us have young children in school, shaky internet connections or cramped workspaces. Yet for weeks we have continued the mission exactly as before. This may continue for months. All of us are committed to the journalism and feel a deep sense of responsibility to our readers, who need the most up-to-date, authoritative information possible. Lives depend on it.

INTRODUCTION: THE GIST

Here we are, well into the 21st century, replete with digital communications technology in our pockets, purses, and briefcases, on our desktops, and perhaps on our wrists or in front of our eyes. Our users, publics, and audiences? They're similarly outfitted: Hello world!

These tumultuous times burst with stories that need telling and events that need explaining, analyzing, and clarifying. The long arc of digital development, still in its infancy, already opens up new directions for all the content-creation industries. Notably, the entire news biz morphs as journalists work in a field teeming with innovation and experimentation. And these transformations promise to continue into the foreseeable future.

Where will you fit into all this? How can you plan your career in journalism in the face of such a rapidly changing environment? One good formula: Explore, prepare, and adapt! While you can't (exactly) plan your future, you *can* equip yourself with the knowledge, skills, and your inquisitive temperament to make the most of whatever future you encounter.

The whirlwind of digital technologies brings new opportunities – along with new practices, restraints, and ethical considerations. Continuous innovation demands constant learning to stay current with ongoing change. As generations of emerging journalists before you, you will need to understand the core principles and traditions of this profession. These fundamental precepts provide needed guidance to meet widely shared expectations for gathering and reporting news. This book also advocates close adherence to the large body of received wisdom (often garnered from painful experience) that guides working journalists and enables them to responsibly serve their audience, publication, public, and history.

When we first decided to create this text, we soon realized that each of us wanted to help journalists succeed, whether they were novices or seasoned journalists. We believe that we can help students most by:

- Adhering to the revered truisms of journalism – truth, accuracy, fairness, independence, and public service.
- Acquainting you with those skills that you can acquire now.
- Suggesting how you can shape and hone needed skills.
- Imparting a journalism-oriented digital vocabulary.
- Preparing you to anticipate and embrace the near future with its myriad opportunities and challenges.

We've strived to create a text that isn't boring or hidebound. Many chapters include sections called *Vox Verbatim,* quotes from one-on-one interviews for the book, featuring Mary Murphy asking working journalists and news content creators about their work. You may already know many of them: David Fallis, Deputy Investigations Editor at the *Washington Post*; CNN digital producer and correspondent Ashley Codianni; *Guardian* reporter Les Carpenter; Gabriel Dance, Deputy Investigations Editor at *The New York Times*; and Brandi Buchman, reporter for *Courthouse News*; and other notable practicing journalists.

We organized chapters to give students a beginning-to-end understanding of how journalists work online:

- **Part I: News Now**
  - **Chapter 1** gives you the view from 30,000 feet, explaining how digitization and global networks changed the overall environment for news and information.
  - **Chapter 2** summarizes how the news industry adapted (and continues to adapt) to the technological changes sweeping the globe.
  - **Chapter 3** examines how journalists work now and what you can expect in the workplace, from pay and hours to story promotion and personal branding.
  - **Chapter 4** covers how to think like a digital journalist, creating digital news stories: Participative and interactive, with embedded multimedia content.

- **Part II: Reporting: Partnering with Processors**
  - **Chapter 5** delves into how online information helps trained journalists discover secrets and uncover stories.
  - **Chapter 6** considers the valuable lessons of traditional shoe-leather reporting and suggests when you should rely on reporting in-person in the real world.
  - **Chapter 7** specifies the truth-in-news requirements that you need to understand to publish accurate stories. And it shows how digital tools offer remarkable ways to verify online media, confirm sources, content, and reports.
  - **Chapter 8** gives you a practical guide to capturing multimedia assets — photographs, videos, audio podcasts and clips, data visualizations, and interactive opportunities.

- **Part III: The Digital Assembly Line: Newsrooms to News Pages**
  - **Chapter 9** describes how you can transform story assets, including all the multimedia content, into content that works in online articles and publications.
  - **Chapter 10** outlines how journalists put all the pieces together so that multimedia stories travel over networks to platforms, sites, and users. It's a packaging job that demonstrates how digital distribution differs from traditional paper-based circulation.
  - **Chapter 11** analyzes what it means for news organizations and journalists that users access news primarily from their mobile phones. It shows how to write and package news stories and how newsrooms adapt to publishing for mobile devices.
  - **Chapter 12** stands by itself, summarizing the main points of the book: The importance of journalism, the primacy of user choice, the pervasiveness of ongoing change, the professional skills required to "do" digital journalism, and how new journalists entering the news industry can handle the demands of such an important job and seize the opportunities journalism offers.

INTRODUCTION

We tried to bring innovative presentation modes into the text. We broke up each chapter into readable chunks; sections labeled *Chapter Learning Objectives*, *The Gist* (a summary of what to look for in the chapter), and *Takeaways* and *Key Concepts and Terms* (what you should know after reading the chapter). We end each chapter with an *Advancer* to prepare you for the next one. These chunks help focus your attention on the most important ideas and topics and let you know what to expect. We carefully designed *Exercises and Activities* to encourage experimental, practical activities that bring the most important concepts, resources, and skillsets into the realm of your personal experience.

Throughout the book, we show how digital journalists adhere to (but sometimes adapt) long-standing journalistic standards in the real-time reporting environment of now. We sprinkled *Pro Tips* in the chapters to inform you about common practices. There's a more informal side to this book, too. We wrote section headings that will remind you of internet phraseology, and livened things up with some fun puns, alliterations, and jokes. (And we shared some tall tales and clever tricks of our trade.)

You'll find other resources on the website: www.routledge.com/9780240824185. We hope that you will share some of the resources you discover with your present and future colleagues.

And we wish you all the best as you claim your future!

Warm regards,
Joan Van Tassel, Mary Murphy, and Joseph Schmitz

PART I

NEWS NOW

1

BE HERE NOW: THE VIEW FROM 30,000 FEET

Chapter Learning Objectives

After reading this chapter, students will be able to:

1. Understand how the COVID-19 global crisis highlighted the importance of accurate and timely news reports.
2. Describe the current media and communication environment of the news industry.
3. Evaluate the effects of many-to-many communication.
4. Analyze how new communication technologies and new media platforms enable news reporting and responding in real time.
5. Summarize the crisis of credibility that journalism faces today.
6. Appraise proposed solutions to the decline in trust of the news media.
7. Consider the role of verification in the news.

> The coronavirus is a fierce reminder of just how much we need credible journalism, especially in times of crisis.
>
> – Mark Hertsgaard, March 25, 2020

THE GIST

In the opening months of 2020, journalism stepped up. The world reeled as a contagious, lethal virus challenged the lives and economic well-being of hundreds of millions, perhaps billions, of people. Journalists sounded the alarm publicly before anyone else, including world leaders, public health officials, and medical professionals. They used every tool in their kit – new tech, old tricks – to wake people up to the growing threat and held leaders accountable for their actions and failures to act. That's their job and they fulfilled their mandate.

This first chapter begins by describing the decisive role that journalism played as the coronavirus crisis unfolded. That clarion call by journalists to focus public attention on an existential danger provides a vital lens for this textbook, demonstrating why students must master the methods that online, multimedia journalists use to produce accurate, timely, and trustworthy news reports. In addition, the consequential coverage of the unfolding pandemic also highlights the importance of the global communication networks underlying the reach and impact of 21st-century news.

Chapter 1 covers how real-time digital communications transformed many aspects of traditional journalism. Modern fiber optic infrastructure dramatically increased the speed of all communications. But that's not all. In addition to a faster network, it's a two-way network, enabling interactive public conversations among billions of people that take place in near real time. For journalists, the advance in real-time delivery of news from media isn't new (think TV's live satellite transmission). However, *on the record written responses to the news* by potentially anyone on earth have never occurred in real time before.

Now we're all adapting to **many-to-many** *interactive* communication, or **M2M**, bringing with it a multiplicity of ideas, perspectives, and beliefs that challenge the worldviews of just about everybody, including national leaders and mainstream journalists. By 2016, the virtually instantaneous spread of viral news over the internet was commonplace old news. The powerful effects of M2M exchanges astonished leaders everywhere as it became clear that this communication form could re-shape social and political realities with unprecedented speed.

At the same time, the stark economics of digital publishing caused many local publications to downsize or close their doors altogether. People in many locales lost their connections with familiar sources of news – they couldn't see themselves or their lives reflected in the big-city news. Quite naturally, individuals tend to privilege the views of their own social network – family, friends, and colleagues – over those far-away elite news media journalists.

The rapid changes in the communication environment and the empowerment of anyone with an internet connection created a crisis of credibility for the news industry – its audience no longer passively accepted editorial pronouncements. The M2M network enabled people to seek their own sources and to do their own research from the largest information archive in history. Journalists increasingly faced demands for transparency about how they gather, produce, and publish news, requiring answers to such questions as: "What do you know?" "How do you know it?" "How did you verify the information?"

News organizations realized that they must face and find solutions to the decline of public trust in mainstream journalism. Many newsrooms explored powerful new ways of gathering, explaining, and telling news stories to foster public trust in the news. Ironically, the critical needs of the public for accurate information during the coronavirus crisis may offer journalists the opportunity to enhance the credibility of professional journalism.

And in the midst of all this transformation, essential elements of the profession *have not* changed: The responsibilities that journalists have to the public and reporters' commitment to long-held values of accuracy and timeliness remain obligatory.

Rarely has journalism been more integral to people's survival around the world. Stay tuned.

INFODEMIC: REPORTING IN THE AGE OF COVID-19

Early in 2020, governments and their citizens around the world struggled to understand the danger posed by COVID-19. They needed to know the basics – how the virus spread, how to recognize the symptoms of infection, what to do in case the symptoms appeared, and where to go if their symptoms worsened. Some people required the answers to even more detailed concerns, such as immune-compromised individuals, medical professionals, hospital administrators, and local officials.

In many countries, the governments couldn't or wouldn't provide accurate, timely information. In the vacuum, misinformation and disinformation about the coronavirus pandemic inundated the internet, circulated by governments, agencies, organizations, and individuals to dodge blame or to support their particular aims. The maelstrom led the World Health Organization (WHO) to characterize the resulting confusion as an "infodemic."

The rapid spread of the coronavirus crisis raised the stakes for accurate news. The crisis stands as a stark indicator of just how important professional, trustworthy journalism is when reality bites. Get accurate news – and social distancing "flattens the curve" of a rising number of cases. Get fake news – and beach-going spring breakers spread the virus around the world, as shown in this heat map posted on Twitter.com at https://tinyurl.com/wtrmav7.

The press stepped up to meet the crisis head-on. News organizations scrambled to sort fact from fiction, science from opinion, and reality from hope. Newsrooms struggled to find qualified experts so they could report the known facts to a frightened audience. They also recognized their responsibility to convey the seriousness of the spread of COVID-19. Equally important, ethical journalists took care to prevent public panic by avoiding sensational language and images, speculation, and mere rumor (Kwan, Wardle, Webb, Townes, & Chen, 2020).

By downplaying the significance of events unfolding in January and February of 2020, administrations in the United States and the United Kingdom made reporting on the growing threat more complicated (Sullivan, 2020). For example, U.S. President Trump characterized COVID-19 as a "hoax" (Schlesinger, 2020) and the U.K. Prime Minister Boris Johnson insisted that people should wash their hands and go about their "business as usual" (Guardian Staff, 2020). As a result, the public faced conflicting messages about the virus: The press reported a serious evolving danger; leaders seemed to regard the stories as overblown.

Despite the casual dismissal of the risk by some leaders and conflicting messages blanketing the internet, news organizations continued to report the unfolding crisis. As more reports of the virus' impact in Italy surfaced, journalists awoke people to the growing threat. Compelling stories and images from China, South Korea, and Italy, combined with warnings from public health experts and medical professionals, finally convinced substantial segments of the population to demand action.

As the crisis came into focus, strong disagreement about how reporters should cover leaders' remarks came to the fore. How should journalists cover press conferences when leaders make misleading and false statements that can have deadly consequences? Should they confront speakers? Should they fact-check in real time or wait until after the presser? These questions were particularly salient for broadcast, cable, and live-streamed video coverage.

Some argued that by simply retransmitting incorrect information, journalists were complicit in the "fake news." *Washington Post* media ethicist and columnist Margaret Sullivan explained the dilemma the press faced:

> The reflexive media urge, deep in our DNA, is still to quote the president without offering an immediate challenge. That's why we continue to see headlines and chyrons that parrot his [Trump's]words directly, no matter how misleading: That the virus will disappear, that it's not inevitable that the disease will spread, that a vaccine is coming along "rapidly," [that the United States is] "very, very ready" to deal with whatever happens.

Sullivan wrote that media *do bear the responsibility to report in the public interest* rather than simply repeating and amplifying inaccurate statements – even if the speaker is the president:

> It's a dumbfounding notion, especially given Trump's proven propensity for lies and false-hoods. But now as a deadly disease, the coronavirus, threatens to turn into a full-blown pandemic, it's not simply bizarre in a way that can be easily shrugged off. It's not just Trump being Trump. And it's definitely not funny. It's dangerous.

Informing the public about danger on their doorsteps is the very heart of journalism – always has been. Journalism is our distant early warning system: Journalists are the scouts, monitoring the environment, scanning the horizon, and fanning out to the edge of the known world to bring back accounts of lurking menace and surprising delights. Sometimes the tigers really roam out there and no one would know they were being stalked as they worked, played, sang, and slept – except for the reports from those journalist-scouts.

The passionate words of journalist Brandi Buchman, reporter for *Courthouse News,* serve as a reminder of this most sacred responsibility of journalism.

Vox Verbatim: Brandi Buchman, Reporter, *Courthouse News*

When journalists think about covering coronavirus, one of the most crucial things they can do to inform their reporting overall is to understand - with great clarity - that every word they put onto a page or shoot into the social media stratosphere is consumed by a living, breathing human being and that human being may very well use that reporter's words to inform decisions they make regarding their most precious commodity: their life.

Know that. Own that. Respect that. Write accordingly.

Though this next part should always be the case, it cannot be reiterated enough during a public health crisis: Take time with information, even if it is five minutes more and it means you won't get that "breaking news" tweet or won't be "first" to publish. It is infinitely more important to be accurate and accurate the first time. This builds trust, credibility and reliability. Readers aren't stupid, they see this effort, they appreciate this effort and they respect this effort.

And lastly, during a pandemic, remember this - solutions come faster when transparency is prioritized. Hold powerful, influential people to account by asking the "impolite" questions that force them to address possible flaws in logic or policy. No, this often isn't comfortable for you as the person behind the pad and pen. But please remember: It was never, at any time, in your job description to make powerful people feel warm and fuzzy. You are there, as all great reporters have ever been, in service of the public.

THE GLOBAL BABEL-SPHERE: EVERYBODY CONNECTED TO EVERYBODY

Today may be the most exciting time to be a journalist since the mid-19th century, when the telegraph and photography brought new speed and power to news reports. Huge opportunities and challenges abound in our new many-to-many (M2M) communication environment. It's a new world: news at the speed of light, directly and personally to the world's billions of users.

Throughout history, people could communicate to each other in one-to-one (1-to-1) conversations and in small groups, few-to-one and few-to-few exchanges. In the 15th century, mechanical print technology expanded communication modes to allow one source of information to reach many people via books, newspapers, and magazines. This then-new form of public communication – one-to-many or few-to-many – sparked massive cultural and political change. Five centuries later, the 20th century brought radio and television, creating vast public audiences, using broadcast satellites to deliver news to global audiences in real time. Now there's the internet.

Audiences everywhere feast avidly at this information banquet. Social media platforms harnessed the internet's capabilities – making receiving, sharing, and participating in the flow easy and fun. At first, Facebook and other free platforms centered on everyday interactions between friends and family. Then social media exploded, pouring all kinds of information and news onto real-time platforms, including Facebook, Twitter, Instagram, Snapchat, WeChat, Weibo, VKontakte, XING, Taringa!, and others.

Social media platforms exist to serve diverse needs and attract users who then create their own content and messages. A broad array of people now create news: Eyewitnesses, citizen-journalists, activists, social and political elites, ordinary people, and journalists themselves all put the new news on the network. Immediate responses to breaking reports flood the web, sometimes also generating news, cramming ever more information about news events into ongoing (but fragmented) global conversations. Suddenly, trending topics and changes in public discussion become transparent to all who look.

With little hesitation, people meet, greet, comment, compliment, argue, and yes – threaten and bully – using social media platforms. Users post ideas, comments, jokes, complaints, recipes, and sometimes their most personal experiences and thoughts. Responses come from everywhere, sometimes from hundreds, thousands, and occasionally millions of people. Never before in human history has there been near-instant global communication among billions of people that allows constant information discovery, discussion, and conversation. *Never!*

MOBILE PHONES: PERSONAL PUBLISHING IN YOUR POCKET OR PURSE

Presto, join the convo! It's taking place everywhere, right now. And it's going on anytime for anyone with a mobile phone and an opinion. A smartphone (or other device), a network, a connection, and a social media account and you're in. Write or create media and hashtags and keywords index postings, allowing social media platforms and search engines to search them in near-real-time (and to archive them ... memorializing them, maybe forever).

Of the nearly 8 billion people in the real world (IRL), more than 60 percent have mobile phones; almost 3 billion of those phones are smart (Statista, 2019). In developed countries, about 87 percent of people use smartphones (Poushter, Bishop, & Chwe, 2018). Each day, some of these billions of people join ongoing conversations, publishing

FIGURE 1.1

On the job, on the scene
Credit: Tina Rencelj, istockphoto.com

gazillions of messages each day from home, work, café, car, bus, sidewalk, or crime scene.

This complex communication ecosystem calls for journalists who can thrive in the digital world. *The New York Times* observed in their impressive study of the news media landscape (2014, p. 90):

> We need more reporters and editors with an intuitive sense of how to write for the web, an interest in experimenting with mobile and social storytelling, a proficiency with data, a desire to engage with readers on and off our site, and a nuanced understanding of the shifting competitive landscape.

Fortunately for today's students, that description fits them well!

SOCIAL MEDIA PLATFORMS: HOSTING THE PARTY

Social media can originate news and also enable users to **amplify** it and discuss it. Recent examples of the speed and reach of news include The Fukushima nuclear reactor meltdown in 2013; the civil war in Syria; the massing of Russian-supported troops and tanks in the Ukraine during 2014 and 2015; the 2015 terrorist attacks in Paris; and the 2016 Orlando, Florida mass shooting. M2M platforms played essential roles in enabling sociopolitical upheavals like the UK's Brexit vote, Donald Trump's successful presidential campaign, and the rise of populism in Europe. In 2019, governments trembled before the internet's power, with Iran, Russia, and 18 other countries limiting access to the network by its citizens (Sherman, 2019).

In each case, social media facilitated the speed, reach, and effects of the story. The power of M2M to alter the global status quo became apparent early in its development. During 2009, a student uprising that began in Tehran and later spread throughout Iran, shocked people around the world. This failed uprising presaged the future spreadability of news, a harbinger of the connected world to come.

A College Student Dies on the Internet: How the World Came to Understand The Power of Crowdsourcing, Texting, and Flash Mobs

It started with one phone call.

According to *Guardian* newspaper reports (Tait & Weaver, 2009), an Iranian living in the Netherlands answered a call from his friend in Tehran, who said he had just taken part in a student uprising. The friend recorded – on his mobile phone – a video showing the horrific shooting of a lovely, vibrant young woman standing next to him. She bled-out from the shot and then died in front of him and subsequently millions of others. He uploaded his video to YouTube and Facebook. The video went viral when it was posted online, and "became one of the most potent threats faced by the Iranian regime in 30 years."

The Iranian students first protested a controversial presidential re-election. They used mobile phone texts to coordinate flash mob rallies, scattering as police arrived – and warning others on the way. Students used Facebook and Twitter posts to send out riveting reports for others to see. Soon, Iranians of all ages joined with the students, causing political turmoil throughout Iran for nearly a year. First-hand descriptions from eyewitness protesters – of police dispersing crowds by using weapons against unarmed students, while thugs-for-hire beat-up protesters – amplified the ensuing international condemnation of the Iranian government for its brutality.

Iran's government tried to block protesters' messages to Facebook and Twitter. But it couldn't shut down the entire Iranian internet because key government operations were tied to the net. Hearing of Iranian students' difficulties in posting to social media, U.S. university students established blind IP addresses that masked senders' identities and locations so that Iranian student messages could auto-post to Facebook and Twitter and enabled the students to accept contributions.

Although the protesters failed to overturn Iran's election, their savvy web-communication demonstrated the immense political power of the internet's social media. This crowdsourced, real-time M2M medium continued to take on international importance throughout 2010 as riveting stories, describing the Arab Spring, exploded into view. As this turmoil swept across the Middle East much of it was watched via al Jazeera's real-time, breaking news coverage.

FIGURE 1.2

Student protesters in Tehran, Iran, 2009

Credit: Breathing Dead, used by permission under the GNU Free Documentation License

In addition to big events, the **InterTubes** (a snarky term for the internet) continually buzz with socially meaningful events. Groundhog Day, deaths of prominent people within communities, powerful new computer chip designs, inside-the-Beltway political maneuverings, and must-see athletic events each get slivers of fleeting fame on the net.

If you think that only big events and big names make it to the M2M crush, consider the story of Justine Sacco. Not only does it highlight a frenzied amplification of a message, but it also provides an object lesson that demonstrates how focusing the power of M2M on a single person can humiliate and damage that individual. Here's what happened:

> Ms. Sacco, a public relations executive, tweeted from Heathrow Airport in London, UK, to her 170 Twitter followers: "Going to Africa. Hope I don't get AIDS. Just kidding. I'm white!"
>
> When Sacco woke up, she discovered a journalist had re-tweeted her comment to his many followers, and these comments went viral on the internet. Before Ms. Sacco landed, her company had fired her from her PR job. An aunt messaged that she had "almost tarnished the family."
>
> One Twitter comment ironically captured the sometimes mean-spirited, nasty nature of the Twitterverse: "We are about to watch this Justine Sacco bitch get fired. In REAL-time. Before she even KNOWS she's getting fired."
>
> (Ronson, 2015)

HOW THE INTERNET ATE THE NEWS INDUSTRY

The early internet was text-only – only one color (green), and no photos, video, or audio. The first newspaper to go online with a trial digital edition – the *Columbus Dispatch* in Ohio – delivered it to 3,600 subscribers via CompuServe. By 1982, when the experiment had ended, nine publications had joined the effort (Carlson, n.d.). The visual internet, the World Wide Web, arrived in 1989. Some of the news industry pioneers that launched websites included CNN, *The Chicago Tribune*, and the Raleigh, NC, *News & Observer* (Sanburn, 2011).

Online news exploded during the 1990s. By the turn of the century, most large publications had an online presence and more households subscribed to internet news services than to print newspapers (Sanburn, 2011). But losing subscribers made print publications less attractive to the advertisers that had begun reaching consumers via direct mail and targeted email.

During the past two decades, the loss of subscribers *and* advertising dollars ravaged the news industry. Not only did news organizations lose their profit-sources, but they also had to pony up large sums of money to address growing demands for online news. Users expected to choose from a wide array of stories, receive engaging multimedia content – and then respond, participate, and share their personalized news. These offerings required digital production equipment, content management systems and servers, and all the bleeding-edge software needed to put the·machines to work. News publications needed journalists who possessed multimedia and data skills and could adapt to the new digital processes, as they do now.

Many publications closed – battered by impacts from the dizzying rates of change that decimated much of the legacy news biz. Between 2005 and 2015, working journalists in the U.S. declined by 50 percent (Doctor, 2015). The rise of social media pressured many news organizations to make deals with platform companies like Facebook, Google, Twitter, and Instagram to gain online distribution. But news organizations paid huge prices for putting third parties between themselves and their users; they sacrificed their own unique branding and watched helplessly as distribution platforms gobbled-up the lion's share of news revenues.

At the same time, sources of news for online users proliferated with abandon. In addition to the platforms, web startups further segmented news audiences. All-online news sites and mobile sites competed for audience shares, gaining traffic and influence. Just a few of these services include *Buzzfeed, Breitbart, HuffPost, Politico, Drudge Report, FiveThirtyEight, Vox, Slate, Salon, Vice, ProPublica, The Verge, Axios, Newsmax,* and many others.

Users voted with their fingers to access the news they wanted. Although many large legacy media outlets remain among the most popular news sites, their users demand snappy home pages and stories with all the clickable bells and whistles that digital technology offers. Multimedia stories – done well – give digital users new richness while fostering a deeper understanding of complex stories.

For journalists, digitization wielded a two-edged sword: Traditional print and broadcast news organizations faced greater competition – but it also provided new, powerful tools for carrying out traditional newsgathering and reporting activities. Journalists can access information, images, and data online, making it available without trips to university, government, or corporate facilities. They can search public records and build backgrounds on companies and individuals. They can report compelling, information-rich stories by adding links, audio, video, data, graphics, and interactive elements to online articles, just as they use digital tools to enhance paper-based publications.

Since the founding of the United States, journalists have contributed to our public discussions. They continue to participate in our increasingly raucous conversations about – well, everything. Reporters appear on television and cable news shows, participate on social media, and in their publication's comment sections.

FIGURE 1.3

News now
Credit: Frimu Films via Creativemarket.com

But jobs in journalism, even when they are rewarding and interesting, are not easy. Making multimedia stories means more work hours, adding time-consuming and complex tasks to journalists' workday. In many newsrooms, there are fewer hands to share the work. News companies continue to downsize, laying off people and scaling back their operations. Even many profitable, internationally recognized media companies have cut budgets and shed staff, sometimes replacing former full-time journalists with freelancers working in the **gig economy**.

Table 1.1 maps the adaptive responses of three key news industry stakeholders to the ongoing industry metamorphosis.

TABLE 1.1 Digital changes everything

Type of Change	*News Industry*	*Practitioners*	*News Users*
Information Environment: Abundance of information			
Summary	Uncertainty over demand, economic, and market conditions	Lack of job stability Portfolio careers Perishable skillsets	Wide choice of news sources, publications, and formats; Broad range of users' actions
Economics	Consolidation of large news organizations; Local "news deserts" as publications downsize or close	Declining wages; More freelancers and contract employees in the gig economy	Decrease in leisure time and disposable income; Economics of limits for users' attention
Business Models	Freemium, Tiered pay models; Paywalls; Digital cross-platform distribution; Native and programmed ads; Sponsored news content	Entrepreneurial attitudes; Greater individual initiative; Less peer interaction	Willingness to pay for news unclear, except for premium brands or specialized news outlets; Will purchase financial information

(continued)

Type of Change	News Industry	Practitioners	News Users
News Production	Digital Assembly Line, from production through consumption; Automation	New skillsets to handle digital workflows; Lifelong education and skill acquisition	Users input via instant polls, comments, social media, and email
Distribution	Offline and multiple online channels; Algorithmic match of content to user; Copyright enforcement schemes	Create and remix content for multiple platforms and consumer devices; Solicit user content for inclusion	Proliferation of reception devices: mobile devices, and web-connected TV services; Individually tailored content – received when, where, and how desired
Content	Stories not limited in length; Multimedia stories; Virtual Reality (VR); Augmented Reality (AR)	Time-consuming, technology-intensive gathering of media assets and story creation	Immersion Interaction Buy new devices to keep up Share Information overload
Format Proliferation (text, audio, animation, graphics, video, data, interactives)	Capital expenses for equipment and software for multiple platforms and consumer devices; Urgent need for staff with high-end skill sets	Advanced technical skills needed to create finished content for distribution across multiple platforms and consumer devices	Constant electronic device and app upgrades to receive desired content
User Behavior	Need constant market surveillance to monitor trends in user and audience media use	Monitor user-generated and bottom-up content, as well as press releases and wire services; Journalist reports not always more privileged than user-generated content	Fragmented by media habits, age, lifestyle, interests, attitudes, and beliefs Comments Emails Share and retransmit content; Create and co-create content (UGC)

Source: Joan Van Tassel

REAL-TIME REPORTING

The lines between news, breaking news, and real-time news keep getting blurrier for journalists. Even when there's plenty of time to report and write a news story, when it's published, it can generate a torrent of follow-up stories that roll in almost immediately – as real-time as it gets. For example, Julie Brown investigated for several years to prepare her *Miami Herald* stories about the mysterious Jeffrey Epstein's sexual predation of underage girls (Hsu, 2019). She published story after story. Once news of Epstein's arrest in New York broke in 2019, the story went national. Brown then published stories about new developments, backfilling the articles with information she already had (and others lacked). Although most major publications chased the story as it unfolded in near-real-time, Brown kept her advantages over competitors through her unique contacts, insights, and her treasure trove of documents that filled a spare bedroom (Mazzei & Rashbaum, 2019).

Court proceedings provide good examples of near-real-time reporting because most courts prohibit using mobile devices or computers in the courtroom. Reporters take careful notes and report the events as soon as possible, during breaks, or when the proceedings finish. Adam Klasfeld live tweeted reports of the Epstein bail hearings for *Courthouse News* as soon as the hearing ended, then collected the documents, wrote an article describing the event, and added excerpts from court records. Bloomberg and CNN also covered the hearing live from outside the courtroom.

The public loves a good trial. Jim Armstrong, reporting for a CBS-affiliate, was a pioneer of live tweeting before so many judges imposed bans on the practice. Covering the trial of Whitey Bulger, the re-captured mobster who had eluded arrest for many years, Armstrong posted gripping real-time reports from the courtroom (Rogers, 2013). He was first to send the announcement of Bulger's guilty verdict – right as it happened. Considered novel and innovative at the time, Armstrong's real-time reporting increased his Twitter following bigtime.

For online journalists, this real-time reporting is part of the new normal: Writing on-the-fly comments, posting to Twitter (sometimes with photos or links to audio), taking notes, and writing up and filing a story in a few hours. Prospective journalists can develop these skills enough to move smoothly through the process. Practice makes it possible to observe carefully, take notes, take pictures, compose and post short messages, and promote the forthcoming story – all without compromising the reportage of the longer story.

It's daunting. Yet real-time reporting via an instant internet opens new possibilities for storytelling. The ability to bring your followers along with you is exciting, even thrilling "you are there!" journalism. But it also poses difficult problems for journalism enterprises.

For editors and reporters whose training and early careers took place in traditional media outlets, such real-time reporting is controversial. They generally accept the characterization of journalism as "a discipline of verification" (Kovach & Rosenstiel, 2014). Most journalism schools also emphasize this view of ethical practices. The bottom line for traditional practitioners: Stories do not leave the newsroom before they have been corroborated and verified as thoroughly as possible to determine the truth and accuracy of the "facts on the ground."

FIGURE 1.4

M2M and verification meet head-on

Credit: By Damnsoft 09 at English Wikipedia, CC BY 3.0, https://commons.wikimedia.org/w/index.php?curid=11802152

VERIFICATION: MEET PARTICIPATION

The new M2M pathway for real-time news emerged about a decade ago. *Guardian* journalist Matthew Weaver (Stelter, 2009) described it:

> Participants post on social media, more participants post pictures, then they upload videos on YouTube. It's only after a few hours that mainstream media confirm the story. Four or five hours – that's forever in Internet time … well, not really, but it's a long time for information to be pouring out before with everyone talking about the breaking news – and a news organization isn't going to publish it?

As more breaking news stories originate from real-time platforms, traditional requirements for "verification before publication" smack right into the windshield of the speeding M2M internet. It's the journalist's speed trap – a story gains wide exposure before anyone knows the underlying truths of the matter. Now journalists discover news in real time, along with everybody else. Reporters and newsrooms are caught between the rock of instantaneous communication and the hard place of verifying that breaking stories are accurate and complete.

WARNING: DON'T TRUST, VERIFY

News organizations have long relied on the scoop ("We're the first with the latest!"). Fierce competition plus the tyranny of online click-counting makes being first even more important. Yet journalistic values of accuracy and corroboration demand reliable verification and fact-checking processes. So, newsrooms try to handle news from social media carefully. They may stress that they have incomplete information and that the story isn't yet verified. Without journalists in the field, reporters can follow participants or citizen-journalists using mobile phones. With multiple eyewitnesses texting and tweeting, journalists may corroborate via incoming social media content.

Within newsrooms, conversations among journalists about stories often focus on how journalists may best fulfill commitments to accuracy and truth. (Chapter 7 describes cutting-edge techniques to corroborate, verify, or challenge news elements in digital environments.) Working journalists hold differing positions about verification – how to do it, how much is enough, and so forth.

News organizations use somewhat different criteria and standards that employees must meet before publishing. Some news professionals feel profound discomfort with changes to traditional processes, believing the most complete verification feasible should precede story publication. These journalists privilege the "discipline of verification" and the expertise needed to verify properly.

As Hermida (2012) wrote:

> Verification is widely considered to be at the heart of the occupational ideology of journalism. Yet, as Brennen contends, "facts are messy, difficult to determine and they are often dependent on interpretation," (2009, p. 301). The process of determining the facts traditionally took place in newsrooms, away from the public eye, as journalists considered conflicting reports, weighed up incoming information and made decisions on what to publish. Arguably, some of the process of journalism is taking place in public on platforms such as Twitter.

But the need for speed makes reflective approaches to stories difficult. When print, broadcast, and online journalists are co-located with online journalists, friction often arises between these different media types. Newspaper reporters don't "go to print" until they have the whole story – right and tight. Live television and cable journalists report breaking stories before all the information is known, so they must follow less restrictive policies than print journalists. But they try valiantly to nail down information before repeating it, emphasizing the partiality of eyewitness reports. Both legacy groups may disdain the verification of online reporters, who constantly update stories as information emerges. Three camps of opinion roughly correlate with the three industry segments. Not surprisingly, each viewpoint corresponds to the opportunities, constraints, and the distribution realities that these respective new segments face.

- *Traditional*: Verify first, publish later
- *Broadcast live – be careful, but publish*:
  - Publish in real time
  - Verify as much as possible
  - Carefully and frequently explain the lack of complete verification
  - Continuously update
  - Place journalists on the ground to verify as close as possible in real time
- *Online – get used to real time*: Publish in real time, continuously update, verify as you can, and report results and make corrections in updates.

BREAKING NEWS! JOURNALISM SUFFERS CREDIBILITY CRISIS

When the Edelman Trust Barometer, the Knight Foundation and Gallup, and the Pew Research Center for Journalism and Media agree that trust in the news media had dropped to historic lows – it's time to gather information, think – and act.

1. The Edelman Trust Barometer (2017) annually surveys worldwide levels of trust that people report about social institutions, including the news media. The Edelman, 2017 survey showed that distrust of the press had dropped to historic lows when only one-fourth of 33,000 people in 28 countries said they considered journalists to be "very" or "extremely" credible.

   - Richard Edelman observed: "People now view media as part of the elite ... The result is a proclivity for self-referential media and reliance on peers. The lack of trust in media has also given rise to the fake news phenomenon and politicians speaking directly to the masses. Media outlets must take a more local and social approach."

2. The Knight Foundation and Gallup (2018) survey of more than 1,200 respondents found that nearly 70 percent of American adults said that their trust in the news media decreased during the past decade. These declines showed partisan differences – 95 percent of conservatives reported declining news media trust while "liberals are about as likely to say that their trust in the media has not changed as to say it has decreased."

  * Yet most Americans (with less partisan divergence) believe media trust can be restored – while few respondents trusted all news organizations, most trusted some news outlets. The reasons for media distrust that respondents cited included:
    * Inaccurate or misleading reporting (alternative facts, lies, and fake news).
    * Biased reporting (slanted, unfair, and one-sided stories).
  * Conversely, respondents characterized trusted news outlets as accurate and unbiased, based on their assessments of the reporting:
    * Accurate: truthful, honest, ethical, and reputable reporting
    * Unbiased: fair, nonpartisan, and balanced reporting
  * Most people indicated that dimensions of trustworthiness mattered to them, such as news organizations' commitment to accuracy (89 percent), quickly and openly correcting mistakes (86 percent), and track-record of not publishing false or misleading content (77 percent). Almost 80 percent of respondents sought commitment to fairness, shown by making fact-checking resources available.
  * Respondents (71 percent) sought transparency to improve news organizations – like "providing links to research and facts to back-up its reporting."

3. The Pew Research Center, American Trends Panel, Barthel and Mitchell (2017) surveyed more than 4,000 panel members to compare changes in Americans' attitudes toward news media and news source types over the year from 2016 to 2017. Changes in "a lot" of trust were fairly stable for media source types during the year-long time period.

  * Just 20 percent of the Pew respondents reported "a lot" of trust in national news organizations. Local news was more often trusted "a lot" – by 25 percent of respondents, while 15 percent of respondents trusted news from friends and families "a lot." Only 5 percent of respondents trusted social media "a lot."
  * The picture for "moderate trust" – which combined "a lot" and "some" – greatly increased the level of trust reported for each news source type; it also highlights the growing importance of local news. Moderate trust in local news *increased* to 85 percent of respondents; while moderate trust for national news declined slightly to 72 percent. Three-fourths of respondents continued to moderately trust friends and families' news. Social media moderate trust increased to 37 percent – *but almost two-thirds of respondents don't trust social media news.*
  * Like the Knight-Gallup findings, the Pew Research Center found that Republican and Democratic trust of news after the divisive 2016 election diverged most for trust in national media and much less for local media. But regardless of political identification, three-fourths of the respondents trusted friends and family only moderately and two-thirds of them continued to distrust social media.
  * Pew respondents reported these considerations had "a large impact" on their assessments of news media trustworthiness. Four criteria stood-out: Roughly half of the respondents said the reputation/identity of the source(s) and the story's

publisher each have large impacts on trust. Almost one-third of respondents said, "they used their gut," while one-fourth said the identity of the person who shared the story altered a story's trustworthiness.

Although quantitative news media research tends to attribute differences in news media trust to political partisanship, age cohort, or other demographic attributes – journalists should also recognize their own beliefs, biases, and behavior to ensure their biases don't compromise their reportage. For example, journalist Matt Taibbi (2016) assigned some blame to journalists for the crisis of credibility brought about by lowered public trust in news media.

> We talked to pollsters, think-tankers, academics, former campaign strategists, party spokes-hacks, even other journalists. Day after day, our political talk shows consisted of one geek in a suit interviewing another geek in a suit about the behaviors of pipe fitters and store clerks and cops in Florida, Wisconsin, Ohio and West Virginia. We'd stand over glitzy video maps and discuss demographic data points like we were trying to determine the location of a downed jetliner. […] We were too sure of our own influence, too lazy to bother hearing things firsthand, and too in love with ourselves to imagine that so many people could hate and distrust us as much as they apparently do.

For many people in America, the mainstream media's coverage doesn't reflect their personal experience. It doesn't cover their lives and their problems, and they rarely see what they recognize as accurate portrayals of themselves and the people they know. This vintage quip from early TV comedian Groucho Marx expressed a common cynical view of big-city journalism: "Shall I believe you or my lyin' eyes?"

6 CREDIBILITY-BUILDING WAYS TO HELP JOURNALISTS WIN USERS' TRUST

The decline in public trust calls into question the truthfulness and accuracy of news itself. How do journalists balance speed with corroboration and verification, especially since scoop-speed fuels users' clicks? In newsrooms, in university journalism departments around the world, and in journalism-related foundations – vibrant conversations address news credibility issues. How can the news industry address public concerns, create sustainable business models, yet shore-up trust in news organizations and journalists with high standards for truth and accuracy? Raising public trust would seem to include the following changes (Adler, 2019):

- Fix #1: Publish more locally focused news coverage.
- Fix #2: Take a more "social approach."
- Fix #3: Increase the diversity of information sources.
- Fix #4: Adopt more transparent journalistic processes and practices.
- Fix #5: Redefine journalistic processes to include other methods.
- Fix #6: Assertively counter fake news.

When journalists add transparency to their articles, it adds to the credibility of the journalist, the news organization, and the story. Many students have a jump start on using social media and taking diversity for granted that they can bring into their journalistic practices. As they move into professional jobs, incorporating transparency techniques will help young journalists establish strong reputations for credibility:

- *Fix #1: Publish more locally focused news coverage*
  Every time a reporter meets someone from the community it creates an opportunity to learn about the locale and to develop a source. It's never been more important to stay close to the ground because the loss of small local newspapers has created "news deserts" that leave residents without local news. The Santa Monica *Daily Breeze* won a Pulitzer Prize for its exposure of improper use of public funds by a small-town school district superintendent. He resigned: Local news has weight and impact.

- *Fix #2: Take a more "social approach"*
  Reporters can foster user engagement by taking advantage of the publication's interactive opportunities: likes, comments, and email to editors or reporters. Some news outlets opt for comment moderation to stem noxious user participation – incivility, racist, misogynist, or foul language. News outlets can include new ways for users to offer leads or corrections to stories by providing direct newsroom contacts.

- *Fix #3: Increase the diversity of information sources*: The usual commentariat, a biased cast of characters – think-tank experts, politicians, political staffers, and campaign pros – no longer command automatic belief in their pronouncements by the public. NPR aims to increase the diversity of its sources, including the "gender, geographic, and racial and ethnic diversity of people heard on NPR as outside sources of news and opinion" (Jensen, 2015). If NPR can do it, you can too.

- *Fix #4: Adopt more transparent journalistic processes and practices*: An old TV news maxim to structure news stories said: "Tell 'em what you're going to tell 'em, tell 'em, tell 'em what you told 'em." Greater transparency would suggest: "Tell'em what you're going to tell'em, tell 'em, tell 'em *how* you told 'em." How to do that? Newman (2017) suggests:

  - *Provide work products whenever possible*: Make documents, interview transcripts or audio files, graphics outtakes, links, and databases readily available to users.
  - *Write methodology explainers*: Just as the nut graf explains why the story is important, an "emmo" graf or grafs would explain the reporting *modus operandi* or M.O. used to report news articles. Let users examine the methods reporters use to gather information, corroborate it, and verify factual claims and accounts, and then draw conclusions from the facts. Transparency would include the rationales for editorial decisions about anonymity, factual claims, conclusions, implications, and identification of areas of uncertainty.
- *Encourage the public to provide tips directly to newsrooms by providing training*: Many news outlets now use tip lines, encrypted email links, and other methods for users to give information to journalists and newsrooms. If news outlets offered users online training in best journalistic practices, it could improve the quality and quantity of news tips – and make verification processes more transparent and better understood. Savvy citizen-journalists could then better "partner" with news sites.
  - *Consider crowdsourcing to review and flag materials in databases, governmental materials, reports, court and public recordings, and transcripts*: The Guardian newspaper organized readers to check the expense accounts of British Members of Parliament. Readers examined records and flagged suspicious entries. Staff

journalists followed up, verifying many of those cases. Readers brought forth far more cases than *The Guardian*'s staff would have found without their readers' help: After the story, some MPs resigned and some failed to win re-election (Andersen, 2009).

Andy Carvin pioneered a way to engage users in the verification process. In 2011, Carvin asked his Twitter followers to verify posts that came in during the Arab Spring protests. Reporting for NPR, Carvin's reports made compelling reading. Silverman (2011) described this innovative work as:

> a living, breathing real-time verification system. [...] Carvin's followers are the engine that drives his reporting. They help him translate, triangulate, and track down key information. They enable remarkable acts of crowdsourced verification, such as when they helped Carvin debunk reports about Israeli munitions in Libya.

- *Fix #5: Redefine journalistic processes to include other methods*: The digital world will keep presenting new ways to "do" journalism. Broadcasters pioneered putting ordinary people who were eyewitnesses to an event live on the air. It's risky and things can go wrong, but when it works, it is credible and powerful.
  - **Participatory journalism**: Newer processes include recruiting users to do research, fact-checking, taking pictures, and recording videos and forwarding them to the reporter. Such relationships put the reporter in a role similar to a journalism professor – but the resulting original material, if it meets journalistic standards, can attract other users and spur them to action too.
  - **Curation**: Curation can be useful to users who like to drill down into the details of a topic. Curation is the process of sorting, selecting, and preserving the most valuable items in a collection, as museum curators do with artifacts, separating the wheat from the chaff. When reporters gather research for a project, they can collect a long list of resources that some users would find useful and interesting. Add links to the best of that material – and it's a double win because it shows how much research went into the article, adding to its credibility, and creates a valuable list for users.
- *Fix #6: Assertively counter fake news*: Fake news isn't new and it isn't news. Nevertheless, take disinformation seriously – debunk it whenever possible. Problems with disinformation (deliberately false reports) and misinformation (inaccurate reports) have existed since the dawn of communication, whether whispered, spoken, written, printed, broadcast, or posted. However, President Trump has popularized the term "**fake news**," creating genuine **FUD** (fear, uncertainty, and doubt) in mainstream journalism among ordinary citizens.

New powerful digital tools enable reporters to raise fact-checking and content confirmation to a whole new level. Data embedded in documents, photographs, and audio and video recordings can tell their own story that conflicts with the account of information counterfeiters. For example, check if dates, times, locations, technical details (camera, exposure, etc.), and editing changes conform to the poster's claims about a document, picture, or media clip? The absence or deletion of such data should send up red flags. (Important note: The same data can confirm important claims, as well.)

Software can also corral and map tweets from specific geographical areas: Is a Tweeter where she says she is? Reporters can compare observations and reports from the same event for accurate times, and locations. Different languages and descriptions often reflect reports from different groups, such as protesters and police, Hindus and Muslims, Chinese and Buddhists, left and right, or other opposing factions.

The reality is that one day, a news organization will face a fast-breaking news story coming from multiple sources – that will turn out to be an elaborate hoax, an entirely bogus story, published just for lulz or for more nefarious purposes. That's bad.

But the fake news that occurs as part of the global, real-time, M2M communication stream presents even more serious problems: Attractive lies travel much faster and farther than the plain-faced truth. People forward lies to others in their social networks, making it even more difficult to stop the spread of the misinformation. But follow-up corrections rarely get instant sharing like the shocking first report did.

Reporters who take fake news seriously are in sync with users. A recent Pew Research Center study with roughly 6,000 U.S. adults found that half of them think fake news is a *very big problem* in America (Mitchell, Gottfried, Stocking, Walker, & Fedeli, 2019). Respondents also had serious concerns about fake news effects. Two-thirds of those surveyed said that false news and untrue information "*greatly impacts Americans' confidence in government institutions*," and slightly more than half thought it *altered Americans' confidence in each other*.

Recall that the Knight Foundation and Gallup report (2018) identified similar levels of concern with fake news. *More than half of respondents also feared the fake news problem will worsen in the near future.* The good news (for journalism) is that most people don't blame journalists for fake news. Slightly more than half of the respondents held political leaders and their staff responsible and/or considered activist groups sources of fake news. And the bad news: More than half of those surveyed, expected journalists to fix fake news problems, a thorny task assignment indeed, given the social channels through which misinformation flows.

Disaggregating respondents reveals the expected divides between Democrats and Republicans about fake news: Republicans more often say that fake news is a big problem (62 percent) and that journalists publish much fake news (58 percent), while fewer Democrats (40 percent) think it's a big problem and even fewer Democrats (20 percent) think that journalists publish fake news. Younger respondents – who lean Democratic – are less concerned with fake news than older, Republican-leaning respondents.

When it comes to debunking fake news? Be that reporter!

DISINFORMATION: 6 KINDS OF FAKE NEWS

Claire Wardle (2016), a journalism verification expert, identified six distinct fake news types:

1. *Authentic material used in the wrong context*: Showing or citing factually true content that didn't happen in the claimed context.

2. *Imposter news sites designed to look like known news organizations*: A web site that mimics a familiar news brand, like *The New York Times*, but isn't the NYT site at all.

3. *Fake news sites*: Web sites that look like news sites, have stories like web sites, but don't provide actual news. Rather, these site operators manufacture false stories out of whole cloth or they rip-off and re-publish material from other sites, presenting the material as their original work.

4. *Fake information*: Content placed on a website that contains false information. In the 2016 U.S. presidential campaign, ads falsely told people that they could text an SMS number to vote, instead of showing up at their voting precinct.

5. *Manipulated content*: Digital forgery, altering content so it purports to say or represent something the originator would otherwise not say or show.

6. *Parody content*: Content created for humor or satire that is later passed off as real.

Altered content or authentic material, once taken out of context, can be difficult to spot. Fake news sites also fool people, especially persons who don't follow the news regularly. The growth of online news sites means that fewer users know the most genuine sources of reliable information. Indeed, a careful examination may be needed to recognize the difference between genuine news enterprises and a site established by a one-person opinionator with a keyboard and an attitude.

5 WAYS NEWS ORGANIZATIONS AND SOCIAL MEDIA PLATFORMS CAN IDENTIFY AND EXPOSE FAKE NEWS

1. *Crowdsourcing*: Use the audience to expose false, misleading, and inaccurate information to moderators and news outlets.

2. **Third-party verification**: Highlight false information by referencing specialized services that verify information on the internet, especially trending stories. Third-party verification sites include Politifact.com, Snopes.com, and Factcheck.org (a Project of the Annenberg Public Policy Center).

3. **Embedded data (metadata)**: Examine embedded data (metadata) in documents and media content to confirm or disconfirm accounts of who, where, when, and how the media originated.

4. **Flagging**: Identify debunked false information, fake news, fake sites, and their information to readers.

5. *Look for **bot army** distribution*: Software helpers spread disinformation and fake news across social media networks.

It's not just users who circulate fake news. **Bots** – robots – are executable software files that act without human intervention. Busy bots establish accounts on social media networks, name them, attach images of faces taken from internet sites, supply false geographic information, make up tag lines, and generate keywords. Once established, a bot can follow other bots (and real users), be followed, tweet, retweet, comment, and the like. One way to create a bot army is to have bots mutually follow each other. When these bots are added to the real users that they follow (and are followed by), bot traffic rapidly proliferates across social media networks.

Bots pose threats to users and communities in several ways (Echeverria & Zhou, 2017). These software executables operate on their own to send spam to users that contains computer viruses, malware, and advertising links. Techniques for manipulating opinions are effective because many companies, researchers, and reporters use metrics to track and report opinions on important topics.

Bot masters establish real accounts for bots masquerading as real persons to post and follow others. They use bots to **astroturf**, artificially establishing a false sense of agreement

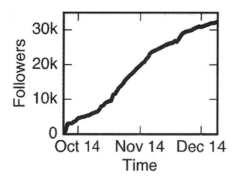

FIGURE 1.5

Bots gain followers quickly

Credit: By Bjarke Mønsted, Piotr Sapieżyński, Emilio Ferrara, and Sune Lehmann [CC BY 4.0 https://creativecommons.org/licenses/by/4.0)], via Wikimedia Commons

among a community. They manipulate opinion by having thousands of bots mention a topic to raise its popularity on social media trending lists. They program bots to follow each other, inflating the number of followers an account shows. Bots also, by voicing opinions from the botmasters' menu, make it (falsely) appear as if support for an opinion is more or less popular than it actually is. Finally, they time tweets so they appear more often in the tweet stream, making a 1 percent increase appear 80 percent more than the real number of tweets on a topic.

Darknet sellers supply entire botnet armies. Researchers have discovered botnets coordinating as many as 350,000 and 500,000 bots (Echeverria, Besel, & Zhou, 2017). During the 2016 presidential election cycle, both the Trump and Clinton campaigns deployed bots, both to increase their followership and to carry their messages (Guilbeault & Wolley, 2016).

Techniques to identify bots:

1. *Identity test*: Username or @name doesn't match image well.
2. *Ratio test*: The ratio of posts to follows and/or followers, when an account has tweeted or posted many times.
3. *Follower test:* Many followers are other bots, as bot-2-bot communication serves to build the impression of an active human network.
4. *Snark test*: Bots' inability to respond appropriately to humor, snark, irony, and sarcasm.
5. *English 101 test*: Poor English usage.
6. *Time zone test*: Timing of tweets indicates foreign time zone origins.

MISINFORMATION: EVERYBODY MAKES MISTAKES – SOME PEOPLE MAKE MISCHIEF

The problem with false news coming out and circulating at the speed of light is a new version of a much older problem. As humorist Mark Twain put it: "A lie can travel halfway around the world while the truth is still putting on its shoes." When news organizations discover they have published inaccurate information, they issue corrections. These correction processes don't always work effectively, especially for proliferating online news. It might take days, weeks, or even months to investigate the issue and publish a correction – with no assurance that original online users will ever learn about the correction.

Some online news venues provide corrections by proliferating corrections the way they reach many users – over their social media networks. Recently, researchers experimented to see if online corrections might work (Gillmor, 2019). The News Co/Lab at Arizona State University partnered with three McClatchy newsrooms, including the *Kansas City Star*, to find out if they could initiate viral news corrections using social media.

Here's how it worked: A story from the *Star* required correction. The research team used the Chrome browser plugin CrowdTangle by Facebook to learn who had shared the original story to their followers on Facebook and Twitter. The *Star* sent out corrections on their own Facebook and Twitter accounts. They sent Direct Messages to Twitter users and posted corrections on the timelines of Facebook users.

This experimental trial got mixed results. Researchers found that they *could* use the same social networks that first spread the incorrect *Star* story, to spread corrections. And many users who originally forwarded the original *Star* story later forwarded the *Star's* correction, but many other users did not. The test showed that the experimental processes were cumbersome and time-consuming. The researchers later encouraged Facebook to automate a one-button process in the CrowdTangle software and they requested the other social media platforms to integrate similar functionalities.

WHEN WILL USERS' HEADS EXPLODE?

Too much information (TMI) says it all. The production of knowledge and information from governments, companies, celebrities, universities, and media overwhelms almost everyone. One headline put it: "Knowledge Doubling Every 12 Months, Soon to be Every 12 Hours" (Schilling, 2013). The vast abundance of information about the world is new. During most of human history, people only had their senses, reports from people in their social group, and orally transmitted tales and their myths from past history.

But information abundance doesn't reduce our need for an accurate, timely, fact-based, depiction of the environment we inhabit. Indeed, history informs us that catastrophic failure often stems from poor choices, based on false beliefs. Given our politically divided, economically inequitable, technologically sophisticated, and relentlessly changing world – there may never be a greater need for timely, important, and accurate information than right now.

Increasingly, this is an excellent time for younger journalists to find work in online news. The business environment favors people who have fresh digital skills. The industry faces many challenges that will benefit from their energy and dedication to formulate innovative solutions.

People raised with digital devices and educated well after the computer revolution have experience forming relationships with others using social media. These competencies will be critical going forward as the news industry seeks new ways to understand and fulfill people's information needs.

The next chapters in this book seek to provide today's students with the digital tools they will need in the online news of tomorrow. This is a practical compendium, organized to bring together the ways of working that have evolved in today's newsrooms. From the new ways that reporters uncover information and data, use the new tools of analysis and verification, handle sources and conduct interviews, acquire and shape multimedia to tell interactive stories, and manage portfolio careers – we invite you to read the black print on the white pages and learn to create those wonderful colorful news pages on the web.

Buckle up.

TAKEAWAYS

- The advent of three technologies changed the media landscape: Digitization, global networks, and mobile, connected end-user devices. These three innovations gave rise to the many-to-many internet – a global, two-way, interactive network. An infinite number of users with their personal devices take information from and contribute information to the internet. Its size and reach amplifies news events. At the same time, it allows users to cocoon themselves in bubbles of information that they already agree with, confirmation bias that reassures them how right they are.

- More 24/7 coverage comes from more places, in more media formats, supplied by more people. Eyewitnesses to news events report before the journalists can. Reporters curate incoming user information posted on social media and on the internet until reporters arrive. Important breaking online stories require even more team coverage than print or broadcasting media, fully engaging staff in the newsroom and in the field. In the information explosion, curation becomes a really big deal.

- Journalists, experts, officials, celebrities – who cares what they think? In the past two years, social institutions in many countries and regions of the world have suffered large losses of authority and trust. Information from horizontal connections between peers is now valued more highly than information that is passed down vertically from privileged elites. Elites are bewildered. Non-elites are angry. As of yet, no one knows how this will play out. We are seeing a political game-changer in the making.

- Professional communicators – journalists, public relations and advertising practitioners, government officials and functionaries, and celebrities – are all trying to figure out how to communicate in this media environment. The loss of credibility particularly troubles journalists, who commit themselves to conveying truthful, accurate, and fair reports. Regaining trust is important because it's the value that journalism adds to the information mix. News publishers can no longer survive by selling consumers' attention to advertisers for a handsome revenue stream. Now they must attract users, based on the relevance, importance and trustworthiness of their news product: Trust is the new news business.

- Suggestions to increase the public's level of trust in journalists' accounts include:
  - Publish more locally-focused news
  - Take a more social approach and allow the audience to participate in the news-making and news distribution processes
  - Increase the diversity of information sources
  - Be more transparent in journalistic procedures and processes while reporting and publishing a story
  - Verify on-the-scene eyewitness reports from social media and include them in reports
  - Take vigorous steps to counter fake news

- The problem of fake news and online bots masquerading as humans is a serious one. Wardle (2016) identified six types of fake news:
  - Authentic material used in the wrong context
  - Imposter news sites designed to look like known news organizations
  - Fake news sites

- Fake information
- Manipulated content
- Parody content
- Six clues to suspect that bots may have delivered a news story, comment, or tweet are:
  - Username or @name does not match image well.
  - An account that has many posts or tweets, with a small number of follows and/or followers.
  - Many followers are other bots, as bot-2-bot communication serves to build an impression of the active human network.
  - Inability to respond appropriately to humor, snark, irony, and sarcasm.
  - Poor English usage.
  - Timing of tweets indicates a foreign time zone.

KEY CONCEPTS AND TERMS

- Characteristics of the news industry
- M2M, many-to-many communication
- Reporting in real time
- Journalism's crisis of credibility
- Solutions to stem the decline in trust of the news media
- Verification as part of journalists' jobs

EXERCISES AND ACTIVITIES

1. How do you expect the digital transformation of the news industry to affect your career in journalism?
2. How have social media many-to-many platforms changed society? The news business? Your life?
3. Find a recent report on how users can identify social media bots, written within the past two years. Describe what bots are, who uses them, how they work, and why users should be aware of them. Write a short 2–3-page story that warns student journalists about bots and informs them how to identify them.
4. If you don't have a Twitter account, this might be a good time to open one. Link your account to your mobile phone. Note how to send tweets to your account from your phone. In the next day or two, go to an event. Be sure to take a pen and notebook. From the event, text tweets to Twitter.com as it unfolds. Stay until it is over. Take notes, including going to the hosts or presenters and getting their names and correct titles. Finally, *immediately* write a 400–500-word story about the event.

ADVANCER

Now that we have looked at high-level differences between traditional news and the new news, we turn to see how the news industry works (and doesn't work so well) in the digital, networked environment. Chapter 2 begins by taking a closer look at the "people formerly known as the audience" and their news habits. Then it explores how the redefined relationship between journalists and users leads publications and reporters to adopt new processes and procedures.

Chapter 2 looks at how news organizations have tried to adapt to the M2M communication environment. Some organizations have changed their practices, while others have altered almost everything about how their operations function. Yet home delivery declined, subscriptions went down, while news advertising revenues migrated to internet and online companies. Now many news organizations struggle for revenues needed to support high-quality journalism.

Finally, the news industry faces intense competition. Trust is crucial. News professionals believe the public needs professionally verified news to raise the levels of trust, but the industry finds itself unsure how to adapt to prevailing news market conditions. Chapter 2 shows how market forces have made a difficult business environment for many news organizations – until the news media organizations find ways to develop reliable revenue streams.

2

NEWS BY THE NUMBERS

Chapter Learning Objectives

After reading this chapter, students will be able to:

1. Understand the changing business model of news media.
2. Compare the news habits and consumption of today's fragmented audiences with those of 20th-century mass audiences.
3. Analyze the implications of information bubbles.
4. Explain how audience behavior changes impact the business decisions news organizations make.
5. Describe the causes and consequences of increased competition on news organizations.
6. Consider how emerging new technologies may impact the news industry.

A highly centralized media system had connected people up to big social agencies and centers of power but not across to each other. Now the horizontal flow, citizen-to-citizen, is as real and consequential as the vertical one.

– Jay Rosen, *The People Formerly Known as the Audience*

THE GIST

Journalists and the public look at successful news organizations in human terms. They see journalism as bringing people important information that they need about the social, political, intellectual, and artistic events of the times. They think good news organizations have:

- A reputation for accuracy and reliability
- Influence

- Scoops and exclusives
- Insider sources
- Entertainment value

It takes professional expertise and organizational resources to build a reputation for excellence. And market conditions affect all organizations – organizations must have the resources to support management, coordination, infrastructure, and workers. With the right people and a healthy budget, they can reach more people faster on more types of media platforms. By attracting talented people in high-level positions to engage in their publication – public officials, influencers, and other journalists and news outlets – a successful news organization can help shape public opinion and policies.

Success doesn't come easily in the M2M global communication system. The adoption of digital technologies by both media enterprises and news consumers brings changes to all aspects of news work. Under the lash of technological advance, news organizations and journalists continue to adapt to meet the wants, needs, and behaviors of their audiences. It hasn't been easy. Complex news organizations find making these changes expensive, frustrating, and prone to unexpected failures. This chapter examines how the M2M internet, with its expanded possibilities, transforms the market conditions that, in turn, shape news operations, user reception and consumption, and the social influence effects of news media.

However difficult, news organizations must find ways to exist within a highly competitive global market economy. Although everyone who plays a role in a news company takes pride in journalistic accomplishments, a news organization's managers answer to boards of directors that demand financial metrics to evaluate performance. For media management, the metrics that matter include: 1) size and loyalty of the audience(s), 2) capitalization, 3) revenues, 4) operating costs, 5) profitability, and 6) **viability** (staying power). Chapter 2 looks at how managers, directors, investors, and donors assess the operation of news organizations.

Chapter 2 also looks at how the audience changed the news industry. It examines the current economic environment for news organizations and how they are responding to continuous technological change to remain viable. And it analyzes how market conditions frame the business decisions news organizations must make to survive and prosper.

PEOPLE GOT ① THE INTERNET, ② SMARTPHONES, AND ③ SOCIAL MEDIA ... AND THEN WHAT HAPPENED?

The short answer: Once these three innovations gained wide use – they rocked the conventional media world. Fire up the Way Back machine to the 1990s:

- Peer-to-peer sharing over the internet gobbled up the bricks-and-mortar retail music stores – moving music-buying almost entirely online.
- Online Netflix cratered Blockbuster retail stores and took down the video rental industry. Now we rent or buy films and whole seasons of TV shows online.

News media! It's your turn to face disruption. The creative destruction taking place for newspapers and magazines is a familiar scenario. And all these industries struggle before changing, crying, "You're killing me, internet!"

A Pew Research study (Barthel, 2019) captured the numbers from 2018:

- U.S. daily newspaper circulation declined 8 percent and Sunday circulation dropped 9 percent between 2017 and 2018, to the lowest level since 1940.
- Cable news was a bright spot for news, with revenues going up 4 percent since 2017, and 36 percent since 2015.
- Network evening news viewership held steady, but local news viewership dropped 10 percent between 2017 and 2018.
- Comscore StationView Essentials® data reported that in 2018, local news viewership declined 10 percent for morning news and 14 percent for late-night and evening news.
- Digital ad spending reached 49 percent of all advertising revenue, increasing from 43 percent in 2017. (However, about half of that revenue went to Facebook and Google.)
  - Mobile ad spending will grow at about 17 percent year-over-year between 2017 and 2022 (Marketing Charts, 2018).

The 2018 figures reflect substantial declines in newspaper circulation and local television news viewing, caused by changes in user media habits that precipitated the devastation of local news in the U.S. As viewers "shifted to a news consumption model that offers little revenue for the actual producers of local news stories, the business model for local journalism has collapsed. The drying up of ad revenue has accelerated waves of consolidation, cost cutting, and closures, further squeezing out locally owned outlets" (Tofte & Husain, 2019, p. 27).

Losing the News, an authoritative report by PEN America (Tofte & Husain, 2019), found that since 2004, the U.S. lost more than 1,800 local newspapers – leaving at least 300 U.S. counties without *any* local newspaper. Moreover, many local news outlets were acquired during waves of local newspaper consolidation – often backed by hedge funds with scant interest in small town residents' well-being. Thus, thousands of communities lost ongoing surveillance by journalists with deep roots in the community, assigned to a local beat and able to tap knowledgeable sources.

The coronavirus pandemic revealed the dangers of losing local news. Most closures shuttered publications with circulations of less than 5,000, creating "news deserts" for 3.2 million people, many in rural counties. In such deserts, people could not find breaking news about nearby COVID-19 threats, guidance from local officials to help counter the pandemic, nor emergency community public health resources.

The pandemic hit local journalism with even more economic bad news. As states restricted residents' movements, small businesses furloughed or let go many workers. More than ten million people in the U.S. applied for unemployment in the last two weeks of March 2020. Stay-at-home public health directives deprived local businesses of revenue. As they closed their doors, local advertising revenue collapsed (McEleny, 2020), taking down local news outlets – just as they were most needed. Waldman and Sennott (2020) warned: "A news desert combined with a pandemic is another public-health disaster waiting to happen. Such communities will either have no local information or rely entirely on gossip and social media."

Over the longer term, broadcast news revenues showed moderate growth – a 6.5 percent compound annual growth rate from 2011 to 2016 (Parker, 2016). Broadcasting properties don't bring in the spectacular profits of TV's heyday. But at least they're profitable, especially during election years, doing better than most internet-impacted industries:

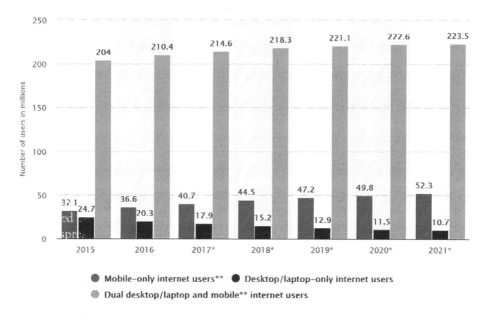

FIGURE 2.1

Growth of number of internet users, 2011–2016
Credit: Joan Van Tassel, using data from Internet Live Stats (2016)

The 2016 political season boosted cable TV news viewership 8 percent overall – CNN jumped an amazing 38 percent. Overall cable news revenues increased 10 percent.

However, a legion of new "cable cord-cutters" and internet-based subscription services such as Hulu augur some uncertainty for cable news in the future. In the U.S., internet usage went up, despite the 2008 recession dip, as shown in Figure 2.1. By 2012, as the economy improved, the internet reached 80 percent of the U.S. adult population; by 2016, nearly 90 percent of U.S. adults had home internet access. In 2019, the number of people in the world using the internet had surpassed 4.4 billion (Internet Live Stats, 2019). Equally important, the widespread diffusion of high-speed broadband connections fundamentally changed the nature of internet access.

Now people get media content from many devices. The precise number varies as new consumer devices come to market and push older technologies aside to make room for the rambunctious new media platforms. (Some fine day we may reach device singularity!) Table 2.1 shows the number and percent of people who used each device (type) to access content at least weekly during 2016.

Changing consumer behaviors make media companies, including news organizations, alter how they produce and deliver material. People want the content they want, where and when they want it on whatever device is most convenient for them. Consider how the distribution of TV entertainment programming has changed because of the proliferation of different kinds of consumer devices. One show that aired only via broadcast and cable now reaches its audiences in many ways (Lynch, 2015):

NEWS BY THE NUMBERS

TABLE 2.1 Percentage of U.S. adults reached each week and size of audience/user base, by consumer device category

Device	* Audience Size (in millions)	** Percentage of U.S. Adults Reached Weekly
TV	214	87%
Radio	225	93%
Connected TV	106	43%
PC	124	49%
Smartphone	187	82%
Tablet	83	37%

Credit: Based on data from Nielsen Research (2016, 2017)

- 45 percent of this episode's audience watched during its live airing
- 32 percent watched it via DVR within seven days after it aired
- 2 percent watched it on DVR between 8 and 35 days after it aired
- 7 percent watched it on video-on-demand within 35 days
- 6 percent watched it using a connected TV device, and
- 8 percent watched it digitally, streaming it on a PC, mobile device or tablet

People want to receive news wherever they are. According to the Pew Research Center (Mitchell, Gottfried, Barthel, & Shearer, 2016), more than 70 percent of U.S. adults follow national and local news somewhat closely, or very closely. And about 65 percent of adults attend to international news. The American Press Institute (2014) found that most Americans use as many as five devices or technologies to access news each week.

With all these devices, the following news habits stand out (Mitchell, Stocking, & Matsa, 2016):

- The popularity of accessing news on TV increases with age. About one-fourth of people 18–29 watch it, while 85 percent of people 65 and older do.
- Only 5 percent of young adults 18–29 get news from newspapers; but almost half of people 65 and over do. This low number of young newspaper readers portends trouble for newspapers in the future. And it suggests that one reason newspapers have declining revenue stems from advertisers' lower interest in reaching older people.
- About half of adults 18–49 access news often online (via PC, smartphone, and tablet). Then adults' preferences for online news access drops sharply for people 50–64 (28 percent) and even more for those 65+ (20 percent). Still, nearly one-third of people aged 50–64 get news online and one-fifth of the 65+ people do.
- Surprisingly, the largest group of users frequently accessing news via tablet fall in the 35–49 group (56 percent). Perhaps they are most likely to use tablets in the workplace.

- While the weekly reach of radio is high (93 percent of U.S. adults), only one-fourth of them often listen to news. Causes for the dearth of news listening could be that other programming is more interesting to listen to in cars than news, that many markets don't have news radio stations and that news formats on stations may need an overhaul to become more relevant and interesting to drivers.

The most frequent news consumers prefer their news on one kind of screen or another (Mitchell et al., 2016). Only 20 percent access news from traditional newspapers. It's an age-related phenomenon; nearly half of people over 65 still receive paper and ink editions, while only 5 percent of young adults 18–24 do. This ongoing digital disruption gives a new meaning to the old expression: "Hold the presses!"

HOW MOBILE MOVED THE NEWS NEEDLE

The Knight Foundation and Nielsen Research examined new mobile users' access and use of mobile news (Knight Foundation, 2016a, 2016b). These research findings are particularly useful because they don't have the serious limitations of self-reported behavior. Rather, software meters, installed on users' phones, automatically collected these users' *actual behavioral data*.

Eighty-nine percent of the 162 million mobile U.S. users (144 million) accessed news on their smartphones or tablets, while only 11 percent didn't (Knight Foundation, 2016a). The diverse mobile audience reflected U.S. population demographics with respect to gender, race, and ethnicity. Adults who use their mobile phones for news were slightly older with higher incomes and more education than the overall U.S. population.

The most popular three categories of news account for 69 percent of mobile users' news content choices:

- Weather – 32 percent
- Current events (including international news) – 22 percent
- Reference and education – 15 percent

Mobile newsflash 1: News is now personal – literally. Mobile phones go with us in hand or in our pockets or purses, always on or near our person.

Mobile newsflash 2: News is an important way for people to use social media sites and chat apps, especially diverse, young adult audiences (18–24). Seventy percent of Facebook users navigated from that site to a news site every day (Knight Foundation, 2016b). BuzzFeed, Reddit, Instagram, Pinterest, and Snapchat also create bridges for millennials to reach mobile news sites. In addition to these social sites, it is important to note that Wikipedia plays an important role in this emergent news ecology. One-third of mobile users visit Wikipedia each month to dive deeper into subjects they first encountered on other sites. Traditional digital users also use the site. The growth of traffic to Wikipedia from news sites has an important side-benefit – it directs news traffic to fact-based information in an era of fake news.

WHO TO WHOM FOR NEWS?

M2M communication and social media afford new, big pathways (more like expressways) for news. According to Mitchell et al. (2016), nearly two-thirds of adults said that friends and family were important sources of news; but only 10 percent saw them as the most important sources. Professional online news organizations remain important too – roughly one-third of the persons who accessed news online got it from established news organizations, while only one-fifth just relied on people close to them.

Quick Poll! What are Your Go-To News Categories? Celebrity, Sports, Fashion, Politics (Pick Your Party), Business, Personal Growth, Science, Beauty, Sports, Local News, Or ...

Just kidding, there's no poll. However, when people go to the same sites, read stories from the same perspective or writer, they surround themselves with an info-bubble. This fragmentation of the audience becomes important when it occurs with events and topics that concern large numbers of people. As discussed in Chapter 1, people don't share or trust mainstream media as much as in previous decades and there are many niche sources for them to choose from. Thus, they draw more news from their **information bubbles, filters,** and **echo chambers** – all similar ways to describe this phenomenon.

Information bubbles occur when users choose the information they access or when automated curation software uses computer algorithms to filter content to match user preferences. Both human and software filters have similar results: Individuals encounter only material they tend to agree with or content that comes from people who are much like themselves and share similar beliefs. (This tendency for people to associate with similar others is called **homophily,** or "love of the same.") People usually believe information that agrees with their worldview, a phenomenon called **confirmation bias.** Selecting news and opinion that conform to their own viewpoint reassures them that their perception of reality is correct – at least about the parts that matter to them.

When people don't get information from different perspectives, they believe there is only one correct way to look at facts and that valid opinions are more uniform than actually is the case. The American Press Institute (2014) conducted a telephone survey using a nationally representative sample of 14,500 adults. The study found that most respondents used as many as five devices or technologies to access news. Most importantly, respondents typically reported accessing multiple news sources – both on and off the internet. However, that finding may no longer hold true. As the previous chapter noted, rising mainstream media distrust has spiked sharply since 2016. One consequence of widespread distrust seems that some people now seek news that is more consistent with their own pre-conceived views. (There's that reassuring confirmation bias again!)

The vast amount of information on the web includes news sites for just about everybody ... but wait! There's not just one site: Multiple news sites exist with almost any topic or perspective. Take politics.

- Conservatives can move from Fox News to drudgereport.com, redstate.com, breitbart.com, Newsmax.com, Independent Journal Review (ijr.org), *Conservative Daily News, National Review, The Wall Street Journal,* and *National Enquirer.*

- Progressives and liberals can get their news at talkingpointsmemo.com, *HuffPost,* dailykos.com, dailybeast.com, *Slate, salon, The Nation, The Guardian, The Atlantic,* and *Mother Jones.*

- Moderates who want more nonpartisan stances can go to many mainstream media outlets (regardless of what political partisans think!) such as *Reuters* and reuters.com, fivethirtyeight.com, *The Christian Science Monitor, USA Today, The Washington Quarterly, Foreign Affairs,* the *Wilson Quarterly,* or even the BBC.

OKAY, NEWS CONSUMERS CHANGED – SO WHAT?

The rapid change in how people get news raises important questions. And we don't have answers to most of them yet: Do users absorb news when riding on public transportation differently than when they sit at home? Do distractions in public spaces diminish reading comprehension or recall? Does it make a difference that many online news sites and mobile sites deliver many articles in short bites?

As consumer behaviors changed, news organizations and journalists have adapted. They have embraced digital infrastructure, online information gathering, electronic delivery, and the host of processes that these new methods entail. They have learned to tell stories in different ways, adopting new formats and multiple media types. But journalism struggles with the fragmentation of the mass audience, the increase in popularity of stories that feature a subjective viewpoint, and the new roles reporters have with respect to their subscribers and followers.

WHICH NICHE?

For journalists used to reaching mass audiences who have few news choices, the splintering of news audiences seems ominous. In a world of nearly infinite information choice, people get what they want, but they may not get the information they need – or that others think they need. Journalists (and political scientists) fear that, depending on the media ecologies they favor, different groups form an understanding of news events that may be quite dissimilar, even contradictory from one another.

Journalists who report for publications serving an audience segment that consumes media only from a sharply defined perspective may face some difficulties. If they come across information that does not conform to the pre-existing beliefs of their users, they may hesitate to publish, fearing users will reject the report and even the publication itself. No editor or reporter wants to wake up and find hundreds of comments accusing them of publishing "Fake news!" Obviously, such concerns affect publications that reflect every political persuasion. Ironically, the most affected are publications that provide information to wide audiences – they receive intense criticism from all points across the spectrum of strongly held opinions.

ABOUT ME AND HOW I FEEL: THE RISE OF SUBJECTIVITY AND EMOTION IN JOURNALISM

Social media enabled users to comment and publish material about their lives, friends, and family. The mobile phone made digital technology personal and individualized content ubiquitous. These changes in how people receive and send information made it routine for people to express how they feel through "likes" and "shares." This personal nature of people's means of communications, especially smartphones and the social connection of networks, makes them a nexus of emotional attachment:

> In the context of a changing media culture, the omnipresence of technology and media in everyday life as people's lives are increasingly lived in media, and the emergence of journalism as a profoundly precarious profession, we see both a challenge and an opportunity for journalists. [...] At the heart of all of this, we argue, is emotion. Emotion drives people's increasingly intimate relationships with technology, fuels engagement with news and information, and inspires professionals to pursue careers in an industry that offers anything but reliable rewards for work well done. It inspires connection.
>
> (Beckett & Deuze, 2016, p. 2)

The movement toward narrative journalism as popular storytelling has been building for decades. Schmidt (2019) contends that corporate media boosted the success of more emotional and subjective stories because it "offered a new news logic, embodied a new media regime, and repositioned the news as a cultural institution."

However, news organizations and many journalists are not always entirely comfortable with this heightened role of emotionality and its narrative counterpart, subjectivity. Steeped in the tradition of the humanities, they learned to value objectivity, the acknowledgment and suspension of personal bias to report with fairness and impartiality. They believed in the notion of progress in the advance of the arts, philosophy, civil discourse, and civil society.

In most cases, only the most extreme personal stories and experiences make the news. By definition, they are unusual and don't apply to the experience of the vast majority of people. Yet stories steeped in emotion increase engagement by affecting how long people stay on the pages of these stories (de Los Santos & Nabi, 2019). As a result, stories that increase user engagement gain approval from news managers for many business reasons, including engagement's link to greater brand loyalty (Chen & Pain, 2019).

WHO IS THE REPORTER, WHO IS THE AUDIENCE?

Of all the changes to news work, probably nothing has changed more than the relationship between journalist and audience. Back in the old days of mass media, journalists dominated crafting news stories and (mostly) had the final word on information published in their media outlets. Typically, letters to the editors, a news program's executive producer, or other forms of audience feedback had little or no influence on mass media news content.

In the internet era, traditional barriers to feedback from the audience have been reduced. The once one-way flow of communication now goes both ways and many reporters still find that interaction challenging. Reporters face second-guessing, fact-checking, even denunciation and name-calling from disgruntled readers.

Reporters often learn about events the same time that users do. Citizen 'journalists' direct online feedback to media reports and reporters blurs the professional lines between users and reporters. Users report their research to supplement, enhance, contradict, or even criticize journalists' stories or practices.

Ordinary users post eyewitness accounts and personal experience to news stories. Some journalists revel in close interactions with their readers, as the lead character in Michael Hastings' novel does when he begins posting:

> And then I'm off, and I get a full sense of the power of the blog, like I'm walking a tightrope, a live piece of performance art. Hundreds of thousands of readers out there are responding within seconds and minutes to what I am writing, and I sense this sensation and the only thing I can think of is that it's like crack. This is a powerful drug, having the ability to communicate so freely and widely and instantaneously, and to get a response, yes they are reading my snark, hurrah.

> (Hastings, 2014, p. 311)

Some journalists have scant training or experience with participatory journalism, crowdsourcing, and other user-generated content (UGC). Yet in the complex interaction between journalists and users, all participants can take similar actions: Write, read, add material, bring extensive knowledge to topics, add research results, respond to comments, challenge posited facts, and propose entirely different conclusions.

FIGURE 2.2

Secretary of State Michael R. Pompeo conducts a press gaggle

Credit: State Department photo by Ron Przysucha

Sonia Livingstone (2014) pointed out one important difference between users and journalists:

> readers and viewers, audiences and publics, users and consumers – call them what you will – are not dutifully positioned at the end of a well-planned chain of control, from innovation to production to marketing and diffusion and, finally, obedient receipt of the goods and meanings on offer.
>
> (p. 248)

This is an important point: Professional journalists are usually contextually situated employees, responsible to a hierarchy of control for the reports and articles they write. In contrast, users are free from employment encumbrances or the membership guidelines of professional guilds. They can pretty much say what they want without the consequences that news media employees face.

It's not just the editorial side of news organizations that face a changing environment. Managers face a range of daunting demands.

---

7 Things News Organizations Are Changing ... Oh, Is That All?

The radical transformation of reporter–reader/viewer relationships and the economic changes wrought by digital technologies have combined to create new startups, new business models, and entirely new ways of "doing" the news business. For example, under Lewis D'Vorkin, *Forbes* magazine linked the print publication with www.forbes.com. *Forbes* then restructured the gathering, processing, and distribution of their news content. D'Vorkin wrote extensively about his unfolding plans, articulating a vision for journalists, academics, experts, readers, users, and even marketers – each contributing to the final product.

D'Vorkin envisioned *Forbes* as a participatory platform, with professionalism at the center, one that provided all stakeholders opportunities to voice their perspectives. He re-designed the magazine to reflect his ideas. In its January 2011 issue, *Forbes* opened part of the magazine to the readers, crowdsourcing to identify people who would be important to know. Later that year, a mobile edition was unveiled, and many other changes have taken place. As D'Vorkin put it:

- We collect news and information differently
- We produce it differently
- We present it differently
- We pay for it differently
- We distribute it differently
- We staff our organization differently
- We enable marketers to be active and engaged participants

Why did a venerable publication such as *Forbes* undergo a wrenching re-organization, one that caused several long-time reporters to leave the company? What conditions drove such dramatic changes in this and other newsrooms across the spectrum of news organizations? The next section examines forces that continue to transform the journalistic enterprise at each all level.

AT THE MOMENT, NEWSONOMICS ARE KIND OF LOUSY (*WITH A TIP OF THE HAT TO KEN DOCTOR*)

Ken Doctor writes the 'Newsonomics' column for the Nieman Journalism Lab and regularly contributes to Politico Media. Doctor provided a definitive assessment of the state of the news business in 2016 and its prospects for 2017 (Doctor, December 19, 2016).

The outlook for news media businesses is generally mixed, but not optimistic. And journalism must weather further economic difficulties. Doctor reported that news media have larger audiences than ever before. But larger audiences have not yielded higher overall revenues. Ad revenue from print publications was down while increased web advertising failed to reach many news publications. Another report found that several high-profile newspapers, such as *The New York Times* and *The Washington Post*, increased their paid subscriptions (Bond and Bond, 2017). But many other online publications did not. Overall, uncertain revenue prospects have battered news media company stock prices.

Facebook and Google, not online news sites, captured most of the new revenues from increased web advertising. The online media platform giants (GAFT: Google, Amazon, Facebook, Twitter) make agreements with news sites to re-distribute news content to one or more of their services, often at the expense of news content-producing companies. For example, not only do Google and Facebook deprive content-producing news publications of their own branding and relationship-building opportunities with users, most of the new revenue goes to the GAFT companies.

Doctor (2019) predicts that newspapers will begin publishing digitally, perhaps distributing a paper edition on some days like Sunday, which is often profitable, or some combination of other days. He goes on to say:

> The business-model changes required for this print-to-digital transition have befuddled newspaper publishers for more than a decade. Print is still where most of their money comes from; how can they preserve all those great print ad and circulation dollars *and* build a digital business big enough to support any semblance of truly community-serving newsroom? Thus far, nothing's worked. Instead of any radical shifts, perhaps understandably given human nature, we've seen straddle after straddle. Some admixture of maintaining what might be enough of print while investing what might be enough in "digital." That straddle is what's coming to an end.

Between 2008 and 2018, U.S. newsroom employment dropped by 25 percent, about 28,000 jobs, many of them at newspapers (Grieco, 2019b). While legacy news organizations – newspapers, television, radio, magazines – have steeply declined over the last decade, digital news companies and sites have replaced some of those positions. The Pew Research Center (2014) Report on the State of the News Media found that approximately 500 new digital news organizations created 5,000 new professional jobs. While the number of new positions doesn't approach the number of jobs lost, some journalists are now cautiously optimistic about the outlook for future news industry job growth.

Digital news startups have different business models, ranging from entrepreneurial subscriber-based and ad-supported sites, to crowdsourcing, to philanthropic-supported journalism. Of course, many legacy news organizations put considerable effort into building their brands on digital platforms. Some traditional newspapers see signs of successful paid digital subscription businesses, protected by paywalls. The *New York Times* and *Wall Street Journal* provide high-profile examples. And many newspaper companies and several television groups intend to roll-out digital subscriber plans in some local markets.

Given the somber state of news businesses, this "creative destruction" of their industry distresses many journalists and threatens their organizations. But the news wasn't all bad. Early 2017 brought a "Trump bump" of rising subscriptions to some news media companies. It also increased contributions to non-profit news organizations like ProPublica.com and *The Guardian* newspaper. While recognizing the painful difficulties faced by journalists who have been working for years, Ken Doctor remains optimistic about the journalism profession's future: "As tough as things seem for the mid-career journalists of today, I'm enthused about the energy, skills and determination I see developing in the next generation of journalists," writes Ken Doctor on his web site, www.newsonomics.com.

Doctor also identified regulatory issues now coming up for the industry that might affect the macro news business environment. He expects to see continued news media consolidation, a process that has been ongoing for many years, under **cross-platform ownership** rules, regulations limited the number of news properties that companies can own in any market, thus ensuring multiple sources of news from newspapers and broadcasters by restricting the number and type of properties a news entity could own in one local market. As the Federal Communications Commission relaxes cross-platform regulations, mergers and acquisitions will continue unabated.

This regulatory change can leave smaller communities with just one source of local news, or perhaps none at all. Of course, people can always go online, where there's every kind of news source imaginable, some reliably accurate and truthful. But "local news" on the "world wide web" surely contradicts traditional notions of place and locality.

Net neutrality has also been an important part of public access and discussion of news. Net neutrality has ensured that, across the internet, all bits move equally – yours, mine, CNN's, and Charter Cable's content. In 2017, the Republican-dominated Federal Communications Commission abandoned net neutrality standard that gave larger (deep pocket) content providers preferred network treatment – faster and cheaper internet service. A federal appeals court ruled in 2019 that the FCC ruling was legal, so the new rules can go into effect (Romm, 2019). The fear is that pricing of bandwidth could increase prices for individuals and small users, restricting ease of access to some content, and perhaps slow overall network improvements (Oliver, 2017). The FCC ended Net Neutrality in 2018.

5 REASONS WHY THE NEWS BUSINESS IS TOUGH RIGHT NOW

News organizations' business environment defines and limits the opportunities that each news enterprise faces. The business strategies and decisions available to news organizations influence their: 1) story selection, 2) story coverage, and 3) news distribution. While editors and reporters determine many aspects of story coverage and presentation, these decisions occur within the specific organization's context. Thus, savvy reporters know that they need to understand their own unique organization and its place within the larger news industry.

More intense market competitiveness now shapes the business decisions that news organizations make. Figure 2.3 shows Porter's classic model (1979) of how market

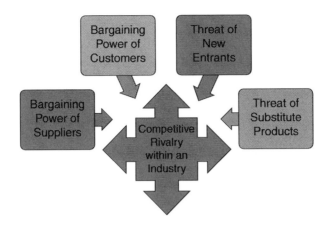

FIGURE 2.3

Forces influencing the competitiveness of a market
Credit: Created by Grahams Child and used under Creative Commons License

forces affect different stakeholders. It's an oldie but a goodie because it brings clarity to the business problems so many news organizations face today. Ongoing internet evolution and **digitization** have enormous impacts on how each of Porter's market forces impacts the news industry – further spurring the greater competition over the past decade.

FORCE 1: THE BARGAINING POWER OF CUSTOMERS

News is everywhere. People can get news from almost an infinite array of sources.

- The internet shifted power to consumers by letting them easily select among many different news sources, available on many media platforms.
- Digitization makes enforcement of sellers' rights of **content exclusivity** (through **copyright**) extremely difficult.
- The internet provides places for consumers to get no-cost news – often high quality, timely news. It's difficult to compete with "free."
- Twitter and other social media bring real-time eyewitness news accounts directly to users. Eyewitness accounts may not be complete, accurate, or objective, but they do impart immediacy, intimacy, and vividness to news stories.

Analysis: Increased bargaining power of buyers = A far more competitive marketplace than before

FORCE 2: THE BARGAINING POWER OF SUPPLIERS

Who supplies news? Sources, reporters, editors, content farms, and now everyone with smartphone access.

- News organizations remain expert suppliers of news. They also remain the most popular news sources, even though their popularity has waned. Some publications retain enough trust from their subscribers and advertisers to support excellent journalism and the resources to survive, and even profit.

- Reporters' sources increase journalists' value and that of their media organizations. Sources provide one of few ways that journalists can gain bargaining power, or leverage. Sources often contact journalists they believe trustworthy, or because they know of a journalist, or of a journalist's reporting. (But now it's more like a two-way street. Instead of "This reporter has a source," it may be that "This source has a reporter.")

- News suppliers have another source of leverage: their specialized knowledge. Specialized knowledge stems from extensive personal experience or the ability to reach experts, perhaps because the journalist and a source share a common language or special expertise. For example, few journalists can understand, explain, or write about credit default swaps. But publications that provide expert investment information must hire writers and reporters who can communicate a complex financial story competently and accurately.

- Reputations drive bargaining power for good and ill. Geography no longer limits outlets' (or journalists') reach. The reputations of news brands and reporters travel the globe and attract followers wherever they may reside.

- Journalists can also increase their bargaining power by developing larger or influential audiences for their work. Twitter, Facebook, and other social media tools help journalists develop personal brands to attract publishers. In business terms, the internet helps journalists to **disintermediate** their own audience from their publishers.

  Disintermediation entails breaking down barriers between layers of action or contact. In traditional media, reporters' work was available only as a condition of being employed by a publisher. With the web, publications can't always stand between reporters and followers – if a journalist has built a strong audience for her work (Cutler, 2011).

- The growth of **content farms**, such as Associated Content and Demand, also disintermediates journalists and writers from publishers. Usually, content farms aggregate content, paying writers $0.02 a word or $10 per article, and then re-sell **buckets** of content to websites that have contractual agreements with these farms. "Content factories" with piece-work labor – provides a more accurate metaphor than "content farm" to describe this power dynamic, one which greatly disempowers journalists.

Analysis: Easy to find suppliers but with some limits = A slightly less competitive marketplace, especially in local and niche news

FORCE 3: THE THREAT OF NEW ENTRANTS

Barriers to entry just aren't what they used to be – now everyone can publish. Washington D.C.-based Gary Arlen (digital business strategy coverage) and former Apple insider, the late Richard Doherty (technology news), provide two examples of individuals who built successful reports, based on their expert knowledge and contacts within the niche news markets that they covered for deep-pocket subscribers.

Yes, incumbent organizations retain big advantages over newcomers. Incumbents already have startup financing and already offer revenue-producing products and services. Incumbents may have differentiated their products to appeal to multiple market segments and perhaps they have developed economies of scale. In many industries, these advantages provide almost insurmountable barriers to new wanna-be entrants. But in the news business – not so much.

Analysis: Significantly lower barriers to entry = A significantly more competitive marketplace

FORCE 4: THE THREAT OF SUBSTITUTE PRODUCTS

Users can find substitute products and services from blogs, social media, and other news suppliers quite easily. Often the substitute's cost is zero, nada, zip ... so users base their choices for existing news and information sources on their current preferences and habits, rather than cost. This presents huge risks when online newspapers put up paywalls but lack compelling reasons for users to pay for content that was previously free.

What's to be done? Groom like-minded audiences. Information bubbles increase users' loyalty to particular news organizations. Many users may scan mainstream media and later bring that information to their **communities of interest** and to their personal blogs. Mainstream media benefits from these page views, but in many cases, users' ideologically compatible sites get more time, attention, and (ultimately) more revenue.

Analysis: Increased number of substitutable products = A more competitive marketplace

FORCE 5: ANALYSIS OF MARKET FORCES 1–4 – COMPETITIVE RIVALRY WITHIN AN INDUSTRY

The interactions of forces 1–4 provide a framework to assess how much competition exists within an industry. In the news industry, three of the four forces lead to more competitive marketplaces. Only an abundance of suppliers – writers, reporters, and editors – reduces competitive pressures on news organizations.

Even so, reporters who work in the trenches can distinguish themselves and protect against interchangeability. Their abilities to cultivate expert sources, develop detailed knowledge, and acquire deep understandings of complex phenomena all erect barriers to easy replacement. Journalists with knowledgeable, reliable sources and access to otherwise unobtainable information can negotiate with greater confidence.

Analysis: Overall impact of forces = A more competitive marketplace

"DIGITAL SECOND ... NOT FIRST" – WHAT IF GOING DIGITAL IS WRONG?

What if news organizations' efforts to go digital was a huge mistake? Hard to believe, yet there is evidence that "digital first" business strategies have not paid off for newspapers. In the wake of digitization, many newspapers invested in "digital first" strategies, plowing resources into converged or all-digital newsrooms. Now, it's even more likely that newsrooms will announce that they are going "mobile first," just like going digital – only on steroids.

Not so fast! Chyi and Tenenboim (2016) make an evidence-based business case that newspapers' digital first efforts have not been very successful. They argue that local newspapers might have been more successful if they had put all that cash into local markets instead – and tried to increase their subscriber base. Chyi and Tenenboim gathered data about the online readership of 51 local newspapers and found:

- Few publications increased online newspaper reading since 2007.
- More than half of the local papers lost online users since 2011.
- Overall, online readers made up about one-third of traditional print newspaper readers.

Bottom line: Print newspapers may be losing readers, but they still reach many more people than digital versions. And online users have not boosted revenues for newspaper publishers. Local subscriptions to print editions still account for 82 percent of these newspapers' revenue. Chyi and Tenenboim found that the true winners in online news were the giant news aggregators – the Google and Facebook news duopoly.

News and information emanate from screens everywhere – including unmeasured venues such as video at gas pumps, cable TV in doctors' waiting rooms, satellite feeds on airplane seat backs, or marquees on shopping carts. No wonder the Pew Research Center, State of the News Media Report found that: "More audience research data exist about each user than ever before. Yet in addition to confusion about what it means, it is almost impossible to get a full sense of consumer behavior – across sites, platforms, and devices," (Rosenstiel & Mitchell, 2011).

Vox Verbatim: Tony Cook, Cook Media

I have spent a career immersed in the world of media as a magazine reporter, writer, editor, screenwriter, TV news producer, internet content executive, web entrepreneur, and owner of a digital marketing company with corporate clients adapting to the new e-way of attracting and engaging customers. I have eye-witnessed the evolution of publishing from linotype printing using hot lead type and £0 ton presses to the present digital age, in which anyone on the globe with a web connection can type 140-characters and tweet to the world. It's been a wild and wondrous ride from copy boy at the *New York Times* to blog jockey on WordPress with a global audience online.

---

4 REASONS THE NEWS INDUSTRY WILL CONTINUE TO CHANGE

Wouldn't it be great if, after a decade of disruptive change, the news business and journalism stabilized? Journalists could spend time working in teams to report and produce fantastic multimedia articles that truly make a difference: Editors could edit, and publishers could even play golf with other influential elites. Users would get all the news that they needed to know, and the world would become wonderful again.

Not going to happen … at least the slowing change part. Change is certain. How things will change – that's not! As Yogi Berra famously said: "It's tough to make predictions, especially about the future." Even if we know some of the dynamics underlying changes, like emerging digital and social M2M technologies, predictions about how

NEWS BY THE NUMBERS

they will unfold often fail. Former Secretary of Defense Donald Rumsfeld called these speculative areas "the known unknowns." And keep in mind that plenty of "unknown unknowns" lurk in this future, too.

CHANGE #1: ARTIFICIAL INTELLIGENCE (AI)

AI is exploding and it's coming to news outlets near you – actually, many sites that you regularly use already use your data to tailor their communication with you. Did Gmail. com identify spam in your email? Have you asked Siri for directions with your iPhone? Been on a foreign language web site and had Google Translate rewrite that page for you in English?

Well, you've been talking with AI in the cloud! And it's talking back.

Definition please: Artificial intelligence is the performance by machines of actions that are normally associated with human intelligence. AI actions include understanding human language and speech, learning, creating tools, planning, creativity, and problem-solving – and beating Chess Grand Masters.

While people have learned to use computers, thanks to AI, computers have learned to speak more naturally and clearly – tailored to each user too. Soon, common consumer devices will use natural speech to interact with their human users. Devices will read news to users and fetch stories that match their users' preferences. Rather than peering at tiny screens, users will hear news, twitters, and texts.

Expect more sophisticated algorithms pushing content at you. Advances in AI will see people change over time and recognize changes in behaviors. Computers will predict new interests, needs, and wants associated with the detected changes – promoting new content to match.

Already busy at work, AI bots currently add millions of "likes" to news sites and make gazillions of comments on social media services. Soon, organizations and even individuals will deploy specialist bots to search the net for news – seeking events, anomalies, and influencers, and fetching that information for their "botmasters." Reporters may use bots to find news in areas of interest and specialization. As experts in a field, journalists often have a sense of the landscape, but bots can seek specific information or provide broad surveillance for new developments.

Journalists spend countless hours using computers. AI-empowered computers can make journalists' work easier and more productive with natural speech processing (NLP). Journalists could then talk and listen instead of using their keyboards all day. AI could make multimedia stories much easier to produce by integrating audio files with text more efficiently. For example, software could harness the user's device camera to track users' eyes so that audio or video would play automatically whenever a user focused on a specific page location.

Precisely *how* new AI capabilities will change journalism requires speculation. But that AI *will affect* the news media industry seems a sure bet. Recall that changes in journalism practices closely track innovations in communication technology. Consider the history of journalism as it adapted to the evolution of the technologies people used for news: stone carvings, ink, papyrus, parchment, paper, printing press, telegraph, photography, moving images, broadcasting, audio and video, computers, and now digital networks. The first architects of communication innovations never quite knew how their inventions would be put to use as the fascinating book by Carolyn Marvin (1988), *When Old*

Technologies Were New, so aptly describes. For example, the inventors of early radio saw it as a person-to-person medium and the first telephone businesses sold it as a broadcast network, sending the same messages to all subscribers.

CHANGE #2: INSTANT APPS

You can use instant apps on your Android mobile phone now – apps that download, no waiting (Canavan, 2017). Until now, apps required users to visit the Google Store to buy, download, and install them before users could – well, use that app. Instant apps download only the part of an app that a user needs at that moment. Apps come to Android Phones on-the-fly complete with a sign-in, allowing users to do something specific – look for an item, buy an item, send an email, find a location, chat with customer service ... – well, there's an app for that! And instant apps reduce the icons on the mobile device screen, as well. Yes! Who doesn't want that?

CHANGE #3: AUGMENTED AND VIRTUAL REALITY

Think of AR as the "Pokemon Effect." With AR, users get digital cues from their devices, which lead them to something in the real world. The success of Pokemon makes it almost certain there will be more fluid interactions between the digital and the real world in the near future. Expect marketers to swarm over AR with hidden messages, special promotions, loyalty rewards, and other lures not yet imagined.

Virtual Reality digitizes the real world (at least the visual aspects of it), then allows users to act in that virtual space. It's immersive, letting users see places they can't go and act in ways that they can't, like leaping tall buildings. These technologies add new arrows to journalists' storytelling quivers to make stories more engaging to their users. Perhaps AR and VR will help news sites' bottom lines. As the costs of virtual reality production and the VR glasses become cheaper, VR and AR will be easier to create and receive – just like previous digital innovations.

CHANGE #4: THE INTERNET OF THINGS (IOT)

Refrigerators, toasters, cars, lawnmowers, U.S. Post Office outdoor mailboxes, children's lunchboxes – who knows what soon will be connected. One thing is sure – more connectivity, more data. For digital reporters, data can make richer stories than traditional coverage of protests or crime scenes. Data captured from the IoT will provide evidence of how people interact with objects, enriching stories in new and exciting ways: tracking illegal shipments and purloined documents on hard drives and verifying key facts of informants' stories by querying a database of automated teller machine transactions, drop-offs at mailboxes, and making purchases, just to name a few ways IoT will provide silent evidence.

To the extent that "things" are connected, retail establishments will transmit data to mobile phones based on the co-location of that mobile device with the store. Proximity enables Location-Based Services (LBS) that allow dynamic offers and promotions to be pushed to users. If news sites act as gateways or can attract users' attention to such messages, this innovation package of IoT and LBS may add sorely needed new revenue opportunities for news sites.

TAKEAWAYS

- It's been a difficult decade for most news organizations, especially print newspapers and magazines. And it hasn't been all that easy for online news sites either. It's a conundrum: Audiences are bigger than ever before. But the news industry is more competitive than ever before. And revenues are too low for many news organizations to survive, let alone thrive. But be sure that where there is an itch for news, someone will figure out how to scratch it – it seems like a new Very Cool news web site pops up every day.

- Audiences have changed too. More and more, they get the news they want, when they want it, where they want it, and how they want it. News habits have changed so that most U.S. adults get news from as many as five devices and check for *their* news several times a day. Generational differences exist – seniors read more newspapers; young adults use mobile phones much more.

- One consequence of people getting only the news they want is that it's increasingly easy for them to surround themselves with information that agrees with their personal worldview. These self-referential choices can be dangerous, both for individuals and for society as a whole, because everyone is wrong – at least some of the time. Attending only to information that a person likes makes badly needed reality corrections far more difficult and unlikely.

- The influence of social media and personal network "likes" and "shares" has grown enormously. Citizen journalists' direct online feedback to media reports and reporters has blurred (even erased) the lines between users and reporters. Now users post eyewitness accounts and personal experience to stories. Reporters often learn about events at the same time that users do.

- Users not only access news anywhere, they also contribute to news from everywhere. Who are the reporters and who are the audiences? To some extent, both reporters and audiences engage in many of the same activities. However, journalists are usually employees of a news organization who work full time and have professional peer groups. These long-standing relationships help journalists develop topic-centered and professional expertise, coupled with professional norms that citizen journalists often lack.

- News organizations have made many changes to respond to the impacts of technology, audience habits, and competition. They have equipped themselves and developed processes to push news across the many platforms their audiences use. They have tried partnerships with news aggregators and social media platforms and developed new content formats. They have built interactive opportunities to further engage users and encouraged (sometimes required) journalists to participate on news sites and on social media services.

- The news industry continues to feel the impact of digitization, M2M, and globalized networks. New means of communication are likely to affect journalism for the foreseeable future. Archeology and common sense tell us that doing well in a changing environment demands continuous learning and adaptation.

- Increased competition requires cost-cutting and creating new forms of advertising and public relations content to increase revenues. Competition encourages more sensational headlines and stories used to attract new users, and it gives them more power in their relationships with news suppliers.

- Emerging technologies that already have impacts on the news industry like big data, algorithms, and bots will become far more sophisticated and continue to extend influence. New technologies that will become more common include artificial intelligence, natural language processing, and machine learning. Instant apps will help publications and consumers, making mobile interaction much easier. Augmented and virtual reality offer journalists new ways to create compelling multimedia reports and stories. Finally, the Internet of Things (IoT) will compile data that will "speak" for these things, giving journalists entirely new sources (and perhaps distribution channels) for information.

KEY CONCEPTS AND TERMS

- Business models, as applied to news organizations
- User news habits and consumption
- Information bubble
- Competition in the news industry
- Digital technologies and change in the news industry

EXERCISES AND ACTIVITIES

1. Find out the name of the company that owns your local paper. Then go to the U.S. Security and Exchange Commission's EDGAR database and get five years of 10-K (annual report) filings and the last available year of 10-Q (quarterly) reports. If your local paper isn't owned by a public corporation, pick the largest newspaper in your state. Write a report that shows the circulation and revenue figures for the local newspaper, or for the parent company's newspaper division. www.sec.gov/edgar/searchedgar/webusers.htm

2. Please go to the story, *On Quora, Journalism and Disintermediation* by Kim-Mai Cutler, on the Quora Review website: http://quorareview.com/2011/02/10/quora-journalism-disintermediation/. Read the story, and then summarize it in 500–700 words.

3. What emerging innovations or technologies do you think will affect journalism in the future? Choose one of them and search the internet to find out more about it. Write a short report that covers: The innovation and how it works, who will use it, how they will use it, and what effects such use will have on journalism, journalists, or on news organizations that adopt it.

ADVANCER

This chapter looked at the business side of news. Chapter 3 examines another side of the news industry – how digitization has changed the ways journalists work. It considers changes to the newsrooms that journalists work in (or don't), and the infrastructure that now supports them (or doesn't).

The processes and practices that define journalism as a profession also define the news industry and the news itself. Journalists generally agree about their need to inform the audience and endorse standards of accuracy, timeliness, and fairness. Although the tools and specific skills may change, good writing and solid reporting remain at the heart of contemporary journalism.

The future will include professional jobs for journalists in rapidly evolving digital news organizations. But many positions will be far different from those in traditional newsrooms; some of these jobs have yet to be invented. The next chapter examines how work in digital news is changing – and also the ways that journalism stays the same.

3

JOURNALISTS @WORK: REMIX & REBOOT

Chapter Learning Objectives

After reading this chapter, students will be able to:

1. Understand the functions of journalism and how they are changing in Western societies.
2. Understand the culture and attitudes of journalists.
3. Analyze journalists' working conditions, including their new roles and responsibilities.
4. Compare legacy (print and broadcast) and integrated newsrooms.
5. Compare traditional and digital news content.
6. Analyze the changing relationship between journalists and users.
7. Understand how newsrooms and journalists receive and respond to data analytics about user behavior.

We cannot make good news out of bad practice.

– Edward R. Murrow

THE GIST

As famed journalist Edward R. Murrow notes, there is an unbreakable connection between means and ends. For that reason, all professions and most trades establish practices that specify how practitioners should carry out their work. When journalists gather information for a story, write it, and publish it, they must observe standards of timeliness, accuracy, and fairness.

Failing to follow these professional standards may hold serious, even life or death consequences for the public as it has during the coronavirus pandemic. In short, bad practice results in bad news.

Robinson (2013, p. 4) describes the five new responsibilities imposed by participation: "A paradigmatic transformation is called for today, shifting the focus from the journalist as a producer to journalist as facilitator, conversationalist, connector, networker, and producer." The COVID-19 pandemic highlighted these new roles, quickly permeating legacy media like television and cable news. For example, when CNN host Chris Cuomo caught the virus, he continued to host or appear on his own show, describing his experiences and conversing with other victims, first responders, and medical caregivers. He used precious news show time to connect with people on the front lines and facilitate deeply personal discussions, a style that resembled the less formal conversations of online discussions.

Digital journalists provided useful links to data bases replete with newly created amazing data visualizations of the spread and consequences of COVID-19. Reporters produced podcasts in conjunction with public health and medical experts. And digital media outlets provided extensive lists of working links to public health agencies, testing facilities, and public health advisory announcements.

The first two chapters ended by examining how the news industry is changing as news workers and organizations adapt to the impacts of many different consumption choices that digital devices enable. Chapter 3 profiles news workers – the values they hold, the work they do, and the practices they follow – because in the digitally networked world, it's not like it used to be. The very roles that journalism has traditionally played in society are being rapidly transformed by these social and technological changes.

Journalists at all levels have mixed feelings about many of these changes yet must find ways of working that meet both their own professional standards and the demands of employment in turbulent times. Many journalists (especially new hires) must take on new roles and greater responsibilities, even as they perform these new tasks in new ways. The chapter compares the similarities and differences between reporting practices for digital news organizations and traditional print and broadcasting news organizations.

Yet, no matter how much journalism has changed in the last decade, it retains many of its most important elements from the past: Both traditional and contemporary journalism adhere to similar objectives and expectations of quality. And although the tools and specific skills may change from year to year, even month to month, solid reporting, good writing, and ethical principles remain at the heart of professional journalism. Thus, the chapter considers the legacies handed down from journalism's past, alongside the new technologies, practices, opportunities, and challenges of today.

Finally, Chapter 3 describes the changing journalistic workplace. It offers a quick look at the 300-year old historical development of newsrooms. It compares legacy, online, converged, de-converged, and self-organized freelancer newsrooms – and even no newsroom at all. One thing is sure: The new newsroom isn't much like the ones in old movies like *All the President's Men* or *Foreign Correspondent*.

TOP 10: WHICH ROLES OF THE PRESS DO *YOU* WANT TO STRENGTHEN?

In the United States, the press enjoys protection under the First Amendment to the Constitution.

Since then, many voices have emphasized the importance of informing people in a democracy about issues that concern them and their communities. Over time, the press evolved along with the larger society, and now plays many additional roles, as shown in Table 3.1.

> "Congress shall make no law respecting an establishment of religion, or prohibiting the free exercise thereof; or abridging the freedom of speech, or of the press; or the right of the people peaceably to assemble, and to petition the Government for a redress of grievances."
>
> If there was debate about the amendment before it passed in the 1st United States Congress, it was not recorded. Consequently, we know little about the intentions of the original legislators.

TABLE 3.1 Ten roles of the press

Ten Roles of the Press	Functions
Inform	To impart to the public items they should know about
Watchdog	To monitor and report the actions of governments and other powerful institutions and organizations
Interpret	To provide context, explanation, and expertise about a given topic or situation
Entertain	To highlight subjects, people, and events of interest
Critic	To offer expertise about the relative value of programs, proposals, actions, activities, and goods and services
Agenda-Setting	To bring important issues forward for wide public consideration
Gatekeepers	To keep unnecessary, unreliable, and redundant information out of respected publications and broadcasts
Afflict the comfortable	To watch for abuses of authority and position
Comfort the Afflicted	To report the plight of the needy
Court of Last Resort	To help free the unjustly accused or imprisoned

Fulfilling many of these roles effectively depends on a strong, vibrant news industry. The decline of the public's trust in the news media may also impair the ability of the press to carry out some of these roles. For example, the rise of social media has weakened one of these functions, that of gatekeeping, according to Shirky (2008, p. 68):

the steady rise of social media is chipping away at the gatekeeping role once played by editors and news directors, empowering the audience to shape the news agenda like never before. The term "audience" itself has fallen out of favor with many online journalism scholars, who believe it conveys an old-fashioned view of the public as passive consumers of news rather than active contributors. [...] This perpetual two-way conversation is producing a culture of participatory journalism "in which vast numbers of strangers contribute directly to something that those journalists alone once controlled." News outlets are hiring social media managers to help facilitate interaction with readers and viewers.

The diminishment of the gatekeeping role has also weakened the ability of the press to set the public agenda. Coverage of issues still exercises influence, demonstrated by such stories as problems with the Veterans Administration hospitals, the Clinton emails, and the Harvey Weinstein sexual harassment scandal. The press, especially the mainstream media, still carry out their traditional roles to some extent, even as the internet erodes their information monopoly.

It's not just trust in the media that has gone down; people place less confidence in the opinions of authorities and experts than they did in previous decades. Consequently, the ability of the press to inform, monitor, and interpret has decreased. Since 2017, tensions between U.S. President Donald Trump and the press exacerbated these problems. Seven in ten Americans reported they felt troubled by the situation, and 73 percent said they believed this tension served as a barrier, which prevented them from receiving important political news and information. These concerns were expressed in similar ways and frequency across party lines – these troubling tensions between the President and the press consistently transcended demographic groups, including age, race, income, and education (Barthel, Gottfried, & Mitchell, 2017).

MEET THE PRESS

The images many people have of journalists come from films like *All the President's Men*, *Parallax View*, *The Mary Tyler Moore Show*, *Foreign Correspondent*, *Killing Fields*, *Wag the Dog*, *Runaway Jury*, *The Wire* (Season 5), *The Paper*, *Spotlight*, and many others that feature journalism and reporters. From many media sources, the public has a dual view of journalists: the Hero and the Villain (Saltzman, 2005). As heroes, journalists are curious, with a strong need to know. They are energetic, determined, sometimes brash, and expressive as they uncover and expose wrong-doing or evil. As villains, journalists are intrusive, ill-mannered, shallow, self-centered, conceited, and sometimes corrupt jerks who mistreat those close to them and mislead the public.

Although actual journalists may demonstrate these characteristics in real life, they are like people in most groups, exhibiting a wide range of traits. Some are shy; others are extroverted. Some express themselves socially; others wait to put it all on the page or the screen. Some journalists are dedicated, and others are lazy or burned out. A few journalists become rich and famous, but most do not.

Regardless of individual reporters' personal attributes and circumstances, the culture of journalism exists, and it encourages certain behaviors. Professional cultures prescribe sets of behaviors that most practitioners understand and accept, as they are in journalism by members of the press (Herkenhoff & Heydenfeldt, 2011). The notion of members of professions as tribes has gained currency, with tribal cultural standards guiding practitioners' activities, behaviors, and attitudes.

Between 2007 and 2011, Hanitzsch et al. (2010) surveyed 1,700 journalists from 18 different countries to compare the cultural attributes of journalists across these nations. The respondents reported that, individually, journalists valued detachment, non-involvement, providing political information, and monitoring their governments. Western journalists reported strongly favoring impartiality, reliability and factualness of information, and observance of universal ethical principles. Such principles typically include accuracy, objectivity, and fairness.

JOURNALISTS @WORK

In addition to identifying values held by individual journalists, Hanitzsch et al. (2010) found four distinct journalistic cultural milieus, e.g., overall social views about the roles and functions of the press:

- Populist disseminators: Voice of the people that gives the audience what it wants and reflects its audience's values.
- Detached watchdogs: Skeptical and critical, journalists monitor leaders and elites.
- Critical change agents: Oppose the status quo and motivate audiences to seek changes.
- Opportunistic facilitators: Support government, business, and leaders by acting as partners.

Western journalists usually saw themselves as watchdogs over government and elites. They did not support an interventionist perspective, declining to promote specific values, ideas, or social change. In contrast, Latin American journalists favored intervention to right wrongs and to bring bad actors to justice.

The view of reporters as watchdogs potentially creates adversarial relationships between reporters and the people they cover. Whether the beat is politics, sports, business, celebrity, or fashion, journalists often seek the very information that newsworthy people wish to minimize or completely hide: conflicts, secrets, and shortcomings. As a result, even people who seek to publicize positive messages through news media (or to spin negative messages) must exercise caution when they talk with reporters. Over time, these divergent goals create a social distance that causes journalists to inhabit a professional world where they are needed by elites, yet pose potential threats to elites' interests.

Reporters assess the stated and potential motivations of their sources and targets, knowing that as journalists they may be "set up" to persuade them or to distract them from the stories that they are actively pursuing. Sources and targets may have altruistic motives: serving justice or fairness, protecting the nation, or aiding the helpless. But sources' motives may also be self-serving – discrediting or destroying enemies, or extending protection to friends and allies. Often, sources and targets have complex mixtures of motives that journalists must evaluate carefully.

In this intricate, risky, and contentious world that journalists inhabit, truth is an elusive delicacy.

Thus, it's not surprising that journalists often develop a skeptical, if not downright cynical, view of others. Journalists are inevitably entangled in our complex social world that includes economics, politics, art, manners, and fashion. The stories that reporters write affect the people, places, and things they cover. When these effects are negative, there can be pushback – resistance that sometimes ranges from murder (of the journalist), to more mundane complaints to the publisher, and letters to the editor. The professional standards that guide journalists stand as one protection for reporters, demanding that they examine the overall fact structure, as well as the motives and actions of all those who are involved. This objective approach, combined with careful documentation, also serves to fend off potential legal threats.

All these circumstances require that journalists make adaptive responses along a spectrum of the professional ideals of accuracy, objectivity, and fairness. Most Western journalists and many practitioners everywhere in the world hold these values. They may be expressed in various ways, depending on censorship practices, publication venue, editorial policies and personalities, time and effort, the story itself, the people in the story, potential consequences of publishing the story, social and cultural mores, and individual psychological factors. All the preceding circumstances spring from their cultural milieu and may influence reporters' journalistic choices and conduct.

Journalists who work for online news media may have more autonomy than traditional news workers. Because they often work as **freelancers** or as **stringers** where there is no communal newsroom, online journalists are under less scrutiny. Digital news sites, particularly startups, sometimes have a smaller editorial staff facing many demands on their attention, resulting in less questioning and fact-checking, fewer reviews by legal counsel, high story counts, and frequent revisions based on real-time analytics – all factors that can reduce editorial oversight.

THE RUNNING STORY OF JOURNALISTS @WORK

A **running story** is one that continues to evolve as it is published in multiple, ongoing accounts – ironically that now applies to the changing ways that journalists work. But disruptive change is not just occurring in journalism: A much larger transformation of the world, societies, politics, economics, and work is underway. Many different factors spur this rapid transformation – scientific, technological, economic, political, and increased competition, as well as changing consumer habits, just to name a few.

The notion that advances in scientific knowledge, technology, and our transportation and communication infrastructures would lead to social change and disrupt many facets of peoples' lives (including patterns of work) is not novel. In the mid-20th century, Buckminster Fuller (Fuller, 1946) showed how the rate of advances in chemistry had accelerated in the then-recent past, as scientists discovered more chemical elements. In the 1970s, sociologist Daniel Bell (1973) observed that society was rapidly evolving into a post-industrial (information) society. By 2002, clarion calls warned us about the unintended and possibly negative effects of the acceleration of the rate of change (Heylighen, 2002):

> It is argued that social and technological evolution is characterized by **ephemeralization**, an accelerating increase in the efficiency of all material, energetic and informational processes. This leads to the practical disappearance of the constraints of space, time, matter and energy, and thus spectacularly increases our power to physically solve problems. However, the accompanying "lubrication" or reduction of friction in all processes creates other, non-physical problems, characterized by the increasing instability, complexity and reach of causal networks, and therefore decreasing controllability and predictability. As a result, individuals are forced to consider more information and opportunities than they can effectively process. This information overload is made worse by "data smog," the proliferation of low quality information because of easy publication. It leads to anxiety, stress, alienation, and potentially dangerous errors of judgment. Moreover, it holds back overall economic productivity.
>
> (p. 1)

Social theorist Zygmunt Bauman draws the picture at a larger level in his many books about the extreme uncertainty of modern life. He describes living in contemporary Western societies as places where things change faster than people can adapt. He calls this social condition **liquid modernity:** "A society in which the conditions under which its members act change faster than it takes the ways of acting to consolidate into habits and routines" (2000, p. 1). In other words, contemporary societies change faster than people can adapt their routines.

Routines are "repetitive, recognizable patterns of interdependent actions, carried out by multiple actors" (Feldman & Pentland, 2003). Interdependence means that changes to work in one part of a process probably require change by workers carrying out tasks in related parts of the process or organization. In addition, a key part of liquid modernity is the relentless advance of communications technologies, which entails discarding old methods and learning new ones.

Vox Verbatim: Megan Finnerty, Journalist and Director, Storytellers Brand Studio

6:30–7:00 am – Up and flipping through Instagram, Facebook, and Twitter for 30 minutes scoping out any stories that seem indulgent or totally "not-worky" – Kardashian and beauty stuff – and then any stories that might lead to other stories or ideas to ponder for stories in the future.

7:00–8:30 am – It takes about 90-minutes to be TV-ready. When I'm putting on makeup, or driving, or cleaning up my apartment, I frequently take calls (hello, speakerphone) for stories for the paper or workshop storytellers.

8:30 am – The days I am on TV, I go to a news meeting in the morning and pitch for that week and that day, and then I go to my print part of the newsroom and work on stories.

9:00 am – Start of the office day. I start with email triage. What has to be responded to immediately? I have an almost-in-box-zero. Once a week, I just go back to some past date – usually a month past – and make sure everything has been deleted, replied to, forwarded, or acted on in some way.

9:45 am – Once I've gotten back to whoever is on fire at that moment, I go through my list of upcoming stories and make sure that they're all still on the stove simmering. I am usually working on several stories of varying lengths at once and coordinating several storytelling nights at once.

10:30 am – If I need to write something complicated then I just do that all day. And I really focus. And everything sits for a week – but not for more than one week. *Deadlines: A few days a week, I file a story of some sort – long or short.

11:00 am – In the digital world stories change every hour, and you have to have the mentality to do that. If you don't, if you get stressed about all the changes, you should get out of the business.

3:30 pm – On days I am on TV I reapply blush and powder and lipstick and head downstairs to the TV studio. If it is a live shoot, I usually leave at 2:30 for a 4 pm shoot in the live truck with the videographer and make story-related calls on the way, or type emails on my phone. I love our shooters, but I couldn't give up that many hours to just sit in the car. So it is awesome that they drive and I work in the passenger seat.

More recently, Bauman and Bordoni (2014) described how liquid modernity changed the workplace: "Forms of modern life may differ in quite a few respects – but what unites them all is precisely their fragility, temporariness, vulnerability and inclination to constant change [...] [in which] change is the only permanence, and uncertainty the only certainty." They characterize the conditions of work in contemporary life as precarious, and term the people who work on contract, by piecework, and by some limited time frame as the *precariat*. Many journalists have become members of this growing group.

Research supports Bauman's theoretical work. A study conducted by IBM (2010), based on interviews with 1,500 Chief Executive Officers from 60 countries, and 33 industries worldwide, found that more than 60 percent of CEOs believe that changes in their industry are the top factors contributing to organizational uncertainty. CEOs said they needed to find innovative ways of managing an organization's structure, finances, people, and strategy. Like those in other industries, many news organizations now seek to adapt to their new environment.

The last chapter quoted *Forbes* magazine Chief Product Officer, Lewis D'Vorkin (2011), writing about why and how the format of the publication was changing. Although he wrote specifically about *Forbes*, D'Vorkin provides a good starting point to compare the differences between traditional news organizations and online news start-ups with respect to their integration of digital technologies in their operations, as shown in Table 3.2.

TABLE 3.2 Differences in news production between traditional and digital, online organizations

Elements of News Work	*Traditional news organizations go digital*	*Online news organizations start digital*
Collect news and information differently	In the library and in the field. Now online as well. Consumers of news do not play a role. The news cycle depends on the publication cycle.	Online sites, databases, and libraries and in the field. Reporters sometimes find new information in user comments to their article. The news cycle is 24/7.
Produce it differently	All mostly digital production but primary output may be channel specific: print, broadcast, etc.	Digital assembly line throughout news gathering, distribution, and consumption processes.
Present it differently	Emphasis on product for primary channel. Less emphasis on other channels. Space and time are limited.	Processes account for product on multiple digital channels. Space and time are unlimited.
Pay for it differently	Ad-supported and subscription business models.	Many different business models, usually with multiple revenue streams: Ad-support (including native advertising), subscription, pay-per (article, issue, etc.), syndication.
Distribute it differently	One distribution process for one channel. Now multiple processes, but often focused on legacy channel.	Multiple distribution processes for multiple channels, but all are digital.

Elements of News Work	Traditional news organizations go digital	Online news organizations start digital
Staff the news organization differently	News organizations hire more freelancers than in decades past, often for less money than full-time employees.	News organizations have small staffs and hire many freelancers. Some use aggregation algorithms and have virtually no staff at all.
Enable marketers to be active and engaged participants	Chinese Wall between editorial and advertising departments.	"Native advertising" is formatted to fit with (and sometimes look like) news articles.
Consumers consume it differently	TV: By appointment Radio: While driving Print: At home or at office direct delivery Consumers are receivers.	On computer and mobile devices (website, email, feed, etc.). Consumers are also participants. News staff monitors comments and responds to them, both directly and indirectly. Increasing consumer engagement is a key goal.

Bauman's ideas also find support from people working in the trenches of journalism. Ornebring, Karlsson, and Fast (2014) examined the conditions of work in the field. They found that traditionally, journalists' work consisted of routines, carried out within guidelines of professional values and standards, acting in their professional roles (rather than personal roles), with great autonomy. Moreover, traditional journalists were employed in stable, full-time jobs within organizations that demanded their full attention.

The researchers then extracted themes from contemporary research in the sociology of work to learn how they applied to the news industry. The newer themes that they found stressed:

- The precariousness of work
- Changing demands for skills (upskilling, downskilling, and reskilling)
- Rapidly changing technological infrastructure

Based on surveys of news executives and journalists, Ornebring et al. found that journalism work is much more precarious now. Profound changes in organizational structures, technology, and the increasing use of contingent labor (part-time, limited-contract, freelance, volunteer, and intern positions) have all contributed to greatly increase uncertainty for the news industry workforce.

News organizations seek many new skills to support digital journalism, requiring them to re-think what they are supposed to do and what is expected of their work. Ornebring and colleagues concluded that there is continued pressure for journalists to multiskill (take photos, shoot video, record audio, create infographics, etc.). However, depending on the individual organizational requirements, upskilling is occurring at the same time as deskilling and reskilling. In other words, ongoing (and often unpredictable) change remains the norm.

5 WAYS THE ROUTINES OF JOURNALISTS ARE CHANGING

It's not like the old days when journalists reported on, wrote assigned stories, and devoted time and energy to seeking out and developing **enterprise stories**. Today, reporters also engage in regular interaction with users, build independent followings, and perhaps grow a community around their stories in a publication. The new participatory regime affects the work roles and responsibilities of individual journalists so that they must develop new routines of working to deal with unfamiliar demands. Many reporting jobs in traditional journalism were already onerous. The added activities that call for interaction with users can overwhelm even experienced reporters, robbing them of time to spend on complex enterprise stories.

Indeed, the demands of participation have added layers upon layers of additional work on journalists. Reporters get used to responding to followers on a website or a blog; then they learn they must involve the public throughout the story, from the time the reporter starts working on it. Last year, journalists mastered Instagram; this year, it's Snapchat. The year before, they wrote keywords so their posts would be optimized for search engines and computer algorithms that re-post their comments. This year, they must learn to write for mobile screens. Next year, they'll tackle how to stream video on Facebook Live and use artificial intelligence scripts in Python language.

Pavlik (2001) thought that participating with users would also change how journalists work in deeper and more subtle ways. An early observer of the ways computers and digital networks had already begun to impact the field, Pavlik advanced ways that journalists' work would change to accommodate a connected public in ways he termed "contextualized journalism."

1. News accounts must be both more accurate and detailed than in the past
2. "Just the facts" is not enough – journalists must also provide context
3. Journalists need to interpret events, as "sense makers of events and processes"
4. Online journalists could play a central role in "reconnecting communities" with similar interests and needs

In a participatory digital environment, journalists lose a measure of the autonomy that they enjoyed in previous decades. Back in the day, reporters gathered information, published their story, and went to their next assignment, the bar, or even home – done and done. Mostly, they received little response to their articles.

Now, online reporters do not finish stories when they type *-30-* at the bottom of the page. (Newspaper reporters typed -30- to signal the end of the story to copy editors.) Today's story cycle is shorter and faster because real-time analytics monitor users' news consumption of pages and individual articles. Based on users' responses, editors task reporters to file quick re-writes, additions, or follow-ups to increase a story's popularity. Thus, the reporter's job isn't over until the users have weighed in.

Journalists experience more demands, while receiving less support than in the past. In part, this pressure stems from the difficulty news organizations have in responding to the rapid transformation of the industry. Deuze (2014) observed that journalists and other media workers often lack the support for carrying out their work that they relied on in previous decades:

as people engage with media in an increasingly immersive, always-on, almost instantaneous, and interconnected way, the very people whose livelihood and sense of professional identity depend on delivering media content and experiences seem to be at a loss on how to come up with survival strategies – in terms of business models, effective regulatory practices (for example regarding copyrights and universal access provisions), and perhaps, most specifically, the organization of entrepreneurial working conditions that would support and sustain the creative process needed to meet the demands of media life.

(p. 1)

Deuze also found that the growing entrepreneurial demands of the job are now added routines, requiring substantial time. For example, today journalists must manage their own careers, rather than working their way up career tracks in stable organizations. They are well-advised to build their personal brands, increase their number of followers, and manage their own professional training so they remain current. In short: Newsie, you're on your own.

Yet learning the skills of professional journalism may not be a solitary effort. Weischenberg, Löffelholz, and Scholl (1998) asked more than a thousand journalists how they had learned to practice their profession. They found that typical news organizations developed consistent routines to deliver consistent products through intense and frequent communication. Through these circular, internal conversations, "editors and journalists constantly reinforce, reiterate, and thus reproduce certain ways of doing things." These conversations foster that elusive characteristic of the best editors and reporters: news judgment.

Vox Verbatim: Joan Van Tassel, A Lesson in News Judgment

When I was new to journalism, I was in the Los Angeles newsroom of ABC Network News around 3 am when the fax machine wasn't in use. Using a battered fax to send more than 100 pages of documents back to New York was slow going in those days.

A report came over the wires, saying that Iraqi troops had crossed the border to launch an attack on Kuwait. Absorbed in my own story, I nodded my head and went back to reading and faxing. But it caught my attention when the shift editor/producer jumped up from his desk and strode around the large room, shouting, "No! No! No!" (Well, actually, the word started with "f.") He knew immediately that this news meant war. That's news judgment. He had it, I didn't, at least not until I had acquired more experience – this night gave me one of my first lessons.

The emergence of new technologies also disrupts journalists' routines. Like other information workers, they must adapt to new machines, applications, processes, and communication platforms. Chen (2019) interviewed 130 *New York Times* reporters, editors, and photographers to learn what they considered their most valuable technologies. Respondents found that the smartphone won hands down. In addition to communications, reporters also used smartphones to record interviews, transcribing them with **artificial intelligence (AI)** aided apps like Trint and Rev. Right up there with the mobile, NYT reporters mentioned the importance of batteries and expressed their wishes for equipment that supported longer battery life. They also used encrypted communications for confidential messages, including Signal, WhatsApp, and ProtonMail. In the field, they may have to add a 360° or 3D scanner camera to their kit, change their laptop, or migrate to a new Content Management System.

Finally, the primary organizational structure that supported intense communication between journalists has been the newsroom, an evolving workspace for the past 300 years. If their colleagues were the source of journalists' professional education, the newsroom was where it occurred. Newsrooms have been the incubators, fostering the ability of new journalists to handle the difficult, contradictory demands of the profession. Given all the changes going on in journalism, it will come as no surprise that newsrooms are changing as well.

NEW NEWS = NEW NEWSROOMS

We have seen that newsrooms are more than infrastructure. They also support vibrant social systems that train, teach, and coordinate the people who work there. However, the increase of **contingent labor** and virtual work teams, means that today's digital journalists may work only in temporary newsrooms at a convention or event. And some reporters may never experience socialization and learning in a newsroom at all. This loss of a stable workplace, surrounded by colleagues (and competitors) is so important, some freelancers pay to join other journalists and writers in "co-op" offices such as the Nieuwsatelier in Amsterdam, Netherlands. Similarly, the Writer's Junction and The Office rent space to writers of all kinds in Los Angeles.

IS THE NEWSROOM AS DEAD AS THE FRONT PARLOR?

The new news has encouraged innovative designs for newsrooms. Historically, newsrooms have changed to allow news purveyors to take advantage of business opportunities. Notably, the rise of modern journalism was fueled by an ever-increasing number of readers, as the Industrial Revolution's explosion of commerce, trade, and markets relied on more and more information. The first daily newspaper in the world was the *Daily Courant*, founded in 1702 by Samuel Buckley (Winston, 2006). Printers could run off text-only broadsheets in the hundreds, which were then passed from hand-to-hand in coffee shops and businesses. As late as the early 19th century, the "newsroom" of the London *Times* was located in the study of a private home. One *Times* writer was a clergyman, another a military retiree, and one *Times* writer was even a prisoner, released from jail on occasional holidays (Bourne, 1887).

Enter then-new technology in the mid-19th century, with the arrival of large-scale movable type printing presses in the 1850s as a driver of massive changes for journalism. The then-newfangled presses could print thousands of copies per hour, enabling newspapers to reach a truly mass audience with long articles, photographs and graphics (Johnson, 2012). This technology brought about centralized newsrooms, with easy-to-navigate workflows between journalists and press production workers. Later, 20th-century broadcast media required entirely different infrastructures: studios, editing facilities, transmitters located on the highest hills to reach a station's entire broadcast range – and eventually – video cameras, and microwave and satellite trucks.

Now, the recent technological **convergence** of digital media, the global internet, social media infrastructures, and consumer mobile devices has brought major transformations in its wake. Newsroom design and infrastructure presently support a news industry that now distributes stories across multiple media platforms. As a result, regardless of their "native" platform, newsrooms mostly use the same technologies: computers, servers, and software for writing, image manipulation, video editing, and content management.

Newsrooms that gather, process, and disseminate news for multiple distribution platforms are called **integrated** or **converged**. Building new facilities enables new configurations of technologies, space, and people that help foster more effective and economically efficient multiplatform operations. It's not easy. Most existing news organizations retained the specialized infrastructure they inherited for as long as they could, as many newspapers did, shown in Figure 3.1.

To meet the demands of distributing news over digital platforms, newsroom production designs in the late 1990s and early 2000s tried to "bolt on" the required technologies. Many television and radio stations, newspapers, magazines, and even internet news organizations adopted this bolted-on approach. It allowed them to experiment and to take advantage of new online distribution channels without completely redesigning workflows and production infrastructure, as shown in Figure 3.1. Such hybrid infrastructure often frustrated newsroom workers with its innate inefficiencies, forcing them to develop their own shortcuts and workarounds.

Some news organizations retain their legacy infrastructure and operate a **web-centric** "separate-but-equal" facilities elsewhere (or, more often, "separate-but-unequal"), but such splintered newsrooms now appear to be on the decline. *The New York Times* started putting together its print-web operations in August 2005. In 2007, *The Washington Post* integrated its news and Web functions "after an internal report called the paper 'Web-stupid'" (Wemple, 2008).

The Washington Post tried several approaches. In 1996, the company established an online newsroom in 1996 in Arlington, Virginia, separated from its D.C.-based print operation. In 2009, *The Washington Post* integrated the two newsrooms in the capitol,

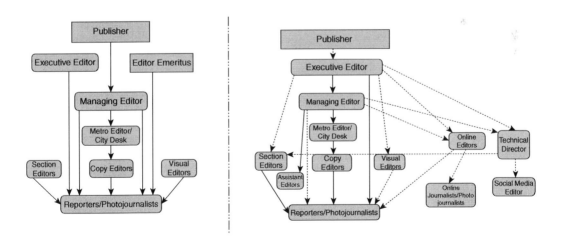

FIGURE 3.1

Legacy newspaper newsroom and early digital newsroom, before IT integration
Credit: Joan Van Tassel

FIGURE 3.2

The BBC Newsroom

Credit: Michal Bělka [CC BY-SA 4.0 (https://creativecommons.org/licenses/by-sa/4.0)]

but retained much of its legacy newspaper-inherited infrastructure. Recognizing a need for a truly integrated newsroom that would enable efficient operation across all the media platforms that the service used to disseminate its news programs and products (Moses, 2014), *The Washington Post* moved into its new converged newsroom in December 2014. Similarly, the British Broadcasting Corporation (BBC) integrated its newsroom, as shown in Figure 3.2.

Many of these expensive new integrated newsrooms support the large news operations that serve large markets. But increasingly, even smaller publications are redesigning their workspaces to accommodate new technologies, new social attitudes about fresh air, greater collaboration, and more mobility (Coester, 2017). *Quartz* (qz.com), *The Virginia Pilot*, *Pittsburgh Post-Gazette*, and the *Bucks County Courier Times* have all designed new spaces for their news operations.

Some shoestring news organizations cannot support a converged infrastructure. They may operate out of cooperative offices or even private residences, supported by high-speed broadband connectivity. In addition, some mobile journalists see themselves in the world and in the wind – the ultimate newsroom without walls.

Now that mobile has become the most popular way for users to receive digital news, newsrooms have adapted once again. Some newsrooms implement a **mobile first** production process; others start with **web first**, depending on the nature of their audience. Whether mobile first or web first, however, they usually integrate mobile story reporting and production throughout the newsroom.

DIGITAL USERS: HOW THEY MOVED FROM PASSIVE TO PASSIONATE

Online users think about news differently than traditional audiences and they engage differently as well. News consumers were long-accustomed to **one-way dissemination** platforms, such as print and broadcast. They knew that to respond to a story, they would need to write a letter to the editor or the broadcast network, only to receive a form letter in response.

Online users see a news environment where they are part of the news process, not just passive consumers, as Robinson (2013) found when she conducted in-depth interviews with about 100 residents of Madison, WI, over a two-year period. Online news users wanted to be able to follow links on stories that mattered to them, so that they could drill down into the details and background of these news reports. Users expected such links. And they wanted the ability to make comments and register their opinions. Robinson concluded that the participation of online users demands a different approach to news: "one that places a new importance on dialogue and deliberation as part of the journalism process itself. This conception should be part of the prep work for new reporters, to learn how to be a 'conversation starter.'"

Users also verify news reports that they find interesting or surprising (Edgerly, Mourão, Thorson, & Tham, 2019). The researchers found that people are most likely to verify news that confirms their existing beliefs, perhaps to make sure it represents their to views in social discussions and arguments. Unlike journalists, the purpose of their verification is *not* to discover if the news is true or not.

HOPING ENGAGEMENT LEADS TO MARRIAGE

Engagement is serious business to online news organizations. Some publications make users partners in every aspect of the news process, from the story pitch, to points beyond publishing (Stearns, 2015). They may invite users to help choose stories, collect information, comment on early forms of the story, and respond to later versions and updates. Other organizations take more limited approaches to user engagement that require listening to users and responding to what they hear (Stearns, 2014). One Chicago radio station, WQEZ, has the Curious City initiative, interacting with users to listen for ideas for news stories. The public can vote on ideas, and journalists are assigned to their choices. Chalkbeat.com has a Reader Advisory Board while NPR maintains a Source of the Week program on its website to encourage sources to come forward with their story ideas.

In the UK, *The Guardian* newspaper listens to understand how people think about issues and how they contextualize news coverage. For example, when the publication explained upcoming changes to commenting policies, they cited user behavior data as the basis for implementation (Hamilton, 2016):

> And we are working to make our comment spaces more welcoming and more connected with our editorial work. We're trialing different ways for journalists to be involved in conversations that can sometimes be overwhelming purely because of the volume of comments, and we're working to make sure that we open comments and encourage conversation only where it can be well managed – and where we can listen. We have started digging deep into the data we have on how users behave in our comment threads, and will be publishing some preliminary findings next week as part of our series, titled *The web we want*.

DIGITAL CONTENT: HOW USERS GOT A SEAT IN NEWSROOMS

Back in the day, journalists defined the news, established the newsgathering parameters, and set the public agenda. In short, journalists didn't just inform the public, they told people what they needed information about. Holding ideals of objectivity and impartiality, many traditional newsrooms subjected the claims of participants, partisans, advocates, beneficiaries, and other interested parties to a rigorous editorial examination. Sometimes their efforts didn't succeed, or, in cases of partisan-leaning publications, yellow journalism, and overt propaganda, they didn't hold those ideals at all. But for the most part, respected publications did their best to reach the ideals of journalistic practice.

Then the interactive internet made it possible for anyone to participate in the public domain to the extent their interests, time, and effort allow. Now individuals set their own news agenda by choosing the news sites and cable channels that most closely approximate the events they consider news. Journalists can define this or that as news, but if an event, personality, or condition becomes a phenomenon on the internet on social media – it's news, no matter what newsrooms may think about it.

The public gets a seat in the newsroom the same way journalists do: They notice something, find out about it, document it, and distribute it. Whether it's a "like," "share," video, podcast, or 120-page screed, users participate in the global public conversation, contributing news content. Unrestrained by journalistic principles and ideals, they judge, opine, and emote freely, bringing their judgments, opinions, and emotions to the daily news stream.

What could go wrong? Some researchers and journalists believe that plenty has already gone wrong. Others welcome the change. And many more ordinary people are now busy fish in a very big news pond that is crowded with more (and more different) fish than ever before.

SHAPE-SHIFTED AND PLATFORM PROMISCUOUS

Characteristics of digital content and networks make participation all so easy. The two-character digital numeric "alphabet," 0s and 1s, provide the building blocks for all digital content – text, pictures, sound, and video. This underlying unity enables servers, networks, routers and switches, software, and services to work together to process and transport digital content. It also fosters transformations between what, at first glance, may appear to be incompatible content types, structures, and formats.

Experience confirms the wide-ranging interchangeability of digital assets. Even novices learn quickly that somewhere, somehow, software exists to turn one kind of file format into another format. Whether it's .docx to .rtf, .txt, or .pdf; .pptx to .pages; .jpeg to .png or .bmp; .csv to .xlsx; or .flv to .mp4 – there *must* be a way to do it.

Information itself is almost as pliable. A picture is worth 1,000 words. A graph replaces a complex, number-filled paragraph. A short video conveys emotions that words cannot fully describe. Armed with the power of Photoshop and other software, just about anyone can shape-shift digital pictures and even audio and video. Don't like blue? Make it yellow. Blood on the concrete isn't real enough? Tweak brightness, hue, and saturation. Want to put a politician's head on a tyrannosaurus? Add in a picture of somebody at a party they didn't attend? There's always a way.

The modifiability of digital content enables news organizations to send material everywhere. In newsrooms, team members assemble stories, pages, and news sites. Integrated newsrooms create multiple versions in advance to meet the different platform requirements, such as automated file packaging and conversion for multiple publications, languages, and end-user devices. More automated software carries out language translations, layout conversion, element resizing, data compression, and a host of other changes needed to get news material to its users. Then through user sharing, content hops around the world at the speed of light, speeding from one social media platform to another and from one user to another.

Users have the power to create information, modify an existing news story, and publish their version of news. In fact, some prominent news organizations have already republished doctored images and fake stories. These problems now loom large for video as well, because software to modify and falsify video images has improved. The speed of digital networks enables media counterfeiters to send their work out just as news organizations can, distributing their content everywhere before anyone can discover the alterations. Individuals, companies, interest groups, and even national governments have all distributed misinformation. It's not surprising: They all have powerful incentives to make sure their versions of events shape public opinion. Welcome to the 21st century.

BEYOND CONSUMPTION: EXPERIENCING THE NEWS

As the last two decades make clear, media and content both change as communications technologies advance. In the past, when people accessed a news source and then took it in, they described people as "consuming news." That consumption still takes place in different ways: On TV, they watch it. Online, the term consumption makes less sense. Yes, people read and watch news, but they also interact with it and create additional content.

However, in **virtual reality (VR)** and **augmented reality (AR)**, users move far from consumption – they experience the news. For this reason, news stories completed in these virtual environments are called **experiences**, rather than articles, reports, or packages. Even when the events took place before the user entered the virtual environment, the subjective experience comes very close to a "you are there" sense of participation.

VR and AR share characteristics, so sometimes they are put together and called **extended reality (XR)** or **mixed reality (MR)**. The images in extended reality stories can include both video and 3D graphic representations. They both include scans of actual objects and virtual objects that the user can explore in 360°.

But VR and AR differ. VR is a 360° world that users experience by wearing a headset that wraps around their eyes and sends sound to their ears. People have to wear the headset to experience it. They open their eyes to a virtual world of 360° – VR is everywhere they look. A person's brain processes the features of this world much as it does in any environment, rapidly assimilating and adapting to "how things work." The feeling of being in a real world that feels natural and all-encompassing is called "presence," a sense of "being there." The quality of the headset, the graphics or video, the speed of responsiveness, the naturalness of motion, and the accessories that allow users to move around the

FIGURE 3.3

Oh, wow! So that's virtual reality!

Credit: Bernd Schray from Pixabay.com

FIGURE 3.4

Augmented reality that you can share with your friends

Credit: Gerd Altmann from Pixabay.com

virtual world are all factors that increase or decrease users' sense of presence in the created environment.

AR, however, may have 3D objects located in 2D space, allowing users to have AR experiences on mobile telephones. Users can rotate an object completely on their mobile phone. They can move through a 3D environment that changes as they move through it. Yet the experience still takes place on their mobile phone screen.

The Reality of Extended Reality

Newsrooms have used AR to offer user experiences, such as *The New York Times*' app that lets mobile users look at the paper's more than 15 AR projects. The Mars InSight rover and the coverage of four athletes from the 2018 Olympics are two good examples of NYT AR (Spinelle, 2019). Throughout 2019, the France 2 TV channel featured AR experiences that show the progress of repair to Notre Dame Cathedral after the tragic fire that damaged the famed structure. *Quartz* produced a much-lauded experience of the Cassini Spacecraft. And *The Washington Post* created a walkthrough of Freddie Gray's altercation with police that ultimately ended with his death in custody from the injuries he sustained.

> "Simply explaining Gray's interaction with police through text can't achieve the same effect as when a user has the ability to choose from which angle and from which point in the altercation they want to experience this encounter," said Francesco Marconi, strategy manager and AI co-lead at the Associated Press.
>
> (Nahser, 2017)

Other publications that have put considerable resources into XR include CNN, *USA Today*, and *VICE*. Publishers are using XR because research suggests that it raises engagement and fosters deeper information seeking about the story (Kang, O'Brien, Villarreal, Lee, and Mahood, 2019; Kline, 2019). Other reasons advanced for using XR experiences are:

- The release of software by Apple and Google to distribute augmented reality on iOS and Android devices created a ready-made audience, so the number of AR experiences may well increase.
- News informs and thus people learn from it.
- News entertains as well as informs, as users find some stories are interesting, exciting, incredible, and inspiring.

Journalists are likely to have more opportunities to work with XR from advances on the near horizon. AR and VR will have increased performance and power as it is enhanced with AI. In addition, these environments will soon link to social networks for even great exposure and engagement.

For newsrooms to make XR an established routine, particularly VR, the cost of creation and display technologies will need to come down even further. That process is underway, with good 360° cameras and 3D sensors costing less than $600 and software innovations. In the next few years, when 5G telephone networks bring faster mobile networks online, newsrooms expect to increase the number of XR experiences they create.

CONCERNS ABOUT CONTESTED CONTENT

When people experience the news through XR, it becomes more obvious that widespread misinformation and disinformation will pose serious challenges to all societies. For journalists, there are more subtle effects of widespread public participation. For example, the social media platforms that enable the rapid transmission of fact-checked news reports also spread inaccurate, unfair, damaging, and misleading content. While decrying the spread of misinformation, journalists have largely accepted the role of social media in shaping coverage, disseminating legitimate news, and building a following. Many journalists participate on social media themselves, particularly Twitter (Broersma & Eldridge, 2019).

For some reporters, citizen journalism may be problematic. Carried out by people who have no training in assessing the accuracy of information, verifying it, presenting it impartially, or providing fairness to subjects, potential exists to cause harm. Thus, although they may have skepticism or reject homegrown reports altogether, they accept citizen journalism as part of the digital environment: People are free to carry out their own research, publish their findings, add to the public store of knowledge, and sometimes attract large followings.

However, the rise of subjective storytelling, and its near cousin, emotion, has generated greater discomfort within newsrooms. Eyewitness accounts and emotion have long been staples of journalism. In accounts of tragic events, journalists may report the observations and emotions of witnesses and participants as objective facts. But the combination of subjective stories, emotional appeals, or opinion raises concerns among some journalists when they appear to violate the traditional journalistic principles of detachment and impartiality.

The RAND Corporation published an analysis of thousands of reports and news programs comparing news before and after 2000 (Kavanaugh et al. 2019). The stories came from multiple media sources, including print, television, cable television, and online sites. The study identified differences between the two periods (pre-2000 and post-2000) in linguistic style, perspective, and word choice in news, documenting the shift toward subjectivity and emotion in the news. Reporting on the RAND study, Owen (2019) noted:

> Even as many aspects of newspaper coverage remained the same, then, there does seem to have been a shift from coverage focused on numbers, authority, and imperatives to coverage that uses storytelling and such contextual details as dates to portray an issue.

Emotional content is of particular concern in extended reality environments. Archer and Finger (2018) found that users have stronger empathetic responses to VR images than to static pictures or text. Subjects said they experienced greater immersion and were more likely to take social or political action than the people consuming static news, especially if they were not very familiar with the story. However, the researchers caution against showing too many scenes of violence, injury, and suffering that can disturb users. Such material can cause some people to disengage from the experience altogether.

The rise of subjective and emotional reportage is disquieting to both journalists and those who support its roles in democracy and public discourse. As news has become more subjective and emotional, public trust of expertise and fact-based evidence has declined. Public discussions of policies increasingly devolve into uninformed opinions and anecdotes about personal experience (Kavanaugh & Rich, 2018).

Even those who believe that journalism must adapt to the rise of subjective/and emotional reportage (rather than ignoring or rejecting it), recognize the challenge it poses to the journalistic enterprise. Beckett (2015) examined how individual journalists adapt to covering emotion-laden events and how newsrooms accommodate them into their workflow processes, as shown in Figure 3.5.

Another reason for journalists' heightened concern about subjectivity and emotion in news is that it directly affects their work. Not only do today's users find accounts of individuals and emotional news stories appealing, but they also engage with them (de Los Santos & Nabi, 2019, p. 53). For example, they click on subjective and emotional stories and spend more time on the pages. It is no surprise that more clicks and longer dwell time drive news managers to encourage reporters and writers to report such stories.

Beckett and Deuze (2016) theorized that these changes in user preferences mean that subjectivity and emotion in news are here to stay. Journalists must find ways to adapt, while maintaining important principles and standards. As the authors put it: "The trend is clear: toward a more mobile, personalized, and emotionally driven news media. The challenge for the networked journalist is clear: how best to sustain the ethical, social, and economic value of journalism in this new emotionally networked environment."

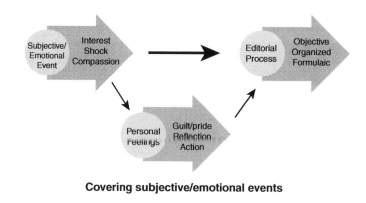

FIGURE 3.5

Journalist and newsroom adaptation to emotional events

Credit: Joan Van Tassel, based on original graphics by Professor C. Beckett, at: https://blogs.lse.ac.uk/polis/2015/09/10/how-journalism-is-turning-emotional-and-what-that-might-mean-for-news/

THE VIRAL IMPERATIVE: USING CONTENT TO MOVE USERS FROM PARTICIPANTS TO PROMOTERS

During the broadcast era, when people turned on the TV for the evening's network news show, the audience came to the channel. But now the media world doesn't work that way. Today, news outlets must reach out to their audiences, providing potential readers with links where they can easily access those stories that interest them.

One reason reporters may spend valuable time interacting with users is to keep them engaged. But an even more important reason is to move users from merely participating-in to promoting stories. For news sites (or stories) to gain more users and followers, they must enlist already engaged users as advocates – unpaid marketers and promoters who can send out content snippets with URLs to other potential users in their personal networks.

Some content goes viral – users share it with friends, families, and followers, who in turn share with still others in their social networks. The appeal of content to would-be sharers is a quality that social media theorist Henry Jenkins calls **spreadability**. In 2009, Jenkins famously wrote: "If it doesn't spread, it's dead." Jenkins, Ford, and Green (2013) studied changes in the way people discovered and distributed digital content in a networked environment. This spreadability meme created new understandings of how the spread of interactive, participatory online media has influenced society and culture. In a networked world, only spreadable content can reach and influence large numbers of people. Thus, stories that don't spread – really are dead.

Jenkins' ideas influenced the ways that news organizations understood their audiences, leading them to measure and track user actions with real-time **analytics**. Ethnographic researcher Angele Christin (2014) spent two years observing newsrooms in the U.S. and France to understand the effects such analytics have on newsroom culture. Christin found that :

- Analytics, usually received by editors in real-time, helps structure the daily routines of newsrooms.

- Reporters and writers receive data about user rankings of articles regularly throughout their workday.

- High rankings on articles by users influence management's promotion and pay decisions.

- Some journalists express disdain for **metrics** – but most journalists regularly monitor the top ten most-read articles on their own initiative.

- For some journalists, getting good numbers is a game – for others, it is an imposition that keeps them from other, more important, work.

For working journalists, Christin's central takeaway is that receiving analytics, particularly those related to user behaviors, affects newsroom routines. Editors now adjust and change page layouts based on analytics, featuring popular stories on the landing page and linking them to less popular ones. Or they may rewrite headlines, add or take out images – whatever actions they think will improve **click-through** or increase the amount of time users spend on stories.

Measures of user engagement are usually part of the analytics package, sometimes called metrics. Measures of user engagement refer to observable behaviors (actions) rather than attitudes, opinions, or feelings. These behaviors are often recorded as time spent on some activity with content – on the news website, the story, the interactive element. The behaviors that organizations measure vary by management requirements, the metrics programmed into site servers, or the analytics provided by such outside vendors as Google Analytics, Newsbeat (by Chartbeat Publishing), SignalNoi.se, or Topsy.

The amount of time spent by users is the key metric, measured in seconds, minutes, hours, etc. (or no time at all). How the user spends that time can mean reading, clicking on interactive content, answering polls, commenting, liking, recommending, sharing, and so forth. Spending little or no time on the site is an important measure, too: the **bounce rate** shows how many users check out a page and leave the publication's site without clicking on any other pages or links on the site. It means that page did not create sufficient interest for the user to continue further on the site.

Clearly time spent is not the only measure of user engagement. Twitter.com's measures of how much a story engages users focuses on actions:

- The number of tweets that are addressed to the journalist's (or perhaps the news organization's) handle
- The number of times the tweets about the story are retweeted to others
- The number of mentions the story gets in tweets

Journalists look at different measures. They usually want to know how many people read their story, how many "likes" and "shares" it received, and the vitality of user comments. Many reporters want to see good discussions that include disagreement, so they are not typically concerned with whether the comments agree with the story. However, few people enjoy comments by mean-spirited online **trolls**, people who deliberately create discord and dismay. Because trolls sometimes post racist, sexist, insulting, and uncivil comments, many news sites moderate comment sections. *The New York Times*, for example, not only moderates comments, but it also selects comments it finds worthy, uprating them in their comment software. *The Washington Post* does not moderate its comments other than to delete obvious profane or hate speech, with the predictable result that now many commenters are trolls who may hate Republicans, Democrats, the plutocrats, the story reporter, politics, government, or all the above.

Vox Verbatim: Monica Guzman, VP of Local at WhereBy.Us

All of the reporters got access to their analytics for their blogs, or whatever they were writing, so we could all have more of a look at how our content was actually being received. So huge! To actually see the numbers and see what was being read and it's also dangerous. I think it's very easy to get too obsessed with that and I have a lot of experience in what happens when it becomes too much of a focus. […] It started to feel like "Okay, maybe if I can check Twitter one more time I can find some little thing I can write a post about that takes me 20 minutes and gets tons of clicks." But that's unfair to users – it's about the quality of news.

The involvement of journalists in social media, whether on the site, blogs, Twitter, Facebook, Instagram, and other social media sites, has surged. A longitudinal study (Kraeplin & Batsell, 2013) sampled more than 200 newspapers and 173 TV stations at

JOURNALISTS @WORK

three points in time: 2002–2003, 2004–2005, and 2011. The authors found that during the first two periods, there was negligible demand for journalists to have social media skills. But by 2011, three-fourths of newspapers and 70 percent of TV stations said that, for new hires, they placed social media skill higher than anything except: 1) the ability to report and write news, and 2) news judgment.

For reporters, the additional duties of anticipating and responding to analytics include writing on social media, sometimes requiring much additional time and focus. Reporters often post enticing snippets of current stories, read and sometimes respond to comments, update stories based on user feedback, and search comments for possible leads or unexplored avenues. Of course, this takes journalists' time away from pursuing other stories, digging up new sources, talking with existing sources, and looking for new stories and leads.

Still, no matter how busy they are, many journalists understand that to be successful, they must participate with users. If users don't share a story, reporters find it more difficult to accumulate a large audience for it. News organizations, sites, journalists, and users together form ad hoc networks of people who have shared but divergent interests in news content. It's the totality of their active engagement that now propels issues to prominence in the public agenda.

Call it the viral imperative with a tip of the hat to Henry Jenkins: If content doesn't spread, it's so dead.

TAKEAWAYS

- Journalism performs many roles in modern societies, with different emphases, depending on culture and other social factors. News informs. It entertains. It monitors important actions and issues, and interprets events. The press brings issues into the public sphere for discussion, thus helping to set society's agenda. Journalists act as critics and gatekeepers against inaccurate information. They sometimes provide the public with a "court of last resort," when injustice occurs. One terse summary of journalistic purpose reads: "comfort the afflicted and afflict the comfortable."

  During the second decade of the 21st century, trust in news media dropped significantly in many societies around the world. The rise of the internet and social media gave people more direct access to events and a much wider array of opinions than before, undercutting the gatekeeper role that the press had earlier played. In today's information-rich environment, public reliance on the news media to: 1) inform, 2) interpret, and 3) set the public agenda has declined as well, particularly in Western societies.

- Journalistic cultures vary across nations and regions. One study found four distinct newsroom cultures that influence the way the press goes about its business while covering and publishing news.

  o *Populist disseminators* act as the voice of the people; news publications express audiences' values and entertain users.

  o *Detached watchdogs* act as monitors of leaders and elites, viewing them with skeptical and critical eyes to ensure they live-up to their expected societal roles.

  o *Critical change agents* generally oppose leaders and elites. Journalists believe that the press must help their country change in order to become fairer and work more effectively on behalf of more people.

○ *Opportunistic facilitators* act as partners with leaders and elites. Journalists generally support leaders' objectives and plans, and they try to help elites implement them.

- Individuals tend to adopt attitudes consistent with the journalistic culture in which they work. In Western countries, journalists tend to value detachment and non-involvement, impartiality, factual accuracy, and careful observance of professional ethical principles. They generally accept the role of watchdog, but avoid promoting specific values, ideas, or social change.

- Many working journalists are part of the new *precariat* in the uncertain reality of "liquid modernity." Journalists often receive below-average earnings and benefits compared to others with similar educational backgrounds and professional expertise. In the downsized world of news media – part-time, limited-contract, and freelance workers (who have few rights) have replaced full-time employees.

  The social environment is difficult as well. Professional relationships with the people a reporter covers are often laced with manipulation and suspicion on both sides. And the profession itself is highly competitive. Journalists must find balances between ambition and service, competition and camaraderie, self-sufficiency and accountability, objectivity and empathy, and between rigorous judgment and open-mindedness.

  Jobs in journalism have changed to become far more demanding, requiring learning new skills, and adopting new routines. In addition to traditional journalistic skills of uncovering information, finding sources, and fluent writing – digital adaptability and expertise are essential. Identifying locations of and working with online information repositories and databases are important competencies.

  Interacting with users on social media and promoting their work has become another part of the job. Given the job-uncertainty in the news industry, journalists must now promote themselves to develop a following that will make the journalist valuable to their publishers.

- Journalism's workplace has evolved as new technologies for delivering news have become available. The Industrial Revolution created rise of manufacturing, trade, and commerce drove the need for economic and market-related information. Journalism filled that need, although professionally-staffed newsrooms did not develop immediately. The availability of large-scale movable type printing presses in the mid-19th century enabled mass printing, thus supporting centralized mass-subscriber news organizations.

  Through World War II, newsroom design maximized print efficiency. Designs for broadcast facilities then emerged from 1950 to the mid-1980s. The rise of computers and digital distribution networks made single-platform designs inefficient. As news organizations gradually extended their reach across multiple platforms, they tried to extend their existing single-platform newsrooms to accommodate the digital newcomers.

  But most of these early efforts proved ineffective. Newsroom designs gradually incorporated multi-platform functionality during the late 1990s, continuing through the present. Today's newsrooms vary, depending on their specific needs, but they generally extend the legacy facilities to incorporate internet and mobile distribution.

- At its most fundamental level, digital content is expressed in 0s and 1s, enabling compatibility between different types of content, hardware, software, and networks.

Thus, news organizations can produce content in one medium and readily transport it for modification and use on multiple platforms: print, broadcast, computers, and mobile devices. But the ease of transforming digital content transcends news organizations: Users, especially those with excellent computer skills, can also take advantage of digital content's malleability – by photoshopping images, rewriting text, and doctoring audio. The ability to alter all kinds of original digital content probably will increase as computational power, software development, and network speed increase. One key problem persists: Once released, counterfeit content can reach millions of people via digital networks before anyone discovers the alteration.

- The roles of news organizations, journalists, and users are changing. Users feel part of the news process. They expect to: 1) find links to additional material that interests them, 2) make comments, and 3) register their opinions. News organizations encourage (or require) reporters to participate on social media networks, responding to users, and commenting on their stories. Reporters also realize that jobs at a given publication may end at any time through acquisition or reorganization. This uncertainty of employment requires that journalists invest time in building social media followings that are interested in their beat or their style of writing and reporting.

  News organizations have also entered the interactive arena to varying degrees. Most have established new ways for users to get involved: opportunities to write comments, offer news tips and leads, send emails to editors or reporters, enter contests, respond to polls, and even to provide opinions on editorial decisions.

- Data analytics provide measurements of how a publication performs. Perhaps the most important set of metrics (measurements) is user behaviors. These metrics include the number of unique visitors to the news site, time spent on each page, number of click-throughs to an article, time spent on each article, number of click-throughs to advertising from a page or article, and the number of click-aways from an article, section, page, or the site (bounce rate).

  Data analytics may stream continuously throughout the news organization or just appear at certain times during the workday. News organization executives, editors, and reporters usually follow them avidly. Editors often re-position stories and pages and rewrite headlines based on the story's analytics; reporters may congratulate themselves – or their colleagues on successful articles, those much clicked-on stories that hold readers' attention.

  Critics of the "journalism of instant feedback" point to the many stories that do not attract users' attention but nevertheless are important for these users to read. Such stories might be about an expected change in interest rates that fails to materialize, a new state law, or changes in precinct voting places. These stories may be dropped quickly by online publications if they cannot compete with the latest Kardashian news or leaks about a popular TV series finale.

KEY CONCEPTS AND TERMS

- Changes to journalists' work in the last decade include working conditions, roles, and responsibilities
- The culture and attitudes of journalists
- Changes in the news industry in the transition from legacy to integrated newsrooms

- Changes in news content in transition from legacy to multiplatform publication
- Changes in the relationship between journalists and users
- User behavior, metrics and analytics, editorial decisions, and news coverage

EXERCISES AND ACTIVITIES

1. How are news organizations doing financially in your state? Find out which media companies own the two largest papers in your state. Go to the U.S. Securities and Exchange Commission EDGAR database, www.sec.gov/edgar/searchedgar/companysearch.html. Look up the two media companies and examine their latest 10-Q (Quarterly financial report) filing. Locate a section that provides management's overview and the analysis of financial condition and operations. How is each company doing? Which parts of each company are doing well? Which parts are struggling? (You may find additional information from financial analysts' opinions, summarized on Yahoo! Finance.)

2. Examine three ambitious digital-only publications, such as www.qz.com, www.axios.com, and www.vox.com. Compare one of them with your favorite online news source. How do they interact with users? How do they invite users to participate? Describe the "tone" they adopt to establish a connection with users.

3. Consider the following aphorisms often cited in newsrooms: Journalism/journalists should "afflict the comfortable and comfort the afflicted" and "Get it first, get it right, get it done." Answer the following questions:
   a. Who is comfortable? How can the comfortable be afflicted?
   b. Who is afflicted? How can the afflicted be comforted?
   c. What are the potential conflicts between getting it first, getting it right, and getting it done?
   d. What can a journalist do when someone else gets it first?
   e. What can reporters do when they get it wrong?

ADVANCER

Chapter 4 turns to the process of writing stories and creating multimedia articles. It compares the underlying structures of reports and stories and provides details about the ways that journalists write reports and stories. It also examines how the prominence of the people in the story, the publications in which an article appears, and the demands of story topics shape the creation of the final news product. Chapter 4 also describes the various multimedia content types and how they contribute to creating compelling narratives. Finally, it discusses the team efforts required to publish well-crafted, significant reports and stories.

PART II

REPORTING: PARTNERING WITH PROCESSORS

4

WWWORD SLINGING: ONLINE STORY STRUCTURES & STRATEGIES

Chapter Learning Objectives

After reading this chapter, students will be able to:

1. Understand how the internet changes news story creation.
2. Know the structures of news reports and narrative stories.
3. Apply the structures of news reports to online articles.
4. Understand why stories matter to people.
5. Apply narrative storytelling structures to online news stories.
6. Consider how journalists use multiple media types in the digital environment.
7. Analyze how report and narrative story structures affect reportorial strategies.
8. Apply storytelling principles to data-based articles.

There's a reason newspaper articles are called stories. That's what they are most of the time. Stories. A reporter is nothing more than a storyteller when it comes right down to it. He has a limited number of facts to work with, and from those facts he [or she] must weave a tale that will hold. But either way, the facts are not the story. The story lies in the inferences, the color, and the spin. These are what reporters are paid for, and their job – their sacred oath – is to make the news pop. It has to sing. It has to thrill. Without all that, it isn't really news to anyone.

– David Hosp, *Innocence*, p. 113

A word after a word after a word is power.

– Margaret Atwood, *Spelling*

THE GIST

Novelist Margaret Atwood reminds us that written words have power. Fingertips on the keyboard, facing the blank page with only words to tell the tales of the real world – that's an awesome, sometimes lonely place. But it's also a powerful place because when a reporter combines words into a compelling news story, as described by David Hosp. news stories can change the world, or at least a part of it. Journalists' stories – done well – may help a single person, family, community, or industry.

Chapter 4 describes how to structure online reports and stories. As a journalist gathers information for an article, it begins to take shape in the reporter's mind, a kind of natural structure. This half-conceptualized structure then informs the collection of additional information to flesh out the way the story will unfold. But the new information may change the reporter's ideas about the structure that would be appropriate for the story. Thus, these two aspects of reporting – story structure and information gathering – affect one another iteratively as the story comes to life.

For example, when an editor says: "cover the City Council meeting tomorrow night", the reporter will attend, take notes, and probably intend to write a linear report that uses the who-what-where-when of the inverted pyramid. Suppose an observant journalist noticed a series of 3 – 2 votes that indicated a seriously divided City Council. Then the story might become a narrative describing increasing disagreement, political division, and strife between competing municipal factions. These two alternative stories require quite different facts, from disparate sources, and a narrative structure appropriate to the story.

Imagine further that multiple credible sources tell the reporter that the factions actually reflect underlying different characteristics and interests between the voter bases of the city's council districts. The editor agrees this is an interesting enterprise story the reporter should pursue – but in the meantime, she wants that 600-word report covering what happened at the City Council meeting last night. Note that it is not uncommon for a complex narrative to emerge from a routine report: The Watergate investigative reporting came out of a seemingly simple big-city occurrence when the police caught and arrested the miscreants, and hauled them before a municipal night court judge to face charges.

Some stories are so paramount, they have the potential to alter the course of events within countries, regions, or perhaps the entire world. When writing them, *how* journalists tell them may be as important as the information contained in the story: The words and images matter. The 2020 global coronavirus pandemic was such an unfolding story. Reporters learned to exercise care when describing the risks that the virus posed to the public, so as not to incite panic among users and their social networks. Recall that even careful reports led people to hoard toilet paper and hand sanitizer.

Yet compelling journalism demands sound structures and memorable stories if news is to interest and engage users, as well as inform them. This chapter covers the story structures to produce articles that capture and hold users' attention. Drawing from a legacy of powerful and enduring communication forms, these familiar styles help audiences comprehend new events and absorb unfamiliar information. The styles are so vital to journalists' connections with their publics that journalism schools expend huge resources teaching students how to write effective news reports and stories.

The two structures most widely used by news writers are:

- The inverted pyramid format online that dominates writing news reports in both traditional and digital media.

- Narrative formats reveal stories with beginning, middle, and ending sequences that resolve the central conflicts confronting one or more characters.

Chapter 4 describes the purposes, elements, and structures that underlie digitally-distributed news reports, news feature stories, and scenic narrative nonfiction stories. It compares legacy media with online media platforms, showing how crafting reports and narratives differs in online venues. It shows how journalists adapt traditional news writing for digital platforms to incorporate many types of media (text, images, audio, video, and interactives) in their stories. Chapter 4 also examines how user control changes users' experience with digital news, and permits users to co-create articles, based on their own preferences and responses.

Finally, this chapter describes how journalists can take advantage of these new interactive possibilities to enrich and strengthen their articles. Armed with this understanding, reporters can apply the report and narrative structures they already know. And the greater array of media types offers exciting experiences that engage users in ways never before possible. The last section in this chapter will cover the important new opportunities for journalists to make data central to their storytelling.

WELCOME TO THE ONLINE WWWORLD

Chapter 3 covered sociologist Zygmunt Bauman's concept of liquid modernity – defined as a social condition that occurs when change happens faster than people can incorporate it into their everyday habits and routines. People who are battered by rapid social changes often experience a sustained sense of incompleteness, unpredictability, and uncertainty.

No human invention expresses this notion of ceaseless change more than the internet – unrelenting change and unending offerings that impact us for good and ill. Immersion is one of the most common ways that users describe their internet experience. On smartphones, people immerse themselves in the content on their small screens, rather than even acknowledge or communicate with the people around them. They walk without glancing up for traffic lights, cars, other people, barriers, stairs, holes in the sidewalk, and the many other potential dangers that might lurk in their immediate environment.

But for all the change the internet hath wrought … news still starts with the first draft of a series of words, sentences, paragraphs, and pages. And the reason is that words are the journalist's most potent and versatile of all their tools. As Bertrand Russell (1948, p. 74) wrote seven decades ago: "A dog cannot relate his autobiography; however eloquently he may bark, he cannot tell you that his parents were honest but poor." Russell's quote demonstrates how language expresses both specific and abstract thoughts. It conveys ideas and concepts that are not visible; it may even describe things that have never existed.

FIGURE 4.1

Immersed in content on their mobile phones

Credit: Joan Van Tassel

The next section considers how news writers can best adapt their writing for the web, focusing on the way users access and consume content and the special advantages the internet offers content creators. It provides specific tips and techniques to guide journalist storymakers – and how to avoid pitfalls. And it suggests strategies that improve users' experience, encouraging them to engage in the story.

3 THINGS ABOUT THE INTERNET THAT AFFECT HOW TO WRITE NEWS FOR THE WEB

An online search will turn up many suggestions for writing web news content. Crafting stories for the internet should follow from the internet's Big Three properties that make writing for it different from writing for other media platforms:

1. It carries enormous amounts of all types of digital data.
2. It supports many simultaneous or quasi-simultaneous, two-way data flows.
3. It extends agency (control) to the users at the edges of the network.

WEB PROPERTY 1: IT'S A REALLY BIG IMMERSIVE WWWORLD

A global fiber-optic network infrastructure supports the internet. Since the internet is a digital network, it carries any kind of digital content. The network doesn't care what the 0s and 1s stand for; it just pushes them around the world at warp speed! The days of journalists having to squeeze a story into six column inches have passed. Online, stories can be as long as needed to tell the story, enhanced with text, images, audio, video, data, and interactives.

But wait! Doesn't every list of web writing tips emphasize that you have 1.2 nanoseconds to capture user's attention: Write short or you'll lose the user (Rogers, 2019). Yes, that's true too!

Here's the deal: User time and attention drive the user-story interaction. The finest reporting, written with intelligence, passion, and significance means absolutely nothing without users!

The web is so big and so interesting that we are all caught between the attraction of the story in front of us … and the lure of the story we haven't yet seen. Most users skim the headlines. When a story catches their interest, they click on that headline, reading only as much of that story as they want to. Then they move on to the next story, their dental appointment, office, or homework assignment. But some users *really*, *really* care about a story that interests them. These users linger over the report, click on the audio, video, documents, and follow the links to drill down to the background, similar incidents, previous stories, biographies, Wikipedia entries, and social media comments – just like you do when stories matter to you.

Are there ways a writer can take advantage of these properties? You betcha … here are some tips:

- *Tip #1 – Keep your initial report short and succinct and provide an image or two.* Make it easy for those users who want to know what's going on in their world – and just want the facts.

- *Tip #2 – Write long and include all the elements available.* Be transparent. Take users on the journalistic journey that led to your report. Distribute the elements of the story across multiple pages, the links to the artifacts and the media that are connected to the story: previous stories, photo gallery, videos, audio, documents, interview transcripts, data, and interactive data-driven resources. Links help users who want to know more about your story to find these pieces. And links appeal to users who want to know *a lot more* about your story. (To the extent the links take users to another page on the site, they will thrill publishers and editors who want to maximize the time users spend on their sites.)

- *Tip #3 – Write a ticktock or a roundup when it makes sense.* Over time, reporters may write many stories about the same topic. If a story comes up regularly on your beat or if you have an ongoing assignment to report on the same or a related story, codify the story's progression from time to time. Post a **roundup** to the cluster of artifacts you've already posted. Often, an annotated timeline provides an ideal format for a **ticktock**, replete with pop-up links to the story at each point in time. And think big – complex stories may rate both roundups and updated ticktocks.

WEB PROPERTY 2: USERS PARTICIPATE IN STORIES: SHARE THE ROAD ON THE INTERACTIVE INTERNET

The online space has big highways, with many other drivers. Smart reporters know users sometimes provide valuable information and experience that add to a story. No one likes a road hog or a conversational monopolist. Share … if you want to be shared!

- *Tip #1 – Share the road on the interactive internet.* Work the data for a variety of interactives. Interactives can be simple (polls and timelines, for example). A clever, easy-to-use interactive recently launched on the liberal news web site www.huffpost. com. Flip-Side lists current issues in the news. Click on any issue, and the interactive shows a grid of headlines from across the political spectrum. It's a graphically simple, interesting way to help users sample the perspectives that different publications bring to topical issues.

- *Tip #2 – Make room for multiple perspectives.* Offer clear invitations to all users for comments. Even if a news site takes a partisan position, reporters can monitor the comment section for different opinions. Reply to commenters who bring different perspectives – personal experiences, facts, and evidence – to your article. Maybe you missed something – who doesn't? Another look might lead to an excellent follow-up article for an open-minded journalist.

- *Tip #3 – Ask users for help.* Collaboration with users can be an effective and useful strategy to help reporters deal with massive databases or factual uncertainty. And of course, collaboration spurs user engagement.

- *Tip #4 – Don't feed the trolls.* Keep in mind that some **trolls** are bots, not people at all. However, some percentage of human users *are* news trolls, people who attempt to discredit the journalists, reports, and stories they don't like. When engaged in an exchange or two to identify persons who are hyper-partisan (or complete wackos), counter with facts and evidence. Be respectful during the first one or two exchanges – then roll up your windows and drive on. Repeat: Don't feed the trolls.

WEB PROPERTY 3: USERS ARE IN CONTROL – JOURNALISTS HAVE NOTHING TO LOSE BUT THEIR CLICKS

Keep users paramount in your mind. Help them control and co-create their experience of your story. News sites provide information to users. They must also provide *sharable* information and content. And minimize the friction. **Friction** is anything that is a barrier to completing an exchange or process. For content, friction is the anti-spreadability factor, preventing people from internet participation, including receiving, publishing, or sharing news on the net. Zwillenberg, Field, and Dean (2014) identified four kinds of friction.

Sources of Friction

- *Infrastructure friction*: The availability, cost, speed, and quality of networks all dictate if and how much people can access the internet.
- *Industry friction*: This source of friction affects news operations in small communities and in poor regions of the world. Publications need economic and human capital to make internal improvements, and to hire qualified engineers, designers, and expert researchers for data management and quantitative analysis.
- *Individual friction*: Deters people from engaging in online activity. Money, computer skills, literacy, spare time, and security or privacy fears keep people offline.
- *Information friction*: Missing web navigation aids, inadequate user help, messy design, language, government censorship, and surveillance present barriers to users around the world.

Journalists can't do much about most sources of friction. But online news sites can help reduce informational friction in these four ways:

- *Tip #1 – Use clickbait carefully.* **Clickbait** is a lure designed to entice users to click on a link. Everyone needs traffic on the site. But don't overpromise so that users click on headlines and then find stories that don't deliver value on the promoted topic or provide information or entertainment.
- *Tip #2 – Advocate for high- and low-bandwidth desktop and mobile news sites.* Check with the tech staff or editor to see if the publication has dual sites and apps, for both multimedia and text/compressed-graphic versions. Then don't include high-**bandwidth** assets on the low-bandwidth mobile site. There are many users around the world with low-bandwidth service: It's important to serve them too.
- *Tip #3 – Add advisories to links that lead to bandwidth-intensive pages or large files.* It's a nonlinear network, people ... just another reason to distribute your content across multiple pages!
- *Tip #4 – Make the navigation clear and easy.* Don't lead users to pages they don't want or need. Use fast-loading navigational elements.

BREAKING NEWS ON THE WEB

You might think that the more complex and difficult demands of writing on the web might change when news breaks. Not really – users like the same things about breaking stories online that they like about online news generally. Such qualities include (Rich, 2015, p. 230): "Immediacy, interactivity, innovation, and multimedia. Users don't care if the effort required fits in the hard-to-do-box – they want what they want, and they'll head for the news outlet that gives it to them soonest."

Publications must post important breaking news as soon as it appears on the radar because it will spread virally across the web quickly. Journalists race to fulfill users' expectations as fast as they can. Archived interactive wrap-arounds, like likes, sharing, and comments go up with the first post. Perusing social media for first-person accounts and media, then obtaining rights to multimedia may take a little longer but somebody jumps on it right away.

When breaking news covers events that entail severe consequences for many people, reporters must use careful judgment to avoid creating mass hysteria or widespread panic. Consider this cautionary tale from Joe Mandese, Editor-in-Chief of *MediaPost* (2020). Joe's article included an analyst's estimate that hundreds of thousands of people could die from COVID-19.

Responding to users' backlash, Mandese labeled the story: "Warning: This article may contain data sensitive to some people" at the report's beginning. During serious crises, journalists walk fine lines between reporting essential facts and warnings – with the risks of causing mass panic. Merely upsetting users lies on the "report the facts" side of this line. Headlines, images, and copy that evoke hysteria cross the line.

In his blog post, Mandese summed up the dilemma of how to report information that is likely to upset users that faced journalists reporting on the early stages of the pandemic:

> We've never needed clear, factual, accurate reporting more than we do now in our history. But I now realize it is also important to do it in a compassionate way that is sensitive to the amped anxiety of some readers. I apologize for not being more sensitive [...] but the facts are that this will be a crisis like no other one we've experienced before, economically, emotionally, humanistically.

So, Mandese reported accurate estimates of COVID-19 deaths. How did *you* feel when you first heard that news? Were you shocked, surprised, horrified...or did you go to the store and buy 54 rolls of toilet paper before your neighbors could? (That's how many people responded.)

What should an ethical journalist do? A stubborn conflict exists between accurately reporting facts about scary, unpleasant events that affect many people – and potentially creating unnecessary psychological or societal harm. How should reporters report important facts – while minimizing potentially dangerous effects? First Draft, a nonprofit organization created to support delivery of accurate information to users in critical moments, offers useful guidance for journalists to address this question. The First Draft website provides tips for reporting about COVID-19 along with many other useful resources and guidelines for journalists reporting in times of crisis (Kwan, Wardle, & Webb, 2020).

- Ask the questions that your users would ask; then answer them.
- Simplify complex statistical or scientific information so users can understand it.
- When citing studies or incorporating data visualizations, provide original data sources.
- Put maps and graphs in clear context.
- Avoid sensational language or stereotypical images that heighten fear.
- Avoid worst-case scenario speculation.
- Identify specific actions users can take to mitigate harms.

- Provide users with links to official sources of up-to-date information.
- Consult with several different authoritative experts.
- Learn, then ask informed questions that help users to evaluate research studies' accuracy and their applicability to users' lives.

WHEN USERS PUT THEIR OWN STORIES TOGETHER

Before we leave online news writing and turn to story structures in the next section, we should understand how users put their stories together for themselves and their personal networks. Users engage in **social curation**: They collect media elements from the internet and write text to narrate previously chosen elements – other text, quotes, tweets, and embedded audio, video, and interactive resources.

AlNoamany, Wiggle, and Nelson (2015) analyzed almost 15,000 user-curated and created stories on Storify.com. (Storify enables users to collect and string together elements from the internet to build collections or stories.) AlNoamany and colleagues found that for the most popular stories, the median (most frequent) number of resources users included was 28. Links comprised the most frequent resource – in 71 percent of the stories, followed by images in 18 percent of them. Eight percent of stories included users' text, annotating the resources. Seven percent featured quotes, and only 2 percent had embedded videos. The five sites that provided almost 90 percent of the user's resources were: Twitter, Instagram, YouTube, Facebook, and Flickr. Users created most stories in a day or less, although many creators added to their stories over time.

Check out the smart, professional *The Washington Post* Daily 202 columns, written by James Hohmann. His columns resemble users' social curation efforts (as on Storify. com) – with one big exception: Hohmann includes far more narrative text than most users' stories. His brightly-written, entertaining summaries of current news stories, followed by quotes and Twitter snippets, focus on political news but also cover the important national stories for the day.

The next section turns from news writing to the structures journalists employ to build their articles. Broadly viewed, there are two types of news articles: reports and stories. **Story** has two meanings: 1) any kind of news article ("My story was published today!") and 2) a tale that has a beginning, middle, and an end or resolution ("That story had a great plot"). Another useful synonym for the second meaning of story is **narrative**: Narratives provide accounts for the sequence of connected events.

A REPORT RECOUNTS WHAT HAPPENED. A NARRATIVE RECOUNTS WHAT HAPPENED, THEN WHAT HAPPENED AFTER THAT – AND HOW IT ALL ENDED

Reports and narratives both convey information, utilizing facts and description. Both focus on people, places, activities, and things. And both structures help news writers explain complex matters.

Whether a journalist creates an article as a report or a story depends on:

- Nature of the subject or events
- Demands of the assignment
- Audience expectations

However, reports and narratives have different purposes, elements, and formats. Reports inform; news narratives describe and deliver experiences. Reports work well for covering ongoing events that are important to a user community: regular board and council meetings, conferences and conventions, product news, weekly police crime summaries, obits, sports events, and entertainment. Narrative writing lends itself to stories that have an engaging individual at their center, conflict, dramatic choices and actions, and a resolution. Articles about celebrities or prominent local people often mix elements of both reports (what just happened to bring this person to the forefront) and narratives (what they've done over time that makes them well-known).

Reports and narratives intended for digital publication may be quite simple, or they may have many parts. But they tend to be more complicated than print or broadcast stories because they … well, because they can be. The online environment has little or no restriction on length and it permits so many different media types in combination.

Traditional media platforms like print, television, and radio, have routine processes for a limited array of media types. It's quite different for digital journalists. As soon as digital journalists start working on an assignment, they must consider how constellations of media types will work together to draw-in users and improve users' engagement: text, images, audio, video, links, and interactive elements.

On and offline, facts comprise the fundamental elements of **reports**. The most often-used facts fall into one or more of the six categories: Who, What, Where, When, Why, and How, or **5W1H**, the well-known acronym for journalists' categories of facts. Each fact provides another slice of a pie or a layer of a stack. Nonfiction narratives also draw on facts, but they bring facts to light from a specific perspective or from within the narrative (the sequences of events about characters, settings, mood, actions, conflict, and resolution). The narrative provides the perspective that guides the story and the sequences by which it unfolds.

Most news stories are reports. A report summarizes the most recent key facts about persons, places, or events. Often journalists use the **inverted pyramid** structure as a guide, as shown in Figure 4.2. The writer stacks the report elements like layers of a cake, which then provide a complete summary – lede, nut graf, details, and kicker. Longer reports often have other elements in the body of the article, such as background, context, history, analysis, and statistical data. The additional explanation allows users to draw conclusions about how the subject of the news story might affect them personally.

In contrast, the structure of a narrative story provides a sequence of events, real or fictional. Story events happen at different points in time. While story events take place sequentially, the telling of them may not follow a strict chronology. Some stories begin at the end, or at dramatic points near the end. The

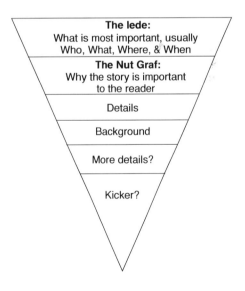

FIGURE 4.2

The inverted pyramid

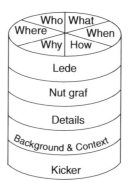

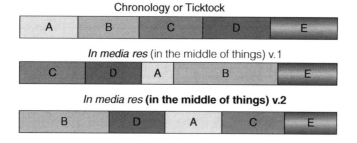

FIGURE 4.3

Comparing structures of reports and narratives
Credit: Joan Van Tassel

end of the story may even come at the beginning: "She survived – and it's amazing how she managed to do it." Another common narrative is one of discovery; the story sequence unearths the events that led to the discovery. Frequently, stories begin *in media res*; they start "in the middle of things," with their beginning explained as the story unfolds.

Consider this familiar childhood story: A young girl in a red cloak walks through the woods to visit her grandmother. In the woods, she meets a wolf. The wolf races to the grandmother's house, ahead of the girl, and eats Grandma. Soon after the girl arrives, the wolf pretends to be Grandma, and eats the girl, too. A hunter comes upon the scene, kills the wolf, cuts the wolf open, and both the girl and grandmother emerge unharmed.

That's the story. But the narrative is something quite different, as shown in Figure 4.3. The narrative defines the story's meaning and the tone by the perspective brought to the story events. Depending on the narrative perspective, *Little Red Riding Hood* might become any of these stories:

- A dark and dire fable, full of fear and misdirection
- The triumph of good over evil, an inspiring saga of hope, kindness, and resurrection
- A rousing adventure focused on the helplessness of women rescued by a heroic male
- A celebration of the primacy of humans over nature.

THINK YOU KNOW WHAT NEWS IS? WHAT'S NEWS DEPENDS ON WHERE YOU CLICK ...

During the era of mass media and broadcasting, mainstream news was *The News* for most people. But in the digital era, users compose their own customized news and information bubble, tailored to their unique perspectives and interests. Users may choose ideological bubbles – *The New York Times*, *Independent Journal Review*, Breitbart.com, or the Christian-oriented OneNewsNow.com. Or they might choose a work-based media menu – such as *Steel Business Briefing*, *MediaPost Marketing Daily*, *Supply Chain Dive*, or *WWD*, formerly *Women's Wear Daily*. What's *your* news?

Online, each site defines news, based on the nature of its audience. Users looking for job-related information about the fishing industry won't sort through the political, entertainment, and sports sections of a large online site. (But they might look at the business section.) More likely, they'll go to web sites that feature the specialized information they need.

These traditional criteria help evaluate the **news value** of topics or stories to any publication's audience:

- **Timeliness**: The story is fresh – it happened recently, or it brings new information about an ongoing story.
- **Impact**: How many people does the story affect? Does it affect the publication's audience specifically? How serious are the effects? Are some places more likely to be affected than others?
- **Proximity**: The general rule – the closer a story is to an audience, the more newsworthy that story is. But what does "close" mean in the connected information world? For online news, close can mean events that are geographically near, but it can also mean economic, political, industry or occupational, emotional, or artistic proximity. Journalists typically emphasize proximity by tying stories to local angles in specific ways that their audiences can relate to.
- **Prominence**: Names make news; big names make big news. Ordinary people care about the lives and drama of powerful, rich, and famous people. In the digital world, that's even truer than before online news! Scandal, incompetence, hypocrisy, and tragedy reliably draw clicks.
- **Conflict**: Conflict gets attention. Bad news travels fast because it's newsworthy. David versus Goliath stories that feature uneven matches with unexpected outcomes are especially appealing to users.
- **Novelty**: There's a reason they call it the "news" – no one has reported it before. "First," "last," "most," and "only" remain effective clickbait, just as when they drew pedestrians to newsstands during the heydays of newspapers. Other "evergreen" attractions remain longest, shortest, smallest, biggest, highest, smartest, etc. New discoveries or new discoveries about old standbys still attract users' attention.

WOULD YOU LIKE YOUR NEWS HARD OR SOFT, WITH OR WITHOUT FEATURES?

Reports and stories fall into four common news types for most journalists in both legacy and digital newsrooms. These basic classifications encompass virtually all reports and narratives: 1) hard news, 2) news features, 3) soft news, and 4) scenic narratives.

- **Hard news** covers breaking news about factual events and occurrences. Traditionally, hard news usually comes to the audience as reports. Generally, "the focus of hard news is mostly on the societal relevance of an issue, with a style that is typically described as rational, impersonal, unemotional, thematically framed, in-depth coverage ..." (Boukes and Boomgaarden, 2015). Online, hard news may come in the form of a tweet or a Facebook post.

- **News features** explore in detail an aspect of a recent or ongoing hard news story. Usually, features provide the human side of a story to help users experience and understand the news in a more emotional or personal way. In news parlance, these articles "hang on the news peg of a hard news story." The softer side of hard news does not necessarily mean fluffy articles; often, the softer aspects of a story illuminate truly serious social issues.

- **Soft news** stories typically cover "entertainment, celebrity, or lifestyle topics." Journalists can write soft news in a report or feature style. Or they may compose features using the narrative form.

- **Scenic narratives** organize feature articles by scenes that are sequentially arranged to unfold a classic storyline. In other words, scenic narratives are classical stories. Longer than reports, journalists rarely use this structure for reports.

FOR A REPORTER, NEWS IS WHATEVER THE EDITOR THINKS IT IS ...

Before beginning to report a story, journalists must get an assignment and approval from an editor. Online and offline, editors decide what reports and stories get reported, written, and published. They may also determine whether a story is covered as hard, feature, or soft news. If the editors think an event, topic, or story is news, it is. If they don't – forget about it – it may be news somewhere else, but not in this publication. If journalists frequently disagree with their editors' decisions, there's always a personal blog – or another job.

Editorial committees often make decisions about which stories to cover. Editors of daily publications usually hold **budget meetings** at the start of the working day to discuss the stories that will appear in the publication. (Of course, the meeting times differ for weeklies, monthlies, or other publishing schedules.) Once produced, the editors will make final decisions about where the story will appear – home page, section, and page. "Today, in most newsrooms, the budget also includes digital stories, assets, and posts that accompany the day's digital stories," (McClure, 2011).

During the budget meeting, the editors also generate the ongoing **news budget**, the lineup of stories, photos, graphics, and information that journalists are still working on. In most newsrooms, journalists pay close attention to the news budget to make sure they deliver the expected copy and assets. Yet, stories sometimes go in an unexpected direction. When they do, reporters keep editors informed so they can post changes to the news budget.

RIDDLE ME THIS: HOW IS A JOURNALIST LIKE A CARPENTER?

Answer: They have similar tools. (Well, not quite. Yes, the craftsman's tools for shaping wood, metal, come from physical substances, while the reporter's brain provides her primary tool for journalism.) However, the names of some frequently used conceptual tools suggest "building" while the labor of proposing, reporting, structuring, and creating often takes some very heavy lifting.

Before editors assign a reporter to work on the story, they evaluate it. The editorial evaluation toolbox has pegs, hooks, and angles. (See the similarity to the building trades?)

- The **news peg**: how stories tie to a currently breaking or running story
- The **news hook**: how reporters appeal to their audience
- The **story angle**: The approach journalists use to tell their story, the first step in developing the reportorial strategy.

These tools for thinking about and assessing stories apply to news reports and news features. They may also apply to scenic narrative nonfiction stories but are not so strictly interpreted. For example, not all scenic narratives need news pegs.

WANT APPROVAL FOR A STORY? HANG IT ON A NEWS PEG

A news peg ties a story to a currently breaking or running story. Hanging a proposed story on a solid news peg is the fastest way to get an article approved, but only if that peg matters to the publication's audience. Stories that are currently part of the social conversation are far more likely to get a green light. Of course, reporters must still find new events or wrinkles.

Information about a current story can provide the news peg for a new story. Reporters look for facts that move the story forward, such as a previously unknown actor, event, or a new comment made by a prominent individual. In the publication-rich online world of niche news, it is difficult to imagine a newsworthy event that can't be pegged to some story somewhere!

FIGURE 4.4

Tools of the trade: peg, hook, and angle

Credit: Peg image public domain. Hook by Fikmik and Angle by Shutswis, licensed from www.123rf.com

WANT USERS' ATTENTION? USE A NEWS HOOK

Why would someone read this story? The news hook describes how and why a story will appeal to an audience. According to Yopp, McAdams, and Thornburg (2010), a news hook is "the most critical piece of newsworthy information that will capture the attention and interest of both the news media and their audiences."

Perhaps a reporter sends an email to the editor of a resort community daily paper, saying, "I want to write about the guy who started shouting in the post office yesterday." The editor replies: "So what?" The reporter answers: "It was Justin Bieber." It could have been any celebrity, prominent local community member, or a wanted felon who was arrested because of his outburst. Each of these events could be viable news hooks. Because not all stories have celebrities conveniently attached to them, journalists must identify the most interesting elements and put them first.

One way to find news hooks? Contemplate the classic Who, What, Where, When, Why, and How elements of the story. For example, on January 22, 2016, three inmates of the Orange County (California) jail escaped. The next day, the main headline on the home page of the *Press-Enterprise*, in Riverside, California, read: "Inmates rappelled from roof to escape Orange County jail." The publication found the "How" aspect of this story (inmates rappelling from the roof) the hook that grabbed readers' attention and encouraged them to read further. This headline also included the "Who" (inmates), the "What" (escape), and the "Where" (the jail). A Google search of this story shows that the "How" headline continued to interest readers for as late as 2020!

Fundamental to all hooks, and to the news itself, is change: "Journalism is about change: no change, no news," wrote Hunter et al. (2011). Strong hooks are especially valuable for online articles because they generate clicks and extend the time users spend viewing a page. Time-proven hooks include: changes for better or worse, danger, conflict, lies, fraud, abuse of power, conflicts of interest, suffering, and many others. Print and broadcast news stories need good hooks because these media have limited space or time, in ways that online news sites do not. Hooks in mobile news stories work more like the print and broadcast hooks because the small screens of mobile devices ensure that only the most compelling stories make the publication's home or splash page.

WANT TO SIMPLIFY THE WRITING JOB? FIND A STRONG STORY ANGLE

The journalist thinks up several potential story angles, and then chooses one. The chosen story angle provides the specific perspective that guides how to tell the story; it determines the most relevant facts. For example, if the story angle is "new discovery," then the article will cover what is new, the specifics of who discovered it, and the when, where, and how the discovery came about. It could include background information about the importance of this discovery, earlier building blocks that led to it, and the effects it will have on people and events in the future.

If the discovery is controversial (such as CRISPR, which enables editing DNA), a long story would likely cover a range of opinions about its value. It could also look at the role of science, engineering, the outcomes of similar discoveries, and commercial interests supporting the new discovery.

However, consider other potential angles. What if the angle were the human (or animal) suffering that the discovery alleviates? Or the relative costs and benefits of producing the innovation compared to existing alternatives? Or grassroots opposition to implementing the discovery? Or it might even focus on mitigating the risks to humans should the technology be misused – perhaps even weaponized (Regalado, 2016).

Choosing the story angle should be a journalist's first step when writing any story. For example:

> A police sting operation arrests an elected city councilman for soliciting a policewoman who he believed to be a street prostitute. The daily print paper takes a purely administrative angle on its web site to bury the story: The headline is at the bottom of the home page, "Official Caught in Sting." It links to a short, bland report on the "Mid-City News" page. Even here, users must scroll down to find the story. The story angle is: Minimize the impact of this story in the local community.
>
> Alternatively, a different local news site has a feistier angle – the headline on the home page says: "City pol John Doe busted for soliciting sex," and features a blurry picture, taken from police surveillance video. There's an audio speaker icon, linking to the audio of "Doe's" proposition. The body of the story mentions the council member's past calls to clean-up the red-light district and punish prostitutes – with links to his earlier statements.
>
> This story's angle: Your city councilman is a sleaze and a hypocrite.

Less salacious stories than a councilman's street bust still offer many potential angles. Suppose a reporter gets an assignment to cover a school board meeting and write a brief report. The story angle can be a standard dispassionate observer's take: so common, this strategy hardly seems like an angle – but it remains a viable (and perhaps the only) choice.

Now suppose that during this mid-year meeting, among many other tasks, the board revises the district budget to repair recent flood damage to several schools. The angle might be to cover these budget changes and the logic behind the board's choices, followed by a summary of the other board actions to end the report. Yet another angle could be to display flood damage images, with an anecdotal lead from a parent about the devastated classroom in her child's school. Here, the angle emphasizes the pressing need to repair the school damage, rather than a narrow focus on school district budget changes.

Regional publications might choose angles that look at all schools in the affected area: "Storm devastates local school budgets." A national nonprofit that supports public education could use its site to publish a news feature with an angle about the flood's effects on classroom learning: "Teachers and students struggle with storm disruption." A school principal association web site might take a financial angle and highlight federal subsidies for student attendance, monies that are lost when students don't attend: "Big winter storms cost districts big dollars."

"An angle always includes an element of surprise," writes Lara (2010), who notes that many editors often don't specify an angle when they assign stories to reporters. This practice frees the reporter to decide how to approach their story. Business journalist and educator Chris Roush recounts *The Wall Street Journal* John Edwards III speaking at an American Press Institute conference (Roush, 2005). Edwards noted that the WSJ published stories about high gas prices from many angles over a brief period:

- A front-pager about how Hurricane Rita affected oil and gas supplies
- Allegations of price gouging
- Reports that oil companies made record profits but minimized the Hurricane Rita story

- How SUV sales declined because of higher gas prices
- Lifestyle changes due to higher gas prices

Freelancers often explore several angles of a single story, so they can make submissions to different publications. One site might want a detailed story; another might take an interview from one of the story's sources; a third might want the ground-level views from consumers, victims, or law enforcement perspectives. This ability to create multiple stories from a single set of reportorial activities helps freelancers succeed in an economically precarious profession. In contrast, staff reporters are more likely to explore possible angles to differentiate their publication from competitors and thereby attract more users.

DIGITAL CARPENTRY 101: 7 STEPS TO BUILDING THE REPORT

There is no shortage of information about news writing: Entire courses, books, articles, presentations, practice modules, and quizzes cover this topic. The next section summarizes basic principles for putting together news reports: Start with the inverted pyramid.

#1 TELL 'EM WHAT YOU'RE GOING TO TELL 'EM: GET YOUR LEDE ON

As with traditional news, in online stories headlines and ledes capture attention. Most online newsrooms want strong ledes that engage users. Most reports use the summary lede. As its name suggests, it summarizes the most important parts of the story – drawn from some combination of Who, What, When, Where, Why, and How. Summary ledes may seem easy to write, and sometimes they are. However, for many writers, ledes are the most difficult paragraphs to compose. *Good* ledes require journalists to understand the most important aspects of the story. Strong ledes also appeal to the publication's audience, stressing those aspects of the story can best capture the attention of the site's users. The lede may be only one sentence or a few sentences. For a short report, the lede should not exceed 40 words; many editors prefer 30–35 words.

Ledes come in many styles. Online editors may want a **punch lede**, one that surprises or startles users, to draw click-throughs to the story page or to maximize user time on that page. **Quote ledes** start with direct or indirect quotes; they begin with quotation marks. An indirect quote lead usually starts with the most striking statement: The MTA will close three more bus lines in the next 60 days due to budget cuts, Mayor Smith announced in his press conference today.

Vox Verbatim: Using Quotes, Joan Van Tassel

"Don't use quotes to state facts," a Newsweek editor told me. "There are only two good reasons for quotes."

I turned a story in and the editor asked, "Why did you put this information in a quote?" I forget what I said to him, but he told me that, as a rule, established facts don't appear in quotes. Rather, writers simply state the facts. Or they state them in an indirect quote with no quote marks, to convey that the facts are accurate. (Of course, in today's political climate, facts themselves are highly contested, and people feel free to advance "alternative facts" they believe should be given the same weight as established facts.)

> Just as important, the editor told me there are two reasons to use quotes: 1) to report opinions or 2) to reveal important information about the person quoted.
>
> - "I think this closure is prudent and necessary," is an opinion – and a reasonable on-the-record quote.
> - "I am very unhappy about this closure because I'm concerned about people who have to get to work from these neighborhoods," – a good quote that gives users information about the speaker's values.

The pressure to attract users' attention drives online sites to allow writers greater latitude in the types of ledes they allow. Journalists compose, contrast, question, direct address, blind, anecdotal, scene-setter (or descriptive), and narrative ledes. Frequently, longer scenic narrative and feature stories begin with quote, anecdotal, scene-setter, and narrative ledes, but journalists may use these lede styles for short reports as well.

#2 NUT GRAF: GIVE 'EM REASONS TO STAY ON THE PAGE

The nut graf follows the lede. Done well, it tells users why they should continue attending to the article. "Why should I read on?" and "What's in it for me?" The nut graf may have one sentence – or perhaps three or four. These two offers have time-tested user appeal:

1. Useful information – stuff users should think carefully about, they can act on, talk about to their friends, family, and co-workers, or increase their social standing. Of course, users can like, forward, or easily comment on nut grafs.
2. Entertainment – interesting, funny, weird, exciting, or perhaps just providing conversational tidbits for sharing. And some people just want to keep up with the Kardashians.

The nut graf establishes the frame of reference, not just by stating why it's important. The writing itself needs to *incorporate* importance; it needs to *be* important. For the article to entertain users, the nut graf must *be* entertaining. Think of it like a supermarket sample. Same deal with the nut graf; if users like it, they "buy" it, and stay engaged with the story.

#3 DETAILS GIVE THE STORY DEPTH AND CREDIBILITY

Early nut grafs show the story's bare bones. The details grafs put meat on those bones, giving depth and breadth to the report. For interested users, nut grafs help stories become more real in their minds – allowing users to see how key facts connect to other facts and circumstances. But the details make the story real.

Journalists usually add details in order of importance, first providing the details that support the most significant of the 5W1H facts stated in the lede. Details about lesser important elements come further down in the story. **Qualifiers** allow language to be flexible and nuanced. They clarify the ideas and pictures in users' minds. And when added to a recitation of facts, they add a layer of specificity that can help users remember them.

> **The Many Qualities of Qualifiers**
>
> The Changing Minds website, http://changingminds.org/techniques/language/modifying_meaning/qualifiers.htm, offers a helpful list of qualifier categories:
>
> - *Qualifiers of relative quality*: best, worst, finest, sharpest, heaviest, etc.
> - *Qualifiers of quantity*: some, most, all, none, etc.
> - *Qualifiers of certainty*: I guess, I think, I know, I am absolutely certain, etc.
> - *Qualifiers of necessity*: must, should, ought, required, have to, etc.
> - *Qualifiers of possibility*: could, may, likely, possible, probable, etc.
> - *Qualifiers of time*: occasionally, sometimes, now and again, usually, always, never, etc.

#4 BACKGROUND, CONTEXT, AND ANALYSIS ONLINE: LINK TO REPLACE (DIGITAL) INK

The opening paragraphs promised readers that the story would give them useful or entertaining information; the rest of the article pays off that promise. The inverted pyramid structure calls for writers to flesh out their stories by adding additional details and background. Some articles include context and analysis as well.

In digital stories, journalists can point to rivers of information for their most avid readers. Links provide efficient ways for engaged users to drill further down into the story, while keeping stories short for the casual skimmer. Internal links let them move around to topics inside the story. Links to other articles let them find information from other net sources. Some publications discourage linking to other sites for supplemental information. Instead, these publications want reporters to link to additional or related information from earlier stories on the site.

Background material takes users deeper into the story elements – history, actors, technical data, statistical findings, government research, trends, and so forth. Context provides frames of reference that define the circumstances surrounding the story, in a sense, the ecology of the story. Understanding a story's context, or even multiple contexts, gives users more ways to evaluate how a story may affect them. Some users drill down; most don't.

A Useful Tool for Background Information

Exploring a story's context is important. One technique to organize context is to build a **ladder of abstraction** (Hayakawa, 1941). Shown in Figure 4.5, the ladder offers an efficient,

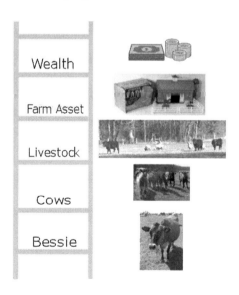

FIGURE 4.5

Take Bessie to the bank

Credit: Public domain images from Wikimedia Commons

systematic process for journalists to think through possible contexts for the story, and then tailor background information to it. (Historical note: By using Bessie the cow as his exemplar, semanticist S. I. Hayakawa gave Bessie lasting fame among writers everywhere.)

Note the ladder of abstraction's bottom step is the individual person, place, or thing. Examples of individual subjects could be: olive farmer Nancy Caswell, Mr. Rivera's appendix surgery, or a truckload load of potatoes from Adalbert Farm going 60 mph north on Highway 84 toward Boise. The second rung includes the singular item on the first rung and other like items: California olive farmers, appendix surgeries, Idaho potato markets. The labels of the ladder's rungs are somewhat arbitrary, so the second rung might also be: women named Nancy, Mr. Rivera's eight surgeries, and vegetables from Twin Falls, Idaho going to markets across the U.S.

FIGURE 4.6

Contexts of a school board meeting
Credit: Joan Van Tassel

Each rung on the ladder of abstraction includes the classes of items from all the lower rungs. The lowest rungs of the ladder are quite specific, close to the ground, and easily visualized. Just about everyone can picture Bessie, a big-eyed black and white milk cow. By contrast, not everyone can summon an image of assets and descriptions of them that include milk cows, all the way up to higher-level abstractions – say, the credit derivative holdings of all global agri-businesses.

Jack Hart (2011) observes that most news reports consist of information that falls within the middle rungs of the ladder. So how might journalists think through the multiple contexts of a report on a Board of Education? Figure 4.6 shows another visual way of thinking about the multiple contexts of a report about a school board meeting. Thousands of news stories this year will focus only on the motions that the local school board approved in a single meeting. Other journalists may venture beyond a few basic facts about a school board, its members, challenges, and immediate past actions. Most editors would eliminate material that jumps to the highest levels of abstraction, like education's purpose in human life.

However, moving down the ladder of abstraction from the middle rungs can offer compelling narrative ledes or even a related feature story. Subjects on the ladder's lower rungs can set hooks that interest readers for even routine reports: "If the School Board doesn't approve this budget request from John Adams Middle School, first-graders Elaine Baer and Bailey Michaels will have to buy their own pencils and all their own art supplies next year."

#5 DON'T LET DETAILS DRIFT INTO OBLIVION

Including details does not mean writing everything the reporter learns. But it does mean including information that's relevant to users, interesting to them, or necessary to understand the "Why" and "How" of the story. Sometimes bullet points can present details efficiently. Timelines may also work well. Sketches and diagrams can simplify complex relationships. Sure, these details are less important than the elements in the lede. But that doesn't mean they should be boring or trivial: If details don't matter, they don't belong in the story!

To help users move from one detail to another, journalists often create **transitions** from the nut graf to the report body. Transitions support user engagement because they smooth users' paths to the next sentence or paragraph. And transitions help users delve further into the story by avoiding abrupt changes that might trigger a user's disengagement from a story.

Transitions – Bridges to Somewhere

After journalists write the explanatory grafs they read the copy and add transitions between graphs and story topics or sections. These transitions tie the story together, building verbal bridges between the topical islands of paragraphs. The two most common transition techniques are: 1) repetition of keywords or phrases, and 2) transitional words. If quotes are tight enough, they may make good transitions, as well.

- Transitional repetition means using a word or phrase that appears at the end of a paragraph and then repeating it (or a synonym for it) at the beginning of the next paragraph. For example, a paragraph may end with: "The Board passed the new budget unanimously." The next paragraph covers dissenters in the community who disagreed with the budget measure. This paragraph might begin: "The Board's new budget provoked some controversy with community (activists, homeowners, or small businesses) because ..." and then include more information about the grassroots opposition in the second paragraph.

- Transitional words clearly imply a transition. These words include: but, as a result, on the other hand, next, so, then, and therefore.

Online, reports aren't just text. Users take multimedia for granted. In April 2015, Anup Kaphle covered the earthquake in Nepal.

> **Vox Verbatim: Anup Kaphle, Editor-in-Chief at *The Kathmandu Post* and Head of Digital Transformation for Kantipur Media Group**
>
> In the past, a story like this may have involved a news story and a second-day analysis. But in a digital world, the readers want (and we try to give) as many angles to a big story as possible. For example, for many who didn't know that Nepal had several UNESCO heritage sites, there was a separate post with photos and videos. Unlike in the traditional print model, an event like this obviously allows us to publish a variety of content in a variety of media formats. [...] To me, it was astonishing how much information was coming from the ground. Despite the big earthquake, cell phone towers were functioning normally, so journalists as well as local citizens were constantly sending a flurry of information on social media.

WHEN LAST COMES FIRST: CREATING HEDS AND DEKS

Headlines and decks attract users. They come last in the creative process because the writer must have a sure grasp of the entire story to write the intriguing, user-motivating prose that will draw people to it. In legacy newspapers, editors wrote these lines. However, reporters and writers at digital-only publications may find they need to write them.

The headline (or hed) is also short, not more than 50–55 characters – shorter, if possible. Use alliteration, rhymes, puns, catchy or trendy words, action words, humor, or other devices to draw attention to the story. (As a historical note, probably the most famous headline ever written was a story about how rural movie-goers didn't attend films about country folk in the Hollywood trade publication *Variety*, back in 1935: Sticks Nix Hick Pix.)

6 TIPS FOR HEADLINES THAT CRUSH THE CLICKABILITY FACTOR

1. *Use numbers* (1, 2, 3, 4, etc.), not one, two, three, four, etc.
2. *Place Search Engine Optimization (SEO) keywords near the beginning of headlines* to maximize results and user hits from SEO.
3. *Arouse curiosity* – "6 Things You Didn't Know About … (interesting topic)"; "The polar bear couldn't make it to the next ice floe – until THIS happened!"
4. *Make a promise* – "3 easy ways to ask for a raise."
   "5 strategies for pain-free tax preparation."
   "Get luscious Lindsay Lohan lips in 1 afternoon."
5. *Use emotion-laden adjectives* – Awesome, compelling, lovable, tragic, thrilling, cutest, etc.
6. *Make sure the headline accurately reflects the story.* Clickbait headlines work – for a while. But after bad experiences, savvy users stop clicking on sites (and reporters) that serve up inaccurate or misleading titles and headlines.

Not all stories need much explanation because many news items are already familiar to users. But if it will attract more users, write a deck (dek or sub-hed). The deck (dek in copy editing lingo) sets up a story. Decks can be longer than the headline with smaller type than the hed. If the story has been in the news for several days, focus on the added information that the article conveys. Examples of such extended stories include well-known political campaigns, ongoing controversies and exposés, high-profile celebrity antics. In these cases, the current article typically relates the most recent event in a longer story that unfolds serially on the front pages, webpages, and mobile screens of news outlets. The never-ending Kardashian Saga provides one example of continuous updating, where readers carry the backstory in their minds already, as did the running stories of Trump–Russia and the COVID-19 pandemic.

DIGITAL STORY CARPENTRY 102: BUILDING FEATURE STORIES

Like so many reports, news feature articles hang on news pegs. Feature articles are designed to illuminate and expand a current news story. They seek to give users insights into human experiences or provide a greater understanding of complex processes, actions, and trends. Just as in reports – images, audio, video, links, and interactives, can enhance users' experiences with a story.

Typically, news features are longer than hard news reports. Features frequently combine aspects of both reports and stories. Feature stories translate well to broadcast and digital media. Online and mobile sites may distribute multimedia elements of the story on different pages to maintain short loading times.

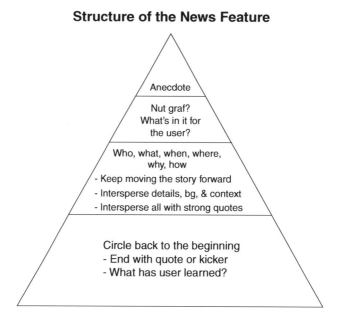

FIGURE 4.7

The news feature structure
Credit: Joan Van Tassel

Before starting to write, identify the news peg, hook, and angle of the story. The angle may suggest a starting point; it also provides a guide for the facts, scenes, persons, and details that should go in the story – and identifies the elements that don't belong. The news feature lede isn't the W5H1 of the report. Rather, the lede usually begins with an introduction that sets the story's tone and purpose. Ledes may be an anecdote, a quote, a saying, a description, the introduction of a person, or a problem. For a feature story, they may run longer than a single paragraph.

After writing the introduction to the feature, a solid nut graf (or multiple grafs) comes next. As in a report, the nut graf tells why they should keep reading. Consider: if users read the story, what promise can the writer make to them? For example, "This story will change everything you ever thought you knew about X (subject)!" tells users they will learn something important. "That he escaped was a miracle. How he did it was a masterpiece of deception and courage" tells users that the story describes compelling bravery in the midst of fear.

But don't tell everything in the nut graf! In fact, when writing a feature story, don't tell everything early in the body of the story either. Withhold some element(s) of understanding exactly how something works, or why it works, or how it all worked out – until near to the story's end. Keep important facts, events, or unexpected plot twists in reserve for surprises that keep users engaged.

After the opening and nut grafs, additional paragraphs follow that highlight and explain one idea per paragraph. Intersperse relevant quotes, context, and examples between the explanatory paragraphs. If multimedia assets and interactive elements add information, excitement, or understanding to the story, insert them between explanatory paragraphs as well. (But remember, inexperienced users need help to navigate through these more complicated stories.)

Journalists have many ways to end news features. A few common endings include surprises, powerful lessons, or the second strongest quote (the strongest one probably should have been used in the opening). Provide a resolution or draw conclusions from the story – but keep it sharp and snappy, not clichéd or soppy. Circle back to show users that the story paid off its earlier promises.

This is a firm rule: Always make the story worth the read for users. Deliver on that opening promise you made at the start of the story! If you've over-promised, make sure you over-deliver.

DIGITAL CARPENTRY 202: GETTING THE SCENIC NARRATIVE FROM SCENE … TO SEEN

We construct descriptive and scenic narrative stories because we know that people avidly seek, read, view, and listen to them every day – and large numbers of people pay for them. Of all types of news stories, nonfiction scenic narratives are the most like classic tales, those "Once upon a time …" fables. Drawing similarities between folk tales and news stories may seem trivial – but it's a useful comparison.

Consider – we humans are a pragmatic lot. People wouldn't expend so much effort to make and attend to stories unless they served important purposes. Stories are useful. Stories play vital roles in human life, in all cultures, because they contain "deep information" about our cultural, social, and personal worlds. News narratives increase users' awareness of their environments and let them benefit from others' experience, knowledge, and insights. Journalism draws from a society's treasury of stories – just as it contributes to that treasury.

Stories explain how our world works. They explain how others faced similar difficulties that we do, made decisions about them, and took actions. Most important, stories reveal how it all turned out. They give us memory pegs that help us remember key facts, absorbed in the context of a narrative. And of course, stories entertain, surprise, and delight us.

Nonfiction narratives reconstruct experiences, events, and processes, allowing users to participate in vicarious experiences. Many scenic narratives hang on a current news story. However, a truly powerful story can *make* news and even spur social change by bringing an urgent event or topic into the public discourse.

FIGURE 4.8

Cave painting from Lascaux, France

Source: DaBler (own work), public domain via Wikimedia Commons

Online and print magazines more often assign scenic narratives than do other news outlets. Magazines have editorial calendars that extend a year or longer, and they can let good stories mature. Editors of daily news sites rarely approve such stories. Not only are they time-consuming and expensive, but there is also uncertainty about when the story will be ready to publish, a factor difficult to accommodate in a daily news budget.

Reporting nonfiction scenic narratives often requires long immersion within the story's environment, the world of the story. Many such narratives originate with a single reporter who undertakes the entrepreneurial project, keeping the story alive by using personal time to accumulate the thick detail that this form demands. These stories may take weeks, months, even years to report and write. Reporters often conduct dozens of interviews, examine thousands of pages of documents and transcripts, and visit many locales and scenes. Even with all that effort and time, the story may turn out quite differently than expected – or it may never come to fruition at all.

According to Hart (2011), creating nonfiction scenic narratives differs from writing news reports because the writer:

- Uses scenes to structure the narrative
- Presents actors as characters, a protagonist and perhaps one or two other actors as supporting players
- Tells the story from an identifiable point of view
- Draws on detailed descriptions of settings, scenes, and participants
- Uses dialog as well as quotes
- Develops a theme

Scenic narrative nonfiction stories can begin anywhere on the ladder of abstraction. However, at some point, they almost always focus on the bottom rungs of the ladder (the individual) and then climb up and down the ladder several times in the same article. For example, a story about a person wrongfully convicted of a crime often starts at the bottom rung of the ladder (someone in prison) and reaches the top rung (the scales of justice). The story could spend time in the middle rungs as well, including DNA testing, the prosecutor's office, the appeals process, the justice system's impacts on families, and even the incarceration nation.

---

5 Things You Should Know From the Science of Stories

- *#1 Stories are universal.* Name one culture that doesn't have stories. (Hint: You can't.) In the 19th and 20th centuries, anthropologists scoured the earth in search of myths and cultural legends. They found that creation myths and other stories existed in each culture they examined. In addition, most families (Kellas, 2005) and individuals (McLean, 2008) create their own stories. There are stories they tell themselves and those they tell others to establish personal and familial identities, maintain their relationships, and strengthen shared views and values.
- *#2 "Real" is compelling,* say neuroscientists. "Real" takes people on more immersive head trips than "less real." In one study, a group watched the full video and a different group watched a 'toon version of ordinary people doing everyday activities (Mar, Kelley, Heatherton, & Macrae, 2007). While each group watched, researchers measured brain waves from areas linked to social

perception and mentalizing action. The realistic video group version showed significantly more brain activity in these centers than did the "toon" group.

- *#3 Stories provide mental transportation systems.* Green (2004) asked people to read a story and then asked them about it. She found that readers engaged in a story, focused attention on it, and experienced thoughts, emotions, and vivid mental images. Green characterized the experience of people entering a narrative world like being "transported" into another place – the story world. In story worlds, people don't just read, watch, or listen to stories, they mentally "visit" that story world. A person's experience with a story was heightened if the person had prior knowledge or experience relevant to the topics or themes covered in the story ... "showed greater **transportation** into the story." A further study demonstrated that story immersion even changed people's beliefs (Green, Chatham, & Sestir, 2012).
- *#4 Stories exist at the center of our social world.* Finally, Rutledge (2011) categorized the specific ways that stories enrich and support social life. Stories:
  - Connect us to universal truths and a larger self by giving us channels to ancient traditions, myths, and legends
  - Provide vehicles to find commonality with others by sharing purpose, meaning, passions, emotions, and problems
  - Function as a primary mode of communication that underlies personal and social identity, learning, decision-making, and persuasion
  - Provide greater certainty by allowing people to experience events vicariously and anticipate outcomes
  - Stimulate imagination and creativity to empathize with others and to think differently
- *#5 Stories prepare us for living.* Another group of neuroscientists studied how people understand and remember stories. By using neuro-imaging, Speer, Reynolds, Swallow, and Zacks (2009) demonstrated that readers don't just follow stories, they reconstruct narratives in their imaginations. Put simply, readers activated their brain centers *as if they were actually participating in the events of the story*. In this way, our brains take stories and use them to build vicarious experiences into our understanding of "What might happen if ..." by using stories as dress rehearsals for possible eventualities.

GETTING THE SCENIC NARRATIVE STORY: IS IT REPORTING OR CULTURAL ANTHROPOLOGY?

Yes. <smile> Sometimes narrative stories seem closer to cultural anthropology or sociology than they do to daily beat reporting! The next chapter covers the cross-fertilization that occurred between journalists and early 20th-century social scientists that contributed so much to reporting for scenic narratives. Through the interaction, both scientists and reporters use formalized observational tools that underpin cultural anthropology *and* journalistic nonfiction scenic narratives.

Keen observation remains one of the reporters' most important journalistic skills. But truly understanding the underlying meanings of what journalists observe often remains impossible unless they become part of the social group over time, through many conversations. An observer might see a crowd of people are all wearing black. If they seem sad, Westerners might guess that the crowd attended a funeral. But in China, mourners typically wear white; thus, a novice American reporter in China might see a crowd dressed in white and completely misread the cultural meaning of the white clothing.

Participant observation methods, which will be covered in detail in Chapter 6, guide observers who become a member of the group under scrutiny – they aren't just detached individuals standing outside the interactions. Rather, participant observers simultaneously attend to unfolding events as they engage in the social world of the story. This role can be quite important to journalists who would write nonfiction scenic narratives.

A journalist can put in words the truths members can't verbalize about themselves and the social worlds they inhabit. Members often take their lives for granted, perhaps without realizing the meanings that underpin their own beliefs and behaviors. Reporters can observe, describe, go back, and verify their understandings with participants. With skill and some luck, the journalist's questions help informants verbalize for themselves the motives, choices, and expected results of behaviors. Then the journalist can write that deep knowledge into the story, transcending detached observation and guesswork.

Vox Verbatim: Joan Van Tassel

Anyone can plainly see how another person acts just by observing them. But if a reporter wants to know the *meanings* of how people act, they have to rub elbows with them – they can't just stand at a distance and hope to have deep understandings about an unfamiliar social group. Once a student in a broadcasting journalism class said she wanted to do a video about the homeless people who lived under a local dock, not far from the university. I told her to get up just before dawn and to go down by the dock at sunrise, for a week or two. There she could take notes, read, and otherwise occupy herself.

Don't tell the first homeless person who comes up to you what you want to do. Be pleasant, ask about their day. Say you are there studying. In a few days, someone else will come to talk to you. You can then tell that person you want to make a video about the people who are living in that community. In a social group, the first contact isn't made by an influencer – typically that will be the second or third person.

The student looked shocked. "Spend two or three weeks there? Ewwww!" She ended up doing a solid story about the three new boutique coffee shops that had just opened in the area. This environment was one she knew well, and she interpreted the meanings of the clientele, baristas, and menu perfectly.

The building blocks for nonfiction scenic narrative stories are ... you guessed it, scenes. Scenes take place in settings, locations that encompass objects (natural and manufactured), characters, actions, and dialog. Everything, even the inanimate objects, tell users much about the story. Does the action occur in a wealthy, exclusive, cultured club room, in a car dealership, a biology laboratory, or in a refugee camp? These settings shape users' expectations of the story that follows.

Online reporters pay special attention to settings. Even if it isn't possible to capture all the scenes, they can and should capture images and video of the settings whenever possible because these images convey so much atmosphere and detail. Of course, when it *is* possible to capture the actual scene, all the better!

Classic narrative stories usually have one protagonist with supporting characters that inform and engage users. Facing the protagonist – (sound of hissing) – is an antagonist and supporters. Sometimes antagonists may be forces of nature or obstacles. The story proceeds within familiar frameworks of right versus wrong, good versus evil, human versus nature, life against death, and the like.

Nonfiction scenic narratives usually feature characters that interact with settings and with other characters. Since they are real, living human beings, characters tend to be complex, contradictory, willful, and nuanced. Characters have physical appearances and presence, manners of speech, and habits. Internally, they have beliefs, opinions, ideas and desires. Characters live their lives immersed in social worlds, where they affect other people, and are affected in turn by others.

Online journalists can avail themselves of the full range of media types to present nonfiction scenic narratives, a vast array of digital resources that were unimaginable just two decades ago. They usually ask for photographs, videos, and even text and telephone messages to and from family and friends. Journalists may also seek surveillance, satellite, broadcast, or law enforcement video. Links to documents and background information may flesh out fully developed narratives. Journalists can add communicative power with evidence generated with interactive databases and user-driven visualizations.

THE NONFICTION SCENIC NARRATIVE STRUCTURE

Writers have a universe of choices when writing a narrative story. Still, the classic structure underlies most nonfiction scenic narratives. Figure 4.9 shows how the classic story starts, builds, develops, and resolves:

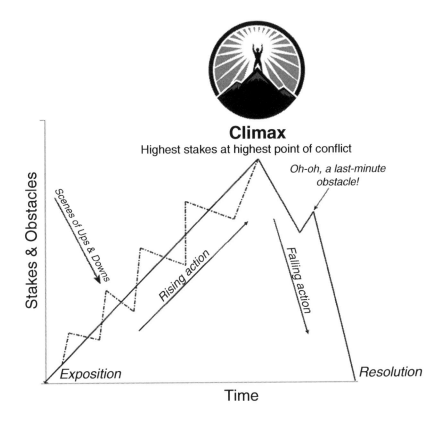

FIGURE 4.9

Narrative structure

First, remember that the chronological storyline is not the same as the narrative, which may start in a place other than the beginning. Starting at the bottom left-hand corner, the story chronology begins with action or **exposition**. Expository writing includes descriptions, explanations, character sketches, mood, and tone that set the stage for a story. So even before the story begins, users may encounter a character immersed in a setting. This character is usually the protagonist, the hero, or heroine: For example: "Once upon a time, there was a beautiful Princess. When she was born, a seer told her parents that she should never show her face in a mirror or disaster would strike. So, she grew up far away, near the edge of a bountiful forest. One day ..." Now our story begins.

Hart (2011) describes a nonfiction scenic narrative story with an unusual main character: merchandise. The business section editor wanted a story about the complexity of global trade that would be understandable to readers by focusing on the journey of a specific load of merchandise, from factory to retail store and buyer, describing the direct experience of traded merchandise. To provide that experience, the reporters followed a lot of manufactured goods, from fabrication in Asia, through their purchase, transport, and final sale in the U.S. These goods were the protagonist. The supporting cast members were the humans who overcame all the obstacles and difficulties of moving the merchandise shipment from the makers to retailers to end-customers.

Sometimes scenic narratives begin with action, rather than with exposition. A story might start *in media res*, right in the middle: "He fought against the water with all his might, clutching his dog Brownie's neck with his left hand. The fury of the swollen creek threw them from side to side, colliding painfully with trees torn out by their roots, and scraping skin off protruding rocks." Then there is usually a bit of exposition: "John Ellis had seen the creek rise and fall all his life – but never like this."

Following the opening action, the writer typically "steps-back" into exposition so users can learn about John's experience with the creek, his dog, the history of the creek, or the decades-old political logjam that ended construction on the upstream dam.

Notice two arrows inside the storyline: **rising action** and **falling action** in Figure 4.9. Rising action means that after the story beginning, users encounter conflict or surprise. This change triggers a need for decision and struggle. Decisions and struggles, winning and losing, only matter if the stakes are high – who cares if the creek rises but doesn't threaten people or buildings? Within scenes, and from one scene to another, as the decisions and struggles mount, the stakes get higher and higher.

Finally, the story reaches the point of maximal struggle: life or death, renewal or ruin, redemption or condemnation. This point, the **climax**, is the apex of the rising action. The struggle ends with the protagonist gaining victory in some sense. Even though a protagonist may die from the struggle, there should be a moral victory, or perhaps a victory for others due to the protagonist's sacrifice. (Know that people typically don't enjoy reading long stories that end in defeat and ruin – at least that's what editors are likely to think.)

The story doesn't end until its **resolution**. After a struggle ends, difficulties making peace may linger. The defeated alligator may take one last lunge at the game warden. Or everyone in the gorge lived happily ever after – once construction of the new dam was finished.

This type of reporting reflects the scenic organizing principle. Writers depict the thoughts, feelings, and actions that attended character's decisions, struggles, climax, setbacks, and resolution – mostly within specific scenes. At each point in the story, key questions to ask participants include:

What happened? How did you feel when that happened? What were you worried about? What did you decide to do at that point? What were your motives? What did you seek to accomplish? What choices did you have? What problems did you see coming anyway? And then what happened?

How did that part of the story end?

The same questions work well with witnesses to understand their perspectives and responses to the events. Witnesses may also corroborate, dispute, or emphasize key points.

Clearly, especially for complex stories, organization of material is vital. Usually, reporters have too much of everything: too many field notes, interview notes and audio files, pictures, documents, data, perhaps even videos. It's critical to log all materials and link each item to specific scenes.

At, or near the end of reportage, writers often construct timelines of events; then they attach the scenes to the events. Online, interactive timelines of events in the published story help users click to different parts of a story. If they wish, they can organize the online material to suit themselves, viewing documents and media assets at their own pace, and revisiting the parts of the story they want to view again.

When writers tell stories by following the timeline, it's called a **chronology**, or a **tick-tock**. Of course, story narratives don't have to follow the timeline. The example of John with his dog in the raging creek demonstrates how it may be a good strategy to start stories with exciting action.

Hunter et al. (2011) note that for some types of stories, the timeline approach effectively conveys how something happened. Timelines work well with investigations, searches, reconstructions, processes, biographies, portraits, and interviews. They also observe that users may be more interested in stories that feature the story participants, what they did, where and how they did it, and what happened.

Even though each story has a timeline, the Odyssey offers an alternative way to approach a narrative without a strict scenic structure. The Odyssey structure allows the presentation of a problem or situation that exists in multiple places, in parallel. It's also good for issues with multiple sides or different aspects. Hunter and colleagues (2011) counsel:

> The picaresque [odyssey] structure allows you to suggest the scope and scale of a given situation more easily than a chronology would do. But a chronology is usually far superior as a means of finding the roots of a given situation.

3 WAYS JOURNALISTS USE DATA TO TELL STORIES

Chapter 8 presents practical methods for designing and producing data and **data visualizations (DVs)**. This section examines how data prove themselves useful in journalists' storytelling in large and small ways. Data may serve to embellish an existing story, adding credibility or authority to reported facts. A chart showing the incidence of measles outbreaks from the Center for Disease Control adds authenticity to a story about anti-vaxxers' activities in the area. Or managers may push the newsroom to increase the number of interactive elements to raise dwell time on pages and user engagement.

In complex stories, DVs can clarify users' understanding. A graph of output or revenues of a company town's major employer can help users understand a story about possible future job losses. A slider showing output or revenues year-by-year makes an engaging interactive for people who live in the area.

Data can also play the starring role in important stories, sometimes offering the only way to tell the story at all. For example, journalists who have quantitative skills may unearth a story that would have remained hidden had they not known their way around a data set. And when large data sets contain information about many aspects of a situation or event or analyzed data collected over time, the findings may allow the reporter to tell the story based upon visualizations of the data itself.

Using data begins by determining if the researcher's methods meet accepted scientific standards. Journalists examine the questions posed in the research and how data collection occurred. Assuming that quality is high, the data analysis and limitations of the research often determine how much trust people should place in any conclusions drawn from the data.

10 STORIES DATA CAN TELL

Once satisfied that the results of the research are credible, journalists may then consider the kinds of stories that they can create around them. According to Davenport (2014), data lends itself to telling ten types of stories, as shown in Table 4.1.

TABLE 4.1 Ten stories journalists can tell with data

Data Category	Types of Data Stories	The Stories Data Tell
Time	What time period does the data cover?	
	1) *Past*: Reporting	Descriptive analytics to tell about what happened
	2) *Present*: Explaining	Explanatory stories about what is going on now. Stories reporting current surveys fit in this category.
	3) *Future*: Prediction	Use past or current data to predict the future. (Note: The best predictor of a future of an event is what happened the last time a similar event occurred.)
Focus	What questions about a situation does the data answer?	
	4) What	Tells about something that happened.
	5) Why	Tells why something happened.
	6) How to address the issue	The data point to ways to improve the existing status quo.
Depth	How many of the key dimensions of the situation does the data address?	
	7) "CSI" projects	Data identify something about why events occurred or are occurring.

Data Category	Types of Data Stories	The Stories Data Tell
	8) Eureka	Usually long, expensive investigations when data point to ways to solve seemingly complex or intractable problems.
Methods	Stories that identify relationships between variables: How one or more things/events change when something else changes.	
	9) Correlation	When X changes, so does Y. The data may not show what caused either variable to change, but they show that variables do change together.
	10) Causation	A change in X caused a change in Y … or both. The data shows that one variable/thing (or event) caused a change in the other. Causal claims typically transcend data; they also require time order (cause before effect), and some "forcing quality" that the causal variable/event exerts on the caused variable/event.

Credit: Joan Van Tassel, based on Davenport (2014)

STRUCTURING DATA STORIES

Almost all articles, even those centered in data, use a combination of verbal narration and visualizations. Castle and LaTorra (2018) list some useful guidelines that will help structure a data story:

- Know your audience
- Begin with a question
- End with an insight
- Tell a compelling story
- Provide context
- Narrate with words, explain with visuals
- Be clear and concise
- Be honest

FROM STORIES TO EXPERIENCES: EXTENDED REALITY (XR) ENVIRONMENTS

After many years of reading, watching, and listening to news and several decades of clicking on and interacting with news, users can now experience the news. The look and feel of augmented reality (AR) and virtual reality (VR) environments seem more akin to 3D video games than to other forms of news. Veda Shastri, video journalist and 360°producer at *The New York Times*, listed the kinds of stories that lend themselves to virtual reality and perhaps augmented reality as well (Nelson, 2018). If the answer to the questions below is "yes," the story may be a good one for XR:

- Space: Is the space visually arresting?
- Scale: Is the size or extent important for the user to know – too big, too small?
- Access: Is it a place that is inaccessible for most users?
- Intimacy: Will users feel like they are having an experience without others present?
- Perspective: Does the experience present a unique view?
- Environment: Does it lend itself to 360° immersion? (VR only)

Archer and Finger (2018) compared how people responded to news stories in text, still photo, and 3D virtual reality formats. Those who experienced VR felt more empathy with the subjects of the story, especially if they had little prior knowledge about the story. They also found that users:

- Rated experiences with one clear protagonist more enjoyable
- Reported feeling more empathy, immersion and engagement when they trusted the narrator
- Trusted a narrator more when they were consistently on the screen

The authors cautioned against "complicated, lengthy experiences or interfaces." They also noted that some users reported discomfort with the VR headset they wore. Finally, they recommended showing people how they can share VR stories with others.

FINDING STORIES

New bombshell stories appear almost every day. Fortunately for journalists, exciting yet-untold stories lurk in many places, too. As we've learned, they even lie in wait for a purposeful data journalist. Learning to spot good stories takes a lively sense of curiosity about people and events. Several characteristics make for a good story: It holds a surprise or two. It has interesting characters. It may cover complex processes, shed light on previously unknown or unseen conditions, or evoke great emotion for participants. Key questions to ask include:

- Is it true?
- Who does it affect?
- Would it make users feel something?
- What does it tell them about themselves, their relationships, their society, or culture?

Reporters seek stories by talking to people, searching the nooks and crannies of the net, reading local stories in *USA Today*, even by examining their own experiences – in conjunction with those of acquaintances, friends, and family. We can't know where the next good story awaits a reporter's discovery.

Sometimes, the story finds the reporter.

TAKEAWAYS

- People can get more news than ever before. The internet communications network provides ways for people to access an amazing repository that stores much of the world's knowledge and many images of human creations. The properties that make the internet unique include: 1) its size and reach, 2) its ability to carry all kinds of digital content, and 3) the many-to-many, two-way communication flows now possible. These characteristics help news organizations and journalists build large audiences and enable journalists (and users) to use engaging multimedia assets in digital stories. Many-to-many communication permits engagement between journalists and users. Users can provide feedback, make comments, and forward stories to their personal and professional networks. Journalists should adopt writing styles that take advantage of internet capabilities and avoid its pitfalls:
  - Write a story to its natural conclusion – the internet allows stories of variable lengths
  - Create interactions for and with users
  - Make it easy for your users
- Traditional structures enable reports and narratives to foster effective information-sharing among users. The inverted pyramid structure underlies most journalistic reports, particularly the fact-based, straightforward accounts of actions and events. The narrative structure guides some news feature stories and nonfiction scenic narrative stories.
- Writing reports starts with identifying the 5W1H facts: who, what, where, when, why, and how. Reports begin with ledes that highlight the most important 5W1H elements or facts. A nut graf that follows the lede explains why the story matters to users. The following sections provide details that flesh out the bare bones of the 5W1H that were first presented in the lede. After giving some details, reports might include background, context, and analysis. The article ends with less important details. Then, journalists can end reports or, if the story warrants, they can offer additional background, context, and analysis. Often writers add a kicker that summarizes the report in a pithy phrase, sentence, or quote.

  To apply the inverted pyramid, keep in mind the function of each structural element, lede, nut graf, and so forth. The ladder of abstraction can help identify rich contexts for elements in the article. Providing links to this material delights engaged users. It also signals less interested users to move on to the next story. Either way, most publications will want the writer to keep the user on the site. Throughout the story, transitions will make following the story smooth for users.

- Stories are culturally universal because they transmit vital knowledge to the members of any community. Stories let users vicariously experience the people, places, and issues that matter to them. Users don't just read stories and look at pictures. Rather, stories "transport" people into situations they may know little about in ways that give greater appreciation to the human side of news. Something important happened! Narratives provide the sequence of events that precede a key event, along with the consequences that follow from that event. Narratives clarify how people respond to important situations – giving users life-lessons for their futures.

- Nonfiction scenic narrative stories have beginnings, middles, and endings. The story is chronological, but the narrative is not. The narrative can begin at any point in the story, with the writer later filling in users about the story's beginning as the action progresses. The story structure calls for a protagonist who has a desire or a goal. Challenges and barriers stand in the way of realizing that goal. As the struggle intensifies, the stakes get higher and higher. Finally, the climax of the story reveals the outcome of the conflict. Resolution comes, perhaps with a small bump or two in the road that occur in the falling action and ending.

- Narrative structures work well for feature and nonfiction scenic narrative stories. Think through the story's news peg, tie to a current news topic, news angle, perspective for telling the story, and news hook that grabs users. News features often start with quotes, startling facts, or observations. Nut grafs lay out why this story matters to users. Write a paragraph or more for each important subtopic or idea. Between these paragraphs, intersperse quotes, context, examples, and descriptions. Make sure the story delivers on the promises in the headline, deck, and earlier parts of the story. End the narrative with a kicker, an impactful statement that wraps up the story, giving the user a sense of closure.

- Multimedia and interactive assets in both reports and stories increase user engagement – at least for interested users. For online stories, insert exciting or interesting assets or links to assets. The viewing or interaction can take place within the story, between paragraphs, or on a multimedia page, corralled together.

- Journalists sometimes write reports based on announcements and press releases. An internet search and a few phone calls can flesh out a short, factual story that appears on the news site, perhaps accompanied by a picture or two. Longer reports take much more effort and time; typically, they require intensive research verification, multiple interviews, images, and documentary evidence.

  Reporters assigned feature news stories first evaluate what parts of the story are important. Journalists frequently visit locations, and they conduct multiple, long interviews. Nonfiction scenic narrative stories usually are the most work-intensive stories. These stories may take weeks, months, or even years of on-site observation. Online, this type of story demands photography and video recordings, many interviews, extensive research, and careful verification. A reporter or even a journalism team often works closely with an editor on these stories because they require so many resources.

- Journalists use data to make stories richer and more understandable. Useful and attractive data visualizations increase user engagement, especially when they are interactive. However, using data to find and create stories around research results requires high-level skills in research methodology and data analysis. Otherwise, it is wise to seek professionally trained experts.

- XR experiences are a new kind of story. This generation of journalists will explore how to use them in the news to tell, enhance, and bring stories to life.

KEY CONCEPTS AND TERMS

- News pegs, hooks, and angles
- Inverted pyramid
- Feature story

- Scenic narrative story
- Story structure
- Narrative structure
- Ladder of abstraction

EXERCISES AND ACTIVITIES

1. Find a current local story that features at least one key actor who is a very influential or interesting individual. Conduct at least two in-person interviews, one with the key person. Develop a good question list: Be sure to ask why or how this person got involved, what happened, what is likely to happen, and what colleagues and friends think about this actor and event. Take photos of the interviewees and the places that are important to the story. Write a 350–500 report that follows the inverted pyramid structure, shown in Figure 4.2.

2. Write the same story as a 500–600 news feature story, following the news feature structure, shown in Figure 4.7.

3. Read the two-part scenic narrative story in *WIRED* magazine by Joshuah Bearman and Tomer Hanuka (with additional reporting by Joshua Davis and Steven Leekart), at www.wired.com/2015/04/silk-road-1/; and www.wired.com/2015/05/silk-road-2/.
   a. List the scenes that make up the story.
   b. Make a copy of Figure 4.9. Identify the turning points of the article that match the classic story structure turning points.

ADVANCER

Chapter 5 covers digital and online reporting tools for newsgathering. The treasure trove of online official records from the criminal justice system, and licensing, tax, property, and registration agencies – it's an information-rich environment that makes even non-geeky journalists' hearts beat faster. Search engines provide other important sources of information; they typically have advanced search options that journalists must use expertly.

The next chapter also looks at mining the big social media and professional networks – Facebook, LinkedIn, Twitter, Instagram, Pinterest, Periscope, and YouTube. Using first-person eyewitness accounts of breaking news events that appear on social media sites remains controversial. Chapter 5 presents the case for using eyewitness accounts and the case for opposing their use. And it examines the procedures journalists follow to verify eyewitness accounts.

5

NEWS GATHERING AND REPORTING: NEW TECH, NEW TRICKS

Chapter Learning Objectives

After reading this chapter, students will be able to:

1. Understand how online newsgathering fits into an overall reportorial strategy.
2. Carry out efficient and effective online searches.
3. Use social media as sources of information.
4. Locate and use public records and public information.
5. Gather data and consider its validity and reliability.
6. Understand and comply with copyright law.
7. Understand how 21st-century information wars impact newsgathering efforts.

Our audiences don't care what we think, they care about what we can find out.
– Nancy Gibbs, *TIME* Editor-in-Chief, to Brian Stelter,
host of CNN, *Reliable Sources*

THE GIST

Ms. Gibbs reminds us of journalism's fundamental purpose: to inform people about the important actions and events that they should understand. People typically respond to journalists' analysis and opinion only when they believe these stories reflect reality – real events and facts. Opinion articles and shows may attract an audience, but people make up their own minds, right or wrong, based on what they think is the real deal.

Acquiring accurate information demands that reporters use *all* the tools of their trade, including online and traditional journalistic methods. Chapter 5 describes the array of online sources for information – media coverage, background, databases, and leads. (Chapter 6 explores traditional newsgathering practices, the hard-won professional knowledge handed down over time – practices known as **shoe-leather journalism**.)

Reporters' time is valuable and limited. Gathering information online offers some efficiencies. Many books and articles provide detailed ways to gather online information. However, it's important to stay current, as resources change frequently. The internet itself changes continuously, requiring frequent searches to locate up-to-date ways of finding material.

Digital technologies swept in new information sources, but they didn't sweep away the old ones. In one sense, digital tools save journalists much time and effort. It is seductive to overemphasize these online newsgathering strategies, but important and complex stories will likely require both online *and* traditional professional competencies. Make no mistake about it, journalists' jobs are now more complex than ever because they must master both skill sets.

Earlier chapters described types of news stories. For all but the shortest (and most routine) reports, articles almost always require more than one type of information: facts, actions, likely effects, opinions, context, background, etc. – and this list doesn't include graphics or multimedia elements. The kind and amount of information reporters gather depends on the assignment, its subject, and the planned length of the finished story. (Online length isn't as much an issue as it is in print although editors typically provide target word-counts, indicating how they view the story's importance and audience appeal.)

Next, reporters consider the most effective reportorial strategies available. When a story is breaking, there may not be much information available yet, so publications publish what they have and go on the hunt for more. However, many stories come straight from a wire service. And simple event announcements may require nothing more than straightforward rewrites of a press release. These short informative blurbs may not mean much to reporters, but they often matter to readers, community leaders, and local editors.

Whenever possible, reporters should seek to put meat on the bones of assigned stories with traditional observation and in-person contact and interviews, especially if they have an assigned beat. Spending time to assemble rich background and contextual information about seemingly routine stories can pay exciting dividends. For example, enterprising reporters at the *Daily Breeze*, a Southern California beach city daily, won a Pulitzer Prize by digging deeply into the local Board of Education's budget.

First, the reporter decides where to go for information online. Are public records available? Public and private reports? Hearing transcripts? Comprehensive data sets? Is the information accessible online? Then, consider the traditional methods that will strengthen the story – asking known sources and contacts, friends, and colleagues of known sources, interviewing people in person, or getting information from direct or indirect observation? For example, capturing video taken from a drone, a form of indirect observation, might bring a special vividness to the public's understanding of the story.

It is also essential to consider the barriers that could obstruct gathering information. Reporters must know the requirements of copyright and the usage rules that govern the public domain. The public's growing distrust of news media creates troubling new impediments to gathering news and finding information.

BUT FIRST! BEFORE YOU START GATHERING INFORMATION, 3 HABITS THAT WILL HELP PREVENT PROFESSIONAL EMBARRASSMENT, AGGRAVATION, AND HEARTBREAK

When a reporter crashes onto a story, boring administrative tasks might seem like a mega-buzzkill. But nothing feels worse than mega-storykills such as losing files, failing to locate files, or accidentally erasing files. Journalists who carry out these minimal admin actions automatically will benefit from them throughout their careers.

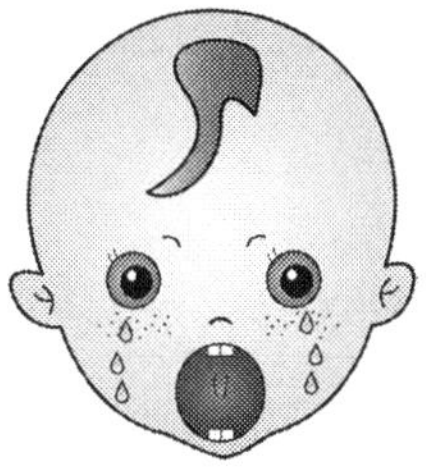

- *Habit #1 Backup everything on an external hard drive or USB thumb drive.* Copy every file, note, picture, audio and video recording, and data set; copy every single 0 and 1, every pixel. ***Go wild and backup your backup.***
- *Habit #2 Create or copy lists of all story materials.*
- *Habit #3 Upload files into the Content Management System (CMS) or other online repository.* Almost all news organizations require uploading and storage of finished assets prior to publishing. Small newsrooms may not have a formal CMS; rather, they manage content using online storage. Freelance journalists working on contract or **spec** must use their own computers, drives, or storage account.

FIGURE 5.1

Don't let this be you

Credit: Image by Cy at Pixabay.com

Table 5.1 displays information-gathering information methods, journalists' reporting strategies, and the genres of articles typically associated with certain kinds of information.

TABLE 5.1 Information-gathering method, reporting strategy, and article type

Information-Gathering Method	e-Reporting Strategies	Type of Article
Facts and background	– Public internet searches; public record search; court and hearing testimony, reports, data – Historical material	Most news genres: reports, news features, explainers, investigative reports, long-form explanatory narratives, long-form scenic narratives, profiles, essays, blogs
Indirect observation	– Social media and news accounts – Observations by others – family, friends, colleagues, admirers, detractors, experts – Photos, film/video footage, audio, and historical documents – Google Earth Maps – Stock footage	Most news genres: reports, news features, vignettes, explainers, investigative, long-form nonfiction narratives, profiles, essays, blogs, tweets

(continued)

TABLE 5.1 Continued

Information-Gathering Method	e-Reporting Strategies	Type of Article
Direct quotes	– Social media and news accounts Online and archived interviews with key insiders, participants, witnesses, experts – Online and archived tape of past press conferences and public appearances – Quotes from preserved documents, Bibles, photos, film/video footage, and audio	Most news genres: reports, news features, explainers, investigative reports, long-form explanatory narratives, long-form scenic narratives, profiles, essays, blogs
Data	– Online official, proprietary, leaked, and dark web databases	Most news genres, but especially investigative reports and long-form explanatory narratives
Breaking news	– Social media sites: Twitter, Facebook, Instagram, Periscope, Snapchat, YouTube Immediate observation, personal stream of consciousness reactions and opinions, images, video, audio	Eye- and ear-witness accounts in reports and re-constructed accounts in feature and nonfiction narrative stories

GATHERING INFORMATION ONLINE

It's easy to see how online sources provide new ways to gather news: Mouse clicks replace endless trips – to the library, the courthouse, the county plat map, and dozens of other collections of records and reports of activities. Indeed, Reich and Godler (2017) found that only 15 percent of the stories they examined from the Israeli press involved **legwork**, traditional shoe-leather reporting. This decline of on-the-scene reporting is worrisome to journalists because of the potential loss of valuable evidentiary reportage and, thus, the credibility of news. When appropriate and possible, a combination of online and shoe-leather reporting serves readers best, as described in Chapter 6.

In the past, information was in short supply, difficult to obtain, and even more difficult to verify. Now information is easy to find, easy to cut and paste – but no easier to verify. Back in the day, reporters spent many hours tracking down information in search of a single pearl of truth. Today, online reporters must spend many hours sorting through a tsunami of information to find that pearl of truth. Filtering out valuable information from inaccurate or entirely fabricated fantasy presents time-consuming challenges and sends even experienced journalists chasing false leads.

NEW TECH, NEW TRICKS **121**

Yet relatively simple searches yield information reporters could have never envisioned in days past – that now just pops up on the screen. Facebook pages paint detailed pictures of billions of otherwise private lives. Following heavy Twitter users can provide a stream-of-consciousness record seemingly directly from their brains to your digital screen.

During 2012, *The Washington Post* published a series of stories about how members of Congress used their power as senators and representatives to further their own financial interests. A team of four reporters asked this simple question: "Have lawmakers helped themselves by helping the country?" After a two-year investigation, the reporters found that 249 lawmakers took public actions that aligned with their private finances. Congressional members claimed these favorable (for them) confluences of financial interests were all coincidences.

The WaPo project required one year for the investigative team to gather its information, and then another year to carry out additional reporting and roll out their stories in four waves:

- Wave 1 focused on earmarks
- Wave 2 looked at stocks and revealed how lawmakers rearranged their personal portfolios after speaking with Fed or Treasury officials
- Wave 3 looked at the laws legislators supported that would benefit businesses in which they or their family members had an interest
- Wave 4 identified how lawmakers sponsored or considered bills that their family members were paid to lobby on.

Vox Verbatim: David Fallis, Deputy Investigations Editor, *Washington Post*

It was a massive undertaking involving four reporters. It included reporting [from] both analog and digital [sources], from shoe leather to intricate database analysis. We mined a vast range of local, state, and federal documents, including the Congressional Record and lobbying reports.

"There are 535 lawmakers in the Senate and House. We divided them among four reporters and vetted all the financial disclosure forms that each member files on an annual basis. Then we compared the forms with other public records. We checked if the disclosures were accurate or missing anything and to see if any of the lawmakers' private financial interests aligned or overlapped with their official actions in office.

The reporting team put together a 10-page list of things to check for each member, including property holdings, financial interest in any companies, and legislative earmarks they had sponsored. For example, we found that Senator Richard Shelby (R-Alabama) and Representative Hal Rogers (R-Kentucky) had both earmarked money to fund public projects adjacent to property they owned. We found that 33 lawmakers had used earmarks to fund infrastructure projects within 2 miles of their property and another 16 had steered earmarks to corporations, colleges, and nonprofits linked to their family members.

If a lawmaker's financial disclosure form said they owned property in anytown USA, we would go into the public record to make sure it was accurate. Did they own other properties? Or did they have an interest in shell companies that owned those properties, but they did not disclose it on the forms? We applied the same rubric to the lawmakers' spouses. For the next year and a half, we went through this process of scrubbing all 535 of these members. We started to find things.

> We were using the Internet to look up property and other databases across the country instead of going to the locations and doing so in person. We could not have done this project in any sort of meaningful or efficient way otherwise. What the Internet can do is it can give you the tools to report from your desk when in the past you would have to go drive or get on a plane and fly somewhere to research a piece of property, a company, or a court case. What it allows you to do is to reach into those jurisdictions and pull those records in an instant and without traveling.

Public records often provide strong evidence to support a fact or set of facts. Reporters should consider the validity of other information sources with greater uncertainty. One way to reduce that uncertainty is to examine sources of **curated** information first. This can save a lot of time. The term "curation" comes from the expert discipline of creating collections for museums. Curating means finding, selecting, and presenting a collection of materials that have value.

Several years ago, the availability of news and other information from online sources gave rise to the concept of journalists as curators (Jarvis, 2009; McAdams, 2008). Jarvis wrote: "journalists need to learn better curatorial skills. Yes, in a sense, they've always curated information, collecting it, selecting it, giving it context in their stories. But now they have to do that across a much vaster universe: the internet."

One important consideration for digital journalists is that gathering information online presents important potential threats to individuals' privacy (Aviles, 2014). One consequence of the very ease of gathering information – reporters can readily find social media comments and pictures that were never intended for public consumption. Journalists must exercise care that, if they disseminate personal information thoughtlessly, they may harm innocent originators. **Cyber-stalking,** even death threats, occurs all too frequently. Some online news organizations may not have implemented codes of ethics or their code may not cover how reporters should handle sensitive information they uncover in day-to-day online newsgathering.

PRIVATE AND INTERNAL NETWORKS

Many independent journalists and small publications lack access to university libraries or large, commercial databases. For example, LexisNexis is a commercial service that provides legal, government, business, and high-tech information sources, including a comprehensive database of stories published by news outlets around the world that stretches back for decades. These curated articles, vetted by professional journalists and editors before publication, provide rich sources of background material. They also enable assessments of the volume of previous press coverage devoted to a specific topic or story, even revealing gaps in past reports that may be relevant now. Other specialized information services cover specific fields – business, finance, geology and raw materials, and medicine.

But access to LexisNexis for many freelance and part-time journalists is prohibitively expensive: Individuals paid more than $440 per month for this service, and most companies paid a great deal more. However, many public libraries offer ways for their patrons to conduct online searches of news databases. Typically, this access includes domestic newspapers, many magazines, and some international publications – depending on the quality of the public library.

The global internet complicates determining how much coverage a story received, since many sites around the world just rewrite or just copy stories from large news outlets. Since users can search themselves, unless the reporter has a specific angle on the story of interest to a subset of users, there is little point in just recapitulating already-known and easily-discovered news. Once the journalist or editor determines a need for additional coverage, the journalist will read as many previously published articles as possible, at the same time developing strategies for gathering new information.

- How did other publications cover the story?
- Do international publications cover the story differently than domestic outlets?
- What important issues does the story raise?
- What contexts or levels of context surround the story; have new, unreported contexts emerged?
- Are key locations, agencies, businesses, hangouts, and experts cited?
- Do previous stories reveal possible sources for the current assignment?

THE PUBLIC INTERNET

The public internet's sheer breadth ensures its broad and potent uses. General internet searches typically suggest people, resources, ideas, and angles that other publications didn't discover or cover. Sometimes a find is just gravy, adding an unexpected twist to a local story. For example, a journalist assigned a short report on local burglaries may learn that thieves took a stuffed owl from a pawnshop or that eight crates of sheer nightgowns disappeared from an upscale lingerie shop.

General Search Engines

Online search services, such as Google, Bing, Yahoo!, and DuckDuckGo enable reporters to uncover different kinds of information that have not surfaced in earlier news reports. In the beginning stage of stories, finding an angle (if one was not suggested) becomes a necessary part of gathering background material. As reporters carry out their initial research, they seek potential angles for the story as well as new information. However, until a reporter analyzes her material carefully, keeping an open mind is essential: Without an open mind it's too easy to overlook small but important discrepancies or disregard counterfactual evidence.

Search returns include links to information from social media and other non-curated web sources that reporters can follow up. But, until other reliable sources confirm this information, it's just that – unconfirmed information. Reporters must maintain a careful balance between being open to intriguing new information and the time-sucking efforts required to check out every possible lead.

Another useful way to find angles requires considering alternative themes for the article. For example, in 2016, local Greek-Americans felt uncertain, fearful, and sad about the predicament of their old country, "Greek-Americans concerned about possible default." Or they may have strong opinions about where to cast blame, "Imposed austerity cripples Greece, say local Greek Americans." Ideas about themes do not need to be specific – or even entirely accurate – at this point in the research. Subsequent reporting and interviews will clarify which, if any, of these themes should frame the final report.

Making a list of a half-dozen or so possible themes for coverage can guide searches of the public internet. Many initial searches will lead nowhere, but others will lead to more ideas for even more useful searches. And perhaps one of these themes will go to the very heart of the matter, leading to further searches that serve up strong returns. Good journalists also try to eliminate potential angles or themes quickly. When their searches show little promise, reporters must use their precious time for productive searches.

In the early stages of research, search engines often provide the only way to locate people and groups to conduct interviews for an assignment. Let's return to the local Seattle angle on the Greek financial crisis: This story clearly needs to include the thoughts and feelings of local Greek-Americans. But who are these persons? An internet search of "Greek community Seattle" returns a Facebook page for Greek Seattle Community and two Greek churches. A link to Yahoo! Answers (https://answers.yahoo.com/question/index?qid=20101117122614AATH9lO) reveals these two comments:

User comment 1: Is there a Greek community in SEATTLE, WA? Because I have contacted www.greekseattle.com, the St. Dimitrios church, various Greek restaurants … and NO ONE ANSWERS. I want to get in contact with the Greek community in Seattle. Please, anyone know how to help?

User comment 2: Go to Mass at St. Dimitrios and pick up the church circular on the way out; it has upcoming events and further opportunities to get to know the Greek community.

This search did the trick: a fast, easy, and useful return. But note the reporter still didn't know what he or she would find. The angle will emerge from the interviews of the newly-discovered sources.

One advantage Google offers is that, although Google displays search returns based on a complex **algorithm**, the number of searches on specific topics also influences the ranking of results. Thus, more popular searches show up higher in the return list (after the paid players and the advertisers). Essentially, Google provides a rough, real-time index of a topic's popularity – very useful data for reporters.

Another reason to use Google lies in the specialized search terms the service provides to users. By changing search requests, reporters can search for exact words, alternative words, or completely exclude certain words from their search. Be sure to check out the tutorials for Google Advanced Search – they offer invaluable options that can make your searches far more efficient and targeted. And visit the Google web page that shows users how to narrow searches to make them more useful at: www.google.com/advanced_search.

In some instances, especially when it involves extremely sensitive information or topics, reporters will want to work with maximum privacy. Savvy journalists know that the Google search engine sees their data and: 1) saves, 2) tracks, 3) mines, 4) distributes, and 5) sells information about searches and users. Google offers an **incognito mode**. However, for more privacy, conduct sensitive private searches with a secure browser that encrypts requests and returns and conceals visited internet sites.

Wikipedia

Wikipedia has proven to be a useful source of information for hundreds of millions of people, who access it for many purposes. The users who post information to the site and those who edit existing information are members of the public. Naturally, posters differ in their expertise, knowledge, and objectivity about their entries. Some Wikipedia entries are self-serving and deceptive. However, community members themselves often flag entries that lack adequate citations, show potential bias, or need updating. As easy and quick to access as Wikipedia may be, some journalists and academics express concerns about the trustworthiness of information on any publicly written and edited knowledge source such as Wikipedia.

Fortunately, we can access substantial research about Wikipedia. Mesgari, Okoli, Mehdi, Nielsen, and Lanamaki (2014) reviewed 110 research studies that examined Wikipedia content. Most studies focused on the amount of material the site carries or the accuracy of the content. Mesgari et al. suggested four criteria for evaluating Wikipedia content when looking at specific topics or subjects:

- *Comprehensiveness*: Health and popular topics are usually very complete; other subject areas receive less coverage and attention.
- *Currency*: Research indicates that Wikipedia is far superior to other encyclopedias with its many contributors and the frequent monitoring and editing of articles.
- *Readability*: Not surprisingly, there is great variation in readability, both within topics and across them.
- *Reliability* (accuracy): While studies have found mixed results, the research finds that Wikipedia accuracy is comparable to the *Encyclopedia Britannica*.

For reporters, the array of topics, even about arcane subjects, make a quick stop at Wikipedia valuable. Journalists often find background information and citations to foundational material that generates helpful leads. In addition, many entries provide historical details not easily found elsewhere.

Despite being Wikipedia users, few reporters formally cite the service in their articles – and certainly not without verifying the information they find there before publishing it. But verification of Wikipedia is easier than it might seem, because most entries provide extensive references and explanatory footnotes. Armed with this information about an entry, journalists and fact-checkers can backtrack to find the information's source(s) and confirm it. Cited material may also lead to interviews with subjects and subject matter experts. So, although journalists don't usually reference Wikipedia, it's easy to see why many use it.

A Dark Day for Online Research

In early 2012, Wikipedia led a fight against proposed legislation that would have made it difficult – perhaps impossible – for websites that rely on collaboration and sharing to continue operating. The House of Representatives' proposed bill, the Stop Online Piracy Act (SOPA) and the Senate version of the bill, the Protect Intellectual Property Act (PIPA), aimed to curb violation of copyright-protected materials through websites based outside of the United States. The legislation would have changed the way people use the internet by restricting public access to websites suspected of piracy. Many tech companies – including Google – feared that adoption of SOPA or PIPA would place onerous restrictions on the many sites (like Wikipedia) that offer information uploaded by users or aggregate content.

Aggregators Reddit and the online compendium of cute cat pictures I Can Has Cheezburger? (http://icanhas.cheezburger.com/lolcats) joined Wikipedia – and went dark for a day to protest the legislation. Other prominent websites, including Google, WordPress, Wired.com, and Mozilla.org (creators of the **open source** Firefox browser) supported the protest in their own ways – redacting words and images while asking users to urge their Congressional representatives to vote against SOPA and PIPA.

FIGURE 5.2

Screenshot: Wikipedia homepage on the day it went dark

Credit: Wikimedia Foundation, via Wikimedia Commons

Beyond the ethical question of censorship, these tech companies argued that such restrictions would end the free and open internet by imposing restrictions that would be too difficult, expensive, or even impossible for them to follow (Farenthold, 2012).

Wikipedia's campaign worked, at least in the short term. Citing an overwhelming response from constituents, the Senate decided to reconsider PIPA five days before its scheduled vote on the bill. Feeling the heat, the House of Representatives drafted an alternative to their SOPA bill, the Online Protection and Enforcement of Digital Trade Act, before throwing in the towel and tabling it indefinitely.

Online Public Records

When journalists get an assignment to do research or write a report, they usually go online. But they typically use internet resources in ways that differ from most people because of their training in locating and accessing public records. Often, these materials are well-documented information, although some of it, especially court documents, may come from parties who have an interest in the outcome of actions. For example, if the assignment requires covering a rash of bankruptcies in Nashville, Tennessee, the court beat reporter may start by calling a friendly local source for background information. (It's a good strategy to interact with this source in a low-cost, genial exchange where the source *is* the expert.)

Now, armed with an informed perspective on the local situation, the next stop is the online U.S. Courts website (www.uscourts.gov) for annual bankruptcy reports by state and county. Anyone can download statistics for the Middle Tennessee District, then of Davidson County. Nashville is the state capitol and regional hub, so most cases will reflect that city's dominance in the area. The records, as shown in Figure 5.3, also report business and nonbusiness filings, by type of filing (Chapter 7, 11, 12, or 13 debt filings).

(December 31, 2014–Continued)

Circuit and District	Total Filings	Total Chapter 7	Total Chapter 11	Total Chapter 12	Total Chapter 13	Predominant Nature of Debt							
						Business Filings					Nonbusiness Filings			
						Total	Chapter 7	Chapter 11	Chapter 12	Chapter 13	Total	Chapter 7	Chapter 11	Chapter 13
TN. M	10.343	5.837	81	1	4.424	217	159	53	1	4	10.126	5.678	28	4.420

FIGURE 5.3

Online record of bankruptcy filings in Davidson County, Middle Tennessee District

Credit: Governmental information in the public domain

NEW TECH, NEW TRICKS

Next the reporter might check the **PACER system (Public Access to Court Electronic Records)** and the **National Archives and Records Administration**. For small fees, anyone can conduct record searches of specific bankruptcy cases and obtain the filed documents. A quick reading could unearth surprising gems that add local color – a topless joint owner or a prominent, thought-to-be-solvent suburban tract developer who recently declared bankruptcy. Or even a respected university professor who is now defending an ongoing civil suit for harassment.

Few people know how to find official records in the fast, focused ways that knowledgeable reporters use. Reporters working on assignments that involve official records have invaluable resources at their keyboards and fingertips – and many journalists expertly employ these tools. To learn effective strategies and resources for searching public records, "must-have" books include: *Investigative Reporter's Handbook* (Houston and Investigative Reporters and Editors, Inc., 2009), and *Computer-Assisted Reporting* (Houston, 2014). These books complement each other, and they provide an astonishing number of ways that journalists can pull together a wealth of data. Brant Houston, author of *Computer-Assisted Reporting*, one of the authors of the *IRE Handbook* was astonished to find that reporter Tim Heider searched for information about him and in short order found:

> the Social Security number of the subject; his height, weight, eye color, current address and driver's license status; property ownership going back three residences; names, addresses and telephone numbers of current neighbors; whether the subject held professional licenses; whether he was subject to tax liens, consumer loans, court judgments or bankruptcy proceedings; and whether he held licenses for controlled substances, airplanes, or boats. Heider also learned the identities of his spouse, who retained her family name, and his children. Through the search, Heider even discovered the name of a relative with a criminal record who had used the subject's address as his own for a while.

Makes you wonder about your own privacy, no?

Personal information is only the start. If journalists need to examine a business or a class of businesses, they can use internet tools to reveal impressive troves of public records and information resources. These handbooks show journalists how to delve deeply into governmental affairs and agencies – their budgets, consultants, and contractors, as well as:

- Federal civil service
- Legislators' campaign finance reports
- Lobbyists and some of their clients
- Court cases – both civil and criminal, from initial filing through verdicts, decisions, and appeals
- Prison systems
- Law enforcement systems – local police, types of crimes, crime databases, personnel, and budgets and contracts
- Education – demographic statistics, educational outcomes, school personnel and facilities, and budgets and contracts

For journalists, scientists, and citizens alike, there is likely to be less data available from the federal government under the Trump administration than in previous years (Harmon,

2017). In early 2017, scientists rushed to preserve data as word spread that many federally-funded databases would be removed from U.S. government websites, especially those concerning climate and the environment. For example, graphics showing the relationship between coal as an energy source and greenhouse gas emissions are no longer available. Similarly, summaries of Interior Department research estimating potential damage from fracking on federal land went missing.

The University of Pennsylvania Program in the Environmental Humanities (PPEH) established a nonprofit group (DataRefuge at www.datarefuge.org/) asking scientists, computer professionals, and librarians to identify, download, and tag valuable government datasets before the incoming administration could take them down (Schlanger, 2017). The group sponsored large Data Rescue events putting the three groups together in venues across the country and storing downloaded datasets on DataRefuge servers. Similarly, the nonprofit Environment Data and Governance Initiative/Code for Science and Society partnered with the University of California libraries to archive government data.

The status of www.data.gov, an Obama initiative to centralize government-funded datasets remains unclear, although the website remains functional with some recent additions. Much of this expensively-gathered and analyzed information is still dispersed across department and agency servers. Journalists seeking government data can contact the various groups that seek to preserve the knowledge and data; they may help journalists find the needed information.

OSINT and COSINT

OSINT stands for open source intelligence, meaning information *in the wild*, available to anyone who figures out where it is on the internet, accesses it, and assesses its value. Find a useful compendium of open source intelligence lies at www.osintframework.com. This site offers hundreds of information sources, including those found on the Dark Web. Equally important, it offers links to public records, operational security sites, and software, and much more. It is well worth an afternoon of exploration and a permanent bookmark.

When looking for OSINT, it pays dividends to ask: "If X happened, what traces of that pre-action/action/reaction cycle would logically exist?" As forensic scientists say, every crime scene has evidence. In a similar fashion, any complex action leaves traces that often reveal the underlying activities. Once a logical starting point to find those traces has been identified, tracking them down on OSINT can result in valuable information or sources. If no information surfaces, consider alternative trace elements, alternative scenarios, or question if the event or activity even occurred.

COSINT stands for Crowdsourced Intelligence or Citizen Open Intelligence. A #COSINT alert on Twitter usually comes from a journalist or citizen journalist who is requesting assistance from other users in finding additional information or verifying already-discovered information. Like OSINT, COSINT almost always refers to information that is available to anyone – usually on the internet. However, it is possible that someone who works in a company or agency would risk providing downloaded information from an organization's internal website or server to respond to a COSINT request. Both OSINT and COSINT attained importance because of the activities of professional and citizen journalists trying to find information about the 2016 Trump campaign, transition, and early months of the administration.

SOCIAL MEDIA

Because Facebook, LinkedIn, and other social networks perform valuable functions for journalists, they have become prime venues from which to gather information for news reports and stories. Social media are now must-check sources for reporters with stories without much information about actors. For one example, Brandtzæg, Lüders, Spangenberg, Rath-Wiggins, and Følstad (2016) interviewed 28 Canadian journalists, asking them how they used social media and verified the information they found there. Brandtzaeg and colleagues cited one reporter's use of social media for an important story:

> The first time I can remember to have used social media very actively in a big incident was the Virginia Tech massacre in 2007. I looked at different student profiles (Facebook) at the school and sent requests to those students who seemed to have been there when it happened. We had several eyewitnesses, via Facebook. We were directly in touch with eyewitnesses.

Reporters now use social media in several ways:

1. To find inside sources, eyewitnesses, and expert sources with unusual knowledge or competencies. Sending messages to groups hastens that search, particularly within medium-sized to small groups that are composed of people in the same occupations or social groups, because these people often know quite a bit about each other.

2. To uncover new stories. Based on the interviews in the Brandtzaeg et al. article, researchers found that journalists routinely used social media to find ideas for new stories.

3. To discover professional and personal information. In addition to specific facts, people's self-presentation enables inferences about their: 1) perceptions, 2) values, 3) social milieu, and 4) actual and aspirational social-economic status. Posted images may contain clues about the environments that a person frequents, the artifacts they value, their social attitudes, and their lifestyle choices in informal settings.

4. To **crowdsource** information-gathering and flagging – by reaching out to groups of people to help find more information or to flag information that needs further investigation. Although infrequent, crowdsourcing has proved useful in some reporting situations. Examples include examining extremely large databases with too much content for a news outlet to review, or digging out information that is known only to small or localized social groups.

Other less obvious uses of social media sites include using them to collect data for analysis. For example, anonymous crowdsourcing occurs when reporters collect comments on a specific topic to get insights about how specific groups feel about a topic or event. (Of course, in these days of bots, trolls, and shills, this procedure can easily produce misleading results.) Reporters can also use SNS Groups to contact narrowly defined groups. They can open lines of communication to find information, solicit opinions, and even initiate quick polls by embedding a survey site questionnaire that could also provide opinions by professional practitioners or from residents of a certain neighborhood.

Social media may also expose journalists in unexpected (and perhaps unwelcome) ways. In 2015, Brian Williams lost his high-status anchoring job at NBC News because of comments posted by military veterans on Facebook. According to *Stars and Stripes*, the publication's Capitol Hill reporter Travis Tritten noticed the comments some vets posted on Facebook. Tritten had a "gut feeling" that there was substance behind these comments (Tompkins, 2015). Facebook also provided leads for Tritten to check the story out, enabling him to follow up with information from new sources with firsthand knowledge of the actual events. (In 2018, NBC News let Williams host *Eleventh Hour* on the network's MSNBC cable channel, which he built into a popular and respected news show.)

Journalists now find social media extremely useful. But the future holds even more strategies, mechanisms, and stories for journalists to wrest from SNS network-level data. Tools to automatically *scrape data* from SNSs to collect personal information from large numbers of users have emerged. Thus, SNS will provide both individual-level and network-level information about people's connections, likes, and shares that can identify sub-cultures, political intentions, social standing, and influencer status in ways we don't yet know (Halpern, 2017).

Twitter

In their interviews with 28 Canadian journalists, Brandtzæg et al. found that Twitter was the most-used social media platform. Twitter affords both individual reporters and news outlets practical benefits for gathering information. The platform is a useful way for journalists to find sources who personally experienced a specific news event or topic. Daniel Victor (2015), news desk editor at *The New York Times*, analyzed five successful searches for such sources and made this helpful suggestion:

> "for successful needle-in-a-haystack-finding, you need to shake your brain out of that mindset and add a new kind of keyword."
>
> You probably skipped right over the most important word used by the five sources above. It's everyone's favorite word, and one you should add to any Twitter search that's seeking personal experiences:
>
> **Me**.
> (And its close cousin "my.")

Victor observed that descriptive search terms that focus on an aspect of the topic or event won't necessarily return tweets from potential sources and eyewitnesses. When analyzing the tweets of people who *experienced* the events a reporter was looking for, Victor found that they had one word in common: "me" and sometimes "my." Thus, a starting search string on Twitter for a burglary victim at a train station might look like: "train, station, robbery, thief, me, my."

Sometimes the short, relevant quotes of live tweet threads from participants and witnesses about news events provide important insights and observations of past occurrences. For example, consider that an editor assigns a report on the re-selling of student loans. Twitter can help the reporter find people whose student loans have been sold, and who were notified only after the deal was done. The search string: "student loans sold me my" returned several tweets that included one person whose loan was sold six times, another whose loan was sold three times, and an individual who could not make automatic payments to the new loan holder.

The reporter can then send a tweet to each potential lead, asking for a phone call to talk about the practice of re-selling student loans. These participants' perspectives may add valuable dimensions to the story that now go far beyond the middle rungs of the ladder of abstraction. In this way, using Twitter helps reporters put human faces on stories that might otherwise roll out as bland accounts of financial processes that hurt otherwise unidentified people.

Another Twitter use involves following organizations of interest to track day-to-day activities. If reporters know of upcoming assignments, they can stay abreast of company-related communications as they occur. This strategy can proactively yield insights into issues of importance to any organization's leaders. Early knowledge of organizational activities and concerns can yield solid leads and scoops. Organizational **retweets** and **follows** provide yet another layer of information and even more potential leads for the Twitter-connected newsie.

Finally, Twitter offers an excellent tool for journalists (and news outlets) to build an audience. Thoughtful, useful tweets attract users to journalists' reports and stories. Many online journalists seek and maintain large numbers of Twitter followers to whom they tweet whenever they have a new story or publication. Chapter 12 will cover how reporters can adopt career-building Twitter strategies to build followings that are independent of their publication's website.

Other Social Media

Other sites journalists use to check for people mentioned in breaking news stories include Facebook, Periscope, Snapchat, Instagram, and Pinterest. It may take 10 minutes to check them all, but diligent reporters can find hidden gems about a person's interests, social network – and perhaps even find a scoop from a user's posts about breaking news. These sites also feature annotated video or photos, opening the possibility of gaining rights to such digital assets quickly.

BLOGS

The blogs that reporters read typically offer specialized knowledge. Experts' blogs provide useful tools to gather information because these blog writers often track narrow parts of an industry, cause, group, or the behavior of other important actors. Networked journalists may follow as many as half-dozen or more blogs about the subjects they cover. Often small blogsites written by bloggers who keep track of events occurring in a small corner of the world report rumors or industry tidbits that provide ideas for new angles on old stories and valuable sources for new stories.

Most of the information published on blogs is not official. It may not be accurate. Some blogs provide pure fantasy. Reporters must verify **UGC, user-generated content**, just as they would any other information they plan to use, whether the author is a renowned expert, a neighborhood activist, or a neighbor with a grudge.

When a reporter relies heavily on a blog's information, they can ask that blogger for an interview. This practice expands the story, builds a relationship with a knowledgeable source, and gives bloggers justly deserved credit for their work. Experts' blogs are particularly useful because they have often written about many issues in their field that can be used to provide leads, background information, and further suggestions.

Other important and useful sites contain mashups of aggregated news, original news, and blogs such as *The HuffPost, The Drudge Report, The Daily Beast*, and *Independent Journal*. These sites give reporters a good sense of topics that other media publish and insights about how media cover them. And a quick read may reveal stories that *aren't* covered.

DATA

Data is more than the self-aware android lieutenant commander and second officer on a Federation starship. Data don't rise to the level of information, knowledge, or wisdom (Bellinger, Castro, & Mills, n.d.). Individual data points are "facts," some of which are not valid. Note that data is the plural of "datum" (one fact); so, data mean more than one fact. However, "data" also means a collection of facts. Thus, "The data is stored on my hard drive." This noun form is called the collective or mass singular. <Author facepalm: Maybe it's time to rewrite the dictionary on data.>

Data come in two distinctive types: qualitative and quantitative data. **Qualitative data** typically describe phenomena: interviews, observations, descriptions of feelings, the contexts of events, and perhaps recounting of personal experience. **Quantitative data** provide numerical measurements of some entity or characteristic. Some measurement process yields a number that can be treated mathematically. Examples include the number of tennis players on a court, the length of a pair of slacks, the price of a gallon of gas, the average price of chicken breasts in New York last month, or the changing favorability ratings of a proposed national policy.

Quantitative and qualitative data often complement each other. Suppose a governmental department proposes an important economic or trade policy overhaul but has not yet released any information. An observant reporter might write about the activity she has seen: "Preparing for the trade agreement, the attaché saw the Commerce Minister eight times last week." She might add the number of last week's appointments to the number of meetings in that month, the month before signing the agreement, and compare them to the year before or after. The number of appointments could be divided into days of the week, averaged across weeks, and compared to the number of appointments with a country not included in the trade agreement – or those with another country that might be included. However, the reporter should probably also add qualitative information from sources – information describing characteristics of these appointments, such as short, demanding, argumentative, exciting, important, or inconclusive.

EXTRACTING INFORMATION AND KNOWLEDGE FROM DATA

The old saying, "garbage in, garbage out" originated during early computer research to remind scientists that computers can only process the information that they are given. Research scientists use it more broadly to warn the unwary about the difficulty of drawing *valid* conclusions from research data. Datasets cannot speak for themselves! Rather, the potency of quantitative data rests in the potential to combine, summarize, and analyze it and thereby *actively create* knowledge about the world.

People need accurate information to act effectively. So, users should be able to rely on researchers' conclusions. The following considerations become paramount during consequential global crises such as the COVID-19 pandemic, regional wars, and

NEW TECH, NEW TRICKS

political upheaval. The information value of data for users increases exponentially *if* researchers have:

- Collected it carefully and systematically
- Created usefully formatted (ordered/arrayed) datasets that faithfully represent the phenomena they purport to describe
- Removed (or identified) problematic data points – incorrect, misplaced, mischaracterized, or otherwise inaccurate observations
- Analyzed the dataset in ways appropriate to the nature and context of the data collection – when, where, and the conditions under which the data was collected
- Identified the limitations of the data, describing processes from data-collection design, through data collection, formatting, analysis and conclusions
- Accurately report results, including any inherent limitations in the research
- Presented research results in clear, understandable, and coherent ways

Sloppy studies, pseudo-scientific reports, and deliberately misrepresented findings intended to persuade, even dupe readers abound – sometimes purveyed through unwitting media outlets. Responsible, ethical journalists must exercise caution when reporting research results: Consider the **provenance** of the research and its data. Provenance – the source or origin of data – identifies the individuals or organization that collected and analyzed the data, their motives, and their chops, verifying that their qualifications for conducting the research and that the topic lies within their expertise. At *minimum,* provenance requires careful review of authors' expertise, qualifications, track-records, and that of their organization(s).

Previously, journalists could presume that data acquired from federal government agencies met and sometimes set gold-standards in the respective fields. Now, given that the present administration – at the behest of political appointees selected for loyalty, not expertise (often from regulated industries) – has fired, transferred, and muzzled so many scientists within federal agencies, presumptions of good faith cannot be sustained (Gowen, Eilperin, Guarino, & Tran, 2020). Many federal and state agencies stopped collecting, analyzing, or reporting data that might constrain preferred, but questionable or politicized policies.

Reporters might find higher-quality research, including datasets, from top-tier scientific journals, experts at topflight research universities, expert fact-driven policy institutes, and select nonprofit groups like the Union of Concerned Scientists and other comparable institutions. Yet, it remains crucial to scrutinize potential conflicts of interest that may exist in light of the authors' funding, research recommendations, research findings, and the objectives of the researchers' organizations.

Drawing information from datasets and creating data visualizations is just one of many ways that reporters work with data. Because reporters routinely report data-driven research findings in their articles, they must consider the large differences in the quality of published research – so that users can heighten or temper the confidence they place in the research conclusions.

Peer-reviewed journal articles are carefully and expertly evaluated by reputable scientists, typically prominent scholars within their scientific or medical sub-discipline. Respected medical journals – like *The New England Journal of Medicine* or *The Lancet* (and its many related journals) typically publish research articles that peer reviewers recommend as providing a significant advance in the respective discipline. *The Lancet* and many other top scientific journals have formal procedures for publishing pre-prints from reputable scholars, in addition to editor's opinions that address important scientific and research concerns for their discipline.

Journalists should exercise caution when reporting information from these as-yet unpublished research pre-prints, even if they have been submitted to peer-reviewed journals: Submission does not mean acceptance. The COVID-19 pandemic increased the pace of curating, hosting, and disseminating coronavirus-related pre-prints given urgent needs to understand viral infection mechanisms, "flatten the curve", and treat coronavirus victims. Pre-prints offered ways to disseminate and crowd-source expert opinions about methodology, findings, and the value of research quickly. Journalists must know that some pre-prints later fail scrutiny by the scientific community.

Often non-peer-reviewed research and expert commentary deserve journalists' scrutiny and reporting. For example, Johns Hopkins University and Medical School Coronavirus Resource Center, *The New York Times*, *The Washington Post*, *Vox*, and other large media outlets internally created and hosted superb, timely, and useful COVID-19 research, curated datasets, and produced stunning data visualizations.

Journalists working for large news organizations have access to in-house expertise to guide reporting of information from datasets and published research papers. Increasingly, specialized data journalists are trained to handle datasets, help create data visualizations, evaluate research methodologies, data analysis, and quantitative findings in research papers. Smaller publications can acquire these competencies from nearby universities and colleges (so make friends with your local university science experts and research methods specialists).

Understanding how to acquire, analyze, and report data demands professional skills that most journalists should have, but more often lack. For journalists who cover business, politics, government, policy, this constitutes essential knowledge. The School of Data Handbook provides a helpful international resource at https://schoolofdata.org/handbook/.

To acquire the most important skills for reporting on data-intensive beats, journalists can take two courses – research methods and statistics. The Massachusetts Institute of Technology (https://ocw.mit.edu) offers excellent courses in quantitative or qualitative research methods and statistics. Students who did solid undergraduate coursework shouldn't hesitate to take graduate level courses at reputable universities.

Validity and **reliability** are two essential criteria for evaluating the quality of data. Validity means that the data reflect what researchers claim they do: The data accurately represent some underlying phenomena relevant to the reporter's knowledge claims. Valid datasets require both accurate and appropriate measurement of the reality they claim to represent. Researchers increase validity by: 1) precisely defining what they measure, 2) using measurements that match this definition (accepted standards or carefully crafted instruments), and 3) accurately measuring the phenomenon.

Reliable measurements provide stable results when repeated. They are consistent. Figure 5.4 reflects how journalists can think about potential threats to the validity and reliability of a dataset. The resulting evaluation would affect the kinds of conclusions reporters could draw from any information resulting from the analysis of the data.

Consider this hypothetical example: A state receives financial data reports from every county in the state, including budgets and contingency funds. Residents can compare their county with others to assess its financial health and to evaluate trends over time. The state database validity depends on: 1) accurate reporting, 2) honest reporting, 3) similar reporting across counties, and 4) elimination of other sources of bias.

The state simply accepts whatever counties file. A team of investigative reporters examines the reports and the data collection process from a mix of large, medium-sized, and small counties. They find that one county political machine is cooking the books, another county hired minimum wage temporary workers for data entry, and a third incorporated inflated estimates from self-interested parties. This dataset can't be valid, because the data doesn't reflect the actual reality of some county budgets.

Suppose that the next year's County Reserve Fund data shows atypical changes. Some counties had great year to year variability, mostly much better financial health, except for one county with a huge decline. Other counties' funds seem to bounce around randomly. The paper's investigating team found:

Unreliable & Invalid   Unreliable, But Valid

Reliable, Not Valid   Both Reliable & Valid

FIGURE 5.4

How validity and reliability affect gathered data

Credit: Nevit Dilmen [CC BY-SA 3.0 (http://creativecommons.org/licenses/by-sa/3.0) or GFDL (www.gnu.org/copyleft/fdl.html)], via Wikimedia Commons

1. After the state legislature quietly relaxed key rainy-day fund reporting provisions as a cynical response to political pressure, most counties showed considerably more funds – but didn't seem to add any actual dollars to their contingency funds. (loss of year to year reliability; reduced validity for second year)
2. Some officials of the troubled county's political machine were jailed; an audit revealed widespread fraud. Unfunded contingency set-asides left the county in dire straits. (loss of year to year reliability; improved validity for second year)
3. High staff turnover, poor training, and lax oversight of budget officials by auditors in many counties. (questionable reliability and validity: both years)
4. No oversight by state auditors or officials. (unknown reliability and validity: both years)

Thus, the statewide county financial health database was neither valid *nor* reliable. Overall, the budget data did not reflect actual budgets or contingency fund set-asides: The dataset was not valid. From one year to the next, even though the overall economy was relatively stable and the budget categories were the same, the data showed wide unexplained and unexpected variability: The dataset was not reliable.

If this example were a real story, the poor data would mean that some residents were systemically misled about the financial status of their communities. In some cases, it might show that those citizens were being defrauded. By identifying deeply-flawed data, followed by investigation to reveal the causes of the problems, the publication could call for prosecutions, important legislative changes, and regulatory and legal accountability. Some of these improvements might even come to pass.

Before writing an article, reporters should understand the limitations of their data – and of the underlying research. All research has limitations including the scope of the research, the underlying assumptions, the data collection, data analysis, and basis for any findings or conclusions. Reporters should consider: Do the findings make sense? Are they likely, or even possible? It is also useful to consider whether, if all the detailed processes involved in carrying out the research were done differently, how would the results change?

As finished articles, data-project stories often take much time to put together and to write. They usually require art, perhaps infographics, charts, maps, and tables. Data journalism demands high levels of skill and care. A team approach – perhaps with professional guidance – adds credibility to the work, particularly when the findings pose problems or challenges for established interests. Typically, newsroom teams composed of several reporters produce data-based or data-dependent articles. Nate Silver provides the seminal example of a hugely successful data journalist who went first to *The New York Times* and then launched a successful media company. See his website http://fivethirtyeight.com and his book (2011), *The Signal and the Noise: Why So Many Predictions Fail – But Some Don't*, for lucid, sophisticated but enjoyable and easily understandable portrayals of data journalism in action.

Clearly, data journalism demands intensive data acquisition and evaluation as part of the newsgathering operations. Crowdsourcing offers new ways for news organizations to handle data analysis tasks that are too great for a newsroom to carry out without help. For example, in the early summer of 2009, *The Guardian* obtained leaked documents that indicated widespread expense fraud on the part of Members of the British Parliament (Andersen, 2009). In the face of public outrage, the MPs sought the appearance of transparency by giving *The Guardian* a huge, unsorted treasure trove of data, totaling more than a million expense claims, submitted over the previous four years. On its own, the paper could never analyze this enormous data tsunami.

The Guardian leadership reached the same conclusion; they were drowning in data. Rather than try to analyze data in-house, they crowdsourced preliminary analysis to readers. On its website, the publishers made the entire dataset available, and invited the public to play a game called "Investigate Your MPs Expenses," complete with points and small prizes. *The Guardian* also recruited help via Twitter – "Investigate your MP's expenses: Use our interactive tools to review expenses claims." Readers accessed expense reports from MPs and examined all the filings. After looking at a claim, the reader would communicate an evaluation of each claim by clicking on one of these four buttons, as shown in Table 5.2.

The paper also posted the usernames of people who had reviewed the most pages, "Top users by line item added," showing the number of pages submitted by the top reviewers. To keep the game going, *The Guardian* would regularly post announcements to show the work in progress:

> We have 466,019 pages of documents. 19,421 of you have reviewed 204,858 of them. Only 261,161 to go ....

The scale of the response was amazing, even for the internet. Within a few days, 20,863 people sorted through 175,119 records, identifying several probable expense miscreants

TABLE 5.2 The Guardian game buttons: Reader assessment of expense claim

Is this expense page interesting?
Should *The Guardian* investigate further?

Joan Van Tassel, based on information in Andersen (2009)

among the Members of Parliament. The collaborative work led to the resignation of at least 28 MPs, criminal proceedings against four of them, and the repayment of 1.12 million pounds by many other MPs. Perhaps some media outlet might develop an American version of this game.

Andersen drew four lessons from *The Guardian's* early crowdsourcing for preliminary data analysis:

- Readers/workers are unpaid, so make it fun
- Public opinion is fickle, so launch immediately
- Speed is mandatory, so use a framework
- Participation will come in one big burst, so have your servers ready

Data Viz – Data Visualization

No matter how well reporters explore or exploit data sets for reports and stories, many people lack the basic numeracy skills to understand formulas, lists of data points, or even follow the reporters' descriptions of what the data show. To bring data to life, make visualizations clear and understandable to all. To increase user engagement with what the data show, news organizations adopt **data visualization** (**DV**) techniques from scientists and artists.

DV presents data in effective ways that allow users to make sense of highly complex data sets that include thousands, perhaps even millions, of data points. Scientists use DV to encourage users to consider the findings of the research, rather than concentrating exclusively on the research methodology or on the presentation graphics. Online, many DVs are interactive, allowing users to delve deeper, or to change parameters, or to see how results change over time or space – particularly in the spaces that users occupy. Some DVs provide opportunities for users to compare findings that rely on different parts of the data set. Thus, visualizations can display alternative levels of detail so that users can explore the finer structures that the data reveal.

DV expert Stephen Few (2013) offers tips to create DVs that help journalists convey the meanings of their datasets:

- Know your data, know your audience, and determine the message you want to communicate.
- Reduce the data to what's needed to communicate your message, remembering that, without context, numbers mean little.
- Determine the best means of expression.
  - Some quantitative messages are best communicated with words, some with tables of numbers, some with specific graphs – bar, line, scatter plot, etc. – and some with a combination of strategies.
  - These principles aren't intuitive; they require training into how our eyes and brains process visual information.
- Consult a data visualization expert on this step (or train yourself).
- Design the display to communicate simply, clearly, and accurately.
  - Don't include anything that isn't data unless it's needed to support the data.
  - Avoid unnecessary color variation and visual effects, or even grid lines in a graph when they aren't needed.
  - Make non-data elements only visible enough to do their job; they should never overshadow the information.
  - Visually highlight information that's most important to the message. Suggest actions in response to the data.

News organizations actively recruit people who have expertise in DV. The specialized type of graphics work that DV entails makes them valuable team members in communicating research findings based on data, analytics and **big-data** applications. News organizations are among many companies that seek both data wranglers and visualizers – and newsrooms are hiring (Bao & Mok, 2013).

Now Hiring: A Different Kind of DJ

DJs aren't just radio jocks anymore. Large news organizations have DJs too – data journalists and sometimes even professional researchers and statisticians in the newsroom as well. Publications actively seek people who understand journalism, coupled with research methods and analysis competencies, a trend that should continue for a long time. Reports and evaluations issued by both governmental, nonprofit, and corporate entities used to be

NEW TECH, NEW TRICKS | **139**

written in straightforward prose, perhaps offering a few percentages. Now, most organizations more carefully evaluate programs and trends using research programs that collect and analyze data, and present precise findings. Increasingly, journalists will need substantial knowledge about how such documents come into existence and what they mean for them to successfully report on their beat.

Data Innumeracy Is Just so Old News!

When news organizations advertise for "data journalists" or "journalists specializing in computer-assisted reporting," they usually mean a person who would recognize instantly the differences between types of data. They would expect this new-hire to handle equally well assignments that might involve both qualitative and quantitative data. Some people may be able to get on-the-job training to reach the competencies required to obtain and hold a data journalist job. But it is more likely that applicants have taken courses in research methods, statistics, data analysis, and perhaps data visualization.

According to one position announcement, the essential functions the data journalist would perform include:

- Acquire, convert, normalize, and migrate data from a variety of databases, text, and image formats; use the scripts and processes best suited for the job.
- Build and improve tools to automate data analysis and manipulation tasks efficiently.
- Develop useful public interfaces to local data collected by metro journalists and third parties. Key content areas include real estate, crime, education, and sports.
- Imagine and develop novel ways for users to interact with information and, where appropriate, contribute to, and edit information.
- Work with the newspaper's database experts, online editorial staff and product development teams to plan and execute online and print database projects.

Another job posting looks for someone who:

- Knows how to identify, obtain, clean, and analyze databases from a variety of sources.
- Is familiar with data visualization concepts and tools.
- Will make data-driven stories accessible and understandable to readers.
- Uses current data tools and can identify new ones to help users to interact with data.
- Uses relevant database and programming tools.
- Has solid writing and reporting skills.
- Has high-level research skills in using digital research tools to find information.
- Does long-range projects solo or as part of a team.
- Can automate workflow, create scrapers, and handle relational database analysis using MySQL, SPSS, SAS, or R.
- May have GIS data skills, or at least be willing to learn and help us come up to speed.
- Has thorough knowledge of public records laws, particularly those dealing with data.
- Is an expert in Excel, Access, and ArcView software.

Note that the first position announcement does not mention reporting skills. It might as well read, "Wanted: Data wrangler." The second announcement at least tips the hat to traditional journalistic skills – it lists reporting and writing skills in sixth place and knowledge of public records as second from the last. News organizations would likely prefer people who are deeply schooled in both journalism and data wrangling. But these people are rare, so they team people with deep data skills and a smattering of knowledge of journalism with others who have deep knowledge of journalism and some ease with drawing conclusions from data analysis and research findings.

NEW WAYS OF DOING OLD-FASHIONED JOURNALISM

The next chapter covers traditional journalistic observation methods. But just as technology opens new ways of finding information, it also opens new ways to conduct time-honored practices. The internet goes beyond online newsgathering because of its real-time communication functions. Observation and investigative collaboration are two examples.

GAME OF DRONES: NEWFANGLED OBSERVATION

In 2016, the Federal Aviation Administration approved limited drone use, for both private and commercial purposes. Since journalism uses probably fall under the commercial umbrella, Will McDonald (2017) suggests journalists who intend to use drones will need to register the drone and get a Remote Pilot Certificate. The FAA rules for drones are a bit complicated and not intuitive. Before launching, check out the Federal Aviation Administration Fact Sheet (2018) for an overview of the rules of the air.

Drones allow journalists – and the public – to observe closely from a distance! The ability to get near otherwise dangerous events such as fires, explosive devices, and conflict, etc., allows drones to gather important and previously inaccessible material. Flying over disaster areas, drones carry digital video cameras that document the location and extent of damage. Similarly, drones can document environmental damage on inaccessible public lands, construction progress from remote sites, and other events and projects that are normally hidden from public view.

Journalists and news organizations using drones will also need to review some ethical and legal practices (Waite & Kreimer, 2016). For example, journalists may not (ethically or legally) fly drones over and publish footage from privately-owned land without permission. Journalists must also take care not to violate the privacy of people who are not in public places.

INVESTIGATIONS: HOLDING THE POWERFUL TO ACCOUNT

Just as journalists communicate with users and users communicate with each other, reporters can collaborate on investigations that could not take place otherwise. Richard Sambrook (2018) points out the reason why newsrooms engage increasingly in collaborative investigations:

- Budget cuts have led to fewer resources in many newsrooms, reducing the money and time spent on investigations.

- Greater scientific and technological complexity mean that many stories require multiple high-level professional knowledge and competencies, some of which most newsrooms lack.
- Strong competitive pressure to attract engaged users with compelling stories.
- More and more issues involve regional or even global coverage, such as climate change, clean energy, clean water supply, antibiotic resistance, and money laundering.
- Increased censorship and threats to journalists.

Several journalist organizations now coordinate such collaborative efforts. Each of these groups has carried out important investigations: International Consortium for Investigative Journalists (ICIJ), Organised Crime and Corruption Reporting Project (OCCRP), Global Investigative Journalism Network (GIJN) and the European Investigative Collaborations (EIC) group. Newspapers in Europe are also collaborating on both investigations and operations strategies, including *Europa* and the European Dailies Alliance (EDA).

COPYRIGHT: A BARRIER TO GATHERING NEWS?

Finding the right assets for a story – relevant information, graphics, video, and data – is an intense activity that almost always takes place under a tight deadline. Nevertheless, journalists must always be mindful of copyright rules even as they furiously search the internet for facts, eyewitness accounts, subject matter experts, and story-related material. Failing to consider copyright issues in the heat of the moment can be costly to both reporters and publications after the story is published.

The basic copyright concept is simple: if the journalist or the publication didn't create it, they don't own it, and they don't have the rights to reproduce it. "It" refers to writings, images, video, film, audio recordings, music, data, computer code (including underlying website code), architectural plans, or any other form of intellectual property.

Journalists may not always respect copyright when they rewrite material reported by citizen journalists or bloggers from social media and use it in their story as if they reported it. Giving credit can be as simple as a phrase like: "as originally reported in the Change Agency blog …" or "as Jim Smith originally posted to Twitter." Print journalists long grumbled that broadcast journalists failed to acknowledge the heavy lifting print newsies have done to break many stories seen on the 6:00 pm news programs. Now online reporters, bloggers, and citizen journalists often complain that print reporters take their work and publish it as their own reporting. Bloggers probably can't expect much better treatment any time soon – but they (too) deserve to get recognition for their original reporting.

To be fair, sometimes digital reporting by bloggers, members of the public, and even online reporters, is not well-sourced, fact-checked, or verified – even when the information turns out to be true. Thus, reporters in major news organizations, whose work must meet these high standards, may believe they have done the complete job, meriting the credit as the reporter of checked, confirmed, and verified news. Nevertheless, crediting the work (and intellectual property) of online sources and citizen journalists needs to improve, as they typically lack adequate redress in the "Wild West" internet.

PUBLIC DOMAIN

Some materials fall outside the rules for copyright protection altogether (Jassin, n.d.). And there are time limits on copyright protection for all intellectual property. When a particular time interval has passed, these works become part of the public domain. They are publicly available to anyone; hence the term **public domain**. Public domain content includes:

- U.S. Government works
- State judicial opinions
- Legislative enactments, and other official documents
- Unadorned ideas and facts
- Blank forms
- Short phrases
- Names, titles, and slogans
- Extemporaneous speeches
- Standard plots and stock characters

FAIR USE

In the list above (fourth from the bottom), notice the copyright exemption for *short phrases*. In some circumstances, **fair use** even allows using materials that have protection under copyright law. The widest interpretation of fair use allowed copying material for limited purposes, such as commenting, criticizing, or creating a parody of the original work. Such uses can be executed without obtaining permission from the copyright owner.

Dubberly (2016) lists the criteria journalists should consider before using material from a copyright-protected document:

1. The purpose and character of the use, including whether such use is of a commercial nature or is for nonprofit educational purposes
2. The nature of the copyrighted work
3. The amount and substantiality of the portion used in relation to the copyrighted work as a whole
4. The effect of the use upon the potential market for or value of the copyrighted work

These criteria apply to social media content as well as to any other work created by someone else, whether published or unpublished. These criteria suggest that journalists in non-profit news organizations might have more latitude in their use of copyrighted material since they can more clearly claim nonprofit educational status. However, fair use allows the press to copy a small portion of the copyrighted work in order to comment on it or to criticize it. And it allows any author to use portions of copyrighted material for critique or parody.

Fair use is particularly defensible when it applies to a small portion of the overall work and it does not affect the original work's market value. Thus, Dubberly suggests reporters ask themselves: "Why are they using the content? What does the content depict? How much are they using?" In addition, since the author has a right to claim authorship, it is important to attribute the work to its creator.

Attribution – giving credit to the original author – is vital for journalists, both ethically and legally. The velocity of online content sharing means that if an article does not cite the original source, a correction will never spread to the degree the article did. Failing to give appropriate credit to the author isn't ... well, fair, and therefore not quite "fair" use either.

NEWSGATHERING ALERT: INFOWAR IN THE 21ST CENTURY

Journalists carry out their work on the front lines of a new struggle that now makes news gathering and publishing challenging, even perilous undertakings. The difficulties that information wars create for journalists cannot be overrated. News media are key targets of extensive information campaigns, crafted to manipulate both journalists and the public at large. These efforts have become highly organized, wide-ranging, and effective at polluting the information environment with misinformation, disinformation, trolling, and other trust-damaging behaviors. Some infowars reflect ongoing state-sanctioned asymmetrical conflict.

Marwick and Lewis (2017) indicate several such activities center around blogs, forums, message boards, social media, and some websites. The motivations of perpetrators vary: ideology, radicalization, status, attention, power, and money. This means journalists need to be careful about the information they gather from social media. Facebook, Twitter, Instagram, and Reddit are hotbeds of false information, part of active disinformation campaigns that target those sites' users.

Typically, perpetrators exploit the internet's participatory culture to form strong networks of similar others. They also form **cybermobs** that acquire information about targets to harass and humiliate them and to push **memes** across the internet. Some software and internet-savvy groups extend their influence by launching non-human actors, **bots** (short for robots). Bots are automated software agents that mimic humans to penetrate social networks, blogs, and other participatory internet venues.

Different categories of individuals and groups foster the distribution of deceptive messages across the internet. Many such disseminators belong to groups and send out messages fully aware of their intent to persuade, misinform, confuse, and deceive. A few people who participate are unwitting, or **unwits**. Marwick and Lewis identify groups that are often responsible for such information pollution:

1. Internet trolls: Baiting others to elicit an emotional response, often for laughs or **lulz**.

2. **Manosphere** participants: Some members of men's rights groups, gamers, computer geeks, fathers' rights groups, paleo men's domination groups, and pickup artists who are vocal anti-feminist, sometimes anti-female. They congregate in blogs, forums, and social networks, often coordinating campaigns to promote their views.

3. Hate groups and ideologues: Typically based on race, religion, gender, or national origin.

4. Conspiracy theorists.

5. Hyper-partisan news outlets.

6. Politicians.

7. Influencers.

According to an Intelligence Community Assessment, published by the Office of the Director of National Intelligence (2017), the U.S. is a significant target of digital propaganda:

> Russian efforts to influence the 2016 US presidential election represent the most recent expression of Moscow's longstanding desire to undermine the US-led liberal democratic order, but these activities demonstrated a significant escalation in directness, level of activity, and scope of effort compared to previous operations.
> [...]
> Moscow's influence campaign followed a Russian messaging strategy that blends covert intelligence operations – such as cyber activity – with overt efforts by Russian Government agencies, state-funded media, third-party intermediaries, and paid social media users or "trolls." Russia, like its Soviet predecessor, has a history of conducting covert influence campaigns focused on US presidential elections that have used intelligence officers and agents and press placements to disparage candidates perceived as hostile to the Kremlin.
>
> (p. ii)

Deliberately disseminated false news is *not* journalism. For example, conspiracy-supporter Alex Jones invited a guest on his show who claimed that the National Aeronautics and Space Administration (NASA) had kidnapped children and shipped them to Mars to become slaves in a colony on the Red Planet. Despite the absurdity of the claim, NASA immediately denied the report to protect itself against the inevitable stories that fake news sites would republish.

Fake news travels fast ... and far. *Buzzfeed* conducted a study of the 40 news stories most circulated on Facebook about the 2016 presidential election (Silverman, 2016). Half of the stories came from mainstream media news sites; the other 20 stories contained false information – fake news. Silverman's results show that in the last quarter, as the election grew close, the number of fake news reports increased dramatically, surpassing mainstream news stories.

> All the false news stories identified in BuzzFeed News' analysis came from either fake news websites that only publish hoaxes or from hyper partisan websites that present themselves as publishing real news. The research turned up only one viral false election story from a hyper partisan left-wing site.
>
> Silverman (2016)

Rogers and Bromwich (2016) also reported that several fake sites published false news stories. One example was traced to the *Denver Guardian*, which claimed that an FBI agent connected to Hillary Clinton's email investigation had murdered his wife and committed suicide. Problem: The *Denver Guardian* doesn't exist. Similarly, the *Conservative Daily Post*, a known purveyor of false news stories, accused then-President Obama and candidate Hillary Clinton of promising amnesty to undocumented immigrants who illegally voted for Democrats. The claim was false: neither politician had made such a promise.

City University of New York Professor and blogger of all things journalism Jeff Jarvis (2017) wrote:

> Our problem isn't fake news. Our problems are trust and manipulation. [...] Media – not just our legacy institutions but also the larger media ecosystem – must become more

equitable, inclusive, reflective of, and accountable to many communities. We must become more transparent. We must learn to listen first before creating the product we call content.

SOCIAL BOTS – INTENT TO DECEIVE

Social bots are a new and specific form of bots. While some bots perform useful and valuable tasks, such as the Siri and Alexa chatbots, the purpose of social bots is to interact with humans, exchanging messages, while not disclosing that they are a bot. In other words, it's full on deception from the outset.

Take the case of Ashley Madison. The site's developers created thousands of female social bots, including profiles and pictures. Some bots acted as sales shills, drawing in customers for pay-to-play. Why bots? Because although the site advertised a 1:1 gender ratio among the under 30 set; in reality only 15 percent of all users were female (Dewey, 2015). Other social bots maintained relationships through emails and chats, engaging users in billable minutes (Newitz, 2015). In order to respond to the messages, the (mostly) men had to pay to chat back. The article's concluding paragraph is chilling and prescient:

> The Ashley Madison con may have played on some of our most ancient desires, but it also gives us a window on what's to come. What you see on social media isn't always what it seems. Your friends may be bots, and you could be sharing your most intimate fantasies with hundreds of lines of PHP code.

In 2015, hackers attacked Ashley Madison and scraped its databases, including the personal information of more than 35 million users. The hackers demanded that the site shut down. When Ashley Madison remained on the internet, the attackers released more than 10 gigabits of users' personal data. In 2016, the Federal Trade Commission fined the Ruby Corp (formerly Avid Life Media) $1.66 million. By 2017, the class action lawsuit on behalf of 37 million users was settled for $11.2 million; documented user's claims might get up to $3,500 (Stempel, 2017) – perhaps several months of alimony for some users.

Meet the Social Bots

How do you know whether a Facebook friend or Twitter follower is a bot or not?

- *Username*: Is the username unusual, weird, and long? (Humans may have funny names, but they are typically understandable, and tend to be shorter than many bot identities.)
- *Profile pictures*: Bots either don't have them (they're still "eggs" on Twitter) or they have to come from somewhere. Copy it to the clipboard and drop it in the Google search box to see if it comes from Wikipedia. If it's from Flickr, Photobucket, or another site, there may be a name match – or not.
- *Profile information*: Examine a suspected bot's followers and following:
  - How many are there? If the account follows hundreds more people than follow the account, it could be a bot.
  - If most or many followers lack photos, remember that bots communicate with bots more often than they do with people, and more frequently than most people do.
- *Communication behaviors*:
  - How long have they been on the SNS? (Bot accounts are often relatively new.)

* How often do they tweet? How often do they retweet? (Bots retweet more than most people do.)
* Look for strange or unnatural syntax, sentences, and spacing.
* Look for too many slang expressions and emojis.
* Consider if responses are too fast – people need to think and plan their replies, not just plugin strings from a data table.
* Look for an exceptionally large number of posts, shares, or tweets.
* Look for tweets and retweets posted at odd hours or at too many hours for most humans.
* *Test with sarcasm, irony, or unexpected questions*: Bots won't be able to answer whether they've ever visited Belgium or Kazakhstan, or respond to "broke my arm, hey, no problemo."

HOW MANY OF THE COMMENTERS ON NEWS SITES COME FROM BOTS? <SHRUG>

Social bots concern most news media organizations. Bots deployed by mischief-makers have already demonstrated the harmful effects they can have. They have been used to:

* Generate hate speech
* Cyberbully and harass individuals
* Spread misinformation
* Attack and smear others
* Generate mass hysteria and panic during emergencies
* Spread propaganda and aid recruitment by criminals and terrorists
* Manipulate stock market prices
* Conduct astroturf campaigns to make it seem like an idea or candidate has far more support than exists
* Manipulate public opinion

Attacked as they are from many sides and social actors, the news media are particularly vulnerable to loss of credibility when bots are programed to sway public perceptions for private gains. The number of bots in **bot armies** and **botswarms** can be in the millions. And when programmed to **follow** other bots, the number of messages they can send grows rapidly.

Journalists find that the loss of trust in the news media is very real indeed, and it constitutes an important hindrance to newsgathering. For example, *Politico* reporter Kyle Cheney sent out a tweet thread describing what happened when he went to the scene of the shooting of Republican lawmakers practicing for a charity baseball game in Alexandria, VA. Not long before, a gunman had shot and wounded Rep. Steve Scalise (R-LA) and four others. Cheney tweeted this from the park:

> I arrived less than an hour after the shooting + overheard a witness – maybe mid-20s – describing the incident in vivid detail by phone.
>
> – Kyle Cheney (@kyledcheney) June 14, 2017

He immediately tensed up, and told me that because I was the media – and he hates all media – he wouldn't tell me a thing.

– Kyle Cheney (@kyledcheney) June 14, 2017

Columnist Callum Borchers (2017) wrote about the incident:

the shooting witness didn't believe or didn't care that information reported by the media could be helpful to the public. Perhaps he was motivated by pure callousness; it seems more likely, however, that he was coming from a place of genuine distrust of the press. […] most people remain willing to speak up in a moment of crisis, even at a time when trust in the media is at an all-time low. But Cheney's experience suggests that some people's regard for the press is so degraded they won't even share information that could help others. That is a rather sad development.

LEVELS OF "NEWS" AND INFORMATION

Evaluating the trustworthiness of information and evidence is a difficult and complex process. Chapter 7 will cover verification as a journalistic competency. For the moment, just compare the levels of reliability that journalists encounter as they work a beat or story:

- Buzz and rumor: No evidence, just "it is said, it is reported, people are saying …"
- Claims:
  - *False claims*: Not true, never happened, made up.
  - *Misleading claims*: Designed to create a false impression.
  - *Biased claims*: Manipulated information that presents the topic in a favorable light, discounting, or ignoring information that would lead to unfavorable opinions.
  - *Inadequate claims*: Claims that may be true or have an element of truth, but with non-existent or weak evidence. There may only be one source, unverified documents, or no indication of fact-checking or verification procedures.
  - *Associative claims*: Seemingly-significant quasi-evidence based on some association: "there at the same place" (party, meeting, convention, city, hotel), "at the same time," "in business with the same company as so-and-so," "knew X who worked with Y," etc.
- Confirmed reports and stories: Evidence provided – at least three sources (best if at least one source speaks on the record), verified documents and/or artifacts, clear indication of careful fact-checking procedures. For data and research articles, solid evidence may include peer-reviewed publications, although these findings are sometimes in dispute between experts who adhere to different schools of thought or reach alternative conclusions about the weight of the evidence.

An important but oft-forgotten lesson from the scientific method: It is not possible to establish never-changing, 100 percent reliable ground "truths." In the end, humans can only approximate the "real" reality. Science tells us to look for associations (often with big data), coupled with causal mechanisms that are plausibly related by their time-order – to establish useful knowledge claims. Science also tells us that to evaluate truth, we should look for evidence that would falsify a knowledge claim. Essentially, this attitude calls for truth-seekers to seek and carefully weigh evidence that would falsify those relationships and factual claims that appear to be true. We might call such attitudes open-mindedness and objectivity.

TAKEAWAYS

- The internet serves as a vast repository for information on nearly every imaginable topic. Finding online sources of information for reports and narratives is relatively easy for most people, although specialized information may require highly developed skills and considerable digging. Search engines, social media, public records and information, and public and private databases provide valuable online sources for journalists.

- Efficient and effective online searches require knowing where to look and how to phrase searches to get useful returns. At a minimum, reporters should carefully review all tutorials from search engine sites. Journalists should be familiar with several books and many articles that provide online sources, methods, and tips. Maintaining a list of sites and search parameters will prove valuable. Persistence works. Sometimes useful results may not emerge without reading many pages of search returns. (For example, one reporter found a source's telephone number on Page 18 of the search results – which showed an application to park a private plane at a local airport. "How the heck did you find me?" the source asked in amazement.)

- Social media platforms enlarge the kinds of information reporters can find. Facebook can disclose a social network of family, friends, and even colleagues. Examining "likes and shares," may reveal attitudes and lifestyle choices. Joined groups may tell reporters about a person's interests or collaborative behavior. Pinterest may reveal important preferences about taste and manners, hobbies, and concerns. Similarly, photo and video sites like Snapchat and Periscope often show a person's location and activities at specific times.

- Skill using public records and information sources opens huge worlds of story possibilities for journalists. Back in the day, reporters had to send individual letters to multiple states and local jurisdictions and wait for the s-l-o-o-o-o-o-w return snail mail responses. It's way quicker now, but ... While it takes some time to click through to the needed information, it takes far more time, effort, and often substantial expertise to weed through and filter all the retrieved information and data. Analyzing the assembled facts isn't any easier than it used to be, either. Books, articles, workshops, and experience all help budding journalists gain the required expertise.

- The internet puts information from public information and records at reporters' fingertips, replacing time-consuming visits to downtown centers, county seats, state capitols, and federal buildings. Working journalists must have a solid grasp of the kinds of data and information available, coupled with the search expertise to find it. Again, books and articles, courses, and workshops all provide paths to the acquisition of these precious skills.

- Data seekers can find both public and private databases. Sometimes, all that is needed is a request for all or even part of the data that some organization has already collected. Trade associations often provide excellent sources, and the press office may also know if private companies have data they might be willing to share. Governmental agencies at each level – federal, regional, state, and local – all need data to manage and oversee their activities. For the most part, these databases are available to journalists, either by simple request, or a Freedom of Information Act (FOIA, pronounced FOY-AH) request.

- Gathering information from data often requires high-level analytical competencies. Understanding research conclusions can require a painstaking assessment of the underlying methodology, assumptions, research questions, sample, measurements, and types of analysis in support of any conclusions. Working with raw data can be even more difficult, because data require an appropriate and fair-minded analysis – and because, in and of themselves, data typically cannot provide actionable information.

- The U.S. Constitution balances the protection of intellectual property for authors with the need for citizens in our democracy to have information to inform the decisions they must make. Thus, while authors own their own works, *fair use* allows other authors to include small portions of original works for the purposes of commentary, critique, and parody. *Public domain* exempts certain works, based on how old they are, and who created them. Generally, the public can access and reproduce government documents, studies, hearings, and other works that fall within the public domain. Journalists must always cite the sources of the content they use, both as direct quotes and as summaries.

- Increasingly during the past decade, information on the internet has become weaponized in wars for the hearts, minds, and wallets of the world. Actors of many different stripes – from governments to organizations to interest groups to individuals seeking advantage or attention – actively disseminate content that supports their goals. Because so many people now receive their news from online sources, the prevalence of inaccurate and false information confuses the public and lowers their levels of trust in *all* authoritative sources. These conditions make trustworthy and trusted online newsgathering difficult. Reporters must take great care to validate the veracity of information and they should make verification a priority.

KEY CONCEPTS AND TERMS

– Online searches for information

– Online sources of information

– Social media as sources for news

– Public records and public information for newsgathering

– Validity and reliability of data

– Copyright law and fair use

– Journalists and the information, misinformation, disinformation in the online environment

EXERCISES AND ACTIVITIES

1. Imagine you have been assigned to report a story with a local angle on a national story. Write a working thesis with three to five questions to which you hope to find answers using a Google search. Determine several search terms for each question and document the results of each search you conduct using various terms or combinations of terms. Which searches were more successful? Which were less successful and why? What did you learn from this experience that could improve future searches?

150 REPORTING

2. Using a story for which you already have a working hypothesis and one or more potential angles, use Google searches to find three or more potential sources who you could interview for your story. Write down contact information and your interview questions for each source. Repeat the process with the same thesis and potential angle for searches on Facebook, LinkedIn, and Twitter.

3. Conduct a LexisNexis blog search on a major news story from the last year. List ten different sources, five from newspapers, five from online-only sites. How do the newspaper stories differ from the online stories?

4. Check out a local car dealership, bank, or grocery store. Has this company been named in any lawsuits in the last three years? Who owns the business? Who owns the property where the business is located? Answer these questions from information you find online, then cut and paste it in a file to turn in.

ADVANCER

Chapter 6 describes traditional newsgathering methods that retain their importance for digital journalists. Nothing speaks louder than the experience of journalists whose work spans the pre-digital and digital eras. It describes in-person interviews, observational methods, spending time in locations, and talking to the people there. Finally, the chapter will examine the processes of fact-checking, checking work for fairness, and monitoring sources of possible biases you might have introduced into your reporting, thinking, and writing.

6

NEWS GATHERING AND REPORTING: TIME-HONORED TECHNIQUES & TOOLS

Chapter Learning Objectives

After studying this chapter, students will be able to:

1. Consider digital and traditional tools of journalism.
2. Know the observational practices of journalism.
3. Prepare for and conduct interviews.
4. Identify and enlist sources.
5. Understand the rules of engagement between reporters and their sources.
6. Manage sources and attribute information to them.
7. Understand how and why journalists adopt security measures.

Digital reporting – the Internet and data analysis – is just one tool in the toolkit. It does not take away the need to vet and verify and talk to people face-to-face. A reporter can use digital tools, but without verifying what they show, they can lead to wrong assumptions and answers. There is no substitute for ensuring accuracy. You must test your analysis and challenge your own assumptions over and over, refining what you think you know and what you actually know. You typically start with a working hypothesis, but often the final story is rarely what you think it was in the beginning. And things that you first thought were very important may be meaningless in the final analysis.

The internet helps you, but it is not a panacea. It is not a band-aid for deeper reporting. For example, using email to interview people is a poor substitute for face-to-face conversation. Email quotes can sound like they were written by a committee. Get face time with people if you can. With email interviews, you can't describe the setting, or hear how the person pauses when speaking. Usually, people don't write like they speak.

– David Fallis, Deputy Investigations Editor, *Washington Post*

THE GIST

Nothing speaks louder than the experience of journalists whose work spans the pre-digital and digital eras. This chapter started with a quote from Mary Murphy's interview with David Fallis of the *Washington Post*. He makes it clear that today's journalist must combine the full array of both digital tools (covered in Chapter 5) and traditional methods: 1) observation, 2) interviewing, and 3) finding and managing sources. These time-honored competencies are all foundational, enabling reporters to find and publish great stories whether through digital or traditional means.

In addition to providing new sources of information and ways to analyze and present it, digital technologies and high-speed online connections can expand reporters' traditional tools. For example, drone cameras, computers, and real-time networks enable remote real-time observation of previously inaccessible sites. Afterward, digital tools also provide effective ways to preserve and publish recordings of the events they capture. Similarly, once limited to in-person and telephone conversations, reporters now conduct interviews with Skype, email, Twitter, and text messages. Getting answers to questions in in-person interviews is preferable to low quality streaming video sessions or non-interactive messages – but these less attractive digital options may turn out to be better than having no answers at all.

Just as observation and interviewing may now take place online, the internet offers bountiful opportunities to identify, contact, and vet potential sources. Reporters can amass valuable information before approaching or interviewing a source. But at some point a reporter may want to meet in person (or on the telephone) if the information provided by the source offers a linchpin for an important story.

Although it is possible to describe situations where a journalist would accept an internet-only relationship, it does not happen often. In face-to-face interactions, people give off clues about their thoughts, feelings, intentions, and values through vocal cues and facial micro-expressions. These small signals give people a "spidey-sense" or a "vibe" about others that they can't put their finger on – signals that might be lost in relationships mediated by technology.

Communication technologies offer new ways for journalists to stay in contact with sources, but they also require new cautions. Maintaining secure contact and preserving anonymity are far more difficult, given modern sophisticated monitoring and surveillance technology. Thus, practicing journalism online demands the adoption of effective security procedures to protect: 1) information, 2) communications with sources and others, 3) personal safety, and 4) exposure to liability.

OBSERVATION: WAY MORE THAN JUST *SEEING*

Given the profound belief that humans have in the phenomena they see, it follows that **observation**, an act of regarding attentively, is central to journalism. Thucydides, recognized as the world's first historian, is also the world's first journalist (Windschuttle, 1999, pp. 52–54). He wrote first-hand reports about the Peloponnesian War in the 5th century BC, which described observation as central to his work:

> And with regard to my factual reporting of events of the war, I have made it a principle
> not to write down the first story that came my way, and not even to be guided by my own

general impressions: either I was present myself at the events which I have described or else I have heard of them from eye-witnesses whose reports I have checked with as much thoroughness as possible. Not that even so the truth was easy to discover: different eyewitnesses give different accounts of the same events, speaking out of partiality for one side or the other or else from imperfect memories.

(Thucydides, translation, 1972, p. 48)

Thucydides' early account brings up a puzzling aspect of eyewitness reports: People may see the same event at the same time yet perceive it quite differently. The Oxford dictionary defines observation is "the action or process of observing something or someone to gain information." Notice that observing is an active process while merely seeing is *not* observing.

Another aspect of observation that is not often discussed is the role of the journalist as a witness to history, to the human condition, and to memorialize people's lived experience in a particular time and place. In the digital era, live satellite feeds and streaming let everyone witness events, but someone has to initiate the feed or stream. When that person is a reporter, it provides credibility to the truth value of the content. And in war, civil strife, and natural disasters, communication networks often go down.

VIRTUALLY THERE: REMOTE AND INDIRECT OBSERVATION

In the past, observation took place concurrently with the event – at the same time and geographic place. But present remote, time-shifting, event-recording, digital observational technologies change that historic limitation. And humans' cultural assumptions about the meaning of time and place have been upended. Time and place are now more fluid constructs. For example, where does the virtual world, *Second Life*, exist? If so, when? When it's live, when there's video of it, when the metadata says it is?

Similarly, virtual "places" (literally) exist in digital storage drives, on servers, or inside fiber optic cables. Are these places and if so for what: the 0s and 1s in the file, the images represented by the digits, or by avatars roaming on 2D screens (or 3D for that matter)? Do these locations really complement the ways people experience virtual places (perhaps) less real than the Real World, yet far more real than just strings of digital data on a machine or network? Perhaps our human perceptions of reality have yet to catch up with digital reality!

OBSERVING WHEN YOU'RE NOT THERE: REMOTE AND INDIRECT OBSERVATION

Observation continues to underpin journalistic practice in both digital and physical realms. As covered in the previous chapter, communications technologies provide many new opportunities for **remote observation**, including video and audio streamed live, video from drones, real-time satellite images, networked surveillance cameras monitor, and user mobile phones. Thus, even when they are not physically present, reporters can "observe" phenomena of all kinds from around the world – earthquakes, weather conditions, flight tracks, traffic, medical devices, bliss on distant beaches, and violent wars.

Technologies and fast digital networks also allow journalists access to **indirect observations** through technical devices. For example, thermometers measure body temperature; measuring a fever provides an indirect measurement of some infections. Similarly, aircraft flight tracks, heart and other medical monitors, barometers, speedometers, galvanometers, or altimeters reveal states or actions that could otherwise remain hidden.

Recordings of remote and indirect observation benefit journalists as well. They can pause to study unfolding events. They can replay recordings multiple times, while focusing on and selecting key elements. These review capabilities enable reporters to increase accuracy and to capture important relationships that would otherwise be missed in the first single pass of recorded material.

Generally, whether observing in person or remotely, reporters record or make careful notes of their observations. This is sound journalistic practice, even if just one or two memorable details about a setting can crystalize the scene in the user's mind ... but which details matter? Journalists record as much as they can when observing because the most relevant aspects of story settings may emerge only while writing, or even later in a follow-up story. Description plays a key role in motivating readers to read the entire article through longer news features, explanatory and scenic narrative stories, so thorough notes or recordings are essential.

2 REASONS NOT TO BELIEVE YOUR LYING EYES

Before examining how to observe carefully and systematically, consider some of the barriers to accurate observation. In the digital world, **deep fakes**, the intentional alteration of audio and video content, lurk on the horizon. Hackers can change the metadata accompanying this material easily, so metadata may not provide adequate defense against false evidence. (A later chapter addresses the challenges newsrooms face in dealing with deep fakes.)

Inattentional blindness causes observers to miss events that happen right in front of their eyes. This blindness occurs when people fail to see phenomena that are fully visible but unexpected because their attention is focused on other tasks, events, or objects (Mack & Rock, 1999). The human brain cannot process all the sensory information it receives. Based on past experience, cognitive filters eliminate "unneeded" information and free us to focus attention on needed information.

Confirmation bias is another powerful impediment to observation. People see the things they expect to see – even if those things are not actually present. Confirmation bias occurs because everyone has beliefs about reality and the world they live in. When observing events through a subjective lens, people tend to look for evidence that confirms these beliefs and then later recall the events that support their subjective perspective.

Cognitive brain scientists stress the intentional quality of observation. For example, Schulte-Ruther, Markowitsch, Fink, and Piefke (2007) consistently found that observation requires rigorous and purposeful mental activity. Observers focus on relevant features and disregard seemingly less salient or important elements. And observers typically integrate what they *see* with what they already *know* or believe to be true. Elizabeth Loftus' acclaimed research program vividly demonstrates how widespread misperceptions and memories of crime and accident witnesses should caution both journalists and juries against uncritical acceptance of uncorroborated witness reports (Costandi, 2013).

The barriers of focus and cognitive integration account for part of the notorious disagreement among observers of the same events. Eyewitnesses to traumatic events often provide inconsistent descriptions of people and actions because bewilderment and shock get in the way of the ability to focus clearly. Another example is the strong disagreement among white and black observers of the same video record of violent interactions between white police officers and African-American citizens: Many whites see police valiantly trying to keep order and protect people and property; many blacks see unnecessary and indiscriminate violence against people of color exercising their first amendment rights of assembly and free speech.

Another common problem with attending to observations is the opposite of inattentional blindness: Seeing something because the observer expected to see it – but it was not actually present. For these reasons, if deadlines permit, after-observational reflection pays dividends to journalists. A reporter characterized Pulitzer Prize-winner Katherine Boos careful reflection this way:

> After a day of reporting, she also immediately writes an email to her husband capturing the emotion of that time, even if it means staying up until 5 a.m. She knows that something will be lost if she sleeps on it.
>
> (Savchuk, 2017)

Science can help journalists sharpen their observational powers. Interestingly, long-time newspaper reporter Robert Park (American Sociological Association, n.d.) was instrumental in the development of systematic observation, especially concerning people and social behavior. Park left journalism to obtain a doctorate in sociology and became a key figure in the influential Chicago School of Sociology. He formulated the basic principles of rigorous observation that led to urban sociologists' careful, documented observation of early 20th-century city life. Through Park, journalism influenced and shaped observation for generations of social scientists.

Over time, sociologists refined these techniques and wrote about them. Testing and publishing observational best practices allowed others to adopt them, a boon to journalists as well as social scientists. Even now Park's advice to budding sociologists well-serves today's journalists who may cover people whose life experiences differ greatly from their own:

> go get the seat of your pants dirty with data ... Go and sit in the lounges of the luxury hotels and on the doorsteps of the flophouses; sit on the Gold Coast settees and on the slum shakedowns; sit in Orchestra Hall and in the "Star and Garter Burlesk."
>
> (McKinney, 1966, p. 71)

The scientific focus on systematic methods of observation gives journalists valuable ways to evaluate observational conditions. Thinking carefully about the conditions and contexts of observation allows reporters to make quick assessments of the advantages and pitfalls of specific situations (Zechmeister, Shaughnessy, & Zechmeister, 2009). Systematic methods include careful attention to the characteristics of the setting, detachment, open-mindedness, and care in drawing conclusions.

HOW TO KEEP YOUR COOL IN A HOT MESS

Astute, systematic observation offers a powerful tool. For many journalists, observing what others prefer to hide entails professional responsibilities and personal risks. People often have something to hide, whether embarrassing personal habits or important institutional missteps. But observing what powerful interests seek to hide entails personal risks. In authoritarian countries and wherever widespread corruption exists, observation can be dangerous. According to Reporters Without Borders (2016), 74 journalists were killed in 2016; 53 of them were murdered or deliberately targeted while 21 died while reporting.

At first glance, observation seems – well, obvious: Just look and listen. However, systematic consideration of the conditions under which an observation takes place helps the reporter to focus on details of the context that makes the meaning of behaviors clearer. For example, seeing groups of buff young men standing around in a large room, has different meanings if it takes place in a prison yard, a military induction center, or a cattle-call for extras for a pirate movie.

What observers see depends on who they are, what they are looking for, where they are standing, and how much social control there is governing actors' behavior (Zechmeister et al., 2009).

1. *Role of the Observer*: **Participant/Nonparticipant**: Participant observation means that the observer is part of the ongoing activity. Nonparticipant observation is carried out by an observer who is not involved with the ongoing activities, other than as an observer. The journalist as participant has a long history, and this form of reportage has gained greater popularity than ever on the Web. But here's a caution: It is easy to get "captured" by participant roles and biases.

2. *Perspective of the Observer*: **Subjective/Objective**: Subjective observation emphasizes the impacts that the activity (and its consequences) have on the observer and other participants. Objective observations stress the activities, persons, or the processes themselves as external to the observer. In digital environments, articles written from a subjective perspective appear frequently: "How I learned to love lipstick from Kim Kardashian," for example. Perspective trade-offs typically center on whether "facts" or "feelings" matter most for an assignment – or perhaps one journalist is a data wonk while another journalist cares more about the emotional impacts upon story subjects and the emotional responses of users.

Objective Observation: "City Council Chair Robert Jefferson banged the gavel, saying, 'I will clear this room if the audience does not remain silent throughout the proceedings!'"

Subjective Observation: "City Council Chair Robert Jefferson banged the gavel angrily, shouting to intimidate the unruly audience members, 'I will clear this room if the audience does not remain silent throughout the proceedings!'"

---

3. *Location of the Observer*: *Direct/Indirect/Remote*: Direct observations are those seen in real time – the reporter is physically present as the event occurs. **Indirect observation** involves observing something that changes with another phenomenon that cannot itself be seen – such as wind on a body of water or instrument monitoring, including flight tracks, heart rate measures, seismometers, spectrographs, as shown in Figure 6.1. **Remote observations** are seen through the "eyes and ears" of a technology – a drone, a camera, a microphone, or live online video. All these types of technology-assisted observation are important advances in giving reporters access to news events; each has its own advantages and limitations.

FIGURE 6.1

Strong south-westerly winds ripple the water
Credit: Jim Champion, CC BY-SA 2.0, via: https://commons.wikimedia.org/w/index.php?curid=12318903

4. *The Behavior of the Observed:* **Controlled/Noncontrolled**: For almost everyone, outside forces control the activities and behaviors that journalists observe. Such outside forces include control by police and emergency personnel, guards, school and detention facilities, authorities, supervisors, parents, and many others. Another example is the scientific observation that often controls the behaviors of subjects. Experimental researchers may ask subjects to carry out specific actions under the direction of the researchers or their agents. In all these situations, experienced reporters stay aware that they are seeing people under unusual circumstances, understanding that authority figures may greatly change the nature of the observations they make.

    Uncontrolled behavior occurs when people can choose how to act. People change their behaviors themselves to adjust to the demands of a given environment, adapting and taking familiar roles. A characteristic of the continuum of controlled-to-uncontrolled behavior is that there are few occasions to observe completely controlled or utterly uncontrolled behavior. Indeed, most such instances take place in private, behind closed doors, where they cannot be observed by nonparticipants. Perhaps the most common relatively uncontrolled behavior occurs when people have consumed too much alcohol or other mind-altering substance.

5. *Type of Setting:* **Natural/Contrived**: Natural settings allow observations of people in their own environments, where they can presumably be themselves. However, the assumption of natural behavior rests on an anonymous presence of observers: Science demonstrates that just the simple act of observation itself changes peoples' behavior.

158   REPORTING

Sometimes contrived settings can be useful as well. Contrived settings include special-purpose offices, police interrogation rooms, laboratories, interview rooms, film sets, and other such venues. People are often unfamiliar with contrived settings. They may not know how to act, having to figure it out or bring behaviors from other settings into the situation. With either choice, the person reveals much about him or herself.

6. *Observational Conditions: Structured/Nonstructured*: Structured observation requires advance planning. It specifies some or all aspects of observation, such as time, place, periodicity, activity, format, etc. Nonstructured observation represents the opposite side of this coin – the observer steps into the situation with little or no prior planning. As observers, journalists sometimes prefer highly structured situations for many reasons, such as control over distractions, compatibility with an angle or a theme, or concerns for physical safety.

Today, widespread monitoring and surveillance make it more difficult to conduct nonstructured observation in many places. Responses in the U.S. to 9/11, the long-standing state of war, and mass murder or killing sprees have given rise to increasing security in many places – schools, shopping malls, youth centers, churches, parks, and other locations where people congregate. These security constraints can make nonstructured observation difficult for reporters, because of increased restrictions on mere presence, photography, or recordings of any kind. There are fewer places journalists can assume freedom of movement and action, so they must carry press cards and business cards, sometimes even badges, whenever and wherever they work.

DRILL DOWN: REMOTE OBSERVATION

Think drones. Think: This is where observation meets the digital age. The last chapter discussed the promise of video footage from drones to allow everyone to see otherwise inaccessible locations. Other advantages of remote observation include the capability to monitor two or more simultaneous events, reduced travel time, and less need to negotiate access. Remote observation also distances the observer from the event, lessening distraction from unimportant sideshows. And the material can be saved, allowing later review.

Journalists at a distance can be less obtrusive. They draw less attention to themselves and are less likely to become part of the story. Depending on the event and its circumstances, the nature of surveillance matters – it may even change the story. Police involved in violent episodes may view individuals streaming these events on Periscope from mobile phones as threatening; attendees of a political cabal leaving a secret meeting will object to reporters streaming video over the internet. In contrast, people at the local PTA meeting probably won't think much about prominent surveillance – although someone might object. But the presence of an overhead camera may well go unnoticed.

Remote observation presents consequential drawbacks for some stories. Remote observation can miss vital texture and insights: A Good Samaritan stops and helps someone injured in a near-riot; a robber hands the cashier a thank-you note before running out of liquor store; or the teen who replaces a purloined lipstick with a used one. Reporters can't count on second-hand reporting to capture crucial anomalies and aberrations in unfolding scenes. In-person direct observation highlights details that make users feel like they were there and experienced the event themselves. Live witnesses bring vitality to reports and stories. Direct observation readily captures the resignation, or hope, or determination of hurricane survivors who have lost all but their lives – in ways that may go unnoticed via remote observation.

FIGURE 6.2

Hi, I'm a dog
Credit: Leung Cho Pan, via www.123rf.com

Remote observation may also make it difficult or impossible to establish the full contexts of the situation. Without being on the scene, journalists may not fully experience the subjective, participant, and perhaps sympathetic contexts for events. It is one thing to watch police attack peaceful demonstrators on a screen. It's a vastly different experience to *be* part of the crowd, *see* blood-covered streets, *stare* down shotgun barrels, *feel* the rising panic of people caught in the crowd crush, and *run* from police wielding batons.

Here are some other concerns journalists might have about remote observations:

- The technology may not show as much as an observer would think. Remote recorders (video, audio, or both) capture signals and scenes; larger or smaller scene angles; or worse audio pickup, etc.
- Remote sensors cannot focus attention the way that people do in real situations; they don't filter and prioritize sensory signals like human brains do.
- It may not be possible to verify the provenance, length, or completeness of recorded material.
- Remotely linked reporters often lack access to important, perhaps crucial events that may have occurred before or after the recording.
- Interpreting behavior remotely entails great difficulties. Indirect and online observation can easily obscure subtle, but vital, cues – gestures, voice tones, smells, muttered words, and other nonverbal interpersonal interaction cues.
- Finally, reporters often can't establish the identities of online participants. People make up usernames; sometimes they use others' photos, symbols, or even their pet cat's image. Thus, confirming accurate information about persons' names, age, gender, marital status, nationality, occupation, or other relevant attributes may be difficult. Wittel (2000) writes: "this uncertainty is particularly problematic in a space that has become famous for its playful possibilities." As cartoonist Peter Steiner famously wrote: "On the Internet, nobody knows you're a dog."

PRACTICAL STUFF: PLANNING OBSERVATION

Nobody in news observes better than photojournalists. Their concentration must be total; their decision processes must be quick enough to let them snap fast. A moment's lapse means losing a brief opportunity for a fantastic shot ... and yet, photojournalists must be flexible, able to respond to what they see through their lens *and* what's taking place in front of their free eye. It's a tricky balancing act.

To start, good photojournalists prepare. They spend time considering how they will observe and record their observation – in advance. They carefully select their kit, often using checklists. In the field, their eyes seldom stop while they assess location features (lighting, distances, angles, colors, etc.) and the types of shots these features will afford. Video shoots typically require multiple vantage points, particularly when an assignment requires edited narrative packages.

Even when there's no need to shoot video or take photos, taking a brief time to consider the right observational "stance" can pay big dividends. A short pause, scanning the overall environment and noting positions of other reporters, will reveal the best spots from which to observe.

Like other newsgathering decisions, the choices reporters make about observations depend on the assignment. A short report needs only the briefest of descriptions. News features and narratives demand more observation-dependent depictions. Enhancing multimedia stories with video and audio might add more and better opportunities for user engagement in the story. These considerations will help structure journalists' planned observational strategies:

- What is the purpose?
- Who is/are the subject(s)?
- What is the central activity?
- What is the focus? What angles or themes seem promising?
- What are the best ways to observe (direct/indirect, natural, structured, controlled)?
- How will I record my observations?

Making the observations as a scene unfolds – choosing what to observe – is a matter of forethought, instinct and luck. It may be difficult to take notes while observing. If possible, at least jot down fragments to spur later memory. After observing, use these fragments to write down everything possible about the observations: Who did what, how they went about it, the setting, the atmosphere, the events, and the consequences. In short, reporters should write up as many details as possible, as soon as possible. Done thoroughly, this is the work that can turn luck into professional opportunity.

~~INTERVIEWING IS EASY~~ ... IT'S NOT

Strong interviews can change the world, an industry or institution, the interviewee, and many of those who experience it. Christopher Hitchens' (2006) eulogy to Oriana Fallaci pointed to her interview with Pakistan leader Zulfikar Ali Bhutto. Fallaci asked him what he thought of Indian Prime Minister Indira Gandhi, and Bhutto replied, "a diligent drudge of a schoolgirl, a woman devoid of initiative and imagination." Insulted, Gandhi demanded a transcript of the interview, and then refused to sign a peace agreement with Pakistan!

The digital world offers many new ways to conduct interviews: Skype, chat, and email, just to name a few. Other than practicing with the technology platform to ensure a smooth process, preparing for an interview may not change a great deal from getting ready for an in-person interview. Good interviews still require planning and research, a balance of purpose with open-minded flexibility, good questions, and careful post-interview analysis.

TRADITIONAL TOOLS & TECHNIQUES

Successful interviewing depends on observational skills, analytical capability, and emotional intelligence. When the reporter adds a dollop of intuition to the mix at the right time, it can turn a ho-hum interview into a headline-worthy adventure. All these competencies help make connections between a person's verbal expressions, nonverbal communication, and their past and present actions. Taken together, these connections bring even seemingly "flat" interviews to life. While it's great to make the links later, perhaps when writing up the interview, eliciting connections in real time lets the interviewer: 1) formulate follow-up questions, 2) know when to depart from the interview plan and explore emerging areas in more detail, and 3) frame questions to illuminate the underlying meaning of an interviewee's previous answer.

Journalists rarely need to ask the interviewed person: Why is he or she giving the interview? The reasons are usually obvious, given the context – although some interviewees have complex or hidden motives. Understanding the subject's motivation is important because it establishes the expected boundaries and limits of the interview. So, why do people give interviews, even when it's risky?

- *A work thing* – The PR person in the organization wants the subject to represent the company. PR will prepare the interviewee and provide explicit direction to try to realize specific objectives.

- *A reputational thing* – Many professionals feel the need to burnish their personal brands.

- *An ego thing* – People grant interviews to further their self-interests, whether it is self-promotion, self-aggrandizement, or simply their desire for attention.

- *A legal thing* – Their lawyer told them to do it – oh, and told them what to say and how to say it, too.

- *A random thing* – The person saw a bank robbery or a police shooting or some other happening of interest and is willing to share the experience as they themselves process their proximity to, and experience with, a news event.

THE "GET"

A "get" means the acceptance of a request for an interview from a newsworthy person who does not often grant interviews. It used to be easy to get interviews; now it's not. In the last two decades, it has become a complex matter to secure an interview and establish the ground rules for interviews with high-profile individuals. Today, publicity and public relations people ("flacks") are wary of exposing a client to an interview that could have less than excellent results for the company, agency, official, or celebrity. That caution imposes many barriers to a successful "get" by reporters.

Larger circulation publications usually have the edge in getting important interviews. This reality puts online journalists at a disadvantage. Unless a reporter works for ESPN, *The Washington Post*, or *The New York Times*, the journalist must figure out a way to create an edge. If they can't argue audience size and reach, they might argue the quality of an audience. Examples include: Reach the difficult-to-reach young demographic or an influential demographic; generate an online buzz bonanza; make a case with a longer-than-usual, nuanced article. Or perhaps the reporter or publication has some specialty that fits with an image the interviewee might wish to project.

Vox Verbatim: Buzz Bissinger, Journalist

FIGURE 6.3

Buzz Bissinger makes a point

Credit: Martin Håndlykken/ Nordiske Mediedager [CC BY-SA 2.0 (https://creativecommons.org/licenses/by-sa/2.0)] (Image cropped, resized, converted to greyscale)

Buzz got one of the biggest gets ever: The bombshell story of Bruce Jenner coming out as Caitlin Jenner, published by *Vanity Fair*. It exploded into virality upon landing. On TV, the story made all three network morning talk shows. On cable, it led the rundown every hour on the hour. On Twitter, it trended for days. But more than that, it was a surprising, solid, fair, and accurate story. Here's what Mr. Bissinger said went into the article:

> You go out and work. So many stories today are about the writer's impression as opposed to the subject and they are often based on a one-hour lunch, half of which the subject is spending on his/her iPhone. They are very superficial, filled with all sorts of judgments that may be right or may be wrong.
>
> Graydon Carter described me as old school and I am proud of that: Old school is the best school, because then you are getting real journalism.
>
> Is everything in the story right? As far as I know. But I can tell you that to make sure that what those kids were saying was true took dozens of conversations, dozens of interviews, dozens of follow-up calls with them, with ex-wives, getting as many sources as I could find to corroborate it – as opposed to taking cheap shots. [It took] getting those kids to be comfortable because they did not have a lot of exposure with the media. Caitlyn Jenner had that kind of experience, but the kids did not. It is not just going to be just one interview, so I spoke to the daughter in person, in text, and phone calls, and email close to 25 times. That is what you have to do to be fair.

PREPARING FOR INTERVIEWS

There are interviews and then there are *interviews*, as shown in Table 6.1. All demand careful preparation. Such work requires reviewing background research, identifying, contacting, and enlisting the person(s) to be interviewed, formulating question lists, and (thoughtfully) ordering questions.

Some interviews resemble speed-dating: short, to-the-point, matter-of-fact, and requiring little preparation. The reporter identifies herself and publication, asks one or two questions, gets the answers, perhaps requests relevant documents or reports, and (with thanks) says goodbye. This type of interview frequently occurs in the news biz: A beat reporter who knows all the important actors and contacts them regularly may already know the necessary background information. Or a reporter from a recognized publication might need a quick quote from a public figure for a breaking news story. Or an editor wants one more quote to provide balance in a report – perhaps a key player's reaction to new story developments.

Other assignments demand more extensive interviewer–interviewee relationships. For example, **ticktock** pieces often require multiple interviews to establish the story chronology and the details of actions and their consequences. Investigative, explanatory, scenic narratives, long news features, special issue lead articles, and celebrity stories often depend heavily on productive interview exchanges. In these cases, formulating substantive

TRADITIONAL TOOLS & TECHNIQUES

163

TABLE 6.1   INTERVIEW PREPARATIONS

Preparations	*"Quick Quote" Interviews*	*Longer-Form Article Interviews*
Background	– Background on news topic	– Background on article topic
	– Other background, as needed	– Background on salient people, places, things, events, actions, motives, feelings, etc.
Negotiation	– Be prepared to set up the interview with a Public Information Officer or public relations person	– Expect to enter detailed negotiations with a Public Information Officer or public relations person
	– Discuss how the information will be sourced	– Discussion can include identity of interviewer, time, length, place, preview of questions or question areas, type of recording equipment, and many other possible issues, such as sensitive areas
Question list	– Ask a few questions from notes	– Prepare question list
		– Sequence questions for "flow"
Venue	– In a media **scrum**, press conference, or by phone	– Best: In person
		– Second best (if fast, stable Net connection): Live video
		– Third best: Mobile phone
		– Fourth best: Skype audio call
		– Last: email
Protocol	– Be professional and be on time	– Be professional and be on time

questions may entail significant background investigation before key interviews can take place. Long articles covering complex issues may demand long interview sessions and even multiple follow-up interviews as the article evolves.

TO TECH OR NOT TO TECH?

That is always a key question. Start with this: When a story is important, nothing beats a face-to-face interview – it remains the gold standard for most reporters and publications. That standard may change when a journalist gets earth-shaking news from someone giving an online interview, but that hasn't happened yet. For the routine "quick quote on an on-going story" or a regular event, the telephone works very well. For that matter, Skype, email, or even text may be enough when the reporter knows the source well.

164   REPORTING

But for important interviews that are essential to the story, reporters will do all they can to conduct these interviews in person. Foundational interviews establish the story's chronology, make some of its essential points, and leave the audience with a sense of personality and presence of someone who is important in the story. The reporter can observe all the conversational **cues** expressed by the interviewee, the cues that include the words, sounds, gestures, and movements that people make. Cues may be visual, **aural**, verbal, nonverbal, and less often, smell, taste, and touch. All types of cues offer insights to interviewees' emotional state, even when they are expressed subtly. **Paralinguistic cues** can bring speech to life, including such actions as raised eyebrows, rolling eyes, snorting, staged coughing, groaning, shrugging the shoulders, and waving the hands. Table 6.2 identifies the available cues frequently used technologies can convey, given their limitations. For example, a synchronous video call is the next best choice if a face-to-face meeting is impossible.

When it is not possible to secure an in-person exchange for a crucial interview, a synchronous online interview with both audio and video (as with Skype, Zoom, Facetime, or other platform) offers the best substitute. The telephone is a less-desirable option – email and text may not work at all. Of course, it is possible to conjure situations where these text-based platforms are the *only* option: The prospective interviewee is at the top of Mt. Everest with a mobile phone that can send text or email, but not video. Or survivalists are holed up in a cabin in the mountains, surrounded by the National Guard with rifles at the ready. (Hey, sure, we can do this interview by email, text, or even Morse code!)

Four reasons to avoid email interviews when possible:

- Subjects see all the questions at once, letting interviewees cherry-pick some questions and avoid answering uncomfortable ones
- Email doesn't permit follow-up questions, immediately after an answer
- People don't write the way they speak
- Reporters can't see the interviewee's spontaneous emotional reactions

TABLE 6.2 Interviewing with tech: Cues, pros and cons

Technology	Available Cues/ Cue Types	Advantages	Tech Limitations and Problems
Face-to-face	Visual, aural, verbal, paralinguistic, nonverbal		
Telephone (landline)	Aural/verbal, paralinguistic	– Easy, well known – Good audio quality audio for use on broadcast, cable, radio, and web outlets	– No visual nonverbal cues – May not be available in natural disasters

TRADITIONAL TOOLS & TECHNIQUES

Technology	Available Cues/ Cue Types	Advantages	Tech Limitations and Problems
Telephone (mobile)	Aural/verbal, paralinguistic	– Easy, well known – Convenient – May work in areas of unrest, accidents, and natural disasters – If important, can use on broadcast and cable news outlets	– Undependable audio quality – Difficult to coordinate conversation because no "backchannel" feed-back between partici-pants exists
Skype (audio only)	Aural/verbal, paralinguistic	– Low cost, especially overseas – If important, can use on broadcast and cable news outlets	– Undependable stream-ing, resulting in gaps and loss of service – Not well known – Many people don't have the software or don't know how to use this service
Skype, Facetime, and online meeting rooms	Visual, aural/some nonverbal, verbal, paralinguistic	– Free or very low cost – Might be able to use video on the web – If important, can use on broadcast and cable news outlets	– May not provide many nonverbal gestural or body language cues – Glitches and gaps in audio and video – May not be available in natural disasters
Chat/IM/SMS text	Textual/verbal, nonverbal, emoticons and emojis	– Occurs in real time – Can ask questions but one at a time	– Text provides few cues – Easy for subject to avoid answering ques-tions and to break off interview
Email	Textual/verbal, nonverbal emoticons and emojis	– May be able to reach persons otherwise unavailable – Person can answer complex questions that require time and thought – Permits sharing attached Word and graphics docs	– Must provide questions in advance – Text provides few cues – Subject can easily avoid answering questions – Subject can delay – email seems less urgent than face-to-face appointments

166 REPORTING

SEQUENCING INTERVIEWS

Interviews for investigative articles call for considerably more thought and planning than other types of stories require. The more the article entails controversy and damage to persons, institutions, or interests – the more it involves pre-planning for interviews. Ideally, key interviews should occur face-to-face, particularly interviews with bad actors or miscreants. It is far too easy for people on the telephone to hang up or to hide their spontaneous emotional reactions.

When interviewing persons whose statements contradict the available evidence, the reporter may schedule one interview to record the lie, then request a second follow-up interview to expose the lie and request an explanation. The first interview covers the story in a non-confrontational manner, drawing out the subject as much as possible. The second interview presents contrary evidence and asks the subject how they account for discrepancies between their explanation and that evidence.

Sometimes both parts in this sequence may occur in the same interview, particularly when the interviewee is a high-ranking, busy individual with whom it is difficult to schedule an interview. In the single interview case, the reporter usually asks the seemingly innocuous questions first, recording falsehoods without comment, even drawing the interviewee out. The tough questions and evidence come second, as they may bring the interview to a rapid, and perhaps angry halt.

FOR THE RECORD

The first rule for any interview is that, unless there is a prior agreement in place, everything is on the record, whether it takes place in person, using Skype or mobile video, or via email. This means that reporters can write about anything that occurs during the interview, if their account is accurate. If the subject gets a phone call from his wife and gets into an argument – it's on the record. Sometimes when an interviewee lets something slip, he or she will say, "Oh, that's off the record!" Actually, it isn't. Depending on the news value of an inadvertent remark, the reporter may or may not use it.

A freelancer for a supermarket counter tabloid conducted an interview with a long-time, well-known TV actor who was the star of a successful new series. When the actor got up for a comfort break, she noticed a prescription on his desk and read it. She recognized the medication as one used for cancer treatment. When the actor returned, she asked him about it. He confirmed her observation, but begged her not to write about it, because he was trying to work for as long as possible to earn money to support his family after he died. He feared he would be replaced on the show if news of his condition leaked out. Yes, the whole thing was on the record. But this reporter did not report the actor's health condition, even though it would have been a juicy, prominent, and lucrative story for her. The actor stayed on the show until a few weeks before he died, 11 months later. Then she wrote the story.

WHAT IS A JOURNALIST'S MOST VALUABLE RESOURCE? (HINT: IT'S NOT INFORMATION)

Remember this: *Inside information that comes from a knowledgeable, live, breathing, human being is like no other kind. These sources are a journalist's most valuable resource because they often tell us where to look for the needle in the vast, global haystack of information.* When reporters say, "I have a source," they usually mean a human source, a person – not a box of documents, online records, or a handwritten diary found in a hidden desk drawer.

Online, information is everywhere. It's good. Competent reporters find it, check it out, share it, receive, and sometimes remix it. That's good too. But the impact of someone speaking out of their own experience: Priceless!

THE 1 PRACTICE THAT CAN MAKE OR BREAK A CAREER IN JOURNALISM

It greatly helps to be a good writer, but writing doesn't guarantee a great career. It helps to be careful with facts and to be an expert at verifying information claims. But they won't guarantee success either. The key ability that keeps a journalist fully employed throughout their career is to develop many high-quality human sources. Journalists find good sources because they look for knowledgeable, well-placed sources and form trusting relationships with them. Sometimes great sources and tipsters find journalists, contacting them over the phone or via email or social media. No matter how busy they are, journalists must make time to follow up on tips, leads, and inside information that seems promising.

Never are sources more essential than when governments and agencies have incentives to prevent troublesome facts from becoming public, like during the COVID-19 pandemic (Cuillier, 2020). Nongovernmental sources proved helpful. For example, The Johns Hopkins University and Medicine Coronavirus Resource Center posted information from (and direct access to) public health and medical experts that journalists might contact for credible information.

Sometimes sources come forward or are brought forward via leaked material, as happened to Captain Brett Crozier, commander of the U.S.S. Theodore Roosevelt aircraft carrier. His letter to the Naval command structure, requesting help for his COVID-19 infected crew, went public (Gafni & Garofoli, 2020). Journalists should make strong efforts to cultivate sources who will call them directly – and exclusively – when potential sources know they have information the public needs.

The Skinny: How Reporters Find and Enlist Sources

There's always the obvious: Call up potential sources to introduce yourself. Start the conversation by asking for an in-person meeting, if possible. Or reporters can attend meetings, conferences, and other events, to find experts and important players in an industry, organization, or topic of interest. For journalists, business cards remain indispensable. But there's way more. Turning on infrared (IR) in mobile phone settings allows for quick exchanges of electronic cards. Reporters should ensure they are easily reached via their publication's staff listing. And make it easy for sources to make contact by publicizing your professional Facebook, LinkedIn, and Twitter accounts.

Reporters answered questions from Lecheler and Kruikemeier (2015) that described how they find sources:

- They go online. The internet offers a common, useful, and important tool for reporters to find sources, especially those who may be unusual or hard to find.
- They review the sites of other established news organizations to see who other journalists have mentioned.
- They rely on traditional methods of finding sources, such as the telephone and press conferences.

- They use Twitter when there is no direct access to information or when they are looking for information about soft and human-interest stories.
- They are not euphoric regarding the democratizing potential of online news sources. Journalists are still gatekeepers, who select sources for their news reporting.

Andrew Jennings covered the Internationale de Football Association for many years. He's the veteran investigative journalist who compiled the story about massive bribes and thievery committed by FIFA executives that broke during 2015 in *The Washington Post* (Miller, 2015). Jennings assembled the damning information in his story by finding the right sources who would blow the whistle.

> From prior investigations and studying organized crime, Jennings knew he would need sources to crack open the secretive soccer association. "You know that everywhere, any organization, if there is any sign at all of how corrupt the people at the top are, there's decent people down in the middle management, because they've got mortgages, they've got children to put through school," Jennings said. "They are just employees, and they will have a sense of proper morality. So you've got to get them to slip you the stuff out the back door. It used to be from the filing cabinet; now it's from the server."

A GUIDE TO HANDLING JOURNALISTS' MOST VALUABLE (RE)SOURCES

It's often not difficult to get people talking. Public relations people, publicists, and organizational information officers have responsibilities to answer reporters' questions as part of their jobs. When journalists contact people who have knowledge about a story, they are often flattered by reporters who seek their opinions. Others quickly see personal advantage in being quoted by influential publications. But sometimes it takes some persuasion to convince potential sources to speak on the record, and not every source will do it. In all cases, it is important for journalists to identify themselves as a reporter and to make their intent to publish the information clear to the source.

Important stories and investigations require a strategic approach. Finding sources who have information is just the first step. The reporter must recruit them to enlist their active help and convince them to provide information. Intelligence services have a similar challenge. They characterize the motivations of potential sources as MICE: money, ideology, compromise, and ego. Reporters have another calculation that could be called FACE: fame, advancement, conscience, and ego. Appeals to these motivations are effective with some sources.

Source Attribution: Who Sez?

Another issue that reporters and sources must settle between them is how to identify the source of the information in the final story. **Source attribution** defines how reporters will identify the source in the published article. Using established ground rules for source attribution, reporters can offer sources alternative ways that offer them greater safety, while still publishing the information they received. Over time, taking great care in handling a source's information offers a vital way to build trusted relationships: Each party knows what to expect when the news organization publishes the story.

Considering source attribution is just part of the daily work for all journalists. Even when someone makes a public statement, precise attribution requires care: Reporters must spell names correctly and provide accurate titles for individuals and names for

TRADITIONAL TOOLS & TECHNIQUES

organizational entities. For professional journalists, identifying an article's sources of information may be just as important as the story itself.

It's equally important for members of the public to know where the story's information came from. Knowing the source(s) of information allows users to assess for themselves the provenance of reported material, the credibility, and quality of the sources. When journalists can't attribute important information to a specific source, many users become skeptical about the story's truth and accuracy.

Anonymous sourcing always raises questions about the information. Many investigative stories necessarily must come from unnamed sources who are close to an interesting situation and have access to important material. (The leaks from the Trump White House provide useful instruction in how reporters attribute information to sources whose names they cannot reveal.) Despite questions that open the information itself to challenge, the lure of learning inside information remains strong: Reporters want to report it; users want to read it.

There are "rules of engagement" between reporters and sources. Negotiations between these parties require careful trade-offs between the credibility of the information and its importance. One reason for careful negotiation is that people often mean different things when they use these terms. Experienced sources in sophisticated media markets know attribution rules as well (or better) than reporters. It's important to establish exactly what the source means by these phrases so that both parties understand precisely the nature of their agreement.

- **On the record** – The reporter can write anything said and attribute it to the source, without restriction.

- **On background** – The reporter can use the information to find out more about the story. The reporter can write and publish the information. However, the original source must remain hidden and attribution is given to someone who states the information on the record.

- **On deep background** – The reporter can use the information but not in direct quotation and not for attribution. The reporter writes it on his or her own or finds an on-the-record source.

- **Not for attribution** – The reporter can use the information but must attribute it to a mutually-agreed-upon, unspecified source, e.g., "a source close to the investigation," or "a high-level administration staffer," precisely as called for by the agreement with the source.

- **Off the record** – The reporter can't use the information at all unless another source provides it on the record.

First, consider on-the-record attribution. Written examples can take several forms, depending on the story and how the reporter received the information.

- According to Englewood School District President Ron Jones, the district will probably exceed its 2015–2016 budget by about 10 percent.

  (*This is president of the school district saying this.*)
- "The district will exceed its 2015–2016 budget by about 10 percent," said Englewood School District President Ron Jones.

  (*This is exactly what the school district president said.*)

- In his report to the Englewood School District, President Ron Jones stated that the district would exceed its 2015–2016 budget by about 10 percent.

  (*This sentence states a main point in a public formal report presented by the school district president.*)

Online journalists can make attributions to on-the-record sources even more informative for users by linking directly to online material about the source. Links to a person's bio and articles about related or recent activities are helpful. Some news sites don't want users to leave their pages, so they discourage the use of online links to other sites. But this practice ill-serves their users, as Phillips (2014) notes: Linking "can provide ways of establishing the provenance of information, offering a simple means of improving ethical accountability."

But suppose the source for the story wasn't School District President Ron Jones. Instead, the information came from his assistant, who called to give the reporter a heads up about the upcoming school board budget meeting. Before she spills the info, Jones' assistant says:

"I'm giving you this information on background."

"OK," the reporter replies, "can I attribute it to a 'knowledgeable source'?"

If the assistant agrees, it's a deal. If she doesn't, the reporter can make a counteroffer. If she doesn't accept any agreement, the reporter will have to call around and try to get someone to comment on the record. In general, it is a bad idea to burn sources.

When they won't agree to go on the record, sources often have sound reasons for wanting to stay far, far away from public disclosure. However, initial reporter–source agreements are not set in stone: They can change if both parties agree. These mutual understandings function as starting places to get the conversation going. As the story develops, agreements remain open to negotiation, even after the discussion or interview. Smolkin (2006a) writes

> journalists negotiate with sources all the time: Can your off-the-record quote be on background? Can I change the way you are identified on background? I know we agreed this will only be on background, but could I possibly use your fabulous background quote on the record?

2 TYPES OF SOURCES REPORTERS WANT: ROUTINE/OCCASIONAL SOURCES AND EYEWITNESSES

Reporters talk to sources almost every day of their professional lives. It goes along with everyday fact-finding and fact-checking, mostly on the computer. Sources comprise all kinds of people – smart/less-than-smart, kind/nasty, truth-tellers/liars, professionals/criminals, God-fearing Christians/immoral degenerates, and of course, rich/poor, old/young, beautiful/plain, and everything in between. It's an ongoing reality show that makes up a good part of the reality of a reporter's daily work life.

Reporters deal primarily with sources who provide them with routine information on a regular basis. These sources usually know about issues a reporter covers regularly or have special knowledge about what's going on in part of the reporter's beat. In addition, occasional or one-time sources provide specific information about an event or action – the usual fodder for the publication.

But mark this: Treat routine and occasional sources well – with respect, courtesy, and appreciation. Because someday one of these sources will come forward with

TRADITIONAL TOOLS & TECHNIQUES

171

not-so-routine inside information and tips. They know you, you treated them well. And you know them, making it easier to evaluate their motivations and resources. This could be the start of something great!

Sources the reporter knows are very different from another kind of important source: eyewitnesses. Think it's easy to remember an unexpected event? Take the eyewitness challenge: What color was the last car that passed you on the road today?

Reporters also seek people with direct experience of an event – eyewitnesses, passersby, and subjects of collateral damage. These sources often agree to discuss their personal experiences, and it can make for compelling journalism. Reporters should know the limitations of eyewitness reports. It is unlikely that they are trained observers. People remember the things they focused on but forget things they attended to in cursory ways. They also recall what they *want* to recall, most often information consistent with their views, while they suppress material that doesn't fit their perspectives. In some cases, they may be in physical shock or in emotional upheaval from what just happened, rendering memory frail and fallible.

The online arena holds several pitfalls for reporters when writing eyewitness accounts. Sometimes sources go home and post their experiences on Twitter and Facebook, making comments that differ from the information they gave earlier to the reporter. Sources may do this for many reasons: They've had time to reflect on their experiences. They embellished their original story to the reporter, or they embellish it later. They faced pressure from peers or others close to them, whose opinions they care about.

No matter why the source changed their story, it puts the journalist in an uncomfortable spot. About the only proper response the reporter can make is: "I stand by my story," since there is usually little reason to initiate an argument with a source. In addition, official accounts usually become known after eyewitnesses have gone home and reporters have filed their story. These reports often differ from the immediate accounts in significant ways. Journalists should not hesitate to do follow-up stories that report meaningful discrepancies between early accounts and later reports.

A second caveat experienced reporters know is that some people like to make themselves the center of events. Attention-seeking eyewitnesses may well exaggerate their danger, their own feelings, or their influence on the event. Some people even go so far as to make things up. At this point, they join the next group of sources: the fake news creators and mischief-makers.

2 TYPES OF SOURCES REPORTERS DON'T WANT: FAKE NEWS CLICK-SEEKERS AND MISCHIEF-MAKERS

Online, everybody's in it for the clicks. This calculus holds true for news organization sites with their own reporting and publishing infrastructure, aggregation sites that republish news and entertainment from other sites to serve niche audiences, individual bloggers, and fake news sites. Shocking, outrageous, and unexpected news gets clicks, even when that news is false. Hence, fake news sites have a financial stake in getting other sites to republish their links, potentially driving hordes of users to their sites.

The creators of fake news manufacture entire stories and supporting material. They forge documents, photoshop counterfeit images, invent data, develop personas that give them fake quotes, and establish social media accounts to republish their own comments. It sounds like a lot of work. But compared to maintaining a fully staffed newsroom of journalists, editors, and digital wizards, the costs of running fake news sites are trivial.

In this environment, it's not surprising that many mainstream media news sites have been tricked by the false stories that first appear on fake news sites. False stories gain credibility as they circulate through social media. For example, well-respected news organizations that have re-published such stories include *The New York Times*, *The Washington Post*, *Los Angeles Times*, *Bloomberg*, NBC Sports, *Boston.com*, and *Engadget.com* (Murtha, 2016).

Journalists would also prefer to do without mischief-makers who pester journalists both offline and online. In live shots, these people sometimes stand behind reporters doing live, on-camera reports and shout while waving their hands. Or they come up and solemnly say, "I don't give you permission to take my picture" and then stand in front of the photojournalist's camera. There aren't a lot of them, but they can sure make a lot of trouble!

Understanding the motivations of mischief-makers is often tricky. Some people just don't like journalists; others hold grudges. Some folks deliberately set out to manipulate, embarrass, or demean reporters. Others want to trick everybody, and the journalist may just provide the first rung on the ladder to their brilliant success; so be it. In these cases, reporters can be, have been, and will be tricked.

The digital world offers vast new arenas for mischief-making because so many people are now accustomed to digital artifacts – images, videos, spreadsheets, and multimedia experiences. It's relatively easy for an "experience engineer" – given resources and motives – to create detailed, convincing materials to support just about any imagined tale. Software to create and alter digital artifacts abounds as does the ability to use these tools. And when built by experts, deconstructing falsified digital documents and objects becomes increasingly difficult as our technology matures.

Gifted amateurs pose some of the same difficulties that professional digital manipulators and scammers do. These pretenders often crave attention. They may create elaborate tales, including believable but bogus evidence to propel them into the public eye and their dreamed-of celebrity status. As such, they can waste the time, effort, and resources of busy journalists.

The first line of defense against bad actors is to stay alert and retain skepticism. Ask: Does the story make sense? If the story were true, what else would have to be true? What other conditions must exist? What would have to be untrue? Over time, as the source spins their story out, a reporter's instinct and experience will kick in and help drop the curtain on an elaborate make-believe play. No matter how alluring a story may be, if it sounds too good to be true – it may well be false.

1 TYPE OF SOURCE REPORTERS ARE AMBIVALENT ABOUT: ANONYMOUS AND UNNAMED SOURCES

Most sources provide information on the record. But in sensitive arenas, they often don't. Such arenas include government, politics, national security, crime, insider business information, and sports and entertainment celebrity activities. These sources will risk disclosure, but not exposure.

And it's never been easier to pass information: Many online news sites encourage users to contact reporters or the publication with a big banner – "Have a tip for us?" "Contact us confidentially" – and provide an easy-to-click link.

Many people (news organizations, practitioners, journalism professors, U.S. presidents) voice concerns about the use of unnamed sources (Franklin & Carlson, 2010;

TRADITIONAL TOOLS & TECHNIQUES

Brooks, Kennedy, Moen, & Ranley, 2011). Critics base their misgivings about anonymous sourcing on the potential for the practice to undermine the credibility of journalism, the publication, and of the reporter. Many publications say they are reluctant to publish articles based on unattributed sources. Yet, despite ongoing criticism, the use of unnamed sources persists.

Why? Because so many important stories might never have seen the light of day without anonymous sources! For example, the Watergate scandal famously depended on "Deep Throat" an anonymous source who revealed himself 31 years later as Mark Felt, Associate FBI Director.

More recently, *NBC News* reported a story from an unnamed national security source who said the intelligence community's assessment was that Russian President Vladimir Putin "personally directed" the campaign of interference in the 2016 presidential election – confirmed by Mueller (2019). In addition, substantial academic and practitioner literature offers support for the idea that use of such sources fosters the publication of stories that ultimately benefit the American public (Spayd, 2017).

In an interview with National Public Radio (2016) about the use of anonymous sources, WaPo reporter Dana Priest said that national security sources never speak on the record. NPR journalist Mary Louise Kelly added:

> Just to give a little bit of insight into that, the people who are agreeing to speak to somebody like Dana or me are people who have security clearances. To keep the clearance, they are regularly polygraphed. And one of the questions that is routinely asked is, have you had any unauthorized contact with the media? These people are risking their jobs, their pensions to speak to us.
>
> (Greene, 2016)

Anonymity may benefit sources. But it is a mixed blessing for journalists and the public: Although it brings otherwise hidden acts and events into the light, it also complicates reporting for journalists and understanding by the public. Attributing important information to anonymous sources places enormous responsibility on journalists. It makes verification more difficult. And it deprives the public key knowledge that would help them weigh the accuracy and reliability of the information and its source.

The journalist must first understand why a source wants to speak out at all. What's the motivation? It might be that the source: 1) has something they want to keep from losing; 2) has little or nothing to lose; 3) has something to gain; 4) represents someone else's interests; 5) wants attention; or 6) genuinely wants to put an end to the wrongdoing. (Note: Be aware that one or more of the other reasons often accompany this last reason.)

The need to assess the motives of sources who request anonymity doesn't mean it shouldn't be granted. More importantly, it doesn't mean the reporter shouldn't publish the information. Rather, reporters (and editors and publications) should consider sources' possible motives when verifying the information, while continuing to look for confirmation.

In addition, there are almost certainly other perspectives on important stories that reporters should explore. In this added reporting, it's important to avoid knee-jerk **othersideism**, **bothsideism**, or **whataboutism**, charges often made against the mainstream media. Nevertheless, it is essential to bring forward mitigating circumstances, alternate points of view, and describe the positions of other stakeholders with conflicting interests that provides users with the tools to make more complete appraisals of the story.

And you thought journalists don't believe in ghosts: Unnamed leakers and whistleblowers

Anonymous sources haunt journalism. Leakers are people who 1) bring themselves forward; 2) provide confidential information; and 3) give their information exclusively to one media outlet or a single reporter. Generally, leakers don't leak for reasons of conscience, but occasionally they do. The Trump administration's controversial actions, such as separating migrating families at the border or non-public contacts with Russia, have been revealed by so many leaks that it seems possible that conscience did play a role in some of them.

Although personal principles may motivate leakers to some extent, they usually want to influence policy, discredit others, or improve their own status. In short, most leakers leak because they believe it will serve them. Frequent leakers have experience using the press to their own advantage. Because a story may accrue to their personal or professional advantage, leakers can push against journalists' ethical boundaries and pose practical problems for information verification – as well as profound risks to the reporter's reputation.

Just because leakers may lack altruistic motives, their self-serving motives don't free reporters from the obligation to honor agreements they made with the leaker. Journalists and news organizations live and die by their word: Their ability to do their job depends on truth-telling and keeping promises. In addition, a reporter's reputation as a trustworthy protector of sources remains vital to obtaining leaked information from key players who have: 1) position, 2) influence, and 3) crucial information – as demonstrated by Mark Felt's "Deep Throat" role in the Watergate scandal.

In contrast, whistleblowers decide to tell journalists what they believe is true to stop practices that they strongly condemn. While they may have mixed motives, righting wrongdoing is prominent among them. When whistleblowers initiate contact, often driven by conscience, they are justifiably reluctant to come forward on the record.

Whistleblowers may have compiled documents and other evidence that they consider proof of others' wrongdoing. Some whistleblower's actions to gather this material may be deemed improper or illegal, opening them up to prosecution. Nevertheless, when whistleblowers seek to expose people in high places or organizations with great power and money, whistleblowers rightly fear that they are jeopardizing their careers, jobs, social influence, and personal privacy.

Ordway (2019) cautions journalists to: 1) use extreme care in revealing details that might compromise the whistleblower's identity, and 2) understand that whistleblowers in the U.S. "are generally protected by law from retaliation, but they sometimes risk their careers and safety to share what they know." So, it's vital that journalists use sophisticated strategies for secure communication and be familiar with the legal framework that applies to each particular whistleblower. Ordway's whistleblower tips located at: https://journalistsresource.org/ provides links to essential information for journalists who work with whistleblowers.

Journalists have ethical obligations to tell whistleblowers that future circumstances could arise such that the source may be identified through other avenues than by the reporter or her news organization. Whistleblowers may be outed by: 1) material available online that points to them as the source of information, 2) ensuing investigations, 3) actions they took while acquiring their material, 4) actions that either the source or the reporter took when communicating about the material, and 5) by an analysis of the

TRADITIONAL TOOLS & TECHNIQUES

material itself. The pact between whistleblower and reporter should include the extent of the journalist's willingness to protect the source – will she exercise care, pay contempt fines, or go to jail? In short, journalists must be completely honest when making agreements with sources who risk severe professional and personal consequences if they are exposed.

Warning: Remember that any source can manipulate, lie, be misled, or be just plain wrong – including leakers and whistleblowers.

Hacking the Code of Attribution to Anonymous Sources

News publications would be far less newsworthy if they only reported information from on-the-record sources. Source anonymity can be the price a journalist pays for insider information and timeliness. Reuters' *Handbook of Journalism* (Reuters, 2019) provides useful, detailed guidelines for journalists.

According to the handbook, Reuters uses anonymous sources "when we believe they are providing accurate, reliable and newsworthy information that we could not obtain any other way." The organization (and reporter) accepts full responsibility for this policy: "Responsibility for reporting what an anonymous source says resides solely with Reuters and the reporter."

An excerpt from the Reuters' *Handbook* (2019) tells reporters how to check the information they receive and offers a delicately nuanced manner of attributing it to unnamed sources, who are sometimes leakers:

Stories based on anonymous sources require particularly rigorous crosschecking.
We should normally have two or three sources for such information.
Unnamed sources rank as follows, in order of strength:

- **An authoritative source** exercises real authority on an issue in question. A foreign minister, for example, is an authoritative source on foreign policy but not necessarily on finance.
- **An official source**, such as a company spokesman or spokeswoman, has access to information in an official capacity. This person's competence as a source is limited to their field of activity.
- **Designated sources** are, for instance, diplomatic sources, conference sources and intelligence sources. As with an official source, they must have access to reliable information on the subject in question.

How Can Reporters Protect Sources?

Whether they are a villain or hero, protecting a source is essential. It is one of the most serious aspects of work in journalism. Reporters differ in how they undertake the protection, care, and feeding of unnamed sources who provide information. But all journalists should know that their reputations depend on taking all possible measures to protect the identities of their sources.

Many reporters have willingly gone to jail rather than disclose the identity of a source. Examples include Judith Miller, a reporter for *The New York Times* who went to jail rather than reveal her administration source who had outed a CIA agent. Another *New York Times* journalist, James Risen, was prepared to go to jail rather than identify the source who gave him information that the government claimed had violated national security. Indeed, investigative reporters have spent days, weeks, and months in lockup for defying U.S. federal court orders to identify their sources. In many other countries, journalists face and undergo harassment, beatings, torture, even death, for protecting sources from government reprisals that sometimes include murder.

Quick Tip: Don't Waver On the Waiver

Government prosecutors established a practice asking defendants or witnesses in a trial to sign **blanket waivers**, thus relieving reporters from previous promises of anonymity. The waiver supposedly allows a reporter to testify in court. Blanket waivers are the subject of much controversy. Even when a source signs a waiver, reporters have gone to jail rather than reveal their source because they understand the coercive power of prosecutors over defendants.

Smolkin (2006b) sent out a survey that asked reporters about how they handle confidential sources. One important question was: "If a source signs a waiver of confidentiality, is that a valid reason to identify the source? Is a blanket waiver enough – or do you need individual, specific permission from your source?" Joe Demma, investigations editor of the South Florida Sun-Sentinel replied:

> No and no. I would need individual, specific and direct permission from the source – in person, naked in a steam room with a heavy metal band blasting and a blindfolded 5-year-old banging on a pot with a soup spoon. No winking and no suggestion that we're not going to tell the whole truth.

MANAGING SECURITY IN THE SURVEILLANCE SOCIETY

Everyone who uses a computer is monitored and surveilled, 24/7. Post a "like" on Facebook for a product and a horde of advertisers know about it in real time. Our smartphones – journalists' most vital work tool (Chen, 2019) – are constantly surveilled. Thanks to *The New York Times* Privacy Project, we know that smartphone apps send vast streams of personalized time-stamped location data to corporate location data aggregators for resale to third parties (Thompson & Warzel, 2019). Smartphone location tracks may then be matched to journalists with high-level sources in government, corporations, law enforcement, and intelligence. Journalists and sources are more likely to be monitored with location data than other persons. Thus, source surveillance may rub off on journalists. So, the new "secs" below have become even more important for news organizations.

Sec-sy Stuff

Operational security (opsec), information security (infosec), and communications security (comsec) and are no longer military or intelligence-only security requirements. News organizations, individual journalists, and an increasing number of computer users need comprehensive control of the data that they generate and receive online. Journalists working in markets and on beats that require confidentiality with sources must understand these issues and stay abreast of constant changes in security hardware, software, and best practices. To enhance journalists' security, the Committee to Protect Journalists (2019b) provides a Digital Safety Kit at https://cpj.org/2019/07/digital-safety-kit-journalists.php#protect. Next, we describe present best practices and identify journalists' resources that address the inevitable changes to come.

Operational Security

Opsec entails following procedures that mask information about persons who might become targets. Typically, such actions include restricting access to personal information, contacts, schedules, activities, and interests. In short, journalists should limit exposure on Facebook and other social media sites. (Note the inevitable trade-offs between opsec and user outreach.) In addition, they should limit the number of SMS text accounts they have and monitor them frequently.

Finally, here's the word about passwords and account access protection: The Committee to Protect Journalists (CPJ) recommends using long, unique passwords for online accounts, changing them regularly, and using a password manager. The CPJ also recommends: 1) locking devices with longer pins or passwords, 2) encrypting devices and storage media, 3) using two-factor authentication (2FA) *and* a security key like a Yubikey, and 4) setting-up remote device wiping.

These guidelines for journalists to protect their actions and communications may seem extreme, but ample reasons exist for them to take care. *The New York Times* Privacy Project analysts easily identified individual phones and then reconstructed their owners' identity and the point-to-point travel routes. Presidential inauguration dignitaries, Woman's March protesters, senior Obama defense officials, and Mar-a-Lago guests were individually identified and tracked – as well as persons who these "target individuals" met along their way.

A report by Thompson and Warzel (2019) has particularly unsettling implications for journalists because reporters' and sources' archived point-to-point location data tracks are now commercially available:

> Reporters hoping to evade other forms of surveillance by meeting in person with a source might want to rethink that practice. Every major newsroom covered by the data contained dozens of pings; we easily traced one *Washington Post* journalist through Arlington, Va.

In another story about surveillance, Thompson and Wezerek (2019) recommend smartphone users stop sharing their personal location trails with data companies by disabling their mobile phone's location-sharing features:

- Stop sharing your phone location with apps
- Disable your mobile ad ID
- Prevent Google from storing your location

They further suggest trying-out the Privacy Pro SmartVPN app to monitor and block apps from other forms of data sharing.

Communications Security

Comsec is particularly difficult because electronic communications are (almost) always vulnerable to interception. Governmental agencies, corporate entities, and non-governmental entities often use sophisticated technology to trace and record communication conducted over computers, tablets, and telephones. Consider the points through which digital messages must pass as they travel from source to receiver: sending computer, router, internet service provider, email server, internet access point, internet backbone, receiving email server, router, and receiving computer. Each point affords collection opportunities and presents vulnerabilities for journalists' communications.

Integrated networks require telephone services to use much of the same network infrastructure as landlines, adding only a short wireless hop from the mobile device to a nearby cell tower. Should a hint of the existence of highly sensitive messages become known, the chances are good that someone in the chain of communication would turn over the who-to-whom contacts and perhaps whole messages in response to a subpoena. Journalists must understand that all their electronic communication platforms – computers, networks, mobile phones, and landlines – are potentially insecure platforms for them to use, even when exchanging constitutionally-protected communication.

Perfect security for communications doesn't exist: Even quiet whispers in a dark garage may be overheard. Nevertheless, all reporters should have a working knowledge of how to enable fundamental digital and physical security measures to protect their communications. One time-honored way to protect journalistic secrets is to mimic the most famous reporter–source meetings of all – Deep Throat and *The Washington Post* reporters who investigated the Watergate scandal by meeting in person in a deserted office building garage after hours.

Quick tip: In the digital era, sometimes it pays to go analog and meet your source in person. But journalists and sources shouldn't bring their mobiles to meetings unless the battery is removed, and/or their phone is carried in a secure Faraday bag that blocks mobile signals.

Journalists can identify a coffee shop, juice bar, library, park, or other public place where they can meet sources for private talks. One reason that the meeting place should be close to the reporter's workplace: Little time is lost if the source has nothing to offer. This meeting place should be public, but not too exposed, affording both privacy and a quick exit, if needed. For meetings with prominent people or those recently in the news, a dingy bar with dark corners may work best. (One enterprising *Los Angeles Times* reporter met sources at a nearby public library, where he reserved small, private study rooms for an hour or four.)

Mobile phones pose multiple, serious comsec problems. They operate on networks that allow them to become always-on microphones, via the long-documented **network SS7-exploit**, which doesn't require that anyone physically handle the phone. The remote eavesdropper can pin down the location of the phone, listen to calls, read messages, and redirect calls or SMS messages to their own device (Gibbs, 2016; Peterson, 2019). Other surreptitiously installed malware (via bogus links or public phone chargers) may permit surreptitious access to a journalist's (or source's) mobile – resulting in even more comsec and opsec compromises, for example, a specialized app that turns mobile phones into "hot mics" that record and re-transmit the audio from conversations.

The only sure ways to prevent a bugged phone from recording is to ensure acoustic isolation by placing the entire phone in a glass jar, by wrapping it in effective muffling material, after removing the battery from the device. Alternatively, Faraday bags block wireless signals and offer protection from most threats. But bag quality varies, and bags degrade with use, so check their reliability by calling your phone when it's in the bag.

Pre-paid phones, sometimes called burner phones, offer other options. But use burners with care; they may not deliver the protection that users imagine. The U.S.

TRADITIONAL TOOLS & TECHNIQUES

government's Hemisphere database preserves historical call records, assembled from all carriers. Hemisphere can match new smartphones and burner phones' patterns against other phones in that database. Know that intelligence and law enforcement agencies can access Hemisphere to construct the network of a target's historical calls. When a new number pops up, the call pattern often enables trackers to discover the environments where that mobile user hangs out (Electronic Frontier Foundation, 2019). And emergency Hemisphere requests may yield results within an hour.

Confidential Communication

Reporters must protect their sources by communicating with them while avoiding being traced. The Society of Professional Journalists operates a website, http://journaliststoolbox.org, that provides useful links to sites that identify secure means of communicating with sources, including The Committee to Protect Journalists, Journalist's Resources, and SecureDrop information (Berret, 2016).

Security methods, technologies, and threat countermeasures change constantly. Journalists who cover beats where they may receive confidential information should stay informed about new methods of detection and protection in order to develop and maintain successful relationships with valuable sources. Careful attention to state-of-the-art tools enable more secure communication with vulnerable sources. Sites that track security technologies include https://eff.org; Reddit thread /r/privacy; privacy-tools.io; and prism-break.org.

Look for services that don't keep logs of connections and interactions – like Signal for SMS (Grothaus, 2019). Signal has strong end-to-end encryption, keeps no records, and provides an option for self-destructing messages; avoid Facebook's WhatsApp. For now, consider encrypted email and VPN services located in Ireland, Sweden, and Switzerland, because they're not subject to U.S. Department of Homeland Security disclosure requirements. Proton encrypted email and VPN services (Switzerland) seem highly rated and secure – and other suitable choices exist.

More mundane comsec practices recommended by the Committee to Protect Journalists – https://cpj.org/2019/07/digital-safety-kit-journalists.php include using the Electronic Frontier Foundation's HTTPS Everywhere browser extension, the Privacy Badger app to block websites and advertisers from tracking the sites that you visit, and an adblocker to prevent malware embedded in popup ads.

Information Security

Infosec, the preservation and storage of material, isn't easy either. How and where can journalists keep information securely? To begin, keeping confidential information on a laptop or desktop computer isn't a good idea unless it's encrypted. So, encrypt storage media and perhaps your devices as well. When traveling, do not carry any information, encrypted or otherwise. Journalists have been detained and threatened to provide passwords and encryption keys to border officers.

The Centre for Investigative Journalism (Carlo & Kamphuis, 2016) notes that others can gain entry through:

- Hardware
- Firmware needed to organize and link components to work together, into working order

- Chipsets, that allow for remote software updates by organizational administrators and
- Operating systems, especially Windows, but others as well

Of the four avenues for threats to computer security, the operating system has a relatively easy fix: Use the *Tails* operating system from a USB drive. *Tails* keeps computing devices from opening the installed OS. Instead *Tails* provides most computers with enough information to run while insuring anonymity through its integration with the Tor browser. According to the *Tails* website (https://tails.boum.org/about/index.en.html), *Tails* installs its own apps and suite of encryption tools: Tor browser, instant messaging client, email client, office suite, image and sound editor. Because Tails only uses the computer's RAM and not its hard drive, it leaves no trace after shutdown and USB stick removal. Note that *Tails* finesses (but doesn't completely eliminate) some of the threats to hardware, firmware, and chipsets. One downside: Tor slows browsing and limits some browser functions.

The Freedom of the Press Foundation also offers SecureDrop, (https://securedrop.org) – presently the most complete, encrypted, and anonymized secure platform for whistleblowers and leakers. SecureDrop provides communication with 50 highly reputable U.S. and international news organizations. End-users interact with SecureDrop by installing and using *Tails* in conjunction with the Tor network (Berret, 2016). Of course, once downloaded, files must reside on encrypted devices to remain secure.

A thorough security update of journalists' laptops or desktop computers that will address all these issues requires a super-nerd or someone with professional security chops to work on the machine. The London-based Centre for Investigative Journalism will help journalists acquire such machines. Contact the organization at: http://www.tcij.org.

Of course, once files are saved to a computer or hard drive, others may read them. Owning an encrypted USB drive, such as the Aegis Secure Key 3.0 or the Kingston 4000 G2

Figure 6.4 The "amnesiac" Tails Operating System doesn't make records of users' activities
Credit: By Les Pounder from Blackpool, UK, CC BY-SA 2.0, https://commons.wikimedia.org/w/index.php?curid=67379379

TRADITIONAL TOOLS & TECHNIQUES

is a good idea to ensure infosec. Recall that SecureDrop includes a secure communication platform for reporters to communicate with sources and receive confidential information.

Physical infosec for mobile phones is important. When reporters are in the field, they can lose their phones, have them stolen, or taken by authorities. Recently, the U.S. government proposed intruding into selected cellphones and computers during border entry. The Freedom of the Press Foundation offers tips and tools for securing mobile phones at https://freedom.press/tools/. This site offers useful opsec and comsec information.

Journalists have one final security need to consider. Call it **emotsec** – the reporter's emotional security. The source-journalist relationship can lead to a professionally intimate linkage. If the sources' identity becomes known and they suffer as a result, the reporter may develop deeply personal regrets. Yet, leaking and whistleblowing are inherently risky, and informing the public is the purpose of journalists' work. Going public may be the only way for a source to vindicate their actions, to right unbearable wrongs or injustices, despite the personal toll it may take. The challenge for journalists is to retain human empathy and decency while distancing themselves emotionally from unavoidable consequences of sound journalism.

Dealing with human sources will always be one of the most difficult parts of any journalist's job.

First, reporters should not let informants do their professional work for them. When dealing with long-time, dependable, and knowledgeable sources, this habit can be easy to fall into. Journalists must always carry out their fundamental tasks of information-gathering, sourcing, verifying, and writing and creation themselves. Revers (2014) interviewed journalists covering state politics in Albany, New York, asking them about their relationships with sources. One editor commented:

> I've seen just bad reporting where people let their sources do too much of the work for them. So you become more of a stenographer than an actual reporter. There's been a lot of that going on.

Second, reporters shouldn't become attached to their sources. Some sources are people that you would dread sharing lunch with while others could be brilliant, good-looking, fun, and appealing dinner companions. Yet all informant–reporter relationships are fraught with conflicts of interest. As one journalist commented: "We always betray them," – sooner or later, reporters will write a story that hurts or offends their sources (Revers, 2014).

Emotional security is an important consideration for journalists covering war and civil unrest, torture, refugees and refugee camps, catastrophes like earthquakes, fires, droughts, etc., and other horrific news events. Reporters can suffer from the same trauma that afflicts other first responders and it often goes unnoticed and untreated within news organizations – and even by the news workers themselves. After covering stories of immense suffering, journalists should consider finding a debriefing partner, trauma therapist, spiritual retreat, or some other form of emotional recovery.

One important warning: Romantic involvement with informants may be toxic for the journalist and perhaps the source (Robertson, 2002). Relationships with sources may become intimate for many reasons: 1) They last a long time; 2) They feature exciting and secret subject-matter; 3) The reporter and source share important interests and perhaps strong mutual attraction.

If information about a liaison becomes public, the journalist and their news organization suffer lost credibility. Even rumors can harm careers. Disenchanted sources also gain unacceptable leverage over "their" journalist. Thus, journalists have obligations to disclose these relationships. Conflicts are particularly acute for married journalists, whose spouse occupies an important position, particularly if the career lies in areas that the reporter covers. In these cases, the news organization will probably remove the reporter from the story, and possibly their beat. Sometimes, reporters must resign or may be fired.

Checklist For Handling Anonymous Sources
- Evaluate the information the source offers.
- Analyze any evidence the source has or can acquire.
- Consider how real are the source's fears if identified – if they are unjustified, the source may be urged to speak for the record.
- Talk with the editor.
- If the editor and the news organization agree that using an anonymous source is justified, look for other sources who will speak on the record.
- Look for corroborating (or disconfirming) evidence of what is going on.
- Develop the most secure means of communication possible. Consider communicating face-to-face IRL (in real life).
- Protect whistleblowers by knowing their legal protections and using SecureDrop, as many large news organizations do routinely.

Finally, sometimes good sources go bad. Real damage or an imagined slight provokes them, and the source of their pain becomes the target of their retaliation. Perhaps the source of pain is the reporter who deserves to be hurt in return. Almost as difficult: the case when the reporter calls to ask someone their side of the story, based on information damaging to that person – and the journalist's question represents the first time that the individual learns about the accusations against them.

Journalists confront intense ethical and psychological dilemmas. Psychological therapists and social workers face many of the same professional boundary issues in their professions. They receive ethical training that provides quite specific guidelines, teaching them to remain helpful, open, and empathetic, even as they refrain from engaging in personally intimate relations with clients. Journalists would do well to adopt a similar code to act ethically and help protect their long-term careers.

TAKEAWAYS

- Observation is the oldest of all journalistic techniques, formally practiced since the 5th century BC when Thucydides wrote about the Peloponnesian War. Observation is more than mere seeing or looking. It is intentional and focused. Barriers to accurate observation include inattentional blindness, the failure to attend to seemingly unimportant or unexpected elements.

  Observation through the "eyes and ears" of new technologies, such as drones, live video chats, and monitoring records of surveillance and measurement devices expand

TRADITIONAL TOOLS & TECHNIQUES

how journalists can observe actions and events. The technologies allow journalists to penetrate places where people cannot travel and reveal aspects of phenomena that the eye cannot see. Remote observation almost always allows recording, so that journalists can review the event as many times as needed.

- Science brings systematic consideration of observational opportunities, sharpening journalists' planning and practice. Observation conditions may be direct, indirect, or remote. Consider all these aspects of the situation:

  1. Role of the observer: An observer is a participant or a nonparticipant during the observed activities or events.

  2. Perspective of the observer: The observer focuses on the activities or events and reports on them directly, objectively and apart from them. Subjective observers focus on both the events *and* their responses to the events, reporting them at least partly from their own subjective point-of-view.

  3. Location of the observer: When reporters observe activities and events in person as they occur, it is direct observation. When they view something that reflects the underlying phenomenon (a thermometer, wind bending trees), rather than the phenomenon itself, it is indirect observation. When they view activities and events through the "eyes and ears" of a technology, it is remote observation or mediated observation (as through a camera lens).

  4. The behavior of the observed: Reporters can recognize that there are many situations where people's behavior is changed by circumstance: school, work, custody and incarceration, presence of authority figures, loved ones, strangers – the list is endless. Absolutely uncontrolled behavior (except in infants) is rarer than one might think. However, people act in relatively uncontrolled ways when they are free to choose how they behave, in familiar surroundings, with people who know them well, and where fewer rules limit them.

  5. Type of setting: Reporters can be aware that whether a setting is natural or contrived affects people's behavior. Their home, workplace, or school, and neighborhoods are natural settings, where they can behave as they normally do. Going to a TV studio for an interview is a highly contrived setting, where few people would behave in a normal way. Of course, one person's contrived setting is another's hometown: The TV studio is comfortable for employees of the station. Similarly, observing a person at a rally would likely be a contrived venue for most people – unless they were a groupie following that attraction for weeks.

  6. Observational conditions: Some observations just happen, while others take place under quite specific conditions. If reporters happen upon an accident or are roaming around an event venue, then their observation is happenstance – there are no structural conditions. However, increasingly reporters work conditionally. Thus, they are constrained by having to attend at a set time (appointment), a special place (a pen for journos at a political event), by activity, such as baseball practice, or by the kind of observations they can make, including using a camera or recorder.

- Successful interviewing depends on observational skills, analytical capability, and emotional intelligence. People give interviews for professional, legal, and personal reasons, that shape the conditions for the journalist to score a "get," a high-profile interview from a newsworthy person.

Technology often becomes part and parcel of an interview. Most reporters record interviews on a digital audio device so that they can have complete transcripts to work from. When necessary, they take notes the old-fashioned way. They wrap-up interviews quickly over the telephone. Video conferencing services allow journalists to conduct interviews with people they couldn't otherwise reach. Generally, email and text are less satisfactory technologies because: 1) Reporters can't see the person's nonverbal cues and 2) Most people don't write the way they speak.

- Before the interview, typical preparations include getting as much background as possible about the topic, including people, places, things, events, actions, motives, and feelings. Consider the negotiation – reporters must work through Public Information Officers or public relations folks before many people in government, large corporations, and celebrities will talk to them. Negotiation issues typically include topic, time and length, and the venue where the interview will take place. The more prominent the interviewee is, the more complicated the negotiation is likely to be.

    Prepare a question list and sequence the questions so they flow smoothly. But during the interview, it's important to: 1) formulate follow-up questions on-the-fly, 2) know when to depart from the interview plan and explore emerging areas in more detail, and 3) frame questions to illuminate the underlying meaning of an interviewee's previous answer.

- Interviews for investigative articles call for considerably more thought and planning than other types of stories require. The more the article entails controversy and damage to persons, institutions, or interests – the more it requires pre-planning.

- Interviews are on the record. Everything.

- Identifying and enlisting sources is a key part of a journalist's jobs. Reporters talk to people. They just walk up to them or call them up, introduce themselves as a journalist, and start asking questions. They check the internet for articles in other publications to see who other reporters mentioned or interviewed. Twitter is particularly important when looking for eyewitnesses or unusual sources. They also attend telephone and press conferences.

    Some sources talk to reporters as part of their job. Others are flattered when asked for their opinion. Other sources require some convincing to talk to a journalist. In these cases, the best appeals are FACE – fame, advancement, conscience, or ego.

    No matter the source's motivation, reporters must make clear from the outset their intent to publish what they learn. Some sources may be reluctant to be publicly identified. In those cases, the reporter can elicit information by making agreements about the rules of engagement and how the reporter will cite the information. Once agreed-to, the reporter may re-open negotiations again to try to change the rules, but both parties must agree to any changes: If the source won't agree, the reporter must stick by the original agreement.

- The first challenge is to get the information according to the rules of engagement, even if the reporter must agree not to publish it at all. (Of course, it's important to make every effort to arrive at an agreement short of not publishing it!) However, just knowing what the source thinks is going on can be useful in asking other people questions.

    - **On the record** – The reporter can write anything said or done and attribute it to the source, without restriction.

TRADITIONAL TOOLS & TECHNIQUES

- **On background** – The reporter can use the information to find out more about the story. The reporter can write and publish the information. However, the original source must remain hidden and attribution given to someone who states the information on the record.
- **On deep background** – The reporter can use the information but not in direct quotation and not for attribution. The reporter writes it on his or her own or finds an on-the-record source.
- **Not for attribution** – The reporter can use the information but must attribute it to a mutually-agreed-upon, unspecified source, e.g., "a source close to the investigation," or "a high-level administration staffer," precisely as called for by the agreement with the source.
- **Off the record** – The reporter can't use the information at all unless another source provides it on the record.
- **Source attribution** is important to all professional journalists. It identifies who made a statement or provided information that appears in a story. Attribution allows the public to know where information came from and to assess for themselves the provenance of reported material and the quality of the source. In writing the story, reporters can attribute information to a source with a direct quote, an indirect quote, or an accurate restatement of something a person said.
- Make sure the information a source offers is valuable before agreeing to provide anonymity. Press for supporting documentation of whatever claims the source makes. Ask: What other evidence exists? Consider whether the source's fears of retaliation or other unpleasant consequences seem justified. Look for other sources for the information who will go on the record and evidence that supports or disconfirms the source's claims. And talk with your editor. Finally, if the information is worth pursuing, establish the most secure communications possible – maybe even in-person IRL.

KEY CONCEPTS AND TERMS

- Traditional techniques from "shoe leather" journalism: observation, interviewing, and finding, recruiting, and handling human sources
- Preparation for interviews and conducting them
- Source handling and attribution of source-provided information
- Rules of engagement for interviews
- Operational security (opsec), information security (infosec), and communication (comsec) for journalists

EXERCISES AND ACTIVITIES

1. Observing a place: Using a good dictionary, sit in a small room (conference room, living room, dining room, bedroom, etc.). Write a list of every object, including architectural features (door handles, latches, frames, etc.) and every other object in the room.

2. Observing people and process: Go to a coffee bar and watch several customers come in, order coffee, pay for it, wait for it, receive it, and drink it (or leave with it). Describe every person and interaction that you observed.

3. Prep for an interview with a high-profile person: Choose a journalist or celebrity whose work you follow. Conduct background research on the person, then compile an interview question list for a 30–45-minute interview with that individual. What would you like to know? Who would be an audience for such an interview and what would that audience want to know?

4. Prep for an interview with an eyewitness: Find someone who has recently attended a sports event, a party, a lecture, or a rally/demonstration. Prepare a question list. Conduct the interview.

5. Choose a subject in your local environment that interests you. Make a list of what you think is going on in that environment. Find and recruit an informant who participates in that environment and ask them what they think is going on. How close is your assessment to your source's views?

ADVANCER

Chapter 7 covers the last step of newsgathering – perhaps the most important step: Verifying information and authenticating digital objects. It examines how journalists and news organizations evaluate the accuracy and credibility of information, particularly information found online. It provides procedures for verifying the reliability of sources. It also presents specific verification methods, including triangulation, multiple sourcing, and crowdsourcing.

It highlights the importance of extracting metadata information from still images and provides state-of-the-art expert resources to authenticate them. Finally, it looks at the limited palette for authenticating video footage.

7

IN VERIFICATION VERITAS

Chapter Learning Objectives

After studying this chapter, students will be able to:

1. Know how journalists assess validity of information and the reliability of sources.
2. Compare and execute methods used to verify information: triangulation, multiple sourcing, and crowdsourcing.
3. Confirm internet use via website ownership, email service, and message routing.
4. Understand the nature and implications of digital information and metadata.
5. Use verification procedures to confirm social media sources and information.
6. Authenticate photographs.
7. Understand proposed techniques to authenticate video footage, in light of the proliferation of deepfakes.
8. Construct a "truth sandwich."

The essence of journalism is a discipline of verification.

– Bill Kovach and Tom Rosenstiel, 2014

THE GIST

Kovach and Rosenstiel's influential text brought a heightened awareness of the need for stringent verification and authentication to professional journalism. They stressed the practice of verifying the accuracy of information by using multiple sources to confirm it, which comprises a fundamental tenet in most newsrooms. Multiple sources can include knowledgeable persons in addition to documentary evidence, such as photographs, official records, and other materials.

Only one segment of news journalism carries out careful fact-checking and verification procedures as a standard procedure: The mainstream news media. Fake news sites don't have to verify. Tabloid papers don't verify, although they usually cover themselves by finding a source who will claim that the tabloid's information is accurate (and sometimes it is). In contrast, professional reporters working for reputable news organizations must verify new or contested information. Reputable journalists do not publish unconfirmed rumors. (Sometimes when rumors or unconfirmed facts have already entered the public realm, careful journalists report it, but make clear in the article that the information is unverified.)

In an era of fake news, explicit verification forms the basis for building public trust in news reports – and in the journalistic enterprise. Phillips (2014) concluded that: "...the gathering of facts, *obtained via a range of identifiable and verified sources*, is the ideal and any departure from this standard is frowned upon as a professional failure. Indeed, verification is the key factor that, according to journalists, separates what they do from unpaid amateur bloggers."

The verification process is time-consuming and sometimes difficult. Thorough verification may delay a story's publication, allowing some other, less diligent fact-checking reporter to get the scoop. Under pressure, reporters may be tempted to rely on the accuracy of sources they trust. But failing to verify key information carries risks: When reportage proves inaccurate, unfair, or even false, journalists' careers may recover – but sometimes they don't.

A Rape on Campus, a longform story published in *Rolling Stone* magazine, described a purported rape at the University of Virginia. It now offers a cautionary tale of the professional consequences resulting from insufficient verification (Erdely, 2014). The sensational article that made an initial splash turned into a journalistic disaster because the reporter and her editors failed to verify foundational information provided by their main source. The result disgraced all the journalists involved – from the reporter through to the editor (Coronel, Coll, & Kravitz, 2015). Retracted in its entirety about four months later, the story spurred multiple successful high-profile lawsuits against the reporter and *Rolling Stone.*

This chapter provides resources to verify facts, photographs, graphics, video, and data. Today's reporters have a vast range and volume of online information that transforms the process of verification. It exponentially expands the number and types of sources available to query and evaluate knowledge claims – right from reporters' desktops.

During the coronavirus pandemic, the importance of accurate and timely information assumed an outsized importance. Yet misinformation and disinformation flourished during the early months of the crisis, causing the World Health Organization to characterize the situation as an **infodemic**, infecting people by means of:

- State media in some nations
- Social media and
- Text messages

Verification, using many of the techniques described in this chapter, emerged as a critical tool for journalists to combat the infodemic. For example, agents targeted African Americans with content that assured them that the melatonin in their skin would protect

IN VERIFICATION VERITAS

them from the virus (Mahadeven, 2020). And a video on Youtube showed a woman in scrubs, claiming to be a nurse, who insisted that 5G cell towers caused the illnesses attributed to virus. YouTube took down that video as well as other false content on the platform. Other social media networks adopted policies and techniques to eliminate such material from their services as well.

Remember this: In addition to the countless lives lost to the pandemic, many, many people lost their lives because of the infodemic. Political leaders prioritizing stock markets over people, minimizing or denying coronavirus lethality, community-transmission, or refusal to direct "social distancing" demonstrably increased both infection and death rates, according to Johns Hopkins University and the Medical Coronavirus Resource Center (2020).

FIGURE 7.1

Created, 1894: Charges of fake news and sensationalism are not new

Credit: F. Opper, extracted from illustration, "The fin de siècle newspaper proprietor.jpg." Retrieved from: Wikimedia Commons.

An old newsroom adage advises, "If your mother says she loves you, check it out." In the excitement of a hot scoop or unfolding drama, it's surprisingly easy to forget this maxim. Nevertheless, whether in doubt, certainty, or rushed: Believe the voice of experience – check it out, even claims of motherly love.

AND THE WINNER OF TODAY'S INTERNET CLICKERAMA IS …

First! Exclusive! Most! Latest! These keywords just keep the clicks coming. The pressure of the 24/7 news cycle, coupled with fierce competition, ensures that many journalists feel pressure to file reports before fully verifying all the information. Sometimes reporters add cautionary notes – "here's what's new, but it's not yet confirmed." Print and some broadcast journalists whose newsroom cultures require that they must wait for confirmation before publishing a story derisively call the rush to publish unverified reports as "never wrong for long." This unresolved professional conflict spurs vibrant but contentious discussions that impact a central tenet of journalism: accuracy. The need for verification is a principle that goes to the heart of the journalistic endeavor.

Some people have a strong suspicion that many reporters do not verify information from their sources and that frequently reporters allow themselves to be played by their sources. Stephen Colbert, in his biting performance at the 2006 White House Correspondents' Dinner (Kurtzman, 2006), captured this cynical view perfectly:

> But, listen, let's review the rules. Here's how it works.
>
> The President makes decisions. He's the decider. The press secretary announces those decisions, and you people of the press type those decisions down. Make, announce, type. Just put 'em through a spell check and go home. Get to know your family again. Make love to your wife. Write that novel you got kicking around in your head. You know, the one about the intrepid Washington reporter with the courage to stand up to the administration? You know, fiction!

UNEASY CONCLUSIONS ABOUT VERIFICATION PRACTICES ...

Shapiro, Brin, Bedard-Brule, and Mychajlowycz (2013) conducted a study that examined: 1) how journalists felt about their own verification practices, and 2) how journalists confirmed information. The researchers asked 28 Canadian journalists to reconstruct the verification process they used for a single newspaper story. Analyses of the reconstructions showed reporters used multiple diverse strategies, including: 1) source triangulation, 2) analysis of primary data sources and official documents, and 3) semi-participant observation. These journalists supported verification. But they also described compromises and limitations inherent in the process, particularly in selecting *which facts* required verification.

Shapiro et al. (2013) found extensive variation in verification procedures. "Proper names, numbers and some other concrete details were typically verified with greater care than some other types of factual statements. Alternatively, statements were frequently relayed, with or without attribution, based on a single subject's word," the researchers concluded. Moreover, journalists typically *did not re-verify information* they had obtained from earlier reporting.

Silverman (2013) confirmed that reporters verify the most basic information carefully, noting that some journalists checked names against official sources. But he also found that reporters differed in how they checked the accuracy of the quotes they used. Some reporters recorded and transcribed their interviews, but others usually don't transcribe interviews unless there are questions, problems, or lawsuits. Most journalists said they avoid allowing their sources to see stories before publishing them, confirming usual newsroom practice. However, that proscription may be changing, as Shapiro and colleagues noted: "Despite some evidence in the literature that partial pre-publication review is not the taboo it used to be (Carr, 2012; Stoltzfus, 2006), our subjects displayed a strong sense that it was a discouraged practice" (p. 667).

One area that reporters typically do *not* try to verify includes facts about subjects' personal experiences. Often, it is simply impractical to verify how someone felt about their elementary school, how good their parents were, or when they first used alcohol or drugs. Thus, facts revealing intimate details of someone's life experiences usually remain shrouded in the mists of memory.

These and other studies find that working reporters are not so cavalier about verification as Colbert mockingly suggests. Still, many reporters aren't always as thorough as they should be. The prevalence of fake news means that the stakes have been raised for mainstream news organizations in all democracies.

Vox Verbatim: Callie Schweitzer, Editorial Director of Audience for *TIME* and Time Inc.

We handle breaking news in the way it should be handled: carefully but quickly. We diligently check our sources and confirm what we can ourselves. We do it with the accuracy that does justice to our readers and with the velocity that keeps us a part of the conversation. We also work to advance the story as much as we can. [...] Ethics are everything in decision- making. We are very cognizant of the power we have when we hit the publish button, and because of that, we spend time discussing what the right approach is for us – whether it's about the use of anonymous sources or showing graphic images or video.

Are the ethical rules different for online? The ethical standards are just as high and important online as they are on any other platform, be it print or on social media. If we make a mistake, we are completely transparent with the audience about it. We issue a correction notice at the very top of the piece.

WHY BOTHER? VERIFICATION DOESN'T SELL PAPERS ...

Oops, maybe it does! In their influential book, *The Elements of Journalism*, Kovach and Rosenstiel (2014) made a systematic and persuasive case for verification as vital to maintain the credibility and success of contemporary journalism:

1. In the networked, digital environment, online journalists must differentiate themselves and their work from the citizen and participatory journalism of the users for whom they work.
2. Journalists' credibility and that of their news organizations more generally demand that journalists not just deliver the news carefully and truthfully – but also that they be *seen* to deliver it carefully and truthfully.
3. Journalists must bring *accurate* information to their readers and listeners, so that users can navigate the complex, interconnected world they live in.
4. The process of verification requires: 1) objectivity of newsgathering methods, 2) transparency about methods and limitations, and 3) respect for the audience's right to evaluate the accuracy and completeness about published news stories and reports.

Some people think that objective reporting requires that journalists cannot have personal opinions or biases. Kovach and Rosenstiel debunk that definition of objectivity. Like everyone, reporters have histories, perspectives, an education, personal quirks, and preferences that inevitably inform their journalistic perceptions and judgments. Kovach and Rosenstiel stress that in professional settings, whether for therapists, scientists, physicians, or journalists, objectivity does *not* mean that they are without opinions. Rather, professional objectivity requires that they employ appropriate objective methods.

Doctors use stethoscopes on patients whether they look healthy or not – or whether the doc likes the patient or not. Similarly, regardless of personal leanings, reporters must bring the same tools, procedures, and principles to their newsgathering, verification, and reporting. The finished news product must be "defensible, rigorous, and transparent," say Kovach and Rosenstiel (2014, p. 10).

THE VERIFICATION TWO-STEP: "THAT OUGHT TO BE EASY!"

Sometimes it is. The two steps sound simple enough:

Step 1: Establish the **reliability** of the source.

Step 2: Verify the **validity** of the information.

The reliability of a source depends upon a source's consistent accuracy. When a source has given a reporter valid information each time they provide it, say ten times, that source is consistent. Thus, reporters consider sources reliable when they:

- Have track records of providing accurate information over time.
- Are in a position to know, such as an eyewitness, official, expert, spokesperson (spox), colleague, and friend or family member.

Valid information requires that the information provides an accurate representation of the "real world" the information purports to describe. Valid information must correspond to an actual situation in the real world. The gold standard for validity: The reporter saw it with her own eyes.

Consider this thought experiment: Someone tells a reporter: "There is a white house with blue trim at 442 E. Lexington Avenue." This statement is either accurate (valid) or not: The white house is there or not; with blue trim. The reporter can physically go to 442 E. Lexington Avenue and establish the validity of the information. Or they might compare the claim with information on satellite-enhanced maps, such as Google.com, or Zillow.com to verify its presence and description. But it's possible those sites haven't updated the Lexington address recently – thus the websites might show a tan house with white trim. Or perhaps the owner painted the trim green after the online photographs or videos of the house were taken. Worst of all, the video might be a deepfake, one that has been altered. In these cases, the validity claim via online sources is second-hand ... and therefore riskier.

Many facts are approximately accurate, not absolutely accurate. The ten-year U.S. Census illustrates this dynamic – it provides a superb statistical representation of the U.S. population – one that's far from perfect. Taking the Census cost about $12.3 billion in 2010. Yet our census systematically under-represents difficult-to-find populations, people who are homeless, on extended vacations outside the country, or somehow become unreachable. Others may not respond for personal reasons or just refuse to be surveyed.

Despite its flaws, the Census provides the most accurate information available about the number, demographics, and living conditions of U.S. residents. Gaps always exist between the perception, appearance, and measurement of most phenomena and their actual states. Thus, claiming that census data provides accurate population descriptions really means that, although census information isn't perfect, this data is as accurate as reasonable resources, human census-takers, government statisticians, and reporters can establish.

Finally, some seemingly factual information may be inaccurate or even entirely false. For example, a source reports: "He was really angry. He yelled, slammed his desk draw shut, then stood up and kicked the wastebasket under the desk." The first sentence conveys an opinion – the reader cannot be sure the actor wasn't pretending (or exaggerating) anger. But the second sentence factually describes behavior.

When verifying information, both reliability and validity (accuracy) matter. But, perhaps counterintuitively, the information's accuracy is more important than the source's reliability – particularly when the reporter–source relationship first begins. Why? Reporters can *only* establish the reliability of their informants for accurate information over time. Thus, *the continued accuracy of information provides a referendum for the source's reliability.*

However, the reverse is *not* true: Reporters cannot guarantee that information provided by a single source (and sometimes even multiple sources) is accurate. Thus, no matter how reliable the source, reporters should always confirm the validity of sources' information by all means possible.

Verifying secret material and/or deliberately hidden information entails surmounting a panoply of hurdles that range from concealing journalistic activities from the government or other powerful actors, to risking severe legal or extralegal retribution, to collaborating with unethical individuals or entities. The 1976 movie *All the President's Men* offers a fascinating window into the creative lengths that journalists sometimes take to confirm vital information that can't be verified by other means.

NOT JUST THE FACTS, MA'AM

Most news articles report verifiable facts. **Facts** are data points: the people, places, things, events, answers, and statements that occur and are subsequently linked together. Even when journalists investigate or provide analysis, they should begin by analyzing the facts.

Inferences, in contrast, are conclusions drawn from known facts. Thus, inferences depend on the accuracy of the facts upon which they rest. We each make inferences throughout our daily lives: We interact with people and infer their purposes, motivations, and even their future intentions. Journalists' inferential processes resemble the ways most people make sense of their worlds, but journalists' processes are more structured, based on systematic examinations of the evidence, logic, and experiences on their reportorial beats. And reporters' inferences are reviewed by editors, publishers, and sometimes lawyers before publication – a system which tends to reduce any undue rush to judgment.

The goal of inferring conclusions from facts and fact-structures is to reveal plausible versions of "the truth." **Truth** captures the reality behind related and relevant facts. Because the underlying nature of reality and truth have been debated by great philosophers for thousands of years, reporters must let the public make final decisions about controversial and contested truths.

As inferences prove to be true, they become known facts. However, facts themselves may be disputed, as well as the relevance of any facts to a given situation. *The Washington Post* columnist, David Ignatius (2017) pinpoints the public's need to know more about the origin of facts:

> The Internet giants such as Google and Facebook should be tuning their systems to establish the **provenance** [bold added] of fact. I'd like to see them using machine learning to interrogate supposed facts to establish where they've been – how they first surfaced, and how they were passed from user to user. If there are gaps in provenance – an unexplained missing link in the chain of evidence, or signs of misattribution – then those anomalies should be flagged automatically.

Party time!

Facts:

Twenty-year-old Erin Cole lives with her parents near the college.
It is 1:20 am on a Friday night (morning).
The front door and living room curtains stand open.
About 40 people in the room are talking, gesturing, and laughing.
Some people have on party clothes.
A dining table has a punchbowl, chips and dip, and cake on it.
A chair has a helium-filled balloon tied to it that says *Happy Birthday*.
In the backyard, six people smoke in a huddled group.
Loud music streams from Spotify.
A few people are dancing.

Provenance:

First-person accounts from party-goers and neighbors

> **Inferences:**
> It's somebody's birthday.
> Erin has quite a few friends.
> Erin's parents are out of town.
>
> **Truth:**
> When her parents left town for a weekend, Erin invited her friends over to celebrate her 20th birthday, and the partiers had a blast.
>
> **Alternative truth (of Erin's parents):**
> When her parents left town for a weekend, Erin's horde of friends came over; they made fools of themselves, raised hell, and kept the neighbors awake.
>
> **Conclusion:**
> The facts are straightforward. The inferences likely are correct. The truth? That depends on the perspective and experience of the person defining the truth.

WHAT YOU NEED TO KNOW ABOUT METHODS TO VERIFY INFORMATION

Verification may simply require contacting multiple sources to corroborate information. It may also involve observation or checking records and online databases. For artifacts – documents, physical evidence, photographs and other graphics, videos, and data sets – a news organization may employ outside experts who use advanced technological tools to verify the accuracy, completeness, provenance, and authenticity of important artifacts.

Even when authentic-looking documents appear to confirm well-known rumors, reporters can pay the price for failing to carry out adequate verification. Just ask former CBS anchor Dan Rather and *60 Minutes II* producer Mary Mapes. Photocopied letters purportedly written by one of George W. Bush's National Guard commanding officers surfaced, and the show aired a segment covering them.

After the broadcast, controversy exploded, sometimes known as Memogate or Rathergate. An independent panel (Thornburgh & Boccardi, 2005), reviewed the verification process and found it inadequate: The letters had not been and could not be authenticated as true copies of original documents. Had appropriate verification taken place, the segment would not have aired and the participants' reputations (including that of CBS News) would not have been tarnished. The ensuing controversy caused Mary Mapes to be fired and may have accelerated Dan Rather's retirement.

THE 2 FLAVORS OF TRIANGULATION: MULTIPLE SOURCES AND MULTIPLE TYPES OF SOURCES

Many news stories begin with a single account of an event or situation. Reporters then place calls to other sources to get confirmation and additional views. If possible, journalists attempt to get independent versions from people without skin in the game, if such persons exist, or perhaps have less at stake than do primary participants. If journalists can get three or four accounts, they sift through them, looking for agreement, differences in perception, areas of disagreement, and inconsistencies.

Even multiple sources may not provide an adequate basis for a definitive account, but perhaps some information can be disconfirmed or falsified. Further, journalists can: 1) share processes of corroboration and verification, 2) lay out evidence, and 3) point out weaknesses, gaps, contradictions, and inconsistencies. Journalists thereby help readers to draw their own conclusions as they seek to understand and interpret important events. And sometimes just falsifying a story can lead to other important stories.

Reputable news organizations regard single-sourced stories with great concern. But sometimes it's not possible for reporters to get more than one source for a story. At Reuters, such a story may be escalated to the top editors within the company. Consider the guidelines for such reports issued by Reuters (2019):

> Stories based on a single, anonymous source should be the exception and require approval by an immediate supervisor, such as a bureau chief or editor in charge. The supervisor must be satisfied that the source is authoritative [...] For a single source story, the informant must be an actual policymaker or participant involved in the action or negotiation with first-hand knowledge, or an official representative or spokesperson speaking on background. Such information should be subject to particular scrutiny to ensure we are not being manipulated.

Verifying information by gathering several different forms of that information is called "triangulation" – and it's a valuable tool for confirming material sources. The term triangulation draws from geometric concepts developed for geographic navigation and surveying by ancient Greeks, as shown in Figure 7.2. By knowing the distance between two known points, ancient mariners triangulated that information with a third point, permitting them to calculate the distance to that third point.

Journalists have adapted the principles of triangulation to corroborate information. To verify accounts of events, reporters seek to confirm what they learn from a second, third, or even more perspectives. **Methodological triangulation** takes this process a step further. It means gathering confirmatory information from additional *types* of sources, such as material from official records, receipts, emails, or even databases – evidence that

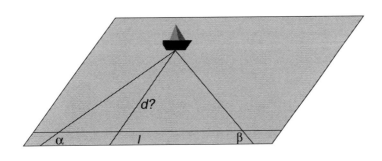

FIGURE 7.2

Triangulation in navigation

Source: Regis Lachaume, Licensed under GNU Free Documentation License

supports accounts from interviewees or other sources. Confirmatory (or disconfirming) evidence comes in many forms:

- Additional interviews with informed individuals.
- Numerical data, such as election results, census data, public and private studies, budgets, and program assessments, etc.
- Documents, scientific studies, public and private studies, and written records such as letters, emails, minutes, agendas, announcements, diaries, receipts, sign-in sheets, etc.
- Legally required public disclosures such as financial filings, individual and corporate disclosures, and public transaction records.
- Official records, including court, business registration, and governmental agency filings.
- Documentary evidence: videos, audio, photographs, maps, and other artifacts.
- Personal observation and records of previous interviews.

Triangulation with expert trusted sources became crucial during the COVID-19 pandemic because of the co-occurring infodemic of false and misleading content on the internet. The U.S. Center for Disease Control was slow to ramp up, so journalists turned to an array of other sources to confirm the facts in their reports. Within two weeks, many sources provided a panoply of information and data that journalists around the world used to verify data they received through their own reporting. These sources included:

- Johns Hopkins University and Medical School (excellent all-around source)
- Johns Hopkins Bloomberg School of Public Health
- *Lancet* (Medical journal (U.K.)) and *New England Journal of Medicine* (U.S.) (widely accepted sources of peer-reviewed research)
- *New York Times* (collection of global data, far surpassing official U. S. government sites in quality and timeliness)
- *Washington Post* (excellent data visualizations and simulations)
- *Vox.com* explainer (excellent comparison of COVID transmission, with and without social distancing)
- JournalistResources.org, FirstDraft.com, and NiemanLab.org (useful sources on how journalists can cover the pandemic that apply to other emergencies as well)

Methodological Triangulation: Uncovering, Documenting, and Confirming the Extravagant Travel Expenses of (Former) Health and Human Services Secretary Tom Price

The story came from a sketchy tip, as part of a "casual conversation with a source" (Diamond and Pradhan, 2017). The lead was that Tom Price, Secretary of the U.S. Department of Health and Human Services, was spending huge sums of money on travel, instead of using less expensive, commercially-available flights. It took *Politico* reporters Diamond and Pradhan months – more than 1,000 hours – to uncover information and verify their story's vital elements. Here is a timeline of their efforts:

- May: *Tip from source that HHS Secretary Tom Price was using private jets for routine travel*
  - Compiled database of Price's trips
  - Meetings and phone calls: contacted sources in and outside of HHS
  - Used news sites to find Price's out-of-Washington, D.C. speeches and appearances
  - Tracked appearances on social media
  - Reviewed HHS summaries of meetings
- August: *HHS staff began sending reporters advance notice of Secretary's travel*
  - Enabled checking with charter services for date/times when commercial flights were available for Price's use
  - Enabled charter airport stakeouts by reporters
- September 15: *Advance notice given that Price would travel to Philadelphia from Washington, D.C. (about 125 miles) via private jet from Dulles Airport. Reporters:*
  - Watched the arrival of two SUVs with police escort. Several people got on the plane but couldn't identify specific individuals
  - Tracked flight on www.Flightaware.com to Philadelphia
  - Tracked Price and Kellyanne Conway in Philadelphia via sources and social media posts; thus, knew when the event ended
  - Staked out the charter terminal at Dulles and saw Tom Price deplane from same aircraft (arriving from Philadelphia)
- Post-September 15: *Reporters gathered information to document cost comparisons of private jet versus commercial air and ground travel*
  - Called charter plane companies to learn costs of private jet trips
  - Checked commercial flight schedules and ticket prices
  - Checked cost of rented SUV to travel between Philadelphia and Washington, DC
- September 18: *Reporters called repeatedly to request meeting or phone call with Price about the story*
  - Requests rebuffed by HHS
  - HHS issued a statement, saying charter travel was used for public health emergencies, and there was no violation of federal travel regulations
- September 19: *Reporters published the first story in Politico*
- Post-September 19 story: *Reporters carried out additional investigation*
  - Examined history of previous trips in database
  - Used U.S. government website (USAspending.gov) to search database to document expenditures on private charter contracts for Price's travel
  - Searched airport data from U.S. airports to gather precise dates and times of Price's departures and arrivals
  - Matched Price's travel dates and times with government expenditure data
- September 21: *Reporters published the second story in Politico*
- Post-September 21 story: *Reporters carried out additional investigation*
  - Examined database for anomalies in Price's travel
  - Found government-paid travel to Simons Island and Nashville, when no events scheduled, apparently for personal reasons
    - Simons Island: Price owned land there and visited with colleagues
    - Nashville: Price lunched with his son, who lives there
  - Examined Price's travel via military aircraft
    - Found such travel cost more than $500,000 and he took his wife with him
    - Compared Price's travel practices with those of previous HHS secretaries
- September 28: *Published the third story in Politico*
- September 29: *Price resigns.*

TAPPING THE WISDOM (AND CAPACITY) OF THE CROWD FOR VERIFICATION

In addition to enabling extensive online verification, the digital age now permits crowd-sourcing efforts to document information that is essential to investigative stories. Verification via crowdsourcing requires providing access to unverified information to many users, who are then asked to find anomalies or to confirm or disconfirm its accuracy. Chapter 1 described how *The Guardian* newspaper, faced with examining a huge dataset of expense reports filed by Members of Parliament of the United Kingdom's House of Commons, crowdsourced the verification of the reports. The publication asked online readers to check each report and to flag suspicious expenses – ones they thought were potentially false, inaccurate, or invalid expense claims. Because *The Guardian* encouraged its users to serve on behalf of the civic good, many readers examined those records and flagged questionable entries. *Guardian* journalists then checked flagged expenses and verified that many of them were indeed improper.

The use of Twitter to provide a real-time verification platform during breaking news events is more controversial. Although Ingram (2012) believes that the benefits of using Twitter can outweigh the disadvantages, he cites two problems with the practice:

1. Serious negative consequences may attend sending out inaccurate information over the internet. Others pick it up and spread it before the correction can catch up – if it ever does. Thus, there is concern among journalists that releasing inaccurate stories does more to propagate misinformation than to disseminate verified news reports. Instances of releasing inaccurate information occurred concerning the shootings at Sandy Hook and the Arab Spring protests in Egypt.
2. Twitter's short messages may make it impossible to send out: 1) the new information along with, 2) cautions about its unverified nature.

It's not possible to reconcile these concerns with the traditional process of holding information inside the newsroom until it can be checked, re-checked, verified, and re-verified. Yet, in the Twitterverse, where so many people have mobile megaphones, especially during emergencies and unrest, information gets out anyway and is *never* verified or corrected. Indeed, governments facing civil disturbance sometimes put out **disinformation** to serve their own ends (Chen, 2015).

Many news organizations now find crowdsourcing useful for newsgathering. But they typically believe that verification requires more careful approaches, carried out by professionals. For example, while *The Guardian* outsourced the first level data analysis – the thousands of pages of expense reports from the Members of Parliament – its journalists handled the final analyses and verification.

THE PROS KNOW: 3 GUIDES TO VERIFICATION

Kovach and Rosenstiel's nine-point guide provides an overview of the verification process, which includes principles and questions for reporters to use. The Protess method tags individual pieces of information and organizes facts by their closeness to reported events – eyewitnesses, documents, hearsay, etc. Finally, European perspectives from two *Verification Handbooks*, including a chapter describing verification policies of the German publication, *Der Spiegel*, offer fully-articulated standards and procedures for reporters to follow.

Steve Buttry (2014) wins the Occam's Razor award for the most succinct confirmation guide with his famed two questions that reporters must ask (and answer) about information they have gathered:

- How do you know that?
- How *else* do you know that? (Buttry credited newsroom coach Rosalie Stemer with the second question)

> **An Awesomely Excellent Starting Point**
>
> Kovach and Rosenstiel (2014) suggest that reporters begin verification procedures by asking themselves four questions, and offer a set of principles they should follow:
>
> Questions:
>
> 1. What does the news audience need to know to make a judgment about the factual accuracy and value of this story?
> 2. Have I explained how I know what I have claimed to know?
> 3. Do any of the ways I have handled this work need an explanation?
> 4. Have I acknowledged what is not yet known?
>
> Principles:
>
> 1. Never add anything that was not there originally.
> 2. Never deceive the audience.
> 3. Be as transparent as possible about your methods and motives.
> 4. Rely on your own original reporting.
> 5. Exercise humility.

THE PROTESS METHOD

As director of the Medill Innocence Project at Northwestern University, David Protess taught students how to find and confirm evidence. His lessons included: "Assume nothing is true. Go directly to the source. Don't rely on just the authorities or officials. Touch all bases. Be systematic" (Dean, n.d.).

The Protess method arranges information into a hierarchy, placing the source of presumed facts into three concentric circles:

- Inner circle: Direct observation or knowledge of report and people who are directly involved in some aspect of the story.
- Middle circle: Primary source documents, e.g., official records, testimony, transcripts, etc.
- Outer circle: Secondary sources, including press accounts.

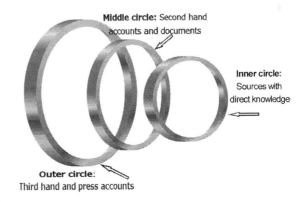

FIGURE 7.3

Protess method information source categories

Credit: Joan Van Tassel

The process involves categorizing the sources of information, starting with sources who have direct knowledge of the events or communications:

Inner circle: Cathy tells a reporter: "I saw Dave erase the email and he said, 'That takes care of that!'"

Middle circle: Second-hand sources of information about what happened: Mary, Cathy's officemate tells a reporter that "Cathy came out of his office and said, 'Dave just erased the email he sent to the commissioner.' I don't think he knows it's stored on the server." Some documentation may be second-hand as well.

Outer circle: Third-hand information from another press account, background information, documentation, or someone who heard about the event from someone who heard it from an eyewitness: Mary's friend tells a reporter that "Mary said that Cathy went into Dave's office and saw him erase the email."

Most facts originate from within the inner circle – from participants, eyewitnesses, or physical evidence. (As Chapter 6 noted, proximity does not guarantee accurate observation.)

However, much of the information journalists acquire falls into the second or third circles: background information, documents and records, the police who arrived on the scene, the neighbor who says the murderer was always such a pleasant guy, or the aggrieved congressional constituent who says her representative is in the tank for special interests.

If they weren't on-the-scene observers themselves, journalists try to reach people who were, talking to as many of the participants as they can. It is riskier to make inferences and assumptions about facts based on information that comes from sources at a distance from the events – from the middle and outer circles. However, documentary evidence and secondary accounts may provide compelling evidence to reinforce information from the inner circle.

Many stories take time to unfold, so journalists may need to construct several sets of concentric circles. A political candidate for office ran in a primary – that's one set of circles. After winning, the candidate goes statewide or national and suddenly there is a new cast of characters, new events, and a new set of Protess rings.

THE VERIFICATION HANDBOOKS

Every discussion of the verification of news information in the online environment benefits from an examination of the *Verification Handbook* (Silverman, 2014) and the *Verification Handbook for Investigative Reporting* (Silverman, 2015), both published by the European Journalism Centre (EJC). The EJC intended the first handbook to help journalists verify information about emergencies, when initial coverage has been notoriously inaccurate (Sood, Stockdale, & Rogers, 1987).

In addition to providing an excellent summary of best journalistic practices for verifying information emergencies, this handbook helps journalists covering many types of breaking news events. In one chapter, Silverman and Tsubaki (2014) lay out the elements of a powerful process that serves as a starting point. Although some parts focus on disaster coverage, the Silverman and Tsubaki checklist is well worth reading in its entirety. Users can download both handbooks in a .pdf file format.

The second handbook, the *Verification Handbook for Investigative Reporters*, offers invaluable resources – every aspiring digital reporter should download a free copy (available at http://verificationhandbook.com/downloads/verification.handbook.2.pdf). It shows how to do advanced Google searches using operators that enable thorough, efficient searches. It also provides a guide to unearthing a wide range of information about persons, corporations, and social media posts that will allow journalists to verify information both about sources and the content of their claimed facts.

Der Spiegel, German Weekly Magazine

Writing in the *Verification Handbook for Investigative Reporting*, Jannsen (2015), described verification procedures that *Der Spiegel* follows. This publication provides an excellent example of best practices for fact-checking and verification. How thorough is the magazine's editorial team?

> A 2008 thesis produced at the University of Hamburg counted all the corrections made by the documentation department in a single issue of *Der Spiegel*. The final count was 1,153. Even if we exclude corrections related to spelling and style, there were still 449 mistakes and 400 imprecise passages, of which more than 85 percent were relevant or very relevant.

Jannsen noted that the key elements of the *Der Spiegel* guidelines include checking all facts with reliable sources or experts, sourcing factual corrections and quotations, and notification and acceptance of corrections by the author. Editors confirm times, dates, locations, names, and titles. Editors also maintain a written record of each step in the process to assure that they have followed the procedures.

FACT-CHECKING IN REAL TIME

Fact-checking of all news reports matters. But in the heated news cycle of the digital age, what value does reporting the results of a fact check in a week or two, a day or two, or even an hour or two really offer? Journalists ponder that question as the public faces a whole new menu of stories by the time the fact check comes out. Journalist and educator Bill Adair at Duke University, founder of PolitiFact, led a team to develop software that could carry out fact-checking in real time.

The software, called *Squash*, translates spoken language into written text, analyzes it for factual claims, then reaches out to databases to assess the validity of the claim. If the analysis includes live speech, the program posts a rating of the accuracy of the claim. Such software may have additional uses for rapid fact-checking of written texts as well. Reporter Jonathan Rauch vividly described his experience watching results of real-time fact-checking carried out by software. This could be a glimpse into a future of artificial intelligence-enhanced live news.

Vox Verbatim: Jonathan Rauch, Contributing Writer at *The Atlantic* and *National Journal* and a Senior Fellow at the Brookings Institution

It's February 2019, and I'm waiting to see whether a robot will call the president of the United States a liar.

At the appointed time, President Donald Trump comes into view. Actually, not at *precisely* the appointed time; my feed is delayed by about 30 seconds. In that interval, a complicated transaction takes place. First, a piece of software – a bot, in effect – translates the president's spoken words into text. A second bot then searches the text for factual claims, and sends each to a third bot, which looks at an online database to determine whether the claim (or a related one) has previously been verified or debunked by an independent fact-checking organization. If it has, the software generates a chyron (a caption) displaying the previously fact-checked statement and a verdict: true, false, not the whole story, or whatever else the fact-checkers concluded. If Squash, as the system is code-named, works, I will see the president's truthfulness assessed as he speaks – no waiting for post-speech reportage, no mental note to Google it later. All in seconds, without human intervention. If it works.

[...] Monitoring from my kitchen table in Washington, D.C., I grew uneasy as the first minutes of Trump's speech ticked by and no fact-checks appeared on the screen. Finally, about five minutes in, the first one popped up. It was laughably off-target, bearing no relationship to what the president was saying. Several more misses followed. But then came several that were in the ballpark. And then, after about half an hour: bull's-eye.

The president said, "In the last two years, our brave ICE officers made 266,000 arrests of criminal aliens, including those charged or convicted of nearly 100,000 assaults, 30,000 sex crimes, and 4,000 killings or murders." It was a claim he had made before, in similar words, and the software recognized it. As Trump spoke, a chyron appeared quoting a prior version of the claim. Alongside, this verdict: "Inflates the numbers."

A few minutes later, a second bull's-eye. Trump:

> The border city of El Paso, Texas, used to have extremely high rates of violent crime, one of the highest in the entire country, and [was] considered one of our nation's most dangerous cities. Now, immediately upon its building, with a powerful barrier in place, El Paso is one of the safest cities in our country.

Beneath his image appeared, again, a prior version of the claim, plus: "Conclusion: false."

[...]

> Of course, outrage addicts and trolls and hyper-partisans will continue to seek out fake news and conspiracy theories, and some of them will dismiss the whole idea of fact-checking as spurious. The disinformation industry will try to trick and evade the checkers. Charlatans will continue to say whatever they please, foreign meddlers will continue trying to flood the information space with junk, and hackers of our brains will continue to innovate. The age-old race between disinformation and truth will continue. But disinfotech will never again have the field to itself. Little by little, yet faster than you might expect, digital technology is learning to tell the truth.

(Rauch, 2019)

VERIFYING USER-GENERATED CONTENT AND EYEWITNESS MEDIA

When important news breaks, reporters will lurk on Twitter, Facebook, and Instagram, waiting for eyewitnesses to post comments, pictures, and videos. In breaking news situations, newsrooms must decide very quickly whether to use user-generated content (UGC) such as tweets, photos, videos, and posts to blogs and social media sites. Users can provide evidence not otherwise available to establish the facts of the story or to add dimension to it with personal experience. However, reporters must exercise restraint and caution in the wild environment of the internet. Wardle (2014) suggests that reporters begin from the position that the information is incorrect. However, when Anthony de Rosa (2014) was Editor-in-Chief at Circa.com (since closed by Sinclair Media), he wrote that he used information from social networks and a tweet as "a lead to follow in a more traditional way."

News organizations increasingly use UGC in their reports. Researchers at the Eyewitness Media Hub, located at the Columbia Journalism School's Tow Center for Digital Journalism, provide evidence demonstrating that TV news, web news sites, and newspapers routinely use UGC (Wardle, Dubberley, & Brown, 2014). Many TV channels use UGC at least once a day; some use it much more than that. For example, the 24/7 TV news channels average more than 11 uses of UGC per day; Al-Jazeera used 51! Newspapers were even more varied in their use of UGC.

Wardle and colleagues (2014) also interviewed journalists who expressed five areas of concern with using UGC in news reports:

1. **Workflow**: News professionals are not sure how to set up the organizational infrastructure to routinize the use of UGC, in terms of processing the material and staffing. Reporters and editors obtain UGC content through one of four ways:
   * Finding people already on the scene who have or can take or get footage at the location of the news event
   * Asking viewers directly to send photographs or videos to the newsroom
   * Searching social networks to locate material themselves and embedding, downloading, or screen grabbing it
   * Negotiating with agencies or other professionals to secure the rights to material and obtain it

2. **Verification**: Journalists are skeptical about one-size-fits-all models of verification. "The question of checklists and systemized processes was asked of every interviewee. There was resistance about the need for standardized verification systems, with people arguing that every piece of content is different and on desks where UGC is regularly used, there was an acceptance that staff just knew which checks had to be completed."

3. **Rights clearance**: Rights clearance calls for obtaining permission from legal copyright holders to use and distribute their original material, expressed as terms and conditions. Publications may not be clear about when fair use governs publishing UGC.

4. **Crediting**: Although credit should be given to users who upload content, such recognition occurs sporadically and inconsistently, both on-air and online. The research found that:
   * TV channels credited about 15 percent of UGC footage. There was wide variation – CNN came in highest, crediting UGC slightly more than half of the time. Interviewees cited time pressure, workflow difficulties, screen clutter, and viewers' lack of memory for failing to credit original sources, as best journalistic practice requires.
   * Newspaper sites were more likely to credit UGC uploaders, identifying half of all UGC content uses, either by an explicit mention on their site (30 percent) or by embedding the link and taking their users to the site where the uploader posted the material (19 percent).
   * Inaccurate credit presents problems. Wardle et al. found content attributed to platforms, and thus inappropriately credited the material to a platform: YouTube, Flickr, Storyful, etc. Even worse, some vague credits included: "Image courtesy: Procured via Google search" or "Source: Internet image."

5. **Labeling**: Labeling UGC as eyewitness video, photograph, comment, or tweet is important because it offers a way for the audience to assess the material's credibility. The research found that TV news channels labeled UGC only about one-fifth of the time. Newspaper sites were much better, labeling UGC about four-fifths of the time.

Wardle and colleagues called for journalists and newsrooms to take a more careful and ethical approach to the use of UGC. Such an approach would include careful consideration of the most appropriate manner to treat uploaders, the audience, and the newsroom staff. More attention should go toward obtaining rights clearances, crediting, and labeling.

TOOLS OF THE TRADE FOR VERIFYING UGC ON SOCIAL MEDIA PLATFORMS

In addition to its usefulness in newsgathering, UGC from social networking sites also provides resources for verification. Pay services such as Geofeedia (www.geofeedia.com) and Echosec (www.echosec.com) help identify the time, username, and sometimes the geographic location of tweets, Facebook posts, YouTube videos, and Instagram posts. For some platforms, Geofeedia and Echosec may also confirm the user's content through the historical lookbacks. Finally, when user settings allow it, GeoSocial Footprint (www.geosocialfootprint.com), lets reporters find social media activity by location and see Twitter users on a map.

When confirming facts about someone's background, paid services may help turn up information, such as Spokeo (www.spokeo.com), that offer paid-service searches for people on multiple databases, including some official records, social networks, and even dating websites. Just enter a name, email address, or username and let the search site do the rest. However, many investigative journalists become experts at searching public databases, which yields much of the same information as the paid services uncover.

Another option is to use the multi-search tool from Storyful, if reporters install a browser plugin for Chrome that enables the entry of a search term, such as a username. Returns include results from Twitter, Instagram, YouTube, Tumblr, and Spokeo. Each site opens in a new browser tab with the relevant results. However, the news organization must subscribe to Storyful. Most social media platforms have individual search tools, so journalists can opt to carry out this detective work themselves.

(All these readily available sites, engines, and apps should make thoughtful persons reconsider their social media footprints. Remember: The internet never forgets!)

CONFIRMING EYEWITNESS ACCOUNTS POSTED ON SOCIAL MEDIA

Consider when a reporter needs to assess the reliability of a self-identified eyewitness who tweets a thread about a massive earthquake that just occurred in Uruguay. How can anyone be sure this self-identified eyewitness isn't sitting on a patio in Tucson? How about the embedded photo – is it real? Did it come from Uruguay around the time of the earthquake? Who originally took it? Who owns the rights to the photo? All these questions need answers before a publication can publish the information and photo.

It's not so much finding and identifying a needle in a haystack as it is searching for a star in the universe. "Accidental journalists," people who are at the scene of a news event by happenstance and snap a photograph or shoot video with their mobile phone, are one kind of eyewitness. People who are part of the scene because they have a stake in the event – a member of Green Peace, aid group worker, a border watcher – are a different kind of eyewitness. Each observer has a unique perspective, a distinctive social reference group, and perhaps an agenda for recording, uploading, and disseminating the event.

VERIFYING ONLINE INFORMATION: SITE-SEEING ON THE NET

Who says something is almost as important as *what* they say because knowing the source of information allows an assessment of the source's expertise and motives. In the 18th century, when the framers of the Constitution wrote the First Amendment, most speech took place in person. But the rise of the printing press added anonymous writing to speech, making it possible for the fractious colonists to elude capture by the British authorities. The internet further separates the speech from the speaker, the writing from the writer, and the video from the shooter.

However, governments (and network-aware journalists) often pull together the resources to discover the identities of people online, even when they try to hide who they are. For example, the internet Wayback Machine (http://archive.org/web/web.php) works against any regular poster, providing many clues that lead to unmasking writers' real-world identity. Searches of this historical archive by social media platform, related topics, language, and usage may uncover earlier messages when network members were not so careful. Mapping the target account's links to others (and those links to still others), thus building an online personal network, can point to potential candidates. Finally, information about the owners of websites can also lead to the discovery of a user's identity.

Where information surfaces is important as well. Many people assume that information published by schools, colleges, universities (.edu sites), and organizational sites (such as nonprofit groups; .org sites) is accurate. It usually seems reasonable to assume that websites operated by government units and agencies (.gov) take care to provide reliable information.

In truth, a degree of skepticism is essential no matter where the material comes from: Although a reporter can be reasonably sure that the information published on many of these sites is correct, that is not always the case. Technological systems are not perfect, and they may make errors or break down altogether. People make mistakes. They also might fudge records or hide and suppress evidence of their own and others' mistakes.

Reporters must assess the usefulness and accuracy of the information on each site on a case-by-case basis. Most sites' home pages provide information about the identity of the creator, whether individual or organizational. If that information is not immediately apparent, look for an "About" button. Of course, the creators of the site also write their own "about" pages or biographies; nevertheless, a quick read often reveals the objectives of the site's owners. When establishing the credibility of a website, a good rule of thumb: If something seems weird or "off" – it probably is.

A reporter's career depends on a clear-eyed view of the authenticity and provenance of information. Journalists recognize that there are vast differences in the quality of the information provided by *all* entities, whether their domain ends with .edu, .org, or .com., or .fun. Here's a great example:

1. Navigate to this URL: https://archive.org/web/ (the Internet Wayback Machine)
2. Input this Uniform Resource Locator (URL) into the "Browser History" field: http://departmentofhumanmanagement.org/

It's a .org site, so it appears to be a quasi-governmental or nonprofit site that anyone could rely on, right? Visually, it looks right, too. *Not!*

This was a spoof-site for the *Strain Trilogy* book series. It instructs humans how to donate their blood to the victorious vampire nation that won an earlier fictional war between the humans and the vampires. It looks authentic because the graphic designers modeled the site after the U.S. government's site for the Social Security Administration, www.ssa.gov. *Remember this: Every government and many people around the world can create this kind of online spoof.*

"*Our site is at the corner of Google and Facebook.*"

It's important to learn how to navigate the internet – it's not always easy, since there are no corner signposts on the internet. But there are internet addresses; each website has an **IP address**, where "IP" stands for Internet Protocol. These addresses are all numbers, so to make it easier for people, websites register a readable text name called a **URL, Uniform Resource Locater**, such as Google.com, amazon.com, or ucla.edu. The URL identifies a unique website; users type the URL into the address bar of a web browser to get to the site.

URLs have three basic parts: the **protocol**, the **server name**, and the **resource ID**. Look below at the Pew Internet's URL to see these three parts. The protocol is shown at the beginning of the URL before the double slash (//); the server name is between the double slash (//) and the first single slash (/); and the resource id is everything after the first single slash (/).

Let's examine each part of this URL:

- **Protocol** (http://)The protocol identifies the method (set of rules) by which the resource is transmitted. All web pages use HyperText Transfer Protocol (**HTTP**) or HyperText Transfer Protocol Secure (**HTTPS**). Thus, all web URL's (including Pew Internet's site) begin with http.//or https.//.
- **Server name** (www.pewinternet.org/)

The server name identifies the computer on which a resource is found. This part of the URL commonly identifies which company, agency, or organization may be either directly responsible for the information or is simply providing the computer space where the information is stored. (Web server names often begin with the letters **www**, but not always). The acronym "www" stands for World Wide Web, which is one network of networks, commonly called the internet. However, private networks of networks (internets) also exist.

The server name for the example (pewinternet.org) belongs to the Pew Internet organization, part of its Pew Research Center (www.pewresearch.org). **Servers** are specialized computers that store and "serve up" web pages. The server name may also be the name of a **website**, but it doesn't have to be. A web site is a complete group of web pages that are organized as a comprehensive set. Web sites can be either all the pages on one server (computer) or all pages under a specific subdirectory.

The server name always ends with a dot and a three-letter or two-letter extension called the **top-level domain name**, or **TLD name**. The top-level domain name is important because it usually identifies the type of organization that created or sponsored the

IN VERIFICATION VERITAS

resource. Sometimes it indicates the country where the server is located. The most common top-level domain names are:

- .com which identifies company or commercial sites
- .org for non-profit organization sites
- .edu for educational sites (accredited schools of all kinds are eligible)
- .gov for government sites
- .net for internet service providers or other types of networks

Most searches pull up websites with the .com suffix, because they are the most common TLD. The websites of most news organizations have a .com suffix, as do most blogs and commercial sites – including the publisher of this book. However, fake news organizations can have a .com domain, as do most sites that plant malware on visitors' computers. In other words, a website's authenticity may require verification. Only .edu sites and .gov sites must provide proof of their status before they can reserve a URL with those TLD extensions.

If the top-level domain name is two letters, not three letters, it identifies a country, e.g., **.us** for the United States, **.uk** for the United Kingdom, **.au** for Australia, **.mx** for Mexico or **.ca** for Canada.

- **Resource ID** (2017/10/19/the-future-of-truth-and-misinformation-online/)

The **resource ID** provides a roadmap to a specific file, listing all subdirectories under which it is located on the server. The Pew Internet web site consists of all the web pages on that server, organized into the subdirectories, /2017 and /10 and /19 where the organization stores this resource: /the-future-of-truth-and-misinformation-online/. (By the way, it's well worth reading!)

A **homepage** is the main page for a web site that provides links to all the other pages on the site. The part of the resource ID after the last slash (/) is the individual **file name** for the specific page or other resource. The file name ends with a three or four-letter designation that specifies the **file type**. Common file types on web sites include **.htm** or **.html** to bring up standard Web pages, **.jpg** or **.gif** to display pictures, and **.pdf** and **.docx** to view or download documents. The forward slash at the end of the URL signifies the end of the URL.

WWWHO OWNS AND OPERATES THAT WWWHERE?

It is often possible to learn a great deal about a website through an internet website **whois lookup** on the Internet Corporation for Assigned Names and Numbers (**ICANN**) website http://whois.icann.org. Another resource is the Pwhois.org utility at http://pwhois.org/index.who. Both services list a great deal of information about a website, as shown in Figure 7.4.

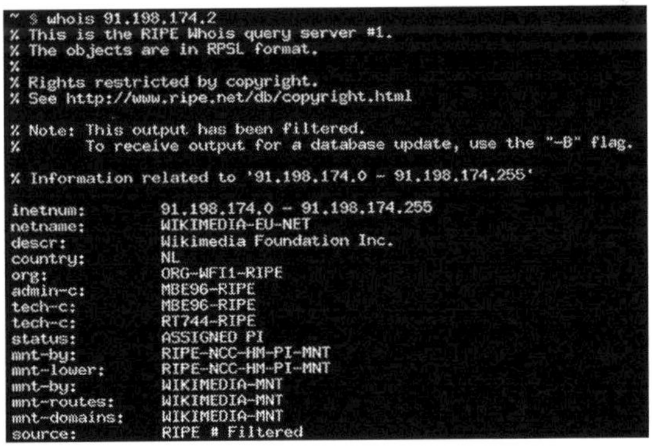

FIGURE 7.4

Screenshot: Whois domain lookup page

Credit: By Zeroos – Own work, Public Domain, https://commons.wikimedia.org/w/index.php?curid=3443598

Internet searches on the terms listed below can prove helpful. A paid service, DomainTools, provides a list of information reporters might seek. A free site offering many of these tools is: http://viewdns.info/.

- **Whois Lookup** – Provides the most current ownership record for a domain name. This service is free on domaintools.com and many other sites.
- **Whois History** – Search historical domain ownership records to reveal prior owners or aliases, and it can help journalists establish timelines.
- **Reverse Whois** – Search the Whois database by name, phone number, email address, or other information to link domain names to the search information.
- **Reverse IP Lookup** – Key in an IP address, and it will return all the domain names hosted by the web host at that IP address.
- **Reverse NS Lookup** – Key in a nameserver and receive all domain names that use the same nameserver.
- **Reverse MX** – Provide the name of the email server and receive all domain names served by this email server.

EVALUATING DIGITAL EVIDENCE: DIGITOLOGY 101

Verifying and authenticating information from the internet, including UGC content, requires a level of knowledge about computers and digital artifacts – pictures, audio, video, and so forth. Without this foundation, the procedures for analyzing photographs and videos sound more difficult and complicated than they are, at least for journalists to make preliminary judgments whether a piece of content is genuine or fake. The next section provides that background "under the hood" information.

Everywhere, it's digital this and digital that. In modern usage, the word "digital" applies to the system of binary representation used in computer processing. Before computers, it just referred to fingers and toes: the first human calculator! According to Webster's dictionary, digital also means counting, and now it brings other ideas to mind, such as "binary," and "high-quality, clear pictures and sound." **Analog** is an alternative system for representing information. Analog is a shortened form of "analogous," which means "similar to or comparable with."

One way to understand the difference between analog and digital is to think of them as alternative ways of representing information. Analog data is **continuous**, reproducing information in a smaller form. Digital is **discrete**, one point of data at a time. Consider the analog and digital watch faces in Figure 7.5.

On the clock, if people know that the little hand represents the position of the sun, and that "6" is either early morning or late afternoon, they can then make a rough estimate of the time

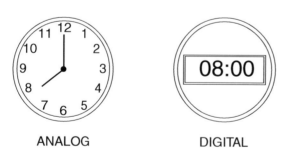

FIGURE 7.5

Analog and digital: Two ways to measure and present the same underlying reality

Credit: James Bromley

without reading the Arabic numerals. In contrast, the digital display shows a single minute in time, in Arabic numerals only. If the person isn't familiar with these numerals ... well, they're flat out of luck, because they lack the visual cues of the point-for-point representation that the analogic system provides.

Not only does the analog watch give the time as 8:00, within a visible continuum of points – it's really an analog (analogous) to the sun moving around a sundial, approximating the 12 hours of sunlight, then the 12 hours of darkness. The digital watch shows 8:00 as a discrete, isolated point in time. "Discrete" does not refer to a person who doesn't gossip (spelled discreet); rather, it means separating something into distinct categories. Once again: Analog data is continuous; digital data is discrete, as shown in Figure 7.6.

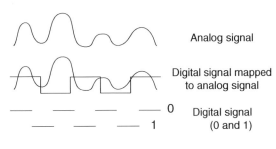

FIGURE 7.6

Making continuous information into discrete digital data

Credit: Joan Van Tassel

Analog is everywhere too. In fact, the world itself is an analog place and the human perception system is inherently analog. (You're not going to dance to a stream of 1s and 0s unless it is converted to analog sound.) Information about the analog environment is converted into digital data, manipulated at warp speed, and then re-converted back into an analog form so that people can see and hear it. One reason it is so hard to protect digital content is that digital data streams must eventually come to an analog device.

VERIFYING PHOTOGRAPHS ... DIGITOLOGY 102

Someone took a specific picture, at an exact time and place, using a specific camera, adjusted to particular settings, and saved it in a predetermined format. Today's digital cameras encode this information and sometimes more, into every picture at the point of capture. Reporters who know how to find this information can use it to evaluate the authenticity of pictures posted on the internet.

This information embedded within the picture itself is called **metadata**. Metadata means "data about data." ("Meta" means "about," so metadata literally means "about data." And since metadata is itself data, the usual definition of the term becomes "data about data.")

Figure 7.7 shows how important metadata is, even in the analog world. Otherwise, people wouldn't know if they're buying black beans, olives, or coconut milk ... OK, maybe it's "metacannedgoods."

FIGURE 7.7

Metadata makes life easier

Credit: Joan Van Tassel

2 WAYS TO VERIFY DIGITAL PHOTOGRAPHS

A reporter wants to use a photo posted on a social media service. The poster claims they took the picture at some time and place. How can a journalist verify those claims? There are two issues of concern:

- Are the described circumstances of taking the photograph true?
- Has the photograph been altered since it was taken?

And there are two fundamental ways to try to answer those questions. The first is to use the metadata. It tells you a great deal both about the means of taking the photograph and whether someone might have altered it afterward. The second technique is to examine the picture itself. The photo should conform to weather reports, position of the sun, topography, cultural artifacts like dress, signage, architecture, and so forth.

TECHNIQUE #1: START WITH METADATA

Digital cameras embed metadata as they save pictures. Many cameras save several types of metadata, each describing different characteristics of the photographic event and the picture, as shown in Table 7.1. After the photo leaves the camera, some external-to-the-camera applications can add even more metadata.

There are two types of metadata.

- *Structural metadata* from the camera describes technical information about the photograph, embedded within the picture itself as the camera saves it. It is a permanent part of the picture (Krawetz, 2015).
- *Informational (or descriptive) metadata* may come from the camera as well. Depending on the camera and its software, it can include the camera type and settings, lens type, many technical details about the picture, and the date the picture was taken (important for establishing copyright). Some camera software allows users to add descriptive metadata, such as titles, comments, tags, credits, and other annotations.

In addition, many photo editing applications add informational metadata that documents modifications to the picture after it left the camera.

TABLE 7.1 Metadata types and sources

	Origins of Metadata	
From Cameras	*From Applications*	*From Either*
MakerNotes	ICC Profile	File EXIF
PrintIM	IPTC	JFIF
	Photoshop	APP14
	XMP	

Credit: Based on table at: http://fotoforensics.com/tutorial-meta.php#IPTC by Hacker Factor, FotoForensics

It is possible to "strip" informational metadata from the picture (Krawetz, 2015). Photos posted on Facebook, Twitter, and other services have metadata stripped out automatically. However, if an individual claims a photograph is an original, the very absence of metadata is itself suspicious.

A horde of users know how to remove metadata as well. Editing metadata to make a false image appear as if it were taken at a news scene doesn't take a genius. Anyone can find a metadata editor to change any of the data in a metadata field and geo-tag a batch of photographs manually. Internet searches for "strip metadata," "manually input geo-tags in metadata," or "metadata editor" will bring up many such utilities and programs, including professional metadata editors requiring supergeek knowledge level.

Journalists can find many metadata reader services online. One site is FotoForensics.com, which also provides useful expert tutorials about authenticating photographs. On the home page of most of these online sites, users upload a photo, as shown in Figure 7.8.

The online service reads the metadata attached to the photo and returns the results to the user in clear text, revealing much information about the photograph. There is an alphabet soup of metadata types: EXIF, IPTC, Maker Notes, File, PrintIM, ICC Profile, JFIF, and SBIM, and other proprietary metadata embeds. The tutorial on metadata at FotoForensics.com offers information about many of these types of photographic metadata.

The results for the graphic analyzed in Figure 7.9 displayed five metadata types, as well as a composite photo profile. The figure shows three of the metadata reports.

GeekSpeak Alert!

The **file metadata** provides information about the data structure of the photograph. Here goes: It is a **JPEG (Joint Photographic Experts Group)** image type, 2,007 pixels wide and 2,434 pixels high. A clever coding scheme made the overall file size of this picture smaller than it would be in RAW format, in a manner described by 8 bits per sample, the three color components (Y-Cb-Cr, 4:4:4), and chrominance subsampling. Later metadata says the resolution is 300 pixels per square inch. Hmmm, maybe Table 7.2 will help.

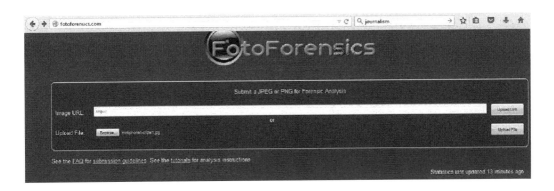

FIGURE 7.8

Screenshot: Home page with input fields for www.fotoforensics.com

Credit: http://fotoforensics.com/tutorial-meta.php#IPTC by Hacker Factor, FotoForensics

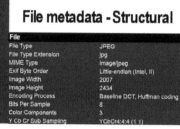

FIGURE 7.9

Screenshots: Metadata structural file, IPTC, and EXIF
Credit: Screen grab with permission from Hacker Factor, FotoForensics

TABLE 7.2 An informal translation of technical jargon

	Geekspeak Deconfabulator
File (black banner)	"File" indicates that all data that follows (until the next black banner) is structural metadata.
JPEG (Joint Photographic Experts Group) image type	A bunch of (mostly) guys sat around a table and decided: "This is how we'll do it!" The same fellas also standardized JFIF (JPEG File Interchange Format) so all machines could read .jpeg files.
EXIF Byte: Little-endian (Intel, II)	Describes the sequential order of the bits and bytes (8 bits) for the camera information, whether bytes arranged from big-to-small or vice versa.
2,007 pixels wide and 2,434 pixels high	The photograph is 6.7" by 8" at high resolution.
Baseline DCT, Huffman coding	A lossless compression scheme to reduce the picture's file size.

Geekspeak Deconfabulator	
JPEG image described by 8 bits per sample	Tells how the device created the jpeg image with 8 bits for each sample (usually **pixels,** contraction for "picture element").
This JPEG picture was encoded in the YCbCr color space, 4:4:4	The device then subsampled the color information for greater color fidelity.

Conclusion: The metadata describe this iPhone Snapchat as a JPEG-compliant photograph. It is a good-sized picture with adequate resolution to look good online and in print. (The size and resolution are probably not high enough to blow up for a highway billboard, though.)

EXIF Metadata

The most common type of informational metadata is **Exchangeable Image File (shortened to Exif or EXIF)** because many camera manufacturers use it. EXIF embeds informational metadata about the camera settings used at the time the photograph was taken, such as the camera make and model, the lens settings, the creation date and time, resolution, and a great deal more. If the camera is GPS-enabled, it will also add location data. In addition, if anyone altered the photograph, it shows the program they used and the date they modified the picture.

IPTC Metadata

The press has its own metadata, standardized by the International Press Telecommunications Council (IPTC). In addition to technical information, the metadata includes the photograph byline, description, location, and more, shown in Figure 7.9. It also allows entry of copyright information.

Not all digital cameras provide a way to enter the photographer's name, photo description, and other details. To add that information, photographers enter the IPTC metadata using application software, usually with the same program used to edit the photo. A photo accompanied by detailed text fields in the metadata may indicate someone might have modified the picture.

XMP Metadata

XMP metadata refers to the Adobe Extensible Metadata Platform, a widely compatible text block that furnishes information included in EXIF and IPTC records. Apple's iPhoto and Quicktime programs also generate XMP records, but they are not nearly as extensive as the ones generated by Adobe applications. Since XMP metadata shows the original EXIF data, if someone modified the photograph – cropping, resizing, etc. – the XMP data will differ from the EXIF data, revealing that the photo has changed from the original. XMP data provide considerable information about any modifications to the photograph, including:

- *Tool identification*: XMP typically includes the name and version of software that was used to edit the file and when these edits occurred.

- *History*: XMP records may include a summary of modifications, such as a record of each time the file was saved or converted. This does not specify *what* happened; it only indicates that *something* happened. But a long history of edits implies that the photograph was manipulated.

- *Sources*: When multiple pictures are combined, the XMP block will record this photograph as coming from multiple sources. Such a designation does not identify the precise combination, only that there is data from more than a single, original photograph. If a user combined material from more than one source, but then deleted it, the XMP record will indicate additional source data, but will not indicate the removal.

"METADATA EMERGENCY, PAGING DR. KRAWETZ ..."

Dr. Neal Krawetz is the founder of HackerFactor.com, which hosts the FotoForensics site. An expert on authenticating photographs, Krawetz described the value and limitations of using metadata to carry out verification:

> Although metadata does not identify the exact changes made to the picture, it can be used to identify attributes, inconsistencies, additional sources, edits, timelines, and a rough sense of how the photo was managed. In effect, metadata provides clues about a photo's pedigree ... Metadata analysis is one of many different types of analysis. The interpretation of results from any single analysis method may be inconclusive. It is important to validate findings with other analysis techniques and algorithms.

In other words – triangulate, agrees computer scientist Dr. Krawetz.

He also lists common pitfalls of metadata analysis. More complete descriptions appear on the FotoForensics website:

- *Timestamps*: Timestamps can be wrong – they may never have been set properly or adjusted for local time. The camera clock may not be accurate.

- *Misleading*: It is easy to confuse metadata field labels as metadata itself. Be sure to read the actual value that pairs with the data in the field.

- *Inconsistent*: Some digital camera manufacturers do not follow the established rules for metadata fields and labels.

- *Stripped*: Some people strip metadata from photographs. It's easy to do.

- *Hosting*: If the photograph came from Facebook, Twitter, and Imgur, and other social networking sites, there's no metadata – they stripped it. Photobucket and Picasa change it. Forget it – as far as metadata is concerned.

- *Faked*: Metadata editors abound and anyone with a computer and a will can change photograph metadata.

- *Residues*: Be careful with photographs modified in Adobe. When someone brings up a photo in Photoshop, then covers that picture with a second image, the metadata will still reflect the picture from the first photo or it will provide scrambled data.

- *Scanners*: Depending on the settings and the software, the metadata may indicate the scanned photograph came from a camera or an application – not a scanner.

IN VERIFICATION VERITAS

AUTHENTICATING PHOTOGRAPHS: SOMETIMES THE EYES HAVE IT

So far, this section has examined using metadata as a method of authentication and shown that this analysis only goes so far. Journalists can also learn a great deal from the content of photos, as shown in Table 7.3. To find where and how someone might have modified the picture, they may need to zoom into the picture to the pixel level. Or they may need an expert with a microscope.

TABLE 7.3 Finding fakery

Look at ...	Look for ...
1. Lighting	The light that falls on people and objects in a photograph comes from a source and a direction. Look for the most lit part on a shape, then draw an arrow from that lit portion straight away from it, showing where the light had to have been to fall on the shape in that manner. If the area of light on the shape is large, draw several arrows from it. Then, draw one or more arrows for all the main shapes. • Is the light coming from a consistent direction? • If different shapes are clearly lit from different sources, is there a discernible pattern to the different sources: two windows or other apertures, shadows obscuring one shape from the source, two artificial sources? If sources of light come from multiple directions that have no obvious explanation, based on the picture itself, it may be a composite of more than one photograph.
2. Eyes and Positions	When seen straight on, the iris, the colored part of the eye is always round. As the eyes turn to the side, up, or down, they change into a more oval (elliptical) shape, as shown in Figure 7.10. 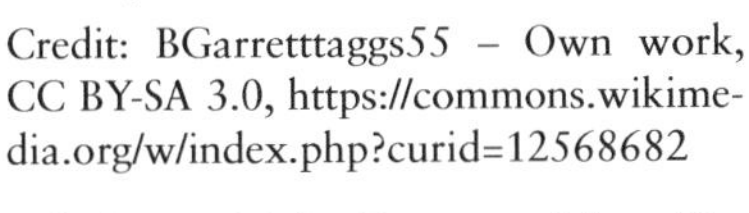

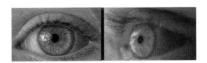

FIGURE 7.10

Blue eye

Credit: BGarretttaggs55 – Own work, CC BY-SA 3.0, https://commons.wikimedia.org/w/index.php?curid=12568682

Figure 7.10 Eyes straight/round iris. Eyes to side: elliptical iris
No attribution required, via www.pixabay.com

Carrying out this process for each person in the photograph should show a consistent "camera center," revealing whether the same camera recorded each person in the picture. If an object in the picture has a known shape and dimensions, an analyst can make the same calculations with it, comparing it to another part of the photo.

Look at …	Look for …
3. Specular Highlights	A close second look at the eyes in Figure 7.10 also show the positions of the light source(s) aimed at the subjects. The eyes of any two people should have consistent specular highlights or there is a chance someone spliced people from different photographs to make them appear together in the same picture.
4. Cloning	This technique is a powerful and not-too-difficult technique for manipulating a photograph. A photo faker wants to take something out that should be there to prove someone is lying. Tools in powerful software programs do the trick – lasso or draw around the part of the picture that comes out, use a clone stamp and a pattern stamp to replicate the background from other parts of the picture, clean it all up with a little erasing and painting and – voila! That object (or person) has disappeared. Carefully done, cloning is difficult to detect, but not impossible. By analyzing blocks of pixels, expert software finds identical and near-identical blocks that are statistically unlikely or do not match adjacent blocks. These findings become clues to consider in the context of other clues.
5. Camera Fingerprints	Retouching a photograph is easy for many people, so fraudsters often re-touch a photo to erase unwanted details. If they do a great job, no one can see it with the naked eye – even by enlarging the photo to the pixel level.
	However, every camera model adds pixel information in a specific way, a recognizable "fingerprint." Retouching changes that information and substitutes added pixel information in the manner of the retouching application. Expert-level software and statistics can unearth significant clues to any retouching, although a scanned photo wouldn't work: the scan would replace the camera fingerprint with the scanner's fingerprint.

Credit: Table based on Farid (2008)

As Dr. Farid's photo identification discussion indicates, authenticating photographs is a complex matter. Savvy new media journalists have three ways to go about photo verification:

- Develop these skills for themselves – take courses, attend workshops, and spend time practicing
- Find an expert in-house maven in the organization
- Contract a trustworthy outside expert to authenticate the photo, hopefully at a price the journalist or their organization can afford.

AUTHENTICATING VIDEO

The Blair Witch Project debuted at the 1999 Sundance Film Festival, held in Park City, Utah, from January 21–31, 1999. The film purportedly told its story through shaky, amateurish "found footage," shot by a group of film students while pursuing the mystery of the Blair Witch. In June 1998, eight months before the festival, the producers established a web site, www.blairwitch.com that chronicled the myth of the Blair Witch from 1785 through 1995. The web site generated buzz before the festival, and it went viral after Sundance – before viral was viral.

The film launched before fake was fake. The entire website was entirely fiction. Made up. Invented. And the film's co-producers and editors, Eduardo Sánchez and Daniel Myrick, created both the spoof site and the supposedly "amateur video" as a money-making publicity stunt. Costing less than a million dollars, the film grossed almost $250 million worldwide (Box Office Mojo, 2015).

The Blair Witch Project changed the horror film genre (Marsh, 2014):

FIGURE 7.11

Recreation of opening shot of film, "The Blair Witch Project"

> The difference is that The Blair Witch Project was conceived around the illusion of authenticity, and a great deal of effort went into sustaining it. Most obviously, it looked real enough: The film was shot and edited as if it genuinely were a work of nonfiction, and, while it was not the first fiction feature to adopt the form of a documentary, it was among the most prominent to do so convincingly.

This, remember, is about a decade before "found footage" entered the lexicon and exhausted its welcome.

Like deceptive photographs, false video is a fact of internet life. It isn't nearly as pervasive, possibly because it requires a higher level of technical skills and investment in computer resources and software to create such frauds. (More than 50 years ago, some people were certain that John Glenn and other astronauts never landed on the moon – that the government produced the video in a studio.)

In the last few years, concern has increased about videos in the news. For example, news organizations around the world used video produced by ISIS that claimed to show the beheading of Kenji Goto, a Japanese journalist. No one disputes the sad fact of the beheading. But questions abound about whether the group shot the video as claimed. Doubts about the authenticity of the video prompted a lively debate. Some weighed in that video was authentic. Others claimed to see evidence that ISIS actually shot the video in a studio in front of a **"green screen"** and substituted a different background (Mendoza, 2015).

In war zones, where journalists may not be able to travel freely, counterfeit videos

FIGURE 7.12

Where is he? A green screen lets editors substitute any image behind the person

Credit: By Whitelamb526 (Own work) [CC BY 3.0 (http://creativecommons.org/licenses/by/3.0)], via Wikimedia Commons

serve the purposes of combatants. When the resources of a government or a well-funded insurgency turn to propaganda and fakery, the stakes go up. On a lighter note, in 2015, a counterfeit video of a drone supposedly striking the wing of a Southwest Airlines aircraft became near-news but turned out to be a nothing more than a publicity stunt. According to *The Dallas Morning News* (Maxon, 2015): "The video shows a winglet colliding with a drone on ascent near LaGuardia Airport. The winglet has SWA colors and branding, but if you look closely it says 'Branit.com,' which is a portfolio site for a special effects artist."

DEEPFAKES: NOW YOU REALLY CAN'T BELIEVE YOUR LYIN' EYES

In 2018, journalists could deal with false or fake videos, such as those mentioned above. However, 2019 brought an unexpected and unwelcome change – **deepfake** videos emerged on the internet in force. The term "deepfakes" get their name by combining "deep" machine learning (a form of **artificial intelligence** or **AI**) with "fake" videos. The first known videos appeared on Reddit.com in 2017, which showed the faces of celebrities instead of the porn stars who actually performed in the videos (Metz, 2019b). In December 2018, a count of deepfakes reached 7,964. One year later, the count rose 84 percent to 14,678, of which 96 percent of porn videos focused on women.

At present, many deepfakes do not look realistic, but improvements in the software used to create them has developed more rapidly than expected. Fake audio is coming too, using computer-generated speech to recreate a person's voice that sounds authentic. Some software developers of deepfake audio-visual creation software have posted their source code on the internet, so companies, researchers, and hackers around the world can collaborate to make rapid progress.

In 2016, an innovative technique called GANs, **generative adversarial networks**, offered the kind of progress that researchers had hoped for. GANs uses two neural network processing architectures to train one another – iteratively implementing changes until the desired change from the source video appears in the target video. GANs are much less processor-intensive than previous techniques. Consequently, in the near future any technically adept person could create do-it-yourself deepfakes with their desktop computer at home. In 2019, even more improvements to deepfake generating software became available: faster, simpler, better. Indeed, startups in the Philippines, India, and other countries offer to generate deepfake media manipulation services for hire (Kumar, 2019).

Internet giants Google and Facebook have invested heavily in programs to identify deepfakes. For example, Google researchers created hundreds of deepfakes with paid actors to learn how to find deepfakes posted on YouTube and other sites (Metz, 2019a). Facebook issued a Deepfake Detection Challenge, funding $10 million in grants and awards for AI researchers to develop algorithms that will uncover deepfake content. Facebook, Google, and Microsoft are also working with the Defense Advanced Research Projects Agency (DARPA) to spur research into deepfake detection as part of the battle against disinformation campaigns.

Researchers at the University of California at Berkeley and the University of Southern California have developed techniques that compare the natural movements and microexpressions of individuals. These techniques, when comparing the same person pictured in a deepfake, detect deepfakes more than 90 percent of the time. In spite of this track-record, Dr. Hany Farid, a professor of computer science at Berkeley, and an expert in image forensics said: "We are outgunned. [...] The number of people working on the video synthesis side, as opposed to the detector side, is 100 to 1" (Harwell, 2019).

IN VERIFICATION VERITAS

Unfortunately, successful efforts at automated detection involve using artificial intelligence to detect flaws in the GANs process have an ironic side effect: Formulas to detect the flaws act to teach the GANs to improve their fake-making process! As Engler (2019) put it: "It's a cat-and-cat game." Engler proposes two ways of combating deepfakes that do not rely on automated detection by AI:

- Create an online public reverse video search service (like current reverse image search services) to allow discovery of the original used to create the deepfake and
- Verify video through block-chain registration that establishes an unchangeable ledger of the original. This process would allow copyright owners and people in deepfakes to access and display the original content to counter the counterfeit.

WHAT'S A JOURNALIST TO DO?

Journalists' verification of video can't stop while experts seek methods for identifying deepfakes. But they can warn news users that they cannot guarantee that a given video is completely real – a true representation of the reality that it depicts. They can "walk" viewers through the verification procedures available to them. These procedures include examining the metadata, considering the context of the scenes, analyzing the video itself frame by frame, and identifying the uploader.

Video metadata is stored on the first frames of the video called the **header**. Professional video machines can read the header, which includes the technical information to allow machines to decode, decompress, and display the video. For journalists, MediaInfo (https://mediaarea.net/en/MediaInfo) is a free, open-source software program that reads and reports out the stored metadata. MediaInfo reads structural metadata from a wide range of audio and video media types. It includes information about the video format, track number, date, duration, bit rate and depth, codec, language, chapters, title, author, director, and tags. The header may also include non-technical text data, such as the title, author, and tags that are added by whoever created, edited, or transferred the video. The MediaInfo software is free, although the creator requests a donation.

Metadata might be useful in identifying the sources of users' original videos posted to the internet, especially to the most popular services. However, when people upload videos to social network sites, such as YouTube, Facebook, and Twitter, these sites' conversion algorithms strip the header and its metadata. Fortunately, other tools permit a determined journalist to verify and authenticate the video.

THE RIGHT TOOLS FOR THE JOB

The *Verification Handbook for Investigative Reporting* and the earlier *Verification Handbook* have sections on authenticating video that offer highly useful and detailed processes to journalists. Any journalists who want to authenticate video should read Malachy Brown chapter on video verificaton (Brown, 2014a). The companion case study (Brown, 2014b) examines a video depicting the horrific aftermath of a reported Ivory Coast massacre. Brown describes in painstaking detail the important questions reporters should ask. He also lists the steps reporters can take to identify and verify the video, particularly for clips posted on social networking sites.

- **Gather context on the video:** Collect as much information as you can about the situation that led to the video. Identify people in the video and those who figure in ongoing political, economic, and social issues. Match the video to the known geography and current infrastructure of the area. Consider past and current conflicts, as well as likely future struggles.
- **Provenance:** Answer the question: Who uploaded the original video? Video footage is often **scraped** from a site and uploaded again by another user. Try to locate the original upload. Use keyword searches (place names, event descriptors, and the names of people, companies, and governmental agencies) to find other copies of the video in question. Use Google Translate to input both the native language and English to make the keyword search.
  - When the keyword search results come back, use the YouTube filter menu to sort the results by "Upload Date," in order to get chronologically-ordered results. Look for identical thumbnails.
- **Verify the uploader:** Each video on YouTube, Twitter, and Facebook has a unique code. On Facebook and YouTube, the code follows the "v=" at the end of the URL in the address field. If the video is on someone's YouTube channel, that unique identifier will be preceded by UC, standing for "user channel." The title will have the name of an uploader, underneath it. Clicking on the uploader's username will take you to the uploader's page. If you click on "About," you will see a description of the uploader or uploading organization – if anything is present.
  Search for that username across other social networking sites. Malachy Brown asks these valuable questions:
  - Are there other accounts, a blog, or website listed on the video profile or otherwise affiliated with this uploader?
  - What information do affiliated accounts contain that indicate recent location, activity, reliability, bias, or agenda of the account holder?
  - How long have these accounts been active? How active are they?
  - Who are the social media accounts connected with and what does this tell us about the uploader?
  - Can we find whois information for an affiliated website?
  - Is the person listed in local phone directories, on Spokeo, Pipl.com, WebMii, or LinkedIn?
  - Do the source's online social circles indicate proximity to this story/location?

- **Locate the video:**
  - Examine any text accompanying the video and clues within the video picture.
  - Within the video, look for features you can locate through searches:
    - Landmarks: rocks, hills, buildings, prominent towers, churches, mosques, universities
    - Infrastructure: roads, bridges, railroad tracks, signs, poles
    - Geographical features: vegetation, mountains, hills, fields, ports, rivers, streams, trees
  - Use the tools:
    - Wikimapia: A crowdsourced version of Google Maps where users outline and describe local identifiable landmarks and features
    - Google maps: Each view – maps, terrain, satellite, and street, and user photographs – helps identify where a photograph or video was recorded with additional confidence.

- **Verify the date:**
  - The upload date is not necessarily the creation date of the video
  - Weather reports for the area on the day purported to be the creation date are clues, but not sufficient to verify a claimed date. (See www.wolframalpha.com to search past weather reports.)
  - To know the time of day the video was recorded, look for shadows. Go to www.suncalc. net, which shows the position of the sun at a particular place and time. The sunlight casts a shadow from objects opposite from the position of the sun.
  - Amnesty International released and maintains the YouTube Data Viewer. It will provide the unique code for the video, the upload date and time, and accompanying text.

An account of an actual verification process by Eliot Higgins (2015) helps us understand how making assumptions about the video and how to use some of the tools works in tracking down the provenance and location of a video clip:

> These videos were on social media accounts and several different websites, all of which belonged to different individuals. They were uncovered by first geolocating the initial videos we found, then using that to predict the likely route those vehicles would have taken to get from each geolocated site. Then we could keyword search on various social media sites for the names of locations that were along the route the vehicle would have had to travel. We also searched for keywords such as "convoy," "missile," etc. that could be associated with sightings.

FRAME-BY-FRAME ANALYSIS

Victor Ribiero (2015) wrote an account of how the careful frame-by-frame analysis of a video freed an innocent man in Brazil. On October 15, 2013, the police arrested activist Jair Seixas, who was marching in a protest, for allegedly setting fire to a police car and a minibus. Another activist livestreamed a video of the arrest on his mobile phone.

To prepare for his trial, the defense team examined three hours of the archived livestream, frame by frame (324,000 frames). One frame proved Seixas innocent: It showed that the vehicle in which police took him away was the very vehicle they accused him of setting on fire!

Frame-by-frame analysis shows camera stops and points to edits in the footage. Most amateur videos, especially when shot on mobile phones, are shaky and full of movement, some of it random. Sometimes single frames of these movements reveal surprises, as one did in the Seixas case.

The right tool for this job is video editing software, although the VLC media player will also work. There is usually a toggle button, switch, or setting to enable stepping through the video one frame at a time. The VLC media player, the free Avidemux video editor, and prosumer software like Final Cut Pro, Adobe Premiere, and Vegas Pro will all work.

EXPERTS

When all else fails, the news organization can call on experts to weigh in. These analysts usually work at major universities that offer advanced programs in signal and image processing, where they work in specialized laboratories. As of 2019, they can identify many kinds of altered video. However, presently no tools consistently and reliably identify deepfakes.

Consolidated Verification Checklist

- Make a plan – listing each story element that needs verification.
- For each fact, ask:
  - How do you know that?
  - How *else* do you know that?
- Triangulate:
  - Draw on your human sources.
  - Consult credible sources and experts.

> - Consider where there might be supporting evidence: official records, meeting agendas and minutes, documents, emails, and surveillance cameras, etc.
> - Check if maps, satellite shots, or weather reports corroborate the story's account?
> - Draw from online sources and social media, compare user-generated content to other sources, then contact story actors and witnesses to talk with them.
>   - Use the technical tools available to you to examine digital objects – stills, video, etc.
> - Use the right tools for the job: Stay current.
> - Verify the provenance of all digital objects – photographs, graphics, data and data analysis, audio, and video recordings.
> - Verify *both* the source and the content.
> - Be skeptical when something looks, sounds, or seems too good to be true.
> - If you need help, ask for it.

NEW VERIFICATION INITIATIVES

In the past decade, awareness of fake news has spurred efforts to support the verification of reported information. In 2005, the First Draft Coalition (FDC) formally initiated intensive collaboration to establish procedures, training, and support services for journalists who use social media and need to arrange for and verify UGC and eyewitness content (Sargent, 2015). The FDC is a joint initiative supported by companies and groups with UGC verification expertise, including Bellingcat, Eyewitness Media Hub, Emergent, Meedan, Reported.ly, Storyful, and Verification Junkie. The FDC tries to promote robust discussions within the journalistic community that center on journalistic ethics, verification, copyright, and content protection for journalists and their news organizations when they use UGC or eyewitness content.

Supported by the Google News Lab, the FDC creates training materials, a database of case studies, and other resources including tools for journalists. The FDC makes these resources available online along with information about discovering content, verification, and using best practices for ethical and legal guidelines. One of the FDC members, Meedan, makes open-source software called Check that enables collaborative sourcing and verification of social media content (see https://meedan.com/en/check/).

The same day that the First Draft Coalition announced its presence, two members of the FDC, Google News Lab and Storyful, launched another new initiative. Journalists seeking eyewitness video can obtain footage pre-verified by Storyful, if their organization pays for the service. Just as the traditional paid wire services, like the Associated Press or Reuters, fed stories to print publications, Storyful now provides verified social media videos to online sites and broadcasters.

Lichterman (2015) wrote: "Since its founding, Storyful has verified more than 100,000 different videos on the platform [YouTube]." Storyful works with YouTube to cover breaking news in several areas, particularly politics; the two companies have partnered in various capacities since 2011. Together they've worked on projects such as CitizenTube and the Human Rights Channel. Storyful also worked with YouTube to cover breaking news and elections around the world through dedicated channels. Now owned by the parent company of Fox News, News Corp., Storyful-managed videos have accumulated more than 2 billion views.

"I'LL HAVE A TRUTH SANDWICH ON A PLATE OF EVIDENCE"

When the evidence indicates that misinformation or outright disinformation has circulated, what can journalists do? There's a format for that called the Truth Sandwich. It's a useful way to identify inaccurate information when it needs to be debunked – without amplifying the false material.

Linguist George Lakoff formulated the Truth Sandwich to address such situations (Sullivan, 2020). He advised journalists to structure the exposure of false information in the following way:

1. *State the truth.* (The first statement shapes users' understanding.)
2. *State the misinformation/disinformation and its source.* (It's important to debunk the source as well as the claim.)
3. *Repeat the truth.* (It's worth repeating and important to speak the truth more often than the lies.)

TAKEAWAYS

- Verification is the process by which journalists assess the reliability of sources and the accuracy of information. Reliability means that a source has consistently provided accurate information in the past. In addition, reporters verify that the person has the requisite expertise or is positioned to know the information's validity.

  Establishing the accuracy of basic, concrete facts such as name, title, educational and work histories, date and time, and location, is usually straightforward. Confirming a source's account or second-hand information may often prove difficult; and verifying reports of purposefully hidden facts and activities typically takes persistence, time, and ingenuity. Similarly, authenticating photos, videos, documents, and signatures often requires specialized expertise – often news organizations obtain expert analysis for important stories.

  Journalists may make inferences from verified facts. Inferences are not facts; they are judgments and conclusions based on the overall fact structure and knowledge of the particular situation. Later, facts may emerge that confirm inferences as true or false. The ultimate truth of any situation may never come out entirely, and the perception of truth may rest on the perspective view of the truth-seeker. Typically, journalists write about facts; occasionally they present inferences; rarely do they attempt to define "grand" truths beyond the facts in their reports.

  Two questions posed by Steve Buttry (2014) provide an excellent frame for the verification process: 1) How do you know, and 2) How *else* do you know? Three important sources for detailed verification procedures are: Kovach and Rosenstiel (2014); the Protess Method by David Protess, from the American Press Institute (Dean, n.d.); and the two *Verification Handbooks* from the European Journalism Centre, edited by Craig Silverman (2014, 2015).

- Methods in journalism for verifying information include triangulation and crowdsourcing. Triangulation means verifying a fact by finding other sources that confirm it, including two types of triangulation: 1) source triangulation, finding multiple sources that confirm the accuracy of the information; and 2) methodological triangulation, confirming the accuracy of the information with at least two different *types of sources* – records and other documentary evidence, reports and transcripts, pictures, data, etc.

Crowdsourcing is another method of verifying information, used less frequently. Crowdsourcing is asking members of the public to come forward with any information they may have about a news event or story. (As law enforcement professionals know, publicizing a need to identify, locate, or confirm a fact, person, place, or date and time can yield needed evidence.) However, journalists are cautious when publicizing unconfirmed information because they risk placing the false information into wider circulation.

- Contemporary news organizations often use information from social media sources. Once reporters know a poster's identity, paid services can provide background information on individuals. But with sufficient knowledge and expertise, some journalists can search the same public databases used by paid services.

   Verifying social media content may entail paying for specialized services to identify the name, time, and geography of a post or tweet, and obtain copyright clearance to use it. When journalists do it on their own, their news organizations must verify any material they use: the photos, videos, audio, or original texts. Thus, journalists take on verification tasks that include learning who created and uploaded the material, assessing their motives, and confirming the location, time, and date of acquisition for media such as photos, videos, and audio files. Finally, news organizations should get permission to use social media information from its creator.

- Verifying information from an internet website begins with learning its origins – from whom and where it came. Many tools provide information about any website (the information's origin), including who owns and operates the site, its IP address, the location of the site's name servers and mail servers, and other information. Knowing the purpose of web sites begins with examining their missions. Useful online tools to examine internet records include: whois lookup, whois history, reverse whois, reverse IP lookup, reverse NS, and reverse MX.

   After compiling the available information on a site, find additional material about the names or companies mentioned on the site. Look for articles that mention the site and note if patterns of agreement or disagreement emerge. Examine the site for any statements about its purpose. How do they shape the site's content? Is content accurate, fair, and complete? If not, do the articles and posts reflect a consistent bias?

- Digital information consists of 0s or 1s, or some other numbering system: Thus, digital information doesn't resemble the phenomenon it describes. Instead, digital data inevitably separates the digital representation from the original source phenomena. Digital data provides information *about phenomena* in abstract, digital form. The human brain's perceptive system is analog. *Analogous* means "similar to"; thus, our perceptions include such phenomena as alphabet letters, light, colors, and sounds. Strings of 0s and 1s are useful for computational purposes, but they won't let human beings see a Van Gogh painting, watch a classic movie, or hear a favorite song. In short, for people to see or hear digital content, it must be represented in an analog form.

- Metadata is data about the content data. It provides information about: 1) the process of coding the phenomenon into a digital format, and 2) an instruction set for a computer to reconstitute the phenomenon in human-perceptible form. Digital content always has metadata attached to it, whether that content is text, pictures, video, or audio. Without metadata, computers lack instructions to "understand" the data or select proper applications needed to manipulate and display the digital data.

- Two distinct processes work together to verify that photographs are genuine:

  1. *Examine the metadata* to the extent it is present. Structural metadata will show the size, resolution, and other technical details about the photo. Descriptive metadata shows information about the camera, the camera settings, and perhaps even the geolocation of the capture. It may also indicate if anyone altered the photo after it left the camera.

  2. *Examine the picture itself* for consistent lighting, the eyes of people in the picture, for consistent eye positions and specular highlights, cloning artifacts, and camera fingerprints. In addition, the content of the picture must conform to weather reports, sun position, topography, and cultural artifacts like dress, signage, architecture, and the like.

- Digital video also has metadata, stored in the header, the first frame of the video. Similar to photographs, both structural and descriptive metadata are present: Structural metadata provides basic technical information about the file, size, resolution, and encoding methods; descriptive metadata may include title, author, and tags and comments. Typically, social media platforms strip the header with its metadata. Other ideas for authenticating video include:

  - Understand the context of the video and how it came to exist
  - Establish the provenance for the video, by looking for other instances of it to make sure it has not been scraped from another site or another user's upload
  - On social media platforms, look for the video's unique identifier. The information will include the name of an uploader and perhaps additional information about the person or organizer who uploaded the material
  - Look for the uploader's accounts on other social media platforms and try to discover the real-world identity of the uploader
  - Examine the video itself, frame by frame, for clues within the pictures and audio. Check for landmarks, infrastructure, weather reports, the sun's position, and geographical features
  - Verify the dates and times for the video creation and the upload
  - Triangulate: Seek supporting or disconfirming evidence and additional user-generated content.

KEY CONCEPTS AND TERMS

- Validity of information
- Source reliability
- Verification methods: triangulation, multiple sourcing, and crowdsourcing
- Factual confirmation of internet sources and messaging: website ownership, timestamps, email service, mapping, and message routing
- Digital information, content, and metadata
- Confirming social media information and sources
- Authenticating visual content: photographs and video footage

EXERCISES AND ACTIVITIES

1. Compare the Protess Method of Verification with the Kovach and Rosenstiel guidelines for verification.

2. Using the *Verification Handbook for Investigative Reporters*, conduct a search on Google.com, using at least six of the special operators listed in Chapter 2 of the handbook.

3. Search the internet to find a description of how reporters verified information in a complex news story. List the verification procedures and confirmatory evidence. Did the journalists provide multisource triangulation and, if so, how many sources did they have? Did they use methodological triangulation by finding other types of confirming evidence? What were these other types of evidence?

4. Shoot a photo and a video from a mobile phone. Go to FotoForensics.com or other photo metadata service, then copy all the information. Use MediaInfo (downloaded from https://mediaarea.net/en/MediaInfo) to copy the header information from your video. From each set of metadata, classify the kinds of metadata present: structural, descriptive, or both?

5. Find a website that offers controversial social, political, or religious opinions. Collect information about the site: its ownership, creation date, whois history, IP address, its purpose and mission. Background the contributors and follow leads to other sites to which they contribute or support.

ADVANCER

Report and verify, of course – but before journalists can put together digital stories, they must consider other assets. (No, not their personal assets!) Rather, they must inventory the multimedia and interactive assets that they have already gathered (text, pictures, video, audio, data resources, links, and interactives) to put together their story. If most information for the story came from telephone conversations, they probably need more material to heighten user-engagement in the story. Chapter 8 describes how digital journalists acquire these digital assets.

8

ACQUIRING STORY ASSETS

Chapter Learning Objectives

After reading this chapter, students will be able to:

1. Compare differences between traditional newspaper pages and section elements with those of online news sites.
2. Analyze how multimedia assets enhance stories.
3. Consider how news organizations use content assets, including text, pictures, audio, video, streaming media, data visualizations, interactive features, and extended reality experiences (augmented reality (AR) and virtual reality (VR)).
4. Plan for the acquisition of multimedia, interactive, and 3D story assets.
5. Understand the equipment and skills needed to acquire content assets.
6. Evaluate how journalists acquire data for informational and interactive assets.

So, when you go out to cover an event, don't bring back a product, a widget, a good, a 10-inch inverted-pyramid story. Use multimedia and interactivity to bring your audience along for the ride. Make them feel like they're in the room with you. Cover the event live, and then repackage your live coverage to attract the search engine audience.

– Ryan Thornburg (http://ryanthornburg.com/category/multimedia-journalism)

THE GIST

Ryan Thornburg advises journalists to consider enhancing their stories by live tweeting, streaming audio or video, publishing audio or video, establishing a scheduled podcast, and posting to the news site using Storify. This chapter opens the media asset creation toolbox lid for digital journalists.

Chapter 8 covers how journalists decide to include multimedia in an article and describes the planning that goes into acquiring content, whether pictures, audio, video, or data-driven interactives. It contains basic information about how to take photographs, shoot video, record audio, set up live streaming videos, and produce podcasts. Sub-sections describe the equipment needed to acquire, save, and send different content materials. Mentors, professional articles and books, and workshops will be of immense help. However, these complex skills will require practical experience working with the equipment in the field to develop professional-level competence.

THE EASY GUIDE TO THE VOCABULARY OF NEWS CONTENT

Content assets, or just "assets," are media files such as text, pictures, audio and video clips, streaming media, virtual reality, and interactives. Other terms include **multimedia assets** and, when prepared for use in stories, **story assets**. Story assets accompany articles, enhancing users' experience, and understanding of stories. Each medium **affords** specific types of story assets. Afford, in this context, means that each medium can deliver only specific types of content assets to users. Thus, the print medium affords text but cannot afford the use of audio, film, or video as television does. TV affords a small amount of text but cannot display book-length prose well, while radio affords audio but not pictures or text.

In contrast, the internet medium affords all digital media types. Thus, online journalists gather much more than just raw information for their stories. As reporters get stories, they also capture such content assets as tweets and posts, photographs, audio and video clips, live streaming audio and video, and now 3D graphics for extended reality experiences.

Online journalists also acquire data. They find it from many sources or generate it on their own. Analyzing data and confirming conclusions takes time and expert skills. And transforming analyses into engaging assets – graphics or interactives – often requires highly specialized training in interactive design.

Here are some common terms, often used interchangeably:

- *Asset*: Goods, benefit, resource, treasure
- *Content assets*: Digital objects (pictures, video clips, etc.) designed for inclusion in a story
- *Media assets and multimedia assets*: Images, audio and video edited packages, 2D and 3D graphics, streaming audio and video, animations, and infographics
- *Interactive assets*: **Navigation elements** include links, buttons, comments, interactive maps, infographics, and data-driven charts and graphs. Interactive opportunities appear in a wide range of forms: polls, 2D and 3D simulations (extended reality), games, buttons, and upload functions for users to respond to crowdsourcing requests

ONLINE NEWS DESIGN: SITES, PAGES, STORIES, AND ASSETS

For online news sites, **web designers** choose the menu of elements for the site's pages, but they rarely select the stories. Senior editors select and sometimes slot stories into pages, often using pre-existing templates, while section editors typically choose and place those stories that fall in their areas of responsibility.

ACQUIRING STORY ASSETS

To fit content for so many varied sizes and shapes of today's many screens, news sites use the latest version of the internet's Hypertext Markup Language, HTML5. It enables **responsive designs** that automatically reformat web pages to fit users' devices on the fly. HTML5 revolutionized how websites and pages handle audio, video, and some interactive assets, thereby making embedding and using content assets far easier than was possible before.

Design elements used by websites to compose home and section pages include:

- *Navigational elements*: Login entry or link, menus, sidebar(s), sections, blocks, or modules, links, footer (corporate/organizational links, site feedback, policies, etc.)
- *Text assets*: Masthead title, copy, headline, ticker (breaking and latest news, information), section sub-headlines, links (internal and external)
- *Graphic assets*: Graphical menus (photos or drawings as menu choices), login box, masthead logo, lead photo(s), other photos and photo thumbnails, illustrations and illustration thumbnails, static maps and infographics, section breakers, search, and link boxes, icons
- *Animation effects and assets*: Animated text, GIFs, ads, banners, marquee
- *Video and animated packages*: Embedded video (HTML5), streaming video, embedded player, video thumbnails
- *Audio assets*: Embedded audio clips (HTML5), streaming audio, embedded player
- *Interactive assets*: Search, share icons (Facebook, Twitter, Pinterest, Instagram, etc.), comments, interactive maps, infographics, data visualizations, polls, 2D and 3D simulations, games and game-like activities, crowdsourcing requests and upload capability for documents, photos, videos, verification help

COMPARING NEWSPAPER FRONT PAGES TO INTERNET HOME PAGES

Newspaper front pages have design elements long familiar to home delivery newspaper subscribers. Some of these traditional elements carry over to online news sites – headlines, photos, and copy – but online news site layout differs from print newspaper layout, as shown in Figure 8.1, on the next page.

Online news outlet home pages carry many more stories and elements than do traditional newspaper pages. For example, the Southern California local newspaper *Daily Breeze* home page has links to more than 20 stories, many of them with pictures, including a larger lead image **above the fold**. (Online, "above the fold" means the part of the web page users can view without scrolling, particularly important to digital publications.) The home page also has links to several **photo galleries**, with one lead photo and other blog photos. In addition, online pages have interactive assets: User polls, links to reporters, user comments, local businesses links, sharing icons to link to social media sites, RSS feeds, sidebar menus, and front-page coupons.

3 PRELIMINARY STEPS TO TAKE BEFORE PLANNING ASSET ACQUISITION

Step #1 – Identify existing multimedia assets.

Step #2 – Gather multimedia while gathering information. Capture content assets as part of the reporting process. Visits to public places (and private ones with permission) provide

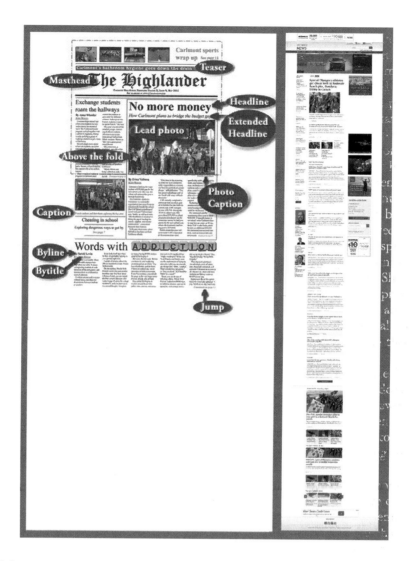

FIGURE 8.1

Difference between a newspaper front page and the *Daily Breeze* online homepage

Credit: Reprinted with permission from Justin Raisner. Reprinted with permission from the Southern California News Group.

opportunities to obtain scene-setting photographs. Telephone interviews (within legal limits) offer ways to record audio. Often journalists capture audio, video, and snap photographs during in-person interviews.

Reporters gather realms of information on their computers. So, download and screen-capture items needed to document important factual claims but be mindful of **copyright law**. Know that web pages, pictures, and prose are all copyrighted material. Still, journalists may claim **fair use** to publish protected material (including website content) without permission when the copied material is appropriate, timely, and newsworthy. Journalists may also use "fair use" to:

- Paraphrase source material
- Provide proof of, or illustrate assertions
- Engage in comment or critique

Step #3 – Write an outline, timeline, or preliminary draft of the story as you understand it. To start, identify the news peg, hook, and angle of the story. Answer the 5W1H questions. Then write a nut graf to answer: Why should users spend time on this story; what will they get from it?

If the available information has gaps or lacks adequate verification, identify missing material but keep going. Add notes that identify places where *existing* multimedia, documents, and data provide evidence for factual claims, support for inferences, offer differing perspectives, or improve user engagement. Remember: The story is fluid at this point. So, stay open-minded about how it may unfold later.

Three key stakeholders' points of view and the questions they raise concerning multimedia assets guide asset planning:

1. *Reporter perspective*: Reporters choose assets they believe explain and enhance the story. Reporters ask how an asset will assist and inform users.

2. *User perspective*: Users click on stories and multimedia assets because something attracts or interests them or increases their understanding of the story. Questions from this perspective ask if multimedia assets will get users' clicks, boost their understanding, and increase their engagement in the story.

3. *Newsroom editors and organizational management perspective*: Decision-makers take a cost/benefit approach. They ask if the *benefits* of adding multimedia assets to a story (to users and the publication) outweigh the *costs* of acquiring the assets.

4 MUST-HAVES BEFORE PLANNING ASSET ACQUISITION

These key pre-planning documents make it possible to develop solid plans. Trying to forge ahead without them runs the risk of inadequate planning, resulting in chaotic, ad hoc acquisition. At worst, it may jeopardize bringing back needed assets altogether.

1. Written rough draft or story outline
2. Inventory of existing multimedia
3. List of available data assets
4. List of existing 3D, 360°, AR, and VR assets

Acquiring assets often requires substantial investments in money and time. That is why planning for acquisition (beyond routine photographs and audio interviews) typically begins after much of the reporting is already finished. Reporters can anticipate explaining to editorial management: 1) The angle and arc of the story, 2) How multimedia assets will strengthen the impact of the story on users, 3) What interviewees might say that will add to the story, and 4) How the reporter can gain access to the location, database, or hard evidence.

BEFORE MEETING WITH AN EDITOR, KNOW WHAT MULTIMEDIA ASSETS CAN AND CAN'T DO

Studies show that the "right assets" attract users, increase users' engagement, and dwell time on stories. In a metric-obsessed environment, these numbers matter. But what *are* the right assets? It's a complicated question because it's not possible to say: "This asset does this and causes users to feel that." Marketers answer this question by conducting focus group and survey research. But journalists have deadlines, so they try to make thoughtful choices, based on available data and their own experience. Some considerations that affect these decisions include:

- *Technologies*: Their speed, display and play capabilities, and sophistication of the typical users' devices
- *Users*: Their information processing styles, especially their analytical and emotional responses
- *Social environment*: Communities and custom play overarching roles in framing individuals' views about evidence, proof, beauty, manner, reasonableness, and justice.

However, don't over-think the choice of assets. With or without multimedia assets, stories rule the news (Lehmann, Castillo, Lalmas, & Baeza-Yates, 2017). The first rule is: The asset you already have is best. The second rule: Imagined assets are (almost) always better than the ones that you eventually get.

Zimmerman and Koon-Stack (n.d.) offered guidelines that describe how different media types advance multimedia stories.

- *Text works well for*: Abstract, complicated aspects of stories; background and analysis; policy development or choices; headlines and photo captions.
- *Pictures work well for*: Emblematic, important moments; evoking users' emotions (reunions of long-lost siblings, soldiers returning from war); objects that don't move; environments.
- *Graphics work well for*: Numbers and statistics, trends, and relationships; diagrams showing how things work or specific causal processes; maps; interactive maps or data; and ticktocks, especially those with key actors' faces.
- *Video works well for*: Live events – what's happening now; action and movement; strong emotions; engaging users.
- *Audio works well for*: Linear narratives; emotions and feelings; capturing speakers' authenticity (or lack thereof); a sense of place.
- *Live streaming works well for*: Visuals and audio of events, with simultaneous user comments; eyewitness, on-scene updates during breaking news; unusual or unexpected events unfolding in real time; performances, with behind-the-scene perspectives (O'Neill & Echter, 2016).
- *Interactive data visualizations*: Game-like experiences; user-directed data exploration that displays contingent effects of users' "what-if" inputs.
- *Extended Reality (VR and AR) attract and hold users when*: They feature a visually appealing, little-known environment (or an unusual look at a known one), an on-screen narrator, and a single protagonist. Extended reality experiences should not be too long or focus entirely on negative topics. Virtual reality 360° video can present a first-person experience through complete immersion in the story world that offers "you are there" perspectives of places and events (Sullivan, 2018). AR works on mobile devices and doesn't require special goggles.

4 SMART QUESTIONS TO ASK BEFORE PLANNING ASSET ACQUISITION

Winston Churchill said when preparing for battle "Plans are of little importance, but planning is essential." This maxim applies to acquiring multimedia and interactive assets because they demand substantial time, effort, and resource investments; journalists need clear plans identifying the prospective assets that will enhance the story for users. In addition, before shooting any kind of video, even 2D or 360° video, the reporter must write a draft script that lays out the expectations for the resulting footage.

Question #1 Specifically, how do outlines, timelines, or draft scripts reflect what the proposed multimedia asset delivers to help the viewer understand, engage in, or experience an event or topic?

Question #2 Is the acquisition opportunity a planned event?

- Events take place at specific times and places, with known actors, thus permitting advance preparation.
- Topical stories come alive in multiple locations that require scheduling and possibly pre-shoot visits to acquire content: interviews, explainer material, scene-setters, and immersive experiences.

Question #3 What level of quality does the multimedia asset require?

Consider this counter-intuitive idea about quality: The less a story concerns important hard news, the higher quality the associated multimedia assets must have. Stories about culture, and celebrities usually demand entertainment value and high quality. Of course, if a reporter gets a blurred shot of the lead singer from today's popular boy band sneaking into a drug rehab facility, quality goes out the window in favor of immediacy.

And when important news breaks, journalists take the multimedia assets they can get. If the assets are high quality, great! If not, news organizations make do. For example, the compelling low-quality home-movie Zapruder footage of the President Kennedy assassination remains one of the most-watched content assets ever created!

Digital journalists routinely make tradeoffs between portability and quality. Mobile phone cameras and audio recorders are useful multimedia capture devices, but they may not produce the high-quality content needed for many purposes like the 3D content in augmented reality (AR) experiences. For midlevel quality, prosumer, highly portable equipment does a decent job. But it's important to remember: The higher the asset quality, the greater the asset acquisition costs – due to more expensive equipment and software, more processing, labor, plus added costs for outside consultants.

Question #4 What resources are needed to acquire each multimedia asset?

The equipment is a given: Cameras, microphones, computers, and memory cards provide a standard asset acquisition kit. In some cases, asset acquisition also requires added money for: 1) specialized professional consultation and work, 2) specialized acquisition equipment, such as a 360° camera for virtual reality (VR) experiences, 3) licenses for copyrighted materials, 4) additional workspaces, and 5) permissions for access to events/venues. Staff reporters do much of this work, but sometimes expert professionals lend a hand. Freelancers often self-finance the work and then carry out most tasks themselves.

Part of the answer to this question is to consider: Do I need expert help? Unless they have special training and experience, journalists often need help with dataset analysis and XR projects. There's a very good reason most XR experiences to date are "special projects," with participation from specialized companies that have pioneered new equipment and techniques. Unless the newsroom has people who have professional skillsets in these two areas, plan to bring in others to work on XR projects. People who have created XR experiences need the draft script and will make solid suggestions to ensure the acquisition of appropriate assets.

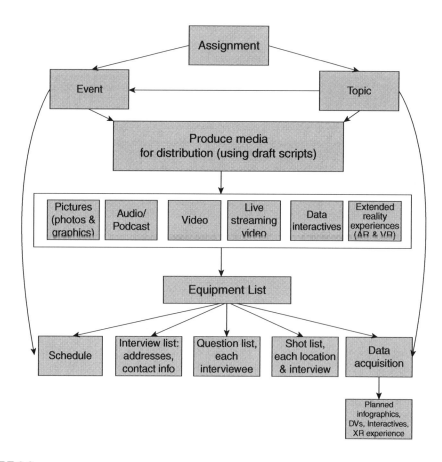

FIGURE 8.2

Preparing to acquire multimedia story assets
Credit: Joan Van Tassel

ACQUIRING STORY ASSETS 235

> ## Vox Verbatim: Gabriel Dance, Deputy Investigative Editor at the *New York Times*
>
> I was the Interactive Editor at *The Guardian*. I hired a team of four interactive reporters, who have much the same responsibilities as traditional reporters – report on, pitch, and tell a story through visual means, data visualization, maps, games, as needed. When the NSA [US National Security Agency] story broke, in June 2013, reporting started as bite-size stories. After a couple of months, we found ourselves with a rather large set of stories that all were related, but no story that held the greater context and held the stories together. People were saying 'I don't understand'. The story was technologically complicated, and it had to do with encryption and wire tapping, and legally complicated as well with FISA court and NSA material.
>
> So, we launched an ambitious interactive project to explain the stories and how they were connected to one another.
>
> The outline was the secret sauce to this project. We came up with an outline, the same way you would outline a written story, a documentary, anything – an overview of the issue, what wireless tapping and encryption mean. Sections and bullet points: This is the bones of the story we want to tell. [...] We asked, "What is the best way to tell that story?" We were completely open to use all the storytelling means and methods available on the internet to make things relevant to people. We shot video. We used rollover interactives where bubbles of explanatory text would pop up.

THE TEN COMMANDMENTS OF KIT

No equipment? No digits, no multimedia story. Digital reporters who just carry their mobile phone in one pocket and their notebook with pen in the other can skip this section. But when journalists transcend that simplicity, their needs for sensitive advanced equipment rapidly escalate, as do the tasks of setting up, operating, and caring for that equipment. So, here's the skinny on kit:

1. *Know your equipment* – every piece.
2. *Use quality equipment bags to stay organized.*
3. *Be kind to your equipment.* Don't throw equipment around, shove things into pockets, drop things, spill coffee on them, or leave cords loose or untethered from devices. Label everything, especially cords and chargers.
4. *After using equipment, clean it!* ... every time, even before you sleep or celebrate your killer shots.
5. *Use the right stuff to clean your equipment.* And don't cheat unless you must keep working. Then spit works fine.
6. *Always carry tape.* Duct tape rocks!
7. *Always have pen and paper.* Irreplaceable equipment breaks or stops working; you just keep observing and writing.
8. *Always have power!* Check rooms for electrical outlets; carry chargers, extra batteries, and extra storage media.
9. *People covet cool equipment.* So be discreet with yours. Don't flash it in rough areas. But if you do and "get braced," don't get brave: Be ready to give up your stuff without pushback.

10. *Someone always has better equipment than you.* If you are nice to them, they might let you test drive it.

In the Field: Scoops, Cops, and Compliance

Before you start acquiring multimedia material, please know: While the First Amendment gives the press much freedom, that freedom has limits, including following the orders and directions of law enforcement officers. At some locations – fires, accidents, and crime scenes – police may deny access to photojournalists. *When force on the ground demands compliance, agree and seek alternative points of access or other workarounds.* When your personal safety depends on obeying orders to stay put, comply. Be especially careful in fast-moving fire areas, crime scenes, and war zones.

Other types of threats may exist as well. Mosquitoes and insects may carry illnesses and food-borne bacteria can sicken anyone. The COVID-19 pandemic highlighted the serious risk of psychological peril from vicarious trauma. "On top of the nature of the story itself, with reporters interviewing survivor families, photographing victims, and looking at distressing data, it can have a direct impact personally" (Morrish, 2020).

As much as possible, take steps to mitigate the risks that reporting in the field may pose to you. In dangerous conditions, try to eat well and sleep regularly, use protective equipment and medications, and seek medical attention promptly when needed. Do your best to stay in contact with colleagues, friends, and family. Take time off, if you can. Give yourself time to recover, even if all you can do is spend a few minutes by yourself in self-reflection, meditation, or prayer.

Remember: If you get hurt or have a nervous breakdown, your editor will probably ~~kill~~ replace you. LOL.

ACQUIRING PHOTOGRAPHS

Photographs capture instants in time. Photographs may not tell you why a car accident happened, but they convey the carnage. Written stories can explain who, what, and why, but still fail to communicate the depth of human tragedy of a single perfect picture. A moment that conveys strong emotions, often elicits strong emotional responses from viewers. And when photographs capture events or feelings that are emblematic of larger truths, they may reach millions of people. Much of the emotional potency of photos stems from their perceived realness, giving them immediate credibility.

The ability to take good photographs demands technical knowledge. Studying excellent news photographs, attending workshops and classes, and careful reading all add to a journalist's knowledge. But only consistent practice enables reporters to avoid fumbling with their camera and missing key shots. For reporters still learning to shoot, the best strategy in high-pressure situations may be to just concentrate on camera stability and image composition, while using the camera's automatic settings for light, speed, and focus.

4 KEY CAMERA SETTINGS FOR GREAT PICTURES

Take photography classes or attend workshops. Discuss photos with colleagues and learn how the pros shoot photographs. And practice with the camera used in **shoots**. Four settings matter: three in the camera and one on the lens. Well-lit photographs result from the interaction between:

1. **Aperture**: Exposure, regulating how much light goes into the camera
2. **Shutter speed**: How long the shutter stays open, another way to control how much light goes into the camera
3. **ISO**: Sets how sensitive the sensor is to light
4. On the lens, the **focus ring** makes the main subject sharp: Try not to use autofocus.

A few tips: Use a **tripod** whenever possible, even in exciting or dangerous situations. If you lack a tripod, steady the camera on a flat surface or hold the camera as steady as possible – then press the shutter release with constant pressure to reduce camera shake. When possible, shoot subjects against clean, uncluttered backgrounds. Compose shots in the camera but leave adequate **crop** room.

A change in one setting usually requires changes in one or more other settings. The only way to learn how the three in-camera settings interact requires you to practice, experiment, examine your results, and re-adjust the settings … then wash, rinse, and repeat until shooting becomes instinctive.

FIGURE 8.3

Controlling lens settings
Credit: Photographer: Mark Sweep, Licensed under CC BY-SA 3.0 via Wikimedia Commons

B4 THE SHOOT

Make sure the equipment is ready – always. For example, erasing previously uploaded photographs from memory cards ensures you have maximum space to store additional photos. Charge all batteries before putting them in accessories bags so that cameras, phones, computers, and other equipment have enough "juice" to operate.

The Day B4 the Shoot

- Print the location's address, phone number, map, and clear directions to the site.
- Check the equipment bag for camera and backup camera, storage cards, computer, chargers and extra batteries for all equipment, and USB and other cables. Don't forget an extra mobile phone battery. (If it *might* rain, take equipment covers, an umbrella, or even plastic grocery bags to keep your equipment dry.)
- Double-check that all batteries are charged.
- Bring any specialized clothing that you might need.
- Put your press pass, ID, and other useful credentials *where you can find them!*

Day of …

Set out your press pass, map, address, and contact information, equipment bag (verify it has all the needed items). Leave early. Arrive early.

Near the location, park in a safe place, if possible. Store unneeded equipment in the car but know that storing expensive electronics at unknown or unguarded locations is foolish; use the vehicle's trunk. Consider putting high-quality equipment bags inside dingy, banged-up bags as camouflage.

At the location, introduce yourself to people who might help you. Survey the environment – just to get a sense of that place. Mentally note unusual, memorable, and pictorial features of the area that might show its ambiance and purpose. Locate all the electrical outlets: You may need them to recharge depleted batteries while shooting with a second camera. Ask if Wi-Fi is available; if so, request an access login and password.

3 pro tips to get the money shot ... and 3 more for the beauty shot

The term **money shot** refers to capturing a difficult-to-get picture that becomes the highlight of a story or film. Arthur "Weegee" Fellig, a famous New York street photographer of the 1930s and 1940s used the much-honored Speed Graphic camera to capture acclaimed money shots of his era. Fellig's advice to news photogs has guided several generations of photojournalists:

1. *f/8 and be there!* The first part of Fellig's advice to photojournalists: Set the camera aperture at f/8 as a default. (The best aperture setting for digital cameras now is f/11, f/8, or f/5.6 – each camera has its own sweet spot. (For the Speed Graphic, f/8 was the sugar.)
2. *Be there!* The second part of Fellig's advice still holds true: If you aren't *there*, you can't get the shot. It's the decisive moment, that exact time and place which defines the event.
3. *Being close* is part of the *be there* adage. Good photojournalists try to be as near as possible to key events, while keeping just enough distance to capture the context of their shots.

FIGURE 8.4

Rule of thirds, vertical and horizontal

Credit: By Chaky (Own work) [Public domain], via Wikimedia Commons

Beauty shots, rooted in the fashion and beauty industries, refer to stylized shots that put a person or product in the best light. In news, beauty shots typically appear in feature stories and articles covering travel, home and garden, society events, and relationships. The key to getting good beauty shots lies in thoughtful composition and lighting.

- Use the **rule of thirds** as a composition template. The four circled intersections of lines, shown in Figure 8.4 mark the *power points* in the image. Photos are typically more interesting when their main subjects aren't centered in the photograph.
- Use the *light to advantage* by finding the right balance of light and shadow.
- Use *focus to create focus*. Photographers use a shallow **depth of field (DOF)** and **bokeh** to separate a subject from its background, as shown in Figure 8.5.

After the Shoot

1. *Browse all your shots*: Inspect each one for sharpness.
2. *Jot a note for each shot*: Write the number or name of the SD memory card, in-camera ID number of each shot, names of people in the image (moving from left to right), and a short descriptive caption. Star the best shots; cross out bad shots.
3. *Save backups of best shots*: Save the backups in a dedicated folder.
4. *Transmit the best shots to the newsroom from the field if needed*: Determine the most efficient transmission method considering your location, organizational policies, and equipment.

FIGURE 8.5

Example of shallow depth of field and bokeh

Credit: By Gregory F. Maxwell gmaxwell@gmail.com [GFDL 1.2], via Wikimedia Commons

The Mobile Darkroom

Photography and camera operation aren't the only technical skills that digital journalists must develop. Since laptops, tablets, and mobiles often serve as photojournalists' digital darkrooms in the field, savvy computer skills become even more essential. At a minimum, reporters must be able to: 1) open, save, and backup files in appropriate drives and directories, 2) transfer and save images to their computers, 3) operate photo editing software to sharpen, **dodge and burn**, **crop**, and caption images, and 4) shut down frozen applications (or their entire computer) and re-boot.

USING LICENSED PHOTOGRAPHS

To find existing photos, search the content management system of your organization's image database. Searching Wikimedia Commons (https://commons.wikimedia.org/wiki/Main_Page) sometimes yields photographs or illustrations that work well with a story's text. And check out free internet sources for images.

When there's a commercial angle, press contacts at companies or institutions often provide photo assets. If the story's context provides neutral or positive coverage, they may email an image upon request. But if they think a story might portray their company or industry in a negative light, fuggedaboudit. Journalists can also crowdsource photo requests, asking users to send pictures, then verifying photos' provenance, getting the user's permission, and providing appropriate credit, as Chapter 7 describes.

LICENSING ILLUSTRATIONS

Illustrations provide images of places, processes, and even ideas that photographs cannot. For example, the visualization of alteration of messenger RDNA in cellular processes by genetically based medications requires illustrations even for knowledgeable and interested readers. Or consider a story describing the supply and pre-positioning of diverse types of war armaments in an operational theater before a military offensive – clear, powerful illustrations can help users comprehend the enormity, complexity, and scope of these efforts in ways that words cannot.

Some large news organizations have staff illustrators, but most hire freelancers for specific pieces. Picture editors often peruse illustrators' online portfolios to locate someone with the desired expertise. Contracts specify the agreement's terms between the commissioning organization and the artist – including payment, copyright, and usage rights. International law dictates that image creators own the images they make, even when they create them as paid work. Sometimes it is cheaper to buy unlimited usage rights than to purchase an image outright.

The Graphic Artists Guild provides its members with **boilerplate** contracts and agreements which form one basis for final contracts. Check out the Graphic Artists Guild Handbook for standard agreements and prices (www.graphicartistsguild.org/) and note that illustrators sometimes place portfolios on this site.

THE MANY LIVES OF VID

The ubiquitous forms of internet video news range from protesters' shaky handheld videos, taken in the middle of riots, to cinematic-quality experiences of enthralling beauty and heart-wrenching pathos. That variability partly stems from the vast array of technical options. Creating a video can just entail starting-up the camera or Periscope app on a mobile phone, focusing on the subject, and tapping the record button to begin recording. Or video-creation may entail shooting video with full cinematic RED or Blackmagic camera rigs, using 12 to 30-person production teams.

Although it's easy to capture quick clips on mobile phones, other types of news video production are very time-consuming. One news video producer estimated that it takes nine hours of work to create just one minute of well-shot and edited video. And because video has become so familiar to users, viewers expect high-quality video when they see news stories reported by known news organizations.

News sites' use of video has increased. One Pew Research survey found that 60 percent of U.S. adults watched videos online. About one-third (36 percent) of them watched news videos (Mitchell, Holcomb, & Vogt, 2014). These researchers also found that established news organizations such as *The New York Times*, *The Washington Post*, and *Detroit Free Press* added staffers expressly to publish online video. Digital-first news sites, *ViceNews*, *Newsy*, *HuffPost*, *Mashable*, and *MediaStorm* have invested heavily in video capabilities.

But, the Reuters Institute for the Study of Journalism (Kalogeropoulos, Cherubini, & Newman, 2016) found less use of video news online than the Pew Research. Three-fourths of the Reuters respondents reported they just occasionally or never viewed online video. Yet when important news breaks, some users avidly seek video. For example, when BBC online news covered the 2015 attacks in Paris, the 2016 Reuters study found that the percentage of users who watched video doubled from the daily average of 10 percent to slightly more than 20 percent.

Online news video conveys additional knowledge to viewers. Wise, Bolls, Myers, and Sternadori (2009) found that readers of online narratives learned additional information by the addition of online video. Respondents described reading like *getting there* – following the story to understand it, while subjects felt watching video was more like *being there* – experiencing the situation much like someone present while those events occurred. One useful way to view these findings lies in considering reading and viewing as alternative forms of mental "transportation." Reading describes the journey, while viewing video transports users to the destination.

Visual media, including video, reach viewers on emotional levels. When viewers watch pictures of others experiencing strong emotions, they often recognize those strong emotions and often generate intrapersonal physiological "mirroring" responses. Lagun and Lalmas (2016) found that video assets increased users' engagement in stories even though they didn't change user bounce rates. *The Washington Post* staff (2019) claimed that video op-eds shifted users' emotional responses to important events – the Hong Kong riots, U.S. Travel Ban and family separation policies, and the impeachment controversy, for example. Thus, pictures of migrant toddlers being torn from their mothers give rise to more compelling emotional impacts than descriptive written stories.

Vox Verbatim: Joan Van Tassel

I was a freelance journalist in Baghdad in 2003, one week after the U.S. invaded Iraq. My contract with ABC News *Nightline* specified that I produce, conduct interviews, and shoot videos of private aid to Iraqi hospitals. I was on my own, carrying 30 pounds all day in more than 90° heat, often accompanied only by one representative from the Ministry of Health, Dr. Mona Nasir. I was totally off the U.S. grid, far from the safe Green Zone military headquarters.

Frightened people, without electricity, wandered Baghdad's streets. I recorded video of everything I could – in the streets, hospitals (including temporary field hospitals), neighborhood clinics, maternity wards, labs, and even in hotel lobbies, where several physicians set up clinics for patients who couldn't get around Baghdad, suddenly with no buses and few taxis. After dark, I reviewed my footage, made detailed notes, and emailed both to ABC's New York producer. My unexpected experiences profoundly changed how I viewed the impact of war on civilians, the aching loss of familiar ways of life, and the profound uncertainty brought about by threats to personal safety.

VIDEO AS A MULTIMEDIA ASSET

Some users like video, especially those who watch soft news and videos that they access on social media. Kalogeropoulos et al. (2016) surveyed 30 publishers, and found that most users watched video via Facebook and other platforms: "Some individual viral videos we studied for this report have had 75–100 million views, far more than they [publishers] could ever have expected using their own websites; however, many other videos sink without a trace." The researchers also found that most of the viral videos were under one minute and appealed to emotion.

Most news organizations have in-house resources for original video (Tu, 2015). Interviews with experienced news site producers, editors, and reporters yielded five recommendations to help publications maximize videos' value on news sites:

- Put the focus on the topic itself, not the medium or user device.
- Breaking news videos have short life spans. After showing the video, save it to re-purpose for later stories.
- Develop consistent patterns of video use to establish users' expectations.
- Clips, short-form, and long-form videos may each do well – or not. Popular videos succeed because of their content, not their length.

- Use two complementary approaches: Post raw mobile phone clips to accompany text to social media and sharing apps. Then have a second team create high-quality, edited video packages.

Video and Other Visual Realities – VR and AR

Virtual and augmented reality incorporate both 2D video and 3D objects. Virtual reality features 360° environments that fill the user's visual field with video or computer-generated images as well as 3D objects. These experiences demand a careful draft script prior to acquisition. From the script, producers list precisely the shots needed for the final experience (called a **script breakdown**) and use it to guide the production. When outside vendors provide computer-generated 3D objects and environments, they will need the draft script to shape their project's design.

5 VIDEO EQUIPMENT OPTIONS

1. *Camera and lenses*:
   - *DSLR (digital single lens reflex) and cinematic video cameras*: Handle with care. These high-end pieces of equipment deliver stunning images, but they aren't for novices and they have very steep learning curves.
   - *Broadcast television video cameras*: Operating these machines takes technical chops. They're large, heavy, and delicate – but they've got great zoom lenses!
   - *Prosumer video cameras*: These cameras hit the sweet spot between quality and ease of use. Except for extremely long shots, their video images are almost indistinguishable from broadcast cameras.
   - *Pocket 4K or HD video action cameras*: GoPro type cameras have better resolution and lenses than mobile phones – but that's not saying much. GoPro type cameras just can't match high-quality prosumer cameras but they're great for point-of-view action shots.
   - *360° video*: 360° cameras capture panoramic views from a complete circle around the camera. They offer varying degrees of quality. The camera should feature at least 4K resolution and capture genuine 360° video.
   - *Mobile phone video cameras*: For short, lively online video clips, these cameras work fine. Just. Despite substantial improvement, the lens remains the weak point. But for important news stories – that clip will run everywhere: Get the shot.
2. *Digital video storage: Memory cards and drives*. Get storage media fast enough to record video, about 90 megabits per second or faster. Oh, and get a lot of it for big 4K or HD video files.
3. *Camera support: Tripod, monopod, or harness*: A steady video picture separates pros from newbies. Yes, shaky footage has that edgy contemporary look, but it doesn't work for long-form documentary or video news packages. Pros support their cameras on parking meters, fences, tables, or any available stable surface.
4. *Microphones*: Microphones come in two flavors: condenser and dynamic. Condenser mics provide rich sounds, often indoors. In the field, dynamic mics can also provide excellent sound quality and they continue to work, even with moisture and equipment-killing abuse.

ACQUIRING STORY ASSETS

5. *Cables, power, white card, and gizmos*: You must have the (often mission-critical) miscellaneous bag: cables, batteries, chargers, paper clips, pen, dimes to twist large screws, rubber bands, etc.

DELIVERABLES: CAMERA SHOTS

Amateurs shooting video often think they have to deliver a video, a package, or an opus. But that's not the case. They are tasked with delivering compelling, well-produced, usable shots that cover the event.

Please memorize this sentence: The shot is the fundamental building block of moving images (Eisenstein, 1942). The photojournalist's central concern rests with identifying and recording the individual shots. Later, the editor must build a sequence of shots, a **montage**, from the footage that the photojournalist delivered. Taken together, the shot, and the montage constructed from multiple shots, create the sense of "being there" that viewers experience as they watch moving images.

The definitions for shots have been well-established in the media industries, although gray areas remain. One group of labels classifies shots by the framing of a scene and how much of the scene or area of interest the shot includes: long shot, medium shot, close-up, etc. Another way of describing shots uses the number of people in it: a two-shot, three-shot, family shot, the group shot, and so forth. Alternatively, sometimes the camera's position and perspective define the shot: high-angle (from above the subject) or low-angle shots (yes, from below the subject). For example: "It's a wide, high-angle, long-shot of the group" or "I want a tight 3-shot of the team."

Shooting video for edited news packages isn't easy; even short packages require multiple shots and angles. Because it's so easy to forget items on a mental shot list, journalists should prepare written shot lists that will likely include many of the following shot types:

- Establishing/wide shot (WS), location
- Several long shots (LS) of principal elements of environment and scenes
- Medium (MS) and long shots of key people, technologies, tools, and communication devices
- Close-up (CU) shots of signs, décor, restraints, and other event artifacts, people using key techs, tools, and comm devices
- Extreme close-up (ECU) shots of expressive faces (excitement, joy, pain, fear, rage, despair, etc.)
- Insert (cut-in) shots – close shots of techs, tools, and devices in use or in-hand

VIDEO – A MOVING EXPERIENCE

People and cars move – as do video cameras. Photojournalists can move their entire camera, or they may use **in-camera moves**. Video production books, video production workshops, or college courses describe classic camera moves such as pans and tilts, arc, dolly, trucking, tracking, and follow. In contrast, in-camera moves don't require camera motion; only parts of the camera lens move.

- **Zoom** or move in
- **Pull-back (PB)**: mooz or move out
- **Rack focus**: Picture goes from out-of-focus to in-focus

MORE ABOUT THE NEW VIDEO

For journalists, it's possible for users to experience both AR and VR video on their mobile devices, although users cannot immerse themselves on them as completely as they do when using headsets. Further, virtual and augmented reality haven't flooded the web because the tech isn't quite there yet. There's a bewildering array of products that capture different information, in different ways, use proprietary software to view, stitch, and edit the results, and play on specialized equipment or software windows. Discarded hardware and software products litter the landscape like dead satellites still circling the Earth in space – outdated, unused, and unusable.

Creating VR and AR content that meets professional expectations is (for now) difficult, time-consuming, and often expensive – an exemplar of the exponentially increasing, consequential technological changes that continue to disrupt online news journalism.

To begin, creating a world for an immersive virtual reality experience requires an animated scene or a 360° **camera**. This device includes at least two cameras, often four, six, or even more grouped in a single housing. By placing wide-angle lenses on multiple sides of the housing, the "camera" shoots a sphere of video that completely circles the camera – instead of a rectangular image of traditional video. Because there is a separate recording of the information from each lens, the different POVs (points of view) must be **stitched** together in post-production. It's a painstaking, difficult, and time-consuming process, so when a product came out in 2019 that stitched the video in-camera, many hoped the feature would catch on.

And the 3D scanners that capture reality in graphic animation – is it video or is it animation? They produce, you decide.

The **3D scanners** start with a laser that measures depth, recording the distance from the scanner to the surface of an object (or space) in tiny increments. It creates so many data points that the resulting information is called a **point cloud**. A second scanner maps light and heat. At the same time, many units include a linked high-resolution video camera that records the color and visible surface **textures**. Finally, a **tracking camera** records the 3D orientation of objects (height, width, and depth) and **skeletal tracking** to define human motion movement.

- Depth measurement
- Color and surface features
- Motion tracking

Artificial intelligence puts these three data sets together to create the virtual environment and objects, allowing them to change positions in relation to users as they "move through" the space. The software accomplishes this computing-intensive process by using the data to build a **mesh model** of the space and objects. Information from the video overlays the mesh with color and surface features. And motion tracking makes it all move, even altering the perspectives of the objects and overall environment to provide the user with the experience of **being there**. Creating virtual environments requires mad creative skills and an abundance of computer processing!

How-To: Shoot 360° and Scan the World

Journalists know how to shoot video. But shooting 360° and 3D scanning are like knowing the difference between rowing a boat and driving a submarine. For example, when you shoot 360°, you can't see the shot. (Well, if you have the app, perhaps you can see it on your phone from behind the tree where you are hiding from the camera, so the top of your head doesn't block the shot.) You need a different kind of tripod, you shoot from a different place, you shoot different kinds of shots in special ways. Oh, and that 5.2K resolution is so exciting? But that resolution is distributed across 360° of panorama instead of a 60° rectangular window, so the high-rez isn't nearly as high as it might seem.

Within a year, new cameras and formats will emerge. And so it goes. Fortunately, plenty of information about it awaits you on the net. "How to shoot 360° video" would be an excellent Google search when you have a project and a camera. Check it out www.immersiveshooter.com/about-immersive-shooter/ by Sarah Redohl for a start.

It's much the same story for scanning and capturing moving images. A scanner to capture 360° objects works well for AR. For VR, a combination light or heat scanner must also have motion tracking capability for high-quality experiences. Although this field is developing rapidly, 3D VR equipment and software need more development to become more cost-effective and easier to use. Again, the internet will provide valuable resources to find up-to-date gear and techniques to shoot, edit, and publish XR. In 2019, the basic rules: 1) scan slowly several times, 2) notice whether the scanner works outside as well as inside, 3) keep the required distance from the scanned object, and 4) avoid reflective objects like chrome and windows.

VIDEO – HEARD AS WELL AS SEEN …

Video images comprise just part of this influential, persuasive, and pervasive medium. Video's boon companion – audio – requires close attention, because of hidden but powerful effects that audio exerts on video users. Vossen (n.d.) writes that: "Choose the wrong music, and your video will be cheesy or simply wrong. Make a bad selection for a sound effect, and the only effect you've made is – ruining your video."

Some professionals argue that sound quality matters more than the video quality (Wilbert, 2016):

- Of our senses, hearing may be the most crucial for communication: Try turning off the soundtrack while watching a scary movie and it's not so frightening – it may even become hilarious without the sound.
- Several media studies show that audiences tolerate poor video accompanied by excellent audio much more than they do excellent video with poor audio.

Audio is equally important for AR and VR experiences. While standard audio techniques may work for AR, VR needs sound that approaches 360° **volumetric** audio. Again, this field changes continuously, so look for current information products and recording techniques on the internet.

AUDIO: SOUNDS LIKE NEWS

Audio remains the least-used multimedia element on the internet. Radio and podcast producer Nate DiMeo (2011) wrote:

> Audio Never Goes Viral. There's something much more intentional about choosing to listen to something than choosing to click on a video or article. If you posted the most incredible story – literally, the most incredible story that has ever been told since people have had the ability to tell stories, it will never, ever get as many hits as a video of a cat with a moustache.

News organizations often add audio clips to individual news stories and provide audio interactivity on their sites. Sometimes news sites link to external audio resources. And they may even post audio clips and stories to an internet aggregator service where users can discover, search for, share, and like audio content. Some news organizations, notably NPR and specialized sites like *538* or *Foreign Policy* also create podcasts.

The online user-experience when hearing news differs from reading news. Readers can return to or reread the material. Listeners must pay attention and piece together the story as it emerges, filling in or guessing about the information that they do not yet have. And listeners can't skim material – at most, listeners can speed up audio playback about 25 percent until words become incomprehensible. Importantly, spoken language differs from written language in its informality and greater brevity.

Anyone observing the careers of Rush Limbaugh, Stephanie Miller, Howard Stern, or Dr. David Jeremiah should recognize the impacts that audio can exert on audience members with similar social or ideological opinions. One aspect of audio's influence may be that sounds – particularly human voices – convey close personal and intimate relationships. People can see others from long distances, but we normally just hear nearby conversational-level voices.

Audio's ability to elicit experiences of intimate conversation and social interactions makes it a compelling medium. In relevant contexts, audio helps to:

1. *Carry the narrative*: More than video, audio provides a primary delivery mechanism for narratives (Frechette, 2012).

2. *Establish emotional empathy*: Listeners identify speakers' emotions from their voices alone better than from video and audio or video-only (Kraus, 2017). Audio recordings and transcripts bolster the credibility and impact of stories' quotes.

3. *Increase understanding*: Listening lets users better discern what speakers intend to convey. And the interactions between reporters and their sources further enhance users' understanding.

4. *Foster user engagement*: Audio recordings draw in listeners and raise their levels of interest. Think National Public Radio's *American Life* series.

5. *Increase believability and trust*: Audio clips let users personally hear sources' statements and assess the levels of accuracy and bias in each story.

6. *Add depth and dimension to stories*: Imagine just an announcer's voice, describing a wedding. Now imagine the same verbal description but coupled with the natural sounds of the wedding – the guests, music, greeting line, and the exchange of vows.

7. *Reach people when users' eyes are engaged*: Users can listen when they can't read – when they're driving, walking, standing in line, or working out.

8. *Reach wider audiences*: Everyone can hear audio on mobile phones – and almost everyone (at least under 30) has their mobile close at hand.

ACQUIRING STORY ASSETS

247

AUDIO AS MULTIMEDIA ASSETS

The audio clips that digital journalists often capture include **interview quotes, voiceovers, ambient (environmental) sound,** and **natural sound**:

- *Interview clips* (or **sound bites**) provide responses to a journalist's specific questions.
- *Voiceovers* (or **voice tracks**) are recordings of program hosts or reporters, speaking from scripts.
- *Ambient sound* audio captures the overall background sounds of a specific environment: a bus stop, drugstore, steel foundry, beach, or an election polling place.
- *Natural sounds* are sounds emanating from an environment, such as wind, birds chirping, traffic, etc.

PODCASTS – THE NEW OLD AUDIO THING

Podcasts, audio content expressly created for the internet, are increasingly popular. People in half of all U.S. homes listen to podcasts while one-fifth of respondents listened in their cars (Winn, 2019). Podcast users' demographics skew toward higher incomes, more education, youth, and they're slightly more likely to be male.

Two ongoing trends have spurred podcasting: First, more and larger niche audiences now seek content expressly tailored to their interests – resulting in more user-interest in podcasts. Second, dramatically increased use of mobile devices to listen on the go further broadens the potential user base. Edison Research (2018) found that three-fifths of podcast users had played podcasts from mobile phones connected to their car's audio system. As more new cars come equipped with integral internet connections, potential podcast audiences will steadily increase.

Users often download online podcasts for later listening. Common genres include news and current events, talk and interviews, comedy, crime, technology, health, personal growth – a broad range of audio programming, often comparable to "softer" news in online news outlets.

ACQUIRING AUDIO

It's simple to acquire just audio compared to video with audio, or even video without audio. The low cost of digital recorders and inexpensive mobile apps make recording audio easy for most journalists. But obtaining *high-quality* audio presents challenges because sound-sensitive audio equipment readily picks up extraneous noises in the environment.

Tech and Tools

Most journalists spend a lot of time on the telephone. Those conversations constitute potential grist for the multimedia mill, *but* first know and comply with the law – and your newsroom policies. Even if state law permits, reporters may be subject to civil liability (see the Reporters Committee for Freedom of the Press: www.rcfp.org/wp-content/uploads/imported/RECORDING.pdf).

When reporting audio for a story make sure you have permission from the person to record them – or know the consent laws in the state where the recording takes place.

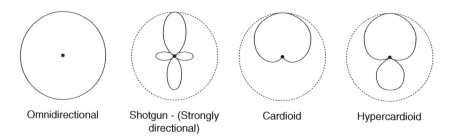

FIGURE 8.6

Microphone pickup patterns
Credit: By Omegatron (Own work) [Public domain], via Wikimedia Commons

(Note: Consent of all parties is required in most states.) Once they have consent, reporters should be ready to roll with their telephone pickup mics, digital audio recorders, and a thoughtful question list.

On the go? Use mobile apps that record calls with decent quality. If possible, find quiet, private places to record in-person audio interviews. Environmental **noise** hampers recording clear audio because the overlapping sounds are difficult to decipher. It's also important to maintain privacy when the reporter's questions evoke difficult, intimate, or threatening issues for an interviewee.

Although professional recording units may be costly, some mid-range DARs ($60–80) can provide excellent quality audio. Mobile phones may not record crisp, clear audio, except (counterintuitively) in noisy places like food courts or coffee shops, when their excellent noise-canceling technology comes into play. Check DAR and phone app comparison reviews such as Perling and Bellamy (2019) on thewirecutter.com.

Recall that mics are either **condenser** or **dynamic** mics. Good condenser mics can produce the highest quality sound, but they require external power. In contrast, high-quality dynamic mics are rugged, not as sensitive as condenser mics, and don't need external power. Microphones of all kinds have different **pickup patterns** that determine how and from where they pick up sound, shown in Figure 8.6. Know the pickup pattern of each mic in your equipment package.

FIGURE 8.7

Handheld microphone
Credit: Joan Van Tassel

- **Omnidirectional** mics, called *omnis*, record sound from 360° around the mic pickup. Most small lapel mics (**lavalier** microphones) used in television interviews are omnis.
- **Shotgun** mics are highly directional; they take-in sound signals from far in front of the mic's pickup and, to a lesser degree, from behind it.
- **Cardioid** mics fall in between omnis and shotgun mics because they are partially directional. They pick up sound in heart-shaped patterns, reducing noise from the sides and back of the mic. Subcardioid mics are less directional; they are excellent handheld mics for interviews.

- **Hypercardioid** and **supercardioid** mics increase pickup sensitivity from the back of the mic to capture sounds from the interviewer. This capability reduces the amount back-and-forth mic handling by field reporters. (Note that moving the mic risks introducing noise from the mic cable and connection.)

Look closely! There's a tiny lavalier microphone pinned to Katie Couric's jacket: See her right lapel?

Most "lavs" are omnidirectional and, in the TV industry, they are usually wireless. A wire runs from the lav to the wireless transmitter, clipped to her waistband, which sends the signal to the receiver on the camera.

FIGURE 8.8

Lavalier microphones
Credit: "Lavaliermic" by Rodrigo Ferrusca – Licensed under CC BY-SA 3.0 via Wikimedia Commons U.S. Navy photo, Katie Couric, in public domain via Wikimedia Commons

Shotgun mic with foam

Shotgun mic with 'dead cat' windscreen

Shotgun mic in action

FIGURE 8.9

Shotgun microphones
Credit: Shotgun mic photos: By Galak76 (own pic) [GFDL (www.gnu.org/copyleft/fdl.html) or CC-BY-SA-3.0 (http://creativecommons.org/licenses/by-sa/3.0/)], via Wikimedia Commons Actividep shoot: by Actividep. Licensed under CC BY-SA 3.0 via Wikimedia Commons

6 Pro Tips for Choosing Microphones

1. Always use the best microphone possible.
2. Use dynamic mics in the field – they are sturdy and reliable.
3. Use condenser mics in controlled conditions, such as studios or performance halls.
4. Use lapel mics for lengthy interviews: Moving a handheld mic back and forth between interviewer and interviewee is tiring and distracting and can introduce line noise.
5. Use handheld mics for short interviews and quick quotes (person-on-the-street material).
6. Use shotgun mics when audio sources are more than 5 or 6 feet away.

Recording for Posterity … or Just for Today's Story

Before picking up your phone or heading to the field … do a soundcheck. Plug in the microphone. Use care when handling it; it's a delicate sensing instrument. Don't touch the grill that covers the mic; it's also delicate. And don't wiggle the mic, connectors, or cord – these actions may cause hiss, crackling, and thumping in the audio recording.

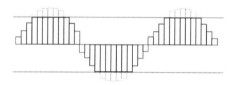

FIGURE 8.10

Clipping in audio is worse than in football

Credit: By David Batley (user:h2g2bob) – Own work, CC BY-SA 3.0, via Wikipedia

Setting and monitoring recording levels is important. If they're set too high, the audio will have **clipping** – losing peak sounds. (Clipping can sound very ugly.) *With digital audio, it's much better to record at too low a dB level than too high a level.* Set DAR sound levels about –12db to –15db for interviews and natural dialog and –10db to –18db for environmental sounds (Ward, 2015). While recording, watch the DAR sound meters and adjust them to hit the mid-point of the range. Before starting to record, stop, and listen to the audio clip. Is it crisp and clear? Do "s" sounds hiss? Or do p's, d's, and t's "pop?" If so, using a **pop filter** over the microphone pickup will help. If it's windy, cover the mic with a windscreen.

It's important to hear what the DAR "hears" – monitor the audio with earbuds or headphones and listen throughout the recording. Both the reporter and interviewee should converse at a normal speaking level. When using handheld mics, position the microphone about 6–10 inches from the speaker's mouth; use the same distance and angle for each person. Encourage speakers to speak *across* the grill and pickup – not down into the mic as novice interviewees might do.

3 Pro Tips for Conducting Audio Interviews

1. Always hold the handheld mic – never let others control your mic.
2. The mic can also serve as a pointer: Let subjects know when to speak by moving the mic toward them.
3. Let people finish their statements. Do not **overlap** speech with the interviewee: Don't interrupt and **step on** a quote – it may become the key "get" from the interview.

RECORDING PODCASTS

Podcasting follows ancient oral traditions of storytelling and conversation. Like those ancient practices, human voices are central to all podcasts. Podcasts unfold in the form of spoken language, rather than written words: "The language in podcasts is seldom very tangled – producers work hard to never leave listeners feeling disoriented, at least not for long or without dramatic effect ..." Weiner (2014). Listening to podcasts requires that listeners create pictures of images in their own minds, thus establishing co-creator relationships between the podcaster's producers and their audience members.

Podcasting Processes

Journalists upload stories to podcast aggregation sites and thereby create libraries for their stories. And they can create their own shows with scheduled episodes to build an audience. Podcasts often feature long, conventional interviews – a host converses with one or more guests and records their conversations. Podcasts that cover specific viewer-interests, illuminating narrow aspects of a broader topic during sequential episodes, have been successful. Examples include modern design, ethics for everyday life, running, and personal investments.

Podcasters typically post shows at regular, scheduled intervals, so listeners know when to tune in or download the pod. Episode lengths vary widely, from less than a minute to an hour. For most shows, episodes usually run about the same length. Podcasts may have multiple segments, covering various aspects of the same topic, multiple topics, or interviews with multiple guests.

The host's question list provides the secret sauce for successful podcasts. Careful preparation that enables the host to ask questions that evoke entertaining, thoughtful, and knowledgeable answers from guests. In contrast, superficial questions elicit superficial answers.

Four indispensable items for podcast production are:

1. *Find or construct a "quiet room"*: Quiet rooms are **sound-proofed** to reduce or eliminate noise. Sound-absorbing materials that cover the walls, floors, ceilings, furniture, and fixtures render quiet rooms acoustically dead.

2. *Microphone*: Use a desktop microphone if your podcast is longer than two or three minutes. The gold standard podcast mic is the legendary Shure SM-M57 with professional XLR connectors. Even this oldie-but-goodie now has an optional XLR-to-USB adapter.

3. *Mixer or two DARs*:
   * A **mixer** takes in multiple audio signals (e.g., reporter and interviewee) and permits the independent setting of sound levels. If one speaker's voice has a big booming bass while the other has a breathy almost-whisper, plugging each person's mic into different mixer inputs and adjusting each speaker's sound level helps to solve that problem.
   * Alternatively, two DAR's will create separate audio tracks if the podcast is an interview with the reporter and one interviewee. (And two DARs cost less than a DAR and a mixer.)

4. *Headphones or good earbuds*: Always monitor the raw podcast sound to hear, identify, and fix problems when they occur.

LIVING OUT LOUD: GO LIVESTREAMING!

Journalists have been live tweeting from the field and posting tweets to publications and social media sites for almost a decade. One reporter likened live tweeting to "using Twitter as his reporter's notebook" (ScribbleLive, 2013). An early example of live multi-media occurred during the explosive Arab Spring of 2011 on the Aljazeera.com website. Simultaneous broadcasting of TV anchors, live shots, and social media feeds from reporters, activists, and experts were all fused into a dynamic, exciting, and up-to-the-minute saga of massive political upheaval. Now everyone livestreams.

But live-streaming also creates problems: The inherent difficulty in curating live social media coverage of breaking hard news may lead to inadequate verification and thus inaccurate reports. Over the past decade, news organizations, editors, and journalists have collaborated to address these issues. Those efforts paid off in 2013 in the aftermath of the terrorist bombings at the Boston Marathon finish line.

The *Boston Globe*'s coverage of that tragedy was so impressive that their *entire staff* won a Pulitzer Prize and an Online News Association award for their live coverage of breaking news (Pulitzer, 2014). While dozens of journalists tweeted, filed stories, and posted videos and photos on Twitter, Vine, and Instagram, all hands in the *Boston Globe* newsroom matched reporters' information, official announcements, and torrents of tweets, photos, along with emails from eyewitnesses to verify reports from multiple sources. Their guiding purpose was not just to receive, repackage, and repeat information, but to ensure accuracy across this panoply of fast-changing live coverage. The Boston.com editorial team used *ScribbleLive*, a software program that lets newsroom editors monitor incoming social media posts from many sources to cross-verify information before publishing it on their news site.

Large news organizations can use *ScribbleLive* or other curating software, but these programs cost too much for most freelancers. Cheaper alternatives can help reporters schedule posts to multiple social media accounts that editors can monitor and publish upon verification. *Hot tip:* If you see something, tweet something. When media companies see steady news reporting from a freelancer using social media, they sometimes negotiate deals to post these tweets and social media streams on their websites.

THE POWERS OF LIVE MEDIA STREAMING

Like live television and radio, live social media put the audience *"there"* ... *right there, as it happens*. Live streams provide a more free-form, behind-the-scenes, personal experience than does broadcast television. They also provide better ways to engage users because of their interactivity: Not only do users see the events happen, both hosts and users see each other's actions and comments.

Live streaming media conveys the importance, urgency, and immediacy of breaking news. Hosts can introduce, frame, and summarize events as they unfold. Combining a news desk with many incoming sources of user reports and comments offers fascinating combinations of observation, speculation, and emotion. Thus, engaging live streaming provides long-form content with the potential to capture users' attention for *hours* instead of just minutes or seconds. Journalists and users can then share these unique, memorable experiences together and thus build followers for individual reporters and for their news sites. These relationships may then create and fortify lasting bonds of trust between users and news organizations.

LIVE STREAMS AS MULTIMEDIA ASSETS

Live streaming offers news sites the potential to scale up their publications by attracting large audiences – audiences that may reach 2 million people or more – if the live-streamed news appeals to broad audience segments. While this technology and the distribution aren't free, it's far less expensive than high-end studios and the satellite time that television broadcasts require to reach comparable (but less engaged) audiences.

Live video and audio streams are particularly effective for breaking news, live events, and live interviews. News organizations can also publish live streams much faster than they can prepare edited video – and they can share the excitement of participating in unfolding events as they happen. Finally, news sites can archive live streams and later re-use this content to provide background, context, and even entertainment for later news stories.

Live streaming requires a computer, camera, live streaming software, and a destination site. Most news organizations use their own sites as destinations. Freelancers also have options to stream-cast live video since YouTube Live and Facebook Live began providing platforms for long-form streaming. And since Twitter's integration of the Periscope app into their social media platform, virtually anyone can live stream video to their personal timeline or to trending topics just by using an appropriate Twitter hashtag.

10 SUGGESTIONS FOR LIVE STREAMING SUCCESS!

Based on several years of live streaming events via social media, journalists should consider these best practices (Power, 2017):

1. Don't try to make the live stream look like broadcast television. (Take advantage of the digital platform.)
2. To build readiness for big breaking stories, make live tweeting and social media part of the job – every day.
3. Live webcasting or short single-scene clips may not require a shot list – but it sure won't hurt.
4. Report the sources of information immediately as the story unfolds.
5. Be *extremely cautious* when reporting anything to users that you haven't personally verified.
6. Don't make assumptions.
7. Admit when you don't know something; live-streaming provides one of the few times that you can learn on the job without embarrassment.
8. Update stories; make corrections to any inaccuracies in earlier reports.
9. Establish a track record for accuracy and candor. Don't remove incorrect earlier posts. Keep the original record even if it's later corrected.
10. Save and share videos after live streams so that they become reusable assets for subsequent stories.

"DATA, DATA EVERYWHERE, BUT NOT A THOUGHT TO THINK." – MATHEMATICIAN JOHN ALLEN PAULOS

Amazing fact: 90 percent of all the world's data was collected during the past two years, according to IBM researchers in 2016 (IBM, 2016). IBM estimated that each day during that 2014–2016 period, humans generated 2.5 quintillion bytes of data. This data-flood originated everywhere: remote sensors, log files, clickstreams, posts to social media sites, digital pictures, video streams, purchase records, credit card transactions, mobile phone GPS signals, and even from AI bots.

Although data may be everywhere, data differ greatly from information. Data are records of observations. Some data, especially quantitative data, come from the **observation** and **measurement** of carefully defined aspects of specified objects (and subjects). Measurement procedures often (and should) dictate exactly what observers look for during observation. Each observation might provide many different, measured, quantitative data points. Alternatively, observations might yield qualitative data in the forms of

---

Example: A research team interviewed a random sample of 1,500 adults over three days to assess the impacts of respondents' age and gender on their confidence in Congress to protect constituents' interests using these questions:

> On a scale of 1 to 5, how confident are you that Congress will protect your interests? Please use the scale below in which 1 means "very little," 3 means "neutral," and 5 means "very much." "What is your gender?" "Finally, what is your age?"

- *Pro tip*: All **variables** *vary* – that is, they change across the individual cases and often from one observation to another.

The dataset below displays the variables: CASE (respondent's identification), ZIP (code), DATE of interview, AGE, GENDER (coded as either 1 or 2; note the hidden assumptions about GENDER in constructing this coding system), and CONFIDENCE that Congress will protect the respondent's interests (coded from 1 to 5).

On a spreadsheet, the data might like this:

CASE	ZIP	DATE	AGE	GENDER (1 or 2)	CONFIDENCE
1	03032	10/15/18	29	1	5
2	60412	10/15/18	52	2	1
3	90405	10/16/18	76	2	3
4	70372	10/16/18	47	1	4

(1,500 cases)

The spreadsheet above would contain much data, but little information. Yet, data analysts using this data could discover important information about how trust in Congress may be influenced by age, gender, and respondents' location. And if the respondents' zip codes were linked to other (pre-existing) zip-code location datasets – and datasets that further linked respondents' zip codes to RURAL-URBAN, STATE, AND 2016 PARTY VOTE variables, the resulting (combined) dataset could provide very important information – especially for journalists covering national politics (and for political operatives).

This example illustrates one reason to hire expert data wranglers as staff or project consultants.

descriptive, contextual, or experiential information rather than more precise (but sometimes less important) quantitative numerical data.

DATA AND ONLINE NEWS NARRATIVES

Online news stories often present data. Cushion, Lewis, and Callaghan (2016), using a large sample of stories (4,285), found that United Kingdom online publications included statistics in almost one-third of their stories. In contrast, traditional media – TV, radio, and print news – only used statistics in about 20 percent of their news stories.

Online users like data. One study assessing visualizations' impacts on user engagement found that articles containing charts and infographics increased users' social participation, length of time on the site, and their article completion rates (Elia, 2015):

- 16–34 percent more comments and shares
- 65–100 percent increase of average session duration
- Up to a three-fold increased depth of scroll (article completion)

Yet, excellent research indicates that news organizations should improve how they use data in stories. Cushion et al. (2016), found that UK journalists too-often presented statistics in vague or incomplete ways – a whopping 75 percent of the time. Sadly, only 25 percent of these stories provided adequate detail and context for their data-based information. And just slightly more than half of these stories included sources for statistical information.

Journalists often just added statistical information that supported the story's dominant perspective. Less than 5 percent of stories included sections that addressed limits of data, its analysis, or an appropriate contextual interpretation of the data. Cushion and colleagues noted:

> Far from data supporting a more diverse information environment, the sources drawn upon for statistical data reinforce the institutional perspectives typically found in news coverage. [...] In other words, the imbalance in statistical sources are not compensated by journalistic scrutiny.

Whatever the shortcomings, data journalism now flourishes. Large organizations like the Associated Press, the BBC, *The New York Times*, and *The Washington Post* have created extensive, expert data teams and acquired the sophisticated tools needed for data analysis and visualization. Lewis (2015) asserted that the ability of users to "search, scrutinize, and visualize" public data shifts journalism from informing users through storytelling to inviting (and guiding) users to explore the data. As publishers gain more experience with data journalism, they can (and should) develop better understandings of users' needs, employ more expert analysis, and formally adopt best data journalism practices (boyd & Crawford, 2012).

The Scientific Revolution in Europe during the 15th century, was grounded on understanding the importance of systematic observation, collection, and analysis of data. Once underway, it led to rapid advances in virtually all scientific and technological realms – changing most aspects of modern life. Carefully collected, analyzed, and shared information derived from data can:

1. *Reveal patterns*: Humans navigate their worlds by recognizing physical, social, and psychological patterns (Kurzweil, 2012). Pattern recognition makes thinking efficient (Ashton, 2013). For example, chess grandmasters require far fewer thoughts to make chess moves than beginners do. Why? Because beginners face huge information jumbles while grandmasters immediately recognize most chess patterns.

2. *Reveal (otherwise invisible) phenomena*: Computers and the internet provide access to timely information about aspects of modern life that were previously hidden: What people do, where they go, how they work, how much they make, what they buy, and thousands of other aspects of daily life. Computers let us collect, store, analyze, and distribute data (and thus information) in near real time.

3. *Guide decisions*: Fast cycles of focused data collection and analysis offer continuous information about what works – and what doesn't (Syman, 2015). Data illuminates the effects of past actions, predicts the likely outcomes of contemplated future actions, and provides insights into real-time processes – thus helping decision-makers chart paths toward desired goals.

4. *Add credibility to narratives*: Narratives often focus on a single person, group, or locale. Data can demonstrate the frequency or salience of issues described in a narrative and can establish links to related problems that interest users.

5. *Bolster factual claims*: In the present environment of "alternative facts," data may not carry the authority it once did. But journalists can offer users ways to drill down into evidence that supports (or fails to support) the central claims in a story.

6. *Tell a story*: Stories have beginnings, middles, and ends. Good stories often have surprises. A sequential analysis of data can help create good stories, revealing unexpected information and shifty, twisty turns – that end with compelling conclusions.

LIMITATIONS OF DATA

Data-based articles are tough to write. Journalists who expect to cite quantitative research routinely should take a research methods course that reflects their beat: business, economics, sociology, psychology, communication, or perhaps a medical/clinical focus. Valid data collection and analysis require specialized expertise – a good contacts list that includes knowledgeable researchers should be among a journalist's prized resources. Even gifted amateurs face pitfalls:

- *Over-quantification*: Although it's always possible to quantify subjective realities, it's rarely clear what the resultant numbers actually mean. For example, researchers may ask people how strongly they approve or disapprove of domestic violence, rated between 1 and 7, but the resulting data can't possibly capture the divergent realities (and trauma) of people's lived experiences.

- *Measurement issues*: Researchers may not measure what they purport to measure. Some measures are straightforward: bank account balance, farm acreage (but not land quality), and income in dollars are numeric (quantitative) measures. Subjective phenomena are far squishier and often less valid or reliable. For example, two people may check "Strongly disagree" on a survey ... but do they mean the same thing by "Strongly" and "disagree." What if one respondent meant "hate," while the second felt "deep concern" or perhaps "disgust"?

- *Sampling issues*: How did researchers find, select, and recruit respondents? Many studies use problematic "convenience" samples – finding anyone willing to answer the researchers' questions. Sometimes unethical researchers select sampling designs that ensure their study results will support researchers' hidden purposes.

- *Analysis issues*: Ronald Coase (1995) wrote: "If you torture the data long enough, it will confess." Coase refers to the many statistical analyses that researchers can use to tease-out findings and thereby support conclusions favored by analysts (or sponsors) that advance personal, organizational, or commercial interests.

- *Reporting issues*: Research reports from academic institutions and government agencies typically follow formalized, professional guidelines – but not always. Sometimes research published by organizations deliberately distorts or describes research findings in self-serving ways. Journalists should seek and report the motivations organizations have for conducting and publicizing research results. When governmental agencies (at all levels) change how they report data; savvy reporters ask themselves the question: "Cui bono?" – "Who benefits?"

ACQUIRING DATA AND DATASETS

Many internet data hubs offer descriptions and extensive resources that help novices (and pros) find complete, publicly available data sets that address the journalist's needs. Careful searches will reveal many such websites. The Journalist's Resource at the Harvard Kennedy School Shorenstein Center on Media, Politics and Public Policy (https://journalistsresource.org) maintains excellent resources for data journalists along with extensive government and non-governmental data for "hot" media topics.

Although federal, state, and local governments and agencies have troves of useful data, only some of this data is readily available, notably at the U.S. Government's Open Data website (www/data.gov/). Too often useful datasets and records have been blocked from public access. Here the **Freedom of Information Act (FOIA)** enables journalists to obtain unreported and even difficult-to-acquire material. Any journalist who plans to produce investigative stories or cover public agencies needs to become a FOIA expert!

Alternatively, a Google search will reveal many sources of datasets available to the public. Academic entities and other nonprofit organizations produce and make available data and sometimes complete datasets. Journalists' organizations also provide data or resources to gather them. There's just no shortage of data for journalists to acquire, analyze, and write about. Now the journalists' problem has become selecting pearls from dross.

News publications can also generate data from their users. These data aren't random samples from the general population or even the publication's user-population – because respondents self-select their participation and, thus, aren't typical of the other users who don't participate. While that bias shouldn't prevent gathering data, it *does* limit the ability to generalize to broader swaths of individuals. Journalists should respect the limitations inherent in their data collection methods to report valid conclusions that take these constraints into account. Even so, a publication's users often become intrigued by stories that link a story's topic with the other users' situations or opinions.

Any process that demands such sophisticated, complex technical skills requires patience, formal courses and workshops, mentors, and practice to transform data into information that can enhance stories. The International Journalists' Network (www.ijnet.org) offers excellent data journalism tutorials and articles. Understanding research methods takes study and careful thought, but it's necessary for journalists to evaluate and report on the quality of data and research. Knowledge of basic statistics is essential. Sometimes, outside experts may save valuable time and money because they can: 1) professionally analyze data, 2) recognize limitations of the research design, and 3) draw solid conclusions from complex research designs and datasets.

Read these three indispensable books to become a proficient data journalist:

- The classic, *Investigative Reporter's Handbook: A Guide to Documents, Databases, and Techniques*, 5th Edition, by Brant Houston and Investigative Reporters and Editors, Inc. Published by Investigative Reporters and Editors, Inc., 2009.
- *Data for Journalists*, 5th Edition, by Brant Houston. Published by Routledge, 2019.
- *The Data Journalism Handbook 2*, 2019, edited by Jonathan Gray and Liliana Bounegru. (in progress but available online). Produced by the European Journalism Centre and Google News Initiative (https://datajournalism.com/read/handbook/two).

TAKEAWAYS

- When news organizations first developed websites, they resembled newspapers with limited space for pages and articles. Now online news sites tailor their designs and layouts to take full advantage of the unique characteristics of online, digital, networked platforms – to deliver a host of features that paper-based publications can't provide. Sites display many stories and pictures on their pages on webpages of variable length (limited only by users' patience). They offer new, powerful ways to engage users, including links, interactive elements, and archives.

- Only online news websites can provide multimedia stories that include text, pictures, audio, video, live streaming media, and data interactives. Most digital content assets provide more information and opportunities for user engagement. Further, online sites combine and remix digital assets for a vast multitude of purposes. Studies confirm that multimedia assets attract users and increase their dwell times on articles when they allow users to experience, explore, and express their opinions.

- Most news sites feature photographs, illustrations, and picture galleries. Combined with headlines, these navigational elements allow users to scan a home page to find the articles they want to access. Audio clips are the least-frequently used multimedia assets, but news organizations often re-purpose radio content for their online sites. Both radio and online, audio-only reports reach people when their eyes are otherwise engaged – when driving or doing other visually-demanding tasks. Audio podcasting has become a popular strategy to reach users on the move and build audiences.

- Digital journalists use the broad palette of media types available as diverse routes to inform users about the people, settings, places, events, and conditions mentioned in a story. Stories thus seem more real, nuanced, entertaining, understandable, interesting, exciting, serious, or even alarming – depending on how the story assets frame and support the article's narrative.

ACQUIRING STORY ASSETS

- *Text* more easily explains complex, abstract ideas, subjects, processes, and actions. Users can scan text and reread it. Users describe the process of reading as "getting there" to understand the story.
- *Pictures* capture important moments and strong emotions in ways that prose cannot. Pictures also provide visual context for stories.
- *Graphics* simplify and clarify numbers, statistics, trends, processes that take place over time, and relationships – including spatial orientation and relationships depicted by maps.
- *Video* adds action, movement, and emotion; it provides a sense of "being there" for stories. 360° video "places" users in the center of a story's environment.
- *Audio clips* increase authenticity and add depth, dimension, and a sense of place to stories. They can also reveal speakers' attitudes, expertise, and emotions. Podcasting lets users download or stream programs for listening on mobile devices, perhaps when driving.
- *Live streaming* lets users receive files bit-by-bit, instead of downloading entire files and saving them on local devices. This lets audiences experience live content – as it happens. When downloading previously created content, live streaming technologies enable users to consume content as it plays out, without lengthy waits.
- *Data content* reaches users in prose, graphics, or designed interactive activities that help people explore diverse ways of looking at data.
- Four key questions about potential content assets guide the asset planning and production process.
  1. What content assets will best enhance the user experience for the story?
  2. Is the story about a planned event or does it take place over time in multiple locations?
  3. After identifying whether a multimedia asset involves covering an event or illuminating a topic, what level of quality does the story require?
  4. What equipment, skills, and time will it take to capture each multimedia asset at the desired level of quality?
- Multimedia equipment needed for content assets includes hardware (camera, microphone, digital audio recorder, and accessories) and software. User manuals describe the proper operation and care of these valuable tools. The skills required for professional-level content acquisition remain formidable, requiring serious study and repeated practice.
- Journalists get data from a host of governmental sources, nonprofit organizations, online data hubs, private companies, and via their own data collection. But raw data isn't nearly enough: Analysis and clear presentation convert data into relevant and useful information. While journalists sometimes use data as click bait or story decorations, *informing users should drive data use*. Sometimes necessary information about the: 1) source of the data, 2) data gathering context, and 3) limitations of the data are *not* provided to users. Research shows that few journalists challenge the accuracy or provenance of data that they provide. These shortcomings in data reporting do not withstand the scrutiny of professional data journalists and discriminating users who are now familiar with appropriate data gathering, analysis, and presentation techniques. These users' comments may reflect poorly on both reporters and publications.

KEY CONCEPTS AND TERMS

- Multimedia assets in online news
- Handling content assets within news organizations
- Multimedia assets and the news creation process
- Planning acquisition of interactive and multimedia assets
- Equipment for the acquisition of multimedia assets
- Content acquisition: Processes, activities, and skillsets
- Data acquisition

EXERCISES AND ACTIVITIES

1. Go to two news websites, one operated by a large news organization and one operated by a local news organization. Count the number of stories on their home pages. Count the images. Identify navigational and interactive elements, such as menus, polls, ads, and notices. Then compare the two home pages.

2. Bring two video cameras, a prosumer or broadcast video camera and your mobile phone, plus a tripod to an event. Shoot several minutes of footage with each device. Use both cameras shooting similar shots, with and without the tripod. Draft a short report, comparing the footage of both video recording devices, with and without the tripod. How do those images compare to the ones you took with your phone?

3. Visit a camera store and "test drive" at least two still cameras, two video cameras, and two microphones. Bring headphones or decent quality earbuds and your own memory card with you. Talk with an experienced salesperson if they have time. Write the manufacturer's name, model number, and price. Take shots and record sound with each camera (including the still cameras). Write short notes about the: 1) quality of the footage and sound, 2) price/performance tradeoffs, and 3) ease of use.

4. Navigate to www.databasic.io/, then click on Connect the Dots. Select "use a sample" and then choose 'Trump's World.' Hover your cursor over the question marks near 'Degree' and 'Centrality,' to understand what they mean. Based on this data, if you wanted to get a message to President Donald Trump, would you try to reach him through Betsy DeVos or Kellyanne Conway? Who would be the best person in the President's circle to go through? Explain your answers.

ADVANCER

Chapter 9 describes how to best process acquired raw material into publishable content assets that add value to stories. Each type of asset requires specialized tools to prepare assets for integration into articles, pages, and sites. In our digital world, most tools include hardware, software, coupled with specialized skills and know-how. Chapter 9 also covers the workflows that journalists devise to manage multimedia assets.

PART III

THE DIGITAL ASSEMBLY LINE: NEWSROOMS TO NEWS PAGES

9

PROCESSING WORKFLOWS: TRANSFORMING ASSETS INTO CONTENT

Chapter Learning Objectives

After reading this chapter, students will be able to:

1. Understand how process workflows transform acquired multimedia files into publishable content.
2. Use metadata to locate story assets.
3. Know the importance of tagging assets for efficient search and retrieval in downstream processing.
4. Choose story assets that enhance users' understanding and engagement in the story.
5. Identify the processing required for individual story assets.
6. Specify the resources needed for processing each type of story asset: hardware, software, utilities, and vendor activities.
7. Develop processing plans for each story asset type, including establishing personal workflows to process each type of story asset copy (text), still images, audio, video, XR, data, interactives, and experiences).

Everything that can be automated will be automated.
— Shoshana Zuboff, *In the Age of the Smart Machine*, 1988

THE GIST

More than 30 years ago, Professor Zuboff proposed three laws for the emerging digital environment. Her prescient first law is much-quoted now that automation is replacing more and more work processes formerly performed by humans. Back in the day, journalists didn't think about automation, let alone "processing workflows." Reporters talked to sources, took or licensed a photograph, wrote the story, and then saw the paper on newsstands several hours later – they just did their job.

They didn't have to download information and upload what they've found to an enterprise Content Management System. They didn't have to work on Content Management Systems (CMS) to write articles, receive edits, and distribute updates. And they could walk down the hall to confer with a colleague instead of Skyping, Zooming, Slacking, or texting a member of the "distributed work team."

Now it's a far more complicated job. Journalists still play foundational roles in the creation of digital news, but they now must integrate their efforts within complex processing workflows. If they work for a media enterprise of any real size, that work will take place using Content Management System, the digital assembly line that depends on metadata to glue the team together. The work product composed by journalists and automation software must work together to produce and distribute a story that can travel around the world to users on many kinds of digital devices.

This chapter breaks down the work of online reporters to initiate the transformation of raw information and media assets into publishable content. The raw files include all the unedited material captured for the specific story: notes and text, graphics, audio, video, and data sets. Each asset type requires media-specific expertise and specialized software tools.

Many news organizations use their Content Management Systems throughout news production and distribution processes to handle today's massive volume of information. All content assets and articles must conform to the formats specified by the CMS for ingesting, tagging, and storing them. As new communication technologies emerge, such as VR and AR, the CMS may not have the capability to accommodate these content assets.

The breadth of skills involved in the preparation is one reason why it takes a team to create complex multimedia stories. For the moment, the creation of XR experiences tends to occur on separate systems because they require specialized expertise, software, and infrastructure to handle the massive data that XR entails.

Workflows provide formalized sequenced steps that ensure completion of complicated content asset processing, from start to finish. This chapter provides comprehensive overviews of these processes and workflows, and describes the competencies needed to process various types of multimedia files.

Most publications use editorial style guides for writing and design, such as the use and placement of story assets as parts of multimedia stories. These organization-specific style guides give the news website a professional, unique, and consistent user experience.

Professional organizations, media companies, and newsrooms also provide ethical guidelines for preparing multimedia and interactive assets. *Some* processing and alterations are acceptable *if* they shape the material to more *closely conform* to the event(s) they purport to represent. For example, if a reporter has a picture or video that took place on a dark, overcast day. If the settings were wrong and the pictures came out too bright, it's usually acceptable to remove some of the brightness from them. But it's not OK to brighten a picture when it faithfully represents a dark, overcast day.

As a story wends its way through the newsroom, from reporter to photo editors, interactive designers, artists, video producers, and section and copyeditors – each team member adds their expertise, often using specialized software to create their work.

Detailed instructions on how to process assets with specific software, such as editing audio or video, color correcting pictures, and creating XR experiences, go well beyond the scope of this chapter. Indeed, entire books are devoted to teaching practitioners these skills. However, interested students can find many online resources to further their learning. Software companies provide helpful video tutorials. And often nearby universities or community colleges offer inexpensive credit and non-credit courses in digital photography, audio processing, and data manipulation – some taught by industry professionals.

PROCESSING RAW ASSETS FOR CONTENT READINESS

As part of the overall news production workflow, processing story assets is a complex activity that takes place between news gathering and publishing, as shown in Figure 9.1. When reporters write the first draft of the story, the thrust of the story becomes clearer and the value of some assets may change. Most important, throughout the production process, journalists should remain mindful of their mission to bring useful information to users and to authentically convey the importance and meaning of the story.

Preparing and processing multimedia demands journalistic, creative, and technical sensibilities. It requires both heart and head, encompassing professional norms, aesthetics, and science. Many reporters come with the norms, the heart, and the art. However, only a select few master the technical and scientific aspects of this work; the rest of us mostly depend on specialists' expertise to prepare multimedia content for publication.

WORKFLOWS IN THE DIGITAL NEWSROOM

A **workflow** is the step-by-step execution of a set of tasks that, if followed, leads to accomplishing a task or goal. Workflows specify the beginning-to-end procedures of what it takes to get a job done. Online news workflows are far more complex than legacy news media workflows because of:

- Greater complexity in the choice of assets to enhance storytelling
- Requirements to prepare multiple media types
- Ever-changing standards, compatibility issues, and regulatory frameworks
- Continuous disruption from technological innovation and change

The advantages of developing workflows for producing multimedia news include greater speed, efficiency, and effectiveness by routinizing decision-making sequences for recurring tasks. In addition, computerized workflows improve finished articles because each stage concludes by checking the work for accuracy and quality (Hardy, 2017). Editors regularly

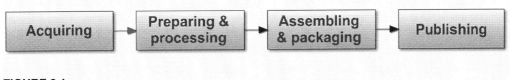

FIGURE 9.1

Transforming information to news
Credit: Joan Van Tassel

check stories to see how far the article has proceeded in the workflow to estimate when it will reach their desks. For news executives, explicit workflows provide transparent ways to estimate costs and budget the resources (time, work, and money) a project will require.

The need for speed is part and parcel of today's competitive digital news marketplace. No one in the newsroom is unaffected by the drive to get the scoop. As this digital reporter's tweets express, being fast and first is a powerful incentive:

Tweet 1: Good news. My #FOIA request for the #MuellerReport was just granted expedited processing.

Tweet 2: I'm totally gonna get it first and beat all you scrubs.

Despite the lure of the scoop, the flood of available information demands careful, orderly handling by journalists, no matter how quickly they want a story published. Reporters must take the time to store and provide keywords that help other team members find and work on assets for the story. CMSs differ in their capabilities. Some CMSs may not handle some types of multimedia content, such as AR, VR, or social media streams – requiring these assets to be managed outside the CMS until the next update. Updates come frequently, a familiar aspect of an ever-changing communications environment that requires newsrooms to revamp work routines continuously.

Metadata Makes Workflows Work

Recall that metadata is data attached to data (including assets such as documents, photographs, videos, datasets, etc.). Metadata is information about the asset files as they move through the Content Management System, from newsgathering through distribution. Metadata information includes the format and size of each file, the creator and creation date, all subsequent changes (when and by whom), descriptive keywords entered by the various individuals who touched it, and many other pieces of information. Without this metadata trail, it would be impossible for the many individuals who work on the story to find and retrieve the assets, know who previously worked on them, and track the sequence of changes that have been made to the asset.

The CMS isn't just an annotated repository for story assets. File metadata provides the informational glue that enables the management and coordination of the work of many people by telling team members what each of the "players" has done, when, and how. CMSs differ and some news organizations design and build their own systems. But CMSs all have this in common: Every participant who touches the story must operate within the constraints of the installed CMS to work in any specific online newsroom.

THE BIG REVEAL: PRE-PROCESSING WORKFLOW

Most journalists develop their own personal habits and workflows to facilitate information-handling, given the increased complexity and speed of online news. Short and simple stories often let reporters hold everything in their brains, using a few notes or material that needs little or no **pre-processing**. Reporters turnaround a 300-word article quickly: It's a routine, well-oiled workflow. One fast way to create these stories is to create a combined research/field notes file, write the lede and nut graf from it, grab several verbatim quotes from the digital audio recorder, and choose a photo … dabba-dabba-do – done in a half-hour or less … now ready to write and publish the story in short order.

Many important stories have more complex structures and workflows: Stories may take place over long time-spans, involve many actors, have wonderful or terrible effects, or affect many people. These stories take much digging and fieldwork to bring

PROCESSING WORKFLOWS

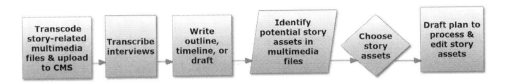

FIGURE 9.2

Pre-processing workflow: Getting ready to get rolling
Credit: Joan Van Tassel

together all the different news articles, documents, pictures, messages, data, interviews, maps, diagrams, and other artifacts that enable the reporter to present and explain the relevant dimensions of the story. For complex stories, the **pre-processing workflow** shown in Figure 9.2 helps journalists organize all the material they may have available for the story. In addition to the complexity, the sheer volume of material often makes it too time-consuming and too expensive to process it all.

Pre-processing lets journalists separate gold from dross, cull material, and select the content that they need to further process a complex story. The six pre-processing workflow steps:

1. *Transcode and upload all story multimedia files to CMS. Transcode all files to usable formats.* Transcoding means converting files from one format to another. Devices capture media files in specific formats such as .jpeg or .raw for photos, .mov, .mts, .mpg for video, .xls for data, .stl files for 3D objects, and so forth. Enterprise content management systems and software applications usually specify the unique file formats that they can import and process. If the acquisition device can't save an asset in the necessary format, the reporter must transcode it from the acquisition format to the CMS-required format. Data files require careful formatting to import them into very specialized analysis and visualization software and services. If required by the news organization, upload all media files to the CMS; otherwise, upload only the material that will go into the story package.

2. *Transcribe all written, audio, and video interviews.* Transcripts provide verbatim text documents of all the questions, answers, and comments that occurred during an interview. If it's a rush job, listen, and just transcribe potential quotes and clips. Time permitting, complete transcripts are better.

3. *Create a **timeline (chronology)**, **mind-map**, outline, or rough draft of the story, as it now stands*, as shown in Figure 9.3. Timelines are particularly helpful for stories that unfold chronologically, from beginning to end. Mind-mapping works well for hierarchical and nonlinear story structures. Topical outlines with bullet points work well for descriptive stories, moving from one aspect of the story to another. Classic rough drafts always work. The best initial structuring document may just depend on which type the writer favors.

4. *Identify potential assets to enhance the story for users.* First, review research, notes, interview transcripts, pictures, and available data. While reviewing, mark, and add notes about material that will enhance the story: quotes, pictures, and data

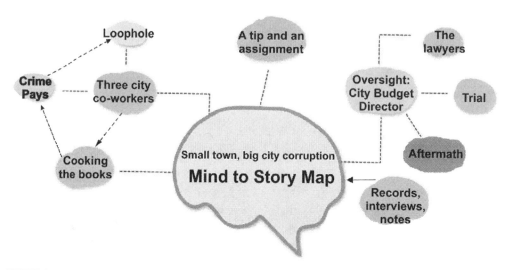
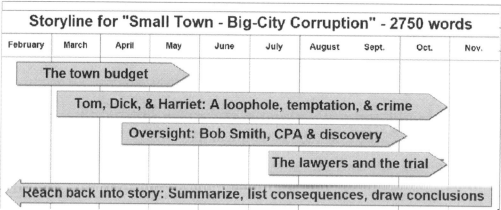

FIGURE 9.3

Story structuring apps: Mindmap and timeline software
Credit: Joan Van Tassel

visualizations. Link potential multimedia assets to related story points in the outline, timeline, mind-map, and/or rough draft. (You may need to go back and forth between identifying potential assets and uploading them to the CMS.)

5. *Choose assets for further processing.* Review the annotated storyline and evaluate whether a multimedia asset will make users' experiences better – or the story clearer or more compelling. Keep only the best and most useful material – hold the rest in the "potential" folder.

6. *Draft plan to process and edit chosen assets.* Assess the processing needed for the chosen assets with an eye toward editing them in the finished article.

A WORD ABOUT CHOICE

Pre-processing requires reporters to face facts: They look squarely at exactly what they have, piece by piece, fact by fact. Then they step back to consider their story and their available assets. Just as reporters must sort relevant facts from unimportant ones, they must also find the most compelling story assets – the one quote, picture, video sequence, audio clip, or interactive data visualization that brings an essential story point into sharp focus for the user.

Taken together, both the copy and the multimedia content should flow together to unfold the story in complete and (hopefully) memorable ways. Even short stories may benefit from related content that offers interested users alternative views and opportunities to drill deeper. Well-executed slideshows, 30-second audio clips, relevant data visualizations, and one-minute explainer videos can raise user engagement.

3 WAYS TO CHOOSE MULTIMEDIA ASSETS

The selection of assets is complicated because journalists must take three differing perspectives into account: the story perspective, the user perspective, and the publication's perspective:

- *The story perspective* examines choices about the best way to tell a story that is consistent with journalistic values. Journalists bring their professional judgment to decide whether an asset buttresses the accuracy, clarity, and completeness of their article. Some questions that arise from the story perspective include:
  - How important is this story; which parts of the story are most important?
  - How many multimedia assets are needed or desirable? Are text and a picture or two sufficient to tell it?
  - Which assets best strengthen the story and make it compelling?
  - Which assets have the greatest technical and aesthetic quality?
  - Where are the optimum places for multimedia assets in the story?

- *The user perspective* focuses on user needs, interests, and wants, including their desire to share stories with others. One part of the journalistic mission charges reporters to understand users and to create stories that satisfy them. If an article covers a current, serious, and weighty issue – users may want context, background, evidence, and analysis. In feature and informational stories, many users want dollops of excitement and entertainment.

  How much users already know from previous stories matters greatly, as does the nature of the coverage that has already appeared in the publication. And up-to-date information about the publication's users always helps journalists, including:
  - **Demographics**: age, gender, socioeconomic status, education, etc.
  - **Values**: religion, spiritual beliefs, personal philosophies, basic political beliefs, cultural norms, ethics, etc.
  - **Lifestyles**: urban/suburban/rural, professional/trade/service workers, full time workers/part-time workers/students/unemployed, retired, stay-at-home spouse, etc.
  - **Interests**: national or world affairs, computers/information technology, politics, business, sports, local news, hobbies, etc.

Users share and forward the news stories they like to their contacts and followers, who share and forward some stories to others in their social networks. Potentially, stories can reach huge numbers of users. One challenge in creating a spreadable multimedia story lies in motivating users to forward it, forward a link to it, post it on their Facebook and Pinterest pages, send out tweets and blog about it, or mention it on their other social networking sites.

Reporters can ask: Is there something in this story that could surprise or delight users? If so, feature it and take aim for going viral! Even without obnoxious clickbait, interesting and engaging articles can go viral – around the world in 80 clicks, perhaps in 80 seconds.

- *The publication's perspective* considers the costs and benefits (reach, reputation, user satisfaction, and revenue) of stories. Executives evaluate these factors to make decisions about the resources that they will allocate to specific projects and stories.

THE PROCESSING MEMO

The processing memo to editors serves as a request for the resources needed to publish a complex, labor-and resource-intensive story. Each of the three previous perspectives should help structure that memo to the editorial team.

The memo begins by affirming the story's importance or interest value (story perspective). It then covers how the additional content will add depth, dimension, and detail – linked to raising user engagement, story dwell time, and increase potential for a wider audience for the site (story and user perspective). Finally, the memo identifies the resources needed to prepare the requested assets (publication's perspective).

Here's what editors and management want to know about resources and costs:

- How many photographs require processing and how long will it take to **crop**, resize, color correct, and caption them? (cost/resources)
- Are there enough photos to comprise an engaging gallery or slideshow? (benefit)
- How much video and audio editing will the project require and how many hours will it involve? (cost/resources)
- How much value will audio and video clips add to the article in terms of revealing important information or providing entertainment, surprise, humor, or beauty? (benefit)
- What data best illuminate the facts presented in the story? Would an infographic or data-based interactive visualization most engage users? (benefit)
  - If interactive, how much time and outside resources will it require? (cost/resources)

The longer the finished story, the more work and resources (time and money) it takes to organize, write, process, and package (assemble) the final story. Some rules of thumb include: Photo processing usually takes minutes to hours. Processing and editing audio and short video clips can take several hours. In contrast, editing a complete package or video segment may take several days, at the rate of about two hours per story-minute. Preparing data for an interactive data visualization may take many hours, perhaps days, depending on the complexity of the story, its data, and the nature of the visualizations.

Creating AR and VR experiences often takes place outside the CMS because they depend on substantial input from in-house or outside experts and require specialized development software.

An attachment to the memo provides detailed information:

1. List of chosen multimedia assets
2. Estimate of resources needed to process each type of story asset:
   * Software
   * Hardware
   * Personnel required
   * Estimate of time required
   * Outside consulting or labor

Newsroom management will get back with approval, a counter-proposal (usually a reduction), or a denial. An approval with reduced resources is a go-ahead. The best strategy is to start work right away. Two good responses to a denial are: 1) Forget about it and move forward; or 2) Gather more information, interviews, and facts and come back again with the new goods, a strengthened case, an attractive appeal to the publication's audience, and a renewed request. Sometimes perseverance pays off; chalk it up to a learning experience when it doesn't.

THE PROCESSING PLAN

The story got the green light – it's a go. The raw assets are ready and available – bagged and tagged. A thoughtful processing plan saves time, effort, and confusion later, especially for long or complex stories. Solid plans include:

1. Lists of approved assets, including the location where each asset resides (drives, directories, files, Content Management System)
2. Processing requirements for each asset
3. Lists of persons responsible for processing
4. Assigned processing priorities for each asset
   * Send out anything that requires work by others as soon as possible – colleagues, other staff or departments, vendors, and consultants: Get them started right away!
5. Lists of resources needed: time, money, software, outside services, etc.
6. Lists of actions/resources needed to acquire any additional assets: hardware, software, outside professionals, etc.

Resources – Human and Nonhuman

Activate the team right away: It's crucial to involve all the people who will create the finished multimedia story content immediately after approval. Get all the new players on the same page by sending the story outline, timeline, mind-map, or rough draft and any storyboards to everyone – editors, departments, colleagues, and perhaps consultants or other specialists. The reporter has already lived the story from gathering information and acquiring assets, to creating story elements. In contrast, the people coming into the story at the processing stage typically need information and time to absorb the story's requirements and consider how to best contribute their own knowledge and expertise.

Even the roughest draft of the copy or a hand-drawn storyboard enables colleagues to start thinking about how to help. Reporters who anticipate their colleagues' needs often find themselves pleasantly surprised by others' ideas and strategies. Prompt assignments to others gets stories published faster because contributors can add more granular estimates of time-to-completion. Freelancers who put together multimedia stories by themselves often find their time estimates considerably more challenging, depending on their level of training and experience in producing the story element packages.

Identify and gather all the resources needed for processing before beginning work on assets. Once the asset processing work begins, it's easy to lose creative ideas or your train of thought when Googling "free audio software" and then downloading, installing, and figuring out how the software works. So, get all the required resources before starting if you can – this later saves you time and eases your mental stress. Three last actions:

1. Locate all needed hardware
2. Download and install any required software – and check out each demo or tutorial
3. Create a list of sites that offer instructions and/or free software and utilities

WRITING AS A WORKFLOW

"In the beginning was the Word ..." and that's the gospel truth for multimedia stories because all else depends on the writing. Even if an article turns out to be mostly info-graphics, lists, photographs, data, audio, or video – the story's copy provides a necessary spine. A written text clarifies the internal sequence of multimedia news articles in ways that no other form of communication can.

Journalists develop their own personal workflow to support the way they write, the topics they write about, and the demands of the contexts in which they work: genres, technologies, industries, societies, and cultures. Of course, digital writing toolsets change frequently as companies roll out software revisions and updates. New apps appear and older apps disappear.

THE COPY WORKFLOW (TEXT)

When a reporter submits copy to a news operation, it goes through an editorial process mandated by the newsroom governing the sequences of writing, editing, rewriting, and re-editing. A generic copy processing workflow is shown in Figure 9.4. However, don't be surprised if a newsroom adds a few of its own wrinkles to the process.

The basic writing requirements for any online story: Make the article readable, engaging, and clickable (BBC, 2017). The short article needs a lede, a nut graf, a little background and context, a quote or two, and a summary. A picture or two and perhaps a video or audio clip can make a five-paragraph report come alive. If the reporter captured interesting, rich visuals, a slide show, or photo gallery – readers may become even more engaged. The multimedia assets used for short stories require little in the way of processing. Reporters draw on their notes, a few documents, and their camera roll to write these articles. Most of the information they need resides in their heads – spreading out the

PROCESSING WORKFLOWS

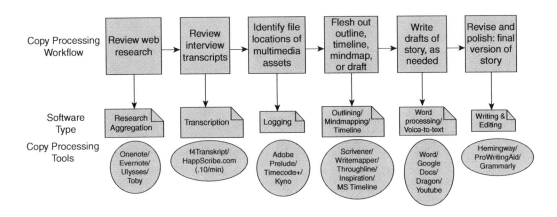

FIGURE 9.4

Copy processing workflow
Credit: Joan Van Tassel

materials that go into the story may be all the content management they need. If writing the headline, make sure it appeals to the audience – curiosity, action, or emotion often drive clicks.

THE COMPLEXITY CHALLENGE

Complex stories demand exceptional skills. The reporter becomes a sculptor, shaping parts of the story into a coherent whole. It takes discipline, intelligence, and artistry to mold storytelling prose and story assets into an article that engages and informs. From the start, the most important question is: What about this story warrants the time and

FIGURE 9.5

Watch those hyphens: This headline went viral on the Net
Credit: Clker-Free-Vector-Images from Pixabay.com

expense to prepare multimedia and data visualization assets? Okay, let's say the story *is* worth it – it's important, meaningful, entertaining, or all that and more.

For a complex story, start the writing process by going back to the initial timeline, outline, mindmap, or draft. That early end-to-end document provided descriptions of facts and events and perhaps a chronology. Now expand it by adding details. Go through the corpus of articles and documents, summarizing their content. If the software allows, link to the source of the information; otherwise, copy that in as well. (The link should provide the location and file name of each source of information.) Indicate in the expanded draft ideas about where multimedia assets might go.

These annotations make it possible to more easily discern the shape of the story: The expanded draft becomes a roadmap to the final multimedia story. An annotated outline for a strongly narrated story about a demonstration in front of a government building in a medium-sized town might look like this:

Lede: Who, what, where, when

Police arrested 22 demonstrators today when they broke through barriers placed in front of the county Department of Human Services office downtown. Six demonstrators sustained injuries as police pushed against the crowd.

Photo: n:\1-18-16 demo\demonstration.tif

Caption: Ann Johnson, helping Lucille Newton, 83, stand

Nut graf summary: Increasing tension between DHS and welfare recipients, shown by recent altercations between agency, clients, and police. Recount political consequences affecting the upcoming election cycle. 350 words

INSERT VIDEO PACKAGE HERE (FILENAME):

(**Title:** Demonstration at DHS. User clicks on video arrow to play)

Video: 2 min. edited package, vid on Tape #3, 090615, shots @
18:27:24 –18:30:04

Audio: Voiceover (VO) and nat. sound on #3 with pix – Crowd
breaks through, pushed back, arrests, etc.
090615, 17:18:31–17:19:40:
Johnson, "Let me help you … stand with me."

Topic 1 text: The budget cuts hit hard – cover federal and state-level cuts that have impacted the poorest of the poor.

Interactive data-viz: *Embed DV showing* "Areas of city clickable to show percentage of the population receiving welfare or food stamps, by year"

Photo: Close-up: Child's lunch box with only potato chips

INSERT AUDIO CLIP HERE (FILENAME):

Title: A Second Grader's Lunch – [User clicks on sound icon to play]

Audio: VO and nat sound.

Clip: on DAR file 090217, 07:37:29–07:38:09:

Robby: "My lunch box … Yeah, I'm hungry."

Text: Topic 2 summary, Topic 3 summary, Topic 4 summary, etc.:
>   (Keep going with key topics.)

Text: Conclusion summary
>   **INSERT: 05 VIDEO HERE**
>   Roll vid of Robby eating potato chip to FREEZE FRAME
>   **INSERT: 05 AUDIO HERE (see previous audio clip): (FILENAME)**
>   **VO**: Robby: "Yeah, I'm hungry."
>   **Audio music or sound effect stinger.**

Figure 9.6 shows a mind-map or workflow process diagram of this multimedia story. Using the detailed document, identity the copy elements needed for the story from beginning to end: lede, nut graf, setups, and transitions. In this story, the freezeframe of Robby and his statement "Yeah, I'm hungry" serve as the kicker. Now sit down and write those copy elements! Then rewrite them. Then polish them.

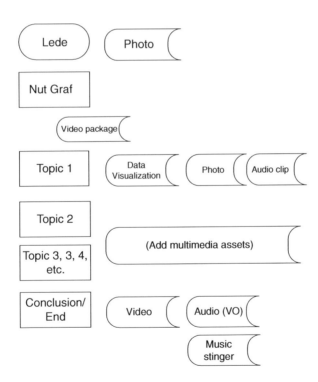

FIGURE 9.6

Mind-map or workflow process diagram of annotated story outline
Credit: Joan Van Tassel

WHY 1,000 WORDS DESERVE A PICTURE

Why use pictures in the first place? How can they enhance a story? Prose provides sequence, causation, and nuance in ways pictures cannot. However, pictures add information in ways that prose typically does not (Coleman, 2010; Powell, Boomgaarden, De Swert, and de Vreese, 2015). Research shows that pictures in news reports:

- Arouse different parts of the brain than written words – apparently two channels *are* better than one
- Add and concretize details
- Evoke emotion
- Provide context
- Clarify and simplify understanding of complex processes and events
- Create a memorable emblem or symbol of a moment, predicament, an entire situation or set of events.

The choice of photos for a story often starts with this decision: Should the image mirror the text or complement it? When a photo repeats in a visual form what the copy says in text, the photo is said to **mirror** the copy. When a picture **complements** the text, it enhances or augments the text. Both strategies have benefits, although many advise that complementing is better than mirroring because it introduces new information.

THE PHOTO PROCESSING WORKFLOW

Almost all photos need (several) adjustments to reproduce the scene that the photographer saw when taking the shot. When journalists file photos from the field, they often do preliminary processing on location before uploading or emailing them. In newsrooms, journalists upload them to their publication's CMS from the photo editing software. When journalists are responsible for final preparation of the photos, they usually analyze the image first and make notes. Then they open each photo and make the necessary adjustments, shown in Figure 9.7.

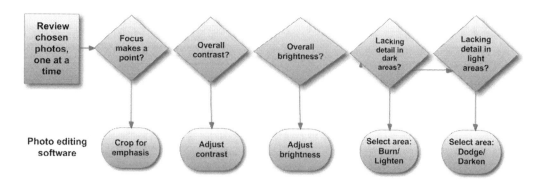

FIGURE 9.7

Photo processing workflow
Credit: Joan Van Tassel

PROCESSING WORKFLOWS

1. **Framing** – cropping the photograph: Photographers do some framing when taking the photograph. However, refining that framing more clearly defines the intended subject of interest to viewers (Smith, 2016). Figure 9.8 shows alternative cropping of pictures of the Passion Façade of the Sagrada Familia Basilica in Barcelona, Spain.

   * Picture 1 of the full Western façade would mirror a story about the austere style that architect Antoni Gaudi envisioned.
   * Picture 2 shows the four towers and would mirror a story describing how long it took to construct them (139 years and counting) if the article was about the team of sculptors who created the figures crowning the towers.
   * Picture 3 might complement the story by helping users focus on these artistic elements.
   * Other reasons to crop photos include: cutting out distracting elements, telling a story with pictures, creating a consistent look and style, and creating balance within the picture.

FIGURE 9.8

Cropping to the story

Credit: By Bernard Gagnon – Own work, CC BY-SA 3.0, https://commons.wikimedia.org/w/index.php?curid=9029528

2. **Exposure**: Most software offers several tools to adjust contrast and brightness. The basis for adjusting an image for the amount of lightness and darkness, or **luminance**, is usually a **histogram**. In photography, a histogram shows the left-to-right distribution of pixels from dark-to-light that fall on the luminance range between 0 and 255 (Orion, 2014). Too many pixels on the left? Picture is too dark. Too many pixels on the right? Picture is too light. Too many pixels in the middle? Picture is washed out because it lacks blacks and whites.

   The "before" and "after" histograms in Figure 9.9 show that some of the darkest pixels were shifted slightly right toward the middle (lighter) and some of the lightest pixels on the right were shifted left toward the middle. Take a close look at the histogram on the right: Notice that the "sawtooth" structure of the second histogram greater diversity in the distribution of luminance values.

   Figure 9.10 shows a house cat's picture, the photograph underlying the values displayed in the first histogram: The spikes at the dark and the fall-off at the light end reflects how the dark parts of the cat's head blend in with the carpet in the first picture.

   In the second picture of the cat, look closely at the cat's ears, especially on the cat's right ear. Notice how much more detail exists in the brightened and raised gamma version. Now go back to the histograms in Figure 9.9. The light frequencies on the right are raised – the cat is brighter. The extreme darks and lights at the ends of the

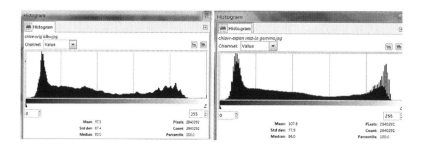

FIGURE 9.9

Histograms of cropped grayscale image, before and after adjustment
Credit: Joan Van Tassel

FIGURE 9.10

Original photo and photo corrected for exposure and detail
Credit: Laurie Rennie

luminance spectrum show a sawtooth in the values. It means there is more discrimination in the values – more luminance detail. The mid-tones follow the same range of values but the spikes are smoother, a result of lowering the gamma to expand the range of mid-tones.

3. **Adjusting color**: Users' devices bring up pages in vibrant color – and users click on images and the articles they accompany. When journalists add color pictures, they need them to display properly on the web, which uses a **color space** called **sRGB**. A color space is a system for converting data (numbers) to visible colors.

The first step in editing pictures is to get the settings right. Most reporters shoot RAW photos, which is all data – there is no "color space" for this data. However, photo editing software converts RAW images to .jpg or .png, using the color space setting in the software "Preferences" or "Settings." Another setting is for **gamma**, a measure of the range of light and dark output by a computer screen monitor. The appropriate setting means the lights and darks will display properly on the monitor, which also enables vibrant color.

To begin, make sure the equipment is set up for the job:

- **Calibrate** the computer monitor: Check the User Guide to find out how to calibrate the device used for photo editing.
- Set color space and gamma for the monitor: Look for the "Color Management" setting and select sRGB. If there is a gamma setting for the screen display, set it to 2.2.

In addition to cropping, the adjustments that maximize the display of color pictures on the web include:

- **Saturation** is the intensity of the color that ranges from freakishly intense and weird to washed-out color to black, white, and gray.
- **Hue** is color – red, blue, yellow, magenta, green, etc. It is possible to adjust all hues together or one at a time.
- **Contrast** makes lights lighter and darks darker, maximizing the contrast between light and dark. Low contrast makes a photograph look gray and washed out.
- **Brightness** affects the mid-tones in a picture. (Compare to contrast, which affects the lights and darks.)
- **Filters** are the fun ways to change pictures like in Snapchat and Instagram on mobile phones. Most photo editing software comes with many filters. Unless the article is about fashion, culture, or humor, filters probably aren't too useful in news.
- **Screens and overlays** bring transparent effects to a picture, floating over everything in the picture. Most of these effects are uniform colors or patterns.

PERMISSIBLE ALTERATIONS OF PHOTOGRAPHS

News professionals have limits on how and how much they may process photographs. One key limit is **fidelity to reality**. That is, a photograph must remain as much like the reality it purports to represent as possible. (Other images, such as drawings, illustrations, and other graphics and human-created graphics, are clearly constructions so they are explicit fabrications.) Many news organizations have formal guidelines that editors and reporters follow. Specific policies depend on the publication, the nature of the story, and the abilities of the reporter or photo editor. The key principle: When substantially altered photographs appear in non-hard news contexts, any alterations must be obvious and labeled so users know how these images have been edited.

Photo enhancement, alteration, and manipulation have become growing concerns in many newsrooms. The digital revolution raises profound ethical issues about how to handle photographs. The National Press Photographers Association's *Code of Ethics* (n.d.) states: "Editing should maintain the integrity of the photographic images' content and context. Do not manipulate images or add or alter sound in any way that can mislead viewers or misrepresent subjects."

The New York Times advises in its long-held *Guidelines on Integrity* (2008):

Photography and Images. Images in our pages that purport to depict reality must be genuine in every way. No people or objects may be added, rearranged, reversed, distorted or removed from a scene (except for the recognized practice of cropping to omit extraneous outer portions). Adjustments of color or gray scale should be limited to those minimally necessary for clear and accurate reproduction, analogous to the "burning" and "dodging" that formerly took place in darkroom processing of images. Pictures of news situations must not be posed.

No "World Court of Journalistic Ethics Violation" or "News Image Police" exist to punish or jail guilty journalists. Still, it pays to play by the rules, especially when reporting hard news. Thus, there should be no special effects, no sharpening, nor morphing without clear and prominent disclosure to users. The journalistic community will more likely respect colleagues who work within the guidelines of the profession.

STYLIN' THE VID: 4 DISTINCT STYLES OF ONLINE NEWS VIDEO

Online vids aren't your father's television. "Great!" say most young adults – that old stuff isn't interesting anyway. Research backs up this judgment, at least when it comes to news. In 2016, TV news viewership fell for the first time in decades. This decline occurred among all age groups but was substantially greater for young users in the UK, the USA, and France (Nielsen & Sambrook, 2016). The same period showed that a slow but steady rise in viewing online news video occurred in most Western countries (Kalogeropoulos, Cherubini, & Newman, 2016), not including the rapid increase in repurposed news videos on YouTube, Facebook, and other social media sites.

Back in 2012, *The New York Times* set the standard for cinematic-style news production with its iconic publication of a Pulitzer Prize-winning multimedia feature story, *Snow Fall*. This story covered a series of avalanches, using video, photographs, and data visualizations to enrich the copy. It created a user experience described as: "so beautiful it has a lot of people wondering if the mainstream media is about to forgo words and pictures for a whole lot more, or at least a new Times redesign" (Greenfield, 2012). *The New York Times* team that produced the piece included 11 people working on the visuals: graphic artists and designers, a photographer, three video specialists, and a researcher – in addition to the reporter and editors. Even with all these people working on it, *Snow Fall* took six months to complete.

Four genres account for most contemporary online news videos:

1. **Cinematic documentary video**: Often high-quality production and editing that allows news subjects to play prominent narrative roles. It's designed to engage users at subjective aesthetic and thematic levels, in addition to conveying knowledge.

2. **Traditional TV news video packages**: News networks and stations often upload video packages online that previously ran on scheduled television news shows. Shot with high-quality equipment and precisely edited for clarity and news value, these packages present current news events and happenings of interest to the public.

3. **Native online video**: Made for the internet, most vids are less than 2.5 minutes that depict unscripted behind the scene material. Often short and minimally edited, they're designed to elicit user engagement and interaction. Increasingly, user-repurposed news videos are uploaded to Facebook and other social media sites.

4. **User-generated video (UGV):** Digital video produced and uploaded by users. Users post original videos as well as remixes that they create from existing footage.

The list shows the wide range of video content that appeals to users. Journalists can draw from any of them to best tell their story. For example, a special project may call for a long-form cinematic documentary. Or the reporter who works at a multi-platform news operation can repurpose one-to-three-minute television-style news packages for the website. A package destined for a social media site shouldn't be much longer than 75 seconds: The average length of Facebook native news videos (Kalogeropoulos et al., 2016). And when journalists and users post video from their mobile phones for Instagram or Snapchat, they should format the video to fit the vertical and square formats for vids posted on those sites.

THE VIDEO PROCESSING WORKFLOW

Preparing edited video requires a broad, valuable skillset to cope with exacting, complex, and often difficult work. This highly complicated workflow is shown in Figure 9.11. Video processing begins with a first-draft script. The script serves as a roadmap because it:

- Shows the journey from beginning to end.
- Shows the incremental steps to reach the destination.
- Indicates points of interest, rest stops, and construction zones.

The first-draft script guides the way to an edited video, especially for long packages that unfold complex stories. This chapter has already covered the preparation needed before processing video material, including logging the footage and transcribing interviews. Now, this "tripod of materials" (logs, transcripts, and script) buttress each other to make the

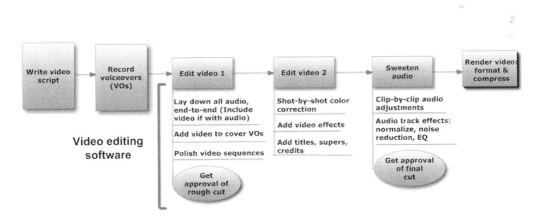

FIGURE 9.11

Video asset processing workflow
Credit: Joan Van Tassel

editing process go smoothly, saving untold hours of frustration hunting for materials and re-doing edits.

A shooting script, as suggested in Chapter 8, provides a good starting point. Otherwise, start from scratch. Here, function trumps form; video editing scripts need not be perfectly crafted or formatted documents – they can even be handwritten.

Sample Rough Cut Video Script

Story: Sold Out

VIDEO	AUDIO
ONCAM STANDUP	If you were hoping to get tickets to Fringe Benefits when
DISS IN: EXT SHOTS, Dark Knight Club	they play at Dark Knight next month on the 10th, 11th,
ONCAM: Dark Knight manager	and 12th. Sorry ... you're already too late.
SUPER: Frank Almorra, Dark Knight Manager	VOICEOVER NARRATION: Dark Knight's management told us that they're all gone, even for standing room only.
DISSOLVE IN: MUSIC VID/FRINGE BENEFITS	ALMORRA: We know how popular this local group is, but we were surprised to sell out in two days. (MUSIC
ONCAM fan	VID SOUND UNDER :05)
SUPER: Emmy Jackson	(MUSIC VID SOUND UP :15–:20)
B-ROLL SHOTS:	EMMY: No-o-o-o, I'm totally bumming ... say it ain't so!
ONCAM/Almorra, Dark Knight Mgr	VOICEOVER NARRATION: But it is ... and Fringe
DISS IN MUSIC VID/BROKEN GLASS	Bennies is hitting the road for a two-month tour right after.
	ALMORRA: The week after, we've booked Broken Glass, so get your tickets for them soon!
	VOICEOVER NARRATION: There ya go – Early bird gets the word!
	OUT: MUSIC VID FADE UP

Editing, Sweetening, and Rendering

Making videos is an intensely creative enterprise. It can take much time to acquire both the technical chops and visual storytelling sensibilities. Journalists who want to work with video should take classes, workshops, and sit-in with professionally trained editors to advance their skills. But after mastering these skills, creating a flowing, living story out of a bunch of disparate clips can be one of the most fun, exciting, and satisfying parts of creating multimedia stories.

Almost everyone begins with the script ... but only if they want to bring in the story by the deadline! Scripts identify for placement the likely-to-be-used clips in a dedicated directory. Then individual journalists have their own way of assembling their story from the script, to make the video/audio editing workflow go smoothly, as shown in Figure 9.12.

Editing is a process almost impossible to describe with words. Ask an experienced editor to show you how she edits. Some editors first assemble all the audio end-to-end (with video if it is there), and then record and slug-in voiceovers on the audio track. Next, they edit the audio without reference to the picture – leave the picture blank and let the voiceovers or other sound-only stand alone.

PROCESSING WORKFLOWS

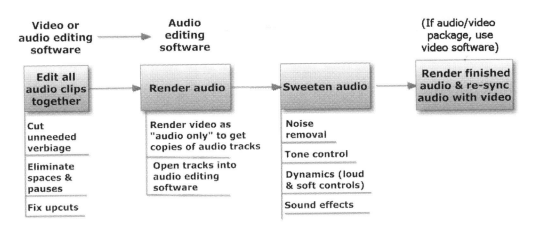

FIGURE 9.12

Editing workflow for video and audio
Credit: Joan Van Tassel

After the audio track tells a good story, beginning to end, look carefully at the video. Are there any weird cuts or blank spots in the video track, where there is narration or voiceover on the audio track? Now backfill the empty places on the video track where there are weird edits (because of cuts on the audio track) or there's no video at all (such as covering audio narration and voiceovers) – and lay down new video where needed. Finally, adjust the video track to make transitions (dissolves, wipes, etc.).

Sometimes editors also build visual montages separately and drop them on the video track, allowing the audio to run under the montage. (A montage is an editing technique that uses a series of short shots to show several aspects of an event or character. They compress time and information in a short period.)

As with photographs, journalists refrain from altering video or adding effects, unless the piece is clearly entertainment. For hard news, credibility rules – even when shots are faulty, perhaps unsteady or out of focus. Yet it is permitted (and often desired) to adjust color, contrast, and brightness to depict how the scene looked to the videographer who took the shot. (Fidelity to reality remains the standard for journalists' stories.)

One unexpected benefit of hands-on editing: It sharpens journalists' performance in planning and shooting because they better understand how their shots will fit together as a narrative in the edit bay. It's hard to estimate the time it takes to edit video because editing depends on so many different factors. This imprecise guide provides ball-park estimates of the time required to edit video:

- *Edit short video clips* (30–45 minutes total)
- *Edit video news package* (half an hour to one hour per finished minute)
- *Edit documentary-style video* (two hours per finished minute)
- *Edit cinematic video* (as long as it takes)

Sweetening is the process that makes audio sound full and clear – pleasant to the ears, as shown in Figure 9.13. It's important because the credibility of a video depends on the sound more than the picture! Hard to believe, isn't it? OK, sure the picture matters a lot. But audio is the dealmaker ... or the deal-breaker. Users look at pictures from a perspective, at a distance. They listen to sound that comes to them and surrounds them. (Notice: People look *at* a screen; they listen *to* a soundtrack.) For users, if a picture isn't exactly right, it's annoying or amusing, but users can typically live with it. Bad sound? They're outta there.

The clarity of spoken words is all-important in news: Listeners must be able to hear what people say. Thus, audio sweetening might include four common adjustments that improve clarity of speech (Robertson, 2012). Audio news clips rarely get the attention that images do – so too many journalists remain unfamiliar with even basic audio editing tasks. Fortunately, as with photographs, only a few alterations should be made to audio clips – and they have similar purposes: to eliminate distraction, focus attention, and improve listenability.

- **Normalization** adjusts the overall loudness or volume of several clips edited together, so that users don't have to change the volume control for each new clip. Compared to photo editing, normalization resembles raising or lowering overall brightness or contrast of a picture.
- **Noise reduction** (NR) eliminates distracting sounds that make spoken words hard to hear or understand, much as cropping eliminates unnecessary content in a photograph. NR functions include frequency smoothing to make distracting sounds less prominent, de-essing (to lower the hiss inherent when people speak words with "s" in them), and high- and low-pass filtering to remove very high and low noises such as

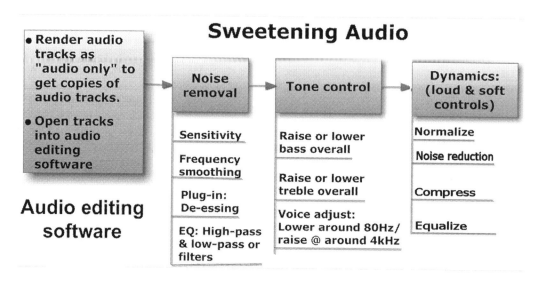

FIGURE 9.13

Details of sweetening workflow
Credit: Joan Van Tassel

PROCESSING WORKFLOWS

air conditioning, fans, traffic, airplanes, and wind. (Use NR sparingly because it can degrade the overall audio quality.)

- **Compression** limits the range of loudness and quiet, making loud sounds quieter and quiet sounds louder.
- **Equalization** raises or lowers specific frequencies to separate spoken words from environmental sounds, making statements more prominent in the clip. In photography, this process resembles burning and dodging areas of a photograph to bring out detail. Muddy voices may become clear by raising a swathe of frequencies around 40Hz. And flat or thin voices brighten with raised frequencies around 4,000Hz.

The two audio alterations used infrequently in news are sound effects and music. Some audio pieces open and close with an audio **sting,** a short set of tones. When in doubt, don't use music because the fundamental rule is: If it wasn't there when you recorded the clip, don't add it. However, entertainment, and coverage of culture and society, often permit exceptions to this rule.

Rendering: The final step in the process is to **render** the finished and audio video into the appropriate format for publication. The format selected depends on the publication outlet and the destination(s) where the online video will reside. Rendering may also involve wrapping the output along with a player to display it and provide user controls (play/pause/stop/audio level).

Processing and editing cinematic-style documentaries are the most demanding of all the video genres. All other forms are *much* easier. An example of the demanding workflow to process and edit shows the complexity of that task. Editors of these videos possess a broad array of exceptional creative and technological skills. Consider this professional editor's description of his sophisticated workflow (Sturm, 2016), listing the software (that costs thousands of dollars) used to prepare high-quality videos:

1. DaVinci Resolve v12.5 – Dailies
2. Avid Media Composer v7.0.3 – Offline
3. Apple Compressor v3.5.3 – Encodes
4. Nuke Studio/NukeX 10.0v3 – Picture conform, Online, VFX
5. DaVinci Resolve v12.5 – Color correction
6. Nuke Studio 10.0v3 *or* After Effects CC 2015 – Motion graphics
7. Final Cut Pro v7.0.3 – Audio conform
8. Soundtrack Pro v3.0.1 – Audio editing and sweetening
9. Final Cut Pro v7.0.3 – Final output

AUDIO-ONLY STORY PROCESSING: EDITING, SWEETENING, AND RENDERING

When radio broadcasters post stories online, they are audio-only. Infrequently, a few online news sites publish audio-only stories. For example, the BBC experiments with audio-only pieces in its BBC Stories section (Southern, 2018). More often, publications intersperse audio clips between sections of copy, using clips as **"receipts,"** to prove that the person speaking made the statements and the journalist has reported the quote accurately.

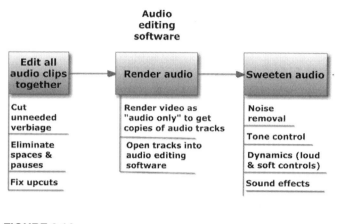

FIGURE 9.14

Audio-only processing workflow
Credit: Joan Van Tassel

Since video usually includes audio, it's important for journalists to know how to edit and process audio, too: The audio processing and editing workflow remains the same, with or without video, shown in Figure 9.14. As with photographs and video, news publications permit only limited alteration to audio clips. Again, a story that is clearly intended to entertain may legitimately include more effects, humor, and surprises than stories with audio documenting hard news. Thus, processing audio usually entails re-creating the sound that existed when the recording occurred.

EDITING AUDIO

The first consequential alteration which occurs in audio editing is choosing to include some parts and excluding others (while taking care to present the speakers' statements faithfully). The fastest method of editing (a necessary skill in newsrooms): create the multimedia piece by cutting together all the audio **bites**, from beginning to end. (Notice that audio bites aren't bytes. Bytes refer to multiple digital information bits.) Many editors use a quick **fade in** at the start of an audio clip and a fast **fade out** at the end.

If the audio is part of a video, put both video and audio together on the timeline. Forget about the video for a minute: Focus on the audio. Review the audio from beginning to end for story continuity. Now review it again and take notes, looking for changes that affect the overall length of the piece because these changes can affect the visual sequence if the piece includes video. Time-affecting changes include:

- Extra verbiage? Make interview bites as succinct and crisp as possible. Eliminate extended interjections, such as hmmm, ahhh, ohhhh, welllll.
- Remove spaces between audio edits that are too long.
- Fix upcuts, which are the opposite of spaces. **Upcuts** occur when an edit cuts off a person's statement before she finished speaking. When ending a sentence, the voice "rests." When there is an upcut, the voice tone does not go lower, as it usually does, so the bite sounds like it was cut off too early (which it was). Possible solutions: Let the bite run longer, cut audio earlier, cover content in voiceover, or acknowledge the upcut in voiceover narration.

Before starting the sweetening process, play the audio and listen. Then listen again and make notes for the sound shaping adjustments shown in Figure 9.14. When people listen, their brains focus on speech, add information from memory, and filter out unimportant sounds: But recordings don't. They recreate the sound received and processed by the equipment – microphone, cords, and recorder – and often sound quite differently from what the humans in the room originally heard. Sweetening recreates an approximation of the sound that the listeners experienced.

TRANSFORM DATA INTO INFORMATION

Charts, graphs, and infographics appear on many online news webpages that cover current events, business and economics, politics, and sports. Static figures such as bar charts and line graphs are commonplace. Interactive data visualizations appear in most major publications, like *The New York Times*, *The Washington Post*, *The Wall Street Journal*, *National Geographic*, and *The Guardian*. Increasingly, large online news sites employ data journalists and interactive designers to create attractive and engaging data visualizations (DVs).

Static DVs show readers simple relationships between variables at a glance. For example, the polio vaccine virtually wiped-out polio in four decades. Inoculation started in 1973 and reduced the number of polio cases (almost) to worldwide extinction by 2012. Compare this partial list of number of reported polio cases by year with the line graph, shown in Figure 9.15:

1973	49,000
1979	52,000
1984	38,000
1990	30,000
1995	8,000
2001	1,000

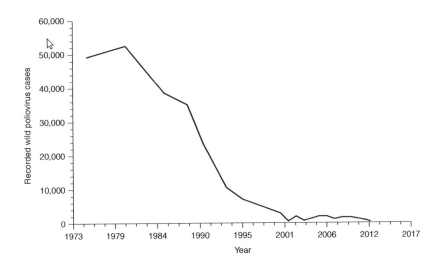

FIGURE 9.15

Effect of polio vaccine on incidence of polio worldwide

Credit: By Microchip08 [CC0], from Wikimedia Commons Licensed under the Creative Commons CC0 1.0 Universal Public Domain at: https://commons.wikimedia.org/wiki/File:Polio_cases_over_time.svg

The visual line graph helps users instantly grasp the dramatic reduction of polio cases in less than 30 years after the vaccine's introduction. In the era of Big Data, DVs help users make sense of huge, complex data sets with many important variables that may have millions of data points. DVs allow users to comprehend the most important research findings. Dense paragraphs explaining complex research findings make tough reads for most people. But lines trending up or down provide comprehensible results instantly, so users remain engaged with the article, and focus on what the data reveal about their world (Tufte, 2001).

THE DATA PROCESSING WORKFLOW

The previous chapter covered how journalists acquire data. The workflow for turning that data into usable information DVs involves three phases, shown in Figure 9.16:

1. Data wrangling: Create the database
2. Data analysis: Understand the data and its context
3. Data visualization: Design visual representations of the data that are relevant to the story

DATA WRANGLING

Data is often just a string of numbers, signifying little or nothing. Data must be defined, labeled, and formatted prior to analysis. Investigators first define each variable and its possible values. Are they text, numeric, string, or date variables? Typical dataset layouts use grids – a matrix in which **columns** display the states (or values) of **variables** (something that changes), and **rows** that display each **case** in the dataset. Cases may be subjects (Republicans, hurricanes, tagged elephants, or widows and orphans). Cases might also be observations, events (car accidents, Ferris wheel rides, incarcerations, or new jobs).

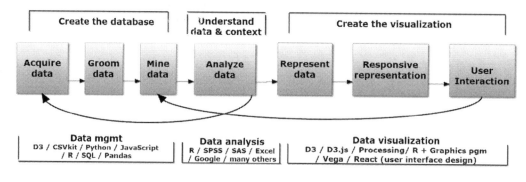

FIGURE 9.16

Data processing work flow
Credit: Joan Van Tassel

The top of each column displays the label for each variable; a (variable) codebook specifies the variable's exact definition (e.g., 2017 household income, 2018 FBI crime rate, Rotten Tomato Movie Critic score). Codebooks should also specify the permissible ranges for each variable – which depends on the variable's metric in the dataset (yes, no, maybe, exact Fahrenheit degrees, strongly agree, don't know, etc.). Codebooks often specify how missing values will be treated during analyses because the nature and extent of missing data may reveal a dataset's quality or perhaps the limits to conclusions that the dataset might support.

Even meticulous data-gathering yields datasets with missing data. For many reasons, respondents fail to answer interview or survey questions. Observers may miss or fail to report some behaviors. So expert data analysts adopt defensible, consistent procedures to treat missing data. Sometimes observers have incentives to *not report* some cases, such as failed Afghanistan civil aid projects, police-involved shootings, or perhaps immigrants' medical emergencies while in federal custody. Savvy journalists and data analysts may discover deliberate bias and might even use that bias to write a hard-hitting follow-up story!

Once gathered, cleaned, groomed, and formatted, the dataset is ready to be analyzed. Early analysis – **mining data** – or a **data dredge**, uses preliminary searches to find relationships among variables. Data analysis identifies regularities, coordinated patterns of change among variables that differ from ordinary random (unassociated) variation. Data analysts seek patterns of relationships among variables that regularly happen. Examples of patterned change include:

- **Positive co-variation** – Variables change together, in similar ways. As values of one variable increase (or decrease), so do those of another variable. The variables change together in tandem. For example, the socioeconomic status of parents and their children's SAT scores demonstrate positive co-variation: The higher the parent's status, the higher their children's SAT scores.

- **Negative co-variation** – Variables may also change together, but in opposite directions. Examples of negative co-variation include persons' socioeconomic status and the likelihood of incarceration: The lower a person's socioeconomic status, the higher the probability of incarceration. We jail opioid users but not the corporate decision-makers who quietly created the necessary conditions for the opioid epidemic.

- **Causation** – Changes in a variable(s) *cause* changes in another variable(s). Importantly, co-variation alone *does not* establish causality. Beware! This trap awaits unwary journalists or naïve readers. Claiming causality requires plausibly asserting these stringent conditions:

  1. Time-order: the causal variable(s) must change first, and
  2. Alternative causal mechanisms should be eliminated, and
  3. Some "forcing" quality enables the independent (causal) variable(s) to alter the dependent (caused) variable(s).

Causation is a tricky business. For example, one or more other variables may mediate the positive co-variation between socioeconomic status and teens' SAT scores. Perhaps the higher scores result from better schools, family resources for private tutors, and/or expensive SAT test preparation. These third (mediating) variables matter – especially if the story describes how users might improve failing school systems!

Just as mining gold extracts valuable metal from dross, analyzing data extracts useful (and sometimes subtle or complex) information patterns hidden within the rows of observations and the columns of variables. Data analysts explore how variables interact with each other – or not. Analysts wrest information from data, but information alone does not confer meaning on findings – meaning depends on another layer of understanding.

A second layer of understanding helps researchers and journalists understand the findings of data analysts. The particular contextual framework from which the data were drawn gives added meaning to data analysts' findings. Questions that reporters might ask include: From what social context and environment did researchers gather the data? Do the findings and conclusions make sense? If results are unexpected, are they still reasonable? Under what conditions? If results don't seem reasonable, what else might explain the findings? Was bias introduced during data collection? The analysis? How might these biases be addressed? Unexpected or surprising results may call for different methods, different questions, or completely different assumptions about what's really going on. Answering these questions can clarify what the research shows and what it means.

HOW JOURNALISTS MIGHT USE DATA TO CREATE NEW INFORMATION

Table 9.1 displays fictitious data about aircraft operations at the Santa Monica Airport (SMO) that nearby residents love to hate – due to its aircraft noise and ultrafine particulate pollution.

The fictitious (but realistic) data in Table 9.1 describe all aircraft operations at SMO that took place, beginning early one Sunday morning. Dataset variables include the date, time, type of FAA tower clearance (takeoff or land), if the flight was conducted under FAA Visual Flight Rules (VFR) or Instrument Flight Rules (IFR), and the aircraft's registration (tail) number.

Here's a thought experiment: Imagine that many residents in this beach city loathe the early Sunday morning airport traffic – and formed a mythical Santa Monicans for Sleep-in Sundays, SMSS. The group organized a petition, presented it to the City Council, and claimed that airport traffic (particularly jet takeoffs) had greatly increased during the last three years. SMSS then demanded that the City Council curtail airport operations on Sunday mornings until 9.30 am.

TABLE 9.1 Fictitious aircraft flights at the Santa Monica Airport (SMO)

Flight Op.	Date	Day *	Time	Operation Takeoff - 1 Land - 2	Clearance IFR - 1, VFR - 2	Engine Jet -1 Prop - 2	Tail Number
1	4/5/20	Sun	8:01	1	1	1	N66L0
2	4/5/20	Sun	8:05	1	1	1	NX372
3	4/5/20	Sun	8:11	1	2	2	C881B
4	4/5/20	Sun	8:14	2	1	1	N737C4
5	4/5/20	Sun	8:16	1	2	2	NB842
6	4/5/20	Sun	8:20	1	1	1	XB738
...N cases							

* Variable created during data analysis

PROCESSING WORKFLOWS

A reporter assigned to write a story for the *Santa Monica Daily Press* sought to factually confirm or debunk the SMSS claims of increased SMO morning jet aircraft operations. She discovered and downloaded airport data from the City data website portal that covered three years, averaging 70,000 aircraft operations per year. The dataset web page had label descriptions which headed the variable columns. Each row began with a unique number identifying an aircraft operation. She wanted to compare jet takeoffs on different days of the week at different times, but a weekday variable wasn't in her dataset. So, she used the "Date" variable to create a "Weekday" variable – easy with any stat package.

The reporter mused: Do the times between operations seem reasonable? She recalled frequent takeoffs during her earlier unobtrusive Sunday morning visit to the Santa Monica airport. She remembered some jet takeoffs – so the SMSS claims seemed OK at first glance.

Then, the reporter called the SMO Airport Manager and asked him about weekend aircraft flights and jet operations. The official told her that jet operations typically peaked on Sunday afternoons, Monday mornings, and Friday afternoons. She asked: "How often are there IFR-flights compared to VFR-flights at SMO? And what's the difference between the two types?" He told her: 1) IFR clearances usually direct jets to other airports, 2) jets almost always fly IFR, and 3) private propeller aircraft usually fly using VFR. Then, she mentioned seeing several jets taking off one Sunday morning. The Airport Manager said, "Oh, those jets are heading back to the East Coast for Monday so they takeoff earlier."

So far, her dataset conformed with other information she had gathered. She reconsidered her original question: "Can I confirm or debunk SMSS claims that (jet) aircraft takeoffs increased during the past three years?" She thought and answered:

> With the data I have, yes, I believe I can. And I can go further. I can also report if jet or propeller aircraft increased most – and which days of the week (and times of day) experienced the greatest increases. I might even use the aircraft tail numbers to discover if the weekend (morning) traffic increases come from local aircraft or from out-of-town departing jets that riled-up the SMSS Santa Monica residents.

Can the dataset tell her all about SMO operations and their impacts? *Absolutely not*! It can't possibly convey the scope of the airport's human impacts. Because this reporter has "done" data, she knows that her dataset inevitably reduces the activities and consequences of a busy urban general aviation airport to a set of numbers – that can't capture the lived experiences, meanings, and actions of the people who fly airplanes, work at SMO, or live in the surrounding neighborhoods. But she *can* compare the variables' frequencies, and she *can* discover associations among the variables in the data. And combined with what else she finds, information from the data *can* add evidence to her story.

In the end, her story describes the modest three-year increases in Santa Monica aviation operations and a rapidly increasing number of early Sunday morning jet takeoffs. She will include interview quotes from the Airport Manager and quotes from aggrieved nearby residents – including an SMSS member who regularly measured the jet takeoff noise with his mobile phone's decibel-level detection app. Data journalism is a complex process – no one knows that better than expert data journalists.

This example shows how reporters can assess data analysis results, combine them with other relevant information, and use this information to describe news events that impact, engage, inspire, or interest their users. Savvy users and editors want to know the provenance of the dataset: the *source*, *who* collected it, *how*, and *why* it was created. Data journalism is a complex process – no one knows that better than expert data journalists.

DATA-VIZ: DATA AND DESIGN

After analysis, the dataset is ready for additional processing that can transform usable information into publishable news assets – data visualizations. Depending on the nature of the data and the findings, these assets could be static charts, graphs, infographics, or perhaps an engaging interactive graphic that enables users to explore the data.

DV experts' advice for journalists seeking to create visualizations that convey the meanings, findings, and conclusions about datasets to users includes:

- Understand the data
- Know your audience
- Reduce the data and findings to focus on the key points that the DV clearly demonstrates
- Determine the best means of presenting the data: bar, line, or scatter plot graphs, pie charts? Timelines? Should the DV be animated, or fully interactive?
- Keep the DV simple and accurate
- Make the DV easy to understand; visually highlight the most important information
- Consider seeking expert advice to help design data visualizations, especially for interactive DVs.

Static charts, graphs, and timelines offer straightforward ways to present important information to users. User-friendly displays make important relationships intuitively obvious. One way to explore data and create DVs: use Google Docs and Sheets to import a small dataset, then experiment. Try out displaying data and variable relationships in different configurations – bar graphs, pie charts, scatterplots, and so forth. Infographics require thoughtful design for clarity, accuracy, and attractiveness. Many free online sites let users create static DVs in the cloud and then embed them on web pages. Data-viz websites typically provide helpful instructions and often videos to clarify procedures for new users.

Interactive, Dynamic DVs

Interactive DVs are much more complex undertakings that typically require expert design processes to structure how users can explore alternative presentations of research results. The design of these interactives presage the new UX field that centers on user experience, a much-discussed area which has become an important part of web site and web page design. Colleagues who design interactive DVs often go by the title of **UX designer**.

Online DVs let users delve deeper, change parameters, or see how results may vary over time, location, or alternative conditions. In essence, dynamic DVs allow users to change the inputs (the interactive part) to visualize the resulting changed outputs (the visualized part). Some DVs help users compare findings that rely on different parts of the

PROCESSING WORKFLOWS

dataset. For example, one type of DV makes visible alternative levels of detail, so users can delve into ever more granular information-structures, often hidden in the data.

Design entails purpose. Meaningful DVs must address these important questions: What relationships must the DV show? How many (and which) variables are relevant to this story? Which variables co-vary (summer, sunbathing, geographic location, and skin cancer)? Does the data show causation, when changes in one variable force changes in one or more variables (giant rock hits car, pushes car into other lane, resulting in an accident)? Recall the pitfalls of causal claims. Causal questions may be trickier than they first appear: Do gas prices affect the miles that people drive? Does increased summer or holiday travel increase the miles driven and thence affect gas prices? Hmmm …

Relationships between variables often don't demonstrate causation. Rather, they may represent co-variation, resulting from other causal variables – some known, perhaps others unknown. View a good model (DV) of co-variation in the *CNN Money* Millennial Diversity Chart at http://cnnmon.ie/1zyQXqI. Users can compare racial and economic differences between and within cohorts: boomers, Gen X, Gen Y, and Millennials. As users move their cursors across the *AGE* variable (on the horizontal x-axis), the DV displays the number of people in that specific age cohort (on the vertical y-axis) and the racial distribution for that group.

Some DVs provide simple comparisons under changing conditions, like *The New York Times* calculator which compares whether buying a home or renting a residence is more financially advantageous, posted at http://nyti.ms/1jWrZqs. The user experience is much like filling out an interactive infographic: Users' supply their data by answering questions about the housing market that they seek to enter, type of mortgage, taxes, etc. Based on the user's answers and baked-in algorithms, the calculator estimates and compares the cost of renting versus buying a comparable home. This interactive visualization demands that users take the time to consider carefully many possible alternatives and future contingencies, such as changes in interest rates. For potential home buyers or renters, these automated comparisons can aid (and engage) persons confronted with complex decisions.

Such sophisticated interactive graphics, when well executed, provide lasting value to the online venues that host them and for subsequent stories that include this DV asset. The ability to create these resource intensive, interactive DVs provides substantial competitive advantages to large media enterprises like *The New York Times*, *The Washington Post*, and *The Wall Street Journal*.

Interactive graphic design involves tradeoffs between the capabilities and limitations of DV software, content platforms and services, and users' equipment. Rigdon (2016) notes the existing compatibility issues between different computer systems, browsers, and content types. In addition, some interactive DVs require intensive computation, a problem for some users' computers and mobile phones. In short, far more can go wrong with interactive DVs than with static ones.

Necessity: the mother of invention creativity

On December 31, 2019, China notified World Health Organization about the outbreak of a mysterious contagious illness that left patients with pneumonia-like symptoms. That same day, journalists at the *South China Morning Post* broke the story, reporting there were 30 cases. Four days later, reporter Dennis Normile from *Science.org* published a similar story, but by then there were 59 sick people in the provincial Chinese city of Wuhan, Hubei, population 11,000,000 (Normile, 2020). One day later, on January 4, the *South China Morning Post* posted video of the first patients on YouTube.

Then the virus spread. And spread further. And coverage by the media continued for the next two weeks. But it wasn't until January 16, 2020 that the U.S. Centers for Disease Control and Prevention went public with information about the growing epidemic. So, during those two weeks, journalists published reports from public health experts describing the virus and its potential risks to the public. Thanks to dedicated journalists and news organizations, people learned about the possibility of a worldwide pandemic that might put billions of people at risk of infection and kill countless millions.

News organizations quickly realized that they needed to find ways to tell this story. But how is it possible to convey the enormity of a global outbreak, a pandemic? The speed of its transmission? The differences in the number of cases between one neighborhood, city, country, race, sex, or age group and another?

Imagine a table of numbers with 150 countries and 30,000,000 data points and hundreds of variables – probably big enough to cover the grounds of a football stadium! And that information, although important, wouldn't answer the most important questions users would ask: Can I protect myself, loved ones, country? What can leaders do *now* to save us, bolster public health, save our jobs?

Data journalism took center stage of the online media effort as COVID-19 created worldwide demands for reliable, *trusted* content. But users needed more than just reams of written information. Data visualizations provided a solution for newsrooms because DVs *show* people what is going on instead of just *telling* them about events. News organizations created targeted, user-centric interactive DVs that made even unfamiliar, scientifically-complex, life-saving information understandable to almost everyone.

The largest digital news organizations with their in-house data vis expertise, vast digital archives, deep journalist benches, and sophisticated CMSs, notably *The New York Times* and *The Washington Post* opened their paywalls for COVID-19 resources with interactive data visualizations leading the way. By leveraging the internet's capacity for global distribution, using their specialized DV expertise, and extensive health information from datasets amassed around the world, these large companies gained large global audiences that sought just that information.

Amazing interactive DVs flourished on the internet. Even private, for profit, data-wrangling and data vis outfits like informationisbeautiful.com made amazingly useful COVID-19 data visualizations. (And made their COVID-19 #Coronavirus Information Data Pack available for download, free for all to use or share). Initially, as users migrated to these big picture stories, local news organizations saw traffic and advertising drop calamitously. But, as the virus spread within the U.S., many people turned to local news, as well as national news, to learn what was happening in their neighborhood and communities.

TOOLS OF THE TRADE

Open-source software offers valuable resources for journalists with statistical and programming skills. Standard data analysis programs include Excel, SAS, SPSS, R, and Python. While R and Python remain open-source products, SAS and SPSS are quite expensive commercial products. RStudio installs a free graphical user interface (single user's desktop), but for novice data analysts, R has a steep learning curve. Python users (named after Monty Python's Flying Circus) must enter code on a command line; Python is not too difficult for users with some programming code chops. All these programs require either understanding basic statistics, advice from a statistician, or the willingness to court ridicule from informed editors, colleagues, or users.

Some data analysis tools such as R can create the database and convert it into an open-source database, SQLite. Several other open-source database management programs exist. Of them, MySQL is probably the most well-known. MongoDB, and MariaDB provide other options.

To display a DV embedded on a website, the database must exist on a server with access to a free DV creation tool like Tableau Public. Other sophisticated DV tools include D3 and D3.js, Javascript, and Highcharts. Reporters with programming skills also use web programming languages to format DVs, including Javascript, HTML, CSS, Python, and PHP.

Software programs provide tools that journalists use to make DVs. Each software package has program-specific ways to: 1) format the data as input, and 2) create the resulting data visualization. Usually, some design elements are baked into the software while retaining some customization options for the final DV. Software reviews are helpful, but there is no substitute for trying out the different software packages – most offer trial versions that provide adequate test drives. One very important consideration: Ensure that the software creates **responsive** DVs. This requires that visualizations will adjust in size and layout to fit many different screens, including desktop, laptop, tablet, TV, and mobile phone shapes.

Publications that analyze and display data to their users usually have in-house tools and expect journalists to use them. Very small publications rarely have such DV tools and they don't budget for them. They depend on journalists who can master open-source software, create charts and graphs using free website services, or use the ubiquitous, rapidly evolving, and often free Google cloud software.

Searches for "statistical analysis software" and "data visualization software" will bring up many products that are suitable for anyone who seeks to analyze and represent data in interesting ways. For example, Timeline[JS] (at URL timeline.knightlab.com) makes timelines that allow the use of multiple media types – text, graphics, online maps, audio, and video – that journalists can **embed** on web pages.

And the (free) Google Charts Excel service provides formatting options that yield adequate DVs, although they aren't interactive. Novices might consider using Google's one-stop-shop approach to free DV creation. Input data into Google Sheets – limited to 2 million cells. Add the Statistics plug-in. Analyze the data. Display the output in Google Data Studio to create many types of charts, including interactive DVs, and then embed the resulting DV on a web page.

When you think you're done: Test, revise, and retest and revise ....

Be sure to test it with several people who did *not* develop it. Ask them detailed questions about their experience and what they learned from the DV. These additional sets of eyes will find problems and mistakes that developers may not. And they can usually offer suggestions that improve the DV's clarity and usability. Just a half-hour of systematic testing often provides the crucial investment needed to learn if the DV actually works and to validate that it gives users the understanding sought by the journalist.

REALITY BYTES

Newsroom technologies usually don't adapt as quickly as new forms of storytelling do. Thus, many newsroom Content Management Systems accommodate 3D models and augmented reality, but probably not virtual reality experiences. Reporters will need to organize and label files carefully to ensure they are available throughout a long project, especially if their work is saved to an outside repository or migrated to a new system in mid-project.

Another area where VR experiences differ from other multimedia types: they require special user devices to view them. Users can see AR content on mobile phone apps, but not in internet browsers – at least not yet. Experiencing VR content, typically in a 360° environment, requires wearing a headset.

Because of their 3D visualizations, extended reality assets for AR and VR require extensive processing that 2D video does not. If the asset has 360° video for virtual reality, it may need to be *stitched* together, either in the camera or with post-production software. Even when the 360° camera stitches the video, the resulting "seams" usually need fine-tuning. Scanned 3D objects and environments may also require designers to clean up the data cloud of excess data points to: 1) reduce the computational load, 2) emphasize strong vertical and horizontal lines, and 3) smooth surfaces in the image.

After stitching the 360° VR video and scanning 3D objects for both AR and VR, much of the editing is similar to 2D video editing. Many XR creators fashion experiences using well-known editing programs like Final Cut Pro and Adobe Premiere. However, XR post-production does have some differences according to media executive John Fragomeni, immersive creator and director, Andy Cochrane (NewscastStudio, 2017):

> The single hardest aspect to 360° video production is review. Outside of the headset, it is impossible to judge anything – the VR POV affects time, scale, distance, even color and blocking. [...] Outside of this time-consuming hurdle, there are a lot of roadblocks that you encounter with each piece of software having different levels of support for VR, requiring awkward round trips and workarounds to get the images rendered and manipulated correctly. A good example of this is color correction – none of the established grading tools supports VR, so we have to develop methods for getting the footage in and out without creating seams or other issues.

Software for AR editing includes Unity (often used for developing video game environments), Unreal, Vuforia, and others. The AR content is put together with Apple's ARKit (iOS) and Google's ARCore (Android). These apps link the phone's camera image of an environment to a virtual object or graphic overlay (texture) onto that environment, thereby mixing a physical environment with virtual images, objects, and textures.

Three key functionalities of modern mobile phones make AR possible. The phone can track user motion. It can estimate the source and brightness of environmental lighting and modify a virtual object to look as if it were naturally lit. Finally, phones can recognize real-world environments, objects, and people. A developer then creates an AR experience by inputting images of whatever they want the phone to detect into a database. When the phone camera "sees" any of these objects, it follows developers' instructions to insert a virtual image to replace the one in the real environment. For example, a user might send an image to a furniture store and, one by one, users see the images of the sofas the retailer is selling in living color within the image of their own living room.

PROCESSING WORKFLOWS

The steps to build a ready-for-distribution AR app are:

- Build a database of images of environments and objects in the real world.
- Train the software to recognize them.
- Trigger the phone to replace the real-world environment or object with a virtual image, whether it's a building or a sign. The virtual image may be an animation that can move in the real-world environment.
- Render the app for use by specific end-user devices – mobile phones and tablets.

As AR becomes more widely available and AR sharing more desirable, it should become more popular. Learning how to build AR apps requires a thorough understanding of computers, substantial training with software, and a willingness to test, revise, and retest how the app is working in user devices. A few tech-savvy people might be able to pick up AR creation by themselves, but most people will need some combination of videos and software tutorials on YouTube, workshops, and courses to learn how to do it.

Creating a VR experience is even more demanding. Professional looking content in VR requires expert knowledge of high-powered software, high-speed computing resources, and a lot of time – even for people who make their living creating VR. If the newsroom doesn't have a resident VR team, the publication probably should partner with a VR production company to handle their production and post-production work.

TAKEAWAYS

- Workflows guide the transformation of raw material into publishable content assets by laying out the steps, processes, and tools required to accomplish these tasks. Each media type requires a specialized workflow, specific hardware, and appropriate software tools to make possible a smooth and efficient preparation process. News organizations often have preferred tool sets that they may require journalists to use. However, internet searches can reveal many free or open-source tools that journalists from small newsrooms or freelance journalists often find useful to augment newsroom software.

- In a world of easily available information, journalists must organize the information they gather, so they can curate it, save it, find it, select from it, and prepare it for publication in an efficient manner. Create a directory for each story with subdirectories for the topics of multi-part articles. For multimedia content, identify potential story assets within each acquired file. Note and tag the timecode for the locations of video and audio clips. Complex stories may require multiple directories for different parts of the story.

  Multimedia assets require careful organization. For long articles, interview transcripts are essential. Similarly, when stories call for edited video and audio, this material should be logged. Without these basic procedures, it's difficult to locate vital materials: Journalists spend time hunting down clips instead of creating strong multimedia assets.

- Identifying story assets that require preparation demands knowing how they will fit into the overall article. Choosing assets begins with transcribing interviews and logging video and audio files. After reviewing the collected research material, interview transcripts and media logs, the next step entails creating an outline, rough draft, or some other type of structuring document.

Once reporters know the available material and understand the story arc, from beginning to end, they can begin an efficient, creative process to place multimedia content where it best adds value to the online article. Research indicates that multimedia assets enhance users' understanding and increase their engagement in online articles.

Pictures, videos, and audio add information that users can't glean from the story's text. The multimedia assets can provide a sense of place, details of settings, expressions of emotions, social context, and other important elements. Interactive content allows users to control the information they receive, especially with data visualizations. Users can explore different dimensions of the data that interest them, and thus become participants in their news experience.

- The kind and amount of preparation and processing needed for assets depends on the:
  - Type of asset
  - Desired production quality
  - Complexity of the finished content
  - Availability of resources

Video and interactive visualizations are often complex, compared to photographs and audio clips. They require substantial resources to produce professional, polished assets. While the preparation of photographs and of audio clips is demanding, they don't require the investment of as much time or as many resources. When newsrooms lack substantial digital resources – high-quality, complex multimedia and interactive assets can only accompany their most important stories.

- The essential resources needed to transform raw assets into publishable content include skilled colleagues and experts, specialized hardware and software, and a place to work. Complex stories with multimedia and interactive assets take a talented team to put them together. Even when journalists have the necessary writing, photography, video, audio, and data visualization skills – the demanding hours this work entails create formidable barriers to completing these projects in a reasonable time. Management typically frames resources in monetary terms, so the availability of time, specialists, freelancers, vendors, equipment, and tools often comes down to the financial bottom line.

- Develop plans for processing each type of story asset: establish priorities, set timelines and deadlines, determine staffing, and manage team coordination. If management or editors must approve these resources, write and send a memo explaining the value that the multimedia assets will bring to the story, the resources needed to prepare the added content, and the anticipated effects on users' understanding and engagement. Take care to think through (and avoid temptations to low-ball) the needed resources because the quality of the final story depends on having adequate resources to do a creditable job.

- It takes high-level skills to wrangle data successfully and expert knowledge to report research findings well. Even if they do not aspire to become data wranglers, journalists working beats in business, politics, and sports need to gain solid knowledge of

PROCESSING WORKFLOWS

research methods and statistics, including co-variation and causality. To inform users, they will need these competencies if they are to contextualize research and characterize the findings accurately.

- Newsroom operations typically define the overall workflow and provide both opportunities and limits to the way journalists work. The news organization may provide some or all the needed tools. It may seem that, given the organizational workflows, that there's no reason to develop personal workflows.

  But journalists have individual ways of working that are comfortable for them even while they adapt to specific organizational requirements. If a journalist's employment changes, familiarity with new content creation advances may be vital for their next job. Since yesterday's technology quickly fades, online journalists should monitor the emergence of new presentation styles, online services, and tools – and keep abreast of new practices and techniques. It's easy and fun to try out demos and watch videos of new stuff.

  When working in the field, it's useful to have mobile content creation tools available for rapid production on a personal mobile device. Walked into a breaking story on the boulevard? Grab it on your mobile and get the scoop. Personal workflows for processing all types of story assets give journalists independence and confidence so that, when the news breaks – they are ready to roll.

- Extended reality (XR) is probably coming to a newsroom near you. Journalists can keep their eyes open for stories with interesting objects, especially if they are in difficult to access locations, must cope with conflicting accounts of events and interactions, and deal with issues that users care about. Advances in acquisition, postproduction, industry-wide standards, and better, lower-cost user devices all loom on the horizon over the next few years.

KEY CONCEPTS AND TERMS

- Workflows in news organizations and newsrooms
- Storing, finding, and retrieving content, including multimedia
- Choosing story assets to enhance users' experience
- Transformation of raw assets into publishable content
- Estimate resources needed to process assets for hardware, software, utilities, and vendor activities
- Planning for processing
- The "processing memo"
- Personal workflows
- Datasets and data visualizations
- Extended reality, augmented reality, and virtual reality

EXERCISES AND ACTIVITIES

1. Download the trial version of a mind-mapping software program. Create a mind-map of a story idea, including the topics you would cover, the research you would need to

carry out, multimedia assets that might illuminate the story, and the resources needed to prepare those assets.

2. Take photographs of an event or meeting. Edit the pictures: crop, brightness, contrast, transcoding to .jpg or .png (if needed). Write a three-paragraph story about the event and insert the pictures into the story. At the end of the story, note whether each picture mirrored or complemented the text.

3. Record a short audio interview and edit it. Try to reduce any noise and normalize the track. Write a page that describes the tools you used, the process of editing, and what you learned.

4. Record a short video on a news or feature news topic. Edit it and post it to a social media site: Instagram, Facebook, Twitter, or another site. Write one page that describes how you recorded and edited the video; include the URL to your video.

5. Go to the Tableau website at: https://public.tableau.com/en-us/s/resources and watch the video, Tableau Public Overview (7:10). Take notes and summarize the information in 2–3 pages.

6. Watch a video about building an AR app and take careful notes. Create a PowerPoint presentation that covers the main points of the video. Be sure to place images on your slides.

ADVANCER

The next chapter describes the assembly, packaging, and distribution of online news content. It first explores how journalists assemble written copy and multimedia content into finished stories that are ready for packaging, publishing, and distribution. Just as hardware and software tools underlie the production of individual articles, an array of digital systems underpins the technology for these final processes. In newsrooms, large news organizations' content management system (CMS) handles content production and storage. Electronic distribution entails largely automated complex processes that include on-the-fly programmatic advertising.

10

PACKAGING ASSETS & PUBLISHING ARTICLES

Chapter Learning Objectives

After reading this chapter, students will be able to:

1. Assess the online news editorial workflow.
2. Apply digital narrative structures to assemble digital, multimedia stories and reports.
3. Assemble and package digital media.
4. Appraise the roles of content management systems (CMS) in digital newsrooms.
5. Analyze the affordances of digital media.
6. Understand how newsrooms monitor articles and make changes, based on user behaviors.
7. Build an audience for a story.
8. Compare forms of advertising on news sites.

A newspaper is complete. It is finished, sure of itself, certain. By contrast, digital news is constantly updated, improved upon, changed, moved, developed – an ongoing conversation and collaboration. It is living, evolving, limitless, relentless.

– Katharine Viner, Editor-in-Chief, *The Guardian*

THE GIST

As Ms. Viner aptly describes, online stories are emergent and always changing, making relentless demands on digital journalists. As soon as a newsroom publishes a story and the reporter comments on it, an update often quickly follows. Sometimes editors update an article to add a quick detail but keeping abreast of substantive changes usually rests on the reporter. After filing a story, reporters used to be able to join colleagues at the local pub. Today, online journalists often find themselves reaching out to sources to confirm or deny the new information and updating their article to reflect new information. Welcome to the new news.

Chapter 10 covers how newsrooms assemble and package the processed story assets for distribution. These creative activities meld together the assets into a completed article – copy, pictures, multimedia, DVs, and interactives. After assembly and packaging, the story is ready for transport across networks, through servers, and placement on web pages for users to access. And as updates come in, the newsroom (and journalist) will modify and recreate that package in an endless cycle that reflects the dynamic nature of online news.

This chapter describes that final part of the news editorial process: assembling, publishing, and disseminating news stories. It's a team effort that requires coordination between journalists, editors, designers, multimedia creators, and IT staff. Even short articles in small newsrooms require collaboration with others in the newsroom, although journalists who operate their own micro or personal news and blog sites typically do much of the work themselves.

Journalists put their unique creative stamp on complex stories. Once they have finished, computers carry out much of the final work in this part of the overall process. It's very different from the traditional printing press distribution of legacy paper-based media.

This chapter closely examines how journalists establish the "look and feel" of an article. Narrative structure, navigational guideposts, and interaction opportunities play large roles in appealing to users. Indeed, careful attention to the entire user experience is essential for online publications because it is so very easy for the-people-who-used-to-be-called-the-audience (TPWUTBCTA) to leave an online article or site almost immediately. When users become confused, uncertain, or frustrated, they quickly lose interest, and they bounce – they're "outta here."

Online websites create many ways for users to engage with stories: Users gain information from multiple media types, interact with data, and participate or communicate with others. As a result, a complex technological infrastructure underlies digital content creation and publishing. In today's newsrooms, the **content management system** provides the hardware and software that is central to the digital editorial process. Later, this chapter features a detailed description of CMSs. For now, envision a CMS as analogous to a digital assembly line, an essential tool for managing the many types of story assets and outputs while coordinating the individual contributions of newsroom workers. The CMS plays essential roles in story assignment, research, approval, assembly, packaging, and publishing digital news content.

In addition, the CMS serves as the organizational library and archive – the "morgue" as newspapers used to call it. Mass storage, accessed through the CMS, holds the publication's creative elements, story assets, research material, complete interviews, and published stories. Stored content, via the CMS, comes to new life in follow-up and round-up stories and allows remixing of existing materials in new ways for multiple editions and publications.

The digitization of the newsroom forced journalists to learn new roles and develop skills, like article promotion and direct interaction with users. Editors must now manage multiple releases across multiple media platforms. And after publishing articles, editors (and often individual journalists) swing into action as they replicate the attention-getting efforts of newspaper boys shouting, "Read all about it!" from street corners in the early 20th century ... only now they use Twitter, Buzzfeed, and other news aggregator sites to tout their stories' headlines.

Even then, the story marketing process isn't over. Metrics show the articles that users click and spend time on, providing real-time information about users' behaviors. Based on that feedback, editors re-write headlines and decks, change story position, pages, and sections. These hectic post-publishing changes influence the popularity of articles and publications and affect the news organization, its editors, and the journalists in different and important ways.

@ WORK: THE ONLINE NEWS CONTENT EDITORIAL WORKFLOW

Legacy media are linear, written for readers to consume stories from beginning to end. In contrast, digital technologies help create story structures that allow users to: 1) choose their own paths through articles, 2) separate information they want from information they don't need, and 3) participate actively with interactives, journalists, and other users. Reporters and editors seek a **narrative structure** that attracts users, helps them navigate the article, and maximizes the story's impact – important because these decisions shape the user's experience.

Consider all the stories published in the classic format – headline, graphic, and copy. This popular structure originated in the early 16th century when the scholar Andrea Alciato first published it. His design began with a headline at the top (motto), followed by an image (pictura), and brief text (inscriptio, now called a deck or dek), as shown in Figure 10.1.

Digital multimedia articles online retain the headline and copy, but all else is quite different! To begin, it takes an expanded team to create an online article longer than a few paragraphs or more than a photo or two. Online content includes all the legacy media formats of print, radio, and television, rolled into one package – and then adds interaction, simulations, and navigation. Thus, online newsroom teams may include producers and editors: video editors, audio editors, data analysts and visualization specialists, and interaction and page designers.

Large teams require coordination – meetings, messages, approvals, and revisions – all complexifying the editorial process. The CMS is the glue that ties the team together. Although packaging an article takes place on team members' computers (with specialized software), the results of their work moves to others on the CMS. Each newsroom organizes its work to meet the publication's specific needs. Figure 10.2 shows a generic end-to-end **online news content editorial workflow**.

THE ARCHITECTURE OF ONLINE ARTICLES: NARRATIVE STRUCTURE

After the reporters have finished a final draft of the copy and team members have processed the multimedia assets, it's time to construct a **narrative structure** to tie everything together. The purpose is to find ways to present the information to enhance the user experience. Some

FIGURE 10.1

Structure of Alciato's "Emblems"

Credit: By Andrea Alciato [Public domain], via Wikimedia Commons

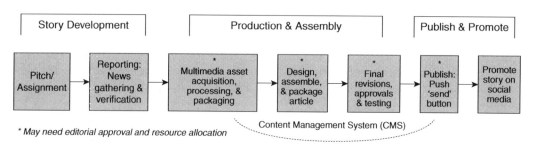

FIGURE 10.2

End-to-end online news content editorial workflow
Credit: Joan Van Tassel

practical matters include anticipating the different choices users might make to navigate the story, whether the article should flow across multiple pages, whether it should flow vertically or horizontally – or both.

Creating a narrative structure hinges on a practical calculus of looking at how the story unfolds on web pages, copy, multimedia, and interactive assets, links, and navigation and branding elements. For short reports, much of this work is routine or even automated. But longer articles require more than the inverted pyramid style provides, especially if they have multiple sections or topics. Providing that structure helps users comprehend and absorb the content. Table 10.1 suggests some criteria that journalists can use to decide how much structure an article needs.

THE STORY STRATEGY NINJA: WHAT'S YOUR STORY?

Every article is different: Narrative structure isn't simply a static container just waiting for journalists to pour a story into it. Rather, it results from a series of decisions to arrive at a logical presentation of the story elements that users can follow – structure

TABLE 10.1 Story and structure

Story Characteristics	*Inverted pyramid → Narrative structure*
Length	Short → Long
Fact Structure	Simple → Complex
Number of events	Few → Many
Chain of events	Simple → Complex
Time span of events	Short → Long
Number of important actors	Few → Many
Number of multimedia assets	Few → Many

Credit: Joan Van Tassel

PACKAGING ASSETS AND PUBLISHING ARTICLES

that the team actively creates and designs. These judgments resolve questions about how to lay out the fact structure, introduce the actors, and recount the events, perspectives, supporting and opposing evidence, analysis, and opinions that all together make up the story.

Reporters can't write a final version of the article until preliminary consensus exists about the narrative architecture of the story. The design of the package, as it will appear on web pages, will determine its final structure. In the end, it will guide the placement of all the story elements, including the amount of copy and the information it conveys.

The team will also keep in mind the proposed answers to these questions:

- What is the overall "look and feel" of the multimedia article?
- Who is telling the story? (There can be multiple storytellers in one story, so what are the indicators of changing perspectives?)
- What is each storyteller's perspective, including the reporter's?
- What is each storyteller's "tone" of voice?

When Leah Gentry served as Editorial Director of the online *Los Angeles Times*, she recommended several steps for evaluating a multimedia story's optimal structure (Rich, n.d.), including making a chronology and a big-picture framework for it, followed by the **deconstruction** of the story, and then the **reconstruction** of it, as shown in Figure 10.3:

1. *List the events in the micro story*: All the events and actions that occurred, from beginning to end make up the **micro story**: This happened, this happened, that happened, so-and-so did this, and then that happened. The result provides a sequential record of what occurred, stated in the simplest language possible so that reporters can relate it using an easy-to-follow, succinct chronology.

2. *Summarize the macro story*: The **macro story** is all the information gathered on the context and background of the story. List the resources that provide related information. (Journalists often enable users to drill down into some of this material by providing links to it, rather than incorporating all the material in the story itself.)

3. *Deconstruction: Break the components of material into chunks*: facts, events, actors/actions, data, context, and background information.

4. *Reconstruction: Link the chunks and micro and macro stories to story assets*: copy, pictures, galleries and slideshows, documents, links, data, video, audio, animations, and simulations. (Multiple links between chunks and assets are fine).

5. *More reconstruction: Organize the chunks + story assets into clusters*, based on similarities such as, events and actions that occurred at the same time, people who belong to the same organizations or groups, and so forth.

6. *Even more reconstruction: Organize the clusters on a storyboard*, linking relationships between clusters.

7. *The last reconstruction step*: Diagram the relationships between clusters.

Figure 10.3 displays the process of organizing the story into larger groupings, the clusters.

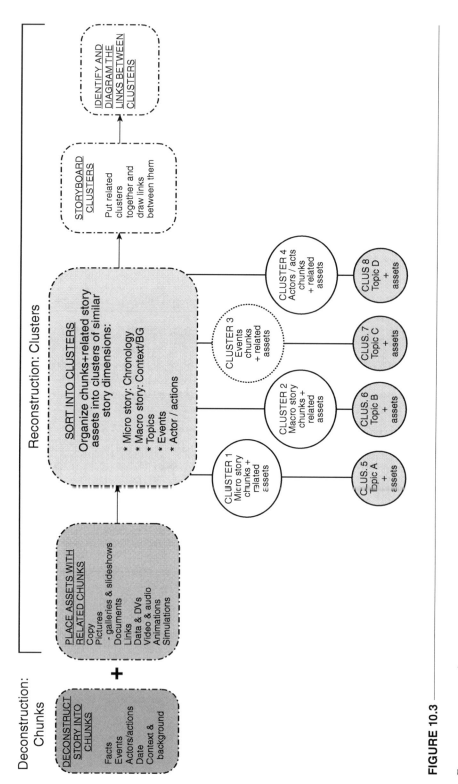

FIGURE 10.3

From story to narrative
Credit: Joan Van Tassel

PACKAGING ASSETS AND PUBLISHING ARTICLES

> **Tools and Tips: Structuring the multimedia story**
>
> TOOL: Arrange and re-arrange narrative chunks and clusters with 3 x 5 cards – yes – actual physical, paper-based 3 x 5 cards work well. So do software programs like Scrivener, Mindola's Supernotecard, Inspiration 9, and similar apps.
>
> - TOOL: Storyboards help users visualize the narrative structure of the story. Storyboarding software works, but so do quick hand-drawn sketches.
> - TOOL: Consider visual organizational software and apps for: Timelines, photo/caption grids, slide shows, carousels, maps, charts and tables, simulations, etc.
> - TIP: Make sure that all multimedia elements drive the story forward, whether together in galleries, sprinkled throughout the story, or linked to specific points in the narrative.
> - TIP: Place visual, multimedia, and interactive elements where they deepen user engagement in the story.

FROM NARRATIVE TO STRUCTURE: DIGITAL ARTICLE ARCHITECTURES

Long stories often require multiple trials and re-sequencing as journalists impose structure on an emerging article. New information pops up and seemingly unimportant facts take-on added prominence. Transitions must be re-thought and reworked. Just seeing the text interwoven with the other story elements often highlights a few tweaks needed to make the story flow more smoothly, as shown in the storyboard in Figure 10.4.

Even though every story is different and there are no pre-made containers where teams can just drop in stories, there are some general narrative structures that might make a good starting point.

Many online digital media packages incorporate one or more of four common structures.

- Linear-embedded
- Hierarchical
- Non-linear
- Combination

FIGURE 10.4

Storyboarding the multimedia story

Credit: Joan Van Tassel

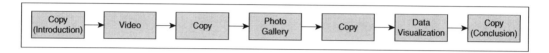

FIGURE 10.5

The linear-embedded article structure
Credit: Joan Van Tassel

LINEAR-EMBEDDED STRUCTURE

Linear-embedded narrative structures resemble a string with multimedia and interactive "knots" located at various points along its length, as displayed in Figure 10.5. This structure works for chronological stories, especially ones with strong cause-and-effect timelines. Linear-embedded structures require: 1) an introduction to start the story; 2) a focus on key events, ordered to move the story forward; and 3) the use of multimedia assets to unfold the entire story. This design works well for narratives with strong sequences of chronological events that tightly wrap other story elements around or between these events in time.

The linear-embedded narrative structure tells the story in a time-ordered sequence, moving the story forward from beginning to end. Like the inverted pyramid style, this copy usually begins with an introduction that reveals a narrative perspective: Who is the storyteller? Why should users read the story? Subsequent section copy can include more context and background, facts, description, explanation, interpretation, and even introduce multiple perspectives.

Linear-embedded narratives often have interstitial copy between sections that introduces new events or actions and may also present and explain a multimedia asset. The purpose of this mid-article copy is to help users stay on track and enhance their experience within the story. Such setups sometimes end by drawing users forward to what happens in the story *after* the multimedia asset, frequently using assets as "previews of coming attractions" or "teases." A good setup is tough to do in a paragraph or two, but that's the goal for well-executed narrative transitions.

HIERARCHICAL STRUCTURE

Hierarchical narrative structures are good fits for articles and sections that require more than one dimension or perspective. One good example of a hierarchical narrative: *The Big Short*, both the book and the movie. Hierarchical narrative architecture is much like a layer cake, using frosting (transitions) between the layers. Each layer contains "slices" of narration that cover some aspect of the layer it is taken from, as shown in Figure 10.6.

The hierarchical structure poses tough challenges for writers – separating the layers and relating each element within them calls for exceptional analytical and creative skills. A copy introduction describes each new layer as it arises within the story *and* includes a setup for the subsections within the layer. Subsections may have copy intros as well – or not. In each subsection, the copy provides new facts and data, adds explanation and context, and transitions to multimedia and to the next section. Note that introductions to the main piece or any section can be a flashback or a quote – which the rest of the copy then backfills from the section's introductory point.

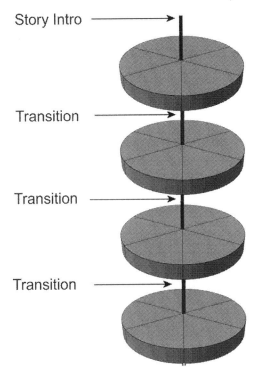

FIGURE 10.6

Hierarchical narrative article structure

Credit: Joan Van Tassel

NON-LINEAR NARRATIVE STRUCTURE

Non-linear narrative structures need an introduction that sets up *all* the pieces for users to choose from. This format engages users by exposing them to the potential riches that lie merely a click away. Some of the story's treasure may be copy, multimedia, interactive elements, or a combination of different story assets.

Sometimes called the "Christmas Tree" structure, non-linear structures present visually rich menus, as shown in Figure 10.7. This structure may offer a menu of titles with brief descriptions or a catalog that lists and describes a mosaic of elements. More people will sample the different multimedia assets when the copy describes each one and encourages users to try the assets out.

COMBINATION STRUCTURES

Combination structures employ multiple narrative structures, tailoring elements for different parts of the article. Writers address each section individually to produce the needed

FIGURE 10.7

Nonlinear narrative article structure
Credit: Joan Van Tassel

copy for the narrative structure used within that section. In addition to advancing the story, both text and navigation must send strong signals that let users know how to navigate each section.

For combination designs, a paramount consideration: label the multimedia elements and make interaction with them crystal clear for users. By now most users know to click on the arrow to play a video – but labels don't hurt and may help some users. Many large news organizations have design documents that specify exactly how to embed and label material. These design documents incorporate the procedures that all writers for the news site must know and follow.

4 ELEMENTS THAT GO IN AN ONLINE DIGITAL PACKAGE

Newsrooms build a digital package for each story, one that includes each story element – functions, apps, and databases needed for interactive opportunities that are presented to users when the story is published. These digital packages require a series of steps to assemble an online article, as shown in Figure 10.8. Unless a story is complex, assembling the package is usually straightforward.

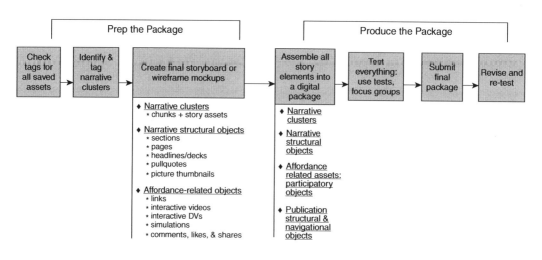

FIGURE 10.8

Workflow to assemble the online news package
Credit: Joan Van Tassel

An online article with its multimedia and interactive assets is an assembled **digital package**. **Packaging** the digital article requires assembling all the story assets into a single entity for distribution to servers, publishing, and display on a web page: **The narrative and multimedia elements (clusters)** – copy, pictures, video, audio, DVs – comprise the story elements, joined by navigation and participation components.

1. **Narrative structural objects** guide users through the story, including its architecture, sections, and navigation. The newsroom staffers who create these objects may be web page designers, specialists in interface, or interaction designers.
   * The **user interface (UI)** offers users alternative ways to navigate and use website features.
   * The **user experience** or **UX**, a design framework that helps users experience and understand the story.
2. **Affordance-related elements** draw on the essential and unique characteristics of online digital media and platforms, offering opportunities to users that other media cannot provide. For example, interactive assets and participation increase user engagement by helping users understand and follow the article. Since users must use mobile devices for AR and headsets for VR, other sites presently host these XR content types. **Interaction design (IxD)** allows users to act, providing ways for them to interact with elements of the material or with other users.
3. **Publication structural, design and navigational objects** are pre-designed assets that the site's publication manual specifies for use with all sections, pages, and articles.

AFFORDANCES: A KEY TO INNOVATIVE DIGITAL PACKAGES

Successful innovative storytelling takes creative thought. It's challenging to come up with something new when so many online articles now exist. One way to generate original ideas for a story relies on the concept of affordances. Analyzing the affordances of design, structure, presentation software, platforms, and devices opens doors to the imagination by linking the possibilities of digital media to alternative constructions of digital stories.

In digital environments, affordances allow (and their absence precludes) how people can use their communications technologies, online services and platforms, and devices. For example:

* An advanced iPod affords searching for audio files, buying them, listening to them, and watching and listening to music videos – in addition to supporting other iPod apps. It affords going online but doesn't afford making telephone calls.
* A digital camera records video and audio. It may also integrate Bluetooth connections, but it doesn't afford surfing the web.
* A mobile smartphone affords placing calls, browsing the internet, messaging, playing games, recording and watching video, and listening to music – but users can't play World of Warcraft with the same wild abandon that they can with a well-designed gaming rig (OK, gamers, please don't @ us.)
* A landline telephone enables voice telephone calls.

Table 10.2 compares the high-level characteristics of print and broadcast with those of the digital internet. This comparison provides useful ways to consider what these media afford – and kudos to Kathleen Reardon and Everett Rogers (1988). Notice the features of internet media describe a panoply of affordances that journalists might harness. When incorporated into news articles, each of these affordances can foster novel ways to engage and delight users with content uniquely tailored to digital environments.

TABLE 10.2 Comparison of communication affordances between non-interactive media and networked digital media

	Print and Broadcast	Digital Internet
Message flow	One to many Few to many	One to one One to few One to many Few to one Few to few Few to many Many to many
Control	Source	Source and receiver
Knowledge of individual audience members	Scant to none	Often scant, but under some conditions, reporters or publishers may acquire far more detailed knowledge
Audience data and segmentation	• Demographics • Psychographics/Lifestyle • Behavioral	• Demographics • Psychographics/Lifestyle • Behavioral • Person-provided (opt-in) • Site user tracking • Micro-segmentation via multiple databases
Interactivity	No	Yes
Feedback	Delayed, receiver to source, inferential feedback	Immediate, reciprocal, direct, or inferential feedback
Asynchronous	Yes, with recording or DVR	Yes
Emotional vs Task-related content	Print: Mostly cognitive Broadcast: Mostly emotional	Both/either
Privacy	Yes	Not much … not yet

Credit: Based on Reardon and Rogers (1988).

PACKAGING ASSETS AND PUBLISHING ARTICLES **313**

The most important affordances of digital networks listed in Table 10.2 are:

- *Messages flow everywhere*: Creators distribute material to 1 or 1 billion users – and users can send messages right back to original creators – and to gazillions of other users.
- *Immediate feedback*: Feedback may be instantaneous, reciprocal, and direct.
- *Recorded actions*: Don't have to "be there to see there" ... *and* the internet is a searchable time machine that preserves past actions.
- *Bits are malleable shapeshifters*: Digitize a paper document, printed picture, old video, historical audio recording, or a book – and turn it into bits. Any bits that hit the network provide fodder for screen grabs, remixes, mashups, and other forms of alteration. Almost everyone has the equipment to alter bits – the computer, the software and the representational devices, give users some control over the bits they receive as well as the ones they create. So digital messages may be saved, altered, and re-sent.
- *Peoples' information becomes public*: Knowledge about individuals is widely available. Much exquisitely detailed "private" information is readily available for commercial resale. As one executive put it: "Privacy? Get over it ..."

BACKGROUNDER ON AFFORDANCES

Perceptual psychologist, James Gibson (1979) developed the theory of affordances which begins with the proposition that humans and their environments are inherently interactive. Environments offer affordances, shaping possibilities for action – and humans take actions that, in turn, may re-shape their environments. Note that media affordances exist only for persons who *can* take the actions made possible by the affordance.

People attend to affordances only when they can identify the possibilities they offer. Of course, previous experience in digital environments helps people recognize and navigate these choices (boyd, 2011). Finally, as in the physical world, users act to take advantage of an affordance when it helps them meet a goal (Steffen, Gaskin, Meservy, Jenkins, & Wolman, 2019).

4 AFFORDANCES OF DIGITAL MEDIA AND SOME MASHUPS

For all environments, affordances lie in the eyes of the beholder. Journalists writing news stories see affordances quite differently than the users who read those stories. Researcher Janet Murray (2011) identified four high-level affordances of digital media that help journalists consider how to best engage users in a story:

- **Procedural**: The ability of a device to respond *flexibly* to users' input. Actions based on the procedural affordance include simulation, interactive data visualizations, searches, image and music, identification services, and games.
- **Participatory**: The things users can do, such as "like," comment, email, share, remix, download, and create their own media and digital artifacts. Murray's formulation of the participatory affordance includes interactions between human users and also human–computer interactions. When persons interact with devices, both have **agency** and can take actions, such as initiating exchanges – sending and receiving messages in response to the *interactive* communications of the other parties.

- **Encyclopedic:** The ability to find, store, retrieve, send, and receive large amounts of information, limited only by connectivity, storage capacity, searchability, and time. One primary constraint on our global encyclopedia are the walled gardens created by governments, corporations, and other powerful actors.
- **Spatial:** Screens, networks, and storage all have a physical presence that exists in space. Other spatial dimensions come from the content on the screen and the words we use to describe our devices such as windows, files, and folders. Descriptions of our internet use also reflect the sense of space: We "surf the Net" by clicking on buttons and links that take us to "sites," traversing access points, nodes, to boundaries at the network's "edge," including the "last mile" to consumers. Now virtual reality represents the bleeding-edge of spatial affordances.

AFFORDANCE MASHUPS

In practice, people create and use digital media in ways that make the simple classifications of affordances more difficult. Digital media implementation often draws on multiple affordances at a single time, as Table 10.3 shows.

AFFORDANCES AND USERS' TECHNOLOGY

Consumer devices – desktop or laptop computer, tablet, phone, phablet, watch, or glasses – afford or limit digital journalism because they provide gateways to the network for users. They determine how (and even if) users can consume online content. Devices both afford and limit every possible user activity, whether it's reading articles or posting Facebook links to stories. And the creation of apps has further expanded the ways content creators and users can take advantage of device affordances.

Device capabilities and network speeds profoundly impact all agents in the news supply chain, from news creation through user consumption. Users' digital devices provide

TABLE 10.3 Affordances play well together

	+ Participatory	*+ Encyclopedic*	*+ Spatial*
Procedural	LinkedIn, Twitter, hookup sites like Match. com, job search sites	Links, search engines: Google, Yahoo!, DuckDuckGo, etc.	Waze & other traffic apps, virtual reality content
Participatory		Links, internet phone & messaging services	Chat & meeting "rooms" like (Zoom), virtual "worlds," and visual game sites
Encyclopedic	Wikipedia editors; crowd-sourcing investigations		Google Maps, weather satellite feeds, maps, & information, FlightAware

Credit: Based on the work of Murray (2011).

PACKAGING ASSETS AND PUBLISHING ARTICLES

a menu of affordances that may be rich or sparse. Networks that carry news sites' content determine connection speed, which affects the affordances the user can actually exploit no matter how many actions the device allows. For example, users can't watch video on their mobile if the device doesn't allow it or runs slowly, or the network is slow. Over time, the speed of devices and networks will increase, but in the interim, it is a concern for news organizations.

Most news sites provide information about the site visitors to reporters. Journalists should learn how users experience their news site by looking at this user data. What reception devices do users have? What are their connection speeds? Can users stream audio or video? How quickly do users' devices download and display images? Formatted text? Do users' devices produce sound, display video, images, color, and format text in ways that can be heard or seen? Figure 10.9 shows how technologies shape how online stories reach users.

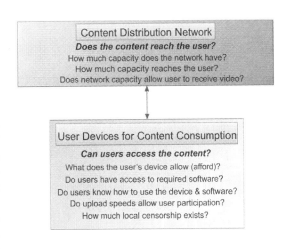

FIGURE 10.9

Technology in online publishing, distribution, and consumption

Credit: Joan Van Tassel

Digital reporters, who typically use topnotch technology, should recognize that many news site visitors don't have the latest, greatest devices or fastest internet services that deliver rich, unlimited content. While it's neat to serve affluent high-tech users, journalists who seek wide audiences must ensure that the broadest array of users can find and access their stories. Sadly, the dearth of U.S. rural broadband limits "mainstream" digital media affordances for heartland users.

MORE ABOUT THE CMS: THE DIGITAL ASSEMBLY LINE THAT JOURNALISTS LOVE TO HATE

An earlier section in this chapter discussed how newsrooms use the CMS as an end-to-end digital assembly line. Consider the CMS as the journalists' workspace. Not only do they upload their research, documents, story assets, and draft articles to it. They receive their editors' comments, requests for clarification, suggestions for revisions, and story approvals on the system. And we have seen that they also assemble articles and receive metrics and user comments.

Journalism students should realize the key role that CMSs will play in their day-to-day professional activities – the CMS will become their virtual workplace. Like physical workspaces, CMS environments should be comfortable, attractive, and functional. It's even better if the CMS environment is inspirational, fun, flexible, and helps journalists exercise their creativity. (Well, good luck with that.)

IF ONLY ... THE DREAMY CMS THAT ISN'T YET HERE

Although journalists appreciate the ability to create digital stories, they're often none-too-fond of the systems that produce them. With good reason: Far too often, CMSs are clunky, silo-ed, sluggish, unattractive, hard to learn, and time-consuming structures of confusing interfaces. Worse, many make assembling news packages a difficult chore. But over time, CMSs have improved. Today's news organizations often opt for customized, open-source systems that allow creators of original content – journalists, editors, and designers – to focus on their work, not on operating the CMS.

Two large news organizations that built their own CMSs have turned these creations into products (Willens, 2019). Vox Media markets its Chorus CMS and *The Washington Post* touts its Arc platform. These systems' designs originated with online news – featuring active, complex daily information input and distribution that serves most forms of large-scale digital publishing. Their price tags are high – both systems cost in the six-figure to seven-figure range, depending on the size and needs of the publishing organization, but they perform the essential online news functions. Vox Media and *The Washington Post* seek additional revenues from the annual licensing fees they receive, perhaps at the cost of aiding their competitors.

CMSs remain a work in progress. Someday, long-form stories will have flexible templates stored in news organization's CMS, even for complex narratives. But that day has not yet arrived. Still, the features of Chorus that make it so well-regarded are instructive (Johnston, 2014; Knight, 2018):

- **Unified workflow**: Repository for information about research, assignments, schedules, and editing throughout the editorial process.

- **Automated resource identification and linking**: Chorus automatically scans stories and conducts background searches to provide links to related articles. It also locates licensed photos and videos that reporters may wish to insert.

- **Rapid customization**: The framework and design of the system allows tech geeks to update it quickly, incorporating shortcuts and better procedures for content creators.

- **System unity**: Chorus isn't silo-ed – separated into different systems, sites, or working groups. People, processes, and content move easily throughout the system.

- **Metrics**: Most news sites measure user behavior through **Key Performance Indicators (KPIs)** like the number of hits, time spent on article, click-throughs, and so forth. Chorus includes a secret sauce which goes beyond Google Analytics.

- **Analytics** add historical data, search trends, and other data to help understand and attract audiences.

- **Integration with advertiser content**: Chorus allows advertisers to post **native advertising**.

However, even the most advanced CMS won't handle the assembly of some complicated articles. For these, web and page designers must assemble the package the old-fashioned way ... manually. Instead of inputting the story assets into a template, designers transform the reporter's hand-drawn storyboards into **mockups** or formal **wireframes** of each page that indicates where everything goes. These pre-assembly documents serve as roadmaps to assemble a digital package that includes story assets and all necessary navigational, structural, and design elements, as shown in Figure 10.10. Upon layout approval, designers assemble the package and publish it.

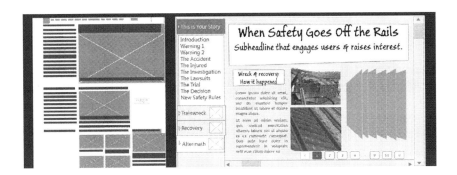

FIGURE 10.10

Web home page wireframe and article page mockup
Credit: Joan Van Tassel

AR and VR experience assets pose challenges for many news organizations and their CMSs. The largest media organizations may have the skilled designers, artists, and software needed to handle large-scale scanned 3D environments for virtual reality, but most newsrooms don't yet have these resources. And virtual reality assembly, packaging, and publishing remains fractured into separate developer eco-systems without standard tools, platforms, or headsets.

While many newsrooms have professionals who can create augmented reality assets, it takes more complicated processes to package, publish, and distribute them. Apps from Apple (ARKit) and Google (ARCore) distribute and display AR experiences to users – crucial processes for publishing AR experiences. However, the CMS has one cost-saving role: store already created 3D assets for reuse in follow-on stories.

A DEEPER DIVE INTO THE CMS STACK: 3 PARTS, 3 PROCESSES

CMSs don't look impressive – just a bunch of computers in boxes with inputs, outputs, and screens. But make no mistake – *CMSs underlie the entire large-scale content and intellectual property industries.* However difficult to use, their importance can't be overemphasized. Without CMSs, news organizations couldn't operate effectively in today's digital environment.

At a bare minimum, CMSs have three parts, connected by a network that allows the parts to "talk to" each other:

1. A searchable repository of digital assets
2. A composition editor for packaging new editions, sections, pages, articles, and updates that allows contributors to edit, comment, notify, save, and version both documents and assets
3. A save-and-send or a save-and-publish button for moving content to a media server or publishing it directly to designated platforms

These parts work together to accomplish three complex and crucial organizational capabilities. Automation, coordination and collaboration, and the reuse of assets make digital news production faster and cheaper. Without these capabilities, incorporating all the media types and formats of digital content would be daunting – perhaps impossible, given the demands of producing and distributing highly complex publications for the diverse multiplicity of user devices.

The Machines Are Industrious This Morning: Automation

CMSs automate many aspects of preparing stories that fit pre-made templates, as many short reports do. Once story creators finish uploading and tagging all the story elements, the CMS assembles the story package, following instructions provided by the story element filenames and tags. Web page and interaction designers have already put together "the look and feel" of the overall website and created design templates for recurrent article types, using programming languages such as **HyperText Markup Language (HTML)**, **Cascading Style Sheets (CSS)**, **Ruby on Rails**, and **JavaScript**.

To allow stories and publication editions to get to users through the many web servers, one task of the CMS is to transcode content into a web-friendly universal XML-based format like **News Markup Language (NewsML)**. This language facilitates the exchange of articles between systems and languages by prescribing the formatting and tagging of news content so that it looks and feels the same everywhere on the internet. For example, NewsML has special tag categories for news-related page elements, such as the headline, deck, byline, teaser, and copyright information, in addition to standard XML metadata for date, version, and other more routine metadata. In the CMS, these tags provide the glue that links all the content assets. A smart, automated CMS system may add: 1) tags that create links between elements and 2) find and link older pages with related information (as indicated by their tags) into the mix.

Team Coordination: Digital Journalists as Collaborators and Cooperators

Back in the day, team up a reporter, an editor, a photog, and a copyeditor with the pressroom – and presto! A big story would be out the door. The CMS replaces the epic inbox snarls of team collaboration with comment streams. The CMS notifies everyone at each stage of article production following copy submission by the reporters. The digital media package and its elements arrive simultaneously in team members' queues so that responses, concerns, suggestions, and revisions can circulate immediately. By streamlining coordination between all the actors, at each point in the process, a CMS greatly speeds up the editorial cycles of creation, revision, and publishing, even with many team members.

Speed is one of the prominent characteristics of the new news. In large media organizations, coordination becomes notoriously difficult. Updating staffers of all media outlets, such as print, broadcast, and multiple online news properties and sites requires reaching across an enormous enterprise with units that have very different competencies and processes. An efficient, well-designed CMS must also track audience comments and other contributions that include the many tweets, photos and videos sent from onlookers' mobile phones. These CMSs allow newsrooms to establish a flow of information inside and outside the organization that can capture the nuances of complicated stories in real time – as they unfold. Recall *The Boston Globe*'s coverage of the marathon bombings in Chapter 4 – and the huge central role that *The Boston Globe*'s CMS digital assembly line played during that dramatic, breaking story.

The Way Cool Library: Remix, Reuse, Reward

The online and nearline storage connected to the CMS adds this important efficiency advantage to large news organizations that cover many stories. The searchable digital library stores all the stories ever published on the news site, complete with their associated assets. If the news outlet holds the copyright, journalists can reuse these assets to add background and context for any story and later reuse them in related, round-up, and retrospective articles – just with a simple click of their mouse. One example: Vox Media's Chorus CMS pulls up such links automatically.

But small-to-medium news operations must often rely on open-source services customized to fit their specific needs. The *Bangor Daily News* (BDN) ran both its web and print editions on a free WordPress website hosting service (Rabaino, 2011). Now the *Bangor Daily News* is one of 12 local news organizations piloting the WordPress.com Newspack, a CMS designed for local news outlets with support from the Google News Initiative and other high-profile news foundations. Newspack will cost about $1,000 per month when released in 2020 (Beatty, 2019).

BUILDING AN AUDIENCE: PREVIEW, PUBLISHING, AND PROMOTION

Shortly before publishing their story, many reporters sign-in to their social media accounts and post a preview of the story-to-come. Reporters may also alert their Twitter followers that they will publish a story soon, usually an hour or two from the first preview post. When Brandi Buchman at *CourthouseNews.com* covered the Paul Manafort trials in 2018, she displayed her preview ninja chops – within minutes of the story link appearing on her timeline, dozens of her followers were all over it.

Publishing? Once again, the CMS plays a starring role. Here's the deal: To publish an article (or an entire publication) – just push the publish button. Click – the material goes everywhere: to servers, aggregators, websites, channels, and devices. The flow to multiple screens is seamless, employing on-the-fly display-sensing software and automated reformatting of the published content to match the screen size and resolution of the many brands of desktop displays, laptops, tablets, mobile phones, and digital TV sets. All the hard work takes place at the CMS front end; just push the button at the back end.

Wait, there's more! After publishing a story, reporters promote it, seeking to maximize readership and foster engagement with users (Batsell, 2015). Journalists now blog, post, and tweet SNSs, such as Facebook, LinkedIn, Instagram, Twitter, Snapchat, Pinterest, and other services as well as on their publication's website. Reporters may post video on YouTube and Twitter, or on other platforms. If it's a strong package – investigative, dramatic, or cinematic – the journalist may write an article on www.medium.com describing the story's origin or an interesting experience while pursuing the story. In short, far more possibilities for promotion and engagement exist than any one journalist can pursue in a few hours.

Then user feedback starts coming in, almost immediately after publishing the story. Users read and respond to the story in its comment section and via email. In turn, digital reporters interact directly with their audience. Long after the package runs, the reporter may still be answering questions and comments about aspects of the story.

HOW TO TELL USERS ABOUT THE STORY BEFORE TELLING THE STORY

For users already interested in a story, a headline and deck may suffice to garner a click. But, in our information-saturated environment, users need good reasons to check out an article. Traditionally, publications or news shows are responsible for promotion. But now reporters promote articles as part of their jobs. Another reason motivates journalists to get involved: They may have to seek another job someday. They promote their own work to build personal followings on social platforms, independent from their publication and thereby give other news outlets incentives to hire them in these uncertain times.

When they promote their articles on SNSs, reporters should recognize that promotion copy differs from news copy in important ways. Although promotions seek to inform, they also seek to influence users' behavior. Promotional copy typically includes most or all these elements:

- The **tease**: The hook – raises interest by appealing to curiosity, increased social status, or admission to a circle of knowledge, etc.

- The **proposition**: Tells users why the story will fulfill personal, professional, social, or civic needs

- The **call to action**: Suggests the user should do something: read the story, share the story, watch the video, etc.

The tease provides a "hook" that highlights the single most interesting aspect of the story. In story promotion, "interesting" means surprising, useful, provocative, outrageous, or shocking. For stories, reports, or digital media packages, the most interesting aspect has been carefully introduced, set up, described, contextualized, and explained. In promotion, all that care and nuance goes by the wayside – drop it. Just cut to the chase.

Check out these CNN.com story promotions written for social platforms in March 2016:

1. *Facebook*: Breaking – He said/she said: Didn't happen, he said – Yale basketball captain sues university over expulsion for a rape. What do you think? Read it at: http://cnn.it/22goFzn

2. *Twitter*: Breaking: He said/she said – B-ball captain sues Yale over rape expulsion. Your opinion? Check it out @ http://cnn.it/22goFzn

3. *Instagram*: Hiker turns over rare gold coin! Really!? See it @: http://cnn.it/22eK4wy

TABLE 10.4 Parsing the micro-promotion

Tease/hook	Proposition	Call to Action
1. He said/she said	What do you think?	Read it at: (link)
2. Breaking and He said/she said	Your opinion?	Check it out @: (link)
3. Rare gold coin	Really!?	See it @: (link)

Credit: Joan Van Tassel

AFTERMATH: DISTRIBUTION AND SURVEILLANCE

Publishing begins the story's public life. It then enters the global communication circulatory system that carries the story's information to the furthest reaches of the world. The story may find its way to individual users via mobile and landline networks, undersea cables, and satellites, reaching many people in just seconds.

Just as the internet's reach gives users windows on the world, it also gives actors with the right resources, software, and expertise the ability to hide their intrusive monitoring of internet users' activities. Many websites and mobile apps surveil users, and quietly sell or share their users' information with unknown others – for purposes never envisioned by the persons who provided that data. But governments in Europe and the United States have fired new salvos in the fight to protect the privacy of online users – probably the first of many to come.

But in the meantime ….

USER BEHAVIOR MONITORING

In the United States, media companies, including news organizations, monitor users' activities on their sites. They would commit business malpractice if they didn't. Media organizations collect individual-level behavioral data whenever users visit their sites. Then, they aggregate data to examine their collective users' behaviors. Real-time data helps news outlets reposition more popular content on their web pages, attract more users, and increase users' dwell times. As internet media businesses increasingly personalize content, they may disaggregate individual-level user data (drawn from data archives) and use it to match users with personalized online content and individually targeted advertising.

To visualize how editors manage news sites, consider the Chartbeat newsroom software package, shown in Figure 10.11, on the next page. The Chartbeat dashboard lets editors see how many people are on the site, which pages they visited, and how long users stayed on each page. Editors can also see how many users are posting to social media or clicking on ads. The dashboard shows from which sites users entered the news site and their departure destinations (Petre, 2015). Chartbeat is used in many large newsrooms, although it has several competitors. Parse.ly markets itself as a data analytics tool specifically designed for editors. Google Analytics, Adobe Omniture, and DemandBase monitor web sites and collect data, but they are more oriented toward marketing efforts. And Mixpanel specializes in monitoring and modeling users' behavior in mobile apps.

These analytics show the stories that are getting the most user clicks. Editors use the metrics to move attention-getting stories into more prominent positions on web pages to encourage even more clicks. They know where to move them through the results of eye-tracking studies of user scanning and reading web pages. The research shows that people typically scan the top of web pages first (Nielsen, 2006) and then pay more attention to the page's left side. This scanning pattern looks like an "F," known as the **F-pattern**, as shown in Figure 10.12, on page 323.

Another common user scanning and reading pattern is the **Z-pattern**, described by Steven Bradley (2011) and shown in Figure 10.13, also on page 323. There are other web page layouts including those that make scanning easier by formatting stories in a *zig-zag* pattern. On mobile pages, users focus first on the upper center of the screen, the so-called **golden triangle** of the mobile display.

322　THE DIGITAL ASSEMBLY LINE

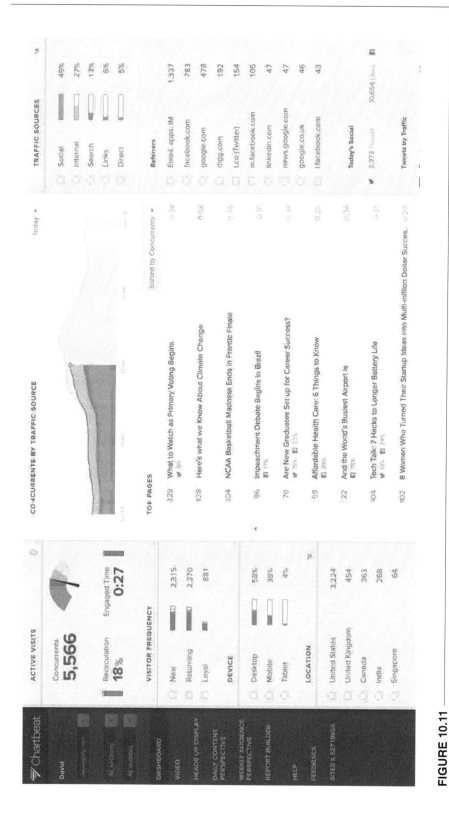

FIGURE 10.11

Chartbeat dashboard mockup

Credit: Reproduced with permission from Chartbeat.

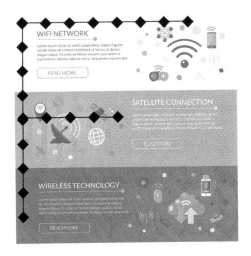

FIGURE 10.12

Eye-tracking user scanning: The F-pattern
Credit: Joan Van Tassel

FIGURE 10.13

Eye-tracking user scanning: The Z-pattern
Credit: Joan Van Tassel

LIMITS ON CORPORATE BIG BROTHERISM

Surveillance of users is now regulated by the European Union's 2018 privacy protection law, the **General Data Privacy Regulation**. The GDPR curtails the collection of data that's presently so commonplace in U.S. media sites. Collecting web analytics does not necessarily violate the GDPR. But online news sites must *first* obtain specific consent from each tracked user before each of these activities:

- Giving behavioral data to advertisers or ad platforms
- Using remarketing markers and tracking codes
- Personalizing content

The GDPR applies to digital content reaching all residents of the EU, even applying to content from companies based outside the EU. The GDPR requires that companies reveal their purposes for collecting user data, whether via website or telephone. Before *any* collection, the company must obtain the user's permission to get data – for each and every purpose. Users can decline to allow data gathering but companies can't then refuse services or increase their prices.

U.S. news companies responded immediately when the GDPR went into effect. *The New York Times* canceled its ad exchange program that made individual behavioral data available to advertisers wishing to target users. In contrast, as many as 1,000 U.S. news publications immediately went dark in Europe to avoid the costly fines for violating the GDPR (Davies, 2019). In contrast. *Business Insider* which draws about 10 percent of its ad revenue from the EU, elected to meet the GDPR requirements. *Business Insider* asked for users' consent to display personalized ads; it reported having high opt-in rates (Davies, 2019).

Eventually, U.S. news organizations became more comfortable with the GDPR. The *Los Angeles Times* now meets the requirements of the GDPR and provides users some articles in the UK and France. When U.S. publications don't comply with GDPR data regulations, they may post notices in EU countries, notifying users that content can't be made available in the EU.

The GDPR forced internet and mobile companies to prepare for the more comprehensive data privacy regulation if they want to publish content online in the EU. In the U.S., the California Consumer Privacy Act (CCPA) went into effect on January 1, 2020, with enforcement scheduled to begin in mid-2020. The CCPA provides many protections much like those in the EU's GDPR. Absent successful legal challenges, California residents can demand that (qualifying) companies:

- Disclose (to each user) the personal data that they have collected, and inform the user the extent to which that company has given or sold the data to a third party. The organization that gathers or processes the information *remains legally* responsible for third-party compliance with both CCPA and GDPR privacy requirements (Deloitte, 2019)

- On request, provide a copy of the personal information collected about users within the past year

- Delete the collected information

- Refrain from sharing the collected information with third parties

- Refrain from retaliation against users for actions they have taken to protect their privacy

Although questions remain regarding how California will enforce the CCPA provisions, they will influence companies' data privacy practices. Since California hosts the fifth largest economy in the world, many analysts believe that companies throughout the U.S. will comply with CCPA provisions so they can operate in California. If users refuse to give permission for use of their data, publishers cannot refuse to let them see the content they make available to those who do give their consent.

To handle the permissions process, large publishers have added consent management platforms (CMP) to their distribution technology array. CMPs collect and store the data which users agree that publishers and their advertisers can have, use, and forward to others for stated purposes. The CMP then feeds this "user-cleared" information to other designated partners in the digital ad supply chain. The central premise: Everyone in the chain knows what personal data may be used, for which purposes, and comply with the CCPA.

The new limits on user monitoring hit news organizations in a tender place: their advertising revenue stream. Advertisers want as much information about users as possible. They'd like to have all their personal information so they can target and pitch them via email, text, and SNSs. Certainly, advertising is as common on news site web pages as it is on other media like TV, radio, newspapers, and magazines. Whether the new privacy rules will affect online news sites' income remains to be seen.

ONLINE ADVERTISING ON NEWS SITES: 4 TYPES THAT EVERY JOURNALIST NEEDS TO KNOW

Depending on the news site's policies, paying subscribers may avoid some advertising. But free riders and incidental visitors inevitably see web pages sprinkled with advertising. Journalists have mixed feelings about news site advertising. They realize that advertising competes with their stories for users' attention. Yet, most accept that advertising revenue covers substantial costs of maintaining their newsroom, the website – and their salaries.

Although advertisers seem to buy web page space, in fact, they buy **impressions**, or ad views. They're buying eyeballs in an attention economy, so to speak. It often requires more than one impression for people to attend to ads. After a few impressions, users may notice the ad and actually process the information it conveys – if the ad displays content that interests the user. To buy impressions, advertisers pay to place their ads on a web site, or even on a specific page. Ads' costs depend on: 1) where the ad appears, 2) its size, 3) its media affordances (print, video, audio, etc.), and 4) its click-through capabilities.

Four types of advertising appear on news site pages:

1. **Native ads** cause some uneasiness in online newsrooms. These ads almost look like the site's news stories – a deliberate strategy to mimic the genuine news articles on the site: Sometimes native ad headlines with a deck and picture appear on the news site's home page. The full article may also look like other site articles, with headlines, bylines, images, copy, and links. But journalists don't write these articles. Rather, advertising copywriters or promotional writers prepare them. Research finds that fewer than 20 percent of users recognize that the article is an ad; users who recognized the misleading article as "highly deceptive" (Wojdynski, 2016).

2. **Programmatic advertising** describes a method to buy and locate ads automatically. In traditional news outlets, advertisers first negotiated price and placement with news organizations, signed contracts, and then mailed their photo-ready art and copy to be inserted into the publication. Programmatic advertising automates all these tasks. Depending on the ad agreement, a news site will accommodate the programmed ad's inclusion by constructing pages on-the-fly. The only human intervention occurs when the advertiser goes online to place the order, agrees to the price, and specifies the size and placement of its ad. Even the billing is automated!

3. **User-tailored ads (mass customized or personalized advertising)** depend on the demographics of each identified user (via account sign-up or other means). The news system then inserts, at pre-specified page locations, an ad tailored to influence users who fit those demographic characteristics. In contrast, personalized ads are tailored to each unique user – often featuring that user's name in the ad. As of 2016, mass customized ads appeared more often than personalized ads, but industry trends favored ad personalization. Yet, increasingly users have become aware of (and dislike) the intrusive individual data collection upon which personalized ads depend (Hitlin & Rainie, 2019).

4. **Static ads** are like unchanging newspaper display ads, the same for every reader.

BARRIERS TO MAXIMIZING AD EXPOSURE

Ad-blocking software creates barriers to ads, particularly for mobile devices. Advertising often annoys users, because it consumes scarce time and bandwidth that users don't want to provide, especially those with expensive data rates. To defend themselves against commercial intrusion, users increasingly arm themselves with ad blocker apps for mobile phones and browser add-ons to prevent ads from appearing. It's an evolutionary process: Browser add-ons disable scripts; sites block content to users who don't allow scripts, leading to stealthy browser ad-blocking add-ons – smarter mice foster development of better mousetraps, thus encouraging the evolution of smarter mice ....

Third-party scripts also slow down users' computers and increase page loading delays. Excessive loading times keep users from seeing stories (and ads), creating ongoing problems for both the site and its users. Some news sites, eager for the revenue from allowing others' scripts, have far too many scripts – driving users to "bounce" from the slower webpages.

To the extent that (enforceable) EU and California data privacy laws spread to other regions, data privacy restrictions will make targeted advertising ever more difficult. Users clearly want to limit ads, as the popularity of ad blockers demonstrates – and they are increasingly concerned with protecting their privacy. Many knowledgeable observers predict that it's just a matter of time before public pressures force political leaders to limit how websites collect user data, track user behaviors, and sell their information to third parties.

TAKEAWAYS

- Online news story creation resembles traditional journalism practice in many ways. An editor assigns a story that comes from a newsworthy happening or a pitch. A reporter gathers information, verifies it, perhaps acquires some assets, processes and prepares the assets, writes copy, and assembles an article. Most workflow steps require editorial approval, followed by revisions. Articles with interactive elements or a complex structure, usually require custom assembly and testing. The news outlet publishes the story on its website, then promotes it if editors think it will attract users. At the same time, the journalist sends out comments, tweets, pictures, and videos to social media sites and blog sites to increase the story awareness and attract more users.

- A story *is not* a narrative. The story provides the chronology of what happened, then what happened next, and so forth, all the way to the end. A narrative is the way the storyteller unfolds the story. For example, a narrative may begin (or end) with a dramatic scene, and then explain how this story came to be. Another well known storytelling strategy begins in the middle – using the narrative structure called *in media res*, Latin for "in the middle of things."

  One way to formulate the narrative story is to deconstruct the story into single chunks of facts, actions, and events, then assemble related chunks into clusters, and finally order the clusters to tell the story. The tools for transforming stories into narratives include storytelling software, digital or cardboard notecards, and storyboards. Before writing the story, journalists should answer four questions: 1) Who is telling the story? 2) What is each storyteller's perspective, including the reporter's? 3) What is each storyteller's tone of voice? 4) What is the story's overall look and feel?

- Digital narrative structures differ from traditional structures because they include multimedia assets and interactive opportunities that other media do not. Journalists have developed four online narrative structures:
  - Linear-embedded format
  - Hierarchical format
  - Nonlinear format, and
  - Combination formats

Linear-embedded formats unfold the story from beginning to end, with related multimedia assets and interactives embedded next to the relevant part of the story. Hierarchical formats work for complex stories that have multiple locations, sets of actors, or time periods. They move from one set to another, each layer adding more information and perspective, until the final layer brings the story to its conclusion, or at least to a jumping-off point for the next story as more information becomes known. Nonlinear formats let users choose how the story unfolds by providing a menu of story clusters. This menu may have thumbnail pictures or simply show a list of choices, linked to each story part. Combination formats take elements from more than one of the other formats, as determined by the best way to tell the story. For example, an article may begin as a linear-embedded narrative, then have interspersed pages with a "Christmas tree" of choices, presented in a nonlinear structure.

- Assembling online articles means putting together all the assets that go into an article to make up a digital media package. The elements and types of assets that go into the package include:
  - **The assets** including copy, pictures, video, and audio, data visualizations, and interactives.
  - **Narrative structural objects** that define the article's architecture, sections, and story-related navigational objects. These objects might include headings, subheadings, pull quotes, and graphic elements. The **user interface** offers users ways to navigate the site and use website features; the **user experience** or **UX** framework helps users experience and understand the story; and **interaction design** (**IxD**) guides the creation of elements to enable user interactions with the article or with other users.
  - **Affordance-related elements** draw on the essential and unique characteristics of online digital media and platforms that allow users to interact – opportunities that other media cannot provide. For example, interactive data visualizations help users better understand and follow the article; participation interactives increase engagement.
  - **Publication structural, design, and navigational objects** are pre-designed assets that the news site's publication manual specifies for use with all sections, pages, and articles.
- Affordances are defined as "possibilities for actions" in an environment. In digital environments, affordances allow (and their absence precludes) how people can use their communications technologies, online services and platforms, and devices. Janet Murray (2011) identifies four broad affordances of digital media:
  - *Procedural*: The **procedural affordance** is the ability of a device to respond flexibly to users' input. Actions based on procedural affordances include simulations, interactive data visualizations, search engines, image and music identification services, and games.
  - *Participatory*: The **participatory affordance** enables human-human and human-computer interactions – both the human and computer parties act as **agents**. **Agency** permits either party to initiate exchanges and send messages that respond to the communication of the other – e.g., *interactive* communication. Coded scripts direct the computer to initiate interacts, invite exchanges, and participate in exchanges with users. In these conversations, each agent influences the actions of the other.

- *Encyclopedic*: The **encyclopedic affordance** means that the internet, individual computers, and linked computers have the capacity to handle vast amounts of information. They take information in, record, store, search, and then display it. Metadata, including keywords, tags, and special markers like the @ sign, and the # hashtag supplement formal classification systems in the digital environment.
- *Spatial*: The **spatial affordance** provides ways that digital devices seemingly recreate spatial dimensions in virtual worlds. The names for ephemeral digital objects evoke "place," such as home, menu, and dock. The physical computer screen affords representing an infinite number of possible and impossible representations of the real world. Digital networks mimic travel in the physical world as we "surf the Net," "visit" web sites, "leave" messages, and "fly" through simulations, as though our computer screens represent 3D space.

- Content management systems comprise the underlying digital assembly lines for content production. Almost all organizations that create large volumes of online content, including news organizations, use CMSs to manage their assets and outputs and to coordinate the contributions of newsroom workers. The CMS plays vital roles in story assignment, research, approval, assembly, packaging, and publishing digital news content. The CMS has at least three parts: 1) a searchable library of stored, digitally-accessible assets, 2) a composition editor to assemble content, save and version documents and assets, and publish content, and 3) a collaboration environment to allow groups and teams to work together to prepare and process content.

  The CMS supports a unified workflow to create digital content that can be shared by workers in multiple departments. Tags attached to all files facilitate searching, retrieving, and linking between similarly tagged items. Much of this work is automated. The system often allows customized workspaces for different categories of workers. Presently some news organizations enable advertisers to post native advertising in the CMS, integrating it with the news outlet's content.

- Responsibility for promoting digital news sites and individual stories no longer remains just the province of sales and promotion professionals. Now editors and reporters must also attract users, build their interest, and engage them to keep them glued to the news site. Writing promotional copy wasn't part of the journalists' job, but now it is. The structure of traditional reports – lede, nut graf, most important facts and events, background, and context – are familiar to journalists. The structure of promotional copy that includes a tease, a proposition, and a call to action demands new skills that require added effort and time.

  - The **tease**: Leads users to click on a story by raising interest and curiosity
  - The **proposition**: Tells users what they will get from the story or extends an offer
  - The **call to action**: Tells users what to do next: read and share the story, watch the video, click the link, etc.

- Large news organizations monitor users' behaviors in real time to maximize site visits and time on the site. Most sites use third-party vendors to format this data into actionable information – usually displayed on continuously updated dashboards that are sometimes integrated with the CMS. Typical metrics of user behavior include the number of hits, bounces, dwell time spent on articles and pages, click-throughs, likes, shares, number of comments, and other data that helps publications to understand current users and attract new users.

PACKAGING ASSETS AND PUBLISHING ARTICLES

- Stories usually have a headline, thumbnail graphic, and short phrase – designed to help users quickly skim the gist of the story to capture their attention and interest. Based on the popularity of an article, editors often design their webpages to encourage more clicks. Editors can use the F-format, Z-format, and mobile page golden triangle to facilitate scanning the page and seeing the appealing content.

- Data privacy laws such as the EU's General Data Privacy Regulation place limits on how U.S. news sites collect and use the data they obtain from users. Prohibitively high fines for violating the GDPR caused some publishers to limit the stories they make available to EU citizens. The California data privacy law (CCPA) went into effect in 2020 with other states in the U.S. planning to follow suit. Publications should expect more such privacy laws in many countries.

- Advertising underpins digital news organizations' business model. In the digital world, marketing, ad placement, sales, and even conferences are geared to special interest audiences. News websites display four types of online advertising:

  - **Native ads** look like news stories, with headlines, images, and copy with a link to the "article" from the front page or section front page news grid. This similarity is deliberate, but native ads *are not* news stories; rather they *are* pitches to buy products or services. News sites often label native ads as "sponsor-provided content" or "content from (company name)."

  - **Static banners and display ads** show the same ad to all site visitors. Banner ads go across the top of the page. Display ads can be placed anywhere on the page.

  - **Programmatic advertising** reaches news sites through a third-party ad distributor. The ad-buying, pricing, and placement is automated, so that the news organization's server collects page information and creates a data sheet of available ad space and a summary of user cookies that specify user characteristics and behaviors. Advertisers look for specific audiences and supply ads tailored to fill the space. All financial details have been defined by contract in advance.

  - **User-tailored ads** that refer to **customized** or **personalized advertising** are a form of programmatic advertising. Customized ads, tailored to match user-demographics identified by sponsors, are inserted to appeal to users who fit that set of demographic characteristics. Personalized ads are tailored to each unique individual user – often the user's name appears in the ad. In 2016, mass customized ads appeared more often than personalized ads; but industry trends favor ad personalization strategies. Recent concerns with laws protecting users' data privacy deter ad personalization.

  - Ad-blocking software represents an important, growing threat to advertising revenue for news websites. As concerns about privacy have grown, more users have installed software that blocks ads or that blocks information-gathering from cookies.

KEY CONCEPTS AND TERMS

- The online news editorial workflow
- Transformation of stories to narratives
- Narrative structures in news reports and stories
- Assembling and packaging the digital story

- Content management systems in digital newsrooms
- Affordances of digital media
- Building the audience for your story
- Types of advertising on news sites

EXERCISES AND ACTIVITIES

1. Do a search on "news organizations and content management system." Read three articles written in the past 5 years and write a short 2 to 3-page paper comparing them. Include the following characteristics in your comparison: Brand, type, and size of CMS; name, type, and size of news organization; how journalists use the CMS; journalistic needs addressed by CMS; and organizational needs addressed by CMS.

2. Describe the affordances of mobile smartphones.

3. Sign up for an account on at least one of the largest five social media networking sites (SMSs), such as Facebook, Twitter, Instagram, Snapchat, or LinkedIn. Follow ten journalists for a week and collect their posts. Analyze and critique their promotional effectiveness.

4. Write a 2 to 3-page paper about programmatic advertising. Include a description of what it is and how it works, recent advances in programmatic ad technologies, and continuing problems as it now functions. Use at least four authoritative sources in your paper.

ADVANCER

The next chapter covers mobile journalism and how to create stories with and for mobile devices. It discusses how mobile journalists (mojos) use their phones to gather information and to capture and edit multimedia content – photos, audio clips, and videos. It's a big adjustment for news organizations to accommodate mobile formats and integrate them with their existing distribution channels – especially when they must handle breaking news. Most newsrooms have redefined and redesigned their workflows to accommodate these additional formats. Finally, Chapter 11 presents the characteristics of mobile infrastructures, including how they impact the audience's reception of stories.

11

MOBILE JOURNALISM: NEWS ON THE MOVE

Chapter Learning Objectives

After reading this chapter, students will be able to:

1. Understand the rise of the mobile market.
2. Consider how mobile users access, consume, and use news.
3. Analyze the mobile workflow of reporters in the field.
4. Put together a mobile kit for field reporting.
5. Analyze mobile device affordances.
6. Understand how journalists use mobile infrastructures.
7. Produce and design news content with mobile devices for global audiences.
8. Identify how newsrooms incorporate mobile workflows within their overall system.

> Currently the smartphone is the most powerful reporter's notebook yet invented, and journalists must be trained to use it to capture the full power for themselves and their audiences. Mobile journalism is a core competency for field reporting elements of a story with small, connected devices. Mojos report in audio, photo, and video. [It is] about working with pictures and then knowing how to write to those pictures.
>
> – Robb Montgomery, quoted in Eisenberg (2019)

THE GIST

Mr. Montgomery describes the mobile phone as the wondrous Swiss Army knife of journalism. And he's right: Take notes, take a photo, record video or audio – or take a break and watch a cat video. Phone calls, messages, and email make smartphones a complete comm device too – all in a sleek hand-held pocket-sized package that everyone carries anyway!

Learning to use the phone as a reporting tool is important for every reporter. But mojos must systematically explore and master the full array of smartphone audio, photo, video, and messaging capabilities available to them. It may take a little practice to put all these tools in your personal toolkits so that you can use them instinctively when under pressure.

Most people find mobile devices easy to use. They offer a wide array of features that enable both users and journalists to express their creativity across a broad range of digital actions, including interactions with content and with others. For journalists, mobile phones provide opportunities to deliver important, meaningful, and engaging material that reaches followers who often pay for news they particularly want to receive.

This chapter describes how journalists produce news content for these increasingly valuable mobile audiences. Reporters need an impressive range of digital skills to excel while reporting in today's multiplatform distribution environment. It's challenging to write succinct stories with low word counts per screen, maintain high standards of journalistic quality, and keep the attention of people on the move. Journalists must know the effective tools and techniques that best find and hold the key audiences who feed their news habits on mobiles.

Many journalists use mobile devices to report and produce news. The chapter describes field reporters' workflow and their specialized equipment: web apps and native mobile apps that reporters use to report and file stories. In the field, reporters must write succinctly (and well!), compose and edit photos, shoot and edit videos, and post on social media – all while reporting their stories. Connectivity is paramount. Thus, one section explains bandwidth issues for users' mobile reception so that journalists better recognize their need to minimize bandwidth usage.

As more news is produced in the field, reporters must understand how mobile digital page design can increase readership and engagement. Bringing new content creation skills to mobile platforms provides one key to growing readership and maximizing audiences with mobile stories and packages. Responsive Web Design (RWD) software automates the processes of reformatting webpages to fit story content to today's many screen sizes, ranging from desktop computers to smartwatches. This chapter describes changes that mobile reporting has made to newsroom workflows and operations.

The coronavirus pandemic social distancing imperative drives on-scene reports and interviews toward unaccompanied mojos – well-prepared and equipped for solo reporting. Understand that mojos and others reporting in the field under these conditions must prepare themselves for serious risks: viral hazards, scary and unpredictable environments, and even wrath from participants who try to avoid reporters' scrutiny. Chapter 11 in its entirety describes how mojos can knowledgeably excel as journalists when working in the dangerous, unforgiving, and high-stakes environments that the COVID-19 pandemic and other intense situations entail.

JUST WHEN NEWSROOMS ADAPTED TO THE INTERNET, GUESS WHAT HAPPENED?

The environment changed! Mobile phones (first lurking as curious "bricks" for weird, rich dweebs) were now in everyone's hand – and the news became another app on everyone's mobile. Buh-bye desktop, hello mobile. Wait, there's more! News is everywhere. Hello print, video broadcast, web desktop and laptop, mobile tablet, phone, and watches. Yikes, where will it stop – 3D virtual reality glasses? Implants? (Look, Mom, my fingers are my antenna!)

But ... for mobile phones to spread around the world took several decades. The first mobile phone call occurred in 1973 (Seward, 2013). Like most *successful* communication devices, mobile had modest initial adoption rates that exponentially increased before eventually leveling off, as shown in Figure 11.1. The adoption of new technologies begins with people called innovators. Next, early adopters try-out the technology, and then (successful) innovations enter mainstream usage. Today, almost everyone has a mobile phone. Because the adoption curve looks like an "S" slightly tilted on its side, it's called the **S-shaped curve of adoption** or just the **S-curve**, first described in 1962 by communication scholar Everett Rogers (Rogers, 1995).

Fast forward 35 years: Mobile technology delivers a huge array of services, often through internet connections. In the U.S.:

- 2011 35 percent of adults owned smartphones (Mitchell, 2015)
- 2015 Adoption of smartphones had grown exponentially (Westlund, 2015)
- 2019 96 percent of adults have mobile phones, four-fifths of them – smartphones (Anderson, 2019)
    - One-third of adults (three-fifths of young adults) *mostly* go online via smartphones.

Accessing news with mobile phones had become so commonplace by 2015, that mobile users' visits to news sites outnumbered those by desktop computer users (Lipsman, 2015). Four-fifths of people who have only mobile access are satisfied with it – they say they lack interest in receiving home broadband at all. About half of the people "not

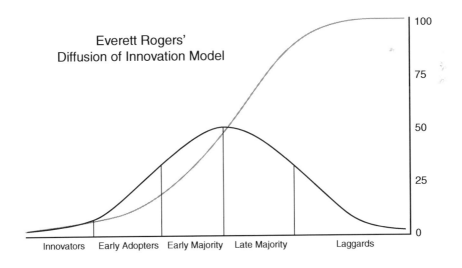

FIGURE 11.1

Diffusion of Innovations: How new ideas and products spread

Credit: By Beat Estermann – Own work, CC BY-SA 4.0, https://commons.wikimedia.org/w/index.php?curid=46617873

interested in broadband" say it's because their smartphone "lets me do everything I need to do online." (Of course, in many rural areas, broadband isn't available or may be quite expensive.)

And many people do use smartphones to do everything they need online. They share on social media, tweet and retweet, comparison shop, checkout at "cash" registers, get directions, map trips, apply for jobs, get health information, track their Fitbit fitness, hail Uber rides, and order delivery of just-in-time meals – reading, listening, and watching the news as they go!

YOU ARE THERE NOW! – MOBILE DEVICES ADD COMPELLING EXPERIENCES OF PARTICIPATION AND IMMEDIACY

A story made possible by a mobile phone in a reporter's hand can translate to viral excitement on social media, especially when the story takes a shocking U-turn in real time. In 2011, reporter Les Carpenter tweeted a thread that captured wide public attention. Formerly a columnist and reporter for *Yahoo! Sports* (now at the *Guardian*), Carpenter covered baseball star Roger Clemen's trial for steroid use. Carpenter described his courtroom experience:

> It was so mundane that I almost didn't go. Of course, cell phones were banned in court and it seemed to be just routine and boring ... even the judge was so bored he took out his Blackberry to check his messages. Then all of a sudden, as I'm following the testimony, the judge realized and then everyone realized that we were watching a volcano erupt.
>
> (Carpenter, 2011)

The eruption occurred when the prosecution committed an error by introducing an affidavit that, prior to trial, the judge had ruled the affidavit wasn't relevant. Just a few of Carpenter's tweets follow here, but thousands of avid sports fans followed his tweetstorm while events unfolded during the first day of the trial:

- Judge Walton is checking his Blackberry   3 hours ago
- Clemens testimony to Congress shows him talking about Pettitte calling him into side room after Jason Grimsley was caught with steroids ...   3 hours ago
- video shows Clemens talking about Pettitte wringing his hands and said: "what are you going to tell them?"   3 hours ago
- video playing Congressman Cummings reading an affidavit of Pettitte's wife remembering her husband telling her Clemens had admitted roid use   3 hours ago

A few tweets later, Carpenter wrote:

- Judge Walton, with jury out of room, is irritated with government for introducing Pettitte's wife's affidavit when he ruled before trial ... that Pettitte's wife's testimony is irrelevant.   3 hours ago
- Walton is taking a break to discuss with a colleague but it seriously looks like he is about to say this is a mistrial   2 hours ago
- Still waiting for judge Walton to return, Rusty Hardin is rubbing Clemens shoulders as they wait   2 hours ago

And then:

- Walton back …   2 hours ago
- Government had offered to Walton that he give strict instructions to jury about ignoring Pettitte's wife's words. Walton didn't buy it   2 hours ago
- uh oh he might be moving toward a mistrial   2 hours ago
- Hardin just asked for a mistrial. Oh boy   2 hours ago
- mistrial declared   2 hours ago

Carpenter wrapped up the Twitter feed with this link to his full story:

- Will have a longer piece later in the day   33 minutes ago
- My Yahoo news story on Clemens mistrial: tinyurl.com/6ek8aon   33 minutes ago

The headline of the 474-word story, as it appeared on Yahoo! was: Clemens case declared a mistrial (Carpenter, 2011). Carpenter used Twitter with great skill in several ways:

- He gave followers an inside minute-by-minute account of unfolding events,
- He created a real-time record of his observations and impressions, and
- By the trial's end, he built an audience for his story on the Yahoo! website.

SMARTPHONES AT THE CENTER OF THE ONLINE NEWS WORLD

Gahran (2016) examined mobile news access using a two-year longitudinal panel of users equipped with a custom smartphone metering app. This Knight Foundation/Nielsen project showed how ubiquitous mobile phone news access had become:

- Mobile was second only to television for people receiving news and information.
- Ninety percent of adult mobile users accessed news via smartphones.
- Mobile users spent 5 percent of their mobile time accessing news and information.
- Wikipedia.com, Reddit.com, and email newsletters became significant drivers toward news.
- Half of the mobile users used social media apps.
- Half of the social media users spent time looking at news on SNS platforms.
  - 70 percent of Facebook users discovered news each day!
  - 80 percent of Facebook, Twitter, and Instagram users liked or shared news with "friends."
  - 60 percent of Facebook and 40 percent of Twitter users talked with others about news.

Gahran (2016) also highlighted the role of social media in news consumption: "Social media apps can be considered news apps, or at least news distribution channels. […] the audience for the news aggregator app Flipboard is the only one that has been steadily increasing. Audiences for other top news apps are flattening."

BACKGROUNDER: THE MOBILE AUDIENCE

Despite the service costs and small screens of most **hand-held** devices, consumers value using the internet whenever they want and wherever they are. Whether they use desktops, laptops, and especially mobile devices, people want to be online. Indeed, staying connected has become an ever-more important aspect of our societies, allowing people to remain in touch with families, friends, and co-workers – and to know what's going on right now!

Who gets news on their phone? Confirming common stereotypes, young adults love their smartphones: Thorson, Shoenberger, Karaliova, Kim, and Fidler (2015) found that younger persons more often used mobile devices to access news – and felt less loyalty to traditional news sources than did older users. Presently, roughly three-fifths of *all* U.S. users access news via mobile devices – with youth, education, and affluence pushing mobile news access rates even higher (Walker, 2019). Mobile users meet their information needs with their mobile devices – now making news *and* the global internet encyclopedia accessible 24/7/365.

HARNESSING USER ENGAGEMENT

For journalists and news organizations, mobile users have transformed news distribution: *The audience itself distributes news articles and the links to their pages, spreading the news to other users.* **User Distributed Content (UDC)** is commonplace for mobile users – enhancing the spreadability of news content. Villi and Matikainen (2015) surveyed more than a thousand respondents in mobile-rich Finland. They discovered that almost three-fifths of mobile internet users forwarded at least one online news link or article. About half of mobile users alerted others to photographs, pointed to (or sent) newspaper content. And three-fourths of mobile internet users received (and read) online news and received photographs.

Users like to share content (and links to content) to family members, friends, and contacts. All this user distribution matters to journalists: Users make excellent marketing partners for journalists and their news outlets. Once published, a publication's audience may spread an article, photograph, video, or recording far and wide across the Net.

Apps make sharing easy because they enable:

> horizontal, intra-audience connections in disseminating media content [...] by enclosing the content within social relations. Currently, the most prominent UDC tools are interpersonal means, such as e-mail and IM (instant messaging), as well as social plug-ins such as the Facebook Recommend, Google +1, and Twitter buttons, which the legacy news media have integrated into their webpages.
>
> (Villi, Matikainen, and Khaldarova (2016)

In other words, friends don't let friends miss important news.

APPS LET USERS SET LIMITS TOO

Mobile users don't like ads. Resentment over intrusive ads and popups taking over their mobile screens has grown. For consumers, the problem was mainly interruption. But for advertisers, the objective is to collect as much data as possible because user data is itself

MOBILE JOURNALISM

a valuable commodity. Advertisers particularly try to access users' geolocation information to target people near their places of business, as well as compile detailed records of users' movements. They also fear restrictions of their further use of that data, since some companies make additional money selling their customer's data.

But there's an app for that. Increasingly, users installed adblocking software on mobile devices – over 600 million people worldwide, most often in Asian or Pacific nations such as China, India, Pakistan, or Indonesia (Courtland, Ryan, & Shaw, 2017). Relatively few U.S. and EU mobile users adopted **adblockers** for a while, but now that's rapidly changing. Of course, advertisers develop software to block the adblockers from blocking ads by requiring that users turn off adblock software to see a page. Now, roughly three-fourths of users don't enter websites with adblock walls, a problem for both news publications and advertisers.

For mobile devices as well as other online activities and actions, governments have begun to respond to user discontent with measures like the European Union's GDPR and California's CCPA. Presently, the advertising industry feels pressure to make all advertising more relevant, useful, attractive, and tolerable for consumers including **in-app ads**, common on mobile phones. These limits concern news organizations because they pose yet another threat to their already precarious business models. Ad revenues from mobile devices are important to them.

FIGURE 11.2

Smartphones give users a gazillion ways to share content

Credit: Cienpies Design via www.123rf.com

MOBILE VELOCITY: NEWS TO VIEWS

Just as mobile devices have emerged as a handy way to receive news, they have also proved themselves as indispensable Swiss army knifes to gather it. Breaking news brings opportunities to mojos that more traditional reporters sometimes adopt as well. By themselves, mojos can gather, edit, and upload multimedia content quickly with their own lightweight equipment and professional apps. If they see an ongoing newsworthy event, they can even capture it first and later ask for the assignment.

For any reporter, acquiring the right material at the right time to tell an important story constitutes the secret sauce of exciting journalism. Accomplishing this goal takes some luck, but more often, planning and preparation provide the ticket to the reporters' luck lottery. Being prepared ensures that when the reporter is positioned at the right place and time – and the right thing happens, *if* the reporter recognizes this event – she brings back the goods.

Earlier chapters stressed that many compelling multimedia stories required planning and high-quality media. Journalists who create complex,

FIGURE 11.3

Users just say no!

Credit: Bram Janssens, via 123rf.com

long-form stories spend time capturing perfectly framed photographs, and high-quality audio and video. These stories win awards, but there's a price to pay. Dedicated equipment forces reporters to carry heavy, bulky stuff – professional cameras, lighting equipment, batteries, chargers, cords, adapters, and many other gizmos: Reporters must accept trade-offs between high production values or increased mobility and speed.

Most newsrooms and users place some importance on perfect production values, subtle lighting, careful framing, interesting angles, stable shots, etc. But the more immediacy and importance a story has, the less attention anyone pays to exquisite production values. Sharp focus, adequate light and framing, and clear sound – the basics do the trick. What characteristics can make stories so important that production values take a back seat?

- Fleeting memorable events – accidents, compelling human interactions
- Events or people of great interest to many users
- Events that impact many people's lives or that have far-reaching consequences
- Footage that captures unusual aspects of exciting or meaningful topics

There *are* stories that mobile devices absolutely crush – when a smartphone makes a reporter's day. For many breaking stories, smartphones deliver. And when the news team coverage and the crowdsourced material come together, mobile phones can capture and publish the scoop – first and fastest. For example, the award-winning *Boston Globe/ABC* coverage of the 2014 Boston Marathon bombings displays journalism magic made with the clever use of reporters' and users' mobile phones. Similar breaking stories involve notable events that take place in riots, protests, large fires, hostage situations, or multi-unit police operations.

Professor Judd Slivka, who teaches mobile journalism classes at the University of Missouri, thinks that mobile technologies offer the best ways for journalists to report for mobile users (Wenger, 2015) because they:

1. Let reporter teams cover big stories and quickly upload copy, images, and video.
2. Provide a single production platform in the field – no more shooting or recording on a mobile device, returning to the newsroom to upload material to computers, edit offline, and finally upload results to the news site and social media.
3. Allow reporters to upload material directly to a wide audience on social media platforms.
4. Include apps that enable journalists to post unique, creative material.

MOBILE WORKFLOW FOR REPORTERS IN THE FIELD

While mojos' workflows begin and end much like those of other digital reporters, their middle processes differ, as shown in Figure 11.4. Mojos follow well-known journalistic practices for research, reporting, and verification processes. But in the field, mojos often work single-handedly, without support from the newsroom for graphics, multimedia, or copy-editing. When alone, the mojo writes the article, records and edits multimedia content, assembles the assets, then connects and uploads their finished article. To cap it off, mojos may also handle the social media promotion.

MOBILE JOURNALISM

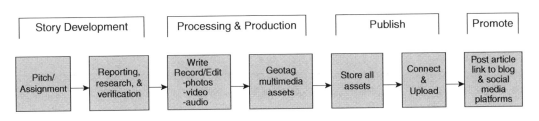

FIGURE 11.4

Workflow for mojos in the field

Credit: Joan Van Tassel, adapted from workflow model presented by Allyssa V. Richardson in Massive Open Online Course (MOOC) on mobile journalism, from the Knight Center for Journalism in the Americas (Weiss, 2014).

Two workflow steps, geotagging, and content storage are important. These two capabilities let mojos find content efficiently on a smartphone, essential keys to assembling stories in the field. Mojos need a robust filing system structure for each story, complete with descriptive folder names. Geotags permit quick searches of all the assets related to a story. Expanding smartphone storage with Micro-SDXC cards lets mojos capture photos, graphics, audio, and video, edit their assets, and save the final version. Once time and high-speed connectivity permits, mojos can immediately upload these assets to the newsroom or their publication's Content Management System (CMS).

Some news organizations will accept mobile phone photographs. For a compelling story where no high-quality pictures are available, a newsroom will take what they can get. Of course, they would prefer high-resolution pictures. To capture and upload high-res photos, field reporters can use Wi-Fi-enabled DSLR cameras to first transmit images to their mobile phones, and then upload them for publication. Some cameras send images straight to popular SNSs via wi-fi.

Mojos can stream video from their phones as well, using Twitter Periscope and Facebook Live. Sure, it's low-res ... but it's live! Establish an account and go for it. Notify followers on SNSs to let them know the streamcast is coming. Both platforms allow users to comment – and reporters can respond to comments as well. Facebook Live service offers some advantages: It allows video senders to draw on the screen to point out objects in their video. And it saves higher-res versions of the video to the sender's FB account.

Newsrooms apply similar standards to using video as they do to photographs. If a news outlet can send a TV truck with microwave or satellite capability to the location, high-quality footage can go live-to-air and live-to-online. But in distant locations, mojos can capture breaking news stories when the TV truck can't get there. If available, reporters connect via a reasonably high-speed wi-fi network to stream the vid. Even though cell networks don't yet have the bandwidth capability of high-speed networks, they can still deliver low-rez video. Some mobile phone plans provide connectivity nearly everywhere in the world. As with photographs, when *really* important news breaks, newsrooms will use any video they can. In remote areas, mojos use satellite phones, although video quality suffers. Still it's effective when it's the only way to show what's happening in some remote corner of the world.

GEO-FENCING LETS NEWSROOMS REACH USERS WHERE THEY ARE

Geo-fencing sends notifications to mobile phones identified in a defined location (Andres, 2019). Using latitudinal and longitudinal coordinates emitted from the phone and cell towers, the geo-fencing software notifies users in a specific location that something of interest is happening near them – emergencies, events, and sales and specials. Geo-fencing requires users' permission to receive their location information and to send notifications to them.

The Lensfest Local Lab in Philadelphia ran an intriguing local news experiment with 350 neighborhood residents (Schmalbach, 2019). Researchers developed a mobile app that sent users texts when they walked by places that *The Philadelphia Inquirer* had featured in **evergreen** stories about art, architecture, or real estate. Even with little promotion, of the 100 people passing by these story locations and receiving notifications, about 15 percent engaged with them – four times more than with regular news alerts. The study concluded that geo-fencing offers ways for local news outlets to: 1) engage interested users in local stories, 2) cultivate users' trust, and 3) monetize previously published content.

FIGURE 11.5

Newsrooms can reach mobile users who are in a GPS-defined area

Credit: Joan Van Tassel

GEAR – THE BASIC EQUIPMENT AND APPS

Putting together the right hardware package for mobile reporting presents challenges. There's more to it than just trade-offs between quality and mobility. Smartphones introduce limitations based on their small screens and limited memory. Mobile apps offer fewer features and choices than desktop versions, making them difficult to use.

So, what equipment kit does the mojo need? Their mobile phone, of course. Because it handles calendar, notes, photos, audio and video, media editing, data and statistical analysis, and even visualization – just about every job that mojos need for all stories.

The quality and resolution of a smartphone's camera matters. Fortunately, smartphone manufacturers upgrade their devices' camera routinely during most model releases. (The photo capabilities of iPhone and Samsung receive high ratings.) Reporters can extend their smartphone camera's capabilities with wide-angle and telephoto lenses from third-party vendors. Add a tripod, monopod, or handheld grip, and a selfie stick – and you're ready to mojo like a pro!

Multiple apps for both Android and iOS smartphones support virtually all news-gathering tasks. Apps include sophisticated software for writing, editing for photos, audio, and video, geolocation and mapping, simple data analysis, and visualization creation. A quick internet or app store search will unearth the latest and greatest apps for the continuous parade of new phones, cameras, program updates, and online services. The best way for digital journalists to stay on top of these new tools: Attend professional events like the annual Online News Association Mobile Conferences and use local get-togethers to talk with vendors. Even better – schmooze with colleagues about mojos' challenges and solutions during informal gatherings.

STORIES ON THE SMALL SCREEN: 6 AFFORDANCES (AND SOME LIMITATIONS)

The mechanics of producing and writing news content for mobile devices resemble those for other media. But importantly – the **affordances** of each media platform (and of the technologies that transmit and deliver content) both allow and preclude specific content types that users can receive. Thus, mobile technology affordances – both enable and constrain content creation and consumption for journalists and users.

User devices exert strong influences on mobile news story presentation. Budiu (2015) observes that smartphones:

1. Are small (but increasing in size).
2. Usually show a single window at a time.
3. Often have a touch screen (but many do not!).
4. Are portable.
5. Have differing features, such as GPS, camera, accelerometer, and others.
6. Vary in computational power, differing in the activities and communication speeds they support.

Each affordance influences how journalists produce and create news stories:

- *The Mobile Screen*
  - *Size*: Smartphone screens are much smaller than computer screens. As designers say, "A mobile screen doesn't have much **real estate**." Budiu stresses that using devices with small screens requires users to interact much more with the screen to access the same amount of information as they would with larger devices.

    Small screens limit the room for **chrome** – those navigational elements (buttons, menus, sections) and other design objects that users need to access sites, pages, and stories. Yielding screen space to chrome is necessary, even though users want content. So, the design challenge for small screens: provide the content that users want, while presenting the chrome that users need, a result Budiu calls the "content-to-chrome ratio."
  - *One window*: The small screen size means that users can see one window at a time. Some smartphones let viewers swipe to the next page (or back to a previous page). Some phone software lets users make the edges of several website windows visible, so they can more easily select or change windows. But really viewing content? Mostly just one window at a time.
  - *Touchscreen*: Touchscreens have pros and cons. Touchscreens permit swipes that offer alternative ways for users to interact with devices. Many people like them. But proper swipes can be difficult to discover and remember. And touch areas (including buttons) must be finger-sized – a comparatively large area on mobile phones. With many touchable buttons and touch-defined areas on the small screen, it's easy for users to touch the wrong area and end up confused about what occurred – making undo buttons essential for touch-screen-enabled devices.
- *Portable*: News users carry mobile devices anywhere, so changes in their physical environment interrupts their attention – leading to fragmented attention and shortened sessions.

- *Variable features*: *GPS, camera, accelerometer, voice, graphic and video display, text messaging, document storage, payment services*: Mobile phones have widely differing capabilities that depend on brands and models. These features may come embedded in the phone's hardware; users install **apps** to add other features.
- *Connectivity*: Mobile phones can connect to networks almost anywhere in the world.
  - *Ubiquitous*: Mojos can work anywhere there is a network.
  - *Interactive*: Communication flows two ways on mobile devices. Mojos send and receive calls, emails, and texts to editors, colleagues, followers, and friends and family. They access the internet to download and upload content. And they interact with users in near-real time.
  - *Variable connection speeds*: Mojos must ensure that the essence of their story is covered in the text – not all users connect at the same speed. Connection speeds vary by cell or smartphone type, models, user plans, networks, service provider infrastructures, and geographic locations. Not all users can see video – or even high-resolution still images. Many users won't be able to access audio files or use interactive graphics.

Power on the Smartphone, Open the Phone App, Dial the Number – Guess What Happens Next ...

Yes, those tiny sine waves that your smartphone emits head straight for the cell tower and stream into the access point. The access software decodes the data and pumps the message into the network. Just because wireless infrastructure cuts the cord for users doesn't mean there aren't cords anywhere. In fact, cell signals often follow a quick path to a wired network, joining up with a cable at an access point, or are bundled with other calls and re-transmitted wirelessly to the nearest cable.

Once on the wire, a phone call can go anywhere in the world to any telephone number or internet access point. (It might even take a quick wireless hop on and off a friendly satellite.) On the final leg of the journey, if the message goes to a wireless phone, it takes another air trip to reach the intended receiver via a cellular tower or Wi-Fi router.

Between sender and receiver lie antennas, towers, wires, cables, servers, dozens of software applications, switches and routers, relays, amplifiers, and transmitters. Throughout the process, there is continual grooming and re-grooming of the message stream to conform it to the appropriate protocol and data format of each traversed network. The network then imposes its own requirements – hardware, software, network architecture, middleware, access authorization, security. Whew!

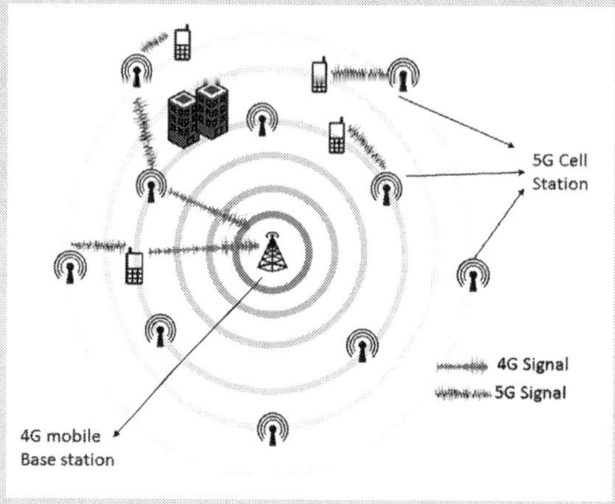

FIGURE 11.6

Welcome to 5G wireless infrastructure!

Credit: Goodtiming8871 [CC BY-SA 4.0 (https://creativecommons.org/licenses/by-sa/4.0)]

Overall, it's a hugely complex technological system that took decades to engineer and build. The demand for mobile communication imposes innovation as a way of life, so that from first generation wireless network (1G), there has been a steady progression to 2G, 3G, 4G, and now 5G waiting in the wings, shown in Figure 11.6. 5G will have greater capacity and transmit information faster than 4G networks.

But what happens when the wireless network goes down? Many mojos working in remote areas carry satellite phones – just in case – because they may offer the only way to report or publish from the field. Delivering live news directly from Syrian battlefields, earthquakes in Bhutan, or refugee camps in the South Sahara has its thrilling rewards – even when communicating via a sat phone capable of transmitting only greatly degraded images.

Using a sat phone isn't as simple or straightforward as using a smartphone because:

- Service must be prepaid
- A satellite must be passing overhead that handles the communications of your service provider
- The sat phone will be larger, may have lower-quality pictures than a smartphone, and will have fewer apps

HOW TO PRODUCE STORIES FOR MOBILE DEVICES

Today's high-end smartphones facilitate storytelling and interaction with users because of their amazing affordances: They're phones, reading devices, notepads, photo albums, music and video players, interview recorders, tutors, and flashlights. And there are the apps. As of May 2019, there were 2.1 million apps in the Google Play store and almost 1.8 million iOS apps in the Apple store (Clement, 2019).

The most important affordance, one that dictates so much of creating content for smartphones, is their size: Devices must fit in a pocket, purse, bag, or hand. They must be light enough to carry around – measured in grams or ounces, rather than kilos or pounds.

A story written for mobile audiences usually begins with a promise, something that gives users reasons to read the story, a snappy headline, a graphic, or a short, intriguing summary. It's an offer to the reader that tempts them to click through to the story on the next page. And it's really important to pay off that promise by delivering on it. A broken promise often results in a bounce – the user leaving the page or even the site.

From this modest start, the news article branches out (usually via links) to some or all the story elements available on desktop or powerful laptop computers. Writing for mobile helps journalists draw on popular features specific to smartphones. For example, they can use their GPS to calculate the distance between the reader and the nearest Kardashian. Or, more seriously, a user's GPS could locate a nearby Superfund toxic waste site that might contaminate that person's water supply. A little creativity goes a long way towards engaging mobile news-users in activities that are important, useful, or just plain fun.

GETTING YOUR HED ON STRAIGHT

For the mobile reporter writing a story, the size of the smartphone screen presents the central challenge. Smartphone screens are smaller than books and way smaller than the newspapers, magazines, or websites displayed on laptops. So, the first (and perhaps only) chance for reporters to get users' attention depends on a striking image, headline, possibly a standfirst, a lede sentence, or summary in the Facebook status area. That's it. Go little or go home.

In most newspapers, copy editors write the headlines and subheads (sometimes called sub-hed, dek, or standfirst). For online and mobile news sites, section editors write them and make decisions about where to place stories on a page. Depending on the publication, mojos also may write headlines for articles and their own blog posts.

Four tech guidelines to launch viral mobile headlines:

1. Mobile first! Write all headlines for mobile from the jump so they fit the smallest screen.
2. Headlines should have no more than 60 characters and spaces for Facebook. Search engines cut off headlines after 67 characters and spaces (think Google), so write heds longer than that and it risks search returns showing an incomplete headline.
3. After publishing an article, check how it looks on your mobile phone: Looking good?
4. Periodically check the latest analytics to see if users are clicking on the story. If the numbers are poor, re-write the hed.

COPY THIS

Common wisdom: Journalists must make the complete storyline available to readers quickly. Users cannot (and won't) crunch through pages of text to find essential pieces of a story. Articles need many points where users can retrieve previous pages and/or drill down to more details. News writers for mobile users should think in screen-size chunks and add interest-raising transitions that lead readers further and further into the story.

Once users start reading, try to keep them reading your story. Consider what appeals to readers to encourage them to continue. The BBC (2017) suggested using graphics and links throughout the story – to take advantage of digital affordances. The BBC also advised that only important or complex articles should exceed 500–600 words. Keep in mind that "important" lies in the eyes of the user. When a story really matters to users, they will read long articles, even on their smartphones.

Research indicates that mobile users have a greater interest in long-form stories than commonly thought. Pew Research Center researchers examined over 100 million anonymous user interactions with almost 75,000 articles presented on 30 news sites (Mitchell et al., 2016). The researchers found:

- Long-form stories averaged as many clicks as the shorter articles. (Of course, there were many more short-form articles, so short stories accounted for more clicks overall.)
- Stories that readers accessed via an internal link (from the same website), engaged people for the longest time-periods, especially for long-form stories.
- News consumers consume news quickly. Users spend a bit less than one minute on articles shorter than 1,000 words. And they spend two minutes on long-form stories.
- Only 3 percent of short-form readers and 4 percent of long-form readers return to a story again – but these returning readers remain engaged in the story the longest of all.

This research offers good news for investigative and long-form journalists: Reporters can present hard evidence to editors that important, complex articles of 5,000 words or more in length will get clicks from mobile users and increase their engagement – measured by the time they spend on these stories. Stories on interesting topics, perhaps crime stories or scandals, may hold readers for as long as eight minutes. Other subjects: Foreign politics, government, domestic affairs, war and peace, economics and business, or entertainment and lifestyle may keep readers' attention between four to five and a half minutes.

WE'VE GOT AN APP FOR THAT

News organizations encourage brand loyalty by building apps that link directly to their mobile news site with one click. Once users are on their site, they offer content designed and tailored for mobile devices' screens – including augmented reality. AR presents mixed reality content that blends "real reality" video from the mobile's camera that is augmented by AR 3D graphics (the "unreal reality"). Mobile devices may also be trained to recognize scenes. Check it out. Try downloading the free *Night Sky* for iOS and Android and point your mobile at the sky on a clear night. The *Night Sky* app will recognize the stars' positions and reveal both the star's names and those of their constellations.

FIGURE 11.7

Mobile users like short *and* long-form stories

Credit: Designed by Freepik at freepik.com

The ability of mobile devices to display AR sparked deepening interest in creating this new form of digital content. Developers can produce experiences wrapped in apps using ARKit by Apple and ARCore by Google. AR enables journalists to tell stories in new ways, enhance multimedia stories, and display both objects and environments that users might otherwise not experience. Eventually, lowering costs and increased quality will enable code-savvy journalists – even at small publications – opportunities to capture 3D images, create user experiences, and "appify" AR experiences.

Mobile phone cameras have other features that reporters can tap to increase user engagement, such as allowing users to contribute to stories if they are close to a scene or take selfies that add to events mentioned in the story. Users can post their added content on Twitter, Instagram, and other social media sites – linking to a story-related hashtag. Finally, smartphone cameras also read barcodes and QR codes – and reporters can use these codes to take users to links that provide other available information, graphics, videos, or interactives.

DESIGN? WHY SHOULD REPORTERS CARE ABOUT IT?

Because they want users to read their stories! Ultimately, both news publications and reporters care about mobile page design because it shapes their users' experiences. Design choices (and their execution) play a vital role in whether users notice a story, read it, stay with it, or even stay on the webpage or the website at all.

Research shows that the right story design boosts readership (Lagun, Hsieh, Webster, & Navalpakkum, 2014). Eye-tracking studies show that mobile users first look at the center within the top half of the screen. Then the user's gaze moves along the rough sides of a triangle, from top down and from left to right; hence the designation "golden triangle" for placement of key information on mobile pages. Darker colored gray areas indicate more intense user gazes, as shown in the screen in Figure 11.8.

FIGURE 11.8

How mobile users check out content

Credit: Joan Van Tassel, heatmap based on findings from Lagun et al. 2014. (Photo of dog): Mathew Hayward, from 123RF Stock Photo, www.123rf.com

FIGURE 11.9

New techs, new models – new screen sizes
Credit: Frikota, www.123rf.com/profile_frikota/123RF Stock Photo

Mobile reading patterns differ from those of desktop and laptop users: The focus on the middle of the screen lets users take in most of the content at one glance. (Recall the section in Chapter 10 that described how eye-tracking studies showed that users scan larger screens in left-hand F-shaped patterns to discover what they want to read on webpages).

WANT USERS' ATTENTION? PUT THE HEADLINE AND AN IMAGE IN THE CENTER OF THE MOBILE PAGE

TODAY'S DESIGN MAKES MEDIA HANDY

Smartphones are carried in pockets or purses, or worn, perhaps as smartwatches. These small interactive communication devices require new approaches to information design and careful exploration of how people use them. Because the interactive devices receive and transmit multiple media types of information, they're particularly complex. The primary design problem: How to best arrange multimedia information so that it's intuitively easy to access text, images, sound, and video. These goals require developing new design principles for websites, page and screen layouts, navigation, menu structures, and affordance optimization.

News companies distribute content to devices with vastly different sizes of screens, from desktop computers to digital watches. Users' devices dictate how publications must lay out and format their content so it will reach the users as intended. One widely adopted method is to install **Responsive Web Design (RWD)** software in content production workflows. RWD automates the reformatting of content to fit the available space of users' devices. In practice, RWD detects the device's screen size and automatically resizes articles (created for consumption across multiple screen sizes) for optimum display on that device – whether it's a large desktop display, a 13"–17" laptop, an 8"–12" tablet, a 3" × 6" smartphone, or a 1.5" × 1.5" smartwatch. It's easy to see why RWD saves news sites both editorial time and costs.

RWD affects the online creative process because mobile users click on articles with short, snappy heds and deks. Such headlines work well in most online news formats. They translate to all screens, unlike longer, more explanatory headlines and sub-headlines that work for print publications. Automated reformatting (coupled with small mobile screen size) requires that online newsrooms write their headlines to accommodate mobile users from the start.

5 Options for News Site and Page Design

Mobile design remains a work in progress; there's no single best choice to create stories and pages for multiple screens (Budiu, 2016). But integrating mobile news operations into existing organizations has triggered new rounds of experimentation that yield five approaches for publishing news across multiple media platforms:

1. *Don't bother with mobile*: Stick with news websites now designed for laptop computers. Mobile users can access the news with their mobile browser.

2. *Create a mobile-dedicated site*: When the news site detects a mobile device, it automatically re-routes it to a mobile site, with a URL that usually starts with an "m," such as "m.SomeNewsSite.com."

3. *Create a publication web app*: Build a stripped-down dedicated mobile site.

4. *Use responsive/adaptive design (desktop first)*. Create the story for desktops first, then adapt the content to fit different users' screen sizes.

5. *Use responsive/adaptive design (mobile first)*:Create the story for mobile screens first, then add information, features, and design elements that enhance users' experience on larger devices – tablets, laptops, and desktops.

The last two designs affect the way journalists structure their stories, although journalists have little say about the story design and creation strategy that their publication uses. When writing stories for a **desktop-first** newsroom, reporters begin by starting large. The entire story comes into being with all the glorious details, including links, multimedia, and the interactive bells and whistles. The sophisticated responsive design employs HTML5 (HyperText Markup Language) to sense the screen size and other features of the displaying device. It then modifies the story to match users' devices, eliminating elements that devices don't support, like Flash or touchscreen features, and perhaps interactives.

In contrast, reporters in **mobile-first** shops start by writing the most succinct, direct version of their story, divided into bite-sized chunks (Johnson, 2019). This strategy requires that reporters focus on the first content and features of a story that users must receive. The whole story can appear on a cascade of mobile pages and the software reformats it to put more on each page for devices with larger screens.

EVEN NEWS GIANTS HAVE IT HARD

Most news organizations struggle to develop workflows that integrate their mobile news distribution (Westlund & Färdigh, 2015). The economics of news production demands that organizations employ multiple media channels that reach economically viable audiences *and* exert influence in the public(s) discourse. But new communication technologies – hardware, software, and apps, just keep coming and further disrupt multimedia news workflows.

Changing production workflows isn't easy. Whether news operations or widget factories, any organization has interconnected parts that change impacts in unexpected ways. To produce professional news at scale for multiple platforms requires complex, expensive digital assembly lines with sophisticated software and hardware. Along with skilled workers, almost everyone in these newsrooms must possess high-level digital media competencies. Moreover, digital news demands continual investment upgrading workers' skill-sets – expensive, time-consuming training – so that news organizations can cope with their rapidly changing business environment.

NEWSROOM WORKFLOWS IRW

In the Real World, the rise of mobile news access gave newsrooms systemic problems when they tried to integrate mobile pages into their workflows. The topic surfaced in a session at the Online News Association Mobile 2015 Conference (Hermann, Banerjee, and Michalski, 2015). *BBC News* Online Editor, Steve Hermann, led discussions about how large news companies are (re-)organizing workflows to respond to the new majority of mobile users. The panel included Subhajit Banerjee, Mobile Editor at *The Guardian*, and Patti Michalski, Managing Editor of Digital/Mobile/Social at *USA Today*.

- For breaking news, at *USA Today*, graphics and video teams give priority to mobile distribution. The company first formed a mobile team, but quickly changed and placed their mobile people throughout the newsroom. They found that when deploying a specialized mobile-only team, mobile became *just that team's* problem. Instead, having all editors focusing on mobile ensures that mobile issues become everyone's concern.

- At *The Guardian*, mobile journalists also hold positions throughout the organization.

- Both organizations begin each day with early morning editorial meetings. Newsroom managers and editors use the latest analytics to understand trends and most-accessed content. These morning meetings address *all* media platforms and content types, including social media.

- Both organizations provide real-time analytics to everyone in their newsrooms.

Coordinating the development and production of digital products is a well-studied and well-practiced activity for software companies. Grier (n.d.) notes that software factories differ from physical *mechanical*, industrial production assembly lines because mechanical assembly lines turn out very similar end-products. They prioritize smoothly coordinated activities, executed in a specified sequential order, performed by (largely) single-skilled workers.

In contrast, newsrooms require specialized, flexible *digital* production architectures. And unlike software products, *each* article, publication, site, or app differs – every day, perhaps every hour or minute! The demands of near real-time production require:

- News-workers with wide ranges of journalistic and digital skills,
- Sophisticated and changing divisions of labor
- Flexible orchestration of work processes
- Well-designed procedures to verify the accuracy of work processes and their outcomes.

Digital newsroom operations require many different people with diverse skillsets to collaborate in the production and dissemination of ever-evolving news content in order to attract and retain users. These operations depend on dynamic processes that are neither linear nor stable and take place under great time pressures. In practice, this means that issues of accuracy, accessibility, readability, navigation, appearance, importance, and user-appeal demand close, expert attention at multiple points during the news-making process.

Each newsroom has unique founding principles and character. The workflows that management adopts reflect the idiosyncratic nature of the organization in its history, organizational culture and goals, and information-handling processes and routines. Thus, no single workflow diagram can fully capture any particular workplace. However, **systems theory** provides lenses to examine dynamic newsrooms by focusing on the essential processes of **input, throughput,** and **output** that enable all organizations to interact within their rapidly changing environments. Figure 11.10 offers a systems view of how newsrooms base their workflows on the processes and purposes of content-creating organizations:

- Input refers to ingestion, acquiring information, assets, and content to be later processed by the people and digital resources within the organization. Much of the digital journalists' work is driven by the demands to: make sense of, acquire, and pre-process information from rapidly changing ambiguous environments.

- Throughput refers to the processes of merging assets, producing, and recreating digital content. Note that newsroom throughput interacts with both the inputs and outputs, a reflection of their interdependencies.

- Output is the content: information, stories, articles, and advertising in the multiple forms that the news organization distributes as products. For newsrooms to function well, they must measure the effects of their output on users to alter input and throughput processes as their news organizations' environment changes.

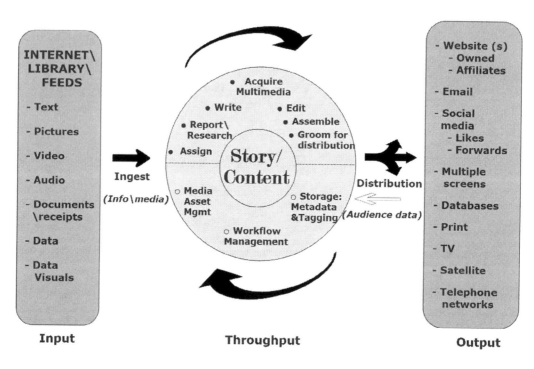

FIGURE 11.10

A general systems model of newsroom workflow

Credit: Joan Van Tassel, with a little help from Dalet (solutions for media workflows)

TAKEAWAYS

- The Knight Foundation (Gahran, 2016) longitudinal study showed that many users accessed news with smartphones and:
  - Mobile was second only to television in connecting people to the news and information
  - 90 percent of adult mobile users employed smartphones to access news
  - Mobile users spent 5 percent of their mobile time accessing news and information
  - Half of mobile users used social media apps and half of social media users looked at news
- Processes of story assignment, information gathering, and verification mimic those of traditional journalists. But mobile reporting and publishing differ in four important ways:
  - Mojos handle more story preparation – they shoot, edit, and assemble stories in the field.
  - Mojos geotag when they record media in the field, at the time they gather it, to locate precisely where they made the recording.

MOBILE JOURNALISM

- Mojos store their material locally in well-named, and located folders, then transfer it to their newsroom Content Management System (CMS) when they have time and adequate bandwidth.
- Mojos need connectivity to download research materials and multimedia, and then to upload their assets, file and publish reports, and promote their articles on social media.

- Putting together gear packages for mobile reporting is a highly individualistic enterprise. Gear usually includes: Smartphones with a high-quality camera, additional high-capacity storage, and useful apps. Serious news video demands a tripod or monopod and perhaps a selfie-stick for standups. Some journalists include lens kits for smartphones, carry higher-resolution DSLR cameras and lenses, and wireless lavalier microphones for interviews.

  Most reporters use sophisticated apps for taking notes, file management, photo, audio, video and audio recording and editing, phone call and voice recording, and mapping and geotagging in their basic package. Some reporters need data analysis and visualization software. Of course, *Minecraft*, *Klondike* solitaire, and other mobile games ease reporters' long waiting periods.

  Talking with other reporters may provide the best way to learn about new equipment. Check-out computer and consumer electronics retail outlets frequently. Search the internet for new ideas from other journalists, news, and trade outlets. Attending mobile journalist workshops, conferences, and taking local university classes provide excellent ways to stay current.

- The two main limits to using mobile news technology are:
  - The small mobile phone screen: There's not much room for copy that inevitably competes for space with graphics, ads, notifications, and navigation elements. Just one window can be read or used at a time, forcing users to remember content on previous screens. Touchscreen features make using mobile phones easier, but small touch areas cause frustrating navigation mistakes.
    Despite their small screens, mobile devices offer mind-boggling arrays of affordances. Especially smartphones – small computers that can compute, transform, store, and communicate information that may display text, graphics, video, audio, animations, and data. Smartphones with expanded memory store huge amounts of data and can connect with telephone, Wi-Fi, local area, personal, and picocell networks and use other wireless signals such as GPS. Smartphone apps enhance the phone's technological affordances, enabling users to do almost everything they could do on a full-size computer – but while traveling and living their lives.

  - Distractions: Mobile devices are carried by people everywhere and users can access content anywhere. But environmental distractions abound, and users' sessions may be cut short. Yet, turning attention to the physical environment may be A Good Thing: mobile's power to distract is too-often manifested by accidents when driving while device-ing.

- Mobile journalists depend on wireless networks. But if there's no network ... there's no breaking news without a sat phone. Mojos working in remote areas carry sat phones to ensure they can report and publish from the field, which bring their own difficulties. To transmit, sat phones need a satellite to pass directly over the mojo that the receiving news organization contracts with to handle field reporters' communications. In addition, most sat phones don't have a high-quality screen, camera, or the same wide choice of apps.

- Writing news for pages displayed on small mobile screens limits the amount of content that will fit. There's only room for three or four elements: A short read headline, a graphic, a succinct summary, and perhaps a nut sentence (a sketch of what happened) that provides a reason for users to read the story. Mobile news stories expand from their first page onto other pages via links or by swipes to subsequent pages, one at a time.

- Page design matters! Position the headline and graphic in the center of the mobile page. The news organization's publishing strategy also matters. If the publication's software incorporates adaptive/responsive web design (RWD), it automates page formatting to fit differing mobile device screen sizes – including tablets, smartphones, and watches. To write stories for all audiences, reporters must know if their newsroom first publishes to its full website. If so, mojos write pages that include the story with all its material; software later eliminates content to fit mobile screens. If their newsroom is "mobile first," then reporters write the mobile version, and the news outlet's CMS software adds material from other pages and sources to fill out larger desktop or laptop screens.

- News organizations must appeal to their mobile users; they are the biggest and fastest-growing market segment. Reaching mobile users requires that publications change their workflows to better compete in ever-faster cycles imposed by newer digital technology. News organizations must take-in information from more sources, produce, and package more complex multimedia content – and do it more quickly. They must also push output (and pull-in users) using multiple networks – while their users employ dozens of different reception technologies.

  The exponential rate of change presents daunting organizational challenges. Building an integrated digital assembly line for high-volume, high-quality content is expensive. So is hiring professionals with the sophisticated digital media skills required to create just-in-time, interactive multimedia content using the complex systems. These costs aren't just one-time expenses; digital newsrooms require continuous investment in innovative hardware and software, and in on-going training for news creators.

  Everyone in digital news organizations must regularly recalibrate their work expectations, habits, routines, and skillsets to better perform their jobs. That's not easy – news professionals (and other workers) toil within deeply held cultural systems of production. Even (or especially) startups have idiosyncratic cultures of digital creation and distribution! Managers must analyze metrics to understand their audiences and direct the work efforts to meet their consumers' demands – which change as their users' devices change. Welcome to the digital world!

- The foundational systems concepts – *input, throughput,* and *output* help identify the basic newsroom workflows required by the integrated digital environment.
  - Input refers to the complex information and content that comes into news organizations, called **ingestion**.
  - Throughput refers to producing, assembling, transforming, and repurposing news content.
  - Output refers to distributing digital news content.

MOBILE JOURNALISM

Over the past few years, newsrooms reached a consensus that, although they need specialized departments and people for different media types (graphics, video, audio, data), they must locate mobile production and publication throughout the newsroom. Mobile audiences now exceed desktop/laptop audiences. In short, everyone in newsrooms must think like a mojo.

Newsroom workflows are neither linear, nor stable – in newsrooms or in the field. Although many traditional journalistic processes have changed, journalistic values have remained remarkably stable. Whether a news organization is centuries old or a startup, even though changes have buffeted the news industries, and even as news industry practices evolve – news organizations that hope to succeed in the trust business must recognize and implement the journalistic values of accuracy and verification, news readability, navigation, appearance, and user-appeal. These issues arise at many points throughout digital news-making processes and they entail thoughtful consideration.

KEY CONCEPTS AND TERMS

- The mobile news market
- Workflows for mobile journalists in the field
- Equipment for mobile reporters
- Affordances of digital media on mobile devices
- The mobile communications infrastructure
- Story creation for mobile users and devices
- Mobile workflows in the newsroom
- The multiplatform digital content creation system

EXERCISES AND ACTIVITIES

1. Go online and search for two recent reports about the mobile phone news market. Compare how these reports characterize news market changes. How does the changing mobile environment affect the news industry and employment in journalism? Writeup your research in a 3 to 4-page paper, based on the news reports that you used.

2. Cover a story using your mobile phone. Take notes, pictures, and record video clips on your phone. Prepare a story: Include photos and at least one video clip, with appropriate captions. Save all your content (notes, photos, videos). Write and edit the story. Insert pictures and video clip. Email it to your editor or instructor. When it is published, promote your story on Twitter.com; write a tweet that includes the headline. Before sending your tweet, upload a photo, and caption it to accompany your message.

3. Go online; search for mobile phone tripods and other camera supports. Read at least two reviews of these types of equipment by professional journalists. Then write-up your findings as a list that describes the brands, models, features, and prices.

4. Write a 2–3-page paper comparing 4G to 5G mobile networks.

ADVANCER

Chapter 12 wraps it all up. The final chapter ties together the main themes in this book: the digital transformation of the news industry, news consumption habits of audiences, rapid and continuous technological change, and journalists' adaptation to these new realities. Most importantly, it reiterates that this new generation of journalists will have chances to reach more people, more quickly, and with greater effect than ever before. Stay tuned.

12

JOURNALISM: "IT'S A GRAND, GRAND CAPER."

Chapter Learning Objectives

This final chapter revisits broad themes covered throughout the book that will affect students' journalism careers including:

1. Understanding the important roles that comprise the journalistic enterprise in our society.
2. Acknowledging users' primacy in the interactive new news environment.
3. Adapting to pervasive change.
4. Recognizing that journalism is an exacting craft.
5. Integrating demands and seizing opportunities in journalism careers.

Beth (in an email to Jennifer): I don't care if they are reading our mail. Bring it on, Tron! I dare you. Try to take away my freedom of expression. I'm a journalist. A free-speech warrior. I serve in the Army of the First Amendment. I didn't take this job for the bad money, and the regressive health care coverage. I'm here for the truth, the sunshine, the casting open of closed doors!

– Rainbow Rowell (2011), *Attachments*, a novel

THE GIST

David Carr characterized journalism as a "grand, grand caper" not only because it's important and influential, but it's also captivating work for curious people – as are most journalists. Rainbow Rowell captures another dimension of reporters' capers in the attitude of the intrepid online journalist who holds to the exciting mission and purpose of journalism. Whether a reporter is a free-speech warrior serving in the Army of the First Amendment or a pixel-stained wretch chained to a mobile device, journalism always involves something new, offering up real-life dramas of truth and consequences. For practitioners, these aspects of their job can alleviate some downsides inherent in the present industry upheaval.

This concluding chapter considers working in journalism in the context of modern life. It summarizes the major ideas in this textbook: 1) Journalism is more important than ever. 2) Users occupy the center of the journalistic enterprise. 3) Change throughout the news industry is transformative, pervasive, and ongoing. 4) Journalism is an exacting profession that calls for passion and commitment. 5) Journalism is fun.

The first section examines the question of whether journalism matters and, if so, to whom? Although it's a truism among journalists that the news media are vital to individuals and society, this belief no longer remains self-evident or even accepted by many persons. Instead, a person's opinions about news often depend on what they consider news, the source of that news, how closely news stories conform with their worldview, and the views of their key reference groups.

Prior chapters recounted how ever-more-powerful computing and networking technologies came together to deliver a deluge of information, driving relentless change in all the information industries. It described the transformations of the news industry and audiences over the past two decades. Legacy news organizations and flashy startups – some flourished while others foundered as journalism reinvented itself with changed technologies, newsrooms, news workers, and journalistic practices during this ongoing digital revolution.

Enter the two-edged sword: Technological and organizational change also delivered powerful tools to the press, enabling journalists to monitor people and events, collect and analyze data, and publish gripping multimedia and data-rich stories. There's a catch (of course): Journalists must commit to continuing professional education to master advanced skills, a challenge when they hold demanding jobs. Reporters don't have reputations for being team players. Yet complex stories demand that expert teams acquire and analyze data and create multimedia news content. This exacting work requires expertise and sweat from journalists working together in the service of news that may have profound consequences for people and society.

Although journalism is serious business, it's also (almost) always interesting. And the people in the news biz! Journalists (even the quiet ones) are usually whip-smart, well-informed, and funny. Most important, journalists derive special satisfaction from working on stories that matter and may improve the lives of people, communities, and perhaps even countries and the world.

But there's more: We journalists love our work. We become mesmerized because it's thrilling to be "in the know," to satisfy our insistent curiosity about what *really happened* and how things *really work*. And it can be such a wild ride – fun, exciting, and dazzlingly rewarding when it isn't darkly depressing.

IS JOURNALISM IMPORTANT?

Many people all over the world check the news on their phones throughout their day to catch current weather forecasts, traffic conditions, economic indices, sports scores, movies, music reviews, recipes, and local event listings. Knowing the events of the day gives attentive users social currency and grist for the conversational mill. And, in the course of getting what they want to know, people often get what they need to know!

Conventional wisdom insists that journalism matters. Political theorists and public intellectuals affirm journalism's key role in democracies. The founders of the United States of America believed journalism was so essential, that they inserted explicit protection for freedom of the press in the U.S. Constitution. Even today, most Very Important People agree. The press has always provided fodder for social discussions, whether in praise or condemnation. A comment attributed to former *Washington Post* owner and publisher, Katharine Graham underscores why people believe journalism is important: "News is what someone wants suppressed. Everything else is advertising. The power is to set the agenda. What we print and what we don't print matter a lot."

FIGURE 12.1

Russia invades Ukraine, May 24, 2018

Credit: Ministry of Defense, Ukraine (Міністерство оборони України) / CC BY (https://creativecommons.org/licenses/by/4.0)

For example, consider the dismal fate of Ricardo Roselló, forced to resign from his office as Governor of Puerto Rico. This story provides a testament to the power of the press (Sullivan, 2019), even in this skeptical age. After ten reporters from the nonprofit Center for Investigative Journalists revealed the rampant cynicism, corruption, and greed within his administration – massive public demonstrations drove him out of office just 11 days after the story broke: The people of Puerto Rico found this journalism awfully important.

"Our reporting connected people's suffering to the administration," CPI's executive director Carla Minet told *Washington Post* media columnist Margaret Sullivan. When journalists tie their stories to the effects they have on users and their communities, these stories can become powerful and compelling. As playwright Tom Stoppard once commented: "I still believe that if your aim is to change the world, journalism is a more immediate short-term weapon" (Billington, 1988, p. 28).

When journalism matters, it's because monitoring our environments is a pressing human need. We inhabit a changing, uncertain, and sometimes dangerous planet. Our ancestors carefully scrutinized environments to respond to both opportunities and threats – that's how they survived to become our ancestors! But as settlements and communities became ever larger, it became impossible to obtain personal knowledge of individuals, local conditions, actions, and events.

Early storytellers served as the journalists of their time, passing down forebears' wisdom to the living and thus preserving the tribe's knowledge about their social and physical worlds. Today, journalists are the storytellers of our time. They give us the scoop on what's happening everywhere, from around the world to our local neighborhoods. And in telling us stories, they extend our knowledge of what matters: situations and outcomes, actions and consequences, life and death.

"CONTENT IS KING," THEY SAY – PERHAPS, BUT USERS RULE

News offers useful and entertaining content for many users. Traditionally, journalists have focused on hard news: war and peace, governments' actions and proposals, political controversy, economic trends, business, corporate behemoths' impacts, non-governmental organizations' activities, public safety, and crime. Journalists get the news out about contemplated actions, the arguments for and against policy choices, and the public's concerns. Over time, public opinion coalesces into camps; factions discuss, negotiate, and enact (or enforce) decisions about how and where to proceed.

Traditional media roles work well when most people believe they can find truthful, accurate news sources. But today, too many people don't believe that mainstream news media provides truthful or accurate depictions of important issues. For others, mainstream reporting is not important to them or their lives; some consider it actively misleads people – perhaps in service of the ruling elites. These people dismiss mainstream journalism; they ignore it, share alternative media within like-minded social networks, and seek different sources for information.

News users have conflicting views about what defines important news. And they/we search for media and information that support personal worldviews. Users find what they seek: The internet hosts media ecosystems for unlimited kinds of constituencies – that, once formed, enact communities akin to virtual worlds. Such online communities include environmental activists, conspiracy theorists, antivaxxers, religious groups, LGBTQ communities, business sector participants, political groups across the spectrum, hate groups, and so many more.

Within their topical arena, news media define: 1) newsworthy events and people, 2) important scenarios that demonstrate causes and effects, and 3) editorial perspectives that publishers, journalists, and users believe or hope to be true. Whatever topic is of interest or concern, from climate change to contrails, news and views meet every need, told in the languages of their audience. Socialists have *The Guardian* and the *Socialist Worker*. Russia-supporters watch Sputnik and RT (Russia Today) channels. Religious readers have *Christianity Today* and many other publications and channels.

Benkler, Faris, Roberts, and Zuckerman (2017) examined the hyperlinking and sharing patterns of stories originating from extreme alt-right websites. The researchers found "a network of mutually-reinforcing hyper-partisan sites [...] combining decontextualized truths, repeated falsehoods, and leaps of logic to create a fundamentally misleading view of the world." This research showed how users who previously accepted mainstream news could become deeply involved within extreme political ecosystems. If new converts continued to read news that expressed more extreme perspectives than their own, they sometimes gradually adopted the new views. Eventually, they adopted a constructed reality achieved by repeating similar stories across many sites with minor alterations or story extensions. Over time, the many sites and stories lent credence to wildly improbable claims.

Studies of links between sites that appeal to people with similar views show how connectivity supports political action. Eddington (2018) wrote:

> Social media has changed the nature of political organization, discourse, and engagement. From likes, retweets, shares, and memes, everyday users have an amplified voice in the online, public-political sphere. [...] Due in part to the access afforded by social media, individual supporters have new ways to engage with, voice concern for, and even criticize political leaders.

It's fine for anyone to read the writings of people they agree with – but it's also important to expose people to good ideas, even ones that they might at first dismiss. Moreover, the simplistic two-sided form of many news accounts obscures the true multiplicity of beliefs and opinions that people hold. Too often, news articles favor the simplicity of yes/no, for/against, rural/urban, right/left, spend/conserve, and love/hate. It's an old lazy practice that ill-serves our knowledge needs.

For people to value the news, they must see themselves, their beliefs, and opinions. Ripley (2018) makes the case that mainstream journalism would become more relevant if stories provided complex depictions of opinions, describing the conflict in detail, rather than reducing its intricacies:

> First, complexity leads to a fuller, more accurate story. Secondly, it boosts the odds that your work will matter – particularly if it is about a polarizing issue. When people encounter complexity, they become more curious and less closed off to new information. They listen, in other words.

Truth be told, many people do not see themselves or their beliefs reflected in the main-stream news: This is a problem … and it's a big one. News about people and events that we don't know about and don't recognize – we don't care about. The important takeaway: A wider, more inclusive lens gains power.

Our tribalized, divided political landscape and contemporary news environment forces journalists to address these two interrelated questions: What constitutes news? Who does journalism serve? If the answer to the second question is "the user," then the answer to the first question differs depending on the publication's audience. Blogs about agriculture policy won't describe new software – but they should discuss the government's responses to trade sanctions for subscribers in ways that mass media channels can't.

The decisions about what constitutes news and which news topics matter rest with individual users making their choices. Users can access virtually unlimited menus of content to build their own personalized story salads. News media outlets may define the range of acceptable perspectives and adapt coverage to attract users, but they're no longer the arbiters of relevant news. In the online world, general topics like weather, traffic, sports, and entertainment evoke widespread agreement about their newsworthiness. But users choose very different sources for news about politics, economics, and social matters, sources that reflect their own worldviews, perspectives, experiences, and values.

FIGHT THE FAKE

Part of the mainstream mission: Counter fake news, even though sometimes people would rather believe an attractive falsity than an uncomfortable truth. For journalists, the reason to tilt at this windmill rests on the sad fact that bad information chases out good information: It's a matter of survival and self-interest. Although users hold different views as to what constitutes fake news, most agree fake news presents serious problems (Dimock, 2019).

Journalists **fact check** to verify claims. And just as digital technologies make it easier to create fake media of all kinds – from documents and images to videos – they also give newsrooms new tools to analyze and verify content. These formidable forensic weapons enable journalists to debunk the bogus. But it's going to be a never-ending arms race between the truth-warriors and the fake merchants.

FIGURE 12.2

News: Breaking it or faking it?
Credit: Pixel2013 on www.pixabay.com

Fake accounts and bot armies also create false impressions of public opinion – almost everyone loves/hates, despises/celebrates, ignores/embraces, or values/discounts this issue, person, group, or policy. Vigilant reporters and news organizations can examine suspicious cases and confirm that accounts, comments, and retweets represent living persons rather than astroturfing bot-swarm propaganda machines or advertising stunts.

Timeliness matters in these analyses because busting a buzz a week or two later is way too late to make a difference. Real-time propaganda needs real-time monitoring and reporting – a tough ask. However, the ability to report on the spread of disinformation in real time is on the near horizon. Some data scientists can follow information as it spreads across the internet, identifying and tracking the disseminating accounts and nodes (Yang, Varol, Hui, and Menczer, 2019).

Although not infallible, DiResta (2018) describes three methods to assess whether a swarm of social media postings stems from an active disinformation campaign or from individual human users:

- *Account authenticity*: Do the accounts appear to reflect authentic human behavior?
- *Narrative distribution pattern*: Does the scale, timing, and number of messages appear manufactured and coordinated, or do messages seem organic, the way humans would spread information?
- *Historical activity*: To the extent that a swarm of messages links to and from websites or accounts, do they have a record of integrity or are their activities suspect or unknown?

News organizations stand on the front lines of ongoing struggles to identify fake news, media, accounts, and sentiments. The traditional roles of journalism won't disappear: Journalists will still work to publish accurate, verifiable facts. They will expose powerful interests and illuminate hidden actions laden with consequences for others to public scrutiny. Journalists will continue to act as a **court of last resort** – the power of the press to ensure that justice prevails.

Julia Brown, a *Miami Herald* reporter, exemplifies journalism's role as a court of last resort. She investigated the years-long sexual predation by Jeffrey Epstein and the sweetheart legal deal that allowed Epstein to continue his illegal activities for a decade (Brown, 2018). The initial police inquiry uncovered more than 50 victims, according to the retired Palm Beach Police Chief. Michael Reiter, who supervised the Epstein investigation, asserted: "This was not a 'he said, she said' situation. This was 50-something 'shes' and one 'he' – and the 'shes' all basically told the same story," according to Reiter, who was appalled by the deal that set Epstein free.

Brown's (2018) introduction to the story eloquently stated the premise of journalism as the court of last resort:

This is the story of how Epstein, bolstered by unlimited funds and represented by a power-house legal team, was able to manipulate the criminal justice system, and how his accusers, still traumatized by their pasts, believe they were betrayed by the very prosecutors who pledged to protect them.

As a result, the investigation uncovered new evidence, Epstein was arrested and charged in New York. And the actions of the U.S. Department of Justice and the Florida state officials who presided over this "deal of a lifetime" came under swift public and Congressional scrutiny.

You can bet that this story matters – to the journalists who uncovered, reported, and published it, to law enforcement officials, the criminal justice system, the attorneys, the witnesses – and most of all, to the young girls who had lodged their complaints, only to have justice denied and delayed, in some cases for more than a decade. And this story has legs, from the subsequent suicide of Epstein, to Prince Andrew's decision to "step-back" from his royal duties "for the foreseeable future" (BBC, 2019).

THE MORE THINGS CHANGE

In times of profound change, the learners inherit the earth, while the learned find them-selves beautifully equipped to deal with a world that no longer exists.

Attributed to Eric Hoffer

Will the news industry continue to change and adapt to the M2M environment? The short answer: "Yes! Expect rapid change in journalism in the foreseeable future." Like other information-based industries, enormous changes have shaped journalism relentlessly for more than 150 years with no signs of slowing down. Indeed, the pace of technological innovation and subsequent adaptation within newsrooms has exponentially increased during recent decades.

"I have a student in Rio working with a student in Hong Kong to produce a video on how journalists cover the COVID-19 crisis," recounts professor and journalist Mary Murphy.

Students work together through video, social media, and Zoom for online meetings and video interviews to provide information about governments, medical crisis, pandemics and, on a less serious note, about the shutdown in Hollywood and how it will impact our culture. They are doing all of this from their bedrooms so we're definitely in a new technological era of journalism. We were heading that way, we were on course, and students and young journalists will point the way we use technology to collaborate across the world.

This ready, worldwide availability of information stems from many different causes. Global increases in literacy, education, computers, scientific research and data, remotely accessible digital repositories, and high-speed digital networks all play roles in creating our present information-rich environment. Recall, during most of human history, informa-tion was scarce. Now our society teems with information. Reports describe this growth as a tsunami, deluge, or glut – not even addressing information's nasty, dark cousin:

disinformation. And all the while, we're accessing vast arrays of news via many different media platforms, channels, and devices.

The information-rich reality turned the economics of journalism upside down and inside out. There's more than enough news supply to meet the demand, both for free and for fee. At the same time, the internet enables just about anybody to enter the game, without buying expensive printing presses, servers, teams of skilled people, or trucks to move the paper. By slashing newcomers' production and distribution costs, the web makes it easy and cheap for potential competitors to attract niche audiences away from broad-interest mainstream publications – without leaving their basement.

In addition, the internet giants, Facebook, Google, Apple, Snapchat, Instagram, and Twitter, have entered the news business. Medium.com built a niche to push long-form multimedia stories to users. Pinterest captures consumers' eyeballs with photo arrays of products coupled with buying suggestions.

These developments undermine established payment models for news outlets. And there's one last cruelty that digital technology inflicted on the news industry: Just as the value of the (news content) product collapsed, so did the money pipe from advertisers. The old business of media companies was to garner readers' attention – *eyeballs* for which advertisers paid handsomely. Now marketers have less expensive, more direct ways to reach consumers – email, text, branded content, social media, influencer marketing – often precisely tailored and targeted to potential customers' demographics and locations.

Unable to compete with easier pathways to customers and easy availability of so many sources of news online, traditional media companies adopted new business models and products to sustain profits. News organizations implemented digital operations. Many downsized – or worse, went out of business altogether. Researchers from the University of North Carolina's Center for Innovation and Sustainability in Local Media found that nearly 1,800 newspapers across the U.S. had closed down between 2004 and 2018 (Abernathy, 2018).

Many of the newspapers that closed had provided news in rural areas. But most new digital-only jobs exist in urban areas. This centralization of news outlets and reporters leads to "news deserts" in areas lacking local news outlets (Abernathy, 2018). News deserts cut-off vital flows of information within rural areas because news outlets in nearby urban centers have few (or no) reporters on-scene to investigate and report on local conditions.

Grieco (2019a) headed a Pew Research Center study which confirmed rural residents' belief that they get less local news now: Six of ten urban dwellers said that news media covers their area compared to only four of ten rural residents. Almost half of the urbanites said that the local news media have a lot of community influence compared to less than one-third of rural inhabitants who believed that local news was influential.

It is clear that the need for journalism remains, even for those who aren't its biggest fans right now. The future is barreling down on us at Mach speed, powered by the multiplier effect of the M2M global communication system. Change is ongoing and continuous. Accurate, timely news is essential for all those who hope to cope with our liquid modernity.

THE TECHS ARE COMING! THE TECHS ARE COMING!

As new technologies emerge during the next decade, they will further transform news production, distribution, and consumption. Get ready for:

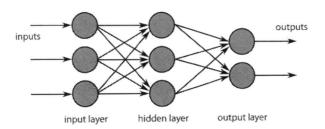

FIGURE 12.3

Artificial intelligence model: Based on brain neural networks

Credit: MultiLayerNeuralNetwork_english.png: Chrislbd derivative work: – HELLKNOWZ |TALK |enWP TALK – MultiLayerNeuralNetwork_ english.png, CC BY-SA 3.0, https://commons.wikimedia.org/w/index.php?curid=11397827

- Quantum computing
- Artificial intelligence and machine learning
- 5G mobile networking and subsequent communication effects
- Wireless electrical power
- Voice user interfaces
- Virtual reality/Augmented reality
- Blockchain
- 3D printing
- Smart robotics
- Autonomous cars
- Internet of Things

Publications might use artificial intelligence to dynamically analyze user data and behaviors to personalize home pages and other offerings, based on the previous individual user-choices – and soon they will. Several newsrooms have already implemented AI automation software to write routine notices and short articles. The Internet of Things (IoT) offers a completely new source of data for reporting and fact-checking. Reporters will need to understand and use blockchain technologies to examine public records. And smart robots may appear in many workplaces.

For users, emerging technologies will deliver: 1) more information, 2) in more formats, 3) many times faster, 4) to more highly connected, more easily powered devices, and 5) with permanently recorded digital payment and access permissions. (Fortunately for news organizations, autonomous vehicles should free-up users' time to access more stories!)

News organizations aren't standing still. They've been investing in technology. They are testing new online and multimedia storytelling forms. Most important, they are experimenting with new ways of producing and distributing news and increasing revenues for users' access to new news products.

New processes are difficult to implement. Online multimedia news organizations adopted radically different workflows within their newsrooms that had important consequences for the way journalists work. Moreover, the range of professional skills needed to create complex digital, data-intensive, interactive multimedia stories requires intensely collaborative environments in order to create satisfying experiences for users (Howe, Bajak, Kraft, & Wihbey, 2017).

The old linear workflow models won't work for multi-brand, fast-moving digital information publishers because: 1) Optimal results depend on decisions made from several perspectives; 2) Key processes must happen in tandem to put multimedia stories together; and 3) Individuals can't possibly acquire all the rapidly changing essential competencies. To produce today's digital news, newsrooms hire people with high-end digital skills who can work well in teams of editors, reporters, web designers, data wranglers, and IT geeks.

Teamwork is expanding beyond the single news organization. Inter-organizational collaboration flourishes in many locales, according to Bunting, Cheung, Preston, Rundlet, and Swyter (2018):

- In Philadelphia, 17 newspapers and broadcasters, Temple University, and the non-profit Resolve Philadelphia joined to promote civic action to address poverty-related issues in the Philadelphia area.

- ProPublica (a nonprofit news organization) established Local Reporting Network Partnerships in 2018 that supported reporters at 20 local news partners to develop investigative projects in their communities.

- Report for America enhanced local journalism in underserved communities. During 2019, they placed 61 journalists in 50 newsrooms across America.

- The Center for Investigative Reporting publishes in national and local news outlets and operates *Reveal*, a platform for multimedia stories that include video, audio, and podcasts. CIR also collaborated with the Google News Lab and local news organizations in New Orleans and San Jose to help create stories that included data journalism, multimedia reporting, and new forms of storytelling for the local markets.

- Cortico, a media technology nonprofit works with the Associated Press, Alabama Media Group, and others to create an ear-to-ground listening tool that systematically identifies and elevates issues that matter to the local community.

- The Knight Foundation teamed-up with contributors including the Democracy Fund, MacArthur Foundation, and Ethics and Excellence, to raise $26 million in 2018. This project supported nonprofit news organizations through the Institute for Nonprofit News.

- The Knight Foundation also joined with the Lensfest Institute in 2019 to support a $20 million fund to transform Philadelphia's local journalism.

- NewsMatch provided almost 200 matching-gifts in 2019 to help local nonprofit news organizations find donors and build audiences.

But the match between nonprofits and news organizations isn't always chill. A study of eight nonprofits by the Shorenstein Center on Media, Politics and Public Policy found glitches when nonprofits partnered with news organizations – double staffing to report and produce stories, and increased coordination costs. Nonprofits also reported trouble getting promised user engagement metrics for their stories – and getting paid (Porter, 2019).

JOURNALISM   **365**

PACE: SUPERSONIC. RATE: EXPONENTIAL. GO TIME: NOW!

In 2019, student journalists blazed a remarkable trail of accomplishments (Stauffer, 2019).

The State, Arizona State University's student publication, scooped the international press when they broke the story of impeachment witness Kurt Volker's resignation. In Pittsburg, Kansas, a high school newspaper forced the principal of their school to resign when they found and wrote about discrepancies in her résumé (Levin, 2019). High school students in Burlington, Vermont, won an important case against their school principal when he censored an article they wrote about an employee charged with unprofessional conduct. Students at *The Graphic* at Amherst-Pelham Regional High in Massachusetts exposed their school's exploitive contract to use prison labor to reupholster the auditorium seats. And in Pelham, New York, middle and high school students own and operate the *Pelham Examiner*, an online news site (DeRienzo, 2019).

The year also saw students take on the big things:

- In partnership with the *Miami Herald* and McClatchy, more than 200 student reporters have contributed to the project: Since Parkland, featuring student journalists writing about the students killed in the 2018 mass shooting at Marjory Stoneman Douglas High School in Florida.
- Olivia Seltzer, 15, founded *The Cramm*, a daily newsletter that covers breaking news for teens.
- The University of Michigan's *The Michigan Daily* investigated charges of sexual misconduct leveled against a professor that led to his early retirement.
- Notably, *The Michigan Daily* has been the only daily paper in Ann Arbor for the past decade. University of Missouri students staff the *Missourian* in Columbia and run local papers in Kearns, Utah, Kearns High School's *The Cougar Claw*. In East Lansing, Michigan and Chicago, Illinois, local news outlets hire students as reporters (DeRienzo, 2019).

Today's students are digital natives, comfortable on and offline. They are well positioned to work and lead in the new news environment. Beyond their technology chops, students are learning the ropes by doing journalism, which has always been the real cool school for reporting.

JOURNALISM: WHEN SEEING IS NOT BELIEVING

> You have to show reality as it is, not as you wish it to be.
>   – Jorge Ramos, reporter for Univision, quoted in Fussman, 2016

Reality is a tough taskmaster. It's hard to see, or to even know if you saw it accurately when you think you have. Even when people *really try* to perceive what's real, **confirmation bias** distorts perception through the filters of pre-existing knowledge, beliefs, expectations, hopes, aspirations, and dreams. Observers tend to give more currency to evidence that confirms these sources of existing biases. Training, experience, and self-awareness can compensate for internal mental processes that otherwise make accurate observation tough. And though one person's fact may be another's opinion – folks who don't die from the measles or get eaten by lions still win.

First and foremost, journalists report facts. Facts are observable and verifiable in some way. Verifying facts requires examining evidence that supports (or refutes) the correspondence of factual claims with observations. For example, a personal scale (if calibrated correctly) provides factual evidence of a person's weight. Similarly, a spectrophotometer (or a good photograph taken today) can confirm reports that a building's color is slate blue with white trim. A video or audio recording or an official transcript of an interview can confirm statements and answers to questions.

But "truth" entails interpreting selected facts, embedded in contexts, and seen from specific perspectives that give our truth its meaning. Consider the Statue of Liberty – a 450,000 pound, 131-foot-tall figure made of steel, cast iron, and copper: all facts. The Statue of Liberty stands for freedom from tyranny – one truth. For some, Lady Liberty represents America's welcome toward new immigrants – another truth. Just as there are infinite numbers of facts, there are ever so many truths. No matter the facts that journalists select, or the perspectives they adopt, some users will strongly disagree, particularly regarding social, moral, and political matters.

Even for issues grounded in factual accuracy, the truth proves elusive, widely disputed in the present partisan, contentious environment of fake news and journalist-bashing. Yet most journalists stand by professional norms and their commitment to accuracy and fairness in the face of partisan bullying or presidential ire. Lakshmanan (2018) wrote of the increasing fury aimed at journalists: Dubbing reporters the "most dishonest people" and urging supporters to jeer at them became a familiar part of Donald Trump's script as a candidate. He riled-up crowds that threatened the press, and occasionally physically intimidated individual reporters. One disturbing t-shirt sold at his rallies evoked lynching: "Journalist. Rope. Tree. Some assembly required."

THE TRUST BUSINESS

As the news industry changed over the last two decades, recurrent questions about the business of journalism arose. Was news just another entry on a corporate spreadsheet? Was it a hallowed enterprise grounded in the Constitution? Were journalists just another kind of content providers?

"Trust, not information, is the scarce resource in today's world," wrote Lorenz, Kayser-Bril, and McGhee (2011), almost a decade ago. Now there is a dawning recognition that being able to trust a news source brings crucial value to users who seek to monitor and understand their environments. Accurate information is critically important for us in this rapidly changing, highly partisan social/political/economic world. World leaders seem to be preparing to "let slip the dogs of war" (William Shakespeare, *Julius Caesar*). Today's behemoth political and profit-driven lions may be far more dangerous than the lions that once roamed African savannas.

Bolstering the case for trust as a viable business models for news, a report from the Reuters Institute, *Journalism, Media and Technology Trends and Predictions 2019* asserted:

> This will be a critical year for both publishers and platforms in terms of rebuilding trust and credibility after years of self-inflicted wounds around quality, privacy, and user experience. A number of fundamentals are beginning to shift and these will be much clearer by the end of 2019.
>
> (Newman, 2019)

JOURNALISM

The COVID-19 pandemic starkly demonstrated that trust must accompany accuracy and timeliness in the journalism canon. Journalists at *The New York Times* analyzed internet usage and found that, during the crisis, people sought information significantly more from mainstream media national and local news sites, while visits to both left and right partisan sites declined (Koeze & Popper, 2020). The lesson? Users seek trustworthy, accurate reports from media outlets when their lives and their communities' welfare depend on access to timely, accurate, and trustworthy news.

For trust to become a new product offering, journalists must be more transparent about their procedures and actions with respect to sourcing, verification of facts, and authentication of documents and multimedia content. The Knight Commission on Trust, Media and Democracy report (Adler, 2019) asserts that building trust in journalism provides an essential key to vibrant civic life and democratic governance. That Commission, composed of corporate leaders, news industry executives, academic researchers of journalism, and journalists – urged news organizations to take four specific actions to build greater trust in media and democracy:

- *Practice radical transparency*: "Develop industrywide, voluntary standards on how to disclose the ways they collect, report and disseminate the news." These standards should include "labeling news, opinion and fact-based commentary; best practices on corrections, fact-checking, anonymous sources and tracking disinformation; and avoiding advertising formats that blur the line between content and commerce" (Adler, 2019).

- *Expand financial support for news*: Explore creating innovative non-profit funding that supports journalism in the public interest, because for-profit organizations may not support the high-quality reporting and analysis that an information-based, modern society needs.

- *Use technology to solve problems of disinformation, misinformation, and lack of information*: Stay current with advanced technology throughout the news production and distribution chain to identify bogus content.

- *Diversify news organizations*: The failure to include underrepresented groups of all kinds limits news coverage and operations.

From a practical perspective, radical transparency might mean changing the traditional inverted style to include "methodology" paragraphs in news stories, as shown in Figure 12.4. An explanatory sidebar would also work well. For working journalists, what does radical transparency mean in practice? Hmmm …

- *Probably won't cut it*: "I called a couple of long-time sources, asked them a few questions, got the quotes, and wrote the article from the press release."

- *Could look something like this*: "Research confirmed all the facts in the story with information obtained from at least two sources. To understand the issues, the reporter called people with differing positions and included their perspectives in the analysis. The data showing public support came from (NAME), a nonprofit group that supports the project; we could find no comparable data available from groups that do not support it."

- *Or this*: The article quotes from Ms. Smith and Mr. Jones came from phone interviews. Transcripts of the entire interviews are posted <u>here</u>. Audio files are posted <u>here</u>.

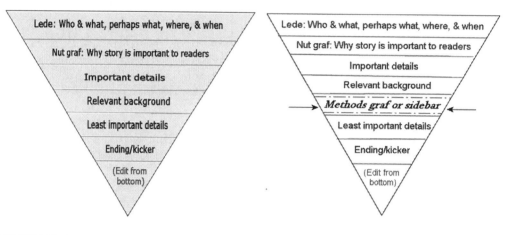

FIGURE 12.4

Open up the inverted pyramid to add a "methods" graf

Joan Van Tassel

When things are going well, it's easy to be complacent about journalism. But history shows that times inevitably come when exceptionally serious events occur – intractable warfare, market crashes, environmental crises, or institutional failures. These kinds of emergencies cast into prominence the crucial, but difficult roles that journalism fills: Commitment to verifiable facts, investigative power, insistence on public disclosure, and transparent accountability.

When hard times come, and things don't go well? Yes, #TruthMatters and #TrustMatters.

FIGURE 12.5

Journalists build a personal brand on social media

Credit: Stux on www.pixabay.com and www.instagram.com

HARD JOB = HIGH PAY (LOL)

Reasonable people might think that a tough job would pay well, but that's often not the case. Teachers, police officers, firefighters, postal workers, and soldiers all perform truly demanding, sometimes dangerous work, for long hours and average pay. These full-time jobs usually come with health and dental insurance, pension or retirement accounts, Social Security, disability, and unemployment benefits. If the journalist's partner also works and if they follow thoughtful budgets, journalists can support middle-class families with their joint income.

You may not yet believe this notion of former President Teddy Roosevelt. He captured

JOURNALISM

the underlying spirit of why so many ordinary people strive to accomplish extraordinary work they care about: "Far and away the best prize that life has to offer is the chance to work hard at work worth doing."

Know that only a few journalists become stars and multimillionaires. It's possible – but not likely. Still, ambitious reporters who devote careful attention to **personal branding** in their publication's comment section, Twitter, Facebook, and Snapchat (and whatever other bright, shiny new platform appears) often find themselves well-rewarded for these efforts. And even if she doesn't reach the top of the prevailing salary scale, such efforts often help a journalist find a new job with more responsibilities, a better beat, a larger market, and higher pay. Recall Brandi Buchman, a reporter for *Courthouse News* who writes illuminating tweet threads as she follows legal proceedings. She has a large following that will stand her in good stead – in her present job, and wherever the future beckons.

The requirement to build personal brands and followings adds yet more time-hogging demands on already hard-working reporters. Another important path that leads to recognition and opportunity for early-career journalists is to carry out enterprise journalism about serious, important stories and submit them for awards. In our experience, recognition from colleagues spotlights a journalist's work and creates wonderful opportunities to meet others. But most of all these honors from colleagues in the trenches of journalism bring lasting personal satisfaction.

Sometimes journalists transform their careers in unexpected directions. One example: After working as an award-winning foreign and then a national correspondent, Sharon Waxman started her own publication.

Vox Verbatim: Sharon Waxman, Founder and CEO, TheWrap

Digital journalism is familiar to me because I started at a wire service – Reuters. There is no deadline in the wires: It's always right now. And you always have competitors breathing down your neck.

To start TheWrap, I had to learn how to write a business plan and hired someone to build a business model – a financial spreadsheet that laid out how the finances would go in the first three years. This was a crash course in business that took about five months. Meanwhile, I started pitching investors. That started as family and friends putting in money and shortly thereafter, I started approaching individual investors and institutions as well.

"We now do 15 magazines a year. It's a different form of content and there is still ample room for magazines in the world."

JOURNALISM … EXCITING, SCRAPPY, AND OFTEN FUN

The dirty secret: journalism has always been horrible to get in; you always have to eat so much crap to find a place to stand. I waited tables for seven years, did writing on the side. If you're gonna get a job that's a little bit of a caper, that isn't really a job, that under ideal circumstances you get to at least leave the building and leave your desktop, go out, find people more interesting than you, learn about something, come back and tell other people about it – that should be hard to get into. That should be hard to do. No wonder everybody's lined up, trying to get into it. It beats working.

(David Carr, quoted in Jahnke & Hahn, 2014)

EXCITING

It's exhilarating to know things that most people don't. Fascinating to learn how something really works. Mind-blowing to know sensational secrets. Intoxicating to get all the details on the down-low.

Another kind of exciting: When an editor or colleague listens to you talk about the progress on a story – and suggests something that opens up a whole new way of thinking about the problem. Suddenly there's a path forward, the curiosity to follow the idea, and the energy to get going. Or in the middle of an interview, your question prompts a comment, a response that is altogether unexpected … and makes big news. Or you find a record with an entry that reveals the "real" truth behind an event – and blows the whole story wide open.

Then there is the adventure and the adrenaline of action upon more action. Say an editor calls and says, "Get on the plane and get the story" – that's how Ashley Codianni started one work week:

Vox Verbatim: Ashley Codianni, Executive Producer, and Global Head of Social and Emerging Media, CNN International

FIGURE 12.6

Protests in Ferguson, Missouri

Credit: Kane Farabaugh/VOA [Public domain]

Monday morning, I woke up, a normal day. Then I got a phone call from my boss, saying go to Ferguson [Missouri]. So instead of going to work, I got up, booked a flight, got to St. Louis, and drove immediately to where the protests were and shot footage from 5:00 pm to 2:00 am. And from 2:00–6:00 am, I edited and posted a video, and my colleague had written a story.

Obviously after that first story, we took a little nap, then we went out about 3:00 pm the next day, and that is when I started to build a bigger picture narrative: Who are the community members? Who are the organizers? Who is this affecting the most? How did this grow into something? And that involved interviewing community members during the day and getting more footage at night. And then, again back to the hotel late at night and editing. In Ferguson and other breaking news stories, especially with digital video, you are that one-man-band. You have to shoot and edit everything yourself and it can be a long process – long but with a quick deadline.

JOURNALISM

SCRAPPY

The movie image of the cynical, wise-cracking reporter goes back past the 1930s and persists to this day. Some journalists act that way in real life and others just adopt that persona. Based on images they've gotten from the media, people often think that journalists are pushy, determined, brash, intense, and thick skinned – and they treat journalists accordingly. Yet it's possible to be a quiet, shy, introverted, polite reporter. (They do exist, even if they don't usually cover crime, political, or sports beats.)

News itself can often be unpleasant. Facts can be horrible, grotesque, surprising, entertaining, or utterly irrelevant. Unearthing (and facing) horrific facts often affects reporters psychologically and spiritually, just as they do to other first responders. For example, when Michael Herr covered small squads of U.S. military troops in Vietnam, his experiences troubled him so deeply that he spent years in therapy. Awful images don't disappear from our minds. Mental images of unspeakable acts linger, unwanted, and unneeded. Police officers, firemen, soldiers, and journalists use dark humor to keep their humanity alive and to keep their profound sadness at bay. Honesty with oneself becomes a necessary policy, even while a breezy or hard-boiled persona offers a handy defense against troubled feelings while continuing the hard work.

Bringing the goods to a big story that almost no one knew about before it broke often gets a reporter into the big time, because it's not easy. That work requires persistence, determination, grit, and luck. Journalists fight for their stories. They wrest facts from the hard rock of articles, records, databases, and the actors who shape important events; it's time-consuming, frustrating work with short deadlines.

Facts remain contentious. Truths are elusive. News stories have consequences, great for some, horrendous for others. Nevertheless, good reporters cover, report, and publish stories that matter.

After the story is published, here come the users. Forget about the cheaters, crooks, and grifters – relationships with users can be rough. Journalists understand that no matter which publication they report for, which topics they cover, how accurate the facts they uncover, and important the acts they discover, some segments of the public will criticize and discount their work. Some users will hate it and respond with vitriol and abuse to unwelcome facts, analyses, or truths. They express their displeasure publicly, in comments sections on social media, perhaps even on the reporter's Twitter timeline for their colleagues to see.

Sincere user comments, even when expressed in an unpleasant or angry way, may merit journalists' calm replies, describing their sources and processes. Reporters can offer more information. Rarely, users might suggest a useful angle for another story. But don't respond to seemingly unhinged users, and *don't feed the trolls*. Block them.

Girl Talk

When women publish their news stories, journalistic landscapes can go way beyond "scrappy." Women, you *are not* overly sensitive: You *are* being targeted.

The Guardian examined its own comment sections to quantify cyberhate against female journalists in online comments sections (Gardiner et al., 2016). Based on 70 million comments from *Guardian* readers, eight out of the ten most abused writers were women – no matter the topic of their article; and the other two "winners" were black men. Conversely, the ten regular writers who received the least abuse were men.

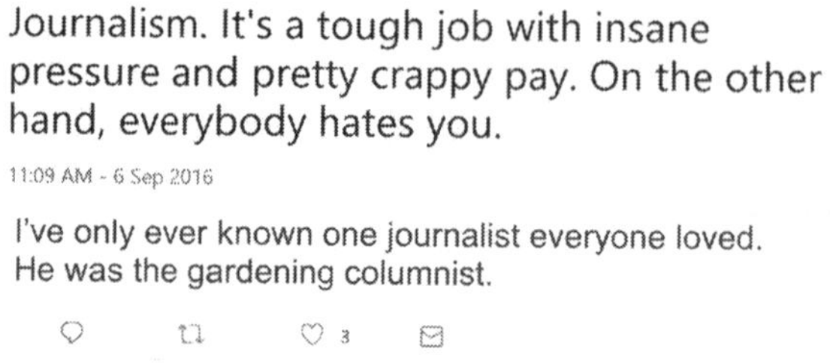

Journalism. It's a tough job with insane
pressure and pretty crappy pay. On the other
hand, everybody hates you.

11:09 AM - 6 Sep 2016

I've only ever known one journalist everyone loved.
He was the gardening columnist.

FIGURE 12.7

Two tweets from journalists (both women)
Credit: Carefully snipped from Twitter by Joan Van Tassel

These *Guardian* findings confirmed the 2014 poll conducted by the International Women's Media Foundation and the International News Safety Institute which demonstrated that rampant hate speech targeted female journalists worldwide (Barton and Storm, 2014). Updated with poll data from 600 women in 2018, nearly two-thirds of these women said they had received threats, intimidation, abuse, or threats online as a consequence of their work (Ferrier, 2018). Roughly six of ten women reported being harassed or intimidated in person, one-fourth experienced physical abuse, and one in ten received death threats.

Those online threats and hate-speech attacks found by the International Women's Media Foundation were immediate and seemed coordinated. Not surprisingly, these threats cause anxiety and deep concern about physical attacks on the journalists, and on the journalists' friends and families. The report also describes measures that one print/online journalist takes:

Mary [a pseudonym] is also careful about the hashtags she uses, so she doesn't alert coordinated attacks from trolls monitoring certain social issues. She shares her location data AFTER the events. She takes explicit threats directly to management, especially if something comes to her desk at the newspaper.

MEN AND #METOO

In newsrooms, males may not realize just how much corrosive abuse their female colleagues receive online and in person. Granted, women may not always appreciate how hostile the atmosphere can be for male journalists either. Although men may not be subjected to as much overt hate as the women, it still isn't a picnic in the park.

That said, it's way better when men in newsrooms don't add to the misogynistic stream of comments that their female colleagues endure. Understand that most women now report unwanted comments and actions as well as online abuse, even those not intended to cause harm. So, if there's a chance that a remark, joke, or suggestion might warrant reporting, consider not saying it. 'Nuff said.

FUN? REALLY?

After the earlier paragraphs, you might ask, "Where's the fun?" But fun in journalism takes many forms. Yes, really.

JOURNALISM

Sometimes a journalist runs across a person, a fact, an event, or just a discordant detail that inspires a nagging hunch, "Hmmm, I wonder if this is a story ..." Then, after some listening and snooping, the reporter finds there *is* a really neat story. This unexpected moment of discovery is *way more fun* than humans are meant to have. It's alive! It's real! And it's waiting just for me! Wow! Enjoy it and savor it, because it may mark the beginning of an amazing ride.

There's the thrill of the chase, too. When a reporter tracks down a story, scavenging the internet for documents, records, and informants, knocking on one door after another, strategizing, pleading, guessing, and pressing limits – those times are fun too.

Writing and producing the story becomes fun – and even more fun when it's over and your story is approved. Sitting around and celebrating with colleagues (some of them drinking) offer great moments for totally unreal conversations. These are the times when you hear the old newsroom tales, spectacular scoops of the past and the ones that never got published, the career high points and the lows ... to say nothing of the big fish that got away.

Vox Verbatim: Mary Murphy, Journalist Educator

Every night reporters told their wildest tales at the Typo Bar across the street from the St. Louis Post-Dispatch. I always loved the one about the reporter and photographer sent to interview a parakeet that had been left $1,000,000 by its owner. As the reporter interviewed the disgruntled relatives, the photographer got a photo of the bird. In those days, cameras let out a huge "POOF" sound as the photog snapped away. The poof scared the bird and it dropped dead of a heart attack. I never got tired of hearing that story, and neither did the photographer, Scott Dine. The photographer, Scott Dine, never got tired of telling that story.

Even when there's no huge breaking story or epic disaster, journalists engage in plenty of hijinks. They work hard, play hard, and share a camaraderie that few other storytellers experience. Journalists like to tell stories: jokes, tall tales, and shaggy dog stories: Just as other first responders – police and firefighters. Journalists let off steam with lively, wry, and often irreverent humor.

Finally, there's publishing your awesome story. Here's what happened right after *Vanity Fair* broke the story Buzz Bissinger wrote about Bruce Jenner coming out as Caitlin Jenner:

Vox Verbatim: Buzz Bissinger

When I saw the cover picture, I said, "This is going to explode! People are going to love it, people are going to hate it, but people are going to talk about it!"

That Monday it was like war. The battle started at 2:00 pm. That is exactly when *Vanity Fair* started to release the pictures to the media. Literally within two to three minutes I was getting emails from all over the place requesting interviews. They just started rolling in, and rolling in and rolling in, and it was a fraction of what *Vanity Fair* was getting. In the course of the day, I probably got close to 50 and they got hundreds and hundreds – we just stopped answering them at one point.

Bissinger went on to do all three national network morning shows and many other interviews. It was a huge story – the first of its kind. How much fun is that!

In their careers, journalists have experiences that transcend fun to reach heights of reward and satisfaction: When a story saves someone's life or changes someone's life for the better (perhaps many someones). Some reports right a wrong or correct the record. Some bring justice, relief, reform to the people who lived them. Some stories make people smile. These are the stories that matter.

Journalism isn't for shrinking violets. Journalism is for people who *really* want to be in the world, to drink it in, taste it, feel it, write it, show it, and change it. Henry Luce (American publisher and editor, 1898–1967) said it best: "I became a journalist to come as close as possible to the heart of the world."

Take care. Be well. Do good.

-30-

KEY CONCEPTS AND TERMS

- Reporters change the world, even when they're young
- In the 21st century change is pervasive for everyone, everywhere
- Users rule
- Journalism is super hard
- Work hard, play hard, and have some fun

ADVANCER

Go forth and get a great job and career!

GLOSSARY

–30–: Back in the day, newspaper reporters typed -30- to signal the end of the story to copy editors.

360° video: A camera or multiple cameras that capture video from all or many points around the camera. Software integrates the various perspectives into a surround-video picture that enables users to see all around the digital environment, using **Virtual Reality (VR)** goggles.

5W1H: Who, what, when, where, why (5W), and how (1H) are the categories that establish the fact structures of news stories.

Above the fold: Folded in half, the top half (above the fold) of the newspaper has a large headline, logo, and a picture from the lead story.

Acoustically dead: A room protected from sounds originating from outside the room. In addition, internal "dead room" surfaces absorb sounds to prevent echoes or reverberation of sounds originating within the "dead room."

Ad blocking software, Adblocker: Software that people use to block ads from appearing on webpages. There are ad blocker extensions for browsers and apps for mobile phones.

Affordance: The classic definition of an affordance is "a possibility for action" in any environment, whether it is physical, social, and technological. In digital environments, affordances allow (and their absence preclude) how people can use communications technologies, online services and platforms, and devices. For example, mobile phones *afford* making calls, accessing the internet, and installing apps. TV technology *affords* the transmission and reception of moving images and sound. **Affordance-related elements** draw on the essential and unique characteristics of online digital media and platforms. As an example, interactive assets and participation increase engagement by helping users understand and follow the news article.

Agency: The ability to take actions.

Aggregation/Aggregator: A website that compiles and reprints material previously published elsewhere online.

Algorithm: A computer program executes commands to accomplish a task. An algorithm provides the specific way that the program directs the computer to reach the solution. For example, the task is to clean a car's exterior. One algorithm would be to take the car to an automated carwash, pay for it, and run it through. A second algorithm would be to take the car to a do-it-yourself carwash, pay for it, and wash it yourself. A third algorithm would be to wash it in your own driveway. A fourth algorithm would be to pay a 14-year-old neighbor to wash it. All four algorithms achieve the objective but use different means to do it.

Ambient (environmental) noise: Background sounds in locations such as wind, birds, and nearby outside traffic. Inside, ambient sounds include heating fans, air conditioners, fluorescent lights, and other noises within the environment.

Amplify, Amplifier effect: Increases in the reach and effect of a news story. The internet increases the effect of news stories because sharing adds to the number of people who receive it. Print, broadcast, online news, and social media play off one another, amplifying and re-amplifying news events.

Analog, analogue, analogous: An analog signal or data is a type of representation in which the representational signal maintains a continuous relationship with the represented phenomenon. An analog signal mirrors the source phenomenon at an infinite number of points – these values are continuous, not discrete.

Analytics: Information resulting from the quantitative assessment and systematic analysis of data, statistics or metrics. Analytics enable news and media organizations to monitor all aspects of a publication's performance. Journalists focus most closely on measures of users' behavior.

Angle, Story angle, News angle: An approach to a journalistic story, a way of framing the story.

Aperture: The opening in a camera lens which allows light to pass through the lens, thus regulating the amount of light reaching sensors or exposing film to capture a picture.

App: Short for applications – refers to software programs for computers; smartphone users adopted a shorter, peppier word to describe these targeted-purpose programs they need to carry-out tasks on their smartphones.

Article pages: Sometimes called the "news hole," these pages on a website belong to a single article. Headings may segment the text into sections. Article pages usually have pictures and may also provide links to multimedia assets and interactive data visualizations. Article pages also may include advertising.

Assets, content assets, designed interactive assets, media assets, multimedia assets, story assets: Assets means goods, resources, or treasures. Digital assets are digital files with economic value. When assets include photos, videos, or audio clips, they are multimedia assets.

Attribution, Attributing: Giving proper credit to story elements, such as photographs, videos, gifs or tweets to the person or individuals who originally produced that content, including user-generated content (UGC). Sometimes credit also goes to the user who uploaded that content to the web and/or to the online platform where that content was originally uploaded, seen or procured. Online attribution can be assigned through digital markers and signifiers such as usernames, Twitter handles, or hyperlinks to the original work, particular when the content has been created by users. **Source attribution** means describing the source of a fact or comment.

Audio mix: In film, the process of preparing a final version of an audio track is called the "mix." Audio mix includes such adjustments as noise reduction, adding music and sound effects, normalization (making volume consistent within a single track), and equalization (making volume consistent across all tracks).

Aural cues: Behavioral sound cues, such as words, but also including grunts, clicks, and other vocalics.

GLOSSARY

Authoritative source: According to the Reuters Handbook, a person who exercises real authority on an issue in question. A foreign minister, for example, is an authoritative source on foreign policy but not necessarily on finance.

Backup: To make an exact copy of a file.

Bandwidth: The carrying capacity of a communication channel, a measure of how much information can flow through the channel. A telephone carries only audio; a television carries audio and video: The bandwidth, or carrying capacity, of a television network must be much larger to accommodate the video.

Barriers to entry: It takes resources to start a business and bring a product to a market. These required resources act as barriers to any market for new providers. Resources, brand, function, design, look and feel, distribution costs, ease of potential customer access – all these and other factors may create barriers for newcomers to entry.

Beauty shot: Originating in the fashion industry, it refers to stylized settings and people – shots designed to make everything in the picture beautiful and appealing.

Big data: Extremely large data sets that provide information about behaviors, connections and links, attributes and traits of actors, and co-variation among variables. People's activities on the internet typically yield finely-grained data, often matched with other data sets (voter rolls, credit card purchases, property ownership, etc.). Mining this data reveals new patterns, trends, and associations that yield insights into people's likely future interactions and behaviors.

Bite: In audio, a single continuous part of a recording of any length, often a statement from an interview.

Blanket waivers: Occur when source relieves a journalist of a promise to shield their role as a source. Prosecutors may then threaten the reporter with a contempt of court for refusing to testify. If necessary, reporters risk going to jail.

Boilerplate: Standard language in documents. The term often describes standardized verbiage in contracts and form letters.

Bokeh: Refers to intentional out-of-focus circular blurs in photographs, leaving the main subject of the picture in sharp focus.

Bothsideism: A rhetorical technique that implies that both sides of an argument have good points, bad points, or equal points. Some criticize the mainstream media for attempting to create an impression of fairness by creating an incommensurate or meaningless "balance," between opposing sides. For example: Statement 1 – "Russia interfered in the 2016 U.S. election." Statement 2 – "On the other hand, the United States has interfered in the elections of other countries too." (Statement 2 is true but doesn't address the important issue raised by statement 1.)

Bots: (see also Socialbot) Bots are executable software files that act without human intervention to automate the performances of standardized digital processes. Bots' programming enable them to establish accounts, collect and save data, send messages, keep scores and tallies, sort, and handle many other routine tasks. Siri is a bot.

Bounce rate: A metric that describes how many users leave a website after viewing only one page: The page did not engage the user enough to entice them to click on another page.

Buckets (of content): Buckets are large collections of content (stories, photos, videos, music, etc.) that are purchased for a single price. For example, theater owners buy single

378   GLOSSARY

movies or have contracts for just a few movies. However, small TV stations buy movies in packages or buckets.

Budget, News budget, Budget meeting: The budget refers to the lineup of news stories that editors plan to use for a specific publication or show. Executives and editors hold budget meetings to: Decide which stories to assign to reporters, set dates for when stories are due, and plan when stories will be published.

Burn: Making part of a photograph lighter to bring out detail.

Buzzfeedication: A mix of hard news, soft news, and no news, such as cat videos or humor, as exemplified by the www.buzzfeed.com website.

Call to action: Suggests something that users should do: Read the story, share the story, watch the video, etc.

Cardioid microphone: The pickup pattern of cardioid microphones readily captures sounds from the front and front sides of the microphone, but few sounds from behind the mic.

Cascading Style Sheets (CSS): A programming language used to design web pages – particularly useful for specifying the appearance of pages.

Case: In a data set, a case is something measured or observed: A person, thing, event, or action. Each case is a row in the dataset.

Causation: A sequence of events over time, wherein changes in one event (cause) act to create changes in another event (effect).

Chipsets: Silicon chips inside every computer that process information. Without chips, computers can't run.

Chrome: Navigational elements on a website or a page – including buttons, arrows, and links to sections.

Chronology or timeline: The listing of events in their time order of occurrence.

Chunks: The individual units of a story: facts, actors and actions, events, causes, consequences, and contexts. Groups of chunks are called **clusters**.

Cinematic video: Video shot in cinematic film style: beautiful, often slow-moving shots that create an atmosphere.

Classic news story structure: Headline, deck, picture, and copy. The inverted pyramid for news copy includes the lede, nut graf, important details and background, additional details, and kicker.

Clean the data: In a record or a database, to remove cases where there is missing, unrelated, or inaccurate data. Sometimes called **grooming the data**.

Clickbait: A lure designed to entice users to click on a link. The lure can be text or an image.

Click-through: When a visitor to a site clicks on a web link or advertisement and the web browser forwards the visitor to the linked website.

Climax: The part of a story when the hero wins, wins some and loses some, or loses all.

Clipping: In audio, when sounds are too loud for a microphone or a recording device, the mic can't reproduce the entire audio wave form. Mics or recording devices cut off or clip frequencies that exceed their capacity. These sounds are permanently lost, thus reducing the sound-quality of the recording.

GLOSSARY

Clusters: Groups of related **chunks**, plus the story assets that go with them, are combined into story clusters.

Color space: A scheme for translating data about color (numbers) into visible colors to instruct computers and other machines how to display or print them.

Combination structure: A article design that may use some elements from linear-embedded, hierarchical, and nonlinear designs to fit the unique narrative structure of the story.

Communication Security (comsec): The ability to communicate with others without surveillance from private or governmental actors.

Communities of interest: Many social bonds create communities: geography, tribal membership, religion, clubs, occupation, etc. By enabling global communication and frequent interaction, the internet fosters "communities of interest," such as beekeepers, quilters, sports, politics, classic car owners, climate deniers – virtually any shared interest now in existence.

Complement: In media, additional content that adds value to an article or story in ways that provide new information or show the content in new ways.

Comprehensives: Users whose style of perusing online pages is to read all the stories from top to bottom.

Compression: In audio, compressing the data reduces the number of frequencies in an audio clip, reducing the loud sounds and increasing the quiet ones. In video, it means reducing the size of the file by removing unnecessary data.

Condenser microphone: More complex and expensive than dynamic microphones, quality condenser microphones reproduce wider ranges of audio signals and add little noise. But they require power and may malfunction in high or low temperatures and high humidity.

Confirmation bias: The tendency for people to believe information that agrees with their personal worldview, including their beliefs, values, ideology, or perspectives. Almost everyone seeks reassurance that they are right in the way they see the world. Usually there are limits to confirmation bias. If people perceive large gaps between the information and their own experience, sometimes the gap triggers a more objective reality check.

Content exclusivity: Companies that publish content can charge more for it if they are the only source. For example, Apple has exclusivity for iPhone and iPad apps. Similarly, only NBC can broadcast certain TV programs – the company has contracts that impose "content exclusivity" for some period of time.

Content farms: Companies that produce large amounts of content (see "buckets"). They usually pay writers small amounts per word, 2–10 cents.

Content hosting: An online repository to which users upload content to store and share with other users. Such sites may accept or specialize in one type of content or allow sharing of multiple types, such as photos, videos, audio, and datasets. Most social media platforms also host user-generated content.

Content Management System (CMS): A system of networked computers, servers, and software that takes in, indexes, tags, stores, and retrieves content files. Most CMSs also track changes to files, called "versioning."

Contingent labor: Often referred to as the "gig economy," it refers to work that is temporary, piecemeal, or services provided on an as needed basis. Workers receive payment or commissions for completed work, instead of a regular salary or company benefits. Freelancers typically work piecemeal.

Continuous data: The basic property that all analog representations yield: data that covaries according to the changing images, sounds, or other perceived qualities of a phenomenon.

Contrived settings: Places that include others' offices, police interrogation rooms, laboratories, interview rooms, film sets, and other venues created for specific purposes.

Controlled behavior: Occurs when a journalist observes people in a situation that imposes controls on behavior. These conditions include control by police and emergency personnel, guards, school and detention facility authorities, supervisors, parents, and many others.

Convergence, convergent: Convergence refers to the integration of networks and user devices so they all handle digital information, whether text, pictures, audio, or data. For content companies, it means a unified digital production workflow to distribute the content over a network that carries any digital or digitally-wrapped electronic media.

Copy workflow: The process that transforms reporting into the text of a finished article. These steps include: research review, interview transcription review, story outline document, complete draft of story, polish and final version of story.

Copyright: Refers to the rights intellectual property owners have to the proceeds from their work. Intellectual property, or IP, includes such original works as writings, designs, other artistic creations, and inventions. In the U.S., copyright and ownership of intellectual property are protected in the copyright clause, Article I, Section 8, Clause 8 of the U.S. Constitution.

Court of last resort: The role of the press to bring justice to wronged persons.

Co-variation (positive) and negative co-variation: Variables that exhibit positive co-variation mirror change such that when values of one variable change in a certain direction, the values of the other variable change in the same direction. In contrast, variables that exhibit negative co-variation also change together, but they change in opposite directions.

Credit, crediting: Attributing story elements, such as user-generated photographs, videos, gifs or tweets to the person(s) or individuals who originally produced that content, the user who uploaded that content to the web, and/or to the online platform where the content was originally uploaded, seen, or procured. Online attribution can be assigned through digital markers and signifiers such as usernames, Twitter handles, or hyperlinks to the original work.

Crop: In editing pictures, cropping means selecting part of the picture and removing all but the selected area. Cropping helps viewers focus on the important parts of a picture.

Crowdsourcing: The online equivalent of the proverb, "Many hands make light work." Crowdsourcing relies on the participation of many people to accomplish a goal or task. It usually refers to using the internet to enlist them and organize their efforts.

Cues: The words, sounds, gestures, and movements that persons make that give others insight into their thoughts and feelings. Cues may be visual, aural (sound), verbal, nonverbal, and less often – smell, taste, and touch.

Curation: The selection, organization, and presentation of content, artifacts, or information needed to create a collection of high-quality related items. **Curated:** To curate means to identify a class of objects, sort and rate them according to their perceived value along a selected dimension, choose the most valuable objects, and then save and preserve them as a collection of those with the highest value.

GLOSSARY

Customized advertising: A form of tailoring ads to user demographic characteristics, based on account sign-up or other means. The system inserts an ad that appeals to users who fit a desired demographic profile.

Cut-in, insert shot: Extreme close-ups of an object or person. Examples include a shot of a mobile phone screen with fingertips pressing numbers, or of a person's eyes.

Cyberbullying: Attempting to bully, intimidate, or silence someone online.

Cybermob: Online harassment and humiliation of a target person by a group of people.

Cyber-stalking: Repeatedly contacting someone online even after the target person has indicated they do not want it. The do-not-contact message may come from a direct written communication, blocking, muting, or other means. In extreme cases, particularly where the cyber-stalker makes threats, expressly referencing violence in the real world, the target should contact law enforcement.

Data: A collection of observed facts that may consist of measurements, observations, descriptions, numbers, symbols, or other representations. **Data analysis** means to examine data to: 1) recognize, distinguish, and describe the distributions of variables' values and, 2) identify and distinguish patterns of co-variation among variables – in contrast to normal random variations.

Database: A set of searchable electronic data.

Data dredge: To run analyses of datasets in search of relationships among variables.

Data journalist (DJ): An individual who has professional competencies in journalism, research methods, data collection, grooming, and analysis.

Data management: Standardized procedures for creating databases, for adding, labeling, indexing, tagging, storing, and retrieving data.

Data visualization (DV): Charts, plots, graphs, or other representations of data and data analysis methods that enable users to visualize the results of data analysis. **Data viz** also refers to the professional field of data visualization. For example: "She datavizzes at Google."

Data wrangling: A popular term that refers to preparing data for analysis: Creating a database and entering, cleaning, grooming, labeling, indexing, tagging, and mining data. A **data wrangler** is someone who specializes in grooming data.

Deconstruction: A process for understanding a story before choosing a narrative structure for telling it. The steps include building a micro story, a list of actors, actions, events, and outcomes. The next stage is to list the parts of the macro story, related information, background, and context. Extracted from the files, research, interviews, data, and past articles, these two lists provide the deconstructed individual chunks of the story.

Demographics: Socioeconomic categories that describe individuals and groups. Common demographic variables include: age, sex, race, educational level, income level, marital status, occupation, religion, birth rate, death rate, average family size, etc.

Depth-of-field (DOF): In photography, film, and video pictures, DOF refers to the amount of the scene that remains in focus. When only one part of the scene is in focus and the rest is blurry, a picture has a shallow DOF; conversely, when an entire scene is in focus, the picture has a deep DOF.

Designated source: Diplomatic sources, conference sources, government spokespersons, and some intelligence sources. As with an official source, the person must have access to reliable information on the subject in question.

Desktop first: A model for digital page design that specifies creating a page for a large, horizontal desktop screen, and then creating alternative pages for progressively smaller screens by eliminating elements.

Digital audio recorder (DAR): A DAR records audio signals, converts them to electrical signals, and then into digital information.

Digitization: Making information digital allows computers to manipulate it as "bits." Digital data has two forms: "0" and "1." Computers process this binary data very quickly, allowing them to sort, save, and represent information efficiently.

Direct observations: Watching and attending to events and activities in person and in real time – the reporter/observer is physically present as the event occurs.

Discrete data: The basic property of digital representation which requires specific values and intervals between values that reliably approximate the changing images, sounds, or other perceived qualities of a phenomenon. Digital data is binary, composed of 0s and 1s. Binary data is discrete in that it can only fit into one of those two separate categories.

Disinformation, deza: Information that is false or misleading, purposefully disseminated to deceive. *Deza* is shortened for the Russian word, *dezinformatsiya*, coined by Josef Stalin. False information that may be publicly announced, planted in the news media, circulated through propaganda, or covertly spread through rumors, with intent to: 1) mislead the public, 2) influence public opinion, and/or 3) obscure the truth.

Disintermediation: There is usually a "division of labor" between segments in a complex structure or process. The resulting layers and slices may reflect differing functions, status, geography, or some other characteristic. Disintermediation means breaking down the barriers between the segments, "flattening" or "shortening" the structure. Often, a function (or actor) is eliminated entirely. For example, buying directly from a manufacturer's web site "disintermediates" the retailer and perhaps other middlemen.

Display ads: Also known as a banner ad, a display ad doesn't change. It shows the same information to all website visitors.

Dodge: Making parts of a photograph lighter to bring out more detail.

Dodge and burn: Changing the lightness or darkness of an area within a picture. To dodge means to lighten the area; to burn means to darken it. For digital pictures, these names describe software editing tools.

DSLR, Digital Single Lens Reflex: A single lens reflex camera captures pictures on a mirror inside the camera that reflects the light coming from the lens and allows it to pass through a prism (costly) or a series of mirrors (not so costly) to the viewfinder. When recording, a shutter pops up and a digital sensor or film (chemical) receives the light waves.

Duct Tape: "Duck tape" was waterproof tape, originally developed by Johnson & Johnson for the U.S. military in World War II to keep ammunition cases dry. Over time, it has become "duct" but it really did mean the tape could shed water like a duck.

Dynamic microphone: A rugged mic often used in the field. Its straightforward design makes it less expensive and more able to withstand knocks, humidity, heat, and cold than condenser mics.

Echo chambers (see filters and information bubble): Similar to an information bubble, an echo chamber results when people who hold similar beliefs and values publish similar

GLOSSARY

383

content, reinforcing the views of similar others. Sometimes refers to the Washington, DC political press.

Editorial workflow, online news content editorial workflow: The stages of creating online news content include pitch/assignment; reporting and verification; multimedia asset acquisition, processing, and preparation; publishing; and promotion.

Embed: On the web, to "call" for content from a remote site and display it on the page of another site where users can view it.

Encyclopedic affordance: Refers to the high capacity of digital devices and networks for handling information. They take in, record, store – then find and display information. The entire internet has this capability as do individual and networked computers.

Enterprise story: A story proposed by or suggested to a reporter with no specific deadline to explore on his or her own time. The journalist investigates enough to understand the potential of the story, find out if the story leads to anything, and whether there is a story at all. If it pans out, editors will assign the story and provide resources.

Ephemeralization: The tendency for digitization of information to lessen the influence or hasten the disappearance of space, time, matter, and energy. An example is the reduction of printing press workers when newspapers and consumers adopt digital distribution.

Equalization: In audio, to adjust the maximum and minimum loudness level of multiple tracks so that the overall sound is the same as it originally sounded in the recorded environment.

Evergreen: Refers to articles or multimedia assets that have lasting value. An example of an evergreen article would be a historical piece about the Alamo or the Brooklyn Bridge.

Exchangeable Image File (shortened to Exif or EXIF): An association of companies that manufacture cameras set the standard for Exif metadata. At the point of capture, Exif data can include the date and time, the camera make, model, and serial number, the camera's shutter speed, aperture, ISO speed setting, lens information, white balance, and the distance to the subject.

Exposition: Prose that explains or interprets something covered in a story.

Exposure: The amount of light that goes into the camera through the lens when a photographer shoots a picture. Allowing in more light results in a lighter, brighter picture.

Fact: Information about people, places, things, or events that is consistent with objective reality and can be verified by evidence. Most news stories report facts.

Fact check: To verify the truthfulness and accuracy of a factual statement or claim.

Fade in/out: In video, a picture gradually comes into view (or goes out of view), pixel by pixel. In sound, the audio rises from silence to normal volume levels, or goes down from a normal level to silence.

Fair use: The U.S. Constitution balances copyright protection for authors of intellectual property with the public's need to know in a democracy. Fair use allows for extracting limited amounts of a work to comment, critique, or parody, thus providing exceptions to copyright protection for authors, including journalists. "The use of copyrighted material must be appropriate, timely, and newsworthy." Journalists may paraphrase material to provide proof, to illustrate claims, and engage in comment or critique under fair use provisions.

Fake news: Refers to news reports that include disinformation (deliberately false reports). Some people characterize any news with which they disagree as "fake news." Others refer to news reports that include misinformation (inaccurate reports) as well.

Falling action: The part of a story after the hero learns his or her fate. Maybe it's a win, maybe not. But there are probably loose ends to tie up or bumps in the road to overcome before the happy-ever-after moment at the story's end.

Feature story: A human-interest or entertaining story that may or may not be related to a current hard news story. Feature stories humanize events, may not be time sensitive, and have a narrative structure.

Fidelity to reality: A faithful representation of the way a phenomenon of interest appeared or occurred in its native context.

File metadata: Information added to a file that provides information about the main file. For example, the metadata added to a picture, as specified by international standards for digital cameras. This information includes data about the photographic file, including its file type, size, type of encoding, etc.

File type: Applications that create and save files adopt varying formats for writing those files. A file name has two parts: the name and the extension. The name is typically user-assigned; the extension identifies common file types, such as .docx, .txt, .pdf, and .jpg. Some file types are rare or unique to the applications that created them, such as .psd, a Photoshop document.

Firmware: Semi-permanent information placed in non-volatile memory of a computer such that it takes special processes to change it. Firmware provides the software glue that governs how the computer components work together.

Flack: A disrespectful term for publicists and public relations people.

Focus, autofocus, manual focus, focus ring: Related to sharpness. The parts of a picture that are sharp – as opposed to blurry – are in focus. The blurry parts remain out of focus. Autofocus relies on camera sensors to make as much of the picture sharp as possible; manual focus requires photographers to look through the viewfinder (or at the screen) and turn the focus ring on the lens until the picture comes into the desired focus.

Follow, following, follows: In social media, to follow someone means to receive their posts, images, videos, likes, and shares. There may or may not be reciprocal followership.

F-pattern or layout: Pages designed to allow users to scan a page by looking at the top, down the left side, in the middle, and then continue down the left side to the bottom of the page.

Framing: In writing, refers to the context of a fact or event. In photography, a manner of focusing on the subject of interest within the picture.

Freelancer: Self-employed individuals who sell their work and/or services by the hour, day, or project, etc., instead of working on a regular, salaried basis for one employer. Freelance journalists are increasingly common in today's media markets. Freelancers are also referred to as contingent labor within a gig economy.

Friction: Conditions and circumstances that make accessing or sharing content on the internet difficult or impossible.

FUD: Acronym that stands for fear, uncertainty, and doubt.

GLOSSARY

385

Gain: Increases an audio signal from the mic as it goes into the amplifier component of a mixer, camera, or digital audio recorder.

Gamma (computer): A measure of the range of light and dark output by a computer screen monitor.

Gamma adjustment (photography): In picture editing, lightening or darkening the mid and some dark tones of the picture, without affecting the lightest tones.

Gatekeeper: An individual or organization that controls access to information.

Get: A "get" is a finished interview with a newsworthy person who does not often grant interviews. Usually "get" also implies that something revealing occurred in the interview.

Gig economy: An economy fueled by the practice of replacing salaried employees with at-will freelance workers, who do not enjoy the benefits, rights, and protections of full-time staff. Freelance journalists have "gigs," not jobs.

Global digital networks: Communication infrastructure designed to carry digital traffic around the world.

Golden triangle: The upper center part of a mobile phone screen, where users first look to scan the page.

Graf: Short for "paragraph," misspelled deliberately to prevent its accidental inclusion in the story.

Green screen: A picture and video editing technique that enables changing a picture's background. An editor can make a person (or digital object) appear to be standing in front of the Taj Mahal, the ruins of Chichen Itza in Mexico, or a collapsed building in Detroit. The background for the foreground subject is a dinosaur-green colored screen. A new background is inserted as a layer below that shot. In editing, a chromakey allows editors to make the green background transparent, allowing any other background colors to show through.

Groom data: To prepare data to be imported into a dataset prior to analysis. Processes include "cleaning" the data to remove cases with missing or inaccurate data, and formatting and defining rows (cases) and columns (variables) to automatically populate the complete dataset.

Hand-held device: As computer technology advanced, devices became smaller. "Hand-held" refers to devices that people carry in their hand or on their person, such as mobile phones and tablets.

Hard news: Breaking or recent news about socially important events that may impact the audience. Hard news often involves political, economic, business, or natural disasters.

Hardware: The metal, plastic, and silicon that make up parts of a computer: case, keyboard, chips, etc. Software is written code; hardware is real "stuff."

Header: Metadata stored on the first frame of a video.

Hierarchical design: A design for an article that accommodates complex stories spanning multiple time periods, topic areas, groups, or sets of consequences. Hierarchical design helps to structure narratives that occur on several levels.

Histogram: A graphic representation of a data distribution. In photography, a histogram shows the left-to-right distribution from dark-to-light of the luminance pixels that compose the picture.

Homepage: A website page that provides links to everything available on the site. Usually, the homepage serves as the visitor's first "landing page" for the site.

Homophily: Refers to the tendency of people to associate with others like themselves. The basis of homophily can be tribe, gender, age, occupation, interests, lifestyle, ideology, values, or some other property. Sociologists coined the word, which means "love of the same."

Hook, news hook: A way to attract users to a story by emphasizing elements that are intriguing, novel, funny, weird, or otherwise interesting.

Hue: Color – red, blue, yellow, magenta, green, etc.

HyperText Markup Language (HTML): One of the first and most fundamental programming languages used to structure and design web pages.

Impression: A single viewing of an ad. In many cases, it requires more than one impression for people to attend to a message.

In-app ad: When users install apps on their mobile phones, free versions often request permission to show ads on the app pages. Many premium versions eliminate in-app ads.

In-camera moves: Camera moves, like pans, involve moving the entire camera body. In contrast, in-camera moves occur inside the lens, such as a zoom – the camera body does not move.

In media res: Latin for "in the middle of things." Writers sometimes start stories in the middle, rather than at the beginning or near the end, a technique also used for narrative news stories.

In the wild: Information that is available on the open internet. It is a reference to the way an animal might escape a cage (silo or server), free to make its way to the wilderness.

Inattentional blindness: Occurs when an observer fails to attend to fully visible but unexpected phenomenon because the observer's focus of attention is on other tasks, events, or objects.

Incognito mode: A browser setting that stores less information in the browser but does not keep websites from gathering and keeping data about your visit. With Google's Chrome browser specifically, the cache of internet sites is a temporary folder, deleted by the browser when the incognito window closes. All history, logins, pages, and downloads disappear. However, tools exist that penetrate the incognito mode and allow network operators to gather information about users' activities.

Indirect observation: Involves observing something that changes with another phenomenon that cannot itself be seen – such as wind on a body of water. It may also refer to the observation of instrument monitoring.

Inferences: Conclusions reached through the analysis and evaluation of facts or evidence.

Information bubble: When people receive information from a particular perspective and do not receive information from other points of view, they may draw their knowledge from an information bubble. Receiving information from a single perspective may occur as a result of personal preferences, online activities and behaviors, filters, feeds, or distribution algorithms.

Information security (infosec): Actions taken to keep information concealed from surveillance by others, whether by private or governmental actors.

GLOSSARY

Informational (descriptive) metadata: Metadata provides information about digital content, such as a picture or video, such as title, date created, camera make, model, settings, and modifications to the original picture, copyright, and comments, to name just a few possibilities.

Input: Something from outside that enters a system. Envisioning newsrooms as systems, newsroom inputs are interviews, media, documents, data, and information from other sources.

Integrated, converged: In media, an organizing concept that breaks down barriers between media channels – print, broadcast, digital, etc. In practice, an integrated newsroom provides a space where media professionals from print, TV and radio, as well as web producers, designers and developers can come together to collaborate on stories, visuals, apps and interactives, across media platforms and channels. Synonym: converged, as in "converged newsroom."

Interaction design (IxD): The practice of designing ways for users to interact with elements of the content or with other users.

Internet Corporation for Assigned Names and Numbers (ICANN, icann.org): A nonprofit organization charged with managing the internet's Domain Name System, including website domain names and Internet Protocol (IP) addressing.

InterTubes: Snarky substitute for the internet.

Inverted pyramid: A style of writing reports that presents the basic facts, the story's importance, details, and possibly additional background, context, and analysis.

IP address: There are two IP address systems, IPv4 and IPv6, with four and six identification groups respectively. In IPv4, the first two numbers designate the network, including the country and the second two numbers designate the host. Although IP addresses will provide an indication of the location of the website or computer location – a region or a country – it does not match precise geographical locations, except in very general ways. Moreover, users may log in remotely from entirely different locations.

IRL: An acronym for In the Real World, not the virtual world on the internet.

ISO: Stands for International Standards Organization. The ISO rating of film stock indicates the sensitivity of that film to light. In digital cameras, ISO settings determine the sensitivity of light on the camera's sensors.

JavaScript: On the web, a programming language embedded within an HTML web page that instructs the user's computer to carry out actions. Thus, it is called a client-side scripting language. An example would be to convert a currency or measurement.

JPEG (Joint Photographic Experts Group): This group is the international committee which developed standards for compressing photographs and pictures to reduce their file size. The JPEG standard permits varying levels of compression, from low to high levels. High levels of compression entail throwing away much of the data, called "lossy" compression, that results in low resolution and the presence of artifacts.

KPIs (Key Performance Indicators): In businesses, measurement of success is important. KPIs differ from one activity to another. For stories, KPIs often include the number of clicks on the headline, time spent on story pages and media, and click-throughs to advertising.

Labeling: In journalism, the description assigned to a piece of news content, that may include such information as the subject, the location, the creator, or the copyright holder. Content management systems may also use the term "tagging," instead of labeling.

Ladder of abstraction: A way to conceptualize how an individual person, place, or thing fits into the ever-broader categories in which it has a place. For example, boxes are part of a larger category of containers. (Containers also include cans, bottles, bags, etc.).

Lavalier, lav microphone: A "lav," or "lapel" mic is small enough to clip onto shirt collars, jackets, or dresses. A cord from the lav mic attaches to the small transmitter worn on a belt loop, waistband, or hidden behind an ear or under clothing.

Lead: A source or piece of information that, if investigated, could add something important to a story.

Lede: The first sentence, few sentences, or paragraph of a news report that provides the important elements readers will need to understand the story. Ledes generally include most or all of 5W1H – who, what, where, when, why, and how.

LexisNexis: A commercial database of articles from academic and professional journals, newspapers, and magazines. Lexis covers legal cases, opinions, and law-related articles.

Licensing: The process by which the licensee gets use of copyrighted intellectual property from the owner or licensor.

Lifestyle: A set of variables that may usefully separate a population into more homogenous segments. While these variables include demographics, they also include geographic data; behavioral information (how persons spend time, interests, hobbies); and personal attitudes, values, and beliefs.

Linear-embedded design: An article design to accommodate a narrative told by relating a sequence of chronological events. The design is likely to have: 1) an introduction, 2) a focus on key events, ordered to move the story forward, and 3) the use of multimedia assets to add additional information and a deeper experience to the story.

Liquid modernity: Zygmunt Bauman's social theory that describes the uncertainty and the precariousness of contemporary life. Liquid modernity exists in "a society in which the conditions under which its members act change faster than it takes the ways of acting to consolidate into habits and routines."

Live Streaming: Contrasted with downloading digital files, live streaming sends the file over a network bit-by-bit. With downloading, receivers can access files after their download; with live streaming, receivers may access files as they come to each user's computer, while the sender is still transmitting.

Lulz: To do something on the internet for laughs (troll someone, for example). The term comes from "laugh out loud," or LOL, made plural with lolz, sometimes expressed as lulz.

Luminance: Scientific term to describe the amount of light emitted or reflected from a surface.

M2M: Abbreviation of Many-to-Many: communication that flows from many people to many other people, as typified by social media.

Macro story: The context and background of a news story, as well as information related it.

Manosphere: Sites, blogs, and forums whose male members are vocal anti-feminist, sometimes anti-female, and who support coordinated campaigns to promote extreme views.

GLOSSARY

389

Medium, media: These terms have multiple meanings. In mass communications, media refers to distribution platforms: newspapers, magazines, books, films, music, television, and radio, and now the internet. Another definition of "medium" defines it as a material that carries information. For example, artists may use paint or glass as mediums; videotape is a medium; and a hard drive is a medium.

Meme: An informational element at the most basic level. The underlying concept is that of a gene to genetics – the biological element that carries the signature for replication. Similarly, a meme carries a signature to replicate an entire message, perspective, or attitude.

Metadata: Data that describes other data, providing information about digital content. Software, users, and applications all provide possible sources of metadata.

Methodical triangulation: A verification method that requires reporters to corroborate information with multiple types of evidence, such as data or documents that confirm a source's account, or a weather report that corresponds to the weather shown in a photo.

Metrics: Measurements of audience-level user engagement with online content, such as the number of page views a story receives, the number of unique visitors to a site, and the amount of time spent with a piece of content. Observable individual-level measures of user engagement include behaviors such as clicking-through, liking, recommending, tweeting, sharing content via email, social media or other digital applications, and embedding content in another site, perhaps personal websites or blogs.

Micro story: The individual components of a story: facts, actors, actions, causes, consequences, and outcomes.

Microphone: A device that translates sound signals into electrical pulses.

Mindmap: A visual way of representing ideas, starting with central ideas, often branched to linked topics that follow from them.

Mining data: Analyzing data for usable information.

Mirror: Choosing a photograph (or other asset) to accompany copy that presents the same information as the text. The opposite, complementing, uses pictures to add new information that goes beyond the copy.

Mixer: Takes in analog or digital sound signals from multiple sources (channels) and allows users to combine them into a single output. A mixer allows users to assign each channel its own volume level, so that sound levels may vary (raise violins, lower drums, for example).

Mobile first: A model for digital page design that specifies first creating a page for the small, vertical mobile phone screen, then creating alternative pages for progressively larger screens by adding content elements.

Mockup: A graphic design tool, a mockup is a carefully drawn model of an article layout.

Mojo: An abbreviated descriptive word for a "mobile journalist."

Money shot: The crucial or climactic moment in a film: Lightning strikes a tree, rain pours, wind batters the tree. The tree falls over – that's the money shot. (Google the term to learn its history.)

Monopod: A camera support on a single leg or pole.

Montage: An edited series of related shots.

Multimedia: Digital content that a computer or media player displays; multimedia can include text, photos and illustrations, video, audio, links, interactive graphics, and data visualizations.

NARA: National Archive & Records Administration is the official records-keeper of the United States. It retains 3 to 5 percent of the material produced by the government every year. NARA tries to keep everything of legislative, social, and historical value – it's worth spending an hour or two looking at the alphabetical list of resources.

Narrative: The way a storyteller unfolds a story. Stories are chronological; narratives may take events out of sequence and present them in non-chronological order.

Narrative structure: Known ways of unfolding stories to audiences. Online, it means how the narrative unfolds on web pages, through copy, multimedia, interactives, including links, and navigation.

Narrative structure objects: Refers to elements of the story that change depending on the narrative structure of the article, such as the specific objects to display sections, pages, headlines and decks, pull quotes, and picture thumbnails.

Native advertising: Ads that look almost like news stories on the site – a deliberate, designed similarity. Native ads have headlines, images, and copy. They link to the "article" from the front page or section front page news grid. Advertising copywriters or promotional writers prepare them for sales or promotional purposes.

Native online video: Video clips made for the web, as opposed to video made for other media, repurposed as-is to post to the web.

Natural settings: Allow observations of people in their own environments, where they can act as they usually do.

Navigation, navigational elements: Provides ways for users to find different sections and pages on websites. Designers embed buttons, menus, icons, arrows, and small thumbnail graphics. They may place explanatory text next to these elements or have text appear when users hover their cursors over a navigational element.

Net Neutrality: A regulatory rule that requires all information that travels across the internet to be treated equally. Net Neutrality ensures that internet traffic from media companies, other corporations, and the government does not dominate traffic from less influential users over the Net. The Trump administration abolished Net Neutrality in 2018.

Network SS-7 Exploit: Provides a way for telephone networks to exchange information about subscribers so they can contact one another on different company's infrastructure. This information exchange leads to many security vulnerabilities to hackers, who use the data to: 1) identify mobile phone subscribers, 2) access their information and their phones, and 3) track and record them. It is also possible to take over the phone microphone and storage remotely to "hot mic" the mobile phone user so that the device will record audio from the user's environment.

News feature story: A type of feature story, based on a current news topic. News features often cover the human side of a hard news article.

News Markup Language (NewsML): Web-friendly XML-based format specifically to facilitate the exchange of news content. It standardizes content formatting to distribute it across multiple systems and languages by prescribing the formatting and tagging of news content.

GLOSSARY

391

News value: A story has greater news value to the extent that it: is timely, affects many people, is close to the audience, involves prominent people, includes conflict, and is unusual or weird.

Noise: Noise is an unwanted sound, such as hiss, static, clicks, and environmental sounds like dogs barking. Analog audio equipment produces more noise than digital recordings, but noise also results from errors introduced when converting analog audio signals into digital data.

Noise reduction (NR): In audio, the process of removing extraneous sounds from a clip. Common sources of noise include air conditioning, traffic, and nearby unrelated conversations.

Nonlinear structure: A non-linear narrative structure presents the elements of the article in a grid or list and lets users choose how they navigate through them. Sometimes called the "Christmas Tree" structure, this format engages users by exposing them to the potential riches that are merely a click away, such as copy, multimedia, interactives, or some combination of elements.

Nonparticipant observation: Occurs when a person who is not involved with the naturally occurring ongoing activities carries out the observation. The person's role is limited to that of an observer.

Nonstructured observation: Occurs when an observer steps into the situation with little or no prior planning.

Normalization: In audio, a technique to raise sounds that are too low and lower sounds that are too loud.

Not for attribution: The journalist can use the information but must attribute it to a mutually agreed upon, unspecified source, e.g., "a source close to the investigation," or "a high-level administration staffer," precisely as called for by the agreement with the source.

Novelty: The property of being new, unusual, or weird.

Nut graf: The paragraph that follows the lede, explaining why users should read the story and why it's important.

Objective observation: Occurs when the observations focus on the activities, persons, or processes themselves, as seen from the outside.

Observation (perceiving): The act or instance of actively noticing or perceiving, regarding attentively, or watching something.

Observations (data): Data points related to a specific subject or case in a data set.

Off the record: The reporter can't use the information *at all* unless another source provides it on the record.

Official source: A source who has access to information in an official capacity, such as a governmental or organizational spokesperson. This person's competence as a source is limited to their field of activity. Sometimes shortened to **spox**.

Omnidirectional microphone: A mic that has a 360° audio pickup pattern.

On background: The reporter can use the information to find out more about the story. The reporter can write and publish the information. However, the original source must remain hidden and attribution given to someone who states the information on the record.

On deep background: The reporter can use the information but not publish it unless they write it on their own or find an on-the-record source. The reporter writes it on his or her own or finds an on the record source.

On the record: The reporter can write anything said and attribute it to the source, without restriction.

One-way dissemination: In media distribution, a means of communication that broadcasts messages to audiences but does not accommodate direct feedback from those audiences.

Open source software: The creators of open source computer software make the source code that underlies its operation available to all. The code typically comes with a license from the copyright owner, allowing others the rights to use, change, and distribute the software.

Operating system (OS): The software inside a computer that governs how it processes information. The MacOS, Windows, and Linux are the three major computer OSs in use today. Hand-held computers called mobile phones use Android or iOS for their OS.

Operational security (opsec): Actions taken by a person, group, or organization to keep others from gathering non-public personal and professional information about them, including attempts by private and governmental actors.

Othersideism: A rhetorical strategy to force people to be on one side of an issue or another. For example: Statement 1: "I voted for Trump because I thought we needed change, even though I didn't agree with his links to white supremacy." Statement 2: "Even so, you must be a racist."

Output: Envisioning newsrooms as systems, newsrooms output news content in the form of articles, pages, and content packages.

Overlap: In audio, when two or more people speak at once and their statements overlap one another, making it difficult to hear any person's statement.

PACER: The PACER system (Public Access to Court Electronic Records) provides the public with access to judicial system records and documents

Package, packaging: Newsrooms build a digital package for each story that includes every element of the article – assets, functions, apps, and back-end data. It requires a precise sequence of steps to assemble and format an online article that will flow through multiple networks and servers.

Paralinguistic cues: Nonverbal cues that accompany and modify verbal statements. These might include raised eyebrows, rolling eyes, snorting, coughing, groaning, shrugging the shoulders, waving the hands. They offer the observer ways to interpret verbal utterances.

Participant observation: A method of learning about people enmeshed within their social environments. Participant-observers are not individuals on the sidelines; rather, observers participate in events as they occur, as well as observe the actions of others. As part of this process, participant-observers observe themselves and their own reactions, the behaviors and communications from other people, and the group's social dynamics.

Participatory affordance: Enables users to participate online, acting to "like," comment, share, remix media, and publish their own digital content. Many news sites incorporate these kinds of participatory affordance. Participation includes interactions between human users, as well as human-computer interactions, in which both human users *and* computers are agents. Either agent can initiate exchanges and send messages that *respond* (interactively) to the other's communication.

GLOSSARY

Participatory journalism: News stories that originate entirely or partially from members of the public depend on participatory journalism.

Peg, news peg: A current news story. Journalists use current news stories to pitch other related stories, hanging it on the "peg" of the current story.

Personal brand: A cultivated reputation to make a person known in a specific way to others beyond their immediate circle of family, friends, and colleagues.

Personalized advertising: Tailoring ads to a unique individual user – sometimes the user's name appears in the ad. In 2016, mass customized ads that draw on characteristics of audience segments appeared more often than did personalized ads, although the industry trended toward more ad personalization. The European Union General Data Protection Regulation (GDPR) and California Consumer Privacy Act (CCPA) may reverse this trend because of their restrictions on user information.

Photo gallery: A section to feature photos or videos. Galleries can be slide shows, carousels, or employ other designed presentation formats.

Pickup patterns: Microphones pick up audio in diverse ways, depending on their design. Omni mics have 360° pickup patterns. A shotgun mic picks up sounds from the narrow direction that it points. Cardioid pattern mics pick up sounds from in front of and from behind the mic. Supercardioids pick up sounds from several points around the mic.

Plosive: The sounds of t, k, p, d, g, and b are plosives. They occur when a person stops the airflow through her mouth, blocking the air by the lips, teeth, or palate … followed by a release of the air. In audio recordings, these releases are noticeable unless a *pop filter* covers the microphone grill.

Precariat: A social class existing under insecure work and living conditions, specifically applied to the lack of job security for individuals in today's modern labor market.

Pre-processing, pre-processing workflow: To organize and ready materials, machines, tools, and raw multimedia assets before creating, editing, and designing them for publication.

Press release: A structured notice to news organizations about a newsworthy event. If the purpose is to draw attendees prior to the event, a series of press releases may preview the event to get publicity and coverage for it. Post-event press releases draw attention to bring credit or public interest to people, places, and organizations.

Procedural affordance: The ability of digital machines to respond flexibly to users' input: Based on what the user requests, the computer sorts through a database of possibilities, returns a set of responses from a database, and displays the requested content. Actions based on the procedural affordance include: simulations, interactive data visualizations, search engines, image and music identification services, and games.

Processing memo: A memo that lays out a quick sketch of an article, its importance, and its audience to obtain the resources needed to prepare multimedia assets for publication.

Processing plan: The details of required steps to prepare multimedia assets for publication, including processes, workers' time, machines, software tools, and vendor services.

Programmatic advertising: Describes a method for buying and locating ads automatically. Programmatic advertising automates ad price, placement, and ad construction on the fly with all elements, such as copy, art, and links, and billing.

Prominence: Refers to the high status, celebrity, or widely recognized person within a social arena.

Promotion: Audience building activities. Journalists promote their stories by posting headlines and brief descriptions on social media and blog sites. Writing promotions (or promos) includes a tease that raises interest, a proposition that tells the users what they will get from the article, and a call to action that tells them how to access the story – usually via a link.

Proposition: In promotional writing, a proposition tells the user why the story will fulfill her personal or social needs.

Protess Method of Verification: A verification method that arranges information into a hierarchy of information, placing gathered information into three concentric circles: inner, middle and outer. The inner circle consists of information that comes from the direct observation or knowledge of a participant or witness. The middle circle includes primary source documents, such as after-incident police reports, official records, testimony, transcripts, etc. The outer circle consists of secondary sources, including press accounts.

Protocol: Protocols are formal sets of standard procedures that, if followed, will result in the achievement of specific desired outcomes. Online, a protocol defines how computers can communicate with each other in a network environment. A communication protocol includes: 1) rules and their syntax, 2) the semantics of data, 3) synchronization procedures to "link up," and 4) methods to identify and fix errors.

Provenance: In journalism, the digital history of a story element, such as who originally created a digital object (photo, video, audio, etc.), who uploaded it, when that individual uploaded it, and the conditions under which it was created and uploaded.

Proximity: Nearness or closeness.

Public domain: Intellectual property, including writings that are not protected by copyright, that anyone can copy, quote, and republish.

Publication structural, design, and navigational objects: Pre-designed assets, such as logos, buttons, arrows, separators, and other frequently-used digital objects, that the news site's publication manual specifies for use with all sections, pages, and articles.

Pull-back, zoom out: In film or video, an in-camera move when a zoom lens moves from a closer shot to a wider one. For example, a shot begins by focusing on the front door and then pulls back to reveal the entire house.

Punch lede: A lede that grabs attention by making an outrageous, unusual, or shocking statement.

Qualifiers: Words that modify the meaning of another word, indicating how the person receiving the message should take it. For example, "That act was illegal." versus "That act was quite illegal," or "That act may have been illegal."

Qualitative data: Qualitative data are typically descriptive, such as interviews, observations, characterizations of feelings, settings or environments, and recounting of personal experience.

Quantitative data: Quantitative data are numerical. Some measurement processes result in numbers that can be treated mathematically. Examples include the number of tennis players on a court, the length of a pair of slacks, the price of a gallon of gas, or the average price of chicken breasts in New York last month. Surveys of individuals or organizations that capture beliefs, values, or experiences with numerical measurements yield quantitative data.

GLOSSARY

Quote lede: Starting a story with a quote.

Rack focus: In film or video, an in-camera move when a shot begins out of focus and blurry and then resolves so that the shot's subject is sharp and clear – in focus.

Real estate: The amount of space on a screen or a page.

Receipts: A slang term for documents and evidence to bolster factual claims in a story, such as copies of official records, photographs, videos, and internet network or server records. For example: "He had two other passports – I've got the receipts from the court filing."

Reconstruction: The process of putting related facts and story assets together into clusters and then ordering them into a narrative.

Reliability (data): In research data measurement, reliability means that measurement consistently yields the same sets of values when measuring the same entities. For example, when measuring crime rates – the same behaviors "count" as crimes over time, across geographic boundaries, and demographic differences. Crimes must be tabulated and reported in consistent manners for crime databases to be reliable.

Reliability (human sources): A source who provides consistently accurate information over time in multiple instances is reliable.

Remote observation: Involves observing at a distance through the "eyes" and "ears" of a technology – satellite, surveillance camera, and/or internet stream.

Render: When editing multimedia objects, many software programs save the instruction set, the edits. The last part of the editing process is to "render" or "render out" the file, means to produce a version of the edited object as a new picture, audio, or video. Saving the object in these programs usually means saving the instruction set, rather than the media itself.

Report: A fact-based news article, usually written following the inverted pyramid format.

Resolution: The end of a story, when difficulties and conflicts reach a conclusion.

Resource ID: A website URL identifies a unique location on the internet. A URL has four parts: 1) the protocol (https://), 2) the server name, 3) the top-level domain (TLD - .com, .org, .gov., etc.), and 4) the resource ID. The resource ID is a specific page or document on a website, usually composed of a collection of pages and resources.

Responsive design: Detects the size of a display (screen) and adapts the content to fit the size, shape, and orientation of that display. Responsive design enables content presentation on large screen TVs, mobile phones, and all the screens in-between. (Sometimes called **RWD**, standing for responsive/adaptive web design).

Retweet: Resend someone else's tweet to followers.

Rights Clearance: Obtaining permission from legal copyright holders to use and distribute their original material, as expressed in specific terms and conditions.

Rising action: In a story, rising action refers to the protagonist's struggle against the obstacles and barriers in striving to achieve a goal or fulfill a dream. At each step in the struggle, the stakes get higher and more serious until the goal is reached – or not. "Rising action" refers to the ever-higher stakes as the conflict continues.

Roundup story: A story that brings users up-to-date on a story that has multiple aspects, events, or facts that have emerged over time.

Routine: A regularly performed sequence of actions that people enact to handle known tasks.

Ruby on Rails: Ruby is a general-purpose programming language. Rails is an application format. Ruby on Rails is a web application framework that uses the Ruby language to implement web apps.

Rule of thirds: In photography, cinema, and video, the rule of thirds provides guidance for framing shots. Imagine a tic-tac-toe grid superimposed over a picture so that it divides the picture into three equal horizontal parts and three equal vertical parts. The rule of thirds favors putting the main subject of the shot off-center to create more dynamic and interesting pictures.

Running story: An ongoing story that continues to evolve as it is published in multiple reports.

Samplers: A user segment, samplers skim a bit of a story to see if they want to go further, quickly abandoning stories that don't interest them.

Saturation: In picture and video editing, the intensity of the colors.

Scanners: A user segment, scanners check out headlines before clicking on a story.

Scenic narrative: A narrative in which the story unfolds through a sequence of scenes. Each scene provides one building block in the overall narrative structure.

Scoop: Getting an exclusive story first, before any other journalist or publication.

Scrape data: To take data from an existing website, either by hand – cutting/pasting or capturing – or through automated scraping software to compile it into a searchable and analyzable dataset.

Scraped: Refers to material (often video footage) uploaded to the internet by one user, that is then "scraped" from the site and re-uploaded to another site by a second user, often without crediting the original uploader.

S-curve of adoption, S-curve: Introduced by scholar Everett Rogers, the S-curve shows the rate of adoption of an innovation. Adoption of something new starts slowly. If successful, an exponentially rising curve reflects the growing number of adopters. The curve levels-off as most people who want to adopt – have adopted.

Search Results Pages (SRPs): Many sites provide an SRP column or utility on their home pages that lets users skim a list for stories that interest them.

Sections: Online publications feature pages devoted to special interests within the news site. For example, the talkingpointsmemo.com website that covers politics has "Editor's Blog," "Livewire," "News," and "Prime" (for paying subscribers).

Segmented pages: Web or mobile pages that are divided into sections. Most news sites use segmented home pages, such as CNN.com, buzzfeed.com, vox.com, and huffpost. com. Usually segments have a headline, a thumbnail image of the story's subject, and a short text block. Some sites group related stories into named sections, such as "Metro" or "Politics" or other categories of articles that interest subscribers and users of the news website. Designers use segmented pages less frequently for mobile page design because of their smaller screens.

Server: A computer optimized for disseminating digital content; i.e., sending out (or serving) content upon request.

GLOSSARY

Server Name: In a website URL, the server name identifies a unique location on the internet: apple.com, mit.edu, and justice.gov. The first part of the server name is just that – the name of the server. The second part of the server name indicates the type of organization that operates the server, called the domain name (.com, .org, .gov., etc.).

Shill: A person who expresses strong approval toward a product, cause, or another person, but fails to disclose a close tie to the object of approval; frequently found in gambling venues, auctions, online reviews, and social network platforms.

Shoe-leather journalism: Reporting the old-fashioned way, searching for information and witnesses by going to places in person, such as visiting centers of original or official documents, and knocking on doors to talk to people in person.

Shoot: To take a shot. As a noun, a "shoot" takes place to capture still photographs or video footage.

Shooting script: A script with scenes in the order they will be shot – as opposed to the linear narrative order. For documentary films and news packages, the shooting script will list the times, locations, correspondent and participating crew members, names of interviewees, and brief descriptions of the shots that journalists hope to capture.

Shot, shot list: A shot begins when the camera rolls and records and ends when the camera and recording stop. The shot is the basic building block for edited films or videos. Editing places one shot after another to tell a story.

Shotgun microphone: A microphone that picks up sounds from a narrow area in front of the mic.

Shutter speed: A camera setting that regulates how fast the shutter opens to allow light to enter the lens and then reach the sensors or the film.

Smartphone: Not all mobile phones are smartphones. Smartphones are essentially multi-purpose portable computing devices. They differ from basic cell phones by employing far more sophisticated chipsets and operating systems that enable complex software, and internet, and multimedia functionalities.

SNS, SNSs: Social Network Service; Social Network Services.

Social curation: Services such as www.storify.com allow users to piece together posts from multiple users and social media networks (SNSs).

Social networking site (SNS): User-generated content sites such as Facebook, Twitter, Instagram, Snapchat, Reddit, YouTube, Weibo, and others. These sites allow user commenting, content sharing, and other services.

Soft news: Refers to articles that do not address news events per se. Soft news may be just for entertainment, such as celebrity happenings, humor, essays, and so forth. Articles may have useful information about personal matters – beauty, fashion, health, décor, cooking, and similar topics. Or they may use human-interest stories to illustrate the important social issues of the day.

Sound bite: A clip from a larger audio file or from the audio track of a video file.

Sound-proofed: A space or room protected from both external and internal noise. Sealed doors, electrical outlets, window frames, and ventilation grates all protect against sounds from outside. Sound-absorbing materials should cover walls, floor, and ceiling to insulate against unwanted sounds and prevent echoes within the sound-proofed space.

Sources: Information obtained from some source, such as documents and records, data, media, and human actors involved in a situation or event.

Spatial affordance: Computers, like other visual media (film and television) have spatial dimensions. Three aspects of this affordance reside in the ways digital environments suggest "place," e.g., home, menus, windows, docks, and the like. Additionally, the screen is a physical area that requires organizational and graphic design. Finally, computer networks feature strong spatial ties and linkages: users "surf the Net," "visit" web sites, and "leave" social network messages for other visitors.

Spec: On spec means working for free in the hopes a publication will like the work and pay the person who submitted the material "on spec." Short for "speculation."

Spox: A shortened term for spokesperson, spokesman, or spokeswoman.

Spreadable media: Content that people want to share with others, a term coined by new media theorist Henry Jenkins. **Spreadability** refers to content that users want to share with others and the extent to which users can spread all or part of a piece of content to other people and places on digital networks. Some factors that encourage sharing include: share buttons, extractability from site, length, file size, topic, and humor.

sRGB: The default color space for pictures on the web. Most pictures do not have a metadata that specifies a color space, so sites will display pictures in sRGB.

Static banners: Ads, usually located across the top of the page. Static means the ads are unchanging so all users visiting the page see the same ad.

Step on: An audio overlap. In recording audio, when one person talks over another, they "step on" the other person's audio.

Sting or stinger: In audio, a few notes of music used at the end of an audio news story. Stings are used occasionally to denote section starts and finishes.

Story: In journalism, there are two meanings for "story": 1) Any news article, 2) A chronological sequence of actions or events that has a beginning, middle, and an end.

Storyboard: A sequence of quick drawings, with directions and dialog or copy, representing the shots or pages planned for content – in movies, TV, or news articles, using paper-based or digital media.

Streaming: Transmitting a file bit-by-bit over the internet. Users receive the file bit-by-bit as well, enabling them to view events live – in real time. For stored files, users can watch right away, instead of waiting to download the whole file. A **Streaming API** is an application that delivers a continuous stream, including video and audio. These apps work mostly in one direction, although player/receivers may allow the connection to deliver real-time comments from users that display in the player.

Stringer: Journalists who are not on staff with a news organization, but contribute stories and content, usually retained on a part-time basis to report on events in a place, region, or topic.

Stripped: Refers to a photograph in which the metadata has been removed.

Structural metadata: Basic information about a photograph or video that describes how it has been captured and stored. This metadata contains instructions to the decoding computer or machine how to reconstitute and display the photo or video content.

Structured observation: An observational condition that requires planning. Prior agreements specify some or all of the conditions of observation, such as time, place, periodicity, activity, format, etc.

GLOSSARY

Subjective observation: Subjective observations focus on the internal responses of the observer to the activity.

Sweetening: In audio, to carry out a set of processes that modify an audio clip to improve its clarity and fidelity to the original sound.

Systems theory: Systems comprise interrelated elements *and* processes that interact to achieve systems' goals. All systems change dynamically. Systems exist within environments – systems both change and are changed by their environments. Systems processes depend on external systems "drivers," internal control mechanisms, and environmental feedback loops.

Tease: In promotional writing, "tease" refers to statements or phrases that raise interest by appealing to curiosity, increased social status, admission to a circle of knowledge, etc.

Thread: Multiple serial posts to Twitter.com, intended to extend remarks past the 140-character limit, often indicated by 1/3, 2/3, 3/3, etc. at the beginning or end of posts.

Throughput: Throughput refers to how dynamic systems take in something from the environment, change it, and then move it out into an environment. Envisioning newsrooms as systems, newsrooms **input** many different forms of information and process it to create or recreate diverse forms of news content for **output.**

Ticktock: A story based on a chronology of events, usually a step-by-step account of how an event or phenomenon developed over time. Such articles often include visual timelines to summarize the chronology.

Timeline or chronology: A way to represent events and actions in the time order that they occurred.

Timeliness: New or especially relevant to current conditions.

Tool identification: Identifying the version of software that was used to edit a file and when these edits occurred.

Top-level domain name (TLD name): There are several kinds of top-level domain names. The most familiar ones identify the kind of organization that operates the website: .com, .org, .edu, .gov, etc. The country code TLD (ccTLD) is also common, an internationally-recognized two-letter extension that identifies the country where the website is registered.

TPFKATA: The People Formerly Known As The Audience, a term coined by journalist and educator, Jay Rosen. It refers to active users in today's digital world, who are *not* the same as the passive recipients of media in the broadcast era: They actively participate in creating and distributing content.

Track: In audio or video, a channel for specific information: right or left channel audio, the video portion of an audio/video signal.

Transcode: To convert and save a coded file into another coding system or file format. A common procedure for all types of content – documents, audio, video, data, and other material. An example is transcoding a .wav file to an .mp3 file. Examples include: myassign1.docx (a Word file), gramrules.pdf (an Adobe file), quicklunch.jpg (a picture file), or grandcanyon.mov (a video file).

Transcribe: In audio, to write spoken words into written words – as occurs when creating transcripts of recorded interviews.

Transition: Places in an article that move the user's focus from one idea to another. A transition may be a sentence, paragraph, heading or subheading, or section.

Transportation: The ability of a story to enable users to experience it, as though on a journey, "transporting" them into the world of the article.

Trial balloon: A plan or idea that a source wants to "float" in public to see "which way the wind blows," or to get a read on the possible reactions of key stakeholders.

Triangulation: Using two points in space to locate a third unknown point. Developed by ancient Greek sailors, in journalism the term means to verify information by confirming it from different sources and different kinds of sources (methodological triangulation).

Tripod: A three-legged camera support.

Troll: Internet slang term referring to individuals who deliberately create discord and dismay by posting inflammatory comments or messages on websites, blogs and/or social media. Trolls use insults, snark, lies, name calling, bullying and other unpleasant behaviors to intimidate or enrage other users.

Truth: The actual state of things, as supported by facts.

TV news package: "Package" is the term for video stories in television news.

Twits: Derogatory term for people who read or post comments to Twitter.com.

Twitter, tweet, tweetstorm: Twitter is a social network service (SNS), which limits posts to 280 characters and spaces. (When Twitter started, posts were limited to 140 characters and spaces.) Each comment is called a *tweet*. A tweetstorm occurs when a person sends out multiple tweets, usually to rant or vent about a deeply-held conviction.

Uncontrolled behavior: Occurs when people can choose how to act for themselves. They may control their own behaviors to adjust to the demands of a given environment, adapting and taking familiar roles. However, they are not controlled by others.

Uniform Resource Locator (URL): A Uniform Resource Locator operates as an address for a website, webpage, and other resources on the internet.

Upcuts: In audio, making a cut when the person hasn't ended the phrase or sentence so that the voice goes up instead of resting down, as it usually does. Upcuts sound like a quote ended prematurely.

User Distributed Content (UDC): News articles forwarded by users who share (distribute) the material to social networks of their friends, family, co-workers, and followers. News organizations encourage UDC because it expands the reach of an article.

User engagement: The extent to which users spend time and interact with the content and activities on a website. Metrics of user engagement for news sites vary from one publication to another, but include: dwell time on the site, article, or page – plus story clickthroughs, ad click-throughs, number of likes, shares, and comments, session duration, return visits, and so forth. "Bounce rate" measures when users leave the site or a page immediately after clicking on it – a metric that captures lack of user engagement.

User experience (UX): The user experience or UX, is a design framework that structures how users experience a story, interactive opportunity, web page, or entire website.

User interface (UI): The UI provides users ways to navigate and use website features.

User-generated content (UGC): Internet content created by users as persons, rather than by professional content creators, such as employees of news, entertainment, and other media companies. Material not published by a branded publishing entity.

User-generated video (UGV): Videos produced by users, often posted to YouTube and other social media sites.

GLOSSARY

UX designer: User designer, UX is short for user experience.

Validity, valid: Valid information accurately represents the underlying phenomenon it portrays. **Validity** is an essential criterion for data-based facts. **Valid** datasets accurately reflect the underlying (quantified) phenomenon that researchers claim to measure. Validity requires: 1) appropriate, 2) consistent (reliable), and 3) accurate measurement of the reality researchers purport to represent.

Values: Personal values reflect what someone holds as important and worthy. Values include "doing the right thing," good character, honesty, accountability, creativity, winning, etc.

Variable: Something that changes – something that varies. In data, variables refer to phenomena that can take on different values. For example, measurements of the weather temperature might be: 1 = very cold; 2 = cold; 3 = cool; 4 = mild; 5 = warm; 6 = hot; 7 = very hot. Alternatively, measurement in Fahrenheit or Celsius provides greater discrimination among degrees of hot and cold.

Verification: To identify corroborating evidence for factual claims. Most newsrooms require two confirmations; in exceptional circumstances, editors and company lawyers may demand more. On the record confirmations matter more than the ones off the record. Similarly, identified sources are stronger than anonymous ones, which require more rigorous confirmation.

Vet, vetting: To check and verify people, places, and information.

Viability: The ability of an entity to survive. To say an enterprise is viable, means that its environmental conditions are such that an entity should survive.

Vignetting: In photography, when the aperture is wider than the barrel of the lens, the corners of the photograph darken, while the center circle (of the lens) remains light.

Virtual Reality (VR): A $360°$ computer simulation of a 3D visual environment (height, width, depth). Requires goggles to see and gloves with embedded sensors to virtually "touch" and move objects in the VR environment.

Voiceover (voice track): An audio recording of a reporter or correspondent that carries the narrative of an audio or video story.

Web first: Newsroom production process where journalists prepare the first version of an article for the news website.

Web production system: Another name for a content management system (CMS).

Web-centric: An application, system, or organization that is designed specifically for the internet.

Whataboutism: A rhetorical device used to defend an action by citing a similar or worse action by another person or organization. For example: Statement 1 – "Donald Trump cheated workers out of money he owed them." Statement 2 – "What about Hillary Clinton's emails?"

Whistleblower: A person who has reached the conclusion that he or she must tell the truth to a journalist to stop a practice they condemn. They may or not come forward. When whistleblowers do initiate contact, it is often a matter of conscience, even if it puts them in personal or professional jeopardy. In many cases, whistleblowers have compiled documents and other evidence that they consider proof of others' wrongdoing.

Who, what, where, when, why, how (5W1H): The most important facts of stories that reporters identify, explain, corroborate, and verify to the maximum extent possible.

Whois, whois lookup: An online service that allows users to find publicly available information about websites.

Wide shot: A shot that captures the objects of interest in a scene, including their environmental context.

Wiki: A user-written and edited site, usually about a specific topic, intended for a particular audience. For example, LyricWiki.com lets users search for lyrics to songs; Rangjung Yeshe Wiki covers Himalayan Buddhism, and WikiEM provides a reference for emergency medicine.

Wild sound: Audio recording of only ambient or environmental sounds, used in audio editing to make the background sound consistent.

Wire service: News services that disseminate feeds to news organizations. Prominent wire services are the *Associated Press*, *Reuters*, and *Agence Presse France*.

Wireframe: A wireframe is a blueprint for the design of a website, page, or article. Sometimes called page schematic or screen blueprint, wireframes arrange the story elements on a page to make clear how to assemble the content, ease users' navigation, and foster pleasing and engaging user experiences.

Workflow: A sequence of steps that, taken in order, lead to completed work.

XLR: A professional audio connector which is more secure and quiet than other types of audio cable connectors.

XMP metadata (Extensible Metadata Platform): Adobe, the application software company, developed and promoted its own metadata format. Since many media professionals around the world use Adobe, most digital cameras record and provide XMP metadata. It is useful to journalists because it records and saves modifications to photographs and pictures.

Zoom, move-in: An in-camera move in which the lens moves, making distant objects appear closer.

Z-pattern or layout: Pages designed to allow users to scan a page by looking across the top left-to-right, then move diagonally right-to-left and down the page to the far-left side, and finally across the bottom of the page, also left-to-right.

WORKS CITED

Abernathy, P. M. (2018). *The expanding news desert: The loss of newspapers and readers*. Center for Innovation and Sustainability in Local Media. Retrieved from www.usnewsdeserts.com/reports/expanding-news-desert/loss-of-local-news/loss-newspapers-readers/

Adler, R. (2019). *Crisis in democracy: Renewing trust in America*. Knight Foundation and Aspen Institute. Retrieved from https://csreports.aspeninstitute.org/documents/Knight2019.pdf

AlNoamany, Y., Wiggle, M. C., & Nelson, M. L. (2015). Characteristics of social media stories. *International Journal of Digital Libraries*, 17(3), 239–256. doi:10.1007/s00799-016-0185-3

American Press Institute. (2014, March 17). The personal news cycle: How Americans choose to get news. *Media Insight Project*. Retrieved from www.americanpressinstitute.org/publications/reports/survey-research/personal-news-cycle

American Sociological Association. (n.d.). *Robert Ezra Park*. Retrieved from www.asanet.org/about/presidents/Robert_Park.cfm

Andersen, M. (2009, June 23). *Four crowdsourcing lessons from The Guardian's (spectacular) expenses-scandal experiment*. Nieman Lab. Retrieved from www.niemanlab.org/2009/06/four-crowdsourcing-lessons-from-the-guardians-spectacular-expenses-scandal-experiment/

Anderson, M. (2019, June 13). *Mobile technology-and-home broadband 2019*. Pew Research Center. Retrieved from www.pewinternet.org/2019/06/13/mobile-technology-and-home-broadband-2019/

Andres, O. (2019, June 28). *What is geofencing? How does it work?* Citizen Truth. Retrieved from https://citizentruth.org/what-is-geofencing-how-does-it-work/

Archer, D., & Finger, K. (2018, March 15). *Walking in another's virtual shoes: Do 360-degree video news stories generate empathy in viewers?* Tow Center for Digital Journalism. Retrieved from www.cjr.org/tow_center_reports/virtual-reality-news-empathy.php

Ashton, K. (2013, July 16). How experts think [Web log post]. Retrieved from https://medium.com/@kevin_ashton/how-experts-think-91b443104b92

Aviles, J. A. (2014). Online newsrooms as communities of practice: Exploring digital journalists' applied ethics. *Journal of Mass Media Ethics*, 29(4), 258–272. doi:10.1080/08900523.2014.946600

Bao, B., & Mok, J. (2013, February 18). Where the jobs are. *Columbia Journalism Review*. Retrieved from www.cjr.org/data_points/between_the_spreadsheets_wnyc_jobs. php

Barthel, M. (2019, July 23). *5 key takeaways about the state of the news media in 2018*. Pew Research Center. Retrieved from www.pewresearch.org/fact-tank/2019/07/23/ key-takeaways-state-of-the-news-media-2018/

Barthel, M., Gottfried, J., & Mitchell, A. (2017, April 4). *Most say tension between Trump administration and news media hinder access to political news*. Pew Research Center. Retrieved from www.journalism.org/2017/04/04/most-say-tensions-between-trump-administration-and-news-media-hinder-access-to-political-news/

Barthel, M., & Mitchell, A. (2017, May 10). *American's attitudes about the news media deeply divided along partisan lines*. Pew Research Center. Retrieved from www. journalism.org/2017/05/10/americans-attitudes-about-the-news-media-deeply-divided-along-partisan-lines/

Barton, A., & Storm, H. (2014). *Violence and harassment against women in the news media: A global picture*. International Women's Media Foundation and International News Safety Institute. Retrieved from www.iwmf.org/wp-content/uploads/2018/06/ Violence-and-Harassment-against-Women-in-the-News-Media.pdf

Batsell, J. (2015). *Engaged journalism: Connecting with digitally empowered news audiences*. New York: Columbia University Press.

Bauman, Z. (2000). *Liquid modernity*. Cambridge, UK: Polity Press.

Bauman, Z., & Bordoni, C. (2014). *State of crisis*. Cambridge, UK: Polity Press.

BBC. (2017). *Writing for mobile: Bite-size basics*. British Broadcasting Corporation. Retrieved from www.bbc.co.uk/academy/en/articles/art20141202144618106

BBC. (2019, November 20). Prince Andrew stepping back from royal duties. *British Broadcasting Corporation*. Retrieved from www.bbc.com/news/uk-50496539

Beatty, S. (2019, April 3). Newspack chooses 12 publishers to drive the creation of the new platform [Web log post]. Retrieved from https://newspack.blog/2019/04/03/ newspack-chooses-12-publishers-new-platform/

Beckett, C. (2015, September 10). How journalism is turning emotional and what that might mean for news [Web log post]. Retrieved from https://blogs.lse.ac.uk/polis/2015/09/10/ how-journalism-is-turning-emotional-and-what-that-might-mean-for-news/

Beckett, C., & Deuze, M. (2016). On the role of emotion in the future of journalism. *Social Media + Society*. doi:10.1177/2056305116662395

Bell, D. (1973). *The coming of post-industrial society*. New York: Basic Books.

Bellinger, G., Castro, D., & Mills, A. (n.d.). *Data, information, knowledge, and wisdom*. Retrieved from www.systems-thinking.org/dikw/dikw.htm

Benkler, Y., Faris, R., Roberts, H., & Zuckerman, E. (2017, March 3). Breitbart-led right-wing media ecosystem altered broader media agenda. *Columbia Journalism Review*. Retrieved from www.cjr.org/analysis/breitbart-media-trump-harvard-study.php

Berret, C. (2016, May 12). *Guide to Secure Drop*. Tow Center for Digital Journalism. Retrieved from www.cjr.org/tow_center_reports/guide_to_securedrop.php

Billington, M. (1988, March 18). Stoppard's secret agent. *The Guardian*, p. 28.

WORKS CITED

405

Bolaffi, G., Bracalenti, R., Braham, P. H., & Gindro, S. (2002). *Dictionary of race, ethnicity and culture*. Thousand Oaks, CA: Sage.

Bond, S., & Bond, D. (2017, February 14). Newspapers welcome more digital subscribers in time of fake news. *Financial Times*. Retrieved from www.ft.com/content/d97bef40-f19b-11e6-8758-6876151821a6

Borchers, C. (2017, June 14). Why a shooting witness refused to talk to the media. *The Washington Post*. Retrieved from www.washingtonpost.com/news/the-fix/wp/2017/06/14/why-a-shooting-witness-refused-to-talk-to-the-media/

Boukes, M., & Boomgaarden, H. G. (2015). Soft news with hard consequences? Introducing a nuanced measure of soft versus hard news exposure and its relationship with political cynicism. *Communication Research*, 42(5), 701–731. doi:10.1177/0093650214537520

Bourne, H. R. F. (1887). *English newspapers. Chapters in the history of journalism* (Vol. 1). London: Chatto & Windus.

Box Office Mojo. (2015). *The Blair Witch Project (1999)*. Retrieved from www.boxofficemojo.com/title/tt0185937/?ref_=bo_se_r_1

boyd, D. (2011). Social networked sites as networked publics: Affordances, dynamics, and implications. In Z. Papacharissi (Ed.), *A networked self: Identity, community, and culture in social network sites* (pp. 39–58). New York: Routledge.

boyd, D., & Crawford, K. (2012). Critical questions for big data: Provocations for a cultural, technological, and scholarly phenomenon. *Communication & Society*, 15(5), 662–679. doi:10.1080/1369118X.2012.678878

Bradley, S. (2011, February 7). *3 design layouts: Gutenberg diagram, Z-pattern, and F-pattern*. Retrieved from http://vanseodesign.com/web-design/3-design-layouts/

Brandtzæg, P. B., Lüders, M., Spangenberg, J., Rath-Wiggins, L., & Følstad, A. (2016). Emerging journalistic verification practices concerning social media. *Journalism Practice*, 10(3), 323–342. doi:10.1080/17512786.2015.1020331

Brennen, B. (2009). The future of journalism. *Journalism*, 10(3), 300–302. doi:10.1177/1464884909102584

Broersma, M., & Eldridge, S. A. II. (2019). Journalism and social media: Redistribution of power? *Media and Communication*, 7(1), 193–197. doi:10.17645/mac.v7i1.2048

Brooks, B., Kennedy, G., Moen, D., & Ranley, D. (2011). *News Reporting and Writing* (10th ed.). The Missouri Group, Boston, MA: Bedford/St. Martin's.

Brown, J. K. (2018, November 28). How a future Trump cabinet member gave a serial sex abuser the deal of a lifetime. *Miami Herald*. Retrieved from www.miamiherald.com/news/local/article220097825.html

Brown, M. (2014a). Verifying video. In C. Silverman (Ed.), *Verification handbook*. Maastricht, NL: European Journalism Center. Retrieved from https://verificationhandbook.com/book/chapter5.php

Brown, M. (2014b). Case study 5.2: Investigating a reported 'massacre' in Ivory Coast. In C. Silverman (Ed.), *Verification handbook*. Maastricht, NL: European Journalism Center. Retrieved from https://verificationhandbook.com/book/chapter5.2.php

Budiu, R. (2015, April 19). Mobile user experience: Limitations and strengths [Web log post]. Retrieved from www.nngroup.com/articles/mobile-ux/

Budiu, R. (2016, February 14). Mobile websites: Mobile-dedicated, responsive, adaptive, or desktop site? [Web log post]. Retrieved from: www.nngroup.com/articles/mobile-vs-responsive/

Bunting, L., Cheung, P., Preston, J., Rundlet, K., & Swyter, N. (2018). *Predictions for 2019: A year of local collaboration*. NiemanLab. Retrieved from www.niemanlab.org/2018/12/a-year-of-local-collaboration/

Buttry, S. (2014). Verification fundamentals: Rules to live by. In C. Silverman (Ed.), *Verification handbook*. Maastricht, NL: European Journalism Center. Retrieved from https://verificationhandbook.com/book/chapter2.php

Canavan, M. (2017, February 6). 11 Questions about Android Instant Apps, instantly answered [Web log post]. Retrieved from http://info.localytics.com/blog/11-questions-about-android-instant-apps-instantly-answered

Carlo, S., & Kamphuis, A. (2016). Information security for journalists. *Centre for Investigative Journalism*. Retrieved from www.tcij.org/sites/default/files/u11/InfoSec%20for%20Journalists%20V1.3.pdf

Carlson, D. (n.d.) A capsule history of online news and information systems. *David Carlson's virtual world*. Retrieved from http://iml.jou.ufl.edu/CARLSON/1980s.shtml

Carpenter, L. (2011, July 14). Clemens case declared a mistrial. *Yahoo! Sports*. Retrieved from https://sports.yahoo.com/news/clemens-case-declared-mistrial-155100424–mlb.html

Carr, D. (2012, September 16). The puppetry of quotation approval. *The New York Times*. Retrieved from www.nytimes.com/2012/09/17/business/media/the-puppetry-of-quotation-approval.html

Castle, M., & LaTorra, J. (2018, March 30). The 8 commandments of storytelling with data [Web log post]. Retrieved from https://twooctobers.com/blog/8-data-storytelling-concepts-with-examples/

Chen, A. (2015, June 2). The agency. *The New York Times*. Retrieved from www.nytimes.com/2015/06/07/magazine/the-agency.html?_r=0

Chen, B. X. (2019, December 19). What we learned about the technology that Times journalists use. *The New York Times*. Retrieved from www.nytimes.com/2019/12/18/technology/personaltech/technology-times-journalists-use.html

Chen, V. Y., & Pain, P. (2019, September). News on Facebook: How Facebook and newspapers build mutual brand loyalty through audience engagement. *Journalism & Mass Communication Quarterly*. doi:10.1177/1077699019876634

Christin, A. (2014, August 28). *When it comes to chasing clicks, journalists say one thing but feel pressure to do another*. NiemanLab. Retrieved from www.niemanlab.org/2014/08/when-it-comes-to-chasing-clicks-journalists-say-one-thing-but-feel-pressure-to-do-another/

Chyi, H. I., & Tenenboim, O. (2016). Reality check. *Journalism Practice, 11*(7), 798–819. doi:10.1080/17512786.2016.1208056

Clement, J. (2019, October 9). *Number of apps available in leading app stores as of 3rd quarter 2019*. Statistica. Retrieved from www.statista.com/statistics/276623/number-of-apps-available-in-leading-app-stores/

WORKS CITED

Coase, R. H. (1995). *Essays on economics and economists*. Chicago, IL.: University of Chicago Press.

Coester, D. (2017, October 18). *A matter of space: Designing newsrooms for new digital practice*. American Press Institute Strategy Studies. Retrieved from www.americanpressinstitute.org/publications/reports/strategy-studies/matter-of-space/

Coleman, R. (2010). Framing the pictures in our heads. In P. D'Angelo & J. A. Kuypers (Eds.), *Doing news framing analysis: Empirical and theoretical perspectives* (pp. 233–261). New York: Routledge.

Committee to Protect Journalists. (2019a). *50 Journalists killed in 2019/motive confirmed or unconfirmed*. Retrieved from https://cpj.org/data/killed/2019/?status=Killed&type%5B%5D=Journalist&start_year=2019&end_year=2019&group_by=location

Committee to Protect Journalists. (2019b). *Digital safety kit*. Retrieved from https://cpj.org/2019/07/digital-safety-kit-journalists.php#protect

Coronel, S., Coll, S., & Kravitz, D. (2015, April). A rape on campus: What went wrong? *Rolling Stone*. Retrieved from www.rollingstone.com/culture/features/a-rape-on-campus-what-went-wrong-20150405

Costandi, M. (2013, August 15). Falsifying memories. *The Guardian*. Retrieved from www.theguardian.com/science/neurophilosophy/2013/aug/16/elizabeth-loftus-falsifying-memories

Courtland, M., Ryan, J., & Shaw, A. (2017, February 1). *The state of the blocked web: 2017 global adblock report*. PageFair. Retrieved from https://pagefair.com/downloads/2017/01/PageFair-2017-Adblock-Report.pdf

Cuillier, D. (2020, April 6). *Governments are using the coronavirus to hide information from reporters and citizens*. NiemanLab. Retrieved from www.niemanlab.org/2020/04/governments-are-using-the-coronavirus-to-hide-information-from-reporters-and-citizens/

Cushion, S., Lewis, J., & Callaghan, R. (2016). Data journalism, impartiality and statistical claims. *Journalism Practice*, *11*(10), 1198–1215. doi:10.1080/17512786.2016.1256789

Cutler, K. (2011, February 10). On Quora, journalism and disintermediation. *Quora Review*. Retrieved from http://quorareview.com/2011/02/10/quora-journalism-disintermediation/

D'Vorkin, L. (2011, November 21). Forbes update: Our strategy comes alive on a new and exciting mobile site. *Forbes*. Retrieved from www.forbes.com/sites/lewisdvorkin/2011/11/21/forbes-update-our-strategy-comes-alive-on-a-new-and-exciting-mobile-site/

Dalen, A. (2012). The algorithms behind the headlines. *Journalism Practice*, 6(5), 648–658. doi:10.1080/17512786.2012.667268

Davenport, T. H. (2014, May). 10 kinds of stories to tell with data. *Harvard Business Review*. Retrieved from https://hbr.org/2014/05/10-kinds-of-stories-to-tell-with-data

Davies, J. (2019, January 16). After GDPR, *The New York Times* cut off ad exchanges in Europe – And kept growing ad revenue. *Digiday.com*. Retrieved from: https://digiday.com/media/gumgumtest-new-york-times-gdpr-cut-off-ad-exchanges-europe-ad-revenue/

de Los Santos, T. M., & Nabi, R. L. (2019). Emotionally charged: Exploring the role of emotion in online news information seeking and processing. *Journal of Broadcasting & Electronic Media*, 63(1), 39–58. doi:10.1080/08838151.2019.1566861

de Rosa, A. (2014). Case Study 2.1: Using social media as a police scanner. In C. Silverman (Ed.), *Verification handbook*. Maastricht, NL: European Journalism Center. Retrieved from https://verificationhandbook.com/book/chapter2.1.php

Dean, W. (n.d.). *Hierarchy of information and concentric circles of sources verification*. American Press Institute. Retrieved from www.americanpressinstitute.org/journalismessentials/verification-accuracy/hierarchy-information-concentric-circles-sources/

Deloitte. (2019). *A quick reference guide for CCPA compliance*. Retrieved from www2.deloitte.com/us/en/pages/advisory/articles/ccpa-compliance-readiness.html

DeRienzo, M. (2019, December 17). Industry Insight: Why news orgs should be collaborating with student journalists. *Editor & Publisher*. Retrieved from www.editorandpublisher.com/columns/industry-insight-why-news-orgs-should-be-collaborating-with-student-journalists/

Deuze, M. (2014). Work in the media. *Media Industries Journal*, 1(2). doi:10.3998/mij.15031809.0001.201

Dewey, C. (2015, August 25). Ashley Madison faked female profiles to lure men in, hacked data suggest. *The Washington Post*. Retrieved from www.washingtonpost.com/news/the-intersect/wp/2015/08/25/ashley-madison-faked-female-profiles-to-lure-men-in-hacked-data-suggest/

Diamond, D., & Pradhan, R. (2017, October 4). How we found Tom Price's private jets. *Politico.com*. Retrieved from www.politico.com/magazine/story/2017/10/04/how-we-found-tom-prices-private-jets-215680

DiMeo, N. (2011, April 6). The memory palace. *Transom*. Retrieved from http://transom.org/2011/the-memory-palace/

Dimock, M. (2019, June 5). *An update on our research into trust, facts and democracy*. Pew Research Center. Retrieved from www.pewresearch.org/2019/06/05/an-update-on-our-research-into-trust-facts-and-democracy/

DiResta, R. (2018, October 10). Free speech in the age of algorithmic megaphones. *WiReD*. Retrieved from www.wired.com/story/facebook-domestic-disinformation-algorithmic-megaphones/#:~:targetText=As%20Americans%2C%20we%20have%20deeply,after%20a%20participatory%2C%20healthy%20debate

Doctor, K. (2015, July 28). *Newsonomics: The halving of America's daily newsrooms*. NiemanLab. Retrieved from www.niemanlab.org/2015/07/newsonomics-the-halving-of-americas-daily-newsrooms/

Doctor, K. (2016, December 19). *Newsonomics: The 2016 media year by the numbers, and a look toward 2017*. NiemanLab. Retrieved from www.niemanlab.org/2016/12/newsonomics-the-2016-media-year-by-the-numbers-and-a-look-toward-2017/

Doctor, K. (2019, August 3). Newsonomics: The "daily" part of daily newspapers is on the way out – And sooner than you might think [Web log post]. Retrieved from https://newsonomics.com/newsonomics-the-daily-part-of-daily-newspapers-is-on-the-way-out-and-sooner-than-you-might-think/

WORKS CITED

409

Dubberly, S. (2016). *A journalist's guide to copyright law and eyewitness media*. First Draft. Retrieved from https://firstdraftnews.com/copyright_handbook/

Echeverria, J., Besel, C., & Zhou, S. (2017, October). *Discovery of the Twitter Bursty botnet*. Cornell University. Retrieved from https://arxiv.org/pdf/1709.06740.pdf

Echeverria, J., & Zhou, S. (2017, June). *Discovery, retrieval, and analysis of the 'Star Wars' botnet in Twitter*. Cornell University. Retrieved from https://arxiv.org/pdf/1701.02405.pdf

Eddington, S. M. (2018). The communicative constitution of hate organizations online: A semantic network analysis of "Make America Great Again". *Social Media + Society*. doi:10.1177/2056305118790763

Edelman. (2017, January 15). *2017 Edelman trust barometer reveals global implosion of trust*. Author. Retrieved from www.edelman.com/news/2017-edelman-trust-barometer-reveals-global-implosion/

Edgerly, S., Mourão, R. R., Thorson, E., & Tham, S. M. (2019). When do audiences verify? How perceptions about message and source influence audience verification of news headlines. *Journalism & Mass Communication Quarterly*. doi:10.1177/1077699019864680

Edison Research. (2018, March 8). The infinite dial 2018 [Web log post]. Retrieved from www.edisonresearch.com/infinite-dial-2018/

Eisenberg, P. (2019, July 29). *Is mobile journalism still a thing?* [Web log post]. Retrieved from www.wochit.com/blog/is-mobile-journalism-still-a-thing/

Eisenstein, S. (1942). *The film sense*. New York: Harcourt Brace Jovanovich.

Electronic Frontier Foundation. (2019). *Hemisphere: Law enforcement's secret call records deal with AT&T*. Author. Retrieved from www.eff.org/cases/hemisphere

Elia, L. (2015, November 30). Study: How the use of data visualization impacts content engagement. *LinkedIn Pulse*. Retrieved from www.linkedin.com/pulse/study-how-use-data-visualization-impacts-content-engagement-elia/

Engler, A. (2019, November 14). *Report: Fighting deepfakes when detection fails*. Brookings Institute. Retrieved from www.brookings.edu/research/fighting-deepfakes-when-detection-fails/

Erdely, S. (2014, November). A rape on campus. *Rolling Stone*. Retrieved from web.archive.org/web/20141119200349/www.rollingstone.com/culture/features/a-rape-on-campus-20141119

Farenthold, D. (2012, January 17). SOPA protests shut down web sites. *The Washington Post*. Retrieved from www.washingtonpost.com/politics/sopa-protests-to-shut-down-web-sites/2012/01/17/gIQA4WYl6P_story.html

Farid, H. (2008, June). Digital forensics: 5 ways to spot a fake photo. *Scientific American*. Retrieved from www.scientificamerican.com/article/5-ways-to-spot-a-fake/

Federal Aviation Administration. (2018, July 23). *Fact sheet: Small unmanned aircraft regulations (Part 107)*. Retrieved from: www.faa.gov/news/fact_sheets/news_story.cfm?newsId=22615

Feldman, M. S., & Pentland, B. T. (2003). Reconceptualizing organizational routines as a source of flexibility and change. *Administrative Science Quarterly*, 48(1), 94–118. doi:10.2307/3556620

Ferrier, M. (2018). *Attacks and harassment: The impact on female journalists and their reporting.* International Women's Media Foundation and Troll-Busters.com. Retrieved from www.iwmf.org/wp-content/uploads/2018/09/Attacks-and-Harassment.pdf

Few, S. (2013). Data visualization for human perception. In: M. Soegaard & R. F. Dam (Eds.), *The encyclopedia of human-computer interaction* (2nd ed.). Aarhus, Denmark: The Interaction Design Foundation. Retrieved from www.interaction-design.org/literature/book/the-encyclopedia-of-human-computer-interaction-2nd-ed/data-visualization-for-human-perception

Franklin, B., & Carlson, M. (2010). *Journalists, sources, and credibility.* New York: Routledge.

Frechette, C. (2012, May 14). *10 tips for using audio more effectively in multimedia stories.* Poynter Institute. Retrieved from www.poynter.org/news/10-tips-using-audio-more-effectively-multimedia-stories

Fuller, B. (1946). *Profile of the industrial revolution: As exposed by the chronological rate of acquisition of the basic inventory of cosmic absolutes – The 92 elements.* [Drawing]. Retrieved from www.rwgrayprojects.com/synergetics/s04/figs/f1903.html

Fussman, C. (2016, July). What I've learned: Jorge Ramos. *Esquire.* Retrieved from: www.esquire.com/entertainment/a45945/jorge-ramos-what-ive-learned/

Gafni, M., & Garofoli, J. (2020, March 31). Captain of aircraft carrier with growing coronavirus outbreak pleads for help from Navy. *San Francisco Chronicle.* Retrieved from www.sfchronicle.com/bayarea/article/Exclusive-Captain-of-aircraft-carrier-with-15167883.php

Gahran, A. (2016, May 16). *Connecting with local mobile news consumers: New Knight research.* Knight Digital Media Center. Retrieved from www.knightdigitalmediacenter.org/blogs/agahran/2016/05/connecting-local-mobile-news-consumers-new-knight-research.html

Gardiner, B., Mansfield, M., Anderson, I., Holder, J., Louter, D., & Ulmanu, M. (2016, April 12). The dark side of *Guardian* comments. *The Guardian.* Retrieved from www.theguardian.com/technology/2016/apr/12/the-dark-side-of-guardian-comments

Gibbs, S. (2016, April 19). The SS7 hack explained: What can you do about it? *The Guardian.* Retrieved from www.theguardian.com/technology/2016/apr/19/ss7-hack-explained-mobile-phone-vulnerability-snooping-texts-calls

Gibson, J. J. (1979). *The ecological approach to visual perception.* Boston, MA: Houghton Mifflin.

Gillmor, D. (2019, February 16). *Can our corrections catch up to our mistakes as they spread across social media?* NiemanLab. Retrieved from www.niemanlab.org/2019/03/can-our-corrections-catch-up-to-our-mistakes-as-they-spread-across-social-media/

Gowen, A., Eilperin, J., Guarino, B., & Tran, A. B. (2020, January 23). Science ranks grow thin in Trump administration. *The Washington Post.* Retrieved from www.washingtonpost.com/climate-environment/science-ranks-grow-thin-in-trump-administration/2020/01/23/5d22b522-3172-11ea-a053-dc6d944ba776_story.html

Gray, J., & Bounegru, L. (Eds.). (2019). *The data journalism handbook 2.* European Journalism Centre and Google News Initiative. Retrieved from https://datajournalism.com/read/handbook/two

WORKS CITED

Green, M. C. (2004). Transportation into narrative worlds: The role of prior knowledge and perceived realism. *Discourse Processes*, 38(2), 247–266. doi:10.1207/s15326950dp3802_5

Green, M. C., Chatham, C., & Sestir, M. A. (2012). Emotion and transportation into fact and fiction. *Scientific Study of Literature*, 2(1), 37–59. doi:10.1075/ssol.2.1.03gre

Greene, D. (2016, December 16). Why the media use anonymous sources (transcript). *National Public Radio*. Retrieved from www.npr.org/2016/12/16/505811892/why-the-media-uses-anonymous-sources

Greenfield, R. (2012, December). What *The New York Times*'s 'Snow Fall' means to online journalism's future. *The Atlantic*. Retrieved from www.theatlantic.com/technology/archive/2012/12/new-york-times-snow-fall-feature/320253/

Grieco, E. (2019a, April 12). *For many rural residents in U.S., local news media mostly don't cover the area where they live*. Pew Research Center. Retrieved from www.pewresearch.org/fact-tank/2019/04/12/for-many-rural-residents-in-u-s-local-news-media-mostly-dont-cover-the-area-where-they-live/

Grieco, E. (2019b, July 9). *U.S newsroom employment has dropped a quarter since 2008, with greatest decline at newspapers*. Pew Research Center. Retrieved from www.pewresearch.org/fact-tank/2019/07/09/u-s-newsroom-employment-has-dropped-by-a-quarter-since-2008/

Grier, D. A., (n.d.). *Software factories*. IEEE Computer Society. Retrieved from www.computer.org/web/closer-than-you-might-think/software-factories

Grothaus, M. (2019, April 19). If you value your privacy, switch to Signal as your messaging app now. *Fast Company*. Retrieved from www.fastcompany.com/90335034/if-you-value-your-privacy-switch-to-signal-as-your-messaging-app-now

Guardian Staff. (2020, March 23). How coronavirus advice from Boris Johnson has changed. *The Guardian*. Retrieved from www.theguardian.com/world/2020/mar/23/how-coronavirus-advice-from-boris-johnson-has-changed

Guilbeault, D., & Wolley, S. (2016, November). How Twitter bots are shaping the election. *The Atlantic*. Retrieved from www.theatlantic.com/technology/archive/2016/11/election-bots/506072/

Halpern, S. (2017, June 8). How he used Facebook to win. *The New York Review of Books*. Retrieved from www.nybooks.com/articles/2017/06/08/how-trump-used-facebook-to-win/

Hamilton, M. (2016, April 8). *The Guardian* wants to engage with readers, but how we do it needs to evolve. *The Guardian*. Retrieved from www.theguardian.com/media/2016/apr/08/the-guardian-wants-to-engage-with-readers-but-how-we-do-it-needs-to-evolve

Hanitzsch, T., Anikina, M., Berganza, R., Cangoz, I., Coman, M., Hamada, B., … Yuen, K. W. (2010). Modeling perceived influences on journalism: Evidence from a cross-national survey of journalists. *Journalism & Mass Communication Quarterly*, 87(1), 5–22. doi:10.1177/107769901008700101

Hardy, R. (2017, October 2). The ultimate workflow for writers obsessed with quality [Web log post]. Retrieved from https://medium.com/better-humans/the-ultimate-workflow-for-writers-obsessed-with-quality-5b2810e1214b

Harmon, A. (2017, March 6). Activists rush to save government science data – If they can find it. *The New York Times*. Retrieved from www.nytimes.com/2017/03/06/science/donald-trump-data-rescue-science.html

Hart, J. (2011). *Storycraft: The complete guide to writing narrative nonfiction*. Chicago, IL: University of Chicago Press.

Harwell, D. (2019, June 12). Top AI researchers race to detect 'deepfake' videos: 'We are outgunned'. *The Washington Post*. Retrieved from www.washingtonpost.com/technology/2019/06/12/top-ai-researchers-race-detect-deepfake-videos-we-are-outgunned/

Hastings, M. (2014). *The last magazine: A novel*. New York: Penguin Group.

Hayakawa, S. I. (1941). *Language in action*. New York: Harcourt, Brace & Company.

Herkenhoff, L. M., & Heydenfeldt, J. A. (2011). A correlational study of professional culture and intraorganizational conflict. *International Journal of Management and Business*, 2(1), 61–76. Retrieved from http://iamb.org/ijmb/journals/vol_2/IJMB_Vol_2_1.pdf

Hermann, S., Banerjee, S., & Michalski, P. (2015, March). *The mobile first newsroom*. Online News Association Mobile 2015 Conference. [Audio recording], London, UK. Retrieved from https://soundcloud.com/onlinenewsassociation/the-mobile-first-newsroom

Hermida, A. (2012). Tweets and truth: Journalism as a discipline of collaborative verification. *Journalism Practice*, 6, 659–668. doi:10.1080/17512786.2012.667269

Hertsgaard, M. (2020, March 25). COVID-19 and the media's climate coverage capabilities. *Columbia Journalism Review*. Retrieved from www.cjr.org/covering_climate_now/covid-19-pandemic-climate-crisis.php

Heylighen, F. (2002). *Complexity and information overload in society: Why increasing efficiency leads to decreasing control*. Retrieved from http://web.archive.org/web/20070103090951/http://pespmc1.vub.ac.be/Papers/Info-overload.pdf

Higgins, E. (2015). Building expertise through UGC verification. In C. Silverman (Ed.), *Verification handbook for investigative reporting*. Maastricht, NL: European Journalism Center. Retrieved from http://verificationhandbook.com/book2/chapter6.php

Hitchens, C. (2006, December). Oriana Fallaci and the art of the interview. *Vanity Fair*. Retrieved from www.vanityfair.com/news/2006/12/hitchens200612

Hitlin, P., & Rainie, L. (2019, January 19). *Facebook algorithms and personal data*. Pew Research Center. Retrieved from www.pewresearch.org/internet/2019/01/16/facebook-algorithms-and-personal-data/

Hosp, D. (2007). *Innocence*. New York: Warner Books.

Houston, B. (2014). *Computer-assisted reporting: A practical guide* (4th ed.). New York: Routledge.

Houston, B. (2019). *Data for journalists* (5th ed.). New York: Routledge.

Houston, B., & Investigative Reporters and Editors. (2009). *Investigative reporter's handbook* (5th ed.). Boston, MA: Bedford/St. Martin's.

Howe, J., Bajak, A., Kraft, D., & Wihbey, J. (2017, May 26). *Collaborative, open, mobile: A thematic exploration of best practices at the forefront of digital journalism*. SSRN. doi: 10.2139/ssrn.3036984

WORKS CITED

Hsu, T. (2019, July 9). The Jeffrey Epstein case was cold, until a *Miami Herald* reporter got accusers to talk. *The New York Times*. Retrieved from www.nytimes.com/2019/07/09/business/media/miami-herald-epstein.html

Hunter, M. L., Hanson, N., Sabbagh, R., Sengers, L., Sullivan, D., Svith, F. T., & Thordsen, P. (2011). *Story-based inquiry: A manual for investigative journalists*. United Nations Educational, Scientific, and Cultural Organization. Retrieved from https://unesdoc.unesco.org/ark:/48223/pf0000193078

IBM. (2010). *IBM 2010 global CEO study: Creativity selected as most crucial factor for future success*. Retrieved from www.03.ibm.com/press/us/en/pressrelease/31670.wss

IBM. (2016, November). *What is big data?* Retrieved from web.archive.org/web/20160530045521/www-01.ibm.com/software/in/data/bigdata/

Ignatius, D. (2017, November 23). How to protect against fake 'facts'. *The Washington Post*. Retrieved from www.washingtonpost.com/opinions/getting-back-to-facts/2017/11/23/ebd6a12e-cfb9-11e7-81bc-c55a220c8cbe_story.html?hpid=hp_noname_opinion-card-d%3Ahomepage%2Fstory&utm_term=.4b8dcbeec44a

Ingram, A. (2012, December). Like it or not, real-time crowdsourced news verification is here to stay [Web log post]. Retrieved from https://gigaom.com/2012/12/18/like-it-or-not-real-time-crowdsourced-news-verification-is-here-to-stay/

Internet Live Stats. (2019, December 1). *Internet Live Stats*. Retrieved from www.internetlivestats.com/

Jahnke, A., & Hahn, D. (2014, March 6). David Carr: Journalism is still serious, just different. *BU Today*. Retrieved from www.bu.edu/today/2014/david-carr-journalism-is-still-serious-just-different/

Jannsen, H. (2015). Organizing the newsroom for better and accurate investigative reporting. In C. Silverman (Ed.), *Verification handbook for investigative reporting*. Maastricht, NL: European Journalism Center. Retrieved from https://verificationhandbook.com/book2/chapter10.php

Jarvis, J. (2009, April 23). Death of the curator. Long live the curator [Web log post]. Retrieved from http://buzzmachine.com/2009/04/23/death-of-the-curator-long-live-the-curator/

Jarvis, J. (2017, June 12). Our problem isn't 'fake news.' Our problems are trust and manipulation [Web log post]. Retrieved from https://medium.com/whither-news/our-problem-isnt-fake-news-our-problems-are-trust-and-manipulation-5bfbcd716440

Jassin, L. J. (n.d.). *New rules for using public domain materials*. Author. Retrieved from www.copylaw.com/new_articles/PublicDomain.html

Jenkins, H. (2006). *Convergence culture: Where old and new media collide*. New York: New York University Press.

Jenkins, H. (2009). If it doesn't spread, it's dead (Part one): Media viruses and memes [Web log post]. Retrieved from http://henryjenkins.org/2009/02/if_it_doesnt_spread_its_dead_p.html

Jenkins, H., Ford, S., & Green, J. (2013). *Spreadable media*. New York: New York University Press.

Jensen, E. (2015, December 8). NPR's on-air source diversity: Some improvement, more work to be done. *National Public Radio*. Retrieved from www.npr.org/sections/ombudsman/2015/12/08/458834769/nprs-on-air-source-diversity-some-improvement-more-work-to-be-done

Johns Hopkins University & Medicine (2020). Coronavirus Resource Center [Website]. Retrieved from https://coronavirus.jhu.edu/map.html

Johnson, H. (2012, May 20). *A brief history of journalism.* Retrieved from https://web.archive.org/ (Go to the archive site and input the URL to find this resource). www.slideshare.net/hollykatharine/a-brief-history-of-journalism

Johnson, J. (2019, July 23). Mobile first design: Why it's great and why it sucks [Web log post]. Retrieved from https://designshack.net/articles/css/mobilefirst/

Johnston, M. (2014, May 12). Singing the praises of Chorus [Web log post]. *CMSCritic*. Retrieved from www.cmscritic.com/singing-the-praises-of-chorus/

Kalogeropoulos, A., Cherubini, F., & Newman, N. (2016). *The future of online news video.* Reuters Institute for the Study of Journalism. Retrieved from https://ora.ox.ac.uk/objects/uuid:b712713d-5429-4a91-862b-badb41803338/datastreams/binb6f1be9e-7fbc-4052-952a-014aaa90e608

Kang, S., O'Brien, E., Villarreal, A., Lee, W., & Mahood, C. (2019). Immersive journalism and telepresence. *Digital Journalism*, 7(2), 294–313. doi:10.1080/21670811.2018.1504624

Kavanaugh, J., Marcellino, W., Blake, J. S., Smith, S., Davenport, S., & Tebeka, M. G. (2019). *News in a digital age: Comparing the presentation of news information over time and across media platforms.* Santa Monica, CA: RAND Corporation. Retrieved from www.rand.org/pubs/research_reports/RR2960.html

Kavanaugh, J., & Rich, M. D. (2018). *Truth decay: An initial exploration of the diminishing role of facts and analysis in American public life.* Santa Monica, CA: RAND Corporation. Retrieved from www.rand.org/pubs/research_reports/RR2314.htm

Kellas, J. K. (2005). Family ties: Communicating identity through jointly told family stories. *Communication Monographs*, 72(4), 365–389. doi:10.1080/03637750500322453

Kline, K. (2019, August 26). Journalism needs help – And mixed reality is coming to the rescue. *Venture Beat*. Retrieved from https://venturebeat.com/2019/08/26/journalism-needs-help-and-mixed-reality-is-coming-to-the-rescue/

Knight Foundation. (2016a, May 11). *Part 1, Mobile America: How people use smartphones to access information.* Author. Retrieved from https://medium.com/mobile-first-news-how-people-use-smartphones-to/news-goes-mobile-how-people-use-smartphones-to-access-information-53ccb850d80a

Knight Foundation. (2016b, May 11). *Part 2, News goes mobile: How different audiences tap mobile news.* Author. Retrieved from https://medium.com/mobile-first-news-how-people-use-smartphones-to/mobile-america-how-different-audiences-tap-mobile-news-1c72525210d7

Knight Foundation, & Gallup. (2018, September 11). Indicators of news media trust. *Knight Foundation and Gallup*. Retrieved from https://knightfoundation.org/reports/indicators-of-news-media-trust

WORKS CITED

Knight, J. (2018, November 20). *Is it finally time for media companies to adopt a common publishing platform?* NiemanLab. Retrieved from www.niemanlab.org/2018/11/is-it-finally-time-for-media-companies-to-adopt-a-common-publishing-platform/

Koeze, E., & Popper, N. (2020, April 7). The virus changed the way we internet. *The New York Times*. Retrieved from www.nytimes.com/interactive/2020/04/07/technology/coronavirus-internet-use.html

Kovach, B., & Rosenstiel, R. (2014). *The elements of journalism: What news people should know and the public should expect* (3rd ed., revised). New York: Three Rivers Press.

Kraeplin, C., & Batsell, J. (2013). Web-centric convergence replaces media partnerships. *Newspaper Research Journal*, 34(4), 68–82. doi:10.1177/073953291303400406

Kraus, M. (2017). Voice-only communication enhances empathic accuracy. *American Psychologist*, 72(7), 644–654. doi:10.1037/amp0000147

Krawetz, N. (2015). Personal communication.

Kumar, S. (2019, November 14). *Q & A with Craig Silverman: Misinformation, deepfakes and democracy*. International Journalists' Network. Retrieved from https://ijnet.org/en/story/qa-craig-silverman-misinformation-deepfakes-and-democracy

Kurtzman, D. (2006). *Stephen Colbert at the White House Correspondents' Dinner*. Retrieved from: http://politicalhumor.about.com/od/stephencolbert/a/colbertbush.htm

Kurzweil, R. (2012). *How to create a mind*. New York: Viking Penguin.

Kwan, V., Wardle, C., & Webb, M. (2020, March 10). Tips for reporting on Covid-19 and slowing the spread of misinformation. *Firstdraft.com*. Retrieved from https://firstdraft-news.org/latest/tips-for-reporting-on-covid-19-coronavirus-and-slowing-the-spread-of-misinformation/

Lagun, D., Hsieh, C., Webster, D., & Navalpakkum, V. (2014, July). Towards better measurement of attention and satisfaction in mobile search. *Proceedings of the 37th international ACM SIGIR conference on research and development in information retrieval, 113–122*. Queensland, Australia. doi: 10.1145/2600428.2609631

Lagun, D., & Lalmas, M. (2016, February). Understanding and measuring user engagement and attention in online news reading. *WSDM '16: Proceedings of the Ninth ACM International Conference on Web Search and Data Mining*. doi: 10.1145/2835776.2835833

Lakshmanan, I. R. A. (2018, June 30). *Can journalists counteract hatred toward the press? It starts with explaining what we do*. Poynter Institute. Retrieved from www.poynter.org/ethics-trust/2018/can-journalists-counteract-hatred-toward-the-press-it-starts-with-explaining-what-we-do/

Lara, A. (2010, December 7). Find an angle to bring your subject to life. *Writer's Digest*. Retrieved from www.writersdigest.com/writing-articles/by-writing-goal/improve-my-writing/find-an-angle-to-bring-your-subject-to-life

Lecheler, S., & Kruikemeier, S. (2015). Re-evaluating journalistic routines in a digital age: A review of research on the use of online sources. *New Media & Society*. doi:10.1177/1461444815600412

Lehmann, J., Castillo, C., Lalmas, M., & Baeza-Yates, R. (2017). Story-focused reading in online news and its potential for user engagement. *Journal of the Association for Information Science and Technology, 68*, 869–883. doi:10.1002/asi.23707

Levin, D. (2019, October 19). When the student newspaper is the only daily paper in town. *The New York Times.* Retrieved from www.nytimes.com/2019/10/19/us/news-desert-ann-arbor-michigan.html

Lewis, S. C. (2015). Journalism in an era of big data. *Digital Journalism, 3*(3), 321–330. doi:10.1080/21670811.2014.976399

Lichterman, J. (2015, June 18). *Google and Storyful are launching YouTube Newswire, feed of verified user-generated videos.* NiemanLab. Retrieved from www.niemanlab.org/2015/06/google-and-storyful-are-launching-youtube-newswire-a-feed-of-verified-user-generated-videos/

Lipsman, A. (2015, September 25). Good news for digital publishers: Audiences are on the rise thanks to mobile [Web log post]. Retrieved from www.comscore.com/Insights/Blog/Good-News-for-Digital-Publishers-Audiences-Are-on-the-Rise-Thanks-to-Mobile

Livingstone, S. (2014). Identifying the interests of digital users as audiences, consumers, workers, and publics. In T. Gillespie, P. J. Boczkowski, & K. A. Foot (Eds.), *Media technologies: Essays on communication, materiality, and society* (pp. 241–250). Cambridge, MA: MIT Press.

Lorenz, M., Kayser-Bril, N., & McGhee, G. (2011, March 1). *Voices: News organizations must become hubs of trusted data in a market seeking (and valuing) trust.* NiemanLab. Retrieved from www.niemanlab.org/2011/03/voices-news-organizations-must-become-hubs-of-trusted-data-in-an-market-seeking-and-valuing-trust/

Lynch, J. (2015, October 20). A first look at Nielsen's total audience measurement and how it will change the industry. Retrieved from www.adweek.com/tv-video/first-look-nielsen-s-total-audience-measurement-and-how-it-will-change-industry-167661/

Mack, A., & Rock, I. (1999). Inattentional blindness. *Psyche, 5*(3). Retrieved from http://journalpsyche.org/files/0xaa59.pdf

Mahadeven, A. (2020, March 27), *Does COVID-19 discriminate based on skin tone? This needs a fact-check.* The Pointer Institute. Retrieved from www.poynter.org/fact-checking/2020/does-covid-19-discriminate-based-on-skin-tone-this-needs-a-fact-check/

Mandese, J. (2020, March 23). Covering the ad industry in the time of COVID-19. *MediaPost.com.* Retrieved from www.mediapost.com/publications/article/348857/covering-the-ad-industry-in-the-time-of-covid-19.html

Mar, R. A., Kelley, W. M., Heatherton, T. F., & Macrae, C. N. (2007). Detecting agency from the biological motion of veridical vs animated agents. *Social Cognitive and Affective Neuroscience, 2*(3), 199–205. doi:10.1093/scan/nsm011

Marketing Charts. (2018, June 25). US online and traditional media advertising outlook, 2018-2022 [Web log post]. Retrieved from www.marketingcharts.com/featured-104785

Marsh, C. (2014, October 6). 15 years later, How *The Blair Witch Project* tricked the world, changed a genre. *Details.* Retrieved from https://web.archive.org/ (Go to the archive site and input the URL to find this resource). www.details.com/blogs/daily-details/2014/10/blair-witch-project-anniversary.html

WORKS CITED

Marvin, C. (1988). *When old technologies were new*. New York: Oxford University Press.

Marwick, A., & Lewis, R. (2017, May 15). *Media manipulation and disinformation online*. Data & Society Research Institute. Retrieved from https://datasociety.net/pubs/oh/DataAndSociety_MediaManipulationAndDisinformationOnline.pdf

Maxon, T. (2015, June 23). Southwest Airlines deals with fake video of a drone not hitting a Southwest Airline jet. *Dallas Morning News*. Retrieved from www.dallasnews.com/business/airlines/2015/06/23/southwest-airlines-deals-with-fake-video-of-a-drone-not-hitting-a-southwest-airline-jet/

Mazzei, P., & Rashbaum, W. K. (2019, July 6). Jeffrey Epstein, financier long accused of molesting minors, is charged. *The New York Times*. Retrieved from www.nytimes.com/2019/07/06/nyregion/jeffrey-epstein-arrested-sex-trafficking.html

McAdams, M. (2008, December 3). 'Curation,' and journalists as curators [Web log post]. Retrieved from http://mindymcadams.com/tojou/2008/curation-and-journalists-as-curators/

McClure, J. (2011, December 14). Newsroom culture of excellence, foundational document No. 4: Story budget aims toward digital [Web log post]. Retrieved from https://yorkblog.com/ydrinsider/newsroom-culture-of-excellence-foundational-document-no-4-story-budget-aims-toward-digital/

McDonald, W. (2017, April 21). *How to fly drones for journalism in the U.S.* Poynter Institute. Retrieved from www.poynter.org/educators-students/2017/how-to-fly-drones-for-journalism-in-the-u-s/

McEleny, C. (2020, March 5). Coronavirus will impact ad spend but could drive shift to utility, e-commerce and live-streaming. *The Drum*. Retrieved from www.thedrum.com/news/2020/03/05/coronavirus-will-impact-ad-spend-could-drive-shift-utility-e-commerce-and-live-streaming

McKinney, J. (1966). *Constructive typology and social theory*. New York: Appleton-Century Crofts.

McLean, K. C. (2008). Stories of the young and the old: Personal continuity and narrative identity. *Development Psychology*, 44(1), 254–264. doi:10.1037/0012-1649.44.1.254

Mendoza, J. (2015, January 24). ISIS video: Is this Japanese beheading real or fake? *Christian Science Monitor*. Retrieved from www.csmonitor.com/World/Global-News/2015/0124/ISIS-video-Is-this-Japanese-beheading-real-or-fake-video

Merrifield, C. (2020, March 20). *Crowdsourcing truth and how journalists can avoid spreading coronavirus misinformation: Q and A with MIT professor David Rand*. Journalist's Resource. Retrieved from https://journalistsresource.org/studies/society/social-media/coronavirus-misinformation-crowdsourcing-truth-mit-david-rand/

Mesgari, M., Okoli, C., Mehdi, M., Nielsen, F. A., & Lanamaki, A. (2014). The sum of all human knowledge: A systematic review of scholarly research on the content of Wikipedia. *Journal of the Association for Information Science and Technology*, 66(2), 219–245. doi:10.1002/asi.23172

Metz, C. (2019a, November 24). Companies prepare to fight the 'deepfake' future. *The New York Times*. Retrieved from www.nytimes.com/2019/11/24/technology/tech-companies-deepfakes.html

Metz, R. (2019b, October 7). The number of deepfake videos online is spiking. Most are porn. *CNN Business*. Retrieved from www.cnn.com/2019/10/07/tech/deepfake-videos-increase/index.html

Miller, M. (2015, June 3). How a curmudgeonly old reporter exposed the FIFA scandal that toppled Sepp Blatter. *The Washington Post*. Retrieved from www.washingtonpost.com/news/morning-mix/wp/2015/06/03/how-a-curmudgeonly-old-reporter-exposed-the-fifa-scandal-that-toppled-sepp-blatter/

Mitchell, A. (2015). *State of the news media 2015*. Pew Research Center. Retrieved from www.journalism.org/2015/04/29/state-of-the-news-media-2015/

Mitchell, A., Gottfried, J., Barthel, M., & Shearer, E. (2016, July 7). *The modern news consumer: News attitudes and practices in the digital era. 1. Pathways to news*. Pew Research Center. Retrieved from www.journalism.org/2016/07/07/pathways-to-news/

Mitchell, A., Gottfried, J., Stocking, G., Walker, M., & Fedeli, S. (2019, June 5). *Many Americans say made-up news is a critical problem that needs to be fixed*. Pew Research Center. Retrieved from www.journalism.org/2019/06/05/many-americans-say-made-up-news-is-a-critical-problem-that-needs-to-be-fixed/

Mitchell, A., Holcomb, J., & Vogt, N. (2014, March 26). *News video on the web: A growing, if uncertain, part of news*. Pew Research Center. Retrieved from www.journalism.org/2014/03/26/news-video-on-the-web/

Mitchell, A., & Rosenstiel, T. (2011, May 9). *Navigating news online: Where people go, how they get there and what lures them away*. Pew Research Center. Retrieved from www.journalism.org/2011/05/09/navigating-news-online/

Mitchell, A., Stocking, G., & Matsa, K. E. (2016, May 5). *Long-form reading shows signs of life in our mobile news world*. Pew Research Center. Retrieved from www.journalism.org/2016/05/05/long-form-reading-shows-signs-of-life-in-our-mobilenews-world/

Morrish, L (2020, March 17). How to stay mentally well while reporting on the coronavirus. *First Draft News*. Retrieved from https://firstdraftnews.org/latest/how-to-stay-sane-while-reporting-on-the-coronavirus/

Moses, L. (2014, August 5). One year in: 10 ways *The Washington Post* has changed under Jeff Bezos. *Digiday*. Retrieved from http://digiday.com/publishers/one-year-bezos-washington-post-changed/

Mueller, R. S., III. (2019, March). *Report on the investigation into Russian interference in the 2016 presidential election* (Vol. 1). Washington, DC: U.S. Department of Justice. Retrieved from www.justice.gov/storage/report.pdf

Murray, J. (2011). *Inventing the medium: Principles of interaction design as a cultural practice*. Cambridge, MA: The MIT Press.

Murtha, J. (2016, May 26). How fake news sites frequently trick big-time journalists. *Columbia Journalism Review*. Retrieved from www.cjr.org/analysis/how_fake_news_sites_frequently_trick_big-time_journalists.php

Nahser, F. (2017, November 2). A reality check about augmented reality in journalism [Web log post]. Retrieved from https://medium.com/global-editors-network/a-reality-check-about-augmented-reality-in-journalism-93c69cf4d8f8

WORKS CITED

National Press Photographers Association. (n.d.). *Code of ethics.* Retrieved from https://nppa.org/code_of_ethics

National Public Radio. (2016, December 16). *Why the media use anonymous sources.* Retrieved from www.npr.org/2016/12/16/505811892/why-the-media-uses-anonymous-sources

Nelson, J. (2018, September 24). *Seven lessons for immersive storytellers from the RJI Innovation Series.* Reynolds Journalism Institute. Retrieved from www.rjionline.org/stories/seven-lessons-for-immersive-storytellers-from-the-rji-innovation-series

New York Times. (2008, September 25). *Guidelines on integrity.* Retrieved from www.nytco.com/wp-content/uploads/Guidelines-on-Integrity-updated-2008.pdf

New York Times. (2014, March 24). *New York Times innovation report.* Retrieved from https://ia902500.us.archive.org/31/items/nyt_innovation_2014/The-Full-New-York-Times-Innovation-Report.pdf

Newitz, A. (2015, September 8). How Ashley Madison hid its fembot con from users and investigators [Web log post]. Retrieved from http://gizmodo.com/how-ashley-madison-hid-its-fembot-con-from-users-and-in-1728410265

Newman, N. (2017, January 1). *Journalism, media and technology trends and predictions 2017.* Reuters Institute for the Study of Journalism. Retrieved from https://reutersinstitute.politics.ox.ac.uk/our-research/journalism-media-and-technology-trends-and-predictions-2017

Newman, N. (2019, January 10). *Journalism, media and technology trends and predictions 2019.* Reuters Institute for the Study of Journalism. Retrieved from www.digitalnewsreport.org/publications/2019/journalism-media-technology-trends-predictions-2019/

Newman, N., Fletcher, R., Levy, D. A. L., & Nielsen, R. K. (2016). *Digital news report 2016.* Reuters Institute for the Study of Journalism. Retrieved from https://reutersinstitute.politics.ox.ac.uk/our-research/digital-news-report-2016

NewscastStudio. (2017, December). Q&A: The evolving workflows of VR creation and production [Web log post]. Retrieved from www.newscaststudio.com/2017/12/19/qa-evolving-workflows-vr-creation-production/

Nielsen, J. (2006, April 17). F-shaped pattern for reading web content [Web log post]. Retrieved from www.nngroup.com/articles/f-shaped-pattern-reading-web-content-discovered/

Nielsen Research. (2016, March 1). *The Nielsen comparable metrics report: Q3 2015.* Retrieved from www.nielsen.com/us/en/insights/report/2016/the-comparable-metrics-report-q3-2015/

Nielsen Research. (2017, March 9). *The Nielsen Nielsen comparable metrics report: Q3 2016.* Retrieved from www.nielsen.com/us/en/insights/report/2017/the-comparable-metrics-report-q3-2016/

Nielsen, R. K., & Sambrook, R. (2016). *What is happening to television news?* Reuters Institute for the Study of Journalism. Retrieved from www.digitalnewsreport.org/publications/2016/what-is-happening-to-television-news/

Normile, D. (2020, January 3, updated January 6). Novel human virus? Pneumonia cases linked to seafood market in China stir concern. *Science.* doi:10.1126/science.aba7672

O'Neill, C., & Echter, B. (2016, September 15). *F*ck it, we'll do it live: Workshopping the hows & whys of live stream (Part 1)*. Retrieved from https://docs.google.com/presentation/d/1bcBUdaDVrA1cAmFcFCPpQJ0DBfL5rN26bwtvCBX1XnI/pub?start=false&slide=id.p

Office of the Director of National Intelligence. (2017, January 6). *Intelligence community assessment (ICA 2017-01D): Assessing Russian activities and intentions in recent US elections*. U.S. Government Publication. Retrieved from www.dni.gov/files/documents/ICA_2017_01.pdf

Oliver, A. C. (2017, January 26). What the end of net neutrality means for you. *InfoWorld*. Retrieved from www.infoworld.com/article/3161784/what-the-end-of-net-neutrality-means-for-you.html

Ordway, D.-M. (2019, October 1). *Covering whistleblowers: 6 tips for journalists*. Journalist's Resources. Retrieved from https://journalistsresource.org/tip-sheets/reporting/whistleblowers-tips-journalists/

Orion, G. (2014, April). What is a histogram and why do photographers use them? Why every photographer should understand histograms [Web log post]. Retrieved from www.creativelive.com/blog/every-photographer-understand-histogram/

Ornebring, H., Karlsson, M., & Fast, K. (2014, October). *The labor of journalism: Challenges of technological and economic restructuring*. Paper presented at University of Missouri, Columbia Conference on Digital Disruption to Journalism and Mass Communication, Brussels, Belgium.

Owen, L. H. (2019, May 14). *U.S. journalism really has become more subjective and personal — at least some of it*. NiemanLab. Retrieved from www.niemanlab.org/2019/05/u-s-journalism-really-has-become-more-subjective-and-personal-at-least-some-of-it/

Parker, S. A. (2016). *The future of broadcasting V: The search for fundamental growth*. Accenture. Retrieved from https://slidex.tips/download/the-future-of-broadcasting-v-the-search-for-fundamental-growth

Pavlik, J. V. (2001). *Journalism and new media*. New York: Columbia University Press.

Perling, A., & Bellamy, S. (2019, March 18). The best voice recorders [Web log post]. *The Wirecutter*. Retrieved from https://thewirecutter.com/reviews/the-best-voice-recorder/#iphone6

Peterson, A. (2019, April 11). *Why the US still won't require SS7 fixes that could secure your phone*. Ars Technica. Retrieved from https://arstechnica.com/features/2019/04/fully-compromised-comms-how-industry-influence-at-the-fcc-risks-our-digital-security/

Petre, C. (2015, May 7). *The traffic factories: Metrics at Chartbeat, Gawker Media, and The New York Times*. The Tow Center for Digital Journalism, Graduate School of Journalism at Columbia University. Retrieved from https://towcenter.columbia.edu/news/traffic-factories-metrics-chartbeat-gawker-media-and-new-york-times

Pew Research Center. (2014, March 26). *State of the media*. Author. Retrieved from www.journalism.org/2019/06/25/archived-state-of-the-news-media-reports/

Phillips, A. (2014). *Communication and society: Journalism in context: Practice and theory for the digital age*. Florence, KY: Taylor & Francis.

WORKS CITED

Porter, C. (2019, January 10). *Quid pro quo(te): The rise of partnership journalism*. Shorenstein Center on Media, Politics and Public Policy. Retrieved from https://medium.com/single-subject-news-project/quid-pro-quo-te-the-rise-of-partnership-journalism-e5e22f8dfd6e

Porter, M. E. (1979). How competitive forces shape strategy. *Harvard Business Review*, 57(2), 137–145.

Post Opinions Staff. (2019, December 17). These video op-eds shifted the way we see the world. *The Washington Post*. Retrieved from www.washingtonpost.com/opinions/2019/12/17/video-op-eds-make-you-think-well-maybe-cry/

Poushter, J., Bishop, C., & Chwe, H. (2018, June 19). *Social media use continues to rise in developing countries but plateaus across developed ones*. Pew Research Center. Retrieved from www.pewresearch.org/global/2018/06/19/social-media-use-continues-to-rise-in-developing-countries-but-plateaus-across-developed-ones/

Powell, T. E., Boomgaarden, H. G., De Swert, K., & de Vreese, C. H. (2015). A clearer picture: The contribution of visuals and text to framing effects. *Journal of Communication*, 65, 997–1017. doi:10.1111/jcom.12184

Power, R. (2017, January). 10 live streaming video tips to help build your business. *Inc.* Retrieved from www.inc.com/rhett-power/10-live-streaming-video-tips-to-help-build-your-business.html

Pulitzer. (2014). *The 2014 Pulitzer Prize - Breaking news reporting*. Author. Retrieved from www.pulitzer.org/citation/2014-Breaking-News-Reporting

Rabaino, L. (2011, June 17). How to run a news site and newspaper using WordPress and Google Docs. *Adweek*. Retrieved from www.adweek.com/fishbowlny/how-to-run-a-news-site-and-newspaper-using-wordpress-and-google-docs/245737

Rauch, J. (2019, June). Fact-checking the president in real time. *The Atlantic*. Retrieved from www.theatlantic.com/magazine/archive/2019/06/fact-checking-donald-trump-ai/588028/

Reardon, K. K., & Rogers, E. M. (1988). Interpersonal versus mass communication: A false dichotomy. *Human Communication Research*, 15(2), 284–303. doi:10.1111/j.1468-2958.1988.tb00185.x

Regalado, A. (2016, February). Top U.S. intelligence official calls gene editing a WMD threat. *MIT Technology Review*. Retrieved from www.technologyreview.com/s/600774/top-us-intelligence-official-calls-gene-editing-a-wmd-threat/

Reich, Z., & Godler, Y. (2017). Being there? The role of journalistic legwork across new and traditional media. *Journalism & Mass Communication Quarterly*, 94(4), 1115–1129. doi:10.1177/1077699016687723

Report for America. (2019, December 2). *Report for America to place a record 250 journalists in 164 local newsrooms in 2020*. Author. Retrieved from www.reportforamerica.org/2019/12/02/report-for-america-to-place-a-record-250-journalists-in-164-local-newsrooms-in-2020/

Reporters Without Borders. (2016). Round-up 2016 of journalists killed worldwide. Retrieved from https://rsf.org/sites/default/files/rsf_2016-part_2-en.pdf

Reuters. (2019). *Essentials of Reuters sourcing. Handbook of journalism*. Author. Retrieved from http://handbook.reuters.com/index.php?title=The_Essentials_of_Reuters_sourcing

Revers, M. (2014). Journalistic professionalism as performance and boundary work: Source relations at the state house. *Journalism, 15*(1), 37–52. doi:10.1177/1464884913480459

Ribiero, V. (2015). Combing through 324,000 frames of cellphone video to help prove the innocence of an activist in Rio. In C. Silverman (Ed.), *Verification handbook for investigative reporting*. Maastricht, NL: European Journalism Center. Retrieved from https://verificationhandbook.com/book2/case-study1.php

Rich, C. (2015). *Writing and reporting news: A coaching method* (8th ed.). Belmont, CA: Wadsworth.

Rich, C. (n.d.). Online writing process [Web log post]. Retrieved from www.lehigh.edu/~jl0d/J198-98/storyboard.html

Rigdon, S. (2016). Print vs. web, static vs. interactive. In T. Chiasson & D. Gregory (Eds.), *Data + Design*. Retrieved from https://trinachi.github.io/data-design-builds/ch16.html

Ripley, A. (2018, June 27, updated 2019, January 11). Complicating the narratives. *Solutions Journalism*. Retrieved from https://thewholestory.solutionsjournalism.org/complicating-the-narratives-b91ea06ddf63

Robertson, H. (2012, August). Audio sweetening. *Videomaker*. Retrieved from www.videomaker.com/article/c4/15356-audio-sweetening

Robertson, L. (2002, May). Romancing the source. *American Journalism Review*. Retrieved from http://ajrarchive.org/Article.asp?id=2520

Robinson, S. (2013). Teaching "journalism as process": A proposed paradigm for J-School curricula in the digital age. *Teaching Journalism and Mass Communication, 3*(1), 1–12. Retrieved from https://aejmc.us/spig/2013/teaching-journalism-as-process-a-proposed-paradigm-for-j-school-curricula-in-the-digital-age/

Rogers, E. M. (1995). *The diffusion of innovations* (5th ed.). New York: Free Press.

Rogers, K., & Bromwich, J. E. (2016, November 8). The hoaxes, fake news and misinformation we saw on election day. *The New York Times*. Retrieved from www.nytimes.com/2016/11/09/us/politics/debunk-fake-news-election-day.html

Rogers, S. (2013, August 14). Live-tweeting from the Whitey Bulger trial [Web log post]. Retrieved from https://blog.twitter.com/2013/live-tweeting-from-the-whitey-bulger-trial

Rogers, T. (2019, October 19). Writing news stories for the web: Keep it short and break it up [Web log post]. Retrieved from www.thoughtco.com/writing-for-the-web-2074334

Romm, T. (2019, October 1). Appeals court ruling upholds FCC's canceling of net neutrality rules. *The Washington Post*. Retrieved from www.washingtonpost.com/technology/2019/10/01/appeals-court-upholds-trump-administrations-cancelling-net-neutrality-rules/

Ronson, J. (2015, February 15). How one stupid tweet blew up Justine Sacco's life. *The New York Times*. Retrieved from www.nytimes.com/2015/02/15/magazine/how-one-stupid-tweet-ruined-justine-saccos-life.html?_r=0

Rosen, J. (2006, June 27). The people formerly known as the audience. *PressThink*. Retrieved from http://archive.pressthink.org/2006/06/27/ppl_frmr.html

WORKS CITED

Rosenstiel, T., & Mitchell, A. (2011). *The state of the news media 2011*. Pew Research Center. Retrieved from www.pewresearch.org/wp-content/uploads/sites/8/2017/05/State-of-the-News-Media-Report-2011-FINAL.pdf

Roush, C. (2005, December 8). Writing the same story from different angles. *Talking Biz News*. Retrieved from http://talkingbiznews.com/1/writing-the-same-story-from-different-angles/

Rowell, R. (2011). *Attachments*. New York: Dutton.

Russell, B. (1948). *Human knowledge: Its scope and limits*. London, UK: George Allen & Unwin, Ltd.

Rutledge, P. (2011, January 16). The psychology of storytelling. *Psychology Today*. Retrieved from www.psychologytoday.com/us/blog/positively-media/201101/the-psychological-power-storytelling

Saltzman, J. (2005, August). *Analyzing the images of the journalist in popular culture: A unique method of studying the public's perception of its journalists and the news media*. Paper presented at the annual conference of the Association for Education in Journalism & Communication, San Antonio, TX. Retrieved from www.ijpc.org/page/resources_–_recommended_books_and_web_sites.htm

Sambrook, R. (Ed.). (2018). *Global teamwork: The rise of collaboration in investigative journalism*. Oxford, UK: Reuters Institute for the Study of Journalism. Retrieved from https://reutersinstitute.politics.ox.ac.uk/sites/default/files/2018-03/sambrook_e-ISBN_1802.pdf

Sanburn, J. (2011, February 1). A brief history of digital news. *Time*. Retrieved from http://content.time.com/time/business/article/0,8599,2045682,00.html

Sargent, J. (2015, June 18). Introducing the First Draft Coalition. *First Draft Coalition*. Retrieved from https://medium.com/@FirstDraft/introducing-the-first-draft-coalition-e557fdacd1a6

Savchuk, K. (2017, July 25). *Pulitzer Prize-winner Katherine Boo's 15 rules for narrative nonfiction - now this is a "must-read"*. Nieman Storyboard. Retrieved from http://niemanstoryboard.org/stories/katherine-boos-15-rules-for-narrative-nonfiction-now-this-is-a-must-read/

Schilling, D. R. (2013, April 19). Knowledge doubling curve [Web log post]. Retrieved from www.industrytap.com/knowledge-doubling-every-12-months-soon-to-be-every-12-hours/3950

Schlanger, Z. (2017, January). Rogue scientists race to save climate data from Trump. *WiReD*. Retrieved from www.wired.com/2017/01/rogue-scientists-race-save-climate-data-trump/

Schlesinger, R. (2020, March 9). Trump's Nero fiddling tweet is too close to the coronavirus reality for comfort. *NBC News*. Retrieved from www.nbcnews.com/think/opinion/trump-s-nero-fiddling-tweet-too-close-coronavirus-reality-comfort-ncna1153521

Schmalbach, S. (2019, April 1). Local news is all around us: How to turn city streets into a true homepage [web blog post]. Retrieved from https://medium.com/the-lenfest-local-lab/local-news-is-all-around-us-how-to-turn-city-streets-into-a-true-homepage-530a1ecb2d1d

Schmidt, T. (2019). *Rewriting the newspaper: The storytelling movement in American print journalism*. Columbia, MI: University of Missouri Press.

Schulte-Ruther, M., Markowitsch, H. J., Fink, G. R., & Piefke, M. (2007). Mirror neuron and theory of mind mechanisms involved in face-to-face interactions: A functional magnetic resonance imaging approach to empathy. *Journal of Cognitive Neuroscience, 19*(8), 1354–1372. doi:10.1162/jocn.2007.19.8.1354

ScribbleLive. (2013, Septermber 17). Scribble chat: How real-time media covered the Boston bombings [Web log post]. Retrieved from http://chats.scribblelive.com/Event/How_real-time_media_covered_the_Boston_bombings?Page=0

Seward, Z. M. (2013, April 3). The first mobile phone call was made 40 years ago today. *Quartz*. Retrieved from https://qz.com/70309/the-first-mobile-phone-call-was-made-40-years-ago-today/

Shapiro, I., Brin, C., Bedard-Brule, I., & Mychajlowycz, K. (2013). Verification as a strategic ritual. *Journalism Practice, 7*(6), 657–673. doi:10.1080/17512786.2013.765638

Sherman, S. (2019, June 6). Russia and Iran plan to fundamentally isolate the internet. *WiReD*. Retrieved from www.wired.com/story/russia-and-iran-plan-to-fundamentally-isolate-the-internet/

Shirky, C. (2008). *Here comes everybody: The power of organizing without organizations*. New York: Penguin Books.

Silver, N. (2011). *The signal and the noise. Why so many predictions fail-but some don't*. New York: Penguin Books.

Silverman, C. (2011, April 8). Is this the world's best twitter account? *Columbia Journalism Review*. Retrieved from www.cjr.org/behind_the_news/is_this_the_worlds_best_twitter_account.php

Silverman, C. (2013, February 27). New research details how journalists verify information. *Poynter Institute MediaWire*. Retrieved from www.poynter.org/reporting-editing/2013/new-research-details-how-journalists-verify-information/

Silverman, C. (Ed.). (2014). *Verification handbook*. Maastricht, NL: European Journalism Centre. Retrieved from https://verificationhandbook.com/book/

Silverman, C. (Ed.). (2015). *Verification handbook for investigative reporters*. Maastricht, NL: European Journalism Centre. Retrieved from https://verificationhandbook.com/book2/

Silverman, C. (2016, November 16). This analysis shows how viral fake election news stories outperformed real news on Facebook. *Buzzfeed*. Retrieved from www.buzzfeed.com/craigsilverman/viral-fake-election-news-outperformed-real-news-on-facebook?utm_term=.sbVa8znO6#.teyk5DyQl

Silverman, C., & Tsubaki, R. (2014). When emergency news breaks. In C. Silverman (Ed.), *Verification handbook*. Maastricht, NL: European Journalism Center. Retrieved from http://verificationhandbook.com/book/chapter1.php

Smith, T. (2016, January). 5 tips for adding impact using the right crop. *Layers Magazine*. Retrieved from https://layersmagazine.com/5-tips-for-adding-impact-using-the-right-crop.html

WORKS CITED

Smolkin, R. (2006a, December/January). Reporters and confidential sources. *American Journalism Review*. Retrieved from http://ajrarchive.org/article.asp?id=4039

Smolkin, R. (2006b, February/March). Waivering. *American Journalism Review*. Retrieved from http://ajrarchive.org/article.asp?id=4038

Sood, R., Stockdale, G., & Rogers, E. M. (1987). How the news media operate in natural disasters. *Journal of Communication*, 37(3), 27–41. doi:10.1111/j.1460-2466.1987.tb00992.x

Southern, L. (2018, June). How BBC Stories experiments with audio to reach younger audiences. *Digiday.com*. Retrieved from https://digiday.com/media/bbc-stories-experimentsaudio-reach-young-audiences/

Spayd, L. (2017, February 18). The public editor: The risks of unnamed sources? Unconvinced readers. *The New York Times*. Retrieved from www.nytimes.com/2017/02/18/public-editor/the-risk-of-unnamed-sources-unconvinced-readers.html

Speer, N. K., Reynolds, J. R., Swallow, K. M., & Zacks, J. M. (2009). Reading stories activates neural representations of visual and motor experiences. *Psychological Science*, 20(8), 989–999. doi:10.1111/j.1467-9280.2009.02397.x

Spinelle, J. (2019, January 7). How journalists are using AR for next-level news. *AR Post*. Retrieved from https://arpost.co/2019/01/07/journalists-using-ar-next-level-news/

Statista. (2019, November 11). Number of smartphone users worldwide from 2016 to 2021. *Statista*. Retrieved from www.statista.com/statistics/330695/number-of-smartphone-users-worldwide/

Stauffer, R. (2019, December 31). The future of the news industry, according to student journalists. *Teen Vogue*. Retrieved from www.teenvogue.com/story/student-journalists-future-news?utm_social-type=owned&utm_source=twitter&utm_brand=tv&mbid=social_twitter&utm_medium=social

Stearns, J. (2014, November 10). Five kinds of listening for newsrooms and communities [Web log post]. Retrieved from https://medium.com/the-local-news-lab/five-kinds-of-listening-for-newsrooms-and-communities-67c373c25df8

Stearns, J. (2015, January 20). *Building journalism with community, not for it*. Local News Lab. Retrieved from http://localnewslab.org/2015/01/20/building-journalism-with-community-not-for-it/

Steffen, J. H., Gaskin, J. E., Meservy, T. O., Jenkins, J. L., & Wolman, I. (2019). Framework of affordances for virtual reality and augmented reality. *Journal of Management Information Systems*, 36(3), 683–729. doi:10.1080/07421222.2019.1628877

Stelter, B. (2009, June 28). Journalism rules are bent in news coverage of Iran. *The New York Times*. Retrieved from www.nytimes.com/2009/06/29/business/media/29coverage.html?searchResultPosition=2

Stempel, J. (2017, July 14). Ashley Madison parent in $11.2 million settlement over data breach. *Reuters*. Retrieved from www.reuters.com/article/us-ashleymadison-settlement-idUSKBN19Z2F0

Stoltzfus, D. (2006). Partial pre-publication review gaining favor at newspapers. *Newspaper Research Journal*, 27(4), 23–37. doi:10.1177/073953290602700402

Sturm, D. (2016, August 29). My post-production workflow [Web log post]. Retrieved from https://doingthatwrong.com/home/post-workflow

Sullivan, M. (2019, July 27). How one small news organization's investigative reporting took down Puerto Rico's governor. *The Washington Post*. Retrieved from www.washingtonpost.com/lifestyle/style/how-one-small-news-organizations-investigative-reporting-took-down-puerto-ricos-governor/2019/07/26/ec7e3ab6-af09-11e9-a0c9-6d2d7818f3da_story.html

Sullivan, M. (2020, March 1). Trump is pushing a dangerous, false spin on coronavirus – and the media is helping him spread it. *The Washington Post*. Retrieved from www.washingtonpost.com/lifestyle/media/trump-is-pushing-a-dangerous-false-spin-on-coronavirus--and-the-media-is-helping-him-spread-it/2020/02/28/1d136dde-5a60-11ea-ab68-101ecfec2532_story.html

Sullivan, T. (2018, February). VR gives journalism a new dimension. *PC Magazine*. Retrieved from www.pcmag.com/article/358864/vr-gives-journalism-a-new-dimension

Syman, K. (2015, January 9). The power of data to create powerful change [Web log post]. Retrieved from www.newprofit.org/fast-company-the-power-of-data-to-create-powerful-change-by-kim-syman/

Taibbi, M. (2016, November). President Trump: How America got it so wrong. *Rolling Stone*. Retrieved from www.rollingstone.com/politics/features/president-trump-how-america-got-it-so-wrong-w449783

Tait, R., & Weaver, M. (2009, June 22). How Neda Agha-Soltan became the face of Iran's struggle. *The Guardian*. Retrieved from www.guardian.co.uk/world/2009/jun/22/neda-soltani-death-iran

Thompson, S. A., & Warzel, C. (2019, December 19). Twelve million phones, one dataset, zero privacy. *The New York Times*. Retrieved from www.nytimes.com/interactive/2019/12/19/opinion/location-tracking-cell-phone.html?action=click&module=Opinion&pgtype=Homepage

Thompson, S. A., & Wezerek, G. (2019, December 19). Freaked out? 3 Steps to protect your phone. *The New York Times*. Retrieved from www.nytimes.com/interactive/2019/12/19/opinion/location-tracking-privacy-tips.html

Thornburgh, D., & Boccardi, L. D. (2005, January 5). *Report of the independent review panel on the September 8, 2004, 60 Minutes Wednesday segment 'For the Record' concerning President Bush's Texas Air National Guard service*. Retrieved from www.image.cbsnews.com/htdocs/pdf/complete_report/CBS_Report.pdf

Thornburg, R., (2013, November 13). How to cover live events: Create an experience [Web log post]. Retrieved from http://ryanthornburg.com/category/multimedia-journalism

Thorson, E., Shoenberger, H., Karaliova, T., Kim, E., & Fidler, R. (2015). News use of mobile media: A contingency model. *Mobile Media & Communication*, 3(2), 160–178. doi:10.1177/2050157914557692

Thucydides., Finley, M. I. (Ed.)., & Warner, R. (Translator.). (1972). *History of the Peloponnesian War* (Rev. ed). New York: Penguin Books.

Tofte, S., & Husain, N. (2019). *Losing the news: The decimation of local journalism and the search for solutions*. PEN America. Retrieved from https://pen.org/wp-content/

WORKS CITED

uploads/2019/11/Losing-the-News-The-Decimation-of-Local-Journalism-and-the-Search-for-Solutions.pdf

Tompkins, A. (2015, February 4). Veterans force NBC's Brian Williams to apologize. *MediaWire*. Retrieved from www.poynter.org/reporting-editing/2015/veterans-force-nbcs-brian-williams-to-apologize/

Trask, R. B. (1994). *Pictures of the Pain: Photography and the assassination of John F. Kennedy*. Danvers, MA: Yeoman Press.

Tu, D. L. (2015). *Video now*. Tow Center for Digital Journalism. Retrieved from https://web.archive.org/web/20160310035208/http://videonow.towcenter.org/

Tufte, E. R. (2001). *The visual display of quantitative information* (2nd ed.). Cheshire, CO: Graphics Press.

Victor, D. (2015, April 27). The one word journalists should add to Twitter searches that you probably haven't considered. [Web log post]. Retrieved from https://medium.com/@bydanielvictor/the-one-word-reporters-should-add-to-twitter-searches-that-you-probably-haven-t-considered-fadab1bc34e8

Villi, M., & Matikainen, J. (2015). Mobile UDC: Online media content distribution among Finnish mobile users. *Mobile Media & Communication*, 3(2), 214–229. doi:10.1177/2050157914552156

Villi, M., Matikainen, J., & Khaldarova, I. (2016). Recommend, tweet, share: User-distributed content (UDC) and the convergence of news media and social networks. In A. Lugmayr & C. Dal Zotto (Eds.), *Media convergence handbook, Vol. 1. Media business and innovation* (pp. 289–306). Berlin, Germany: Springer.

Vossen, C. (n.d.). The importance of audio...in video [Web log post]. Retrieved from www.522productions.com/the-importance-of-audio-in-video

Waite, M., & Kreimer, B. (2016). *Drone journalism lab operations manual*. University of Nebraska, College of Journalism and Mass Communications Faculty Publications, 96. Retrieved from http://digitalcommons.unl.edu/journalismfacpub/96

Waldman, S., & Sennott, C. (2020, March 25). The coronavirus is killing local news. *The Atlantic*. Retrieved from www.theatlantic.com/ideas/archive/2020/03/coronavirus-killing-local-news/608695/

Walker, M. (2019). *Americans favor mobile devices over desktops and laptops for getting news*. Pew Research Center. Retrieved from www.pewresearch.org/fact-tank/2019/11/19/americans-favor-mobile-devices-over-desktops-and-laptops-for-getting-news/

Ward, C. (2015, August 12). How to set audio levels for video [Web log post]. Retrieved from www.premiumbeat.com/blog/how-to-set-audio-levels-for-video/

Wardle, C. (2014). Verifying user-generated content. In C. Silverman (Ed.), *Verification handbook*. Maastricht, NL: European Journalism Center. Retrieved from https://verificationhandbook.com/book/chapter3.php

Wardle, C. (2016, November 18). 6 types of misinformation circulated this election season. *Columbia Journalism Review*. Retrieved from www.cjr.org/tow_center/6_types_election_fake_news.php

Wardle, C., Dubberley, S., & Brown, P. (2014). *Amateur footage: A global study of user-generated content in TV and online-news output*. Tow Center for Digital Journalism. doi: 10.7916/D88S526V

Weiner, J. (2014, December). Toward a critical theory of podcasting. *Slate*. Retrieved from www.slate.com/articles/arts/ten_years_in_your_ears/2014/12/what_makes_podcasts_so_addictive_and_pleasurable.html

Weischenberg, S., Löffelholz, M., & Scholl, A. (1998). Journalists in Germany. In D. H. Weaver (Ed.), *The global journalist: News people around the world* (pp. 229–256). Cresskill, NJ: Hampton Press.

Weiss, J. (2014, September 9). Mobile journalism workflow: Seven basic steps. *Digital Journalism*. Retrieved from https://ijnet.org/en/story/mobile-journalism-workflow-seven-basic-steps

Wemple, E. (2008, February15). One mission, two newsrooms: A river runs through the struggle for the future of *The Washington Post*. *Washington City Paper*. Retrieved from www.washingtoncitypaper.com/articles/34569/one-mission-two-newsrooms

Wenger, D. (2015). What mobile journalism should be and why it isn't. In D. Halpern-Winger & D. Potter (Eds.), *Advancing the story: Journalism in a multimedia world* (2nd ed.). Retrieved from www.advancingthestory.com/2015/05/11/what-mobile-journalism-should-be-and-why-it-isnt/

Westlund, O. (2015). News consumption in an age of mobile media: Patterns, people, place, and participation. *Mobile Media & Communication*, 3(2), 151–159. doi:10.1177/2050157914563369

Westlund, O., & Färdigh, A. M. (2015). Accessing the news in an age of mobile media: Tracing displacing and complementary effects on mobile news on newspapers and online news. *Mobile Media & Communication*, 3(1), 53–74. doi:10.1177/2050157914549039

Wilbert, M. (2016, May 10). Why audio matters most for audiences [Web log post]. Retrieved from web.archive.org/web/20160720041834/www.dacast.com/blog/audio-matters-audiences/

Willens, M. (2019, July). The CMS war between Vox Media and *The Washington Post* is heating up. *Digiday*. Retrieved from https://digiday.com/media/cms-war-vox-media-washington-post-heating/

Windschuttle, K. (1999). Journalism and the Western tradition. *Australian Journalism Review*, 21(1), 50–67.

Winn, R. (2019, June). Podcast stats & facts (new research from June 2019). *Podcasting Insights*. Retrieved from www.podcastinsights.com/podcast-statistics/

Winston, B. (2006). *Messages: Free expression, media and the West from Gutenberg to Google*. New York: Routledge.

Wise, K., Bolls, P., Myers, J., & Sternadori, M. (2009). When words collide online: How writing style and video intensity affect cognitive processing of online news. *Journal of Broadcasting & Electronic Media*, 53(4), 532–546. doi:10.1080/08838150903333023

Wittel, A. (2000). Ethnography on the move: From field to net to internet. *Forum for Qualitative Research*, 1(1). Retrieved from www.qualitative-research.net/index.php/fqs/article/view/1131/2517

Wojdynski, B. W. (2016). The deceptiveness of sponsored news articles: How readers recognize and perceive native advertising. *American Behavioral Scientist*, 60(12),

WORKS CITED

1475–1491. doi:10.1177/0002764216660140. Received from https://journals.sagepub.com/doi/full/10.1177/0002764216660140#articleCitationDownloadContainer

Yang, K. C., Varol, O., Hui, P. M., & Menczer, F. (2019). Scalable and generalizable social bot detection through data selection. Cornell University. Retrieved from https://arxiv.org/pdf/1911.09179.pdf

Yopp, J., McAdams, K., & Thornburg, R. (2010). *Reaching audiences: A guide to media writing* (5th ed.). Boston, MA: Pearson/Allyn & Bacon.

Zechmeister, J. J., Shaughnessy, E. B., & Zechmeister, J. S. (2009). *Research methods in psychology* (8th ed.). Boston, MA: McGraw-Hill.

Zimmerman, E., & Koon-Stack, C. (n.d.). How to incorporate multimedia into your storytelling [Web log post]. Retrieved from https://storytelling.comnetwork.org/explore/172/how-to-incorporate-multimedia-into-your-storytelling

Zuboff, S. (1988). *In the age of the smart machine: The future of work and power.* New York: Basic Books.

Zuo, M., Cheng, L., Yan, A., & Yau, C. (2019, December 31). Hong Kong takes emergency measures as mystery 'pneumonia' infects dozens in China's Wuhan city. *South China Morning Post.* Retrieved from www.scmp.com/news/china/politics/article/3044050/mystery-illness-hits-chinas-wuhan-city-nearly-30-hospitalised

Zwillenberg, P., Field, D., & Dean, D. (2014). *The connected world: Greasing the wheels of the internet economy.* Boston Consulting Group. Retrieved from www.icann.org/en/system/files/files/bcg-internet-economy-27jan14-en.pdf

INDEX

Page numbers in **bold** refer to content in figures; page numbers in *italics* refer to content in tables.

360° cameras 244, 245
5W1H 89, 94, 97

Abernathy, P. 362
accuracy 191–192
Adair, Bill 201
adblocker, ad-blocking software 179, 325, 337, 374
advertising (online) 14, 33, 41, 324–326, 336–337; display ads 325; native ads 325, 329, 390; programmatic ads 325, 329; revenues 30, 33, 41, *60*; types 325; user-tailored ads 325
affordances 311–315, *312, 314*, **315, 342,** 375; digital affordances 313–314; users' technology 314–315; mobile devices 341–343
aggregation/aggregator 171, 251, 379
Al-Jazeera 203, 252
AlNoamany, Y. 88
altering images 279–280
alt-right websites 358
American Press Institute (API) 35, 37
American Trends Panel (ATP) 20–21
analog, analogue, analogous 208–209, **208, 209,** 224, 376; analog vs. digital 208–209, **208, 209**
analytics 62, 73–75, 316, 321–323, **322,** 344, 348, 376
Andersen, M. 23, 136, 137
Anderson, M. 333
anonymous sources 169, 172–176
apps 48, 336–337, 345

Archer, D. 71, 112
Arlen, Gary 44
Armstrong, Jim 17
artificial intelligence (AI) 47–48, 63, 363, **363**
Ashley Madison 145
asset acquisition 228; audio 245–251, **248–250;** data 257–258; equipment management 235–236; live streaming 252–253; photographs 236–240, **237–239;** podcasts 251; preliminary steps 230–234, **234;** videos 240–245; virtual and augmented reality 244–254; *see also* processing workflows
Associated Press 70, 222, 255, 273, 364
Atlantic, The 37, 201
attribution (source) 143, 168–170, 190, 391; attribution agreements 168–169; misattribution 193; to anonymous sources 175
Atwood, Margaret 82
audience behavior 34–37, **34, 35;** consumer devices 34–36, *35;* print vs. digital readership 46; relationship with journalists 39–40; sources of news 36–37
audio acquisition 247–251; clipping 250, **250,** 378; digital audio recorder (DAR) 248, 250, 251, 382; noise 247, 248; podcasts 247, 251; *see also* microphones
audio processing 283–287; editing **286;** mixing/sweetening adjustments **284;** with video 282–285, **283**
augmented reality (AR) 48, 111–112, 242, 244–245
Axios.com 14

background information 98–100, 112, 125–127, 131–132, 224; *see also* PACER
Bangor Daily News, The 319
Barthel, M. 20–21, 33, 35, 56
Bauman, Zygmunt 58–61, 62–64, 73, 83
BBC 37; audio-only stories 285; data stories 255; integrated newsroom **66**, 348; interview with Prince Andrew 361; users and video 240; writing online stories 272, 344
beauty shots 238
Beckett, C. 38, 72, **72**
Bell, Daniel 58
Benkler, Y. 358
Berret, C. 180
bias 20, 21, 37, 154, 365
Bissinger, Buzz 162, **162**, 373–374
blanket waivers 176
blogs 131–132, 141
Bloomberg 17
Boos, Katherine 155
Borchers, Callum 147
Bordoni, C. 59
Boston Globe, The 252, 338; Boston Marathon bombing (2013) 252, 338
bots 25–26, **26**, 29, 47, 65, 129, 143, 145–146, 254, 377; socialbots 145–146
Bounegru, L. 258
bounce, bounce rate 320, 326, 343, 377
boyd, D. 255, 313
Bradley, Steven 321
Brandtzaeg, P. B. 129, 130
breaking news 18, 86–88, *120*, 131, 190, 200, 202, 222, 348
Breitbart.com 14, 37, 91
Brennen, B. 19
Broersma, M. 71
Bromwich, J. E. 144
Brown, Julie 17, 360–361
Brown, Malachy 219–220
Buchman, Brandi 10, 319, 369
Buckley, Samuel 64
Bucks County Courier Times 66
budget, news 92
Budiu, R. 341
Bunting, L. 364
Business Insider 323
business model changes 41–42, 46–48
business strategies 42–46
Buttry, Steve 199, 223
Buzzfeed.com 14, 36, 144, 302

cable news 34
California Consumer Privacy Act (CCPA) 324, 337
Callaghan, R. 255
Carpenter, Les 334–335
Carr, David 190, 355, 369
Carvin, Andy 23
Castle, M. 111
causation *111*, 289, 293, 378
CBS 194
Center for Innovation and Sustainability in Local Media (University of North Carolina) 362
Center for Investigative Reporting (CIR) 364
Centers for Disease Control and Prevention (CDC) 294
Centre for Investigative Journalism (CIJ) 180, 357
Chalkbeat 67
Chartbeat 321, **322**
Chen, B. X. 63, 176
Chen, V. Y. 9, 39, 198
Cheney, Kyle 146–147
Chicago Tribune, The 14
Chorus (Vox Media) 316, 319
Christianity Today 358
Chronology 89, **90**, 109, 162, 267, 274, 305, 378
Christin, Angele 73
Churchill, Winston 233
Chyi, H. I. 46
cinematic documentary videos 280
classifications of news 92
Clemens, Roger 334–335
clickbait 86
CNN 14, 17, 203, 293, 320
Coase, Ronald 257
Cochrane, Andy 296
codebooks 289
Codianni, Ashley 2, 10, 370, **370**
Coester, D. 66
Colbert, Stephen 189
collaboration 85, 140–141, 318, 364
color adjustment 278–279
Columbus Dispatch, The 14
combination narrative structures 309–310
Committee to Protect Journalists (CPJ) 176, 177, 179
communications security (comsec) 177–179
competition 42–43, **43**, 45

INDEX

confirmation bias 37, 154, 365
Consent Management Platforms (CMPs) 324
Conservative Daily Post 144
Consortium for Investigative Journalists (CIJ) 141
consumer devices 34–36, *35*
content assets *see* asset acquisition; multimedia assets
content exclusivity 43
content farms 44
content management system (CMS) 264, 267, 302, 303, **304**, 315–319, 328, 379; and metadata 266; limits of 296, in mobile reporting 339, 359
contested content 71–72, **72**
contexts, of stories 98–99, **98–99**
Cook, Tony 46
copy processing workflows 272–275, **273**, **275**
copyright: rules 141–143, 230–231; licensing 239–240, 388; public domain 142, 394; rights clearance 203; *see also* creating; fair use
coronavirus *see* COVID-19 crisis (2020)
corrections 26–27
Cortico 364
COSINT (crowdsourced intelligence) 128
Cougar Claw, The 365
Courthouse News 2, 10, 17, 369
covariation 289, 380
COVID-19 crisis (2020) 7–8, 9–10, 54; data visualizations (DVs) 293–294; local news 33; nongovernmental sources 167; peer-reviewed articles 134; psychological trauma 236; reporting ethically 82, 87; trust in news media 367; verification of information 188–189, 196
Cramm, The 365
credibility levels 19–21, building credibility 21–24
crediting 203
cropping photographs 277, **277**
cross-platform ownership 42
crowdsourcing 12–13, 22–23, 25, 39, 40, 129, 136–137, 198
CrowdTangle 27
Crozier, Brett 167
cues 164, *164–165*
culture of journalism 56–58
Cuomo, Chris 54
curation 23, 88, 122
Cushion, S. 255
cybermobs 143; cyber-stalking 122

Daily Breeze 22, 118, 229
Daily Courant 64
Dailybeast.com 37, 132
Dallas Morning News, The 218
Dance, Gabriel 2, 235
DAR (digital audio recording) systems 248, 250, 251
Darknet 26
data: analysis 228, 256–257, 289–292, *290*, 294–295; collection 129, 133, 254–258; data smog 58; data stories 109–111, *110–111*; data visualizations (DVs) 109–110, 137–138, 287–288, **287**, 292–294, 295; data wrangling 288–289; extracting information from 132–137, **135**; privacy laws 323–324; processing workflows 287–295, **287–288**, *290*; rise of data journalism 138–140, 255
DataRefuge 128
Davenport, T. H. 110
Dean, D. 86
decks 100–101, 344, 347
deepfakes 154, 218–219
de Los Santos, T. 39, 72
de Rosa, Anthony 202
Demma, Joe 176
Denver Guardian 144
de Rosa, A. 202
DeRienzo, M. 365
Der Spiegel 201
design 229, **230**, 303, **303**, 345–348, **346**; Responsive Web Design (RWD) 332, 347, 395; website design 228–229; mobile first vs. desktop first 347–348
details grafs 97
Detroit Free Press 240
Deuze, M. 62–63, 72
Diamond, D. 196–197
digital vs. analog 208–209, **208–209**; digital first strategies 45–46; startups 41, *60–61*; technology integration *60–61*; transformation 14–15, *15–16*, 32–36; *see also* digital content
digital content 67–70; contested content 71–72, **72**; online news writing 84–86; users as promoters 73–75
DiMeo, Nate 245–246
direct observation 156
Director of National Intelligence (USA) 144
DiResta, Renee 360
disinformation, deza 9, 23–25, 382; *see also* fake news

disintermediation 44
distribution 14, *16*, *60*, 302, **315**, 321, 347; *see also* packaging assets
distrust *see* trust levels
Doctor, Ken 14, 41, 42
Doherty, Richard 44
DomainTools 208
Drudgereport.com 14, 37, 132
Dubberly, S. 142
D'Vorkin, Lewis 40, 60

echo chambers 37
Echosec 204
Eddington, S. M. 358
Edelmen, Richard 19
Edelmen Trust Barometer (2017 survey) 19
Edison Research 247
editorial online content workflows **283**, 303–311, *303–304*, *304*, *306–310*; audio editing workflow 284, **284**, 286–287, **286**; copy processing workflow 273; data processing workflow **288**, 295, *288*; metadata in workflow 210–211; multimedia acquisition preparation **251**; pre-processing workflow 266–270, **267**; photographs 239, 278–280, **276**; video 221, 270, **281**, 282–283, *283*
editorial oversight 92, 93
Eldridge, S. 71
Electronic Frontier Foundation 179
emotion 38–39, 71–72, **72**, 241
emotional security (emotsec) 181–182
employment, newsrooms 41
Engler, A. 219
Environmental Data and Governance Initiative (EDGI) 128
ephemeralization 58
Epstein, Jeffrey 17, 360–361
ESPN 161
equipment: audio 248–250, **248–249**; mobile journalism 340; photography 235–236; podcasts 251; video 242–243; virtual and augmented 244–245
European Dailies Alliance (EDA) 141
European Investigate Collaborations (EIC) 141
European Journalism Centre (EJC) 200
experiencing news 69–70, 240–241
explanatory grafs 99–100, 103
exposure, image 277–278, **278**
extended reality (XR) *see* augmented reality (AR); virtual reality (VR)
eyewitness accounts 43, 71, 171, 202–204, 222
Eyewitness Media Hub 203

Facebook 12–13, 129; corrections 27; deepfake identification 218, 220; live streaming 253; news gathering 130; revenues 41, 46; videos 241, 281
fact-checking 23–24, 201–202, 359
facts (def) 193, 366
fair use 142–143, 230–231; public domain 142
fake news 23–27, 144, 171–172, **189**, 359–361, **360**
Fallaci, Oriana 160
Fallis, David xvii, 2, 121–122, 151–152
Farid, H. 216, 218
Ferrier, M. 372
Fast, K. 61
Federal Aviation Administration (FAA) 140
Federal Communications Commission (FCC) 42
Federal Trade Commission (FTC) 145
Fellig, Arthur 238
female journalists' abuse 143, 371–372, **372**
Ferguson Protests (2014) 370, **370**
Few, Stephen 138
Field, D. 86
FIFA corruption scandal (2015) 168
filters 37
Finger, K. 71, 112
Finnerty, Megan 59
First Amendment (USA constitution) 54–55, 205, 236
First Draft 87–88, 222
FiveThirtyEight.com 14, 37, 136, 246
flagging 25
flash mobs 12–13
Flipboard 335
Forbes 40, 60
Foreign Policy 246
FotoForensics 211, **211**, 214
F-pattern 321, **322**
Fragomeni, John 296
France 2 TV channel 70
Freedom of Information Act (FOIA) 257
Freedom of the Press Foundation (FPF) 180, 181
freelancers 58, *61*, 64, 96, 232, 240, 253, 272, 298, 379; precariat 59, 76, 393
Fuller, Buckminster 58
future changes in news 46–48, 362–364

Garofoli 167
Gallup 20, 24
GANS (generative adversarial networks) 218, 219
gatekeeping 55–56

INDEX

General Data Privacy Regulation (GDPR) 323–324, 337
Gentry, Leah 305
Geofeedia 204
geo-fencing 340, **340**
geotagging 339
get (interviews) 161–162
Gibbs, Nancy 117, 178
Gibson, James 313
Global Investigative Journalism Network (GIJN) 141
Godler, Y. 120
golden triangle 321, 329, 345, **346**, 385
Google: data visualizations (DVs) 295; deepfakes identification 218, 220; Google News Initiative 319; Google News Lab 222, 364; revenues 46; search results rankings 124; web advertising 41
government data 127–128
governmental privacy regulation 323–324; California Consumer Privacy Act (CCPA) 324, 337; General Data Privacy Regulation (GDPR) 323–324, 337
GPS (Global Positioning System) **340**, 343
Graham, Katharine 357
Graphic, The 365
Graphic Artists Guild 240
Gray, J. 258
Green, J. 73
Green, M. C. 105
green screens 217, **217**
Grieco, E. 362
Grier, D. A. 349
Guardian, The 9, 18, 37, 42, 67, 287, 301, 358; abuse of female journalists 371–372; crowdsourcing 22–23, 136–137, **136**, 198; data analysis 136–137; integrated newsroom 348; Iran election protests (2009) 12; MP expenses scandal (UK, 2009) 22–23, 136–137, **137**, 198
Guzman, Monica 74

Handbook of Journalism (Reuters) 175
Hanitzsch, T. 56–57
hard news 92, 358
Hart, Jack 99, 104, 108
Hastings, Michael 39
headlines 100–101, **273**, 344, 347
Heider, Tim 127
Hermann, Steve 348
Hermida, A. 19
Herr, Michael 371

hierarchical narrative structure 308, **309**
Higgins, Eliot 221
Hitchens, Christopher 160
Hoffer, Eric 361
Hohmann, James 88
homophily 37
hooks 93, **93**, 94, 102
Hosp, David 81, 82
Houston, Brant 127
Hsu, Tiffany 17
HTML (Hypertext Markup Language) 229, 318, 347–348
HuffPost 14, 37, 85, 132, 240
Hulu 34
human sources *see* sources (human)
Hunter, M. L. 94, 109

IBM (International Business Machines) 60, 254
Ignatius, David 193
IJR.org 14, 37, 91
illustrations 239–240
inattentional blindness 154
indirect observation 156, **157**
inferences 193–194
infodemic 9–10, 188–189
information bubbles 37, 45; infowar 143–147; overload 27, 58; security 179–182
Ingram, A. 198
interactive assets 85, 228, 229, 233, 311; *see also* asset acquisition
interactive data visualizations (DVs) 292–293
internal links 98
International Journalists' Network (IJNET) 258
International News Safety Institute (INSI) 372
International Women's Media Foundation (IWMF) 372
internet: overview 83–84; factors affecting web news 84–86; introduction of 14; navigation 205–208; number of users 34, **34**; *see also* online writing principles; social media
Internet Corporation for Assigned Names and Numbers (ICANN) **207**, 387
Internet of Things (IoT) 48, 363
interviews 160–166, *163*, 250; via technology 163–165, *164–165*
inverted pyramid structure 89, **89**, 96–100, 368
Iran election protests (2009) 12–13, **13**

Jannsen, H. 201
Jarvis, Jeff 144–145
Jenkins, Henry 73, 75, 313, 398
Jenner, Caitlin 162, 373

Jennings, Andrew 168
Johns Hopkins University 167, 189
Johnson, Boris 9
Jones, Alex 144
journalism: overview 355–356; changes and adaptations 361–364, **363**; cultures 56–57 exciting, scrappy and fun vocation 369–374; facts, truth, and trust 365–368; importance of journalism 356–357; renumeration and personal branding 368–369, **368**; student publications 365; user-centered journalism 358–361
journalist roles 44, 55–57, 60–64, *60–61*, **368**, 369; routines 63–64, 74–75
JPEG (Joint Photographic Experts Group) 211, *212–213*

Kalogeropoulos, A. 240–241, 280–281
Kansas City Star, The 27
Kaphle, Anup 100
Karlsson, M. 61
Kathmandu Post, The 100
Kavanaugh, J. 71
Kelly, Mary Louise 173
Key Performance Indicators (KPIs) 316
kit *see* equipment
Klasfeld, Adam 17
Knight Commission on Trust, Media and Democracy 367
Knight Foundation 20, 24, 36, 335, 364
Koon-Stack, C. 232
Kovach, Bill 17, 187, 191, 198–199, 223
Krawetz, Neal 214
Kruikemeier, S. 167

labeling content 204
ladder of abstraction 98–99, **98**, 104
Lagun, D. 241
Lakoff, George 223
Lakshmanan, I. R. A. 366
Lalmas, M. 241
Lancet, The 134, 196
Lara, A. 95
LaTorra, J. 111
leakers 174–175, 180
Lecheler, S. 167
lede 96–97, 102 388; punch lede 96, 304; quote lede 96, 397
Lensfest Local Lab, Philadelphia 340, 364
Lewis, J. 255
Lewis, R. 143

licensing 239–240; *see also* copyright
Lichterman, J. 222
linear-embedded narrative structure 308, **308**
links, web 22, 23, 54, 66, 85, 98, 170, 229, *314*
liquid modernity 58–59, 76, 388; ephemeralization 58, 383; precariat 59, 76, 393
live streaming 252–253
Livingstone, Sonia 40
local news 20, 22, 33, 362, 365
Löffelholz, M. 63
Loftus, Elizabeth 154
Lorenz, M. 366
Los Angeles Times, The 65; newsroom 178; multimedia stories 305–307; privacy 324
Luce, Henry 374

Mandese, Joe 87
many-to-many (M2M) overview 8, 11, 12–13, 18, **18**, 24, 32
Mapes, Mary 194
market forces 42–45
Marvin, Carolyn 47–48
Marwick, A. 143
Marx, Groucho 21
Mashable 240
Massachusetts Institute of Technology (MIT) 134
Matikainen, J. 336
McAdams, M. 94
McDonald, Will 140
media assets *see* assets
MediaInfo 219
MediaPost Marketing Daily 97, 91
MediaStorm 240
Mesgari, M. 125
metadata 209–216, **209**, **215**, *210*, *212–213*, *215–216*; camera metadata *210*, **211–21**; content assembly 264, 318, 264, 318, 389; informational metadata 210–211; strip out metadata 211, 214, 219; structural metadata 210, *212*, 219, 225, 396, *212–213*, 219, 266; video metadata 219
methodological triangulation 195–197, **195**
methods graf 367, **368**
Miami Herald 17, 360–361, 365
Michigan Daily, The 365
microphones 242, 248–250, **248–249**; choosing 250; types 248, pickup patterns **248**
Microsoft 218
Miller, Judith 175

INDEX

mind maps 267, **268**, 275
Minet, Carla 357
mischief-makers 172
Missourian, The 365
Mitchell, A. 24, 35, 36, 240, 333, 344
mobile phones: affordances and limitations 341–343, **342**; audiences 36, 336–337; breaking news 337–338; news organization apps 345; newsroom workflows 348–349, **350**; producing stories for 343–345, **345**; recording audio 248; reporting equipment and apps 340; rise in use of 11–12, **12**, 83, **83**, 331–335; security for 178–179, 181; webpage design 345–348, **346**; workflows for field reporters 338–339, **339**
mockups 310, **316, 317**
money shot 238, 389
Montgomery, Robb 331
MP expenses scandal (UK, 2009) 136–137, *137*, 198
Mueller, Robert 173, 266
multimedia assets 228–232, **232**, 247, 253, 258–260, 297–298, 308–311, 326–327, **339**, 376; *see also* asset acquisition
multimedia story construction 305–307; deconstruction 305, **306**; reconstruction 305–306, **306**, 395
multimedia stories, overview 14–15, **15**, 100; processing workflows 265–266, **265**, 273–275, **273, 275**; *see also* asset acquisition
multiple sources 187, 192, 194–195
Murphy, Mary 361, 373
Murray, Janet 313, *314*, 327
Murrow, Edward R. 53

Nabi, R. 39, 72
narrative structures 114, 307, **308**, 326; combination formats 309–310, 326–327, 379; hierarchical format 308, **309**, 326–327, 385; linear-embedded format 308, 309, 326–327, 388; nonlinear format 309, **310**, 326–327, 388
National Aeronautics and Space Administration (NASA) 144
National Archives and Records Administration (NARA) 127
National Press Photographers Association (NPPA) 279
National Security Agency (NSA) 235
native ads 325, 329, 390
National Geographic 287

National Public Radio (NPR) 173; crowdsourcing 23; diversity 22; podcast 246; user engagement 67, 246
NBC News 129–130, 173
Nelson, M. L. 88
net neutrality 42, 390
network SS7-exploit 178, 390
New England Journal of Medicine, The 134, 196
New York Times, The 12, 24, 41, 91, 130, 134, 161, 175, 197, 235, 240, 255, 287; cinematic video 280; comments moderation 74; extended reality (XR) 70, 112; journalist skills 12; interactive data 293, 294; newsroom 65; NYT internal technology study 63; pandemic 294, 367; permissible photograph alterations 279–280; privacy 194, 323; subscription roll-out 41–42
Newman, N. 22, 240, 280, 366, 384
News Co/Lab, Arizona State University 27, 365
news features 92, 101–103, **102**, 114, 154, 160, 390
news gathering 118, *119–120* 121; blogs 131–132; copyright barriers 141–143; data and information 132–140, **135**; information wars 143–146; news judgment 63, 75; observation and collaboration 140–141; online information overview 120–122; public records 126–128, **126**; search engines 123–124; social media 129–131; *see also* sources (human)
news judgement 63, 75
news story types 92–93, 101–103; hard news 92, 358; news feature 92, 101–103, **102**, 114, 154, 160, 390; reports 88–89, **89**, 90; roundup 85, 395; running story 58, 93, 396; scenic narratives 92–93, 103–109, **107**, *119–120*; soft news 92, 241, 397; ticktock 109, 162, 232, 399
news value 91, 391
news work 59–65, **65**; contingent labor 61, 64, 379, 384; changing routines 62–64; freelancer 15, 54, 58, *61*, 270, 384; gig economy 15, *15*, 379; newsrooms 64–66, **65**; precariat 59, 76, 393; stringer 58, 398; working conditions 59–61, *60–61*
News Markup Language (NewsML) 318, 390
NewsMatch 364
Newsonomics 41, 42
newspaper circulation 33
newspaper design 229, **230**, 303, **303**

News pegs **93**, 101, 114
newsrooms 64–68, **65**; mobile workflows 348–349, **350**
Newsy 240
Nielsen Research 35, 36
Night Sky app 345
non-linear narrative structure 309, **310**
nonprofit organizations 87, 95, 128, 205, 364
Normile, Dennis 293–294
NPR (National Public Radio) 22, 25, 67, 173, 246
nut grafs **89**, **90**, 97, 100, 102, **102**, 113–114, 231, 266, 272, **275**, **293**, 391

observation 140, 152–160, 391; controlled/uncontrolled behavior 157, 380, 400; direct/indirect 156–157, **157**, 382, 386; natural/contrived 158, 380, 390; objective/subjective 156, 391, 399; participant/nonparticipant 156, 391, 392; structured/nonstructured 158, 391, 398; *see also* planning observation; remote observation
observational bias 154–155; confirmation bias 37, 154, 365; inattentional blindness 154; expectational blindness 155
off the record 166, 169, 170, 185, 391; *see also* unnamed sources
on the record 147, 166, 169–170, 182, 184–185
OneNewsNow.com 91
Online News Association (ONA) 348, 352
online users profile 66–67, 255
online writing principles 84–86; breaking news 86–88; reports 96–100
operational security (opsec) 176–177, 185, 392
Ordway, D. 174
organizational resources 32
Organized Crime and Corruption Reporting Project (OCCRP) 141
Ornebring, H. 61
OSINT (open source intelligence) 128
Owen, L. H. 71

PACER (Public Access to Court Electronic Records) 127, 392
packaging assets 302, **310–311**, 392
paralinguistic cues 164, 392
participant observation 156, 392
participatory journalism 23, 39–40, 393; *see also* public participation
Pavlik, J. V. 62

peer-reviewed journal articles 133–134, 147, 196
Pelham Examiner, The 365
PEN America 33
personal branding 44, 63, **368**, 369, 393
Pew Research Center: local news 362; mobile news consumption 35, 344; news media consumption 35–36, 46; news media employment 41; trustworthiness and fake news 20–21, 24
Philadelphia Inquirer, The geofencing 340, **340**
Phillips, A. 170, 188
photographs: processing workflows 276–280, **276–278**
Pittsburgh Post-Gazette 65
planning observation 152–154, 159–160, 183
podcasts 54, 246–247, 251
Politico.com 14, 41, 146; Tom Price investigation 197–198
Pompeo, Michael R. 40
Porter Competitive Forces Model 42–45, **43**; new entrants **43**, 44; news suppliers 44–45, 50
Pradhan, R. 196–197
presidential election of 2016 (U.S.) 25–26, 144, 173
President Trump 12, 23, 56, 202, 366
press, roles of 54–56, **55**; amplifying 10, 12–13, 376
Press-Enterprise 94
Priest, Dana 173
privacy 122, 124, 127, 140, 176–177, 179, 313, 321, 323–324, 326, 329, 393
processing memos 270–271, 299, 393
processing plans 271–272, 299, 393
processing workflows 263–266, 393; audio 282–287, **283–284**, **286**; copy 272–273, **273**; data 287–295, **287**, **288**, **290**; extended reality (XR) 296–297; mobile journalism 338–339, **339**, 348–349, **350**; photographs 276–280, **276–278**; pre-processing workflows 266–272, **267**; videos 280–285, **281**, **283**
propaganda 144, 146, 360, 382
ProPublica 42, 364
Protect Intellectual Property Act 125
Protess, D. 199, 223
Protess method 198, 199–200, **199**, **223**, 394
public participation: contested content 71; social curation 88
public records 118, 121–122, 126–128, **126**, 139–140, 146, 363

INDEX

qualifiers 97–98, 394
qualitative data 132, 254–255, 394
quantitative data 132, 254–255, 394
Quartz 66; augmented reality 70

radio news 35, 36, 67, 228, 248
Ramos, Jorge 365
RAND Corporation 71
Rather, Dan 194
Rauch, Jonathan 201–202
Reardon, Kathleen 312
Reddit 143, 179, 218, 335
Redstate.com 37
Reich, Z. 120
reliability 134–136; in data 134–135, **135**, 395; in user-generated content 204–205; *see also* public participation
remote observation 153–154, 156, 395; drones 140, 158, **159**
rendering 282, 285–285, **286**, 296–297, 395
renumeration 368–369
Report for America 364
report structures 88–89, **89**, 96–101
Reporters Without Borders 156
Responsive Web Design (RWD) 332, 347, 395
Reuters 37, 222, 240, 369; anonymous sources 175; single-sourced stories 195
Reuters Institute for the Study of Journalism (RISJ) 240, 366
Revers, M. 181
Ribiero, Victor 221
Rigdon, S. 293
Ripley, A. 359
Risen, James 175
Robinson, S. 54, 62, 66–67
Rogers, Everett 200, 312, *312*, 333, 396; Diffusion of Innovation Model **333**
Rogers, K. 144
Rogers, S. 17
Rogers, T. 84
Roosevelt, Theodore (Teddy) 368–369
Rosen, Jay 31; TPFKATA 399
Rosenstiel, Tom 17, 46, 187, 191, 198–199, 223
rough drafts 231, 267, **267**
roundups 85, 395
Roush, Chris 95
Rowell, Rainbow 355
Russell, Bertrand 83
Rutledge, P. 105

Sacco, Justine 13
Salon 14, 37
Sambrook, Richard 140–141, 280
scenic narratives 92–93, 103–109, **107**, *119–120*
S-curve of adoption 333, *333*, 396
Schmidt, T. 39
Scholl, A. 63
Schulte-Ruther, M. 154
Schweitzer, Callie 190
Science Magazine 294
ScribbleLive 252
search engine optimization (SEO) 101
search engines 62, 123–124, 148, *314*, 344; *see also* Google
SecureDrop 179–180, 182
security management 176–182; communications security; (comsec) 176–179; information security (infosec) 176–181; operational security (opsec) 176–179; emotional security (emotsec) 181–182
Seixas, Jair 221
Sennott, C. 33
Shapiro, I. 190
Shastri, Veda 111–112
Shearer, E. 53
Shorenstein Center, Harvard Kennedy School 257, 364
shot 160, 172, 237–239, **238–239**, 242–245, 276, 283, 338; shot list **234**, 243, 253, 397
Signal 179
Silver, Nate 136
Silverman, C. 23, 144, 190, 200, 223
single-sourced stories 195
Slivka, Judd 338
smartphones *see* mobile phones
Smolkin, R. 170, 176
social curation 88, 396
social media 11–13; as bridge to news websites 14, 36; corrections 27; fake news 360; gatekeeping 55; journalists' use of 74–75; live streaming 252–253; news gathering 129–131; promotion 319, 320; trust in 20; user-generated content (UGC) 71, 202–204; verification 18–19; video viewing habits 241; *see also* Facebook; Twitter
Socialist Worker 358
Society of Professional Journalists (SPJ) 179
soft news 92, 397
sources (human) 57, 166–168; attribution 168–170; multiple sources 195–197; routine

sources and eye witnesses 170–171; source security 176–182; source reliability 191–192, 395; source validity 191–192

South China Morning Post 293–294

Speer, N. K. 105

Spokeo 204, 220

spreadability 73, 75, 86, 336, 398

Stars and Stripes 130

State, The 365

Steiner, Peter 159

Stop Online Piracy Act 125–126

Stoppard, Tom 357

stories (in cultures) 121–123

story angles 93, **93**, 94–96, 102, 123–124

story assets *see* asset acquisition; multimedia assets; processing workflows

story perspectives 269–270, 326

story promotion 319–320, *320*, 325, 394

storyboards 271, 307, 316, 326

Storyful 203–204, 222

Storytellers Brand Studio 59

storytelling 82–83; classifications of news 92; data stories 109–111, *110–111*; extended reality (XR) environments 111–112; headlines and decks 100–101; narrative structures 88–91, **90**; news features 101–103, **102**; online news writing 84–86; pegs, hooks, and angles 93–96, **93**; report structures 88–89, **90**; scenic narratives 103–109, **107**; science of 104–105; subjective narratives 39, 71–72, **72**

student newspapers 365

subheadings *see* decks

subjectivity in news 38–39, 71–72, **72**

subscriptions 14, 41–42, 46

Sullivan, Margaret 9, 10, 223, 228, 232, 357

Supply Chain Dive 91

surveillance 171, 177–180; by journalists 33, 152–153; Hemisphere Project 179; of journalists 158, 177–180; protecting sources from 171, 178–180; of users' behavior 321–324, **322**, 324–325

sweetening audio 284–287, **283**, **284**, **286**

systematic observation 155, 255

systems theory 349, **350**, 399; input 349, **350**, 387; output 349, **350**, 392; throughput 349, **350**, 399

tablets 36, 239, 297, 347, 352

Taibbi, Matt 21

Tails software 180

television news 33–34, 35, *35*

Tenenboim, O. 46

texting 12–13, 18

TheWrap 369

Thompson, S. A. 176

Thornburg, Ryan 94, 194, 227

Thorson, E. 67, 336

Thucydides 152–153, 182

timelines 85, 100, 109, 208, 214, 233, 267, **268**, 292, 295, 307, 399; ticktock 85, 109, 232, 399

traditional organizations vs digital startups 41, *60–61*

transcripts 267, 273, **273**, 281, **281**, 297–298, 367–368, 399

transitions 100, 113, 275, 283, 307–308, 344, 399

transparency 8, 10, 21–23, 36, 191; radical transparency 367

triangulation 140, 195–197, **195**, 400; methodological triangulation 195–197, **195**, 223–224, 389

Tritten, Travis 130

trolls 74, 85, 85, 143–144, 371–372, 400

Trump, Donald J. 9, 23, 56, 201–202, 366

trust levels 19–21, 37; as business model 366–368; and news gathering 146–147; techniques for improving 21–24

truth (def) 193–194, 366, 400

truth sandwich 186, 223

Tsubaki, R. 200

Twitter: corrections 27; human sources 168; Iran election protests (2009) 13; live streaming 253; news gathering 130–131; real-time reporting 17; user engagement measures 74; and verification 198, 220; web advertising 41

URL (Uniform Resource Locator) 206–207, 400; home page 207; internet protocol 206, 387; resource ID 206–207, 395; server name 206, 397; top level domain (TLD) 206–207, 399

unnamed sources 169, 172–176

USA Today 37, 70; integrated newsroom 348; local news 112

user behavior 321–324, **322–323**; engagement 73–74, 400; analytics 73–75, 77, 303, 321, 348, 375–376; metrics 389; scanning 321, **323**, 345, 384, 385, 402

user perspectives 269–270

INDEX

user-generated content (UGC) 39, 71, 131, 202–204, 222, 281; user distributed content (UDC) 336

user participation *see* crowdsourcing, participatory journalism and user-generated content (UGC)

validity: in data 134–136, **135**; in sources 191–192

Vanity Fair 162, 373

variable *111*, 254, 288–291, *290*, 293, 380, 401

Variety famous headline 101

verification 18–19, **18**, 187–191; and crowdsourcing 198; evaluating digital evidence 208–209, **208–209**; facts, inferences, and truth 193–194; multiple sources 194–197; new initiatives 222; of online information 205–208; by online users 67; of photographs 209–216, **209**, **211**, **212**, **215**, *210*, *212–213*, *215–216*; real-time fact-checking 201–202; re-verification 190; third party verification sites 25; three guides to 198–202, **199**; user-generated content and eyewitness media 202–204; of videos 216–222; *see also* fake news

ViceNews 70, 240

Victor, Daniel 130

video: acquisition of 240–245; authentication of 216–222; mobile phones 339; processing workflows 280–285, **281**, **283**

Villi, M. 336

Viner, Katharine 301

Virginia Pilot 66

virtual reality (VR) 48, 111–112, 242, 244–245; Content Management Systems (CMS) 317; emotional content 71; experiencing news 69–70, **69**

Vox.com 14, 134; Chorus CMS 316

Vox Verbatim: Bissinger, Buzz 162, 373; Codianni, Ashley 370; Cook, Tony 47; Dance, Gabriel 235; Fallis, David xvii 121; Finnerty, Megan 59; Guzman, Monica 74; Kaphle, Anup 100; Murphy, Mary 373; Rauch, Jonathan 219–220; Schweizer, Callie 190; Van Tassel, Joan 63, 106, 241; Waxman, Sharon 369

Waldman, S. 33

Wall Street Journal, The 37, 42, 55; interactive data 287, 293; story angle 95–96

Wardle, Claire 24–25, 28–29, 87, 202–204

Warzel, C. 176–177

Washington Post, The xvii, 37, 41, 74, 134, 161, 193, 196, 240, 357; Congress finances investigation (2012) 121–122; COVID-19 resources 294; CMS 316; data journalism 255, 287, 293; extended reality (XR) 70; fake news 10; FIFA corruption scandal (2015) 168; newsroom 65–66; opsec 177–178; source attribution 173; subscriptions 41; user response to video 241

Waxman, Sharon 369

Wayback Machine 205

Weaver, Matthew 12, 18

Weiner, J. 251

Weischenberg, S. 63

Wezerek, G. 177

WhatsApp 63, 179

whistleblowers 174–175, 180, 182, 401

whois lookup 207, **207**, 208, 220, 402

Wiggle, M. C. 88

Wikimedia Commons 239

Wikipedia 36, 124–126, **126**

Williams, Brian 129–130

wireframes 316, **317**

Wise, K. 240

Wittel, A. 159

WordPress 319

workflows *see* processing workflows

World Health Organization (WHO) 9, 188, 293

writing workflows 272–275, **273**, **275**

WWD (Women's Wear Daily) 91

Yahoo! 123, 124, 314, 334

Yopp, J. 94

YouTube 12, 189, 220, 222, 253

Zimmerman, E. 232

Z-pattern 321, **323**

Zuboff, Shoshana 263

Zwillenberg 86

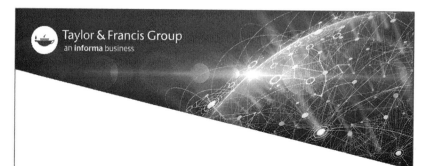